PRAISE FROM THE EXPERTS
FOR
THE PDR® POCKET GUIDE
TO PRESCRIPTION DRUGS™

"Any patient or family member of a patient should have ready access to this book. It is informative, useful and a pleasure to read. . . . Superbly written and understandable by those we wish to help—our patients and their families."

> —Edwin C. Cadman, M.D.,
> Ensign Professor and chairman,
> Department of Internal Medicine,
> Yale University School of Medicine

"A must for every household where there are concerns about the safe use of medications. It is an ideal way to clarify and supplement the information provided by your health-care provider."

> —Jack M. Rosenberg, Pharm.D., Ph.D.,
> professor of clinical pharmacy and pharmacology,
> director, Division of Pharmacy Practice,
> Arnold & Marie Schwartz College of
> Pharmacy and Health Sciences,
> Long Island University

THE PDR® PDR®

FAMILY GUIDES™

POCKET GUIDE

TO PRESCRIPTION DRUGS™

THIRD EDITION
REVISED AND UPDATED

Based on Physicians' Desk Reference®,
the Nation's Leading Professional Drug Handbook

POCKET BOOKS
New York   London   Toronto   Sydney   Tokyo   Singapore

Officers of Medical Economics: *President and Chief Executive Officer:* Curtis B. Allen; *Vice President, Human Resources:* Pamela M. Bilash; *Vice President, Finance and Chief Financial Officer:* Thomas W. Ehardt; *Vice President, New Business Planning:* Linda G. Hope; *Executive Vice President, Magazine Publishing:* Thomas F. Rice; *Senior Vice President, Operations:* John R. Ware

POCKET BOOKS, a division of Simon & Schuster Inc.
1230 Avenue of the Americas, New York, NY 10020

ISBN: 0-671-02585-6

First Pocket Books printing of this revised edition January 1999

10 9 8 7 6 5 4 3 2 1

Publisher's Note

The drug information contained in this book is based on product labeling published in the 1998 edition of *Physicians' Desk Reference®*, supplemented with facts from other sources the publisher believes reliable. While diligent efforts have been made to assure the accuracy of this information, the book does not list every possible action, adverse reaction, interaction, and precaution; and all information is presented without guarantees by the authors, consultants, and publisher, who disclaim all liability in connection with its use.

This book is intended only as a reference for use in an ongoing partnership between doctor and patient in the vigilant management of the patient's health. It is not a substitute for a doctor's professional judgment, and serves only as a reminder of concerns that may need discussion. All readers are urged to consult with a physician before beginning or discontinuing use of any prescription drug or undertaking any form of self-treatment.

Brand names listed in this book are intended to represent only the more commonly used products. Inclusion of a brand name does not signify endorsement of the product; absence of a name does not imply a criticism or rejection of the product. The publisher is not advocating the use of any product described in this book, does not warrant or guarantee any of these products, and has not performed any independent analysis in connection with the product information contained herein.

Contents

Contents

The PDR® Pocket Guide to Prescription Drugs based on the sixth edition of The PDR® Family Guide to Prescription Drugs®

Contributors and Consultants

Editor-in-Chief: David W. Sifton
Director of Professional Services: Mukesh Mehta, R Ph
Art Director: Robert Hartman

Managing Pharmaceutical Editor: Maria Deutsch, MS, R Ph, CDE

Writer: Kathleen Rodgers, R Ph

Assistant Editors: Ann Marevis; Gwynned L. Kelly

Illustrations: Christopher Wikoff, MAMS

Editorial Production: Vice President of Production: David A. Pitler; Director of Print Purchasing: Marjorie A. Duffy; Director of Operations, Production: Carrie Williams; Manager of Production, Annuals: Kimberly Hiller-Vivas; Electronic Publishing Coordinator: Joanne M. Pearson; Electronic Publishing Designer; Robert K. Grossman; Senior Digital Imaging Coordinator: Shawn W. Cahill; Digital Imaging Coordinator: Frank J. McElroy, III

Medical Economics Company

Vice President of Directory Services: Stephen B. Greenberg

Director of Product Management: David P. Reiss

Product Manager: Mark A. Friedman

National Sales Manager, Trade Group: Bill Gaffney; Promotion Manager: Donna R. Lynn

Board of Medical Consultants

Gary D. Koenig, MD
Florissant, MO

Mitchell R. Lester, MD
James F. Murray Fellow, Pediatric Allergy and
Immunology
National Jewish Center for Immunology and Respiratory
Medicine, Denver, CO

Younghee Limb, MD
Assistant Professor of Internal Medicine
State University of New York, Stony Brook, NY

Gardiner Morse, MS
Executive Editor, AIDS Clinical Care, Waltham, MA

Louis V. Napolitano, MD
Senior Attending Physician
Hackensack Medical Center, Hackensack, NJ

Mark D. Ravenscraft, MD
Medical Director, Renal Transplantation
St. John's Mercy Medical Center, St. Louis, MO

Martin I. Resnick, MD
Professor and Chairman, Department of Urology
Case Western Reserve University, Cleveland, OH

Frank Simo, MD
Assistant Clinical Professor, Department of
Otolaryngology
St. Louis University, St. Louis, MO

Karl Singer, MD
Exeter Family Medicine Associates, Exeter, NH

Eugene W. Sweeney, MD
Assistant Clinical Professor of Dermatology
Columbia College of Physicians and Surgeons,
New York, NY

Gary D. Davila, MD
Florissant, MO

Michael B. Lamet, MD
James F. Lander Fellow, Geriatric Medicine and
Internal Medicine Research Unit, Hematology and Respiratory
Medicine, Denville, CA, Illinois

Vaughns Linth, MD
Assistant Professor of Internal Medicine
State University of New York, Stony Brook, NY

Gardiner Morse, MS
Executive Editor, AIDS Clinical Care, Waltham, MA

Pedro V. Napolitano, MD
Senior Attending Physician
Hackensack Medical Center, Hackensack, NJ

Mark D. Eisenberg, MD
Medical Director, Renal Transplantation
St. John's Mercy Medical Center, St. Louis, MO

Michael Reusler, MD
Professor and Chairman, Department of Biology
Case Western Reserve University, Westford, OH

Frank Simo, MD
Assistant Clinical Professor, Department of
Otolaryngology
St. Louis University, St. Louis, MO

Raj Sagar, MD
Dallas Family Medicine Associates, Dallas, MA

Lawrence W. Surman, MD
Assistant Clinical Professor of Dermatology
Columbia College of Physicians and Surgeons
New York, NY

Foreword

Like its predecessors, this new edition of *The PDR Pocket Guide to Prescription Drugs* strives to make the many benefits of modern pharmaceuticals—as well as their undeniable risks—as clear and simple as can be. Unlike other books in the field, *The PDR Pocket Guide* discloses all important side effects specifically attributed to the drug by the manufacturer, no matter how rare. As a safeguard against error, it also provides you with full information on standard dosage recommendations. It tells exactly what to do when you miss a dose of your medication, while alerting you to the warning signs of an overdose. And to help you find all these facts as quickly as possible, it lists each medication under its familiar brand name—with a cross-reference in case the drug is dispensed generically.

Still, despite the depth and detail of the information you'll find here, *The PDR Pocket Guide* is not a replacement for your doctor's advice. Instead, it serves as a reminder of the basic instructions and caveats that all too often are forgotten by the time a patient leaves the doctor's office, as well as providing you with a checklist of the problems and conditions that you must be certain the doctor knows about—facts that might call for a change in your prescription.

In this way, the book is designed to serve as an aid in an ongoing dialogue between you and your doctor—a collaboration that's necessary for any treatment to work. Just as the doctor must tell you how and why to use a particular drug, you must tell the doctor how it affects you, reporting any reactions or drug interactions you suspect you may have. And while it's up to the doctor to devise your treatment strategy, it's up to you to make sure that the right doses are administered at the right times, and that the prescribed course of therapy is completed as planned.

Physicians' Desk Reference has been providing doctors with the information needed for safe, effective drug therapy for over 50 years. Designed especially for healthcare professionals, it presents the facts in a detailed, technical format approved by the Food and Drug Administration. Now, to make the key facts buried in this wealth of data accessible to everyone, *The PDR Pocket Guide* has stripped away the medical shorthand and technical terminology, and presented the core of this information in a simple, standard format designed for maximum convenience and ease of use by the consumer.

Almost all the information you'll find in *The PDR Pocket Guide's* consumer drug profiles has been extracted from PDR itself. When necessary, however, selected facts have been added from other sources—in particular, the databases maintained by PDR's sister company, MICROMEDEX, INC. Generally, this extra information describes uses for a drug that are still awaiting formal FDA approval, or supplies instructions meant specifically for the patient, such as how to make up a missed dose.

Finally, to give you added perspective, the book includes a series of chapters that provide a general overview of many common ailments and the ways they can be treated today. As with the drug profiles, these chapters are designed to supplement the information you receive from your doctor, and to aid you in discussing your treatment.

Modern drug therapy is a vast and complicated field—so complicated that, for many questions about medicines, the answer varies with each patient. *The PDR Pocket Guide to Prescription Drugs* gives you general guidelines for safe drug use; but only your doctor, evaluating the unique details of your case, can give you the exact instructions best suited for you. The goal of this book is simply to alert you to the most pertinent questions to ask, and to help clarify your doctor's answers—in short, to give you the tools you need to supervise your own medical care as effectively as possible. We wish you good health.

Robert W. Hogan, MD
Chair, Board of Medical Consultants

How to Use This Book

Modern medicines spare us all an incredible amount of suffering. If you doubt it, imagine a world without antibiotics to cure infections, analgesics to alleviate pain, or any of the many drugs we use to ease stiff joints and help weakened hearts.

But today's potent medicines are not without their risks. For certain people, at certain times, some drugs can cause problems. And for all people, misusing a medication is an invitation to trouble. The purpose of this book is to alert you to those times and those conditions which should make you wary, and to help you use all of your medications safely and effectively.

This book is not a substitute for a visit to the doctor. Only a doctor can weigh all the diverse aspects of your condition and choose the treatment most likely to meet your needs. What we hope this book can do, however, is help you sort out the facts and questions that deserve further discussion. Your doctor, after all, can respond only to the problems and concerns you mention. And a seemingly unimportant question could turn out to be a crucial aspect of your particular case.

The Drug Profiles

The drug profiles in this section are designed to give you detailed information on the nation's most frequently prescribed prescription drugs, plus a few widely used over-the-counter medications. Though the section covers more than 1,000 products, it is not all-inclusive. If you do not find a profile for a particular prescription you've received, you shouldn't be concerned. There are a number of specialized, yet valuable drugs in current use that have been omitted here due to lack of space.

Most prescription products have two names—a generic chemical name and a manufacturer's brand name. Both are listed alphabetically in this book, with a profile of the drug appearing under the more familiar of the two. In most instances, that means the brand name. In a few cases—such as insulin, for example—the generic name heads the profile. In either case, the drug's other name gives you a cross-reference to the profile.

If there is more than one brand of a drug, you'll usually find the profile under the name that's most frequently prescribed. For example, information on amoxicillin can be found in the profile of Amoxil, the nation's leading brand. Other brands of amoxicillin, such as Wymox and Polymox, are cross-referenced to the Amoxil entry.

The drug profiles begin with correct pronunciation of the name, followed by the other brand and generic names for the drug. The information that follows these names is divided into 10 sections. Here's what you'll find in each.

Why is this drug prescribed?
This section provides an overview of the major diseases and disorders for which the drug is generally given. It names each basic problem, but does not go into technical details. For instance, the information here will confirm that a particular antibiotic is used to fight, say, upper respiratory tract infections. The section does not, however, attempt to list all the specific germs that the antibiotic is capable of eliminating.

Most important fact about this drug
Highlighted here is one key point—out of the dozens found in a typical profile—that is especially worthwhile to remember. We've placed it here for the sake of emphasis. Never regard this section as a definitive summary of the drug.

How should you take this medication?
Some drugs should never be taken with meals. Others must be. This section details such special instructions, including how and when to take the medication, and any dietary restrictions that may apply. Also found here is advice on what to do when you forget a dose, and any special storage requirements that apply.

What side effects may occur?
Shown here are the potential side effects that the manufacturer has listed in the drug's FDA-approved product labeling. Virtually any drug will occasionally cause an unwanted reaction. However, even the most common of these reactions is generally seen in only a small minority of patients. For that reason, presence of a long list of possible side effects does not mean that the drug is unusually dangerous

or trouble-prone. In fact, your odds of experiencing even one of these effects are typically very low. Not listed are the side effects that can be detected only by a physician or analysis in a laboratory.

Why should this drug not be prescribed?
A few drugs are known to be harmful under certain specific conditions, which are detailed here—the most common being hypersensitivity to the drug itself. If you think one of these restrictions applies to you, you should alert your doctor immediately. If you're correct, he or she may decide to use an alternative treatment.

Special warnings about this medication
This cautionary information is presented as a double check. If it includes any problems or conditions that your doctor may be unaware of, be sure to bring them to his or her attention. Chances are that no change in treatment will be called for; but it's worth making sure. In any event, do not take this information as a signal to change your dosage or discontinue the drug without consulting your doctor. Such a change might well do more harm than good.

Possible food and drug interactions
when taking this medication
In this section you'll find a list of specific drugs—and types of drugs—that have been known to interact with the medicine being profiled. Generally, the list includes a few examples of each type. However, it is far from inclusive. If you're not certain whether a medication you're taking falls into one of these categories, be sure to check with your doctor or pharmacist.

Remember, too, that the chances of an interaction—and its intensity if one occurs—vary from person to person. In many cases, the benefits of the two medicines may outweigh the results of an interaction. Don't stop taking either drug without first consulting your doctor.

Special information
if you are pregnant or breastfeeding
Very few medicines have been definitively proved safe for use during pregnancy. On the other hand, only a handful are known to be inevitably harmful. Most drugs fall in-between, in a gray area where no harm has been reported, but neither

has safety been conclusively proved. With many of these drugs, the small theoretical risk they pose may be overshadowed by your need for treatment. This section will tell you whether a drug has been confirmed safe, is known to be dangerous, or is part of that large group about which scientists are not really sure.

Recommended dosage
Shown here are excerpts of the dosage guidelines your doctor uses. They generally present a range of doses recommended for typical cases, and sometimes include a recommended maximum. The information is presented as a convenient double check in case you suspect a misunderstanding or a typographical error on your prescription label. It is not useful for determining an exact dosage yourself. The dose that's best for you depends on numerous factors—such as your age, weight, physical condition, and response to the drug—that can be properly evaluated only by your doctor.

Overdosage
As another safety measure, this section lists, when available, the signs of an overdose. If the symptoms listed in this section lead you to suspect an overdose, your best response is to seek emergency medical attention immediately.

Other Features
The book includes several other sections that you'll find useful when faced with certain specific problems.

The Disease and Disorder Index enables you to quickly identify drugs available for a particular medical condition. Arranged alphabetically by ailment, it lists all the medications profiled in the book.

Also available are the following special sections.

Product Identification Guide
It's wise to keep all your prescription medications in their original bottles or vials. However, if they do somehow get mixed up, you may find this section helpful for sorting them out. It includes actual-size photographs of the leading products discussed in the book, arranged alphabetically by brand name. Manufacturers occasionally change the color

and shape of a product, so if a prescription does not match the photo shown here, check with your pharmacist before assuming there's been a mistake.

The Appendices

This section provides you with several important safeguards that every home should always have handy. One is a brief guide to safe medication use. Another—for ready reference in an emergency—is a directory of regional poison control centers.

Also found in this section are lists of drugs that meet certain special conditions, such as those that are sugar- or alcohol-free, and those that may make you unusually sensitive to light. These lists include prescription and over-the-counter products, and are not limited to brands mentioned in the drug profiles. On the other hand, the lists are not all-inclusive; so even if a medication fails to appear, there's still a chance it may qualify. Check with your pharmacist to be sure.

The Doctor-Patient Partnership

Although doctors today can often work miracles with advanced technology and sophisticated medicines, they still need the help of the patient to make most treatments work. No matter how potent the medication, it can still prove worthless if you fail to take it properly. Likewise, if you react badly to a drug, or have a condition that makes it dangerous, there is nothing any doctor can do about it unless you report the problem.

This book is offered as an aid in this cooperative effort with your doctor. We hope its suggests the right questions to ask, while allaying any unwarranted concerns you might have. Most of all, we hope it helps in some small way to make all of your treatments as effective as they can possibly be.

Drug Profiles

Generic name:

ACARBOSE

See Precose, page 988.

Brand name:

ACCOLATE

Pronounced: ACK-o-late
Generic name: Zafirlukast

Why is this drug prescribed?
Accolate helps prevent asthma attacks. It is prescribed for long-term treatment.

Most important fact about this drug
Accolate will not stop an asthma attack once it starts. You will still need to use an airway-opening medication when an attack occurs.

How should you take this medication?
Accolate should be taken twice every day, whether or not you have had any recent asthma attacks. Do not take the medication with food. Allow at least 1 hour to pass before eating, or wait for 2 hours after a meal. You can continue to take Accolate while using another medication to stop an attack.

- *If you miss a dose...*
  Take it as soon as you remember. If it is almost time for your next dose, skip the one you missed and go back to your regular schedule. Do not take 2 doses at once.

- *Storage instructions...*
  Store at room temperature in a dark, dry place.

What side effects may occur?
Side effects cannot be anticipated. If any develop or change in intensity, inform your doctor as soon as possible. Only your doctor can determine if it is safe for you to continue taking Accolate.

- *More common side effects may include:*
  Headache, infection, nausea

- *Less common side effects may include:*
  Accidental injury, abdominal pain, allergic reactions (hives; swelling of the lips, tongue, face, arms, and legs; rash), back pain, diarrhea, dizziness, fever, generalized pain, indigestion, muscle aches, vomiting, weakness

Why should this drug not be prescribed?
If you have had an allergic reaction to Accolate or to any of its ingredients, avoid this drug.

Special warnings about this medication
While taking Accolate, you should not stop—or even cut down on—any other asthma medication you are using unless your doctor recommends it. Remember that Accolate is not an airway-opening medication. You will still need an inhaler to stop an attack.

If you have been taking an oral steroid drug and your doctor does decide to cut back the dosage, there is a remote chance that complications will follow. Inform your doctor of any new symptoms.

Also call your doctor if you develop any of the following: pain in the upper right abdomen, nausea, fatigue, lethargy, itching, flu-like symptoms, or jaundice (yellowing of the skin and eyes). These are signs of a liver problem—a rare side effect of Accolate. If tests show the problem to be serious, you may have to stop using the drug. The symptoms will disappear after you stop taking the drug.

Possible food and drug interactions
when taking this medication
A full stomach can reduce Accolate's effectiveness. Do not take with meals.

If Accolate is taken with certain other drugs, the effects of either could be increased, decreased, or altered. It is especially important to check with your doctor before combining Accolate with the following:

Aspirin (Ecotrin, Genuine Bayer, others)
Astemizole (Hismanal)
Blood-thinning drugs such as Coumadin
Carbamazepine (Tegretol)
Cisapride (Propulsid)
Cyclosporine (Sandimmune, Neoral)
Erythromycin (E.E.S., E-Mycin, others)

Heart and blood pressure medications called calcium channel blockers,
including Calan, Cardizem, and Procardia
Phenytoin (Dilantin)
Terfenadine (Seldane)
Theophylline (Theo-Dur, others)
Tolbutamide (Orinase)

Special information
if you are pregnant or breastfeeding

Accolate should be taken during pregnancy only if clearly needed. If you are
pregnant or plan to become pregnant, inform your doctor immediately.

Accolate does find its way into breast milk and should not be taken by
nursing mothers.

Recommended dosage

ADULTS AND CHILDREN 12 AND OVER

The usual dose is 1 tablet twice a day.

CHILDREN UNDER 12

Safety and effectiveness have not been studied in this age group.

Overdosage

No overdoses of Accolate have been reported. However, any medication
taken in excess can have serious consequences. If you suspect an overdose,
seek medical attention immediately.

Brand name:

ACCUPRIL

Pronounced: AK-you-prill
Generic name: Quinapril hydrochloride

Why is this drug prescribed?

Accupril is used in the treatment of high blood pressure. It can be taken
alone or in combination with a thiazide type of water pill such as
HydroDIURIL. Accupril is in a family of drugs known as "ACE inhibitors." It
works by preventing a chemical in your blood called angiotensin I from
converting into a more potent form that increases salt and water retention in
your body. Accupril also enhances blood flow throughout your blood vessels.

Along with other drugs, Accupril is also prescribed in the treatment of congestive heart failure.

Most important fact about this drug
You must take Accupril regularly for it to be effective. Since blood pressure declines gradually, it may be several weeks before you get the full benefit of Accupril; and you must continue taking it even if you are feeling well. Accupril does not cure high blood pressure; it merely keeps it under control.

How should you take this medication?
You can take Accupril with or without meals.

Alcohol may increase the effect of Accupril, and could cause dizziness or fainting. Avoid alcoholic beverages until you have checked with your doctor.

Take Accupril exactly as prescribed, and see your doctor regularly to make sure the drug is working properly without unwanted side effects. Do not stop taking this drug without first consulting your doctor.

▪ *If you miss a dose...*
Take the forgotten dose as soon as you remember. However, if it is almost time for your next dose, skip the one you missed and go back to your regular schedule. Never try to "catch up" by doubling the dose.

▪ *Storage instructions...*
Accupril can be stored at room temperature. Protect from light.

What side effects may occur?
Side effects cannot be anticipated. If any develop or change in intensity, inform your doctor as soon as possible. Only your doctor can determine if it is safe for you to continue taking Accupril.

▪ *More common side effects may include:*
Dizziness, headache

▪ *Less common side effects may include:*
Abdominal pain, coughing, fatigue, nausea, vomiting

▪ *Rare side effects may include:*
Angina (severe chest pain), back pain, bleeding in the stomach or intestines, bronchitis, changes in heart rhythm, constipation, depression, dimmed vision, dizziness when first standing up, dry mouth or throat, extremely high blood pressure, fainting, hair loss, heart attack, heart

failure, hepatitis, high potassium, impotence, increased blood pressure, increased sweating, inflammation of the pancreas, inflammation of the sinuses, insomnia, itching, kidney failure, nervousness, numbness/tingling, palpitations, rapid heartbeat, sensitivity to light, severe allergic reactions, skin peeling, sleepiness, sore throat, stroke, swelling of the mouth and throat, vague feeling of illness, vertigo

Why should this drug not be prescribed?

If you are sensitive to or have ever had an allergic reaction to Accupril or similar drugs, such as Capoten and Vasotec, you should not take this medication. Make sure your doctor is aware of any drug reactions you have experienced.

Special warnings about this medication

If you develop swelling of the face, lips, tongue, or throat, or of your arms and legs, or have difficulty swallowing or breathing, you should contact your doctor immediately. You may need emergency treatment.

You may feel light-headed, especially during the first few days of Accupril therapy. If this occurs, notify your doctor. If you actually faint, stop taking the medication until you have consulted with your doctor.

Vomiting, diarrhea, and heavy perspiration can all deplete your body fluid; and dehydration can cause your blood pressure to drop. If this leads to light-headedness or fainting, you should check with your doctor.

Inform your doctor or dentist that you are taking Accupril before undergoing surgery or anesthesia.

Do not use potassium supplements or salt substitutes containing potassium without consulting your doctor.

If you develop a sore throat or fever, contact your doctor immediately. It could indicate a more serious illness.

If you are taking Accupril, your doctor will do a complete assessment of your kidney function and will watch it closely as long as you are taking this drug.

If you notice a yellow tinge to your skin and the whites of your eyes, stop taking the drug and notify your doctor immediately. This could be a sign of liver damage.

The safety and effectiveness of Accupril in children have not been established.

Possible food and drug interactions
when taking this medication

If Accupril is taken with certain other drugs, the effects of either could be increased, decreased, or altered. It is especially important to check with your doctor before combining Accupril with the following:

Diuretics such as Lasix
Lithium (Eskalith, Lithobid)
Potassium-sparing diuretics such as Aldactone, Dyazide, and Moduretic
Potassium supplements such as Slow-K and K-Dur
Salt substitutes containing potassium
Tetracycline (Sumycin)

Special information
if you are pregnant or breastfeeding

ACE inhibitors such as Accupril have been shown to cause injury and even death to the unborn child when used in pregnancy during the second and third trimesters. If you are pregnant, your doctor should discontinue Accupril as soon as possible. If you plan to become pregnant, make sure your doctor knows you are taking this medication. Accupril appears in breast milk and could affect a nursing infant. If this medication is essential to your health, your doctor may advise you to discontinue breastfeeding until your treatment is finished.

Recommended dosage

HIGH BLOOD PRESSURE

The usual starting dose is 10 or 20 milligrams taken once a day. If you have any problems with your kidneys or if you are also taking a diuretic, your starting dose may be lower. Depending on how your blood pressure responds, your doctor may increase your dose up to a total of 80 milligrams a day taken once a day or divided into two doses.

CONGESTIVE HEART FAILURE

The usual starting dose is 5 milligrams taken twice a day. Your doctor may increase the dose from week to week, up to as much as 20 to 40 milligrams daily, divided into 2 equal doses. If you have kidney problems, the dosage will be lower.

Overdosage

Any medication taken in excess can have serious consequences. If you suspect an overdose, seek medical attention immediately.

A severe drop in blood pressure is the primary sign of an Accupril overdose.

Brand name:

ACCUTANE

Pronounced: ACC-u-tane
Generic name: Isotretinoin

Why is this drug prescribed?

Accutane, a chemical cousin of vitamin A, is prescribed for the treatment of severe, disfiguring cystic acne that has not cleared up in response to milder medications such as antibiotics. It works on the oil glands within the skin, shrinking them and diminishing their output. You take Accutane by mouth every day for several months, then stop. The antiacne effect can last even after you have finished your course of medication.

Most important fact about this drug

Because Accutane can cause severe birth defects, including mental retardation and physical malformations, a woman *must not* become pregnant while taking it. If you are a woman of childbearing age, your doctor will ask you to sign a detailed consent form before you start taking Accutane. If you accidentally become pregnant while taking the medication, you should immediately consult your doctor.

How should you take this medication?

Take Accutane with food. Follow your doctor's instructions carefully.

Depending on your reaction to Accutane, your doctor may need to adjust the dosage upward or downward. If you respond quickly and very well, your doctor may take you off Accutane even before the 15 or 20 weeks are up.

After you finish taking Accutane, there should be at least a 2-month "rest period" during which you are off the drug. This is because your acne may continue to get better even though you are no longer taking the medication. Once the 2 months are up, if your acne is still severe, your doctor may want to give you a second course of Accutane.

Avoid consumption of alcoholic beverages.

Read the patient information leaflet available with the product.

Do not crush the capsules.

- *If you miss a dose...*
  Take the forgotten dose as soon as you remember. If it is almost time for your next dose, skip the one you missed and go back to your regular schedule. Do not take 2 doses at the same time.

- *Storage instructions...*
  Store at room temperature, away from light.

What side effects may occur?

Side effects cannot be anticipated. If any develop or change in intensity, inform your doctor as soon as possible. Only your doctor can determine if it is safe for you to continue taking Accutane.

- *More common side effects may include:*
  Conjunctivitis ("pinkeye"), dry or fragile skin, dry or cracked lips, dry mouth, dry nose, itching, joint pains, nosebleed

- *Less common side effects may include:*
  Bowel inflammation and pain, chest pain, decreased night vision, decreased tolerance to contact lenses, delay in wound healing, depression, fatigue, headache, nausea, peeling palms or soles, rash, skin infections, stomach and intestinal discomfort, sunburn-sensitive skin, thinning hair, urinary discomfort, vision problems, vomiting

Why should this drug not be prescribed?

You should not take Accutane if you are sensitive to or have ever had an allergic reaction to parabens, the preservative used in the capsules.

If you are a woman of childbearing age, you should not take Accutane if you are pregnant, if you think there is a possibility you might get pregnant during the treatment, or if you are unable to keep coming back to the doctor for monthly checkups, including pregnancy testing.

Special warnings about this medication

When you first start taking Accutane, it is possible that your acne will get worse before it starts to get better.

If you are a woman of childbearing age and you are considering taking Accutane, you will be given both spoken and written warnings about the importance of avoiding pregnancy during the treatment. You will be asked to sign a consent form noting that:

- Accutane is a powerful, "last resort" medication for severe acne;
- You must not take Accutane if you are pregnant or may become pregnant during treatment;
- If you get pregnant while taking Accutane, your baby will be at high risk for birth defects;
- If you take Accutane, you must use effective birth control from 1 month before the start of treatment through 1 month after the end of treatment;

- You must test negative for pregnancy within 2 weeks before starting Accutane, and you must start Accutane on the second or third day of your menstrual period;
- You may participate in a program that includes an initial free pregnancy test and birth control counseling session;
- If you become pregnant, you must immediately stop taking Accutane and see your doctor;
- You have read and understood the Accutane patient brochure and asked your doctor any questions you had;
- You are not currently pregnant and do not plan to become pregnant for at least 30 days after you finish taking Accutane;
- You have been invited to participate in a survey of women being treated with Accutane.

Some people taking Accutane, including some who simultaneously took tetracycline, have experienced headache, nausea, and visual disturbances caused by increased pressure within the skull. See a doctor immediately if you have these symptoms; if the doctor finds swelling of the optic nerve at the back of your eye, you must stop taking Accutane at once and see a neurologist for further care.

Be careful driving at night. Some people have experienced a sudden decrease in night vision.

Some people taking Accutane have had problems regulating their blood sugar level.

You may not be able to tolerate your contact lenses during and after your therapy with Accutane.

You should stop taking Accutane immediately if you have abdominal pain, bleeding from the rectum, or severe diarrhea. You may have an inflammatory disease of the bowel.

You should not donate blood during your therapy with Accutane and for a month after you stop taking it.

Possible food and drug interactions
when taking this medication
While taking Accutane, do not take vitamin supplements containing vitamin A. Accutane and vitamin A are chemically related; taking them together is like taking an overdose of vitamin A.

Special information
if you are pregnant or breastfeeding
Accutane causes birth defects; do not use it while pregnant. Nursing

mothers should not take Accutane because of the possibility of passing the drug on to the baby via breast milk.

Recommended dosage

The recommended dosage range for Accutane is 0.5 to 2 milligrams per 2.2 pounds of body weight, divided into 2 doses daily, for 15 to 20 weeks. The usual starting dose is 0.5 to 1 milligram per 2.2 pounds per day.

People whose disease is very severe or is primarily on the body may have to take up to the maximum recommended dose.

If after a period of 2 months or more off therapy, severe cystic acne persists, your doctor may prescribe a second course of therapy.

Overdosage

Any medication taken in excess can have serious consequences. If you suspect an overdose of Accutane, seek medical attention immediately.

- *Overdosage of Accutane, like overdosage of vitamin A, can cause:*
  Abdominal pain, dizziness, dry or cracked lips, facial flushing, incoordination and clumsiness, headache, vomiting

Generic name:

ACEBUTOLOL

See Sectral, page 1120.

Generic name:

ACETAMINOPHEN

See Tylenol, page 1297.

Generic name:

ACETAMINOPHEN WITH CODEINE

See Tylenol with Codeine, page 1299.

Generic name:

ACETAMINOPHEN WITH OXYCODONE

See Percocet, page 939.

Generic name:

ACETAZOLAMIDE

See Diamox, page 368.

Generic name:

ACHROMYCIN V

See Tetracycline, page 1224.

Brand name:

ACLOVATE

Pronounced: AK-low-vait
Generic name: Alclometasone dipropionate

Why is this drug prescribed?
Aclovate, a synthetic steroid medication of the cortisone family, is spread on the skin to relieve certain types of itchy rashes, including psoriasis.

Most important fact about this drug
When you use Aclovate, you inevitably absorb some of the medication through your skin and into the bloodstream. Too much absorption can lead to unwanted side effects elsewhere in the body. To keep this problem to a minimum, avoid using large amounts of Aclovate over large areas, and do not cover it with airtight dressings such as plastic wrap or adhesive bandages unless specifically told to by your doctor.

How should you use this medication?
Use Aclovate exactly as prescribed by your doctor and only to treat the condition for which your doctor prescribed it. The usual procedure is to spread a thin film of Aclovate cream or ointment over the rash and massage gently until the medication disappears. Do this 2 or 3 times a day.

For areas of deep-seated, persistent rash, your doctor may recommend a thick layer of Aclovate cream or ointment topped with waterproof bandaging, to be left in place for 1 to 4 days. If necessary, this procedure may be repeated 3 or 4 times. Do not use bandaging at all, however, unless your doctor so advises.

Aclovate is for use only on the skin. Be careful to keep it out of your eyes.

■ *If you miss a dose...*
Apply it as soon as you remember. If it is almost time for the next dose, skip the one you missed and go back to your regular schedule.

■ *Storage instructions...*
Store at room temperature.

What side effects may occur?
Side effects cannot be anticipated. If any develop or change in intensity, inform your doctor as soon as possible. Only your doctor can determine if it is safe for you to continue taking Aclovate.

■ *Side effects may include:*
Acne-like pimples, allergic rash/inflammation, burning, dryness, infection, irritation, itching, pale spots, prickly heat, rash, redness, stretch marks on skin

Why should this drug not be prescribed?
Do not use Aclovate if it has ever given you an allergic reaction.

Special warnings about this medication
Aclovate is for external use only. Do not let the cream or ointment get into your eyes. Avoid using the product on your face, underarms, or groin, unless the doctor tells you to.

Do not use Aclovate to treat diaper rash or apply it in the diaper area; waterproof diapers or plastic pants can increase unwanted absorption of Aclovate.

If your skin is inflamed or you have some other skin condition, tell your doctor. You may absorb more drug than usual.

If you use Aclovate over large areas of skin for prolonged periods of time, the amount of hormone absorbed into your bloodstream may eventually lead to Cushing's syndrome: a moon-faced appearance, fattened neck and trunk, and purplish streaks on the skin. Children, because of their relatively larger ratio of skin surface to body weight, are particularly susceptible to overabsorption of hormone from Aclovate. The drug should not be used on children under 1 year of age or for more than 3 weeks in children older than 1 year.

Possible food and drug interactions when taking this medication
Check with your doctor before combining Aclovate with other more potent steroids, since this could lead to undesirably large amounts of hormone circulating in your bloodstream.

Special information
if you are pregnant or breastfeeding

Drug absorbed from Aclovate cream or ointment into the bloodstream may find its way into an unborn child's blood, or may seep into breast milk. To avoid any possible harm to your child, use Aclovate very sparingly—and only with your doctor's permission—if you are pregnant or nursing a baby.

Recommended dosage

Apply a thin film of Aclovate cream or ointment to the affected skin areas 2 or 3 times daily; massage gently until the medication disappears.

Bandages that block out air may be used to control psoriasis and other severe skin rashes, if your doctor recommends them. Apply as follows:

1. Cover the affected area with a thick layer of Aclovate cream or ointment and a light gauze dressing, then cover the area with a pliable plastic film.
2. Seal the edges to the normal skin by adhesive tape or other means.
3. Leave the dressing in place 1 to 4 days and repeat the procedure 3 or 4 times as needed.

With this method of treatment, marked improvement is often seen in a few days. If an infection develops, the use of airtight bandages should be discontinued. Your doctor will recommend an alternative treatment.

Once your condition is under control, you should stop using Aclovate. If you don't see any improvement within 2 weeks, check with your doctor.

Overdosage

Any medication taken in excess can have serious consequences. If you suspect an overdose, seek medical attention immediately.

In a child, an overdose of Aclovate may cause increased pressure within the skull leading to bulging soft spots (in an infant's head) or headache. If this happens, see a doctor without delay.

Over the long term, overuse of Aclovate can interfere with a child's normal growth and development.

Generic name:

ACRIVASTINE WITH PSEUDOEPHEDRINE

See Semprex-D, page 1123.

Brand name:

ACTIGALL

Pronounced: AK-ti-gawl
Generic name: Ursodiol

Why is this drug prescribed?

Actigall is used to help dissolve certain kinds of gallstones. If you suffer from gallstones but do not want to undergo surgery to remove them, or if age, infirmity, or a poor reaction to anesthesia makes you a poor candidate for surgery, Actigall treatment may be a good alternative.

Actigall is also used to prevent gallstones in people on rapid-weight-loss diets.

Most important fact about this drug

Actigall is not a quick remedy. It takes months of Actigall therapy to dissolve gallstones; and there is a possibility of incomplete dissolution and recurrence of stones. Your doctor will weigh Actigall against alternative treatments and recommend the best one for you.

Actigall is most effective if your gallstones are small or "floatable" (high in cholesterol). In addition, your gallbladder must still be functioning properly.

How should you take this medication?

Take Actigall exactly as prescribed; otherwise the gallstones may dissolve too slowly or not dissolve at all. During treatment, your doctor will do periodic ultrasound exams to see if your stones are dissolving.

- *If you miss a dose...*
  Take it as soon as you remember, or at the same time as the next dose.

- *Storage instructions...*
  Store at room temperature in a tightly closed container.

What side effects may occur?

Side effects cannot be anticipated. If any develop or change in intensity, inform your doctor as soon as possible. Only your doctor can determine if it is safe for you to continue taking Actigall.

■ *Side effects may include:*
Abdominal pain, allergy, arthritis, back pain, bronchitis, chest pain, constipation, cough, diarrhea, dizziness, fatigue, flu-like symptoms, gas, hair loss, headache, indigestion, insomnia, joint pain, menstrual pain, muscle and bone pain, nasal inflammation, nausea, sinus inflammation, sore throat, stomach or intestinal disorder, upper respiratory tract infection, urinary tract infection, viral infection, vomiting

Why should this drug not be prescribed?
Do not take this medication if you are sensitive to or have ever had an allergic reaction to ursodiol or to other bile acids.

Actigall will not dissolve certain types of gallstones. If your doctor tells you that your gallstones are calcified cholesterol stones, radio-opaque stones, or radiolucent bile pigment stones, you are not a candidate for treatment with Actigall.

Also, if you have biliary tract (liver, gallbladder, bile duct) problems or certain liver and pancreas diseases, your doctor may not be able to prescribe Actigall for you.

Special warnings about this medication
Although Actigall is not known to cause liver damage, it is theoretically possible in some people. Your doctor may run blood tests for liver function before you start to take Actigall and again while you are taking it.

Possible food and drug interactions
when taking this medication
If Actigall is taken with certain other drugs, the effects of either could be increased, decreased, or altered. It is especially important to check with your doctor before combining Actigall with the following:

Aluminum-based antacid medications (Alu-Cap, Alu-Tab, Rolaids, others)
Cholesterol-lowering medications, such as Lopid, Mevacor, Questran, and Colestid
Estrogens such as Premarin
Oral contraceptives

Special information
if you are pregnant or breastfeeding
If you are pregnant or plan to become pregnant, inform your doctor immediately. So far, there is no evidence that Actigall can harm an unborn

baby; but to be safe, the medication is not recommended during pregnancy. Caution is needed during breastfeeding; it is not known whether Actigall taken by a nursing mother passes into her breast milk.

Recommended dosage

DISSOLVING GALLSTONES

The recommended daily dosage is 8 to 10 milligrams per 2.2 pounds of body weight, divided into 2 or 3 doses.

PREVENTING GALLSTONES

The usual dose in people losing weight rapidly is 300 milligrams twice a day.

Overdosage

Although there have been no reports of overdose with Actigall, the most likely symptom of severe overdose would be diarrhea. Since any medication taken in excess can have serious consequences, you should seek medical attention immediately if you suspect an Actigall overdose.

Brand name:

ACTRON

See Orudis, page 898.

Generic name:

ACYCLOVIR

See Zovirax, page 1410.

Brand name:

ADALAT

See Procardia, page 1011.

Generic name:

ADAPALENE

See Differin, page 372.

Brand name:

ADDERALL

Pronounced: ADD-ur-all
Generic ingredients: Amphetamines

Why is this drug prescribed?

Adderall is prescribed in the treatment of attention-deficit disorder with hyperactivity, the condition in which a child exhibits a short attention span and becomes easily distracted, overly emotional, excessively active, and highly impulsive. It should be used as part of a broader treatment plan that includes psychological, educational, and social measures.

Adderall is also prescribed for narcolepsy (uncontrollable attacks of sleep).

Most important fact about this drug

Adderall, like all amphetamines, has a high potential for abuse. If used in large doses over long periods of time, it can cause dependence and addiction. Be careful to take Adderall only as prescribed.

How should you take this medication?

Never take more Adderall than your doctor has prescribed. Do not take it for a longer time or for any other purpose than prescribed.

Take the first dose upon awakening. If additional doses are prescribed, take them at intervals of 4 to 6 hours. Avoid late evening doses, which can interfere with sleep.

- *If you miss a dose...*

  If you are taking 1 dose a day, and at least 6 hours remain before bedtime, take the dose as soon as you remember. If you don't remember until the next day, skip the dose and go back to your regular schedule. Do not take a double dose.

  If you are taking more than 1 dose a day, and you remember within an hour or so of the scheduled time, take the missed dose immediately. Otherwise, skip the dose and go back to your regular schedule. Never take 2 doses at once.

- *Storage instructions...*

  Store at room temperature in a tight, light-resistant container.

What side effects may occur?

Side effects cannot be anticipated. If any develop or change in intensity, tell your doctor as soon as possible. Only your doctor can determine if it is safe for you or your child to continue taking Adderall.

■ *Side effects may include:*

Changes in sex drive, constipation, depression, diarrhea, dizziness, dry mouth, exaggerated feelings of well-being, headache, high blood pressure, hives, impotence, insomnia, loss of appetite, mental disturbances, overstimulation, rapid or pounding heartbeat, restlessness, stomach and intestinal disturbances, tremor, twitches, unpleasant taste, weakened heart, weight loss, worsening of tics (including Tourette's syndrome)

Why should this drug not be prescribed?

Do not use Adderall if you have any of the following conditions:

Heart disease
Hardening of the arteries
High blood pressure
High pressure in the eye (glaucoma)
Overactive thyroid gland

Never take Adderall within 14 days of taking an antidepressant classified as an MAO inhibitor, including Nardil and Parnate. A potentially life-threatening spike in blood pressure could result.

Your doctor will not prescribe Adderall if you have ever had a reaction to similar stimulant drugs. The doctor will also avoid prescribing Adderall if you appear agitated or are prone to substance abuse.

Special warnings about this medication

If you have even a mild case of high blood pressure, take Adderall with caution. Be careful, too, about driving or operating machinery until you know how this drug affects you. It may impair judgment and coordination.

Adderall can make tics and twitches worse. If you or a family member has this problem (or the condition called Tourette's syndrome), make sure the doctor is aware of it.

If the problem is attention-deficit disorder, the doctor will do a complete history and evaluation before prescribing Adderall, taking particular account of the severity of the symptoms and the age of your child. If the problem is a temporary reaction to a stressful situation, Adderall is probably not called for.

At present, there has been no experience with long-term Adderall therapy in children. However, other amphetamine-based medications have been known to stunt growth, so your doctor will need to watch the child carefully.

Possible food and drug interactions when taking this medication

If Adderall is taken with certain other drugs, the effects of either could be increased, decreased, or altered. It is especially important to check with your doctor before combining Adderall with the following:

Acetazolamide (Diamox)
Antihistamines such as Benadryl and Chlor-Trimeton
Drugs classified as MAO inhibitors, including the antidepressants Nardil and Parnate
Drugs that make the urine more acid, such as Uroquid-Acid No. 2
Fruit juices and vitamin C
Glutamic acid (an amino acid related to MSG)
High blood pressure medications such as Calan, Esimil, HydroDIURIL, Hytrin, Procardia, and Serpasil
Lithium (Lithonate)
Major tranquilizers such as Haldol and Thorazine
Meperidine (Demerol)
Methenamine (Urised)
Norepinephrine (Levophed)
Propoxyphene (Darvon)
Seizure medications such as Dilantin, phenobarbital, and Zarontin
"Tricyclic" antidepressants such as Norpramin, Tofranil, and Vivactil

Special information if you are pregnant or breastfeeding

Heavy use of amphetamines during pregnancy can lead to premature birth or low birth weight. Avoid taking Adderall unless absolutely necessary. Amphetamines do find their way into breast milk, so you should not take Adderall while breastfeeding.

Recommended dosage

Whether the problem is attention-deficit disorder or narcolepsy, the doctor will keep the dosage as low as possible.

ATTENTION-DEFICIT DISORDER WITH HYPERACTIVITY

Children 3 to 5 years of age

The usual starting dose is 2.5 milligrams daily. Each week, the doctor will raise the daily dosage by 2.5 milligrams until the condition is under control.

Children 6 years of age and older

The usual starting dose is 5 milligrams once or twice a day. Each week, the daily dosage may be increased by 5 milligrams. Only in rare cases will a child need more than 40 milligrams per day.

The doctor may interrupt therapy occasionally to see if the drug is still needed.

NARCOLEPSY

Adults

The usual total daily dose ranges from 5 to 60 milligrams, taken as 2 or more smaller doses.

Children under 12 years of age

The usual starting dose is 5 milligrams daily. Each week, the doctor will raise the daily dose by 5 milligrams until the condition is under control.

Children 12 years of age and older

The usual starting dose is 10 milligrams daily, with weekly increases of 10 milligrams daily until the drug takes effect.

Overdosage

A large overdose of Adderall can be fatal. Warning signs of a massive overdose include convulsions and coma.

■ *Symptoms of Adderall overdose may include:*
Abdominal cramps, assaultiveness, changes in blood pressure, confusion, diarrhea, hallucinations, heightened reflexes, high fever, irregular heartbeat, nausea, panic, rapid breathing, restlessness, tremor, vomiting

If you suspect an overdose, seek emergency treatment immediately.

Brand name:

ADIPEX-P

See Fastin, page 484.

Brand name:

ADVIL

See Motrin, page 795.

Brand name:

AEROBID

Pronounced: AIR-oh-bid
Generic name: Flunisolide
Other brand names: AeroBid-M, Nasalide

Why is this drug prescribed?

AeroBid is prescribed for people who need long-term treatment to control and prevent the symptoms of asthma. It contains an anti-inflammatory steroid type of medication and may reduce or eliminate your need for other corticosteroids. A nasal-spray form of the drug (Nasalide) is available for relief of hay fever.

Most important fact about this drug

AeroBid helps to reduce the likelihood of an asthma attack, but will not relieve one that has already started. To be effective as a preventive measure, it must be taken every day at regularly spaced intervals. It may be several weeks before you receive its full benefit.

How should you take this medication?

Take this medication at regular intervals, exactly as prescribed by your doctor.

■ *Administration technique:*

1. Place the metal cartridge inside the plastic container.
2. Remove the cap; inspect the mouthpiece for foreign objects.
3. Shake the inhaler thoroughly.
4. Tilt your head slightly and breathe out as completely as possible.

5. Hold the inhaler upright and put the plastic mouthpiece in your mouth; close your lips tightly around it.
6. Press down on the metal cartridge. At the same time, take a slow, deep breath through your mouth.
7. Hold your breath as long as you can. While holding your breath, stop pressing down on the cartridge and remove the mouthpiece from your mouth.
8. Allow at least 1 minute between inhalations.

To help reduce hoarseness, throat irritation, and mouth infection, rinse out with water after each use. If your mouth is sore or has a rash, tell your doctor.

Illustrated instructions for use are available with the product.

- *If you miss a dose...*
  Use it as soon as you remember. If it is almost time for your next dose, skip the one you missed and go back to your regular schedule. Do not take 2 doses at the same time.

- *Storage instructions...*
  Store away from heat or cold and light. Keep away from open flames.

What side effects may occur?
Side effects cannot be anticipated. If any develop or change in intensity, inform your doctor as soon as possible. Only your doctor can determine if it is safe for you to continue taking AeroBid.

- *More common side effects may include:*
  Cold symptoms, diarrhea, flu, headache, infection of the upper respiratory tract, nasal congestion, nausea, sore throat, unpleasant taste, upset stomach, vomiting

- *Less common side effects may include:*
  Abdominal pain, chest congestion, chest pain, cough, decreased appetite, dizziness, ear infection, eczema (inflamed skin with sores and crusting), fever, heartburn, hoarseness, inflamed lining of the nose, irritability, itching, loss of smell or taste, menstrual disturbances, nervousness, phlegm, rapid, fluttering heartbeat, rash, runny nose, shakiness, sinus congestion, sinus drainage, sinus infection, sinus inflammation, sneezing, swelling due to fluid retention, wheezing, yeastlike fungal infection of the mouth and throat

- *Rare side effects may include:*
  Acne, anxiety, blurred vision, bronchitis, chest tightness, chills, constipation, depression, difficult or labored breathing, dry throat, earache, excessive restlessness, eye discomfort, eye infection, faintness, fatigue, gas, general feeling of illness, head stuffiness, high blood pressure, hives, inability to fall or stay asleep, increased appetite, indigestion, inflammation of the tongue, laryngitis, moodiness, mouth irritation, nasal irritation, nosebleed, numbness, pneumonia, rapid heart rate, sinus discomfort, sluggishness, sweating, swelling of the arms and legs, throat irritation, vertigo, weakness, weight gain

Why should this drug not be prescribed?

This medication is not for treatment of prolonged, severe asthma attacks where more intensive measures are required.

If you are allergic or sensitive to AeroBid or other steroid drugs, advise your doctor. This medication may not be right for you.

Special warnings about this medication

Your asthma should be reasonably stable before treatment with AeroBid Inhaler is started. AeroBid should be started in combination with your usual dose of an oral steroid medication. After approximately 1 week, your doctor will start to withdraw gradually the oral steroid by reducing the daily or alternate daily dose. A slow rate of reduction is very important, as some people have experienced withdrawal symptoms such as joint and/or muscular pain, fatigue, and depression. Tell your doctor if you lose weight or feel light-headed. You may need to take more oral corticosteroid temporarily.

This medication is not useful when you need rapid relief of asthma symptoms.

Transferring from steroid tablet therapy to AeroBid Inhaler may produce allergic conditions that were previously controlled by the steroid tablet therapy. These include rhinitis (inflammation of the mucous membrane of the nose), conjunctivitis (pinkeye), and eczema.

Contact your doctor immediately if you have an asthma attack that isn't controlled by a bronchodilator while you are being treated with AeroBid. You may need an oral steroid drug.

While you are being treated with AeroBid, particularly at higher doses, your doctor will carefully observe you for any evidence of side effects such as the suppression of glandular function and diminished bone growth in children. If you have just had surgery or are under extreme stress, your doctor will also closely monitor you.

The use of AeroBid may cause a yeastlike fungal infection of the mouth, pharynx (throat), or larynx (voice box). If you suspect a fungal infection, notify your doctor. Treatment with antifungal medication may be necessary.

Since the contents of this inhalant are under pressure, do not puncture the container and do not use or store the medication near heat or an open flame. Exposure to temperatures above 120 degrees may cause the container to explode.

People taking drugs such as AeroBid that suppress the immune system are more open to infection. Take extra care to avoid exposure to measles and chickenpox if you've never had them or never had shots. Such diseases can be serious or even fatal when your immune system is below par. If you are exposed, tell your doctor immediately.

Also, if you have tuberculosis, a herpes infection of the eye, or any other kind of infection, make sure the doctor knows about it. You probably should not use AeroBid.

Possible food and drug interactions when taking this medication
No interactions have been reported.

Special information if you are pregnant or breastfeeding
The effects of AeroBid during pregnancy have not been adequately studied. If you are pregnant or plan to become pregnant, inform your doctor immediately. It is not known whether AeroBid appears in breast milk. If this medication is essential to your health, your doctor may advise you to discontinue breastfeeding your baby until your treatment with this medication is finished.

Recommended dosage
The AeroBid Inhaler system is for oral inhalation only.

ADULTS

The recommended starting dose is 2 inhalations twice daily, in the morning and evening, for a total daily dose of 1 milligram. The daily dose should not exceed 4 inhalations twice a day, for a total daily dose of 2 milligrams.

CHILDREN

For children 6 to 15 years of age, 2 inhalations may be used twice daily, for a total daily dose of 1 milligram.

The safety and effectiveness of this drug have not been established in children under 6 years of age.

Overdosage
Any medication taken in excess can have serious consequences. If you suspect an overdose, seek emergency medical treatment immediately.

Brand name:

AKTOB

See Tobrex, page 1247.

Generic name:

ALBUTEROL

See Proventil, page 1029.

Generic name:

ALCLOMETASONE

See Aclovate, page 11.

Brand name:

ALDACTAZIDE

Pronounced: al-DAK-tah-zide
Generic ingredients: Spironolactone, Hydrochlorothiazide
Other brand name: Spirozide

Why is this drug prescribed?
Aldactazide is used in the treatment of high blood pressure and other conditions that require the elimination of excess fluid from the body. These conditions include congestive heart failure, cirrhosis of the liver, and kidney disease. Aldactazide combines two diuretic drugs that help your body produce and eliminate more urine. Spironolactone, one of the ingredients, helps to minimize the potassium loss that can be caused by the hydrochlorothiazide component.

Most important fact about this drug
If you have high blood pressure, you must take Aldactazide regularly for it to be effective. Since blood pressure declines gradually, it may be several weeks

before you get the full benefit of Aldactazide; and you must continue taking it even if you are feeling well. Aldactazide does not cure high blood pressure; it merely keeps it under control.

How should you take this medication?
Take Aldactazide exactly as prescribed. Stopping Aldactazide suddenly could cause your condition to worsen.

■ *If you miss a dose...*
Take it as soon as you remember. If it is almost time for your next dose, skip the one you missed and go back to your regular schedule. Never take 2 doses at the same time.

■ *Storage instructions...*
Store at room temperature.

What side effects may occur?
Side effects cannot be anticipated. If any develop or change in intensity, inform your doctor as soon as possible. Only your doctor can determine if it is safe for you to continue taking Aldactazide.

■ *Side effects may include:*
Abdominal cramps, breast development in males, change in potassium levels (leading to such symptoms as dry mouth, excessive thirst, weak or irregular heartbeat, and muscle pain or cramps), deepening of the voice, diarrhea, dizziness, dizziness on rising, drowsiness, excessive hairiness, fever, headache, hives, inflammation of blood vessels or lymph vessels, inflammation of the pancreas, irregular menstruation, lack of coordination, liver problems, loss of appetite, mental confusion, muscle spasms, nausea, postmenopausal bleeding, rash, red or purple spots on skin, restlessness, sensitivity to light, severe allergic reaction, sexual dysfunction, sluggishness, stomach bleeding, stomach inflammation, stomach ulcers, tingling or pins and needles, vertigo, vomiting, weakness, yellow eyes and skin, yellow vision

Why should this drug not be prescribed?
Aldactazide should not be used if you have acute kidney disease or liver failure, have difficulty urinating or are unable to urinate, or have high potassium levels in your blood.

If you are sensitive to or have ever had an allergic reaction to spironolactone, hydrochlorothiazide, or similar drugs, or if you are sensitive to sulfa drugs, you should not take this medication. Make sure your doctor is aware of any drug reactions you may have experienced.

Special warnings about this medication

This medication should be used only if your doctor has determined that the precise amount of each ingredient in Aldactazide meets your specific needs.

Potassium supplements (including salt substitutes) or diuretics that leave high levels of potassium in your body should not be used while taking Aldactazide, unless specifically recommended by your doctor.

If you are taking an ACE-inhibitor type of blood pressure medication such as Vasotec, this drug should be used with extreme caution.

If you have liver disease or lupus erythematosus (a disease that causes skin eruptions), Aldactazide should be used with caution.

Excessive sweating, dehydration, severe diarrhea, or vomiting could cause you to lose too much water and cause your blood pressure to become too low. Be careful when exercising and in hot weather.

Notify your doctor or dentist that you are taking Aldactazide if you have a medical emergency, and before you have surgery or dental treatment.

Possible food and drug interactions
when taking this medication

If Aldactazide is taken with certain other drugs, the effects of either could be increased, decreased, or altered. It is especially important to check with your doctor before combining Aldactazide with the following:

ACE-inhibitor blood pressure drugs such as Vasotec
Antigout medications such as Zyloprim
Digoxin (Lanoxin)
Diuretics such as Lasix and Midamor
Indomethacin (Indocin)
Insulin or oral antidiabetic drugs such as Micronase
Lithium (Lithonate)
Norepinephrine (Levophed)
Potassium supplements such as Slow-K
Steroids such as prednisone

Special information
if you are pregnant or breastfeeding

The effects of Aldactazide during pregnancy have not been adequately studied. If you are pregnant or plan to become pregnant, inform your doctor immediately. Aldactazide appears in breast milk and could affect a nursing infant. If this medication is essential to your health, your doctor may advise you to discontinue breastfeeding until your treatment is finished.

Recommended dosage

ADULTS

Congestive Heart Failure, Cirrhosis, Nephrotic Syndrome (kidney disorder)
The usual dosage is 100 milligrams each of spironolactone and hydrochlorothiazide daily, taken as a single dose or in divided doses. Dosage may range from 25 milligrams to 200 milligrams of each ingredient daily, depending on your individual needs.

High Blood Pressure
The usual dose is 50 milligrams to 100 milligrams each of spironolactone and hydrochlorothiazide daily, in a single dose or divided into smaller doses.

CHILDREN

The usual dose of Aldactazide should provide 0.75 milligram to 1.5 milligrams of spironolactone per pound of body weight.

Overdosage
Although there is no information on specific signs of Aldactazide overdose, any medication taken in excess can have serious consequences. If you suspect an overdose, seek medical attention immediately.

Brand name:

ALDACTONE

Pronounced: al-DAK-tone
Generic name: Spironolactone

Why is this drug prescribed?
Aldactone flushes excess salt and water from the body and controls high blood pressure. It is used in the diagnosis and treatment of hyperaldosteronism, a condition in which the adrenal gland secretes too much aldosterone (a hormone that regulates the body's salt and potassium levels). It is also used in treating other conditions that require the elimination of excess fluid from the body. These conditions include congestive heart failure, high blood

pressure, cirrhosis of the liver, kidney disease, and unusually low potassium levels in the blood. When used for high blood pressure, Aldactone can be taken alone or with other high blood pressure medications.

Most important fact about this drug
If you have high blood pressure, you must take Aldactone regularly for it to be effective. Since blood pressure declines gradually, it may be several weeks before you get the full benefit of Aldactone; and you must continue taking it even if you are feeling well. Aldactone does not cure high blood pressure; it merely keeps it under control.

How should you take this medication?
Take Aldactone exactly as prescribed by your doctor. Stopping Aldactone suddenly could cause your condition to worsen.

■ *If you miss a dose...*
Take it as soon as you remember. If it is almost time for your next dose, skip the one you missed and go back to your regular schedule. Never take 2 doses at the same time.

■ *Storage instructions...*
Store at room temperature.

What side effects may occur?
Side effects cannot be anticipated. If any develop or change in intensity, inform your doctor as soon as possible. Only your doctor can determine if it is safe for you to continue taking Aldactone.

■ *Side effects may include:*
Abdominal cramps, breast development in males, change in potassium levels (leading to such symptoms as dry mouth, excessive thirst, weak or irregular heartbeat, and muscle pain or cramps), deepening of voice, diarrhea, drowsiness, excessive hairiness, fever, headache, hives, irregular menstruation, lack of coordination, lethargy, liver problems, mental confusion, postmenopausal bleeding, severe allergic reaction, sexual dysfunction, skin eruptions, stomach bleeding, stomach inflammation, ulcers, vomiting

Why should this drug not be prescribed?
You should not take Aldactone if you have kidney disease, an inability to urinate, difficulty urinating, or high potassium levels in your blood.

Special warnings about this medication

Potassium supplements or other diuretics that leave your potassium levels high, such as Maxzide, should not be used while taking Aldactone, unless specifically indicated by your doctor.

ACE inhibitors (Vasotec, Capoten), used for blood pressure and heart failure, should not be taken while using Aldactone.

If you are taking Aldactone, your kidney function should be given a complete assessment and should continue to be monitored.

If you have liver disease, your doctor will be cautious about using this medication.

Excessive sweating, dehydration, severe diarrhea, or vomiting could cause you to lose too much water and cause your blood pressure to become too low. Be careful when exercising and in hot weather.

Notify your doctor or dentist that you are taking Aldactone if you have a medical emergency, and before you have surgery or dental treatment.

Possible food and drug interactions
when taking this medication

If Aldactone is taken with certain other drugs, the effects of either could be increased, decreased, or altered. It is especially important to check with your doctor before combining Aldactone with the following:

ACE inhibitors such as Vasotec and Capoten
Digoxin (Lanoxin)
Indomethacin (Indocin)
Norepinephrine (Levophed)
Other water pills such as Lasix and HydroDIURIL
Other high blood pressure medications such as Aldomet and
  Procardia XL

Special information
if you are pregnant or breastfeeding

The effects of Aldactone during pregnancy have not been adequately studied. If you are pregnant or plan to become pregnant, inform your doctor immediately. Aldactone appears in breast milk and could affect a nursing infant. If this medication is essential to your health, your doctor may advise you to discontinue breastfeeding until your treatment with this medication is finished.

Recommended dosage

ADULTS

Primary Hyperaldosteronism

Initial dosages of this medication are used to determine the presence of primary hyperaldosteronism (too much secretion of the adrenal hormone aldosterone). People can be tested with this medication over either a long or a short period of time.

In the long test, you take 400 milligrams per day for 3 to 4 weeks. If your potassium levels and blood pressure are corrected with this dosage in this time period, your physician may assume you have this condition.

In the short test, you receive 400 milligrams per day for 4 days. A laboratory test compares potassium levels while you are on Aldactone and after the medication is stopped. Your doctor may then make a diagnosis.

After the diagnosis of primary hyperaldosteronism is made and confirmed by more tests, the usual dose is 100 to 400 milligrams per day, prior to surgery. In those who are not good candidates for surgery, this drug is given over the long term at the lowest effective dose.

Adult Edema (Congestive Heart Failure, Cirrhosis of the Liver, or Kidney Disorders)

The usual starting dosage is 100 milligrams daily either in a single dose or divided into smaller doses. However, your doctor may have you take daily doses as low as 25 milligrams or as high as 200 milligrams.

Your doctor may choose to adjust your dosage after an initial 5-day trial period or add another diuretic medication to this one.

Essential Hypertension (High Blood Pressure)

The usual starting dosage is 50 to 100 milligrams daily in a single dose or divided into smaller doses. This medication may be given with another diuretic or with other high blood pressure medications.

It may be up to 2 weeks before the full effect of this medication is seen. Your doctor can then adjust the dosage according to your response.

Hypokalemia (Potassium Loss)

Your doctor may have you take daily dosages of 25 milligrams to 100 milligrams when potassium loss caused by the effects of a diuretic cannot be treated by a potassium supplement.

CHILDREN

Edema (Swelling Due to Water Retention)
The usual starting dosage is 1.5 milligrams per pound of body weight daily in a single dose or divided into smaller doses.

Overdosage
Although no specific information on signs of Aldactone overdose is available, any medication taken in excess can have serious consequences. If you suspect an overdose, seek medical attention immediately.

Brand name:

ALDOMET

Pronounced: AL-doe-met
Generic name: Methyldopa

Why is this drug prescribed?
Aldomet is used to treat high blood pressure. It is effective when used alone or with other high blood pressure medications.

Most important fact about this drug
You must take Aldomet regularly for it to be effective. Since blood pressure declines gradually, it may be several weeks before you get the full benefit of Aldomet; and you must continue taking it even if you are feeling well. Aldomet does not cure high blood pressure; it merely keeps it under control.

How should you take this medication?
Take this medication exactly as prescribed. Try not to miss any doses. Do not stop taking the drug without your doctor's knowledge.

Drowsiness may occur when dosage is increased. If your doctor increases the amount of Aldomet you take, start the new dosage in the evening.

■ *If you miss a dose...*
  Take it as soon as you remember. If it is almost time for your next dose, skip the one you missed and go back to your regular schedule. Never take 2 doses at the same time.

- *Storage instructions...*
  Keep Aldomet in the container it came in, tightly closed. Store Aldomet tablets at room temperature. Keep oral suspension in the refrigerator. Protect from light.

What side effects may occur?
Side effects cannot be anticipated. If any develop or change in intensity, inform your doctor as soon as possible. Only your doctor can determine if it is safe for you to continue taking Aldomet.

- *More common side effects may include:*
  Drowsiness during the first few weeks of therapy, fluid retention or weight gain, headache, weakness

- *Less common or rare side effects may include:*
  Anemia, Bell's palsy (paralysis of the face, making it look distorted), bloating, blood disorders, breast development in males, breast enlargement, changes in menstruation, chest pain, congestive heart failure, constipation, decreased mental ability, decreased sex drive, depression, diarrhea, dizziness when standing up, dry mouth, fever, gas, hepatitis, impotence, inflammation of the large intestine, inflammation of the pancreas, inflammation of the salivary glands, involuntary movements, joint pain, light-headedness, liver disorders, milk production, muscle pain, nasal stuffiness, nausea, nightmares, parkinsonism (tremors, shuffling walk, stooped posture, muscle weakness), rash, slow heartbeat, sore or "black" tongue, tingling or pins and needles, vomiting, yellow eyes and skin

Why should this drug not be prescribed?
If you have liver disease or cirrhosis, or if you have taken Aldomet before and developed liver disease, do not take this medication.

If you are sensitive to or have ever had an allergic reaction to Aldomet, or if you have been prescribed the oral suspension form of Aldomet and have ever had an allergic reaction to sulfites, you should not take this medication.

If you are taking drugs known as monoamine oxidase (MAO) inhibitors, you should not take Aldomet.

Special warnings about this medication
Before you begin taking Aldomet, your doctor should perform a complete study of your liver function, and it should be monitored periodically thereafter.

Aldomet can cause liver disorders. You may develop a fever, jaundice (yellow eyes and skin), or both, usually within the first 2 to 3 months of therapy. If either of these symptoms occurs, stop taking Aldomet and contact your doctor immediately. If the fever and/or jaundice were caused by the medication, your liver function should gradually return to normal.

If you have a history of liver disease, this medication should be used with caution.

Hemolytic anemia, a blood disorder in which red blood cells are destroyed, can develop with long-term use of Aldomet; your doctor will do periodic blood counts to check for this problem.

Aldomet can cause water retention or weight gain in some people. A diuretic will usually relieve these symptoms.

If you have asthma and are taking the liquid form of Aldomet, you could have an allergic reaction to the sulfite component of the liquid.

If you are on dialysis and are taking Aldomet for high blood pressure, your blood pressure may rise after your dialysis treatments.

Aldomet can cause you to become drowsy or less alert, especially during the first few weeks of therapy or when dosage levels are increased. If it affects you this way, driving or operating heavy machinery or participating in any hazardous activity that requires full mental alertness is not recommended.

Notify your doctor or dentist that you are taking Aldomet if you have a medical emergency and before you have surgery or dental treatment.

**Possible food and drug interactions
when taking this medication**
If Aldomet is taken with certain other drugs, the effects of either could be increased, decreased, or altered. It is especially important to check with your doctor before combining Aldomet with the following:

Antidepressants known as MAO inhibitors, including Nardil and Parnate
Dextroamphetamine (Dexedrine)
Imipramine (Tofranil)
Iron-containing products such as Feosol
Lithium (Lithonate)
Other blood pressure medications such as Catapres and Calan
Phenylpropanolamine (a decongestant used in common cold remedies
    such as Dimetapp, Entex LA, and others)
Propranolol (Inderal)
Tolbutamide (Orinase)

Special information
if you are pregnant or breastfeeding

The use of Aldomet during pregnancy appears to be relatively safe. However, if you are pregnant or plan to become pregnant, inform your doctor immediately. Aldomet appears in breast milk and could affect a nursing infant. If this medication is essential to your health, your doctor may advise you to discontinue breastfeeding until your treatment is finished.

Recommended dosage

ADULTS

The usual starting dose is 250 milligrams, 2 or 3 times per day in the first 48 hours of treatment. Your doctor may increase or decrease your dose over the next few days to achieve the correct blood pressure.

To reduce the effect of any sedation the medication may cause, dosage increases will usually be given in the evening.

The usual maintenance dosage is 500 milligrams to 2 grams per day divided into 2 to 4 doses. The maximum dose is usually 3 grams.

Your doctor will also adjust your dosage of Aldomet when it is taken in combination with certain other high blood pressure drugs.

If you take Aldomet with a non-thiazide high blood pressure medicine, your doctor will limit the initial dosage to 500 milligrams daily divided into small doses.

Dosages will be adjusted, and other high blood pressure drugs may be added, during the first few months of treatment with Aldomet. Those with reduced kidney function may require smaller doses. Older people who are prone to fainting spells due to arterial disease may also require smaller doses.

CHILDREN

The usual starting dose is 10 milligrams per 2.2 pounds of body weight daily, divided into 2 to 4 doses. Doses will be adjusted until blood pressure is normal. The maximum daily dose is usually 65 milligrams per 2.2 pounds of body weight or 3 grams, whichever is less.

OLDER ADULTS

Dosages of this drug are adjusted to each individual's needs. Lower doses may be prescribed by your doctor.

Overdosage

Any medication taken in excess can have serious consequences. If you suspect an overdose, seek medical attention immediately.

■ *Symptoms of Aldomet overdose may include:*
Bloating, constipation, diarrhea, dizziness, extreme drowsiness, gas, light-headedness, nausea, severely low blood pressure, slow heartbeat, vomiting, weakness

Generic name:

ALENDRONATE

See Fosamax, page 526.

Brand name:

ALEVE

See Anaprox, page 63.

Brand name:

ALLEGRA

Pronounced: ah-LEG-rah
Generic name: Fexofenadine hydrochloride

Why is this drug prescribed?

Allegra relieves the itchy, runny nose, sneezing, and itchy, red, watery eyes that come with hay fever. Its effect begins in 1 hour and lasts 12 hours, peaking around the second or third hour. Allegra is one of the new type of antihistamines that rarely cause drowsiness.

Most important fact about this drug

Seldane, an antihistamine related to Allegra, has been implicated in dangerous interactions with the common antibiotic erythromycin, the antifungal medication ketoconazole (Nizoral), and several similar drugs. Allegra poses no such risks. It is also safe for people with liver disease.

How should you take this medication?

Take Allegra only as prescribed.

- *If you miss a dose...*
  Take it as soon as you remember. If it is almost time for your next dose, skip the one you missed and go back to your regular schedule. Do not take 2 doses at once.

- *Storage instructions...*
  Store at room temperature. Protect blister packs from moisture.

What side effects may occur?
Side effects cannot be anticipated. If any develop or change in intensity, tell your doctor as soon as possible. Only your doctor can determine if it is safe for you to continue taking Allegra.

- *Side effects may include:*
  Colds or flu, drowsiness, fatigue, indigestion, menstrual problems, nausea

Why should this drug not be prescribed?
If Allegra gives you an allergic reaction, avoid it in the future.

Special warnings about this medication
If you have a kidney problem, you should take half the usual dose.

**Possible food and drug interactions
when taking this medication**
No interactions have been reported.

**Special information
if you are pregnant or breastfeeding**
The effects of this drug during pregnancy have not been adequately studied. If you are pregnant or plan to become pregnant, inform your doctor immediately. It is not known whether Allegra appears in breast milk. If the drug is essential to your health, your doctor may advise you to stop nursing until your treatment is finished.

Recommended dosage

ADULTS

The usual dosage is 1 capsule (60 milligrams) twice a day. People with kidney problems should take only 1 dose a day.

CHILDREN

Not for children under 12.

Overdosage

An overdose is unlikely to produce serious symptoms. Nevertheless, an excessive dose of any medicine can have serious consequences, so you should seek medical attention whenever an overdose is suspected.

Generic name:

ALLOPURINOL

See Zyloprim, page 1419.

Brand name:

ALORA

See Estraderm, page 469.

Generic name:

ALPRAZOLAM

See Xanax, page 1370.

Generic name:

ALPROSTADIL

See Caverject, page 205.

Brand name:

ALTACE

Pronounced: AL-tayce
Generic name: Ramipril

Why is this drug prescribed?

Altace is used in the treatment of high blood pressure. It is effective when used alone or in combination with other high blood pressure medications, especially thiazide-type water pills (diuretics). Altace works by preventing the conversion of a chemical in your blood called angiotensin I into a more potent substance that increases salt and water retention in your body. It also enhances blood flow in your circulatory system. It is a member of the group of drugs called ACE inhibitors.

Altace is also prescribed for people who show signs of congestive heart failure after a heart attack. It helps prevent the condition from getting worse.

Most important fact about this drug

If you are taking Altace for high blood pressure, you must take the drug regularly for it to be effective. Since blood pressure declines gradually, it may be several weeks before you get the full benefit of Altace; and you must continue taking it even if you are feeling well. Altace does not cure high blood pressure; it merely keeps it under control.

How should you take this medication?

Take this medication exactly as prescribed by your doctor. If you have difficulty swallowing the capsule, you can sprinkle the contents on a small amount (about 4 ounces) of apple sauce, or mix the contents with 4 ounces of water or apple juice. Be sure to eat or drink the entire mixture so that you get the full dose of the drug. You can prepare the mixture ahead of time; it will keep for 24 hours at room temperature or 48 hours in the refrigerator.

■ *If you miss a dose...*
If you forget to take a dose, take it as soon as you remember. If it is almost time for your next dose, skip the one you missed and go back to your regular schedule. Never take 2 doses at the same time.

■ *Storage instructions...*
Store Altace at room temperature in a tightly closed container.

What side effects may occur?

Side effects cannot be anticipated. If any develop or change in intensity, inform your doctor as soon as possible. Only your doctor can determine if it is safe for you to continue taking Altace.

■ *More common side effects may include:*
Cough, headache (in people with high blood pressure); cough, dizziness, low blood pressure (in people with congestive heart failure)

■ *Less common or rare side effects may include:*
Abdominal pain, anemia, angina pectoris (chest pain), anxiety, arthritis, bruises, change in taste, constipation, convulsions, depression, diarrhea, difficulty swallowing, dizziness, dry mouth, fainting, fatigue, feeling of

general discomfort, fever, fluid retention, heart failure, hearing loss, heart attack, impotence, inability to sleep, increased salivation, indigestion, inflammation of the stomach and intestines, irregular heartbeat, itching, joint pain or inflammation, labored breathing, light-headedness, loss of appetite, low blood pressure, memory loss, muscle pain, nausea, nerve pain, nervousness, nosebleed, rash, ringing in ears, skin reddening, skin sensitivity to light, sleepiness, sudden loss of strength, sweating, tingling or pins and needles, tremors, vertigo, very rapid heartbeat, vision changes, vomiting, weakness, weight gain

People prescribed the drug after a heart attack may also experience light-headedness when standing; more severe heart failure is also a possibility.

Why should this drug not be prescribed?

If you are sensitive to or have ever had an allergic reaction to Altace, or if you have a history of swelling of the face, tongue, or throat while taking similar drugs such as Capoten, Vasotec, and Zestril, you should not take this medication. Make sure that your doctor is aware of any drug reactions that you have experienced.

Special warnings about this medication

If you develop swelling of the face around your lips, tongue, or throat or difficulty swallowing, difficulty breathing, swelling of arms and legs, or infection, sore throat, and fever, you should contact your doctor immediately. You may have a serious side effect of the drug and need emergency treatment.

If you are taking Altace, your kidney function should be given a complete assessment and should continue to be monitored.

If you notice your skin or the whites of your eyes turning yellow, notify your doctor. Your liver may be affected, and you may have to stop taking Altace. Your doctor should routinely test your liver function while you are on this drug.

Altace should be used with caution if you have impaired liver or kidney function, or a disease of the connective tissue such as lupus erythematosus or scleroderma.

If you are taking diuretics and Altace, or have congestive heart failure, you may develop excessively low blood pressure.

Do not use salt substitutes containing potassium without consulting your doctor. Altace can cause increased potassium levels in your blood, especially if you have diabetes and kidney problems.

Light-headedness can occur when taking Altace, especially during the first days of therapy, and should be reported to your doctor. If fainting occurs, stop taking the medication and notify your doctor immediately.

Dehydration, excessive sweating, severe diarrhea, or vomiting could deplete your body's fluids, causing your blood pressure to drop dangerously.

ACE inhibitors such as Altace have been known to cause severe allergic reactions in people undergoing desensitization therapy with bee or wasp venom. These drugs have also caused severe reactions in kidney dialysis patients.

Possible food and drug interactions
when taking this medication
If Altace is taken with certain other drugs, the effects of either could be increased, decreased, or altered. It is especially important to check with your doctor before combining Altace with the following:

    Alcohol
    Diuretics such as hydrochlorothiazide (found in many blood pressure
        medicines)
    Diuretics that don't wash out potassium, such as spironolactone
        (Aldactone) and the diuretic component in Dyazide, Maxzide,
        Moduretic, and others.
    Lithium (Lithonate, Eskalith)
    Potassium supplements such as K-lyte and K-Tab
    Potassium-containing salt substitutes

Special information
if you are pregnant or breastfeeding
When used during the second and third trimesters, Altace can lead to birth defects, prematurity, and death in developing and newborn babies. If you are pregnant or plan to become pregnant and are taking Altace, Altace should be discontinued as soon as possible. Contact your doctor immediately. Altace may appear in breast milk and could affect a nursing infant. If this medication is essential to your health, your doctor may advise you to avoid breastfeeding.

Recommended dosage

ADULTS

As a precaution, your doctor may have you take the first dose of Altace in his office. To reduce the risk of a severe drop in blood pressure, the dosage of any diuretic you're taking should be reduced or, if possible, eliminated.

High blood pressure

For patients not on diuretics, the usual starting dose is 2.5 milligrams, taken once daily. After blood pressure is under control, the dosage will range from 2.5 to 20 milligrams a day in a single dose or divided into 2 equal doses. If Altace proves insufficient, the doctor may then add a diuretic.

Heart failure after a heart attack

The usual starting dose is 2.5 milligrams taken twice a day. If your blood pressure drops severely, your doctor will reduce the dose to 1.25 milligrams, then slowly increase it back to the starting dose, aiming for a maintenance dose of 5 milligrams twice a day.

If you have kidney problems, your doctor may prescribe a lower than normal dose.

CHILDREN

The safety and effectiveness of Altace in children have not been established.

Overdosage

Any medication taken in excess can have serious consequences. If you suspect an overdose, seek medical attention immediately.

Symptoms of low blood pressure are likely to be the primary warning of an Altace overdose.

Brand name:

ALUPENT

Pronounced: AL-yew-pent
Generic name: Metaproterenol sulfate
Other brand name: Metaprel

Why is this drug prescribed?

Alupent is a bronchodilator prescribed for the prevention and relief of bronchial asthma and bronchial spasms (wheezing) associated with bronchitis and emphysema. Alupent Inhalation Solution is also used to treat acute asthmatic attacks in children 6 years of age and older.

Most important fact about this drug
Alupent's effects last up to 6 hours. It should not be used more frequently than your doctor recommends.

Increasing the number of doses can be dangerous and may actually make symptoms of asthma worse. Fatalities have occurred with excessive use of this medication.

If the dose your doctor recommends does not provide relief of your symptoms, if your symptoms become worse, or if side effects occur, seek medical attention immediately.

How should you take this medication?
Take this medication exactly as prescribed by your doctor.

- *If you miss a dose...*
  Take the dose as soon as you remember. Take any remaining doses for the day at equal intervals thereafter. Do not increase the total for the day or take 2 doses at the same time.

- *Storage instructions...*
  Store at room temperature. Protect from light and excessive humidity. Keep out of reach of children.

What side effects may occur?
Side effects cannot be anticipated. If any develop or change in intensity, inform your doctor as soon as possible. Only your doctor can determine if it is safe for you to continue taking Alupent.

- *Side effects may include:*
  Bad taste in mouth, cough, diarrhea, dizziness, fatigue, headache, high blood pressure, insomnia, nausea, nervousness, rapid or throbbing heartbeat, stomach and intestinal upset, throat irritation, tremors, vomiting, worsening or aggravation of asthma

Side effects can occur when a new aerosol container is used, even though you have had no trouble with the medication in the past. Replacing the container may solve the problem.

Why should this drug not be prescribed?
If you are sensitive to or have ever had an allergic reaction to Alupent or similar drugs, such as Proventil, you should not take this medication. Make sure your doctor is aware of any drug reactions you have experienced.

Unless you are directed to do so by your doctor, do not take this medication if you have an irregular, rapid heart rate.

Special warnings about this medication
When taking Alupent, you should not use other inhaled medications (called sympathomimetics) before checking with your doctor. Only your doctor can determine the sufficient amount of time between inhaled medications.

A single dose of nebulized Alupent used to treat an acute attack of asthma may temporarily relieve symptoms but not completely stop the attack.

Consult your doctor before using this medication if you have a heart condition or convulsive disorder (e.g., epilepsy), high blood pressure, hyperthyroidism, or diabetes mellitus. Alupent can cause significant changes in blood pressure.

Possible food and drug interactions
when taking this medication
If Alupent is taken with certain other drugs, the effects of either could be increased, decreased, or altered. It is especially important to check with your doctor before combining Alupent with the following:

MAO inhibitors (antidepressant drugs such as Nardil and Parnate)
Bronchodilators such as Ventolin and Proventil inhalers
Tricyclic antidepressants such as Elavil and Tofranil

Special information
if you are pregnant or breastfeeding
The effects of Alupent during pregnancy have not been adequately studied. If you are pregnant or plan to become pregnant, inform your doctor immediately. It is not known whether Alupent appears in breast milk. If this medication is essential to your health, your doctor may advise you to stop nursing your baby until your treatment is finished.

Recommended dosage

ADULTS

Inhalation Aerosol
The usual single dose is 2 to 3 inhalations. Inhalation should usually not be repeated more often than about every 3 to 4 hours. Total dosage per day should not exceed 12 inhalations.

Inhalation Solution 5%
Treatment usually need not be repeated more often than every 4 hours to relieve acute attacks of bronchospasm.

As part of a total treatment program for chronic breathing disorders, the inhalation solution may be taken 3 to 4 times per day, as determined by your doctor.

Inhalation solution is given by oral inhalation with the aid of a nebulizer or an intermittent positive pressure breathing (IPPB) apparatus.

The usual single dose with the nebulizer is 10 inhalations. However, a single dose of 5 to 15 inhalations can be taken, as determined by your doctor. The usual single daily dose with the IPPB is 0.3 milliliter diluted in approximately 2.5 milliliters of saline solution. The dosage range is 0.2 to 0.3 milliliter, as determined by your doctor.

Inhalation Solution 0.4% and 0.6% Unit-Dose Vials
The inhalation solution unit-dose vial is administered by oral inhalation using an intermittent positive pressure breathing (IPPB) apparatus. The usual adult dose is 1 vial per treatment. You usually should not need to repeat the treatment more often than every 4 hours for severe attacks of wheezing. You can use the unit-dose vials 3 to 4 times a day.

Syrup
The usual dose is 2 teaspoonfuls, 3 or 4 times a day.

Tablets
The usual dose is 20 milligrams, 3 or 4 times per day.

CHILDREN

Inhalation Aerosol
Alupent Inhalation Aerosol is not recommended for use in children under 12 years of age.

Inhalation Solution 5%
For children aged 6 to 12 years, the usual single dose is 0.1 milliliter, given by oral inhalation with a nebulizer. Dosage can be increased to 0.2 milliliter 3 to 4 times a day.

The unit-dose vial is not recommended for children under 12 years of age.

Syrup

The usual dose for children 6 to 9 years of age or weighing under 60 pounds is 1 teaspoonful, 3 or 4 times a day.

The usual dose for children over 9 years of age or weighing over 60 pounds is 2 teaspoonfuls, 3 or 4 times a day.

Tablets

The usual dose for children 6 to 9 years of age or weighing under 60 pounds is 10 milligrams, 3 or 4 times a day.

The usual dose for children over 9 years of age or weighing over 60 pounds is 20 milligrams, 3 or 4 times a day.

Tablets are not recommended for use in children under 6 years of age.

Overdosage

Any medication taken in excess can have serious consequences.

If you suspect an overdose, seek medical attention immediately.

■ *Symptoms of Alupent overdose may include:*
Dizziness, dry mouth, fatigue, general feeling of bodily discomfort, headache, high or low blood pressure, inability to fall or stay asleep, irregular heartbeat, nausea, nervousness, rapid, fluttery heartbeat, severe, suffocating chest pain, tremors

Brand name:

AMARYL

Pronounced: AM-a-ril
Generic name: Glimepiride

Why is this drug prescribed?

Amaryl is an oral medication used to treat Type II (non-insulin-dependent) diabetes when diet and exercise alone fail to control abnormally high levels of blood sugar. Like other diabetes drugs classified as sulfonylureas, Amaryl lowers blood sugar by stimulating the pancreas to produce more insulin. Amaryl may also be used along with insulin and other diabetes drugs.

Most important fact about this drug
Always remember that Amaryl is an aid to, not a substitute for, good diet and exercise. Failure to follow a sound diet and exercise plan may diminish the results of Amaryl and can lead to serious complications such as dangerously high or low blood sugar levels. Remember, too, that Amaryl is not an oral form of insulin, and cannot be used in place of insulin.

How should you take this medication?
Do not take more or less of this medication than directed by your doctor. Amaryl should be taken with breakfast or the first main meal.

■ *If you miss a dose...*
Take it as soon as you remember. If it is almost time for the next dose, skip the one you missed and go back to your regular schedule. Do not take 2 doses at the same time.

■ *Storage instructions...*
Amaryl should be stored at room temperature in a well-closed container.

What side effects may occur?
Side effects cannot be anticipated. If any develop or change in intensity, tell your doctor as soon as possible. Only your doctor can determine if it is safe for you to continue taking Amaryl.

■ *Less common or rare side effects may include:*
Anemia and other blood disorders, blurred vision, diarrhea, dizziness, headache, itching, muscle weakness, nausea, sensitivity to light, skin rash and eruptions, stomach and intestinal pain, vomiting, yellow eyes and skin

Amaryl, like all oral antidiabetics, can result in hypoglycemia (low blood sugar). The risk of hypoglycemia can be increased by missed meals, alcohol, other medications, fever, injury, infection, surgery, and excessive exercise. To avoid hypoglycemia, closely follow the dietary and exercise regimen suggested by your doctor.

■ *Symptoms of mild low blood sugar may include:*
Blurred vision, cold sweats, dizziness, fast heartbeat, fatigue, headache, hunger, light-headedness, nausea, nervousness

■ *Symptoms of more severe low blood sugar may include:*
Coma, disorientation, pale skin, seizures, shallow breathing

Ask your doctor what steps you should take if you experience mild hypoglycemia. If symptoms of severe low blood sugar occur, contact your doctor immediately; severe hypoglycemia is a medical emergency.

Why should this drug not be prescribed?
Avoid Amaryl if you have ever had an allergic reaction to it.

Do not take Amaryl to correct diabetic ketoacidosis (a life-threatening medical emergency caused by insufficient insulin and marked by excessive thirst, nausea, fatigue, and fruity breath). This condition should be treated with insulin.

Special warnings about this medication
It's possible that drugs such as Amaryl may lead to more heart problems than diet treatment alone, or treatment with diet and insulin. If you have a heart condition, you may want to discuss this with your doctor.

When taking Amaryl, you should check your blood and urine regularly for abnormally high sugar (glucose) levels. The effectiveness of any oral antidiabetic, including Amaryl, may decrease with time. This may occur because of either a diminished responsiveness to the medication or a worsening of the diabetes.

Even people with well-controlled diabetes may find that stress such as injury, infection, surgery, or fever triggers a loss of control. If this happens, your doctor may recommend that you add insulin to your treatment with Amaryl or that you temporarily stop taking Amaryl and use insulin instead.

**Possible food and drug interactions
when taking this medication**
If Amaryl is taken with certain other drugs, the effects of either could be increased, decreased, or altered. It is especially important to check with your doctor before combining Amaryl with the following:

Airway-opening drugs such as Proventil and Ventolin
Aspirin and other salicylate medications
Chloramphenicol (Chloromycetin)
Corticosteroids such as prednisone (Deltasone)
Diuretics such as hydrochlorothiazide (HydroDIURIL) and chlorothiazide (Diuril)
Estrogens such as Premarin

Heart and blood pressure medications called beta blockers, including
Tenormin, Inderal, and Lopressor
Isoniazid (Nydrazid)
Major tranquilizers such as Mellaril and Thorazine
MAO inhibitors (antidepressants such as Nardil and Parnate)
Miconazole (Monistat)
Nicotinic acid (Nicobid)
Nonsteroidal anti-inflammatory drugs such as Advil, Motrin, Naprosyn,
Nuprin, Ponstel, and Voltaren
Oral contraceptives
Phenytoin (Dilantin)
Probenecid (Benemid)
Sulfa drugs such as Bactrim DS, Septra DS
Thyroid medications such as Synthroid
Warfarin (Coumadin)

Use alcohol with care; excessive alcohol intake can cause low blood sugar.

Special information
if you are pregnant or breastfeeding

Do not take Amaryl while pregnant. Since studies suggest the importance of
maintaining normal blood sugar levels during pregnancy, your doctor may
prescribe injected insulin instead. Drugs similar to Amaryl do appear in
breast milk and may cause low blood sugar in nursing infants. You should not
take Amaryl while nursing. If diet alone does not control your sugar levels,
your doctor may prescribe injected insulin.

Recommended dosage

ADULTS

The usual starting dose is 1 to 2 milligrams taken once daily with breakfast
or the first main meal. The maximum starting dose is 2 milligrams.

If necessary, your doctor will gradually increase the dose 1 or 2 milligrams at
a time every 1 or 2 weeks. Your diabetes will probably be controlled on 1 to
4 milligrams a day; the most you should take in a day is 8 milligrams.

Weakened or malnourished people and those with adrenal, pituitary, kidney,
or liver disorders are particularly sensitive to hypoglycemic drugs such as
Amaryl and should start at 1 milligram once daily. Your doctor will increase
your medication based on your response to the drug.

CHILDREN

Safety and effectiveness in children have not been established.

Overdosage

An overdose of Amaryl can cause low blood sugar (see "What side effects may occur?" for symptoms).

Eating sugar or a sugar-based product will often correct mild hypoglycemia. For severe hypoglycemia, seek medical attention immediately.

Brand name:

AMBIEN

Pronounced: AM-bee-en
Generic name: Zolpidem tartrate

Why is this drug prescribed?

Ambien is used for short-term treatment of insomnia (difficulty falling asleep or staying asleep, or early awakening). A relatively new drug, it is chemically different from other common sleep medications such as Halcion and Dalmane.

Most important fact about this drug

Sleep problems are usually temporary and require medication for a week or two at most. Insomnia that lasts longer could be a sign of another medical problem. If you find that you need this medicine for more than 7 to 10 days, be sure to check with your doctor.

How should you take this medication?

Ambien works very quickly. Take it just before going to bed. Take only the prescribed dose, exactly as instructed by your doctor.

- *If you miss a dose...*
  Take Ambien only as needed. Never double the dose.

- *Storage instructions...*
  Store at room temperature. Protect from extreme heat.

What side effects may occur?

Side effects cannot be anticipated. If any develop or change in intensity, tell your doctor immediately. Only your doctor can determine whether it is safe to continue taking Ambien.

■ *More common side effects may include:*
Allergy, daytime drowsiness, dizziness, drugged feeling, headache, indigestion, nausea

■ *Less common side effects may include:*
Abdominal pain, abnormal dreams, abnormal vision, agitation, amnesia, anxiety, arthritis, back pain, bronchitis, burning sensation, chest pain, confusion, constipation, coughing, daytime sleeping, decreased mental alertness, depression, diarrhea, difficulty breathing, difficulty concentrating, difficulty swallowing, diminished sensitivity to touch, dizziness on standing, double vision, dry mouth, emotional instability, exaggerated feeling of well-being, eye irritation, falling, fatigue, fever, flu-like symptoms, gas, general discomfort, hallucination, hiccup, high blood pressure, high blood sugar, increased sweating, infection, insomnia, itching, joint pain, lack of bladder control, lack of coordination, lethargy, lightheadedness, loss of appetite, menstrual disorder, migraine, muscle pain, nasal inflammation, nervousness, numbness, paleness, prickling or tingling sensation, rapid heartbeat, rash, ringing in the ears, sinus inflammation, sleep disorder, speech difficulties, swelling due to fluid retention, taste abnormalities, throat inflammation, throbbing heartbeat, tremor, unconsciousness, upper respiratory infection, urinary tract infection, vertigo, vomiting, weakness

■ *Rare side effects may include:*
Abnormal tears or tearing, abscess, acne, aggravation of allergies, aggravation of high blood pressure, aggression, allergic reaction, altered production of saliva, anemia, belching, blisters, blood clot in lung, boils, breast pain, breast problems, breast tumors, bruising, chill with high temperature followed by heat and perspiration, decreased sex drive, delusion, difficulty urinating, excessive urine production, eye pain, facial swelling due to fluid retention, fainting, false perceptions, feeling intoxicated, feeling strange, flushing, frequent urination, glaucoma, gout, heart attack, hemorrhoids, herpes infection, high cholesterol, hives, hot flashes, impotence, inability to urinate, increased appetite, increased tolerance to the drug, intestinal blockage, irregular heartbeat, joint degeneration, kidney failure, kidney pain, laryngitis, leg cramps, loss of reality, low blood pressure, mental deterioration, muscle spasms in arms and legs, muscle weakness, nosebleed, pain, painful urination, panic attacks, paralysis, pneumonia, poor circulation, rectal bleeding, rigidity, sciatica (lower back pain), sensation of seeing flashes of lights or sparks, sensitivity to light, sleepwalking, speech difficulties, swelling of the eye, thinking abnormalities, thirst, tooth decay, uncontrolled leg movements, urge to go to the bathroom, varicose veins, weight loss, yawning

Why should this drug not be prescribed?

There are no known situations in which Ambien cannot be used.

Special warnings about this medication

When sleep medications are used every night for more than a few weeks, some may lose their effectiveness. Remember, too, that you can become dependent on some sleep medications if you use them for a long time or at high doses.

Some people using Ambien have experienced unusual changes in their thinking and/or behavior. Alert your doctor if you notice a change.

Ambien and other sleep medicines can cause a special type of memory loss. It should not be taken on an overnight airplane flight of less than 7 to 8 hours, since "traveler's amnesia" may occur.

When you first start taking Ambien, until you know whether the medication will have any "carry over" effect the next day, use extreme care while doing anything that requires complete alertness, such as driving a car or operating machinery. Older adults, in particular, should be aware that they may be more apt to fall.

Use Ambien cautiously if you have liver problems. It will take longer for its effects to wear off.

If you take Ambien for more than 1 or 2 weeks, consult your doctor before stopping. Sudden discontinuation of a sleep medicine can bring on withdrawal symptoms ranging from unpleasant feelings to vomiting and cramps.

When taking Ambien, do *not* drink alcohol. It can increase the drug's side effects.

If you have breathing problems, they may become worse when you use Ambien.

Possible food and drug interactions
when taking this medication

If Ambien is used with certain other drugs, the effects of either drug could be increased, decreased, or altered. It is especially important to check with your doctor before combining Ambien with the following:

The major tranquilizer, chlorpromazine (Thorazine)
The antidepressant drug, imipramine (Tofranil)
Other drugs that depress the central nervous system, including Valium, Percocet, and Benadryl

Special information
if you are pregnant or breastfeeding

If you are pregnant or plan to become pregnant, inform your doctor immediately. Babies whose mothers take some sedative/hypnotic drugs may have withdrawal symptoms after birth and may seem limp and flaccid. Ambien is not recommended for use by nursing mothers.

Recommended dosage

ADULTS

The recommended dosage for adults is 10 milligrams right before bedtime. Your doctor will prescribe a smaller dose if you are likely to be sensitive to the drug or have a liver problem. Never take more than 10 milligrams of Ambien per day.

CHILDREN

Safety and effectiveness have not been established in children below the age of 18.

OLDER ADULTS

Because older people and those in a weakened condition may be more sensitive to Ambien's effects, the recommended starting dosage is 5 milligrams just before bedtime.

Overdosage

People who take too much Ambien may become excessively sleepy or even go into a light coma. The symptoms of overdose are more severe if the person is also taking other drugs that depress the central nervous system. Some cases of multiple overdose have been fatal.

If you suspect an overdose, seek medical attention immediately.

Generic name:

AMCINONIDE

See Cyclocort, page 295.

Generic name:

AMILORIDE WITH HYDROCHLOROTHIAZIDE

See Moduretic, page 782.

Generic name:

AMITRIPTYLINE

See Elavil, page 441.

Generic name:

AMITRIPTYLINE WITH PERPHENAZINE

See Triavil, page 1274.

Generic name:

AMLODIPINE

See Norvasc, page 871.

Generic name:

AMLODIPINE AND BENAZEPRIL

See Lotrel, page 705.

Generic name:

AMOXICILLIN

See Amoxil, page 54.

Generic name:

AMOXICILLIN WITH CLAVULANATE

See Augmentin, page 105.

Brand name:

AMOXIL

Pronounced: a-MOX-il
Generic name: Amoxicillin
Other brand names: Trimox, Wymox

Why is this drug prescribed?
Amoxil, an antibiotic, is used to treat a wide variety of infections, including:

gonorrhea, middle ear infections, skin infections, upper and lower respiratory tract infections, and infections of genital and urinary tract.

Most important fact about this drug
If you are allergic to either penicillin or cephalosporin antibiotics in any form, consult your doctor before taking Amoxil. There is a possibility that you are allergic to both types of medication; and if a reaction occurs, it could be extremely severe. If you take the drug and feel signs of a reaction, seek medical attention immediately.

How should you take this medication?
Amoxil can be taken with or without food. If you are using Amoxil suspension, shake it well before using.

■ *If you miss a dose...*
Take it as soon as you remember. If it is almost time for the next dose, and you take 2 doses a day, take the one you missed and the next dose 5 to 6 hours later. If you take 3 or more doses a day, take the one you missed and the next dose 2 to 4 hours later. Then go back to your regular schedule.

■ *Storage instructions...*
Amoxil suspension and pediatric drops should be stored in a tightly closed bottle. Discard any unused medication after 14 days. Refrigeration is preferable.

What side effects may occur?
Side effects cannot be anticipated. If any develop or change in intensity, inform your doctor as soon as possible. Only your doctor can determine if it is safe for you to continue taking Amoxil.

■ *Side effects may include:*
Agitation, anemia, anxiety, changes in behavior, confusion, diarrhea, dizziness, hives, hyperactivity, insomnia, nausea, rash, vomiting

Why should this drug not be prescribed?
You should not use Amoxil if you are allergic to penicillin or cephalosporin antibiotics (for example, Ceclor).

Special warnings about this medication
If you have ever had asthma, hives, hay fever, or other allergies, consult with your doctor before taking Amoxil.

You should stop using Amoxil if you experience reactions such as bruising, fever, skin rash, itching, joint pain, swollen lymph nodes, and/or sores on the genitals. If these reactions occur, stop taking Amoxil unless your doctor advises you to continue.

For infections such as strep throat, it is important to take Amoxil for the entire amount of time your doctor has prescribed. Even if you feel better, you need to continue taking Amoxil. If you stop taking Amoxil before your treatment time is complete, you may get other infections, such as glomerulonephritis (a kidney infection) or rheumatic fever.

If you are diabetic, be aware that Amoxil may cause a *false positive* Clinitest (urine glucose test) result to occur. You should consult with your doctor about using different tests while taking Amoxil.

Before taking Amoxil, tell your doctor if you have ever had asthma, colitis (inflammatory bowel disease), diabetes, or kidney or liver disease.

Possible food and drug interactions
when taking this medication

If Amoxil is taken with certain other drugs, the effects of either could be increased, decreased, or altered. It is especially important to check with your doctor before combining Amoxil with the following:

Chloramphenicol (Chloromycetin)
Erythromycin (E.E.S., PCE, others)
Oral contraceptives
Probenecid (Benemid)
Tetracycline (Achromycin V, others)

Special information
if you are pregnant or breastfeeding

Amoxil should be used during pregnancy only when clearly needed. If you are pregnant or plan to become pregnant, inform your doctor immediately. Since Amoxil may appear in breast milk, you should consult your doctor if you plan to breastfeed your baby.

Recommended dosage

Dosages will be determined by the type of infection being treated.

ADULTS

Ear, Nose, Throat, Skin, Genital, and Urinary Tract Infections
The usual dosage is 250 milligrams, taken every 8 hours.

Infections of the Lower Respiratory Tract
The usual dosage is 500 milligrams, taken every 8 hours.

Gonorrhea
The usual dosage is 3 grams in a single oral dose.

Gonococcal Infections Such as Acute, Uncomplicated Anogenital and Urethral Infections
3 grams as a single oral dose.

CHILDREN

Children weighing 44 pounds and over should follow the recommended adult dose schedule.

Children weighing under 44 pounds will have their dosage determined by their weight.

Dosage of Pediatric Drops:
Use the dropper provided with the medication to measure all doses.

All Infections Except Those of the Lower Respiratory Tract
Under 13 pounds:
   0.75 milliliter every 8 hours.
13 to 15 pounds:
   1 milliliter every 8 hours.
16 to 18 pounds:
   1.25 milliliters every 8 hours.

Infections of the Lower Respiratory Tract
Under 13 pounds:
   1.25 milliliters every 8 hours.
13 to 15 pounds:
   1.75 milliliters every 8 hours.
16 to 18 pounds:
   2.25 milliliters every 8 hours.

Children weighing more than 18 pounds should take the oral liquid. The required amount of suspension should be placed directly on the child's tongue for swallowing. It can also be added to formula, milk, fruit juice, water, ginger ale, or cold drinks. The preparation should be taken immediately. To be certain the child is getting the full dose of medication, make sure he or she drinks the entire preparation.

Overdosage
Any medication taken in excess can have serious consequences. If you suspect an overdose, seek medical attention immediately.

■ *Symptoms of Amoxil overdose may include:*
Diarrhea, nausea, stomach cramps, vomiting

Generic name:

AMPHETAMINES

See Adderall, page 17.

Generic name:

AMPICILLIN

See Omnipen, page 883.

Brand name:

ANAFRANIL

Pronounced: an-AF-ran-il
Generic name: Clomipramine hydrochloride

Why is this drug prescribed?
Anafranil, a chemical cousin of tricyclic antidepressant medications such as Tofranil and Elavil, is used to treat people who suffer from obsessions and compulsions.

An obsession is a persistent, disturbing idea, image, or urge that keeps coming to mind despite the person's efforts to ignore or forget it—for example, a preoccupation with avoiding contamination.

A compulsion is an irrational action that the person knows is senseless but feels driven to repeat again and again—for example, hand-washing perhaps dozens or even scores of times throughout the day.

Most important fact about this drug
Serious, even fatal, reactions have been known to occur when drugs such as Anafranil are taken along with drugs known as MAO inhibitors. Drugs in this category include the antidepressants Nardil and Parnate. Never take Anafranil with one of these drugs.

How should you take this medication?

Take Anafranil with meals, at first, to avoid stomach upset. After your regular dosage has been established, you can take 1 dose at bedtime to avoid sleepiness during the day. Always take it exactly as prescribed.

This medicine may cause dry mouth. Hard candy, chewing gum, or bits of ice may relieve this problem.

■ *If you miss a dose...*
If you take 1 dose at bedtime, consult your doctor. Do not take the missed dose in the morning. If you take 2 or more doses a day, take the missed dose as soon as you remember. If it is almost time for your next dose, skip the one you missed and go back to your regular schedule. Do not take 2 doses at the same time.

■ *Storage instructions...*
Store at room temperature in a tightly closed container, away from moisture.

What side effects may occur?

Side effects cannot be anticipated. If any develop or change in intensity, inform your doctor as soon as possible. Only your doctor can determine if it is safe for you to continue taking Anafranil.

The most significant risk is that of seizures (convulsions). Headache, fatigue, and nausea can be a problem. Men are likely to experience problems with sexual function. Unwanted weight gain is a potential problem for many people who take Anafranil, although a small number actually lose weight.

■ *More common side effects may include:*
Abdominal pain, abnormal dreaming, abnormal tearing, abnormal milk secretion, agitation, allergy, anxiety, appetite loss, back pain, chest pain, confusion, constipation, coughing, depression, diarrhea, dizziness, dry mouth, extreme sleepiness, failure to ejaculate, fast heartbeat, fatigue, fever, flushing, fluttery heartbeat, frequent urination, gas, headache, hot flushes, impotence, inability to concentrate, increased appetite, increased sweating, indigestion, inflamed lining of nose or sinuses, itching, joint pain, light-headedness on standing up, memory problems, menstrual pain and disorders, middle ear infection (children), migraine, muscle pain or tension, nausea, nervousness, pain, rash, red or purple areas on the skin, ringing in the ears, sex-drive changes, sleeplessness, sleep disturbances, sore throat, speech disturbances, taste changes, tingling or pins and needles, tooth disorder, tremor, twitching, urinary problems, urinary tract

infection, vision problems, vomiting, weight gain, weight loss (children), yawning

■ *Less common side effects may include:*
Abnormal skin odor (children), acne, aggression (children), eye allergy (children), anemia (children), bad breath (children), belching (children), breast enlargement, breast pain, chills, conjunctivitis (pinkeye), difficult or labored breathing (children), difficulty swallowing, difficulty or pain in urinating, dilated pupils, dry skin, emotional instability, eye twitching (children), fainting (children), hearing disorder (children), hives, irritability, lack of menstruation, loss of sense of identity, mouth inflammation (children), muscle weakness, nosebleed, panic, paralysis (children), skin inflammation, sore throat (children), stomach and intestinal problems, swelling due to fluid retention, thirst, unequal size of pupils of the eye (children), vaginal inflammation, weakness (children), wheezing, white or yellow vaginal discharge

Why should this drug not be prescribed?

Do not take this medication if you are sensitive to or have ever had an allergic reaction to a tricyclic antidepressant such as Tofranil, Elavil, or Tegretol.

Be sure to avoid Anafranil if you are taking, or have taken within the past 14 days, an MAO inhibitor such as the antidepressants Parnate or Nardil. Combining Anafranil with one of these medications could lead to fever, seizures, coma, and even death.

Do not take Anafranil if you have recently had a heart attack.

Special warnings about this medication

If you have narrow-angle glaucoma (increased pressure in the eye) or are having difficulty urinating, Anafranil could make these conditions worse. Use Anafranil with caution if your kidney function is not normal.

If you have a tumor of the adrenal gland, this medication could cause your blood pressure to rise suddenly and dangerously.

Because Anafranil poses a possible risk of seizures, and because it may impair mental or physical ability to perform complicated tasks, your doctor will probably warn you to take special precautions if you need to drive a car, operate complicated machinery, or take part in activities such as swimming or climbing, in which suddenly losing consciousness could be dangerous. Note that your risk of seizures is increased:

■ If you have ever had a seizure
■ If you have a history of brain damage or alcoholism
■ If you are taking another medication that might predispose you to seizures

As with Tofranil, Elavil, and other tricyclic antidepressants, an overdose of Anafranil can be fatal. Do not be surprised if your doctor prescribes only a small quantity of Anafranil at a time. This is standard procedure to minimize the risk of overdose.

Anafranil may cause your skin to become more sensitive to sunlight. Avoid prolonged exposure to sunlight.

Before having any kind of surgery involving the use of general anesthesia, tell your doctor or dentist that you are taking Anafranil. You may be advised to discontinue the drug temporarily.

When it is time to stop taking Anafranil, do not stop abruptly. Your doctor will have you taper off gradually to avoid withdrawal symptoms such as dizziness, fever, general feeling of illness, headache, high fever, irritability or worsening emotional or mental problems, nausea, sleep problems, vomiting.

**Possible food and drug interactions
when taking this medication**
Avoid alcoholic beverages while taking Anafranil.

If Anafranil is taken with certain other drugs, the effects of either could be increased, decreased, or altered. It is especially important to check with your doctor before combining Anafranil with the following:

Barbiturates such as phenobarbital
Certain blood pressure drugs such as Ismelin and Catapres-TTS
Cimetidine (Tagamet)
Digoxin (Lanoxin)
Drugs that ease spasms, such as Donnatal, Cogentin, and Bentyl
Flecainide (Tambocor)
Fluoxetine (Prozac)
Haloperidol (Haldol)
Methylphenidate (Ritalin)
Major tranquilizers such as Thorazine
MAO inhibitors such as Nardil and Parnate
Paroxetine (Paxil)
Phenytoin (Dilantin)
Propafenone (Rythmol)
Quinidine (Quinidex)
Sertraline (Zoloft)
Thyroid medications such as Synthroid
Tranquilizers such as Xanax and Valium
Warfarin (Coumadin)

**Special information
if you are pregnant or breastfeeding**

If you are pregnant or plan to become pregnant, inform your doctor immediately. Anafranil should not be used during pregnancy unless absolutely necessary; some babies born to women who took Anafranil have had withdrawal symptoms such as jitteriness, tremors, and seizures. Anafranil appears in breast milk. Your doctor may advise you to stop breastfeeding while you are taking Anafranil.

Recommended dosage

ADULTS

The usual recommended initial dose is 25 milligrams daily. Your doctor may gradually increase this dosage to 100 milligrams during the first 2 weeks. During this period you will be asked to take this drug, divided into smaller doses, with meals. The maximum daily dosage is 250 milligrams. After the dose has been determined, your doctor may direct you to take a single dose at bedtime, to avoid sleepiness during the day.

CHILDREN

The usual recommended initial dose is 25 milligrams daily, divided into smaller doses and taken with meals. Your doctor may gradually increase the dose to a maximum of 100 milligrams or 3 milligrams per 2.2 pounds of body weight per day, whichever is smaller. The maximum dose is 200 milligrams or 3 milligrams per 2.2 pounds of body weight, whichever is smaller. Once the dose has been determined, the child can take it in a single dose at bedtime.

Overdosage

An overdose of Anafranil can be fatal. If you suspect an overdose, seek medical attention immediately.

- *Critical signs and symptoms of Anafranil overdose may include:*
  Impaired brain activity (including coma), irregular heartbeat, seizures, severely low blood pressure

- *Other signs and symptoms of overdosage may include:*
  Agitation, bluish skin color, breathing difficulty, delirium, dilated pupils, drowsiness, high fever, incoordination, little or no urine output, muscle

rigidity, overactive reflexes, rapid heartbeat, restlessness, severe perspiration, shock, stupor, twitching or twisting movements, vomiting

There is a danger of heart malfunction and even, in rare cases, cardiac arrest.

Brand name:

ANAPROX

Pronounced: AN-uh-procks
Generic name: Naproxen sodium
Other brand names: Aleve, Naprelan

Why is this drug prescribed?
Anaprox and Naprelan are nonsteroidal anti-inflammatory drugs used to relieve mild to moderate pain and menstrual cramps. They are also prescribed for relief of the inflammation, swelling, stiffness, and joint pain associated with rheumatoid arthritis and osteoarthritis (the most common form of arthritis), and for ankylosing spondylitis (spinal arthritis), tendinitis, bursitis, acute gout, and other conditions. Anaprox also may be prescribed for juvenile arthritis.

The over-the-counter form of naproxen sodium, Aleve, is used for temporary relief of minor aches and pains, and to reduce fever.

Most important fact about this drug
You should have frequent checkups with your doctor if you take Anaprox regularly. Ulcers or internal bleeding can occur without warning.

How should you take this medication?
Your doctor may ask you to take Anaprox with food or an antacid to avoid stomach upset. Take Aleve with a full glass of water.

Take this medication exactly as prescribed by your doctor.

If you are using Anaprox for arthritis, it should be taken regularly.

■ *If you miss a dose...*
Anaprox: Take the forgotten dose as soon as you remember. If it is almost time for your next dose, skip the one you missed and go back to your regular schedule. Never take 2 doses at the same time.

Naprelan: Take the forgotten dose only if you remember within 2 hours after the appointed time. Otherwise, skip the dose and go back to your regular schedule.

- *Storage instructions...*
Store at room temperature in a tightly closed container.

What side effects may occur?
Side effects cannot be anticipated. If any develop or change in intensity, inform your doctor as soon as possible. Only your doctor can determine if it is safe for you to continue taking Anaprox.

- *More common side effects of Anaprox may include:*
Abdominal pain, bruising, constipation, diarrhea, difficult or labored breathing, dizziness, drowsiness, headache, hearing disturbances, heartburn, indigestion, inflammation of the mouth, itching, light-headedness, nausea, rapid, fluttery heartbeat, red or purple spots on the skin, ringing in the ears, skin eruptions, sweating, swelling due to fluid retention, thirst, vertigo, vision changes

- *Less common or rare side effects of Anaprox may include:*
Abdominal bleeding, black stools, blood in the urine, change in dream patterns, chills and fever, colitis (inflammation of the large intestine), congestive heart failure, depression, general feeling of illness, hair loss, inability to concentrate, inability to sleep, inflammation of the lungs, kidney disease or failure, menstrual problems, muscle weakness and/or pain, peptic ulcer, severe allergic reactions, skin inflammation due to sensitivity to light, skin rashes, vomiting, vomiting blood, yellow skin and eyes

Naprelan shares some of the above side effects, but also has some of its own:

- *More common side effects of Naprelan may include:*
Back pain, flu symptoms, infection, nasal inflammation, sinus inflammation, sore throat, urinary infection

- *Less common side effects of Naprelan may include:*
Accidental injury, anemia, bronchitis, chest pain, cough increased, difficulty swallowing, fever, gas, high blood pressure, high blood sugar, joint pain, joint/tendon problems, leg cramps, "pins and needles" or tingling, stomach inflammation, weakness

- *Rare side effects of Naprelan may include:*
Abscesses, amnesia, angina pectoris (severe chest pain), anxiety, belching, blood disorders, bone disorders, bursitis, certain cancers, confusion, digestive tract inflammation, emotional changeability, enlarged abdomen,

eye or ear problems, fainting, gallstones, heart and blood vessel disorders, kidney stones, loss of appetite, migraine, nail disorders, neck pain or rigidity, nerve problems, nervousness, nosebleed, paralysis, pelvic pain, prostate problems, respiration and/or lung problems, skin disorders, stomach/intestinal/rectal hemorrhage or other disorders, tooth problems, ulcers, urinary problems, vaginal inflammation, vertigo, weight loss

Why should this drug not be prescribed?
If you are sensitive to or have ever had an allergic reaction to Anaprox, aspirin, or similar drugs such as Motrin, if you have had asthma attacks caused by aspirin or other drugs of this type, or if you have ever retained fluid or had hives or nasal tumors, you should not take this medication. Make sure your doctor is aware of any drug reactions you have experienced.

Special warnings about this medication
Remember that peptic ulcers and bleeding can occur without warning.

This drug should be used with caution if you have kidney or liver disease. It can cause liver inflammation in some people.

Do not take aspirin or any other anti-inflammatory medications while taking Anaprox, unless your doctor tells you to do so.

Anaprox and Naprelan contain sodium. If you are on a low sodium diet, discuss this with your doctor.

Use with caution if you have heart disease or high blood pressure. This drug can increase water retention. It also may cause vision problems. If you experience any changes in your vision, inform your doctor.

This drug makes some people drowsy or less alert. Avoid driving, operating dangerous machinery, or participating in any hazardous activity that requires full mental alertness if you find that the drug has this effect on you.

Do not take Aleve for more than 10 days for pain or 3 days for fever. Contact your doctor if pain or fever persists or gets worse, if the painful area becomes red or swollen, or if you develop more than a mild digestive upset.

Possible food and drug interactions when taking this medication
If Anaprox is taken with certain other drugs, the effects of either could be increased, decreased, or altered. It is especially important to check with your doctor before combining Anaprox with the following:

ACE inhibitors such as the blood pressure medication Capoten
Antiseizure drugs such as Dilantin
Aspirin

Beta blockers, including blood pressure drugs such as Inderal
Blood thinners such as Coumadin
Certain water pills (diuretics) such as Lasix
Lithium (Lithonate)
Methotrexate
Naproxen in other forms, such as Naprosyn
Oral diabetes drugs such as Micronase
Other pain relievers such as aspirin, acetaminophen (Tylenol), and
  ibuprofen (Motrin)
Probenecid (Benemid)

If you have more than 3 alcoholic drinks per day, check with your doctor
before using painkillers.

Special information
if you are pregnant or breastfeeding
The effects of Anaprox during pregnancy have not been adequately studied.
If you are pregnant or plan to become pregnant, inform your doctor
immediately. Avoid Anaprox, Naprelan, and Aleve during the last 3 months
of pregnancy. Anaprox appears in breast milk and could affect a nursing
infant. If this medication is essential to your health, your doctor may advise
you to discontinue breastfeeding until your treatment with this medication is
finished.

Recommended dosage

ANAPROX: ADULTS

Mild to Moderate Pain, Menstrual Cramps, Acute
Tendinitis and Bursitis
The starting dose is 550 milligrams, followed by 275 milligrams every 6 to 8
hours or 550 milligrams every 12 hours. You should not take more than
1,375 milligrams a day to start, or 1,100 milligrams a day thereafter.

Rheumatoid Arthritis, Osteoarthritis, and Ankylosing
Spondylitis
The starting dose is 275 milligrams or 550 milligrams 2 times a day
(morning and evening). Your physician can adjust the doses for maximum
benefit. Symptoms should improve within 2 to 4 weeks.

Acute Gout
The starting dose is 825 milligrams, followed by 275 milligrams every 8
hours, until symptoms subside.

ANAPROX: CHILDREN

Juvenile Arthritis

The usual daily dosage is a total of 10 milligrams per 2.2 pounds of body weight, divided into 2 doses. Dosage should not exceed 15 milligrams per 2.2 pounds per day.

The safety and effectiveness of Anaprox have not been established in children under 2 years of age.

ANAPROX: OLDER ADULTS

Your doctor will determine the dosage based on your particular needs. Adjustments in the normal adult dosage may be needed.

NAPRELAN

Rheumatoid Arthritis, Osteoarthritis, and Ankylosing Spondylitis

The usual dose is two 375- or 500-milligram tablets taken once a day. Your doctor will adjust your dose. You should not take more than three 500-milligram tablets daily.

Pain, Menstrual Cramps, Acute Tendinitis and Bursitis

The starting dose is two 500-milligram tablets taken once a day. For a short time, the doctor may increase the dose to three 500-milligram tablets daily.

Acute Gout

The usual dose is two to three 500-milligram tablets taken together on the first day, then two 500-milligram tablets once daily until the attack subsides.

It is not known whether Naprelan is safe for children.

ALEVE

1 tablet or caplet every 8 to 12 hours, to a maximum of 3 per day. For those over age 65, no more than 1 tablet or caplet every 12 hours. Not recommended for children under 12.

Overdosage

Any medication taken in excess can cause symptoms of overdose. If you suspect an overdose of Anaprox, seek medical attention immediately.

■ *The symptoms of Anaprox overdose may include:*
Drowsiness, heartburn, indigestion, nausea, vomiting

Brand name:

ANASPAZ

See Levsin, page 656.

Generic name:

ANASTROZOLE

See Arimidex, page 82.

Brand name:

ANEXSIA

See Vicodin, page 1337.

Brand name:

ANOLOR 300

See Fioricet, page 496.

Brand name:

ANSAID

Pronounced: AN-sed
Generic name: Flurbiprofen

Why is this drug prescribed?
Ansaid, a nonsteroidal anti-inflammatory drug, is used to relieve the inflammation, swelling, stiffness, and joint pain associated with rheumatoid arthritis and osteoarthritis (the most common form of arthritis).

Most important fact about this drug
You should have frequent checkups with your doctor if you take Ansaid regularly. Ulcers or internal bleeding can occur without warning.

How should you take this medication?
Your doctor may ask you to take Ansaid with food or an antacid.

Take this medication exactly as prescribed by your doctor.

If you are using Ansaid for arthritis, it should be taken regularly.

■ *If you miss a dose...*
Take the forgotten dose as soon as you remember. If it is almost time for your next dose, skip the one you missed and go back to your regular schedule. Never take 2 doses at the same time.

■ *Storage instructions...*
Store at room temperature.

What side effects may occur?
Side effects cannot be anticipated. If any develop or change in intensity, inform your doctor as soon as possible. Only your doctor can determine if it is safe for you to continue taking Ansaid.

■ *More common side effects may include:*
Abdominal pain, diarrhea, general feeling of illness, headache, indigestion, nausea, swelling due to fluid retention, urinary tract infection

■ *Less common or rare side effects may include:*
Altered sense of smell, anemia, anxiety, asthma, blood in the urine, bloody diarrhea, bruising, chills and fever, confusion, conjunctivitis (pinkeye), constipation, depression, dizziness, feeling of illness, gas, heart failure, hepatitis, high blood pressure, hives, inflammation of the nose or mouth, inflammation of the stomach, insomnia, itching, kidney failure, lack of coordination, memory loss, nervousness, nosebleed, peptic ulcer, pins and needles, rash, ringing in the ears, sensitivity of skin to light, severe allergic reaction, skin inflammation with or without sores and crusting, sleepiness, stomach and intestinal bleeding, swelling of throat, tremor, twitching, vision changes, vomiting, vomiting blood, weakness, weight changes, welts, yellow eyes and skin

Why should this drug not be prescribed?
If you are sensitive to or have ever had an allergic reaction to Ansaid, aspirin, or similar drugs such as Motrin, or if you have had asthma attacks caused by aspirin or other drugs of this type, you should not take this medication. Fatal attacks have occurred in people allergic to this drug. Make sure your doctor is aware of any drug reactions you have experienced.

Special warnings about this medication
This drug should be used with caution if you have kidney or liver disease. Kidney problems are most likely to develop in such people, as well as in those with heart failure, those taking water pills, and older adults.

If you have asthma, take Ansaid with extra caution. Do not take aspirin or similar drugs while taking Ansaid, unless your doctor tells you to do so.

Ansaid can cause vision problems. If you experience a change in your vision, inform your doctor. Blurred and/or decreased vision has occurred while taking this medication.

Ansaid slows the clotting process. If you are taking blood-thinning medication, this drug should be taken with caution.

This drug can increase water retention. If you have heart disease or high blood pressure, use with caution.

If you want to take Ansaid for pain less serious than that of arthritis, be sure to discuss the risks of using this drug with your doctor.

Possible food and drug interactions
when taking this medication
If Ansaid is taken with certain other drugs, the effects of either could be increased, decreased, or altered. It is especially important to check with your doctor before combining Ansaid with the following:

Antacids
Aspirin
Beta blockers such as the blood pressure medications Inderal and
    Tenormin
Blood thinners such as Coumadin
Cimetidine (Tagamet)
Methotrexate (Rheumatrex)
Oral diabetes drugs such as Micronase
Ranitidine (Zantac)
Water pills such as Lasix and Bumex

Special information
if you are pregnant or breastfeeding
The effects of Ansaid during pregnancy have not been adequately studied. If you are pregnant or plan to become pregnant, inform your doctor immediately. In particular, you should not use Ansaid in late pregnancy, as it can affect the developing baby's circulatory system. Ansaid appears in breast milk and could affect a nursing infant. If this medication is essential to your health, your doctor may advise you to discontinue breastfeeding until your treatment is finished.

Recommended dosage

ADULTS

Rheumatoid Arthritis or Osteoarthritis:
The usual starting dosage is a total of 200 to 300 milligrams a day, divided into 2, 3, or 4 smaller doses (usually 3 or 4 for rheumatoid arthritis). Your doctor will tailor the dose to suit your needs, but you should not take more than 100 milligrams at any one time or more than 300 milligrams in a day.

CHILDREN

The safety and effectiveness of Ansaid have not been established in children.

OLDER ADULTS

Older people are among those most apt to develop kidney problems while taking this drug.

Your doctor will determine the dosage according to your needs.

Overdosage

Any medication taken in excess can cause symptoms of overdose. If you suspect an overdose of Ansaid, seek medical attention immediately.

■ *The symptoms of Ansaid overdose may include:*
   Agitation, change in pupil size, coma, disorientation, dizziness, double vision, drowsiness, headache, nausea, semiconsciousness, shallow breathing, stomach pain

Category:

ANTACIDS

Brand names: Gaviscon, Gelusil, Maalox, Mylanta, Rolaids, Tums

Why is this drug prescribed?
Available under a number of brand names, antacids are used to relieve the uncomfortable symptoms of acid indigestion, heartburn, gas, and sour stomach.

Most important fact about this drug
Do not take antacids for longer than 2 weeks or in larger than recommended doses unless directed by your doctor. If your symptoms persist, contact your doctor. Antacids should be used only for occasional relief of stomach upset.

How should you take this medication?

If you take a chewable antacid tablet, chew thoroughly before swallowing so that the medicine can work faster and be more effective. Allow Mylanta Soothing Lozenges to completely dissolve in your mouth. Shake liquids well before using.

■ *If you miss a dose...*
Take this medication only as needed or as instructed by your doctor.

■ *Storage instructions...*
Store at room temperature. Keep liquids tightly closed and protect from freezing.

What side effects may occur?

When taken as recommended, antacids are relatively free of side effects. Occasionally, one of the following symptoms may develop.

■ *Side effects may include:*
Chalky taste, constipation, diarrhea, increased thirst, stomach cramps

Why should this drug not be prescribed?

Do not take antacids if you have signs of appendicitis or an inflamed bowel; symptoms include stomach or lower abdominal pain, cramping, bloating, soreness, nausea, or vomiting.

If you are sensitive to or have ever had an allergic reaction to aluminum, calcium, magnesium, or simethicone, do not take an antacid containing these ingredients. If you are elderly and have bone problems or if you are taking care of an elderly person with Alzheimer's disease, do not administer an antacid containing aluminum.

Special warnings about this medication

If you are taking any prescription drug, check with your doctor before you take an antacid. Also, tell your doctor or pharmacist about any drug allergies or medical conditions you have.

If you have kidney disease, do not take an antacid containing aluminum or magnesium. If you are on a sodium-restricted diet, do not take Gaviscon without checking first with your doctor or pharmacist.

Possible food and drug interactions
when taking this medication

If antacids are taken with certain other medications, the effects of either could be increased, decreased, or altered. It is especially important to check with your doctor before combining antacids with the following:

Cellulose sodium phosphate (Calcibind)
Isoniazid (Rifamate)
Ketoconazole (Nizoral)
Mecamylamine (Inversine)
Methenamine (Mandelamine)
Sodium polystyrene sulfonate resin (Kayexalate)
Tetracycline antibiotics (Achromycin, Minocin)

Special information
if you are pregnant or breastfeeding
As with all medications, ask your doctor or health care professional whether it is safe for you to use antacids while you are pregnant or breastfeeding.

Recommended dosage

ADULTS

Take antacids according to the following schedules, or as directed by your doctor.

Gaviscon and Gaviscon Extra Strength Relief Formula Chewable Tablets
Chew 2 to 4 tablets 4 times a day after meals and at bedtime or as needed. Follow with half a glass of water or other liquid. Do not swallow the tablets whole.

Gaviscon Extra Strength Relief Formula Liquid
Take 2 to 4 teaspoonfuls 4 times a day after meals and at bedtime. Follow with half a glass of water or other liquid.

Gaviscon Liquid
Take 1 or 2 tablespoonfuls 4 times a day after meals and at bedtime. Follow with half a glass of water.

Gelusil Liquid and Chewable Tablets
Take 2 or more teaspoonfuls or tablets 1 hour after meals and at bedtime. The tablets should be chewed.

Maalox Antacid Caplets
Take 1 caplet as needed. Swallow the tablets whole; do not chew them.

Maalox Heartburn Relief Chewable Tablets
Chew 2 to 4 tablets after meals and at bedtime. Follow with half a glass of water or other liquid.

Maalox Heartburn Relief Suspension, Maalox Magnesia and Alumina Oral Suspension, and Extra Strength Maalox Antacid Plus Anti-Gas Suspension
Take 2 to 4 teaspoonfuls 4 times a day, 20 minutes to 1 hour after meals and at bedtime.

Maalox Plus Chewable Tablets
Chew 1 to 4 tablets 4 times a day, 20 minutes to 1 hour after meals and at bedtime.

Extra Strength Maalox Antacid Plus Anti-Gas Chewable Tablets
Chew 1 to 3 tablets 20 minutes to 1 hour after meals and at bedtime.

Mylanta and Mylanta Double Strength Liquid and Chewable Tablets Antacid/Anti-Gas
Take 2 to 4 teaspoonfuls of liquid or chew 2 to 4 tablets between meals and at bedtime.

Mylanta Gelcaps
Take 2 to 4 gelcaps as needed.

Mylanta Soothing Lozenges
Dissolve 1 lozenge in your mouth. If needed, follow with a second. Repeat as needed.

Rolaids, Calcium-Rich/Sodium Free Rolaids, and Extra Strength Rolaids
Chew 1 or 2 tablets as symptoms occur. Repeat hourly if symptoms return.

Tums, Tums E-X, and Tums Anti-Gas Formula
Chew 1 or 2 tablets as symptoms occur. Repeat hourly if symptoms return. You may also hold the tablet between your gum and cheek and let it dissolve gradually.

CHILDREN

Do not give to children under 6 years of age, unless directed by your doctor.

Overdosage

Any medication taken in excess can have serious consequences. If you suspect an overdose, seek medical attention immediately.

■ *Symptoms of antacid overdose may include:*

For aluminum-containing antacids (Gaviscon, Gelusil, Maalox, Mylanta)

Bone pain, constipation (severe and continuing), feeling of discomfort (continuing), loss of appetite (continuing), mood or mental changes, muscle weakness, swelling of wrists or ankles, weight loss (unusual)

For calcium-containing antacids (Mylanta, Rolaids, Tums)

Constipation (severe and continuing), difficult or painful urination, frequent urge to urinate, headache (continuing), loss of appetite (continuing), mood or mental changes, muscle pain or twitching, nausea or vomiting, nervousness or restlessness, slow breathing, unpleasant taste, unusual tiredness or weakness

For magnesium-containing antacids (Gaviscon, Gelusil, Maalox, Mylanta)

Difficult or painful urination, dizziness or light-headedness, irregular heartbeat, mood or mental changes, unusual tiredness or weakness

Generic name:

ANTIPYRINE, BENZOCAINE, AND GLYCERIN

See Auralgan, page 109.

Brand name:

ANTIVERT

Pronounced: AN-tee-vert
Generic name: Meclizine hydrochloride
Other brand name: Bonine

Why is this drug prescribed?

Antivert, an antihistamine, is prescribed for the management of nausea, vomiting, and dizziness associated with motion sickness.

Antivert may also be prescribed for the management of vertigo (a spinning sensation or a feeling that the ground is tilted) due to diseases affecting the vestibular system (the bony labyrinth of the ear, which contains the sensors that control your balance).

Most important fact about this drug
Antivert may cause you to become drowsy or less alert; therefore, driving a car or operating dangerous machinery is not recommended.

How should you take this medication?
Take this medication exactly as prescribed by your doctor.

■ *If you miss a dose...*
Take it as soon as you remember. If it is almost time for your next dose, skip the one you missed and go back to your regular schedule. Do not take 2 doses at the same time.

■ *Storage instructions...*
Store away from heat, light, and moisture.

What side effects may occur?
Side effects cannot be anticipated. If any develop or change in intensity, inform your doctor as soon as possible. Only your doctor can determine if it is safe for you to continue taking Antivert.

■ *More common side effects may include:*
Drowsiness, dry mouth

■ *Rare side effects may include:*
Blurred vision

Why should this drug not be prescribed?
If you are sensitive to or have ever had an allergic reaction to Antivert or similar drugs, do not take this drug. Make sure that your doctor is aware of any drug reactions you have experienced.

Special warnings about this medication
If you have asthma, glaucoma, or an enlarged prostate gland, check with your doctor before using Antivert.

Possible food and drug interactions when taking this medication
Antivert may intensify the effects of alcohol. Do not drink alcohol while taking this medication.

Special information
if you are pregnant or breastfeeding
Studies regarding the use of Antivert in pregnant women do not indicate that this drug increases the risk of abnormalities. However, if you are pregnant or plan to become pregnant, inform your doctor before using Antivert. Check with him, too, if you are breastfeeding your baby.

Recommended dosage

ADULTS AND CHILDREN 12 AND OVER

Motion Sickness:
For protection against motion sickness, take 25 to 50 milligrams 1 hour before traveling. You may repeat the dose every 24 hours for the duration of the journey.

Vertigo:
The recommended dosage is 25 to 100 milligrams per day, divided into equal, smaller doses as determined by your doctor.

CHILDREN

The safety and effectiveness of Antivert have not been established in children under 12 years of age.

Overdosage
Any medication taken in excess can have serious consequences. If you suspect an overdose of Antivert, seek emergency medical treatment immediately.

Brand name:

ANUSOL-HC

Pronounced: AN-yoo-sol AICH-SEE
Generic name: Hydrocortisone
Other brand names: Hytone, ProctoCream-HC

Why is this drug prescribed?
Anusol is a steroid cream for use on the skin. It is prescribed to treat certain itchy rashes and other inflammatory skin conditions.

Most important fact about this drug

When you use Anusol-HC, you inevitably absorb some of the medication through your skin and into the bloodstream. Too much absorption can lead to unwanted side effects elsewhere in the body. To keep this problem to a minimum, avoid using large amounts of Anusol-HC over extensive areas, and do not cover it with airtight dressings such as plastic wrap or adhesive bandages unless specifically told to by your doctor.

How should you use this medication?

Use Anusol-HC exactly as directed, and only to treat the condition for which your doctor prescribed it.

Anusol-HC is for use only on the skin. Be careful to keep it out of your eyes.

Apply the medication directly to the affected area.

If you are using Anusol-HC for psoriasis or a condition that has been difficult to cure, your doctor may advise you to use a bandage or covering over the affected area. If an infection develops, remove the bandage and contact your doctor.

■ *If you miss a dose...*

Apply it as soon as you remember. If it is almost time for the next dose, skip the one you missed and go back to your regular schedule.

■ *Storage instructions...*

Keep the container tightly closed, and store it at room temperature, away from heat. Protect from freezing.

What side effects may occur?

Side effects cannot be anticipated. If any develop or change in intensity, inform your doctor as soon as possible. Only your doctor can determine if it is safe for you to continue using Anusol-HC.

■ *Side effects may include:*

Acne-like skin eruptions, burning, dryness, growth of excessive hair, inflammation of the hair follicles, inflammation around the mouth, irritation, itching, peeling skin, prickly heat, secondary infection, skin inflammation, skin softening, stretch marks, unusual lack of skin color

Why should this drug not be prescribed?

Do not use Anusol-HC if you are sensitive to or have ever had an allergic reaction to any of its ingredients.

Special warnings about this medication

Avoid covering a treated area with waterproof diapers or plastic pants. They can increase unwanted absorption of Anusol-HC.

If you use this medication over large areas of skin for prolonged periods of time—or cover the treated area—the amount of the hormone absorbed into your bloodstream may eventually lead to Cushing's syndrome: a moon-faced appearance, fattened neck and trunk, and purplish streaks on the skin. You can also develop glandular problems or high blood sugar, or show sugar in your urine. Children, because of their relatively larger ratio of skin surface area to body weight, are particularly susceptible to overabsorption of hormone from Anusol-HC.

Long-term treatment of children with steroids such as Anusol-HC may interfere with growth and development.

If an irritation develops, stop using the medication and contact your doctor.

Possible food and drug interactions
when using this medication

No interactions have been reported.

Special information
if you are pregnant or breastfeeding

The effects of Anusol-HC during pregnancy have not been adequately studied. If you are pregnant or plan to become pregnant, inform your doctor immediately. It is not known whether this medication appears in breast milk in sufficient amounts to affect a nursing baby. To avoid any possible harm to your baby, use Anusol-HC sparingly, and only with your doctor's permission, when breastfeeding.

Recommended dosage

ADULTS

Apply Anusol-HC to the affected area 2 to 4 times a day, depending on the severity of the condition.

CHILDREN

Limit use to the least amount necessary, as directed by your doctor.

Overdosage
Extensive or long-term use can cause Cushing's syndrome (see "Special warnings about this medication"), glandular problems, higher than normal amounts of sugar in the blood, and high amounts of sugar in the urine. If you suspect an overdose of Anusol-HC, seek medical treatment immediately.

Brand name:

ARICEPT

Pronounced: AIR-ih-sept
Generic name: Donepezil hydrochloride

Why is this drug prescribed?
Aricept is one of only two drugs that can provide some relief from the symptoms of early Alzheimer's disease. (Cognex is the other.) Alzheimer's disease causes physical changes in the brain that disrupt the flow of information and interfere with memory, thinking, and behavior. Aricept can temporarily improve brain function in some Alzheimer's sufferers, although it does not halt the progress of the underlying disease.

Most important fact about this drug
To maintain any improvement, Aricept must be taken regularly. If the drug is stopped, its benefits will soon be lost. Patience is in order when starting the drug. It can take up to 3 weeks for any positive effects to appear.

How should you take this medication?
Aricept should be taken once a day just before bedtime. Be sure it's taken every day. If Aricept is not taken regularly, it won't work. It can be taken with or without food.

■ *If you miss a dose...*
Make it up as soon as you remember. If it is almost time for the next dose, skip the one that was missed and go back to the regular schedule. Never double the dose.

■ *Storage instructions...*
Store at room temperature.

What side effects may occur?
Side effects cannot be anticipated. If any develop or change in intensity, tell the doctor as soon as possible. Only the doctor can determine if it is safe to continue Aricept.

The most common side effects are diarrhea, fatigue, insomnia, loss of appetite, muscle cramps, nausea, and vomiting. When one of these effects occurs, it is usually mild and gets better as treatment continues.

■ *Other side effects may include:*
Abnormal dreams, arthritis, bruising, depression, dizziness, fainting, frequent urination, headache, pain, sleepiness, weight loss

Why should this drug not be prescribed?
There are two reasons to avoid Aricept: an allergic reaction to the drug itself, or an allergy to the group of antihistamines that includes Periactin, Optimine, and Nolahist.

Special warnings about this medication
Aricept can aggravate asthma and other breathing problems, and can increase the risk of seizures. It can also slow the heartbeat and possibly cause fainting in people who have a heart condition. Contact your doctor if any of these problems occur.

In patients who have had stomach ulcers, and those who take a nonsteroidal anti-inflammatory drug such as Advil, Nuprin, or Aleve, Aricept can make stomach side effects worse. Be cautious when using Aricept and report all side effects to your doctor.

**Possible food and drug interactions
when taking this medication**
Aricept will increase the effects of certain anesthetics. Make sure the doctor is aware of Aricept therapy prior to any surgery.

If Aricept is taken with certain other drugs, the effects of either could be increased, decreased, or altered. It is especially important to check with your doctor before combining Aricept with the following:

Antispasmodic drugs such as Bentyl and Cogentin
Bethanechol chloride (Urecholine)
Carbamazepine (Tegretol)
Dexamethasone (Decadron)
Ketoconazole (Nizoral)
Phenobarbital

Phenytoin (Dilantin)
Quinidine (Quinidex)
Rifampin (Rifadin, Rifamate)

Special information
if you are pregnant or breastfeeding

Since it is not intended for women of child-bearing age, Aricept's effects during pregnancy have not been studied, and it is not known whether it appears in breast milk.

Recommended dosage

ADULTS

The usual starting dose is 5 milligrams once a day at bedtime for at least 4 to 6 weeks. Do not increase the dose during this period unless directed. The doctor may then change the dosage to 10 milligrams once a day if response to the drug warrants it.

CHILDREN

The safety and effectiveness of Aricept have not been established in children.

Overdosage

Any medication taken in excess can have serious consequences. If you suspect an overdose, seek medical attention immediately.

- *Symptoms of Aricept overdose include:*
  Collapse, convulsions, extreme muscle weakness (possibly ending in death if breathing muscles are affected), low blood pressure, nausea, salivation, slowed heart rate, sweating, vomiting

Brand name:

ARIMIDEX

Pronounced: AR-i-mi-deks
Generic name: Anastrozole

Why is this drug prescribed?

Arimidex is used to treat advanced breast cancer in postmenopausal women whose disease has spread to other parts of the body following treatment with tamoxifen (Nolvadex), another anticancer drug.

The growth of many breast cancer tumors is thought to be stimulated by estrogen. One of the hormones produced by the adrenal gland is converted to a form of estrogen by an enzyme called aromatase. Arimidex suppresses this enzyme and thereby reduces the level of estrogen circulating in the body.

Most important fact about this drug

Arimidex, like many other anticancer medications, may prolong survival and improve quality of life. To keep this medication working properly, it's important to continue taking it even when you don't feel well. If you develop bothersome side effects, call your doctor. He or she can recommend ways to reduce your discomfort.

How should you take this medication?

Take Arimidex exactly as directed.

- *If you miss a dose...*
  Take the forgotten dose if you remember within 12 hours. If it is almost time for your next dose, skip the one you missed and go back to your regular schedule. Never take 2 doses at once.

- *Storage instructions...*
  Store at room temperature.

What side effects may occur?

Side effects cannot be anticipated. If any develop or change in intensity, tell your doctor as soon as possible. Only your doctor can determine if it is safe for you to continue taking Arimidex.

- *More common side effects may include:*
  Abdominal pain, back pain, bone pain, chest pain, constipation, cough, depression, diarrhea, dizziness, dry mouth, headache, hot flashes, loss of appetite, nausea, pain, pelvic pain, "pins and needles", rash, shortness of breath, sore throat, swelling of arms and legs, vomiting, weakness, weight gain

- *Less common or rare side effects may include:*
  Accidental injury, anxiety, blood clots, breast pain, bronchitis, confusion, drowsiness, feeling of illness, fever, flu-like symptoms, fractures, hair thinning, high blood pressure, increased appetite, infection, insomnia, itching, joint pain, muscle pain, nasal or sinus inflammation, neck pain, nervousness, sweating, urinary tract infection, vaginal bleeding, weight loss

Why should this drug not be prescribed?

Do not take Arimidex if you are pregnant.

Special warnings about this medication

Because Arimidex may raise the level of cholesterol in your blood, your doctor may periodically do blood tests to check.

Possible food and drug interactions
when taking this medication

At present, no drug interactions are known.

Special information
if you are pregnant or breastfeeding

If you are pregnant or plan to become pregnant, do not take Arimidex. In animal studies, this medication has caused severe birth defects, including incomplete bone formation and low birth weight; it could be poisonous to your unborn child. Arimidex also increases your chances of having a miscarriage or a stillborn baby. If you should accidentally become pregnant, tell your doctor immediately.

Because of the possibility of Arimidex passing through your breast milk to your baby, you should probably avoid breastfeeding.

Recommended dosage

ADULTS

The usual dose is a 1-milligram tablet taken once a day.

Overdosage

Although there have been no reports of Arimidex overdose, any medication taken in excess can have serious consequences. If you suspect an overdose, seek medical attention immediately.

Brand name:

ARMOUR THYROID

Pronounced: ARE-more THIGH-roid
Generic name: Natural thyroid hormones TC and TD

Why is this drug prescribed?

Armour Thyroid is prescribed when your thyroid gland is unable to produce enough hormone. It is also used to treat or prevent goiter (enlargement of the thyroid gland), and is given in a "suppression test" to diagnose an overactive thyroid.

Most important fact about this drug

Although Armour Thyroid will speed up your metabolism, it is not effective as a weight-loss drug and should not be used for that purpose. Too much Armour Thyroid may cause severe side effects, especially if you are also taking appetite suppressants.

How should you take this medication?

Take Armour Thyroid exactly as prescribed by your doctor. There is no "typical" dosage; the amount you need to take will depend on how much thyroid hormone your body is able to produce. Take no more or less than the amount your doctor prescribes. Take your dose at the same time every day for consistent effect.

Do not change brands of medication without consulting your doctor.

If you are taking Armour Thyroid to compensate for an underactive thyroid gland, you will probably need to take the medication indefinitely.

■ *If you miss a dose...*
Take it as soon as you remember. If it is almost time for your next dose, skip the one you missed and go back to your regular schedule. Do not take 2 doses at the same time. If you miss 2 or more doses in a row, consult your doctor.

■ *Storage instructions...*
Store at room temperature in a tightly closed container.

What side effects may occur?

Side effects are rare when Armour Thyroid is taken at the correct dosage. However, taking too much medication or increasing the dosage too quickly may lead to overstimulation of the thyroid gland.

■ *Symptoms of overstimulation may include:*
Changes in appetite, diarrhea, fever, headache, increased heart rate, irritability, nausea, nervousness, sleeplessness, sweating, weight loss

Although children treated with Armour Thyroid may initially lose some hair, the hair loss is temporary.

Why should this drug not be prescribed?

You should not take Armour Thyroid if you have ever had an allergic reaction to this drug, your thyroid gland is overactive, or your adrenal glands are not making enough corticosteroid hormone.

Special warnings about this medication

If you are elderly, particularly if you suffer from angina (chest pain due to a heart condition), you should take Armour Thyroid at a lower dosage, and your doctor should schedule frequent checkups.

Armour Thyroid tends to aggravate symptoms of diabetes and underactive adrenal glands. If you take medication to treat one of these disorders, your dosage of that medication will probably need to be adjusted once you start taking Armour Thyroid.

Possible food and drug interactions
when taking this medication

If you take Armour Thyroid with certain other drugs, the effect of either drug could be increased, decreased, or altered. It is especially important to check with your doctor before combining Armour Thyroid with the following:

Asthma medications such as Theo-Dur
Blood thinners such as Coumadin
Cholestyramine (Questran)
Colestipol (Colestid)
Estrogen preparations (including some birth control pills such as Ortho-
    Novum and Premarin)
Insulin
Oral diabetes drugs (such as Diabinese and Glucotrol)

Special information
if you are pregnant or breastfeeding

If you need to take Armour Thyroid because of a thyroid hormone deficiency, you may continue using the medication during pregnancy, but your doctor will test you regularly and may change your dosage. Once your baby is born, you may breastfeed while continuing treatment with Armour Thyroid.

Recommended dosage

ADULTS

Your doctor will tailor the dosage of Armour Thyroid to meet your individual requirements, taking into consideration the status of your thyroid gland and any other medical conditions you may have.

Overdosage
An overdose of Armour Thyroid will speed up all of the body's vital processes, causing physical and mental hyperactivity, increased appetite, excessive sweating, chest pain, increased pulse rate, palpitations, nervousness, intolerance to heat, and possibly tremors or a rapid heartbeat.

Brand name:

ARTANE

Pronounced: AR-tane
Generic name: Trihexyphenidyl hydrochloride

Why is this drug prescribed?
Artane is used, in conjunction with other drugs, for the relief of certain symptoms of Parkinson's disease, a brain disorder that causes muscle tremor, stiffness, and weakness. It is also used to control certain side effects induced by antipsychotic drugs such as Thorazine and Haldol. Artane works by correcting the chemical imbalance that causes Parkinson's disease.

Most important fact about this drug
Artane is not a cure for Parkinson's disease; it merely minimizes and reduces the frequency of symptoms such as tremors.

How should you take this medication?
You may take Artane either before meals or after meals, whichever you find more convenient. Your doctor will probably start you on a small amount and increase the dosage gradually. Take Artane exactly as prescribed.

If the medication makes your mouth feel dry, try chewing gum, sucking mints, or simply sipping water.

Artane comes in tablet and liquid form. With either, you will probably need to take 3 or 4 doses a day.

Once you have reached the dosage that is best for you, your doctor may switch you to sustained-release capsules ("Sequels") which are to be taken only once or twice a day. Do not open or crush the sequels. Always swallow them whole.

■ *If you miss a dose...*
Take it as soon as you remember. If it is within 2 hours of your next dose, skip the one you missed and go back to your regular schedule. Do not take 2 doses at the same time.

■ *Storage instructions...*
Store at room temperature. Do not allow the liquid to freeze.

What side effects may occur?
Side effects cannot be anticipated. If any develop or change in intensity, inform your doctor as soon as possible. Only your doctor can determine if it is safe for you to continue taking Artane.

■ *Common side effects may include:*
Blurred vision, dry mouth, nausea, nervousness

These side effects, which appear in 30% to 50% of all people who take Artane, tend to be mild. They may disappear as your body gets used to the drug; if they persist, your doctor may want to lower your dosage slightly.

■ *Other potential side effects include:*
Agitation, bowel obstruction, confusion, constipation, delusions, difficulty urinating, dilated pupils, disturbed behavior, drowsiness, hallucinations, headache, pressure in the eye, rapid heartbeat, rash, vomiting, weakness

Why should this drug not be prescribed?
Do not take Artane if you are known to be sensitive to it or if you have ever had an allergic reaction to it or to other antiparkinson medications of this type.

Special warnings about this medication
The elderly are highly sensitive to drugs such as Artane and should use it with caution.

Artane can reduce the body's ability to perspire, one of the key ways your body prevents overheating. Avoid excess sun or exercise that also cause you to become overheated.

If you have any of the following conditions, make sure your doctor knows about them, since Artane could make them worse:

Enlarged prostate
Glaucoma
Stomach/intestinal obstructive disease
Urinary tract obstructive disease

It is important to stick to the prescribed dosage; taking larger amounts "for kicks" could lead to an overdose.

Your doctor should watch you carefully if you have heart, liver, or kidney disease or high blood pressure, and should check your eyes frequently. You should also be watched for the development of any allergic reactions.

**Possible food and drug interactions
when taking this medication**

If you take Artane along with any of the drugs listed below, your doctor may need to adjust the dosage of Artane, the other medication, or possibly both.

Amantadine (Symmetrel)
Amitriptyline (Elavil)
Chlorpromazine (Thorazine)
Doxepin (Sinequan)
Haloperidol (Haldol)

**Special information
if you are pregnant or breastfeeding**

No specific information is available concerning the use of Artane during pregnancy or breastfeeding. If you are pregnant or plan to become pregnant while taking Artane, inform your doctor immediately.

Recommended dosage

Your doctor will individualize the dose to your needs, starting with a low dose and then increasing it gradually, especially if you are over 60 years of age.

ADULTS

Parkinson's Disease:

The usual starting dose, in tablet or liquid form, is 1 milligram on the first day.

After the first day, your doctor may increase the dose by 2 milligrams at intervals of 3 to 5 days, until you are taking a total of 6 to 10 milligrams a day.

Your total daily dose will depend upon what is found to be the most effective level. For many people, 6 to 10 milligrams is most effective. Some, however, may require a total daily dose of 12 to 15 milligrams.

Drug-Induced Parkinsonism:

Your doctor will have to determine by trial and error the size and frequency of the dose of Artane needed to control the tremors and muscle rigidity that sometimes result from commonly used tranquilizers.

The total daily dosage usually ranges between 5 and 15 milligrams, although, in some cases, symptoms have been satisfactorily controlled on as little as 1 milligram daily.

Your doctor may start you on 1 milligram of Artane a day. If your symptoms are not controlled in a few hours, he or she may slowly increase the dose until satisfactory control is achieved.

Use of Artane with Levodopa:
When Artane is used at the same time as levodopa, the usual dose of each may need to be reduced. Your doctor will adjust the dosages carefully, depending on the side effects and the degree of symptom control. Artane dosage of 3 to 6 milligrams daily, divided into equal doses, is usually adequate.

Artane Tablets and Liquid:
You will be able to handle the total daily intake of Artane tablets or liquid best if the medication is divided into 3 doses and taken at mealtimes. If you are taking high doses (more than 10 milligrams daily), your doctor may divide them into 4 parts, so that you take 3 doses at mealtimes and the fourth at bedtime.

Overdosage
Overdosage with Artane may cause agitation, delirium, disorientation, hallucinations, or psychotic episodes.

■ *Other symptoms may include:*
Clumsiness or unsteadiness, fast heartbeat, flushing of skin, seizures, severe drowsiness, shortness of breath or troubled breathing, trouble sleeping, unusual warmth

If you suspect an overdose of Artane, seek medical attention immediately.

Brand name:

ASACOL

See Rowasa, page 1102.

Generic name:

ASPIRIN

Pronounced: ASS-per-in
Brand names: Empirin, Ecotrin, Genuine Bayer, Halfprin

Why is this drug prescribed?
Aspirin is an anti-inflammatory pain medication (analgesic) that is used to relieve headaches, toothaches, and minor aches and pains, and to reduce

fever. It also temporarily relieves the minor aches and pains of arthritis, muscle aches, colds, flu, and menstrual discomfort. In some patients, a small daily dose of aspirin may be used to ensure sufficient blood flow to the brain and prevent stroke. Aspirin may also be taken to decrease recurrence of a heart attack or other heart problems.

Most important fact about this drug
Aspirin should not be used during the last 3 months of pregnancy unless specifically prescribed by a doctor. It may cause problems in the unborn child or complications during delivery.

How should you take this medication?
Do not take more than the recommended dose.

Do not use aspirin if it has a strong, vinegar-like odor.

If aspirin upsets your stomach, use of a coated or buffered brand may reduce the problem.

Do not chew or crush sustained-release brands, such as Bayer time-release aspirin, or pills coated to delay breakdown of the drug, such as Ecotrin. To make them easier to swallow, take them with a full glass of water.

- *If you miss a dose...*
  Take it as soon as you remember. If it is almost time for your next dose, skip the one you missed and go back to your regular schedule. Never take 2 doses at the same time.

- *Storage instructions...*
  Store at room temperature.

What side effects may occur?
Side effects cannot be anticipated. If any develop or change in intensity, inform your doctor as soon as possible. Only your doctor can determine if it is safe for you to continue using aspirin.

- *Side effects may include:*
  Heartburn, nausea and/or vomiting, possible involvement in formation of stomach ulcers and bleeding, small amounts of blood in stool, stomach pain, stomach upset

Why should this drug not be prescribed?

Do not take aspirin if you are allergic to it, if you have asthma, ulcers or ulcer symptoms, or if you are taking a medication that affects the clotting of your blood, unless specifically told to do so by your doctor.

Special warnings about this medication

Aspirin should not be given to children or teenagers for flu symptoms or chickenpox. Aspirin has been associated with the development of Reye's syndrome, a dangerous disorder characterized by disorientation, and lethargy leading to coma.

If you have a continuous or high fever, or a severe or persistent sore throat, especially with a high fever, vomiting and nausea, consult your doctor. It could indicate a more serious illness.

If pain persists for more than 10 days or if redness or swelling appears at the site of inflammation, consult your doctor immediately.

If you experience ringing in the ears, hearing loss, upset stomach, or dizziness, consult your doctor before taking more aspirin.

Check with your doctor before giving aspirin for arthritis or rheumatism to a child under 12.

Possible food and drug interactions
when taking this medication

If aspirin is taken with certain other drugs, the effects of either could be increased, decreased, or altered. It is especially important to check with your doctor before combining aspirin with the following:

Acetazolamide (Diamox)
ACE-inhibitor-type blood pressure medications such as Capoten
Anti-gout medications such as Zyloprim
Arthritis medications such as Motrin and Indocin
Blood thinners such as Coumadin
Certain diuretics such as Lasix
Diabetes medications such as DiaBeta and Micronase
Diltiazem (Cardizem)
Dipyridamole (Persantine)
Insulin
Seizure medications such as Depakene
Steroids such as prednisone

Special information
if you are pregnant or breastfeeding
The use of aspirin during pregnancy should be discussed with your doctor. Aspirin should not be used during the last 3 months of pregnancy unless specifically indicated by your doctor. It may cause problems in the fetus and complications during delivery. Aspirin may appear in breast milk and could affect a nursing infant. Ask your doctor whether it is safe to take aspirin while you are breastfeeding.

Recommended dosage

ADULTS

Treatment of Minor Pain and Fever
The usual dose is 1 or 2 tablets every 3 to 4 hours up to 6 times a day.

Prevention of Stroke
The usual dose is 1 tablet 4 times daily or 2 tablets 2 times a day.

Prevention of Heart Attack
The usual dose is 1 tablet daily. Your physician may suggest that you take a larger dose, however. If you use Halfprin low-strength tablets (162 milligrams), adjust dosage accordingly.

CHILDREN

Consult your doctor.

Overdosage
Any medication used in excess can have serious consequences. If you suspect symptoms of an aspirin overdose, seek medical treatment immediately.

Brand name:

ASPIRIN FREE ANACIN

See Tylenol, page 1297.

Generic name:

ASPIRIN WITH CODEINE

See Empirin with Codeine, page 451.

Brand name:

ASTELIN

Pronounced: AST-eh-linn
Generic name: Azelastine hydrochloride

Why is this drug prescribed?
Astelin is an antihistamine nasal spray. It is prescribed for the relief of hay fever symptoms such as itchy, runny nose and sneezing.

Most important fact about this drug
Astelin can cause drowsiness. Do not drive a car, operate machinery, or undertake any other activity that requires mental alertness until you know how the drug affects you. Avoid combining Astelin with alcohol, antihistamines, and other drugs that slow the central nervous system; worse drowsiness could result.

How should you take this medication?
Use Astelin nasal spray only as prescribed. Avoid spraying in the eyes.

Before initial use, prime the pump by depressing it 4 times, or until a fine mist appears. When 3 or more days have elapsed since the last use, you should reprime the pump with 2 strokes, or until a fine mist appears.

Relief of symptoms usually occurs within 3 hours and lasts up to 12 hours.

■ *If you miss a dose...*
Take the forgotten dose as soon as you remember. If it is almost time for your next dose, skip the one you missed and go back to your regular schedule. Never double your dose.

■ *Storage instructions...*
Store the bottle in an upright position at room temperature with the nasal pump tightly closed. Do not freeze.

What side effects may occur?
Side effects cannot be anticipated. If any develop or change in intensity, inform your doctor as soon as possible. Only your doctor can determine if it is safe for you to continue taking Astelin.

■ *Common side effects may include:*
Bitter taste, drowsiness, headache, nasal burning, sneezing, sore throat

■ *Less common side effects may include:*
Abdominal pain, abnormal thinking, allergic reaction, anxiety, back pain, blood in the urine, breast pain, constipation, coughing, depression, dizziness, dry mouth, eye problems, fatigue, frequent urination, flu-like symptoms, flushing, herpes simplex infection, high blood pressure, increased appetite, laryngitis, loss of menstruation, loss of the sense of personal identity, loss of sensitivity to touch, mouth and tongue sores, muscle pain, nasal inflammation, nausea, nervousness, nosebleed, overactivity, pain in arms and legs, pinkeye, rapid heartbeat, skin problems, sleep disturbances, stomach and intestinal inflammation, taste loss, throat burning, vertigo, viral infection, vomiting, watery eyes, weight gain, wheezing

Why should this drug not be prescribed?
If you are sensitive to or have ever had an allergic reaction to Astelin or any of its ingredients, you should not take this medication.

Special warnings about this medication
Remember that Astelin makes some people drowsy. See "Most important fact about this drug" for precautions to take.

If you have a kidney condition, make sure the doctor is aware of it. Your dosage of Astelin may have to be reduced.

Possible food and drug interactions
If Astelin is taken with certain other drugs, the effects of either could be increased, decreased, or altered. It is especially important to check with your doctor before combining Astelin with the following:

Alcohol
Drugs that slow the nervous system, including codeine, phenobarbital, and Restoril
Cimetidine (Tagamet)
Ketoconazole (Nizoral)

Special information
if you are pregnant or breastfeeding
The effects of Astelin during pregnancy have not been adequately studied. If you are pregnant or plan to become pregnant, inform your doctor immediately. Because of the possibility of harming the developing baby, you may need to give up the medication. It is not known whether Astelin appears in breast milk. Your doctor may want you to stop breastfeeding while using this drug.

Recommended dosage

ADULTS

The usual dose for adults and children 12 years of age and older is 2 sprays into each nostril twice a day.

CHILDREN

The safety and effectiveness of Astelin have not been established in children under 12 years of age.

Overdosage

A severe overdose is unlikely, and would probably cause no other symptoms than extreme drowsiness. However, if you suspect an overdose, it's still wise to seek medical attention immediately.

Generic name:

ASTEMIZOLE

See Hismanal, page 563.

Brand name:

ATARAX

Pronounced: AT-a-raks
Generic name: Hydroxyzine hydrochloride
Other brand name: Vistaril

Why is this drug prescribed?

Atarax is an antihistamine used to relieve the symptoms of common anxiety and tension and, in combination with other medications, to treat anxiety that results from physical illness. It also relieves itching from allergic reactions and can be used as a sedative before and after general anesthesia. Antihistamines work by decreasing the effects of histamine, a chemical the body releases that narrows air passages in the lungs and contributes to inflammation. Antihistamines reduce itching and swelling and dry up secretions from the nose, eyes, and throat.

Most important fact about this drug

Atarax is not intended for long-term use (more than 4 months). Your doctor should re-evaluate the prescription periodically.

How should you take this medication?
Take this medication exactly as prescribed by your doctor.

- *If you miss a dose...*
  Take it as soon as you remember. If it is almost time for your next dose, skip the one you missed and go back to your regular schedule. Do not take 2 doses at once.

- *Storage instructions...*
  Store tablets and syrup away from heat, light, and moisture. Keep the syrup from freezing.

What side effects may occur?
Side effects cannot be anticipated. If any develop or change in intensity, inform your doctor as soon as possible. Only your doctor can determine if it is safe for you to continue taking Atarax.

Drowsiness, the most common side effect of Atarax, is usually temporary and may disappear in a few days or when dosage is reduced. Other side effects include dry mouth, twitches, tremors, and convulsions. The last two usually occur with higher than recommended doses of Atarax.

Why should this drug not be prescribed?
Atarax should not be taken in early pregnancy or if you are sensitive to or have ever had an allergic reaction to it. Make sure your doctor is aware of any drug reactions you have experienced.

Special warnings about this medication
Atarax increases the effects of drugs that depress the activity of the central nervous system. If you are taking narcotics, non-narcotic analgesics, or barbiturates in combination with Atarax, their dosage should be reduced.

This medication can cause drowsiness. Driving or operating dangerous machinery or participating in any hazardous activity that requires full mental alertness is not recommended until you know how you react to Atarax.

Possible food and drug interactions
when taking this medication
Atarax may increase the effects of alcohol. Avoid alcohol while taking this medication.

If Atarax is taken with certain other drugs, the effects of either could be increased, decreased, or altered. It is especially important to check with your doctor before combining Atarax with the following:

Barbiturates such as Seconal and Phenobarbital
Narcotics such as Demerol and Percocet
Non-narcotic analgesics such as Motrin and Tylenol

Special information
if you are pregnant or breastfeeding

Although the effects of Atarax during pregnancy have not been adequately studied in humans, birth defects have appeared in animal studies with this medication. You should not take Atarax in early pregnancy. If you are pregnant or plan to become pregnant, inform your doctor immediately. Atarax may appear in breast milk and could affect a nursing infant. If this medication is essential to your health, your doctor may advise you to discontinue breastfeeding until your treatment is finished.

Recommended dosage

When treatment begins with injections, it can be continued in tablet form.

Your doctor will adjust your dosage based on your response to the drug.

FOR ANXIETY AND TENSION

Adults

The usual dose is 50 to 100 milligrams 4 times per day.

Children under Age 6

The total dose is 50 milligrams daily, divided into several smaller doses.

Children over Age 6

The total dose is 50 to 100 milligrams daily, divided into several smaller doses.

FOR ITCHING DUE TO ALLERGIC CONDITIONS

Adults

The usual dose is 25 milligrams 3 or 4 times a day.

Children under Age 6

The total dose is 50 milligrams daily, divided into several smaller doses.

Children over Age 6

The total dose is 50 to 100 milligrams daily, divided into several smaller doses.

BEFORE AND AFTER GENERAL ANESTHESIA

Adults
The usual dose is 50 to 100 milligrams.

Children
The usual dose is 0.6 milligram per 2.2 pounds of body weight.

Overdosage
Any medication taken in excess can have serious consequences. If you suspect an overdose of Atarax, seek medical attention immediately.

The most common symptom of Atarax overdose is excessive calm; your blood pressure may drop, although it is not likely.

Generic name:

ATENOLOL

See Tenormin, page 1213.

Generic name:

ATENOLOL WITH CHLORTHALIDONE

See Tenoretic, page 1209.

Brand name:

ATIVAN

Pronounced: AT-i-van
Generic name: Lorazepam

Why is this drug prescribed?
Ativan is used in the treatment of anxiety disorders and for short-term (up to 4 months) relief of the symptoms of anxiety. It belongs to a class of drugs known as benzodiazepines.

Most important fact about this drug
Tolerance and dependence can develop with the use of Ativan. You may experience withdrawal symptoms if you stop using it abruptly. Only your doctor should advise you to discontinue or change your dose.

How should you take this drug?
Take this medication exactly as prescribed by your doctor.

- *If you miss a dose...*
  If it is within an hour or so of the scheduled time, take the forgotten dose as soon as you remember. Otherwise, skip the dose and go back to your regular schedule. Do not take 2 doses at once.

- *Storage instructions...*
  Store at room temperature in a tightly closed container, away from light.

What side effects may occur?
Side effects cannot be anticipated. If any develop or change in intensity, inform your doctor as soon as possible. Only your doctor can determine if it is safe for you to continue taking Ativan.

If you experience any side effects, it will usually be at the beginning of your treatment; they will probably disappear as you continue to take the drug, or if your dosage is reduced.

- *More common side effects may include:*
  Dizziness, sedation (excessive calm), unsteadiness, weakness

- *Less common or rare side effects may include:*
  Agitation, change in appetite, depression, eye function disorders, headache, memory impairment, mental disorientation, nausea, skin problems, sleep disturbance, stomach and intestinal disorders

- *Side effects due to rapid decrease or abrupt withdrawal of Ativan:*
  Abdominal and muscle cramps, convulsions, depressed mood, inability to fall or stay asleep, sweating, tremors, vomiting

Why should this drug not be prescribed?
If you are sensitive to or have ever had an allergic reaction to Ativan or similar drugs such as Valium, you should not take this medication.

Also avoid Ativan if you have the eye disease acute narrow-angle glaucoma.

Anxiety or tension related to everyday stress usually does not require treatment with Ativan. Discuss your symptoms thoroughly with your doctor.

Special warnings about this medication

Ativan may cause you to become drowsy or less alert; therefore, driving or operating dangerous machinery or participating in any hazardous activity that requires full mental alertness is not recommended.

If you are severely depressed or have suffered from severe depression, consult with your doctor before taking this medication.

If you have decreased kidney or liver function, use of this drug should be discussed with your doctor.

If you are an older person or if you have been using Ativan for a prolonged period of time, your doctor will watch you closely for stomach and upper intestinal problems.

Possible food and drug interactions
when taking this medication

Ativan may intensify the effects of alcohol. Avoid alcohol while taking this medication.

If Ativan is taken with certain other drugs, the effects of either could be increased, decreased, or altered. It is especially important to check with your doctor before combining Ativan with barbiturates (phenobarbital, Seconal, Amytal) or sedative-type medications such as Valium and Halcion.

Special information
if you are pregnant or breastfeeding

Do not take Ativan if you are pregnant or planning to become pregnant. There is an increased risk of birth defects. It is not known whether Ativan appears in breast milk. If this medication is essential to your health, your doctor may advise you to discontinue breastfeeding until your treatment is finished.

Recommended dosage

ADULTS

The usual recommended dosage is a total of 2 to 6 milligrams per day divided into smaller doses. The largest dose should be taken at bedtime. The daily dose may vary from 1 to 10 milligrams.

Anxiety

The usual starting dose is a total of 2 to 3 milligrams per day taken in 2 or 3 smaller doses.

Insomnia Due to Anxiety

A single daily dose of 2 to 4 milligrams may be taken, usually at bedtime.

CHILDREN

The safety and effectiveness of Ativan have not been established in children under 12 years of age.

OLDER ADULTS

The usual starting dosage for older adults and those in a weakened condition should not exceed a total of 1 to 2 milligrams per day, divided into smaller doses, to avoid oversedation. This dose can be adjusted by your doctor as needed.

Overdosage

Any medication taken in excess can have serious consequences. An overdose of Ativan can be fatal, though this is rare. If you suspect an overdose, seek medical attention immediately.

- *The symptoms of Ativan overdose may include:*
  Coma, confusion, drowsiness, hypnotic state, lack of coordination, low blood pressure, sluggishness

Generic name:

ATORVASTATIN

See Lipitor, page 673.

Brand name:

ATRETOL

See Tegretol, page 1199.

Brand name:

ATROVENT

Pronounced: AT-row-vent
Generic name: Ipratropium bromide

Why is this drug prescribed?

Atrovent inhalation aerosol and solution are prescribed for long-term treatment of bronchial spasms (wheezing) associated with chronic obstructive pulmonary disease, including chronic bronchitis and emphysema. When inhaled, Atrovent opens the air passages, allowing more oxygen to reach the lungs.

Atrovent nasal spray relieves runny nose. The 0.03% spray is used for hay fever. The 0.06% spray is prescribed for colds.

Most important fact about this drug
Atrovent inhalation aerosol and solution are not for initial use in acute attacks of bronchial spasm when fast action is needed.

How should you take this medication?
Atrovent inhalation aerosol and solution are not intended for occasional use. To get the most benefit from this drug, you must use it consistently throughout your course of treatment, as prescribed by your doctor.

The nasal spray pump must be primed; your doctor will show you how.

■ *If you miss a dose...*
Take it as soon as you remember. If it is almost time for your next dose, skip the one you missed and go back to your regular schedule. Do not take 2 doses at once.

■ *Storage instructions...*
All forms of Atrovent may be stored at room temperature. Do not freeze. Keep the nasal spray tightly closed.

What side effects may occur?
Side effects cannot be anticipated. If any develop or change in intensity, inform your doctor as soon as possible. Only your doctor can determine if it is safe for you to continue taking Atrovent.

INHALATION AEROSOL AND SOLUTION

■ *More common side effects may include:*
Blurred vision, cough, dizziness, dry mouth, fluttering heartbeat, headache, irritation from aerosol, nausea, nervousness, rash, stomach and intestinal upset, worsening of symptoms

■ *Less common or rare side effects may include:*
Allergic reactions, constipation, coordination difficulty, difficulty in urinating, drowsiness, fatigue, flushing, hives, hoarseness, inability to fall or stay asleep, increased heart rate, itching, low blood pressure, loss of hair,

mouth sores, sharp eye pain, swelling of the tongue, lips, and face, tightening of the throat, tingling sensation, tremors

NASAL SPRAY

■ *Side effects may include:*
Blurred vision, change in taste, conjunctivitis ("pinkeye"), cough, dizziness, dry mouth/throat, eye irritation, headache, hoarseness, increased runny nose or nasal inflammation, inflamed nasal ulcers, nasal congestion, nasal dryness, nasal irritation/itching/burning, nasal tumors, nausea, nosebleed, posterior nasal drip, pounding heartbeat, ringing in the ears, skin rash, sneezing, sore throat, swollen nose, thirst, upper respiratory infection

Why should this drug not be prescribed?
If you are sensitive to or have ever had an allergic reaction to Atrovent or any of its ingredients, or to soybeans, soy lecithin, or peanuts, you should not take this medication.

You should also avoid Atrovent if you are allergic to drugs based on atropine. Make sure your doctor is aware of any drug reactions you have experienced.

Special warnings about this medication
An immediate allergic reaction (hives, swelling, rash, wheezing) is possible when you first use this drug.

Unless you are directed to do so by your doctor, do not take this medication if you have the eye condition called narrow-angle glaucoma (high pressure inside the eye), an enlarged prostate, or obstruction in the neck of the bladder.

Keep Atrovent away from your eyes. It can cause blurred vision, pain, or even narrow-angle glaucoma.

If you develop eye pain, blurred vision, very dry nose, or nosebleeds after using the nasal spray, call your doctor.

Possible food and drug interactions
when taking this medication
No interactions have been reported.

Special information
if you are pregnant or breastfeeding
The effects of Atrovent during pregnancy have not been adequately studied. If you are pregnant or plan to become pregnant, inform your doctor

immediately. It is not known whether Atrovent appears in breast milk. If this drug is essential to your health, your doctor may advise you to stop nursing your baby until your treatment is finished.

Recommended dosage

ADULTS

Aerosol or Solution
The usual starting dose is 2 inhalations, 4 times per day. Additional inhalations may be taken, but the total should not exceed 12 in 24 hours.

Nasal Spray 0.03%
The usual dose is 2 sprays in each nostril 2 or 3 times a day.

Nasal Spray 0.06%
The usual dose is 2 sprays in each nostril 3 or 4 times a day. Do not use this strength for more than 4 days.

CHILDREN

Safety and effectiveness have not been established in children below 12 years of age.

Overdosage
There is no information on specific symptoms of Atrovent overdose. However, any drug taken in excess can have serious consequences. If you suspect an overdose of Atrovent, seek medical attention immediately.

Brand name:

A/T/S

See Erythromycin, Topical, page 465.

Brand name:

AUGMENTIN

Pronounced: awg-MENT-in
Generic ingredients: Amoxicillin, Clavulanate potassium

Why is this drug prescribed?
Augmentin is used in the treatment of lower respiratory, middle ear, sinus, skin, and urinary tract infections that are caused by certain specific bacteria.

These bacteria produce a chemical enzyme called beta lactamase that makes some infections particularly difficult to treat.

Most important fact about this drug

If you are allergic to either penicillin or cephalosporin antibiotics in any form, consult your doctor *before taking Augmentin*. You may be allergic to it, and if a reaction occurs, it could be extremely severe. If you take the drug and feel signs of a reaction, seek medical attention immediately.

How should you take this medication?

Augmentin should be taken every 8 or 12 hours, depending on the dosage strength. It may be taken with or without food, but taking it with meals or snacks will help prevent stomach upset. Be sure to take all the medicine your doctor has prescribed, even if you begin to feel better.

Shake the suspension well. Use a dosing spoon or medicine dropper to give a child the medication; rinse the spoon or dropper after each use.

■ *If you miss a dose...*
Take it as soon as you remember. If it is almost time for the next dose, and you take 2 doses a day, take the one you missed and the next dose 5 to 6 hours later. If you take 3 doses a day, take the one you missed and the next dose 2 to 4 hours later. Then go back to your regular schedule.

■ *Storage instructions...*
Store the suspension under refrigeration and discard after 10 days. Store tablets away from heat, light, and moisture.

What side effects may occur?

Side effects cannot be anticipated. If any develop or change in intensity, inform your doctor as soon as possible. Only your doctor can determine if it is safe for you to continue taking Augmentin.

■ *More common side effects may include:*
Diarrhea/loose stools, nausea, skin rashes and hives

■ *Less common side effects may include:*
Abdominal discomfort, anemia, arthritis, black "hairy" tongue, blood disorders, fever, gas, headache, indigestion, intestinal inflammation, itching, itching or burning of the vagina, joint pain, muscle pain, skin inflammation, skin peeling, sores and inflammation in the mouth and on the tongue and gums, stomach inflammation, vomiting, yeast infection

■ *Rare side effects may include:*
Agitation, anxiety, behavioral changes, blood in the urine, change in liver function, confusion, convulsions, dizziness, hyperactivity, insomnia, kidney problems

Why should this drug not be prescribed?
If you are sensitive to or have ever had an allergic reaction to any penicillin medication, do not take this drug.

Also avoid taking Augmentin if it has ever given you liver problems or yellowing of the skin and eyes.

Special warnings about this medication
Augmentin and other penicillin-like medicines are generally safe; however, anyone with liver, kidney, or blood disorders is at increased risk when using this drug. Alternative choices may be available to your doctor.

If you have diabetes and test your urine for the presence of sugar, you should ask your doctor or pharmacist if this medication will interfere with the type of test you use.

Allergic reactions to this medication can be serious and possibly fatal. Let your doctor know about previous allergic reactions to medicines, food, or other substances before using Augmentin. If you experience a reaction, report it to your doctor immediately and seek medical treatment.

If you develop diarrhea while taking Augmentin, inform your doctor. It could be a sign of a potentially dangerous form of bowel inflammation.

Some formulations of Augmentin contain phenylalanine. If you have the hereditary disease phenylketonuria, check with your doctor or pharmacist before taking this drug.

Possible food and drug interactions
when taking this medication
Augmentin may react with the antigout medication Benemid, resulting in changes in blood levels. A reaction with another antigout drug, Zyloprim, may cause a rash. Notify your doctor if you are taking either of these drugs.

Special information
if you are pregnant or breastfeeding
The effects of Augmentin during pregnancy have not been adequately studied. Because there may be risk to the developing baby, doctors usually recommend Augmentin to pregnant women only when the benefits of

therapy outweigh any potential danger. Augmentin appears in breast milk and could affect a nursing infant. If Augmentin is essential to your health, your doctor may advise you to stop nursing your baby until your treatment with this drug is finished.

Recommended dosage

ADULTS

The usual adult dose is one 500-milligram tablet every 12 hours or one 250-milligram tablet every 8 hours. For more severe infections and infections of the respiratory tract, the dose should be one 875-milligram tablet every 12 hours or one 500-milligram tablet every 8 hours. It is essential that you take this medicine according to your doctor's directions.

CHILDREN LESS THAN 3 MONTHS OLD

Children in this age group take 30 milligrams per 2.2 pounds of body weight per day, divided into 2 doses and taken every 12 hours.

CHILDREN OLDER THAN 3 MONTHS

For middle ear infections, sinus inflammation, lower respiratory tract infections, and more severe infections, the usual dose of the 200- or 400-milligram suspension is 45 milligrams per 2.2 pounds per day, in 2 doses, every 12 hours, and of the 125- or 250-milligram suspension, 40 milligrams per 2.2 pounds per day, in 3 doses, every 8 hours.

For less severe infections, the usual dose is 25 milligrams of the 200- or 400-milligram suspension for each 2.2 pounds of weight per day, divided into 2 doses, every 12 hours, or 20 milligrams of the 125- or 250-milligram suspension per 2.2 pounds per day, divided into 3 doses, every 8 hours.

Children weighing 88 pounds or more will take the adult dosage.

Overdosage

Augmentin is generally safe; however, large amounts may cause overdose symptoms. Suspected overdoses of Augmentin must be treated immediately; contact your physician or an emergency room.

Symptoms of Augmentin overdose may include:
Diarrhea, drowsiness, kidney problems, overactivity, rash, stomach and abdominal pain, vomiting.

Brand name:

AURALGAN

Pronounced: Aw-RAL-gan
Generic ingredients: Antipyrine, Benzocaine, Glycerin
Other brand name: Auroto Otic

Why is this drug prescribed?
Auralgan is prescribed to reduce the inflammation and congestion and relieve the pain and discomfort of severe middle ear infections. This drug may be used in combination with an antibiotic for curing the infection.

Auralgan is also used to remove excessive or impacted earwax.

Most important fact about this drug
Discard this product 6 months after the dropper is first placed in the drug solution.

How should you use this medication?
Use this medication exactly as prescribed. Administer as follows:

1. Warm the drops to body temperature by holding the bottle in your hand for a few minutes.
2. Shake the bottle.
3. Lie on your side or tilt the affected ear up.
4. Gently pull the earlobe up.
5. Administer the prescribed number of drops.
6. Avoid touching the dropper to the ear.
7. Keep the ear tilted up for about 5 to 7 minutes.

Do not rinse the dropper; replace it in the bottle after each use. Hold the dropper assembly by the screw cap and, without squeezing the rubber bulb, insert the dropper into the bottle and screw down tightly.

■ *If you miss a dose...*
Use it as soon as you remember. If it is almost time for your next dose, skip the one you missed and go back to your regular schedule.

■ *Storage instructions...*
Store at room temperature.

What side effects may occur?
Side effects cannot be anticipated. If any develop or change in intensity,

inform your doctor as soon as possible. For Auralgan, no specific side effects have been reported.

Why should this drug not be prescribed?
If you are sensitive to or allergic to any of the ingredients contained in Auralgan or similar drugs, you should not take this medication. Make sure your doctor is aware of any drug reactions you have experienced.

Unless directed to do so by your doctor, do not use this medication if you have a punctured eardrum.

Special warnings about this medication
Notify your doctor if irritation occurs or if you develop an allergic reaction to this medication.

**Possible food and drug interactions
when taking this medication**
No food or drug interactions have been reported.

**Special information
if you are pregnant or breastfeeding**
The effects of Auralgan during pregnancy have not been adequately studied. If you are pregnant or plan to become pregnant, notify your doctor immediately. It is not known whether Auralgan appears in breast milk. If this medication is essential to your health, your doctor may advise you to discontinue breastfeeding until your treatment is finished.

Recommended dosage

ADULTS AND CHILDREN

Acute Otitis Media (Severe Middle Ear Infection):
Apply the medication drop by drop into the ear, permitting the solution to run along the wall of the ear canal until it is filled. Avoid touching the ear with the dropper. Then moisten a piece of cotton dressing material, such as gauze, with Auralgan and insert it into the opening of the ear. Repeat every 1 to 2 hours until pain and congestion are relieved.

Removal of Earwax:
Apply Auralgan drop by drop into the ear 3 times daily for 2 or 3 days to help detach and remove earwax from the wall of the ear canal.

After the wax has been removed, Auralgan is useful for drying out the canal or relieving discomfort.

Before and after the removal of earwax, cotton dressing material such as gauze should be moistened with Auralgan and inserted into the opening of the ear following use of the medication.

Overdosage
No information on overdosage with Auralgan is available.

Generic name:

AURANOFIN

See Ridaura, page 1082.

Brand name:

AUROTO OTIC

See Auralgan, page 109.

Brand name:

AVENTYL

See Pamelor, page 904.

Brand name:

AXID

Pronounced: AK-sid
Generic name: Nizatidine

Why is this drug prescribed?
Axid is prescribed for the treatment of duodenal ulcers and noncancerous stomach ulcers. Full-dose therapy for these problems lasts no longer than 8 weeks. However, your doctor may prescribe Axid at a reduced dosage after a duodenal ulcer has healed. The drug is also prescribed for the heartburn and the inflammation that result when acid stomach contents flow backward into the esophagus. Axid belongs to a class of drugs known as histamine H_2 blockers.

Most important fact about this drug
Although Axid can be used for up to 8-12 weeks, most ulcers are healed within 4 weeks of therapy.

How should you take this medication?
Take this medication exactly as prescribed by your doctor.

■ *If you miss a dose...*
Take it as soon as you remember. If it is almost time for your next dose, skip the one you missed and go back to your regular schedule. Do not take 2 doses at once.

■ *Storage instructions...*
Store at room temperature.

What side effects may occur?
Side effects cannot be anticipated. If any develop or change in intensity, inform your doctor as soon as possible. Only your doctor can determine if it is safe for you to continue taking Axid.

■ *More common side effects may include:*
Abdominal pain, diarrhea, dizziness, gas, headache, indigestion, inflammation of the nose, nausea, pain, sore throat, vomiting, weakness

■ *Less common or rare side effects may include:*
Abnormal dreams, anxiety, back pain, chest pain, constipation, dimmed vision, dry mouth, fever, inability to sleep, increased cough, infection, itching, loss of appetite, muscle pain, nervousness, rash, sleepiness, stomach/intestinal problems, tooth problems

Why should this drug not be prescribed?
If you are sensitive to or have ever had an allergic reaction to Axid or similar drugs such as Zantac, you should not take this medication. Make sure your doctor is aware of any drug reactions you have experienced.

Special warnings about this medication
Axid could mask a stomach malignancy. If you continue to have any problems, notify your doctor.

If you have moderate to severe kidney disease, your doctor will reduce your dosage.

Possible food and drug interactions
when taking this medication
If Axid is taken with certain other drugs, the effects of either could be increased, decreased, or altered. It is especially important to check with your doctor before combining Axid with aspirin, especially in high doses.

Special information
if you are pregnant or breastfeeding
The effects of Axid during pregnancy have not been adequately studied. If you are pregnant or plan to become pregnant, inform your doctor immediately. Axid appears in breast milk and could affect a nursing infant. If this medication is essential to your health, your doctor may advise you to discontinue breastfeeding until your treatment with this medication is finished.

Recommended dosage

ADULTS

Active Duodenal Ulcer:
The usual dose is 300 milligrams once a day at bedtime, but your doctor may have you take 150 milligrams twice a day.

Active Noncancerous Stomach Ulcer:
The usual dose is 150 milligrams twice a day or 300 milligrams once a day at bedtime.

Maintenance of a Healed Duodenal Ulcer:
The usual dose is 150 milligrams once a day at bedtime.

If you have moderate to severe kidney disease, your doctor will prescribe a lower dose.

CHILDREN

The safety and effectiveness of Axid have not been established in children.

Overdosage
No specific information on Axid overdose is available. However, any medication taken in excess can have serious consequences. If you suspect an overdose of Axid, seek medical attention immediately.

Generic name:

AZATADINE WITH PSEUDOEPHEDRINE

See Trinalin Repetabs, page 1285.

Generic name:

AZELAIC ACID

See Azelex, page 114.

Generic name:

AZELASTINE

See Astelin, page 94.

Brand name:

AZELEX

Pronounced: AY-zuh-lecks
Generic name: Azelaic acid

Why is this drug prescribed?

Azelex helps clear up mild to moderate acne. The skin eruptions and inflammation of acne typically begin during puberty, when oily secretions undergo an increase.

Most important fact about this drug

You should keep using Azelex regularly, even if you see no immediate improvement. It takes up to 4 weeks for Azelex to show results.

How should you use this medication?

Use Azelex once in the morning and again in the evening. Wash the areas to be treated and pat dry. Apply a thin film of Azelex and gently but thoroughly massage it into the skin. Wash your hands afterwards.

Do not put bandages or dressings over the treated areas. Avoid getting Azelex in the eyes, mouth, or nose. If any of the cream does get into your eyes, wash it out with large amounts of water. Call your doctor if your eyes remain irritated.

■ *If you miss a dose...*
Apply it as soon as you remember. If it is almost time for the next dose, skip the one you missed and go back to your regular schedule.

■ *Storage instructions...*
Store at room temperature. Protect from freezing.

What side effects may occur?

Side effects cannot be anticipated. If any develop or change in intensity, inform your doctor as soon as possible. Only your doctor can determine if it is safe for you to continue using Azelex.

- *More common side effects may include:*
  Burning, itching, stinging, tingling

- *Rare side effects may include:*
  Dryness, inflammation, irritation, peeling, rash, redness

Why should this drug not be prescribed?

Do not use Azelex if it causes an allergic reaction.

Special warnings about this medication

Azelex may cause some itching, burning, or stinging when you first begin treatment. You can expect this to stop as treatment continues. If it doesn't, you should check with your doctor. You may have to cut back to a single application daily, or even temporarily stop using this medication.

Azelex has been known to occasionally have a bleaching effect on the skin. Report any abnormal changes in skin color to your doctor.

Possible food and drug interactions
when using this medication

No interactions have been reported.

Special information
if you are pregnant or breastfeeding

The effects of Azelex during pregnancy and breastfeeding have not been adequately studied. If you are pregnant or plan to become pregnant, notify your doctor immediately. Small amounts of Azelex could appear in breast milk. If you are nursing, use this medication with caution.

Recommended dosage

The usual dose is a thin film of Azelex applied twice a day.

Overdosage

An overdose is unlikely. However, if your skin becomes severely irritated, you should stop applying the medication and call your doctor.

Generic name:

AZITHROMYCIN

See Zithromax, page 1394.

Brand name:

AZMACORT

Pronounced: AZ-ma-court
Generic name: Triamcinolone acetonide
Other brand names: Nasacort, Nasacort AQ

Why is this drug prescribed?

Azmacort and Nasacort are metered-dose inhalers containing the anti-inflammatory steroid medication, triamcinolone acetonide; Nasacort AQ is a metered-dose pump spray. Azmacort is used as long-term therapy to control bronchial asthma attacks. Nasacort and Nasacort AQ are prescribed to relieve the symptoms of hay fever and other nasal allergies. Nasacort is also used in the treatment of nasal polyps (projecting masses of tissue in the nose).

Most important fact about this drug

Azmacort does not provide rapid relief in an asthma attack. Instead, it reduces the frequency and severity of attacks when taken on a regular basis. For quick relief, you must still use airway-opening medications.

How should you take this medication?

Take these drugs on a regular daily basis, exactly as prescribed. With Azmacort and Nasacort, you should begin to see improvement after a week, although it may take 2 weeks or more to achieve the greatest benefit. Nasacort AQ should begin to produce results on the first day, but will take a week to yield maximum benefit.

Shake the canister or bottle before each use. Do not use an Azmacort inhaler more than 240 times. Discard the Nasacort canister after 100 inhalations and the Nasacort AQ bottle after 120 actuations.

If the drug irritates your throat, gargling and rinsing your mouth with water after each dose can help to relieve the problem.

If you are using a bronchodilator inhalant, it should be used before the Azmacort inhalant to derive the best effects from this drug. Use of the two inhalers should be separated by several minutes.➥

Do not spray Nasacort directly onto the bone that separates the nostrils. Avoid spraying either medication in your eyes.

Illustrated instructions for use are available with the product.

- *If you miss a dose...*
  Use it as soon as you remember. If it is almost time for your next dose, skip the one you missed and go back to your regular schedule. Do not take 2 doses at once.

- *Storage instructions...*
  Store at room temperature. Since the contents of the aerosol inhalant are under pressure, do not puncture the container and do not use or store the medication near heat or open flame. Exposure to temperatures above 120 degrees F. may cause the container to explode.

What side effects may occur?
Side effects cannot be anticipated. If any develop or change in intensity, inform your doctor as soon as possible. Only your doctor can determine if it is safe for you to continue taking these medications.

- *More common side effects of Azmacort may include:*
  Back pain, flu symptoms, headache, sinus inflammation, sore throat

- *Less common side effects of Azmacort may include:*
  Abdominal pain, bladder inflammation, bursitis, chest congestion, cough, diarrhea, dry mouth, facial swelling, hives, hoarseness, increased wheezing, irritated throat, mouth infection, muscle pain, pain, rash, sensitivity to light, severe allergic reaction, toothache, urinary tract infection, vaginal infection, voice changes, vomiting, weight gain

- *More common side effects of Nasacort may include:*
  Headache

- *Less common side effects of Nasacort may include:*
  Dryness of the membranes lining the nose, mouth, and throat, nasal irritation, nasal and sinus congestion, nosebleeds, sneezing, throat discomfort

- *Side effects of Nasacort in children aged 6 to 11 may include:*
  Cough, ear inflammation, fever, indigestion, nausea, nosebleed, throat discomfort

■ *Side effects of Nasacort AQ may include:*
Increased cough, nosebleed, sore throat

Why should this drug not be prescribed?
Do not use any of these medications if you are allergic to or sensitive to any of the ingredients.

Do not use Azmacort if:

your asthma can be controlled with airway openers and other non-steroid medications.
you require only occasional steroid treatment for asthma. (Azmacort is not for treatment of prolonged, severe asthma attacks where fast-acting measures are required.)
you have bronchitis not associated with asthma.

Special warnings about this medication
Your doctor will see that your asthma is reasonably under control before starting you on Azmacort. For about a week, he or she will have you take Azmacort along with your usual dose of oral steroid. After that, you will gradually take less and less of the oral drug. If you develop joint or muscular pain, weariness, and depression, contact your doctor immediately. If you feel light-headed or find that you are losing weight, also tell your doctor.

If you are using Azmacort and your airway-opening medication is not effective during an asthma attack, contact your doctor immediately. Also get medical help immediately if your wheezing gets worse after a dose of Azmacort.

The use of triamcinolone acetonide may cause a yeast-like fungal infection in the mouth and throat (Azmacort) or nose and throat (Nasacort and Nasacort AQ). If you suspect a fungal infection, notify your doctor. Treatment with antifungal medication may be necessary.

People using steroid medications such as these are more susceptible to infection. Chickenpox and measles, for example, can be far more serious for children and for adults who have not had them. Try to avoid exposure, but if you are exposed, inform your doctor. Medication may be needed.

Switching from steroid tablet therapy to Azmacort Inhaler may allow allergic conditions to surface that were previously controlled by the tablets. These include rhinitis (inflammation of the inside of the nose), conjunctivitis (pinkeye), and eczema.

If your child is using any of these medications, your doctor will watch to be sure he or she is growing properly. If you have just had an operation, or if you are experiencing extreme stress, your doctor will watch you closely.

Use these medications with extreme caution if you have tuberculosis, an untreated infection, or a herpes infection of the eye.

If your symptoms do not improve or get worse, contact your doctor. If you are using Nasacort or Nasacort AQ, also notify your doctor if you notice nasal irritation, burning, or stinging after using the medication.

Use Nasacort or Nasacort AQ with caution if you have not fully healed from nasal ulcers, or an injury to your nose. Steroids can slow wound healing, and there have been rare cases of perforation inside the nose caused by inhaled steroids.

If you are using Nasacort or Nasacort AQ, contact your doctor if your symptoms don't improve after 3 weeks or if they get worse. Also notify your doctor if you have nasal irritation, burning, or stinging after you use Nasacort.

Possible food and drug interactions while taking this medication
Inhaled steroids such as Azmacort, Nasacort, and Nasacort AQ are not recommended for long-term use while you are taking prednisone (Deltasone).

Special information if you are pregnant or breastfeeding
The effects of triamcinolone acetonide during pregnancy have not been adequately studied. If you are pregnant or plan to become pregnant, inform your doctor immediately. It is not known whether triamcinolone acetonide appears in breast milk. If this medication is essential to your health, your doctor may advise you to discontinue breastfeeding until your treatment with this medication is finished.

Recommended dosage

AZMACORT

The Azmacort Inhaler unit is for oral inhalation only.

Adults

The usual dose is 2 inhalations (about 200 micrograms), taken 3 or 4 times a day or 4 inhalations taken twice a day. The daily dose should not exceed 16 inhalations.

Children 6 to 12 Years of Age

The usual dose is 1 or 2 inhalations (100 to 200 micrograms), taken 3 or 4 times a day or 2 to 4 inhalations taken twice a day. The daily dose should not exceed 12 inhalations.

Children Under 6 Years of Age
The safety and effectiveness of this drug have not been established in children under 6 years of age.

NASACORT

Adults and Children Aged 12 and Older
The usual starting dose is 220 micrograms a day, taken as 2 sprays in each nostril once a day. (One spray is 55 micrograms.) If necessary, your doctor may increase the dose up to 440 micrograms a day, taken all at once, twice a day, or 4 times a day. Once Nasacort has started to work, your doctor may decrease the dose to 110 micrograms a day.

Children 6 Through 11 Years of Age
The usual starting dose is 2 sprays in each nostril once a day, for a total of 220 micrograms a day. Your doctor will adjust the dose to best suit the child.

Children Under 6 Years of Age
The safety and effectiveness of Nasacort in children under 6 years of age have not been established.

NASACORT AQ

Adults and Children Aged 12 and Older
The usual starting dose is 220 micrograms taken as 2 sprays in each nostril once a day. Once your symptoms are under control, your doctor may reduce the dose to 110 micrograms a day.

Children Under 12 Years of Age
Safety and effectiveness have not been established for children under 12.

Overdosage
Any medication taken in excess can have serious consequences. If you suspect an overdose, seek emergency medical treatment immediately.

An overdose is likely to be signaled by an increase in side effects. Accidental contact with the contents of the canister would most likely irritate your nose and give you a headache.

Overuse of Nasacort AQ may upset your stomach and intestines.

Continual overuse of Azmacort inhalation aerosol could lower your resistance; cause weakness; wasting, or swelling; and interfere with healing.

Brand name:

AZULFIDINE

Pronounced: A-ZUL-fi-deen
Generic name: Sulfasalazine

Why is this drug prescribed?

Azulfidine, an anti-inflammatory medicine, is prescribed for the treatment of mild to moderate ulcerative colitis (a long-term, progressive bowel disease) and as an added treatment in severe ulcerative colitis (chronic inflammation and ulceration of the lining of large bowel and rectum, the main symptom of which is bloody diarrhea). This medication is also prescribed to decrease severe attacks of ulcerative colitis.

Azulfidine EN-tabs are prescribed for people with ulcerative colitis who cannot take the regular Azulfidine tablet because of symptoms of stomach and intestinal irritation such as nausea and vomiting when taking the first few doses of the drug, or for those in whom a reduction in dosage does not lessen the stomach or intestinal side effects. The EN-tabs are also prescribed for people with rheumatoid arthritis who fail to get relief from salicylates (such as aspirin) or other nonsteroidal anti-inflammatory drugs (such as ibuprofen).

Most important fact about this drug

Although ulcerative colitis rarely disappears completely, the risk of recurrence can be substantially reduced by the continued use of this drug.

How should you take this medication?

Take this medication in evenly spaced, equal doses, as determined by your doctor, preferably after meals or with food to avoid stomach upset. Swallow Azulfidine EN-tabs whole.

It is important that you drink plenty of fluids while taking this medication to avoid kidney stones.

If you are taking Azulfidine EN-tabs for rheumatoid arthritis, it may take up to 12 weeks for relief to occur.

■ *If you miss a dose...*
Take it as soon as you remember. If it is almost time for your next dose, skip the one you missed and go back to your regular schedule. Do not take 2 doses at once.

■ *Storage instructions...*
Store at room temperature.

What side effects may occur?
Side effects cannot be anticipated. If any develop or change in intensity, inform your doctor as soon as possible. Only your doctor can determine if it is safe for you to continue taking Azulfidine.

■ *More common side effects may include:*
Headache, lack or loss of appetite, nausea, stomach distress, vomiting

■ *Less common side effects may include:*
Anemia, bluish discoloration of the skin, fever, hives, itching, skin rash

■ *Rare side effects may include:*
Abdominal pain, blood disorders, blood in the urine, bloody diarrhea, convulsions, diarrhea, drowsiness, hallucinations, hearing loss, hepatitis, inability to fall or stay asleep, inflammation of the mouth, intestinal inflammation, itchy skin eruptions, joint pain, kidney disorders, lack of muscle coordination, loss of hair, mental depression, red, raised rash, ringing in the ears, sensitivity to light, severe allergic reaction, skin discoloration, skin disorders, spinal cord defects, swelling around the eye, urine discoloration, vertigo

Why should this drug not be prescribed?
If you are sensitive to or have ever had an allergic reaction to Azulfidine, salicylates (aspirin), or other sulfa drugs, you should not take this medication. Make sure your doctor is aware of any drug reactions you have experienced.

Unless you are directed to do so by your doctor, do not take Azulfidine if you have an intestinal or urinary obstruction or if you have porphyria (an inherited disorder involving the substance that gives color to the skin and iris of the eyes).

Special warnings about this medication
If you have kidney or liver damage or any blood disease, your doctor will check you very carefully before prescribing Azulfidine. Deaths have been reported from allergic reactions, blood diseases, kidney or liver damage, changes in nerve and muscle impulses, and fibrosing alveolitis (inflammation of the lungs due to a thickening or scarring of tissue). Signs such as sore throat, fever, abnormal paleness of the skin, purple or red spots on the skin, or jaundice (yellowing of the skin) may be an indication of a serious blood

disorder. Your doctor will do frequent blood counts and urine tests. Use caution taking Azulfidine if you have a severe allergy or bronchial asthma.

If you develop loss of appetite, nausea, or vomiting, report it immediately. The doctor may need to adjust your dosage or change the prescription.

If Azulfidine EN-tabs are eliminated undisintegrated, stop taking the drug and notify your doctor immediately. (You may lack the intestinal enzymes necessary to dissolve this medication.)

Men taking Azulfidine may experience temporary infertility and a low sperm count.

Skin and urine may become yellow-orange in color while taking Azulfidine. In addition, prolonged exposure to the sun should be avoided.

Possible food and drug interactions
when taking this medication
If Azulfidine is taken with certain other drugs, the effects of either could be increased, decreased, or altered. It is especially important to check with your doctor before combining Azulfidine with the following:

Digoxin (Lanoxin)
Folic acid (a B-complex vitamin)

Special information
if you are pregnant or breastfeeding
The effects of Azulfidine during pregnancy have not been adequately studied. If you are pregnant or plan to become pregnant, inform your doctor immediately. Azulfidine is secreted in breast milk and could affect a nursing infant. If this medication is essential to your health, your doctor may advise you to discontinue breastfeeding until your treatment is finished.

Recommended dosage
Your doctor will carefully individualize your dosage and monitor your response periodically.

ULCERATIVE COLITIS

Adults
The usual recommended initial dose of Azulfidine and Azulfidine EN-tabs is 3 to 4 grams daily divided into smaller doses (intervals between nighttime doses should not exceed 8 hours). In some cases the initial dosage is set at 1 to 2 grams daily to lessen side effects. As therapy continues, the dose is usually reduced to 2 grams daily.

Children Aged 2 and Older
The usual recommended initial dose is 40 to 60 milligrams per 2.2 pounds of body weight in each 24-hour period, divided into 3 to 6 doses. For the longer term, the dose is usually reduced to 30 milligrams per 2.2 pounds of body weight in each 24-hour period, divided into 4 doses.

RHEUMATOID ARTHRITIS

Adults
The usual dose of Azulfidine EN-tabs is 2 grams a day, divided into smaller doses. Your doctor may have you start with a lower dose, then raise the dosage to 3 grams after 12 weeks.

Children
Safety and effectiveness of Azulfidine EN-tabs in juvenile rheumatoid arthritis have not been established.

Overdosage
Any medication taken in excess can have serious consequences. If you suspect an Azulfidine overdose, seek emergency medical attention immediately.

■ *Symptoms of Azulfidine overdose may include:*
  Abdominal pain, convulsions, drowsiness, nausea, stomach upset, vomiting

Brand name:

BACTICORT

See Cortisporin Ophthalmic Suspension, page 275.

Brand name:

BACTRIM

Pronounced: BAC-trim
Generic ingredients: Trimethoprim, Sulfamethoxazole
Other brand names: Cotrim, Septra

Why is this drug prescribed?
Bactrim, an antibacterial combination drug, is prescribed for the treatment of certain urinary tract infections, severe middle ear infections in children, long-lasting or frequently recurring bronchitis in adults that has increased in seriousness, inflammation of the intestine due to a severe bacterial infection,

pneumonia in patients who have a suppressed immune system (*Pneumocystis carinii* pneumonia), and travelers' diarrhea in adults.

Most important fact about this drug

Sulfamethoxazole, an ingredient in Bactrim, is one of a group of drugs called sulfonamides, which prevent the growth of bacteria in the body. Rare but sometimes fatal reactions have occurred with use of sulfonamides. These reactions include Stevens-Johnson syndrome (severe eruptions around the mouth, anus, or eyes), progressive disintegration of the outer layer of the skin, sudden and severe liver damage, a severe blood disorder (agranulocytosis), and a lack of red and white blood cells because of a bone marrow disorder.

Notify your doctor at the first sign of an adverse reaction such as skin rash, sore throat, fever, joint pain, cough, shortness of breath, abnormal skin paleness, reddish or purplish skin spots, or yellowing of the skin or whites of the eyes.

Frequent blood counts by a doctor are recommended for patients taking sulfonamide drugs.

How should you take this medication?

It is important that you drink plenty of fluids while taking this medication in order to prevent sediment in the urine and the formation of stones.

Bactrim works best when there is a constant amount in the blood. Take Bactrim exactly as prescribed; try not to miss any doses. It is best to take doses at evenly spaced times day and night.

If you are taking Bactrim suspension, ask your pharmacist for a specially marked measuring spoon that delivers accurate doses.

- *If you miss a dose...*
  Take the forgotten dose as soon as you remember. If it is almost time for your next dose, skip the one you missed and go back to your regular schedule. Do not take 2 doses at once.

- *Storage instructions...*
  Store tablets and suspension at room temperature and protect from light. Keep tablets in a dry place. Protect the suspension from freezing.

What side effects may occur?

Side effects cannot be anticipated. If any develop or change in intensity, inform your doctor as soon as possible. Only your doctor can determine if it is safe for you to continue taking Bactrim.

■ *More common side effects may include:*
Hives, lack or loss of appetite, nausea, skin rash, vomiting

■ *Less common or rare side effects may include:*
Abdominal pain, allergic reactions, anemia, chills, convulsions, depression, diarrhea, eye irritation, fatigue, fever, hallucinations, headache, hepatitis, inability to fall or stay asleep, inability to urinate, increased urination, inflammation of heart muscle, inflammation of the mouth and/or tongue, itching, joint pain, kidney failure, lack of feeling or concern, lack of muscle coordination, loss of appetite, low blood sugar, meningitis (inflammation of the brain or spinal cord), muscle pain, nausea, nervousness, red, raised rash, redness and swelling of the tongue, ringing in the ears, scaling of dead skin due to inflammation, sensitivity to light, severe skin welts or swelling, skin eruptions, skin peeling, vertigo, weakness, yellowing of eyes and skin

Why should this drug not be prescribed?
If you are sensitive to or have ever had an allergic reaction to trimethoprim, sulfamethoxazole, or other sulfa drugs, you should not take this medication. Make sure that your doctor is aware of any drug reactions that you have experienced.

Unless you are directed to do so by your doctor, do not take this medication if you have been diagnosed as having megaloblastic anemia, which is a blood disorder due to a deficiency of folic acid.

This drug should not be given to infants less than 2 months of age.

Bactrim is not recommended for preventative or prolonged use in middle ear infections and should not be used in the treatment of streptococcal pharyngitis (strep throat) or certain other strep infections.

You should not take Bactrim if you are pregnant or nursing a baby.

Special warnings about this medication
Make sure your doctor knows if you have impaired kidney or liver function, have a folic acid deficiency, are a chronic alcoholic, are taking anticonvulsants, have been diagnosed as having malabsorption syndrome (abnormal intestinal absorption), are in a state of poor nutrition, or have severe allergies or bronchial asthma. Bactrim should be used cautiously under these conditions.

If you develop severe diarrhea, call your doctor. This drug can cause a serious intestinal inflammation.

If you have AIDS (acquired immunodeficiency syndrome) and are being treated for *Pneumocystis carinii* pneumonia, you will experience more side effects than will someone without AIDS.

Possible food and drug interactions
when taking this medication

If Bactrim is taken with certain other drugs, the effects of either could be increased, decreased, or altered. It is especially important to check with your doctor before combining Bactrim with the following:

Amantadine (Symmetrel)
Blood thinners such as Coumadin
Methotrexate (Rheumatrex)
Oral diabetes medications such as Micronase
Seizure medications such as Dilantin
Water pills (diuretics) such as HydroDIURIL

Special information
if you are pregnant or breastfeeding

Bactrim should not be taken during pregnancy. If you are pregnant or plan to become pregnant, notify your doctor immediately. Bactrim does appear in breast milk and could affect a nursing infant. It should not be taken while breastfeeding.

Recommended dosage

ADULTS

Urinary Tract Infections and Intestinal Inflammation

The usual adult dosage in the treatment of urinary tract infection is 1 Bactrim DS (double strength tablet) or 2 Bactrim tablets, or 4 teaspoonfuls (20 milliliters) of Bactrim Pediatric Suspension every 12 hours for 10 to 14 days. The dosage for inflammation of the intestine is the same but is taken for 5 days.

Worsening of Chronic Bronchitis

The usual recommended dosage is 1 Bactrim DS (double strength tablet), 2 Bactrim tablets, or 4 teaspoonfuls (20 milliliters) of Bactrim Pediatric Suspension every 12 hours for 14 days.

Pneumocystis Carinii Pneumonia

The recommended dosage is 20 milligrams of trimethoprim and 100 milligrams of sulfamethoxazole per 2.2 pounds of body weight per 24 hours divided into equal doses every 6 hours for 14 days.

Travelers' Diarrhea

The usual recommended dosage is 1 Bactrim DS (double strength tablet), 2 Bactrim tablets, or 4 teaspoonfuls (20 milliliters) of Bactrim Pediatric Suspension every 12 hours for 5 days.

CHILDREN

Urinary Tract Infections or Middle Ear Infections

The recommended dose for children 2 months of age or older, given every 12 hours for 10 days, is determined by weight. The following table is a guideline for this dosage:

22 pounds, 1 teaspoonful (5 milliliters)

44 pounds, 2 teaspoonfuls (10 milliliters) or 1 tablet

66 pounds, 3 teaspoonfuls (15 milliliters) or one-and-a-half tablets

88 pounds, 4 teaspoonfuls (20 milliliters) or 2 tablets or 1 DS tablet

Intestinal Inflammation

The recommended dose is identical to the dosage recommended for urinary tract and middle ear infections; however, it should be taken for 5 days.

Pneumocystis Carinii Pneumonia

The recommended dose, taken every 6 hours for 14 days, is determined by weight. The following table is a guideline for this dosage:

18 pounds, 1 teaspoonful (5 milliliters)

35 pounds, 2 teaspoonfuls (10 milliliters) or 1 tablet

53 pounds, 3 teaspoonfuls (15 milliliters) or one-and-a-half tablets

70 pounds, 4 teaspoonfuls (20 milliliters) or 2 tablets or 1 DS tablet

The safety of repeated use of Bactrim in children under 2 years of age has not been established.

OLDER ADULTS

There may be an increased risk of severe side effects when Bactrim is taken by older people, especially in those who have impaired kidney and/or liver function or who are taking other medication. Consult with your doctor before taking Bactrim.

Overdosage

If you suspect an overdose of Bactrim, seek emergency medical attention immediately.

- *Symptoms of an overdose of Bactrim include:*
  Blood or sediment in the urine, colic, confusion, dizziness, drowsiness, fever, headache, lack or loss of appetite, mental depression, nausea, unconsciousness, vomiting, yellowed eyes and skin

Brand name:

BACTROBAN

Pronounced: BAC-tro-ban
Generic name: Mupirocin

Why is this drug prescribed?

Bactroban is prescribed for the treatment of impetigo, a bacterial infection of the skin.

Most important fact about this drug

If the use of Bactroban does not clear your skin infection within 3 to 5 days, or if the infection becomes worse, notify your doctor.

How should you use this medication?

This drug is for external use only.

- *If you miss a dose...*
  Apply it as soon as you remember. If it is almost time for the next dose, skip the one you missed and go back to your regular schedule.

- *Storage instructions...*
  Store at room temperature.

What side effects may occur?

Side effects cannot be anticipated. If any develop or change in intensity, inform your doctor as soon as possible. Only your doctor can determine if it is safe for you to continue using Bactroban.

- *More common side effects may include:*
  Burning, pain, stinging

- *Less common side effects may include:*
  Itching

- *Rare side effects may include:*
  Abnormal redness, dry skin, inflammation of the skin, nausea, oozing, skin rash, swelling, tenderness

Why should this drug not be prescribed?

If you are sensitive to or have ever had an allergic reaction to Bactroban or similar drugs, you should not use this medication. Make sure your doctor is aware of any drug reactions you have experienced.

Special warnings about this medication

Continued or prolonged use of Bactroban may result in the growth of bacteria that do not respond to this medication and can cause a secondary infection.

This drug is not intended for use in the eyes.

If your skin shows signs of an allergic reaction or irritation, stop using Bactroban and consult your doctor.

Possible food and drug interactions
when taking this medication

There are no known interactions.

Special information
if you are pregnant or breastfeeding

The effects of Bactroban during pregnancy have not been adequately studied. If you are pregnant or plan to become pregnant, inform your doctor immediately. Bactroban may appear in breast milk and could affect a nursing infant. Your doctor may advise you to discontinue breastfeeding until your treatment with this medication is finished.

Recommended dosage

Apply a small amount of this medication to the affected area 3 times a day. Cover the treated area with gauze if you want.

Overdosage

There is no information available on overdosage.

Brand name:

BAYCOL

Pronounced: BAY-call
Generic name: Cerivastatin sodium

Why is this drug prescribed?

Baycol is used, along with a diet, to bring down dangerously high cholesterol levels when other measures have failed. Excess cholesterol in the blood-stream can lead to hardening of the arteries and heart disease. Baycol lowers both total cholesterol and LDL ("bad") cholesterol, while raising the HDL ("good") cholesterol that tends to clear the arteries.

Most important fact about this drug

Although you can't feel any symptoms of high cholesterol, it is important to take Baycol every day. The drug will be more effective if it is used along with a low-fat diet and plenty of exercise.

How should you take this medication?

Take Baycol once a day, in the evening, with or without food. Your cholesterol levels should begin to show improvement within 4 weeks.

■ *If you miss a dose...*
Take it as soon as you remember. If it is almost time for your next dose, skip the one you missed and go back to your regular schedule. Do not take 2 doses at once.

■ *Storage instructions...*
Baycol tablets should be stored at room temperature, away from moisture.

What side effects may occur?

Side effects cannot be anticipated. If any develop or change in intensity, inform your doctor as soon as possible. Only your doctor can determine if it is safe for you to continue taking Baycol.

■ *More common side effects may include:*
Diarrhea, indigestion, joint pain, runny nose, sinus problems, weakness

■ *Less common side effects may include:*
Chest pain, increased cough, insomnia, leg pain, muscle pain, swelling

Why should this drug not be prescribed?

Do not take Baycol if you are pregnant or breastfeeding; it could harm the developing baby. Also avoid Baycol if you have a liver condition or the drug gives you an allergic reaction.

Special warnings about this medication

Contact your physician immediately if you experience any unexplained muscle pain, tenderness, or weakness. Baycol has been known to trigger a muscle-wasting condition that can also affect the kidneys. The drug should be temporarily discontinued if you develop any condition that might predispose you to kidney problems, including a blood infection, low blood pressure, major surgery, injury, a severe fluid disorder, or uncontrolled seizures.

Baycol occasionally causes liver problems as well. If you've had a liver disease in the past, or you regularly drink alcoholic beverages, make sure the doctor is aware of it. Because of Baycol's potential effect on the liver, the doctor will probably test your liver function regularly.

Possible food and drug interactions
when taking this medication

If Baycol is taken with certain other drugs, the effects of either could be increased, decreased, or altered. It is especially important to check with your doctor before combining Baycol with any of the following:

Antifungal drugs such as Diflucan and Nizoral
Drugs that suppress the immune system, such as Sandimmune and Neoral
Erythromycin (E.E.S., E-Mycin, PCE, others)
Fibric acid derivatives such as Atromid-S
Nicotinic acid (Niacin)

Special information
if you are pregnant or breastfeeding

If you are pregnant or plan to become pregnant, stop taking Baycol immediately and inform your doctor. Baycol should not be used during pregnancy or while nursing.

Recommended dosage

ADULTS

The usual starting dose of Baycol is 300 mcg (micrograms) once a day in the evening. If you have kidney disease, the starting dose is 200 mcg.

If your doctor prescribes both Baycol and cholestyramine (Questran), take the Questran first, followed by Baycol at least 2 hours later.

CHILDREN

The safety and effectiveness of Baycol have not been established in children.

Overdosage

Little is known about Baycol overdose. However, any medication taken in excess can have serious consequences. If you suspect an overdose, seek medical treatment immediately.

Generic name:

BECLOMETHASONE

Pronounced: BECK-low-METH-ah-sone
Brand names: Beclovent Inhalation Aerosol, Beconase AQ
Nasal Spray, Beconase Inhalation Aerosol, Vancenase
AQ Nasal Spray, Vancenase Nasal Inhaler, Vanceril
Double Strength Inhalation Aerosol, Vanceril Inhaler

Why is this drug prescribed?

Beclomethasone is a type of steroid used for respiratory problems. Beclovent and Vanceril are prescribed for the treatment of recurring symptoms of bronchial asthma.

Beconase and Vancenase are used to relieve the symptoms of hay fever and to prevent regrowth of nasal polyps following surgical removal.

Most important fact about this drug

Beclomethasone is not a bronchodilator medication (it does not quickly open the airways); and it should not be used for relief of asthma when bronchodilators and other nonsteroid drugs prove effective. Do not expect immediate relief from beclomethasone, and do not take higher doses in an attempt to make it work. It is not intended for rapid relief, but it will help control symptoms when taken routinely.

How should you take this medication?

Beclomethasone is prescribed in an oral inhalant or a nasal spray form. Use this medication only as preventive therapy, and take only the dose prescribed.

Although some people begin to notice improvement within a day or two, it may take 1 or 2 weeks for the full benefits to appear. If there's no improvement after 3 weeks, let your doctor know.

Be sure to take the drug regularly, even if you have no symptoms. Many people will require additional drugs to control asthma symptoms fully, but this drug may allow other drugs to be used in smaller doses.

If you are also using a bronchodilator inhalant, take it before inhaling beclomethasone. This will improve the effect of the second drug. Take the two inhalations several minutes apart.

Spray the inhalation aerosol into the air twice before you use it for the first time and when you have not used it for more than 7 days. Use it within 6 months.

Before you use Vancenase AQ 84 microgram nasal spray, press the pump 6 times or until you see a fine spray. If you don't use it for more than 4 days, reprime the pump by spraying once or until a fine spray appears.

To use the inhaler:
1. Remove the cap and hold inhaler upright.
2. Shake the inhaler thoroughly.
3. Take a drink of water to moisten the throat.
4. Tilt your head slightly and breathe out.
5. While activating the inhaler, take a slow deep breath for 3 to 5 seconds, hold the breath for about 10 seconds, then breathe out slowly.
6. Allow at least 1 minute between inhalations.

Gargling and rinsing your mouth with water after each dose may help prevent hoarseness and throat irritation. Do not swallow the water after you rinse.

Be careful to avoid spraying the medication into your eyes. This medication comes with directions. Read them carefully before using it.

■ *If you miss a dose...*
Take it as soon as you remember and take the remaining doses for that day at evenly spaced intervals. If it is time for your next dose, skip the one you missed. Never take 2 doses at the same time.

■ *Storage instructions...*
Store at room temperature in a dry place, away from heat and cold. Do not puncture the container, store it near open flame, or dispose of it in a fire or incinerator.

What side effects may occur?
Side effects cannot be anticipated. If any develop or change in intensity, inform your doctor as soon as possible. Only your doctor can determine if it is safe for you to continue taking this medication.

■ *Side effects may include:*
Cataracts, dry mouth, fluid retention, hives, hoarseness, increased pressure within the eye (glaucoma), skin rash, wheezing

■ *When using a nasal spray, other possible side effects are:*
Cough, headache, light-headedness, nasal burning, nasal and throat dryness and irritation, nausea, nose and throat infections, nosebleed, pain, pinkeye, ringing in the ears, runny nose, sneezing, sore throat, stuffy nose, tearing eyes, unpleasant—or loss of—taste and smell

Why should this drug not be prescribed?

Your doctor will prescribe beclomethasone only if your asthma cannot be controlled with bronchodilators and other nonsteroid medications.

Beclomethasone is not used for the treatment of non-asthmatic bronchitis, or for intermittent asthma therapy.

If you are sensitive to or have ever had an allergic reaction to beclomethasone or other steroid drugs, you should not take this medication. Make sure that your doctor is aware of any drug reactions that you have experienced.

Although unlikely, immediate allergic reactions to beclomethasone have been known to occur.

Special warnings about this medication

When steroid drugs are taken by mouth they substitute for and decrease the body's normal ability to make its own steroids as well as its ability to respond to stress.

There is a risk of causing a serious condition called "adrenal insufficiency" when people change from steroid tablets taken by mouth to aerosol beclomethasone. Although the aerosol may provide adequate control of asthma during the changeover period, it does not provide the normal amount of steroid the body needs during acute stress situations. If you are being transferred from steroid tablets to beclomethasone and you experience a period of stress or a severe asthma attack, your doctor may prescribe additional treatment with steroid tablets.

Transfer from steroid tablet therapy to beclomethasone aerosol may reactivate allergic conditions that were previously suppressed by the steroid tablet therapy, such as runny nose, inflamed eyelids, and eczema. Inform your doctor if you experience any of these symptoms.

High doses of steroids can suppress your immune system. Take extra care to avoid exposure to measles or chickenpox if you have never had them or never had shots. These infections can be serious or even fatal if your immune system is below par. If you are exposed, seek medical advice immediately.

Symptoms such as mental disturbances, increased bruising, weight gain, facial swelling (moon-faced), acne, and cataracts may occur with orally inhaled steroids such as Beclovent. If you experience any of these symptoms, notify your doctor immediately.

Long-term use of steroids can slow down growth in children. If your child seems to be growing more slowly than normal, call your doctor.

If bronchodilator medications seem less effective after you start taking beclomethasone, be sure to tell your doctor. Do not abruptly stop using beclomethasone on your own.

If you have tuberculosis, a herpes infection of the eye, or any untreated infection, your doctor may not want you to use an inhaled steroid.

Special information
if you are pregnant or breastfeeding

The effects of beclomethasone in pregnancy have not been adequately studied. If you are pregnant or are planning a pregnancy, let your doctor know. Steroids do appear in breast milk and could harm your baby. Your doctor may want you to avoid breastfeeding while you are using beclomethasone.

Recommended dosage

ADULTS

Beclomethasone Oral Inhalant

The usual recommended dose for adults and children 12 years of age and over is 2 inhalations taken 2 to 4 times a day. Four inhalations taken twice daily have been shown to be effective in some people. If you have severe asthma, your doctor may advise you to start with 12 to 16 inhalations a day. Daily intake should not exceed 20 inhalations.

For the double-strength inhalation aerosol, the usual dose is 2 inhalations twice a day. If your asthma is severe, your doctor may have you start with 6 to 8 inhalations a day. The maximum daily dosage is 10 inhalations.

Beclomethasone Nasal Spray

For adults and children 12 years of age and older, the usual dosage is 1 or 2 inhalations in each nostril 2 to 4 times a day, depending on the brand. For the double strength nasal spray, the dosage is 1 or 2 inhalations in each nostril once a day.

The usual dosage of Vancenase AQ 84 micrograms for adults and children 6 years and over is 1 or 2 inhalations in each nostril once a day.

CHILDREN

Beclomethasone Oral Inhalant

Children 6 to 12 years of age: The usual recommended dose is 1 or 2 inhalations 3 or 4 times a day. Four inhalations twice daily have been effective for some children. Daily intake should not exceed 10 inhalations.

For the double-strength inhalation aerosol, the usual dose is 2 inhalations twice daily, with a maximum of 5 inhalations a day.

Beclomethasone Nasal Spray
Children 6 to 12 years of age: The usual dosage is 1 inhalation in each nostril 2 or 3 times daily. Some children may need 2 inhalations. The dosage for the double strength nasal spray is 1 or 2 inhalations in each nostril once a day.

Beclomethasone should not be given to children under the age of 6 unless advised by your doctor.

Overdosage

Any medication taken in excess can have serious consequences. If you suspect an overdose, seek medical attention immediately.

Brand name:

BECLOVENT

See Beclomethasone, page 133.

Brand name:

BECONASE

See Beclomethasone, page 133.

Brand name:

BEEPEN-VK

See Penicillin V Potassium, page 932.

Brand name:

BELLATAL

See Donnatal, page 409.

Brand name:

BENADRYL

Pronounced: BEN-ah-dril
Generic name: Diphenhydramine hydrochloride

Why is this drug prescribed?

Benadryl is an antihistamine with drying and sedative effects. It relieves red, inflamed eyes caused by food allergies and the itching, swelling, and redness from hives and other rashes that are caused by mild allergic reactions. It also relieves the sneezing, coughing, runny or stuffy nose, and red, teary, itching eyes caused by seasonal allergies (hay fever) and the common cold. Antihistamines work by decreasing the effects of histamine, a chemical released in the body that narrows air passages in the lungs and contributes to inflammation. Antihistamines reduce itching and swelling and dry up secretions from the nose, eyes, and throat.

Benadryl is also used to treat allergic reactions to blood transfusions, to prevent and treat motion sickness, and, with other drugs, to treat anaphylactic shock (severe allergic reaction) and Parkinson's disease, a nerve disorder characterized by tremors, stooped posture, shuffling walk, muscle weakness, drooling, and emotional instability.

Most important fact about this drug
Antihistamines may produce excitability in children. In the elderly they may cause dizziness, excessive calm, or low blood pressure.

How should you take this medication?
Benadryl should be taken exactly as prescribed, or follow instructions on the label.

▪ *If you miss a dose...*
Take it as soon as you remember. If it is almost time for your next dose, skip the one you missed and go back to your regular schedule. Do not take 2 doses at once.

▪ *Storage instructions...*
Store at room temperature. Protect from moisture.

What side effects may occur?
Side effects cannot be anticipated. If any develop or change in intensity, inform your doctor as soon as possible. Only your doctor can determine if it is safe for you to continue taking Benadryl.

▪ *More common side effects may include:*
Disturbed coordination, dizziness, excessive calm, increased chest congestion, sleepiness, stomach upset

▪ *Less common or rare side effects may include:*
Anaphylactic shock (extreme allergic reaction), anemia, blurred vision, chills, confusion, constipation, convulsions, diarrhea, difficulty sleeping,

double vision, dry mouth, nose, throat, early menstruation, excessive perspiration, excitation, fast, fluttery heartbeat, fatigue, frequent or difficult urination, headache, hives, inability to urinate, increased sensitivity to light, irregular heartbeat, irritability, loss of appetite, low blood pressure, nausea, nervousness, rapid heartbeat, rash, restlessness, ringing in the ears, stuffy nose, tightness of chest and wheezing, tingling or pins and needles, tremor, unreal or exaggerated sense of well-being, vertigo, vomiting

Why should this drug not be prescribed?

Benadryl should not be used in newborn or premature infants, or if you are breastfeeding your infant.

Do not take this medication if you are sensitive to or have ever had an allergic reaction to diphenhydramine hydrochloride or other antihistamines.

Special warnings about this medication

In general, you should use antihistamines very cautiously if you have the eye condition called narrow-angle glaucoma, narrowing of the stomach or intestine because of peptic ulcer or other stomach problems, intestinal blockage, symptoms of an enlarged prostate, or difficulty urinating due to obstruction in the bladder.

Antihistamines can make adults and children less alert and, in young children, may cause excitability.

Elderly people (60 years or older) are more likely to experience dizziness, extreme calm, and low blood pressure.

Use Benadryl cautiously if you have a history of asthma or other chronic lung disease, an over-active thyroid, high blood pressure, or heart disease.

This medication can cause drowsiness. Driving or operating dangerous machinery or participating in any hazardous activity that requires full mental alertness is not recommended until you know how you react to Benadryl.

Possible food and drug interactions
when taking this medication

Benadryl may increase the effects of alcohol, and alcohol may increase the sedative effects of Benadryl. Do not drink alcohol while taking this medication.

If Benadryl is taken with certain other drugs, the effects of either could be increased, decreased, or altered. It is especially important to check with your doctor before combining Benadryl with the following:

Antidepressant drugs known as MAO inhibitors, such as Parnate and Nardil

Sedative/hypnotics such as Halcion, Nembutal, and Seconal

Tranquilizers such as Xanax and Valium

Special information
if you are pregnant or breastfeeding
The effects of Benadryl during pregnancy have not been adequately studied. If you are pregnant or plan to become pregnant, inform your doctor immediately. Benadryl should be used during pregnancy only if clearly needed. Antihistamine therapy is not advised for nursing mothers. If this medication is essential to your health, your doctor may advise you to discontinue breastfeeding until your treatment with Benadryl is finished.

Recommended dosage
Your doctor will tailor the dosage to suit your needs. Benadryl reaches its peak effect in 1 hour, and 1 dose will continue to work for 4 to 6 hours.

ADULTS

The usual recommended dose is 25 to 50 milligrams 3 or 4 times daily. The sleep-aid dosage is 50 milligrams at bedtime.

Motion Sickness
For prevention of motion sickness, take the first dose 30 minutes before exposure to motion; take the other doses before meals and at bedtime for as long as the motion continues.

CHILDREN (OVER 20 POUNDS)

The usual dose is 12.5 to 25 milligrams, 3 to 4 times daily. A child should not take more than 300 milligrams a day.

This medication should not be used as a sleep aid for children under age 12.

Your physician will determine the best use of the drug in response to its effects on the child.

Overdosage
Any medication taken in excess can have serious consequences. If you suspect an overdose, seek medical attention immediately. Antihistamine overdose has caused hallucinations, convulsions, and death in children.

■ *Symptoms of Benadryl overdose may include:*
Central nervous system depression or stimulation, especially in children, dry mouth, fixed, dilated pupils, flushing, stomach and intestinal symptoms

Generic name:

BENAZEPRIL

See Lotensin, page 702.

Brand name:

BENTYL

Pronounced: BEN-til
Generic name: Dicyclomine hydrochloride

Why is this drug prescribed?
Bentyl is prescribed for the treatment of functional bowel/irritable bowel syndrome (abdominal pain, accompanied by diarrhea and constipation associated with stress).

Most important fact about this drug
Heat prostration (fever and heat stroke due to decreased sweating) can occur with use of this drug in hot weather. If symptoms occur, stop taking the drug and notify your doctor immediately.

How should you take this medication?
Take this medication exactly as prescribed.

■ *If you miss a dose...*
Take it as soon as you remember. If it is almost time for your next dose, skip the one you missed and go back to your regular schedule. Do not take 2 doses at once.

■ *Storage instructions...*
Store at room temperature. Keep tablets out of direct sunlight. Keep syrup away from excessive heat.

What side effects may occur?
Side effects cannot be anticipated. If any develop or change in intensity, inform your doctor as soon as possible. Only your doctor can determine if it is safe for you to continue taking Bentyl.

■ *Side effects may include:*
Blurred vision, dizziness, drowsiness, dry mouth, light-headedness, nausea, nervousness, weakness

Not all of the following side effects have been reported with dicyclomine hydrochloride, but they have been reported for similar drugs with antispasmodic action; contact your doctor if they occur.

Abdominal pain, bloated feeling, constipation, decreased sweating, difficulty in urinating, double vision, enlargement of the pupil of the eye, eye paralysis, fainting, headache, hives, impotence, inability to urinate, increased pressure in the eyes, itching, labored, difficult breathing, lack of coordination, lack or loss of appetite, nasal stuffiness or congestion, numbness, rapid heartbeat, rash, severe allergic reaction, sluggishness, sneezing, suffocation, suppression of breast milk, taste loss, temporary cessation of breathing, throat congestion, tingling, vomiting

Why should this drug not be prescribed?
If you are sensitive to or have ever had an allergic reaction to Bentyl, you should not take this medication. Make sure your doctor is aware of any drug reactions you have experienced.

Unless you are directed to do so by your doctor, do not take this drug if you have a blockage of the urinary tract, stomach, or intestines; severe ulcerative colitis (inflammatory disease of the large intestine); reflux esophagitis (inflammation of the esophagus usually caused by the backflow of acid stomach contents); glaucoma; or myasthenia gravis (a disease characterized by long-lasting fatigue and muscle weakness).

This drug should not be given to infants less than 6 months of age or used by women who are nursing an infant.

Special warnings about this medication
Bentyl may produce drowsiness or blurred vision. Therefore, driving a car, operating machinery, or participating in any activity that requires full mental alertness is not recommended.

Diarrhea may be an early symptom of a partial intestinal blockage, especially in people who have had bowel removals and an ileostomy or colostomy. If this occurs, notify your doctor immediately.

You should use this medication with caution if you have autonomic neuropathy (a nerve disorder); liver or kidney disease; hyperthyroidism; high blood pressure; coronary heart disease; congestive heart failure; rapid, irregular heartbeat; hiatal hernia (protrusion of part of the stomach through the diaphragm); or enlargement of the prostate gland.

Possible food and drug interactions when taking this medication

If Bentyl is taken with certain other drugs, the effects of either could be increased, decreased, or altered. It is especially important to check with your doctor before combining Bentyl with the following:

Airway-opening drugs such as Proventil and Ventolin
Amantadine (Symmetrel)
Antacids such as Maalox
Antiarrhythmics such as quinidine (Quinidex)
Antiglaucoma drugs such as Pilopine
Antihistamines such as Tavist
Benzodiazepines (tranquilizers) such as Valium and Xanax
Corticosteroids such as prednisone (Deltasone)
Digoxin (the heart failure medication Lanoxin)
Major tranquilizers such as Mellaril and Thorazine
MAO inhibitors (antidepressants such as Nardil and Parnate)
Metoclopramide (the gastrointestinal stimulant Reglan)
Narcotic analgesics (pain relievers such as Demerol)
Nitrates and nitrites (heart medications such as nitroglycerin)
Tricyclic antidepressant drugs such as Elavil and Tofranil

Special information if you are pregnant or breastfeeding

The effects of Bentyl during pregnancy have not been adequately studied. If you are pregnant or plan to become pregnant, notify your doctor. Bentyl does appear in breast milk and could affect a nursing infant. Do not use it when breastfeeding.

Recommended dosage

ADULTS

The usual dosage is 160 milligrams per day divided into 4 equal doses. Since this dose is associated with a significant incidence of side effects, your doctor may recommend a starting dose of 80 milligrams per day divided into 4 equal doses. If no side effects appear, the doctor will then increase the dose.

If this drug is not effective within 2 weeks or side effects require doses below 80 milligrams per day, your doctor may discontinue it.

Overdosage
Any medication taken in excess can have serious consequences. If you suspect an overdose, seek medical attention immediately.

■ *Symptoms of a Bentyl overdose include:*
Blurred vision, difficulty in swallowing, dilated pupils, dizziness, dryness of the mouth, headache, hot, dry skin, nausea, nerve blockage causing weakness and possible paralysis, vomiting

Brand name:

BENZAC W

See Desquam-E, page 353.

Brand name:

BENZAGEL

See Desquam-E, page 353.

Brand name:

BENZAMYCIN

Pronounced: BEN-za-MI-sin
Generic ingredients: Erythromycin, Benzoyl peroxide

Why is this drug prescribed?
A combination of the antibiotic erythromycin and the antibacterial agent benzoyl peroxide, Benzamycin is effective in stopping the bacteria that cause acne and in reducing acne infection.

Most important fact about this drug
If you experience excessive irritation, stop using Benzamycin and notify your doctor.

How should you use this medication?
Use Benzamycin 2 times per day, once in the morning and once in the evening, or as directed by your doctor.

Before applying Benzamycin, thoroughly wash the affected area with soap and warm water, rinse well, and gently pat dry. Apply Benzamycin to the entire area, not just the pimples.

- *If you miss a dose...*
  Apply it as soon as you remember. If it is almost time for your next dose, skip the one you missed and go back to your regular schedule.

- *Storage instructions...*
  This medication should be stored in your refrigerator in a tightly closed container and discarded after 3 months. Do not freeze.

What side effects may occur?
Very few side effects have been reported with the use of Benzamycin. However, those reported include dryness and swelling.

Occasionally, use of this medication has caused a burning sensation; eye irritation; inflammation of the face, eyes, and nose; itching; oiliness; reddened skin; skin discoloration; skin irritation and peeling; and skin tenderness.

If any side effects develop or change in intensity, inform your doctor as soon as possible. Only your doctor can determine if it is safe for you to continue using Benzamycin.

Why should this drug not be prescribed?
If you are sensitive to or have ever had an allergic reaction to erythromycin or benzoyl peroxide, or any other ingredients in Benzamycin, you should not use this medication. Make sure your doctor is aware of any drug reactions you have experienced.

Special warnings about this medication
Benzamycin Topical Gel is for external use only. Avoid contact with your eyes, nose, mouth, and all mucous membranes.

Benzamycin may bleach hair or colored fabric. Avoid contact with scalp and clothes.

As you use this antibiotic, organisms that are resistant to it may start to grow. Your doctor will have you stop using Benzamycin and will give you a medication to fight the new bacteria.

If you develop diarrhea after you start using Benzamycin, call your doctor. You may have an intestinal inflammation that could be serious.

Possible food and drug interactions
when using this medication
If Benzamycin is used with other acne medications, the effects of either could be increased, decreased, or altered. Always check with your doctor

before combining any other prescription or over-the-counter acne remedy with Benzamycin.

Special information
if you are pregnant or breastfeeding

The effects of Benzamycin during pregnancy have not been adequately studied. If you are pregnant or plan to become pregnant, inform your doctor immediately. It is not known whether Benzamycin appears in breast milk, but erythromycin does if it is swallowed or injected. If this medication is essential to your health, your doctor may advise you to discontinue breastfeeding your baby until your treatment with this medication is finished.

Recommended dosage

ADULTS

Apply to affected areas twice daily, once in the morning and once in the evening.

CHILDREN

The safety and effectiveness of Benzamycin have not been established in children under 12 years of age.

Overdosage

There is no information available on overdosage.

Brand name:

BENZASHAVE

See Desquam-E, page 353.

Generic name:

BENZONATATE

See Tessalon, page 1222.

Generic name:

BENZOYL PEROXIDE

See Desquam-E, page 353.

Generic name:

BENZTROPINE

See Cogentin, page 249.

Brand name:

BETAGAN

Pronounced: BAIT-ah-gan
Generic name: Levobunolol hydrochloride

Why is this drug prescribed?
Betagan eyedrops are given to treat chronic open-angle glaucoma (increased pressure inside the eye). This medication is in a class called beta blockers. It works by lowering pressure within the eyeball.

Most important fact about this drug
Although Betagan eyedrops are applied to the eye, the medication is absorbed and may have effects in other parts of the body. If you have diabetes, asthma or other respiratory diseases, or decreased heart function, make sure your doctor is aware of the problem.

How should you use this medication?
Use Betagan eyedrops exactly as prescribed. Some people also need to use eyedrops that constrict their pupils.

Administer Betagan eyedrops as follows:
1. Wash your hands thoroughly.
2. Gently pull your lower eyelid down to form a pocket between your eye and eyelid.
3. Hold the bottle on the bridge of your nose or on your forehead.
4. Do not touch the applicator tip to any surface, including your eye.
5. Tilt your head back and squeeze the medication into your eye.
6. Close your eyes gently.
7. Keep your eyes closed for 1 to 2 minutes.
8. Wait 5 to 10 minutes before using any other eyedrops.
9. Do not rinse the dropper.

- *If you miss a dose...*
  If you take Betagan once a day, use it as soon as you remember. If you do not remember until the next day, skip the dose you missed and go back to your regular schedule. Do not take 2 doses at once. If you take Betagan 2 or more times a day, use it as soon as you remember. If it is almost time

for your next dose, skip the one you missed and go back to your regular schedule. Do not take 2 doses at once.

■ *Storage instructions...*
Store at room temperature, away from light.

What side effects may occur?
Side effects from Betagan cannot be anticipated. If any develop or change in intensity, inform your doctor. Only your doctor can determine whether it is safe for you to continue using this medication. You may feel a momentary burning and stinging when you place the drops in your eyes. More rarely, you may develop an eye inflammation.

Beta blockers may cause muscle weakness; weakened muscles around the eyes may cause double vision or drooping eyelids.

■ *Other potential side effects include:*
Burning and tingling (pins and needles), chest pain, confusion, congestive heart failure, depression, diarrhea, difficult or labored breathing, dizziness, fainting, hair loss, headache, heart palpitations, hives, impotence, low blood pressure, nasal congestion, nausea, rash, skin peeling, slow or irregular heartbeat, stroke, temporary heart stoppage, vision problems, weakness, wheezing

Why should this drug not be prescribed?
Do not use Betagan if you have ever had an allergic reaction to it or are sensitive to it.

You should not use Betagan if you have any of the following conditions:
Asthma
Cardiogenic shock (shock due to insufficient heart action)
Certain heart irregularities
Heart failure
Severe chronic obstructive lung disease
Slow heartbeat (sinus bradycardia)

Special warnings about this medication
Betagan contains a sulfite preservative. In a few people, sulfites can cause an allergic reaction, which may be life-threatening. If you suffer from asthma, you are at increased risk for sulfite allergy.

Betagan may be absorbed into your bloodstream. If too much of the drug is absorbed, this may worsen asthma or other lung diseases or lead to heart failure, which sometimes happens with oral beta-blocker medications.

Beta blockers may increase the risks of anesthesia. If you are facing elective surgery, your doctor may want you to taper off Betagan prior to your operation.

Use Betagan cautiously if you have diminished lung function.

Since beta blockers may mask some signs and symptoms of low blood sugar (hypoglycemia), you should use Betagan very carefully if you have low blood sugar, or if you have diabetes and are taking insulin or an oral antidiabetic medication.

If your body tends to produce too much thyroid hormone, you should taper off Betagan very gradually rather than stopping the drug all at once. Abrupt withdrawal of any beta blocker may provoke a rush of thyroid hormone ("thyroid storm").

Do not use 2 or more beta-blocker eye medications at the same time.

Possible food and drug interactions
when taking this medication

If Betagan is used with certain other drugs, the effects of either could be increased, decreased, or altered. It is especially important to check with your doctor before combining Betagan with the following:

Calcium-blocking blood pressure medications such as Calan and
  Cardizem
Digitalis (the heart medication Lanoxin)
Epinephrine (Epifrin)
Oral beta blockers such as the blood pressure medications Inderal and
  Tenormin
Reserpine (Serpasil)

Special information
if you are pregnant or breastfeeding

The use of Betagan in pregnancy has not been adequately studied. If you are pregnant or plan to become pregnant, notify your doctor immediately. Betagan eyedrops should be used during pregnancy only if the benefit justifies the potential risk to the unborn child. Since other beta-blocker medications are known to appear in breast milk, use Betagan eyedrops with caution if you are breastfeeding.

Recommended dosage

ADULTS

The recommended starting dose is 1 or 2 drops of Betagan 0.5% in the affected eye(s) once a day.

The typical dose of Betagan 0.25% is 1 or 2 drops twice daily.

For more severe glaucoma, your doctor may have you use Betagan 0.5% twice a day.

Overdosage
Overuse of Betagan eyedrops may produce symptoms of beta-blocker overdosage—slowed heartbeat, low blood pressure, breathing difficulty, and/or heart failure. Any medication taken in excess can have serious consequences. If you suspect an overdose of Betagan, seek medical attention immediately.

Generic name:

BETAINE ANHYDROUS

See Cystadane, page 300.

Generic name:

BETAMETHASONE

See Diprolene, page 393.

Generic name:

BETAXOLOL

See Betoptic, page 150.

Brand name:

BETIMOL

See Timoptic, page 1243.

Brand name:

BETOPTIC

Pronounced: bet-OP-tick
Generic name: Betaxolol hydrochloride

Why is this drug prescribed?
Betoptic Ophthalmic Solution and Betoptic S Ophthalmic Suspension contain medication that lowers internal eye pressure and is used to treat open-ngle glaucoma (high pressure of the fluid in the eye).

Most important fact about this drug
Although Betoptic, a type of drug called a beta blocker, is applied directly to the eye, it may be absorbed into the bloodstream. Because it may have effects in other parts of the body, you should use Betoptic cautiously if you have diabetes, asthma or other respiratory diseases, or decreased heart function.

How should you use this medication?
Use this medication exactly as prescribed. You may need to use other medications at the same time.

Betoptic S Suspension should be shaken well before each dose.

Administer Betoptic as follows:
1. Wash your hands thoroughly.
2. Gently pull your lower eyelid down to form a pocket between your eye and eyelid.
3. Hold the bottle on the bridge of your nose or on your forehead.
4. Do not touch the applicator tip to any surface, including your eye.
5. Tilt your head back and squeeze the medication into your eye.
6. Close your eyes gently.
7. Keep your eyes closed for 1 to 2 minutes.
8. Wait for 5 to 10 minutes before using any other eyedrops.
9. Do not rinse the dropper.

■ *If you miss a dose...*
Use it as soon as you remember. If it is almost time for your next dose, skip the one you missed and go back to your regular schedule. Do not use 2 doses at once.

■ *Storage instructions...*
Store at room temperature.

What side effects may occur?
Side effects cannot be anticipated. If any develop or change in intensity, inform your doctor as soon as possible. Only your doctor can determine if it is safe for you to continue using Betoptic.

■ *More common side effects may include:*
Temporary eye discomfort

■ *Less common or rare side effects may include:*
Allergic reactions, asthma, changes in taste or smell, congestive heart failure, decreased corneal sensitivity, dead skin, depression, difficulty

breathing, difficulty sleeping or drowsiness, dizziness, hair loss, headache, hives, inflammation of the cornea, inflammation of the tongue, intolerance to light, itching, peeling skin, pupils of different sizes, red eyes and skin, slow heartbeat, sluggishness, tearing, thickening chest secretions, vertigo, wheezing

Why should this drug not be prescribed?

Do not use Betoptic if you are sensitive to or have ever had an allergic reaction to it.

People with certain heart conditions should not use Betoptic.

Special warnings about this medication

Before you use Betoptic, tell your doctor if you have any of the following:

Asthma
Diabetes
Heart disease
Thyroid disease

If you are having surgery, your doctor may advise you to gradually stop using Betoptic before you undergo general anesthesia.

This drug may lose some of its effectiveness for glaucoma after you have been taking it a long time.

Possible food and drug interactions
when using this medication

If Betoptic is used with certain other drugs, the effects of either could be increased, decreased, or altered. It is especially important to check with your doctor before combining Betoptic with the following:

Drugs that alter mood, such as Nardil and Elavil
Oral beta blockers such as Inderal and Tenormin
Reserpine (Serpasil)

Special information
if you are pregnant or breastfeeding

The effects of Betoptic during pregnancy have not been adequately studied. If you are pregnant or plan to become pregnant, inform your doctor immediately. Betoptic may appear in breast milk and could affect a nursing infant. If this medication is essential to your health, your doctor may advise you to stop breastfeeding until your treatment with Betoptic is finished.

Recommended dosage

Your doctor may have you take another medication with Betoptic or Betoptic S.

ADULTS

Betoptic

The usual recommended dose is 1 to 2 drops of Betoptic in the affected eye(s) twice daily.

Betoptic S

The usual recommended dose is 1 to 2 drops of Betoptic S in the affected eye(s) twice daily.

Overdosage

Any medication used in excess can have serious consequences. If you suspect an overdose of Betoptic, seek medical attention immediately.

With an oral beta blocker, symptoms of overdose might include:

Heart failure, low blood pressure, slow heartbeat

Brand name:

BIAXIN

Pronounced: buy-AX-in
Generic name: Clarithromycin

Why is this drug prescribed?

Biaxin, an antibiotic chemically related to erythromycin, is used to treat certain bacterial infections of the respiratory tract, including:

Strep throat
Pneumonia
Sinusitis (inflamed sinuses)
Tonsillitis (inflamed tonsils)
Acute middle ear infections
Acute flare-ups of chronic bronchitis (inflamed airways)

Biaxin is also prescribed to treat infections of the skin, and, combined with Prilosec or Tritec, is used to cure ulcers near the exit from the stomach (duodenal ulcers) caused by *H. pylori* bacteria. The drug can also be prescribed to combat *Mycobacterium avium* infections in people with AIDS.

Most important fact about this drug
Biaxin, like any other antibiotic, works best when there is a constant amount of drug in the blood. To keep the amount constant, try not to miss any doses.

How should you take this medication?
You may take Biaxin with or without food. Take it exactly as prescribed; continue taking it for the full course of treatment.

- *If you miss a dose...*
  Take it as soon as you remember. If it is almost time for your next dose, take the one you missed and take the next one 5 to 6 hours later. Then go back to your regular schedule.

- *Storage instructions...*
  Store at room temperature in a tightly closed container, away from light. Do not refrigerate the suspension.

What side effects may occur?
Side effects cannot be anticipated. If any side effects develop or change in intensity, tell your doctor immediately. Only your doctor can determine whether it is safe for you to continue taking Biaxin.

- *Side effects may include:*
  Abdominal pain/discomfort, altered sense of taste, diarrhea, headache, indigestion, nausea

Why should this drug not be prescribed?
Do not take Biaxin if you have ever had an allergic reaction to it, or if you are sensitive to it or erythromycin, or similar antibiotics such as Tao and Zithromax. Also avoid Biaxin if you have a heart condition or an imbalance in the body's water and minerals; and do not take the drug while taking Orap, Propulsid, or Seldane.

Special warnings about this medication
If you have severe kidney disease, the doctor may need to prescribe a smaller dose of Biaxin. Make sure the doctor is aware of any kidney problems you may have.

Like other antibiotics, Biaxin may cause a potentially life-threatening form of diarrhea that signals a condition called pseudomembranous colitis (inflammation of the large intestine). Mild diarrhea, a fairly common Biaxin side effect, may disappear as your body gets used to the drug. However, if Biaxin gives you prolonged or severe diarrhea, stop taking the drug and call your doctor immediately.

Possible food and drug interactions
when taking this medication

If Biaxin is taken with certain other drugs, the effects of either can be increased, decreased, or altered. It is especially important to check with your doctor before combining Biaxin with the following:

Astemizole (Hismanal)
Bromocriptine (Parlodel)
Carbamazepine (Tegretol)
Cisapride (Propulsid)
Cyclosporine (Sandimmune, Neoral)
Disopyramide (Norpace)
Fluconazole (Diflucan)
Hexobarbital
Lovastatin (Mevacor)
Phenytoin (Dilantin)
Pimozide (Orap)
Tacrolimus (Prograf)
Terfenadine (Seldane)
Theophylline (Slo-Phyllin, Theo-Dur, others)
Valproate (Depakene, Depakote)
Zidovudine (Retrovir)

Biaxin is chemically related to erythromycin. It is possible that other drugs reported to interact with erythromycin could also interact with Biaxin. They include:

Blood thinners such as Coumadin
Digoxin (Lanoxin)
Ergotamine (Cafergot)
Triazolam (Halcion)

Special information
if you are pregnant or breastfeeding

If you are pregnant or plan to become pregnant, notify your doctor immediately. Since Biaxin may have the potential to produce birth defects, it is prescribed during pregnancy only when there is no alternative. Caution is advised when using Biaxin while breastfeeding. Biaxin may appear in breast milk, as does its chemical cousin, erythromycin.

Recommended dosage

ADULTS

Ear, Nose, and Throat Infections

Your doctor will carefully tailor your individual dosage of Biaxin depending upon the type of infection and organism causing it.

The usual dose varies from 250 to 500 milligrams every 12 hours for 7 to 14 days.

Duodenal Ulcers

The usual dose is 500 milligrams three times a day, plus 40 milligrams of Propulsid each morning, or 400 milligrams of Tritec twice a day.

Mycobacterium Avium Infections

For prevention or treatment, the recommended dose is 500 milligrams twice a day.

CHILDREN

Biaxin is not recommended for children under 6 months of age.

The dose for children older than 6 months depends on how much the child weighs. Biaxin is usually given twice a day for 10 days.

Overdosage

Although no specific information is available, any medication taken in excess can have serious consequences. If you suspect an overdose of Biaxin, seek medical attention immediately.

Generic name:

BISMUTH SUBSALICYLATE, METRONIDAZOLE, AND TETRACYCLINE

See Helidac Therapy, page 560.

Brand name:

BLEPH-10

See Sodium Sulamyd, page 1147.

Brand name:

BONINE

See Antivert, page 75.

Brand name:

BRETHAIRE

See Brethine, page 157.

Brand name:

BRETHINE

Pronounced: Breath-EEN
Generic name: Terbutaline sulfate
Other brand names: Bricanyl, Brethaire

Why is this drug prescribed?
Brethine is a bronchodilator (a medication that opens the bronchial tubes), prescribed for the prevention and relief of bronchial spasms in asthma. This medication is also used for the relief of bronchial spasm associated with bronchitis and emphysema.

Most important fact about this drug
If you experience an immediate allergic reaction and a worsening of a bronchial spasm, notify your doctor immediately.

How should you take this medication?
Take this drug exactly as prescribed by your doctor.

The action of Brethine may last up to 8 hours. Do not use it more frequently than recommended.

- *If you miss a dose...*
  Take it as soon as you remember. Then take the rest of your medication for that day in evenly spaced doses. Do not take 2 doses at once.

- *Storage instructions...*
  Store at room temperature in a tightly closed container, away from light.

What side effects may occur?
Side effects cannot be anticipated. If any develop or change in intensity, inform your doctor as soon as possible. Only your doctor can determine if it is safe for you to continue taking Brethine.

■ *More common side effects may include:*
Chest discomfort, difficulty in breathing, dizziness, drowsiness, fast, fluttery heartbeat, flushed feeling, headache, increased heart rate, nausea, nervousness, pain at injection site, rapid heartbeat, sweating, tremors, vomiting, weakness

■ *Less common side effects may include:*
Anxiety, dry mouth, muscle cramps

■ *Rare side effects may include:*
Inflamed blood vessels

Why should this drug not be prescribed?
If you are sensitive to or have ever had an allergic reaction to Brethine or similar drugs such as Ventolin, you should not take this medication. Make sure your doctor is aware of any drug reactions you have experienced.

Special warnings about this medication
When taking Brethine, you should not use other asthma medications before checking with your doctor. Only your doctor can determine what is a sufficient amount of time between doses.

Consult with your doctor before using this medication if you have diabetes, high blood pressure, or an overactive thyroid gland, or if you have had seizures at any time.

Unless you are directed to do so by your doctor, do not take this medication if you have heart disease, especially if you also have an irregular heart rate.

Possible food and drug interactions
when taking this medication
If Brethine is taken with certain other drugs, the effects of either could be increased, decreased, or altered. It is especially important to check with your doctor before combining Brethine with the following:

Antidepressant drugs known as MAO inhibitors (Nardil, Parnate, others)
Beta blockers (blood pressure medications such as Inderal and
Tenormin)
Other bronchodilators such as Proventil and Ventolin
Tricyclic antidepressant drugs such as Elavil and Tofranil

**Special information
if you are pregnant or breastfeeding**
The effects of Brethine during pregnancy have not been adequately studied. If you are pregnant or plan to become pregnant, inform your doctor immediately. It is not known whether Brethine appears in breast milk. If this drug is essential to your health, your doctor may advise you to stop nursing your baby until your treatment is finished.

Recommended dosage

FOR BRETHINE

Adults
The usual tablet dose is 5 milligrams taken at approximately 6-hour intervals, 3 times per day during waking hours. If side effects are excessive, your doctor may reduce your dose to 2.5 milligrams, 3 times per day.

Do not take more than 15 milligrams in a 24-hour period.

Children
This medication is not recommended for use in children below 12 years of age.

For children 12 to 15 years of age, the usual dose is 2.5 milligrams, 3 times per day, not to exceed a total of 7.5 milligrams in a 24-hour period.

FOR BRETHAIRE

The usual dosage for adults and children 12 years and older is 2 inhalations separated by a 60-second interval, repeated every 4 to 6 hours.

Overdosage
Any drug taken or used in excess can have serious consequences. Signs of a Brethine overdose are the same as the side effects. If you suspect an overdose, seek medical attention immediately.

Brand name:

BREVICON

See Oral Contraceptives, page 887.

Brand name:

BRICANYL

See Brethine, page 157.

Generic name:

BROMFENAC

See Duract, page 419.

Generic name:

BROMOCRIPTINE

See Parlodel, page 913.

Generic name:

BROMPHENIRAMINE, PHENYLPROPANOLAMINE, AND CODEINE

See Dimetane-DC, page 386.

Brand name:

BRONTEX

See Tussi-Organidin NR, page 1294.

Generic name:

BUDESONIDE

See Rhinocort, page 1080.

Generic name:

BUMETANIDE

See Bumex, page 160.

Brand name:

BUMEX

Pronounced: BYOO-meks
Generic name: Bumetanide

Why is this drug prescribed?
Bumex is used to lower the amount of excess salt and water in your body by increasing the output of urine. It is prescribed in the treatment of edema, or fluid retention, associated with congestive heart failure and liver or kidney

disease. It is also occasionally prescribed, along with other drugs, to treat high blood pressure.

Most important fact about this drug

Bumex is a powerful drug. If taken in excessive amounts, it can severely decrease the levels of water and minerals, especially potassium, your body needs to function. Therefore, your doctor should monitor your dose carefully.

How should you take this medication?

Bumex can increase the frequency of urination and may cause loss of sleep if taken at night. Therefore, if you are taking a single dose of Bumex daily, it should be taken in the morning after breakfast. If you take more than one dose a day, take the last dose no later than 6:00 P.M.

■ *If you miss a dose...*
Take the forgotten dose as soon as you remember. If it is almost time for your next dose, skip the one you missed and go back to your regular schedule. Never take 2 doses at the same time.

■ *Storage instructions...*
Store at room temperature.

What side effects may occur?

Side effects cannot be anticipated. If any develop or change in intensity, inform your doctor as soon as possible. Only your doctor can determine if it is safe for you to continue taking Bumex.

■ *More common side effects may include:*
Dizziness, headache, low blood pressure, muscle cramps, nausea

■ *Signs of too much potassium loss are:*
Dry mouth, irregular heartbeat, muscle cramps or pains, unusual tiredness or weakness

■ *Less common or rare side effects may include:*
Abdominal pain, black stools, chest pain, dehydration, diarrhea, dry mouth, ear discomfort, fatigue, hearing loss, itching, joint pain, kidney failure, muscle and bone pain, nipple tenderness, premature ejaculation and difficulty maintaining erection, rapid breathing, skin rash or hives, sweating, upset stomach, vertigo, vomiting, weakness

Why should this drug not be prescribed?

Bumex should not be used if you are unable to urinate or if you are dehydrated.

If you are sensitive to or have ever had an allergic reaction to Bumex or similar drugs such as Lasix, you should not take this medication. Make sure your doctor is aware of any drug reactions you have experienced.

Special warnings about this medication

If you are allergic to sulfur-containing drugs such as sulfonamides (antibacterial drugs), check with your doctor before taking Bumex.

Bumex can decrease the number of platelets in your blood. Your doctor should monitor your blood status regularly.

Bumex can cause a loss of potassium from the body. Your doctor may recommend foods or fluids high in potassium or may want you to take a potassium supplement to help prevent this. Follow your doctor's recommendation carefully.

While taking this medication you may feel dizzy or light-headed or actually faint when getting up from a lying or sitting position. If getting up slowly does not help or if this problem continues, notify your doctor.

Possible food and drug interactions
when taking this medication

If Bumex is taken with certain other drugs, the effects of either could be increased, decreased, or altered. It is especially important to check with your doctor before combining Bumex with the following:

Blood pressure medications such as Vasotec and Tenormin
Indomethacin (Indocin) and other nonsteroidal anti-inflammatory drugs
Probenecid (Benemid)

The combination of Bumex and certain antibiotics or cisplatin (Platinol) may increase the risk of hearing loss.

Because Bumex can lower potassium levels, the combination of Bumex and digitalis or digoxin (Lanoxin) may increase the risk of changes in heartbeat.

The combination of Bumex and lithium (Lithonate) may increase the levels of lithium in the body, causing it to become poisonous.

Special information
if you are pregnant or breastfeeding

The effects of Bumex during pregnancy have not been adequately studied. If you are pregnant or plan to become pregnant, inform your doctor immediately. It is not known if this medication appears in breast milk. Your doctor may advise you to discontinue breastfeeding your baby until your treatment with Bumex is finished.

Recommended dosage

ADULTS

The usual total daily dose is 0.5 to 2.0 milligrams a day. For most people, this is taken as a single dose. However, if the initial dose is not adequate, your doctor may have you take a second and, possibly, a third dose at 4- to 5-hour intervals, up to a maximum daily dose of 10 milligrams.

For the continuing control of edema, your doctor may tell you to take Bumex on alternate days or for 3 to 4 days at a time with rest periods of 1 to 2 days in between.

If you have liver failure, your dose will be kept to a minimum and increased very carefully.

CHILDREN

The safety and effectiveness of Bumex have not been established in children below the age of 18.

Overdosage

An overdose of Bumex can lead to severe dehydration, reduction of blood volume, and severe problems with the circulatory system.

■ *The signs of an overdose include:*
Cramps, dizziness, lethargy (sluggishness), loss or lack of appetite, mental confusion, vomiting, weakness

If you suspect an overdose, get medical attention immediately.

Generic name:

BUPROPION FOR DEPRESSION

See Wellbutrin, page 1361.

Generic name:

BUPROPION FOR SMOKING

See Zyban, page 1413.

Brand name:

BUSPAR

Pronounced: BYOO-spar
Generic name: Buspirone hydrochloride

Why is this drug prescribed?
BuSpar is used in the treatment of anxiety disorders and for short-term relief of the symptoms of anxiety.

Most important fact about this drug
BuSpar should not be used with antidepressant drugs known as monoamine oxidase (MAO) inhibitors. Brands include Nardil and Parnate.

How should you take this medication?
Take BuSpar exactly as prescribed. Do not be discouraged if you feel no immediate effect. The full benefit of this drug may not be seen for 1 to 2 weeks after you start to take it.

- *If you miss a dose...*
  Take the forgotten dose as soon as you remember. If it is almost time for your next dose, skip the one you missed and go back to your regular schedule. Never take 2 doses at the same time.

- *Storage instructions...*
  Store at room temperature in a tightly closed container, away from light.

What side effects may occur?
Side effects cannot be anticipated. If any develop or change in intensity, inform your doctor as soon as possible. Only your doctor can determine if it is safe for you to continue taking BuSpar.

- *More common side effects may include:*
  Dizziness, dry mouth, fatigue, headache, light-headedness, nausea, nervousness, unusual excitement

- *Less common or rare side effects may include:*
  Anger/hostility, blurred vision, bone aches/pain, confusion, constipation, decreased concentration, depression, diarrhea, fast, fluttery heartbeat, incoordination, muscle pain/aches, numbness, pain or weakness in hands or feet, rapid heartbeat, rash, restlessness, stomach and abdominal upset, sweating/clamminess, tingling or pins and needles, tremor, urinary incontinence, vomiting, weakness

Why should this drug not be prescribed?
If you are sensitive to or have ever had an allergic reaction to BuSpar or similar mood-altering drugs, you should not take this medication. Make sure your doctor is aware of any drug reactions you have experienced.

Anxiety or tension related to everyday stress usually does not require treatment with BuSpar. Discuss your symptoms thoroughly with your doctor.

The use of BuSpar is not recommended if you have severe kidney or liver damage.

Special warnings about this medication
The effects of BuSpar on the central nervous system (brain and spinal cord) are unpredictable. Therefore, you should not drive or operate dangerous machinery or participate in any hazardous activity that requires full mental alertness while you are taking BuSpar.

Possible food and drug interactions
when taking this medication
Although BuSpar does not intensify the effects of alcohol, it is best to avoid alcohol while taking this medication.

If BuSpar is taken with certain other drugs, the effects of either can be increased, decreased, or altered. It is especially important to check with your doctor before combining BuSpar with the following:

The blood-thinning drug Coumadin
Haloperidol (Haldol)
MAO inhibitors (antidepressant drugs such as Nardil and Parnate)
Trazodone (Desyrel)

Special information
if you are pregnant or breastfeeding
The effects of BuSpar during pregnancy have not been adequately studied. If you are pregnant or plan to become pregnant, inform your doctor immediately. It is not known whether BuSpar appears in breast milk. If this medication is essential to your health, your doctor may advise you to discontinue breastfeeding until your treatment is finished.

Recommended dosage

ADULTS

The recommended starting dose is a total of 15 milligrams per day divided into smaller doses, usually 5 milligrams 3 times a day. Every 2 to 3 days, your doctor may increase the dosage 5 milligrams per day as needed. The daily dose should not exceed 60 milligrams.

CHILDREN

The safety and effectiveness of BuSpar have not been established in children under 18 years of age.

Overdosage

Any medication taken in excess can have serious consequences. If you suspect an overdose of BuSpar, seek medical attention immediately.

■ *The symptoms of BuSpar overdose may include:*
Dizziness, drowsiness, nausea or vomiting, severe stomach upset, unusually small pupils

Generic name:

BUSPIRONE

See BuSpar, page 164.

Generic name:

BUTALBITAL, ACETAMINOPHEN, AND CAFFEINE

See Fioricet, page 496.

Generic name:

BUTALBITAL, ASPIRIN, AND CAFFEINE

See Fiorinal, page 499.

Generic name:

BUTALBITAL, CODEINE, ASPIRIN, AND CAFFEINE

See Fiorinal with Codeine, page 502.

Generic name:

BUTOCONAZOLE

See Femstat, page 493.

Brand name:

CAFERGOT

Pronounced: KAF-er-got
Generic ingredients: Ergotamine tartrate, Caffeine

Why is this drug prescribed?
Cafergot is prescribed for the relief or prevention of vascular headaches—for example, migraine, migraine variants, or cluster headaches.

Most important fact about this drug
The excessive use of Cafergot can lead to ergot poisoning resulting in symptoms such as headache, pain in the legs when walking, muscle pain, numbness, coldness, and abnormal paleness of the fingers and toes. If this condition is not treated, it can lead to gangrene (tissue death due to decreased blood supply).

How should you take this medication?
Cafergot is available in both tablet and suppository form. Be sure to take it exactly as prescribed, remaining within the limits of your recommended dosage.

Cafergot works best if you use it at the first sign of a migraine attack. If you get warning signals of a coming migraine, take the drug before the headache actually starts.

Lie down and relax in a quiet, dark room for at least a couple of hours or until you feel better.

Avoid exposure to cold.

To use the suppositories, follow these steps:

1. If the suppository feels too soft, leave it in the refrigerator for about 30 minutes or put it, still wrapped, in ice water until it hardens.
2. Remove the foil wrapper and dip the tip of the suppository in water.
3. Lie down on your side and with a finger insert the suppository into the rectum. Hold it in place for a few moments.

■ *If you miss a dose...*
Take this medication only when threatened with an attack.

■ *Storage instructions...*
Store at room temperature in a tightly closed container away from light. Keep suppositories away from heat.

What side effects may occur?
Side effects cannot be anticipated. If any develop or change in intensity, inform your doctor as soon as possible. Only your doctor can determine if it is safe for you to continue taking Cafergot.

- *Side effects may include:*
  Fluid retention, high blood pressure, itching, nausea, numbness, rapid heart rate, slow heartbeat, tingling or pins and needles, vertigo, vomiting, weakness

- *Complications caused by constriction of the blood vessels can be serious. They include:*
  Bluish tinge to the skin, chest pain, cold arms and legs, gangrene, muscle pains

Although these symptoms occur most commonly with long-term therapy at relatively high doses, they have been reported with short-term or normal doses. A few people on long-term therapy have developed heart valve problems.

Why should this drug not be prescribed?
If you are sensitive to or have ever had an allergic reaction to ergotamine tartrate, caffeine, or similar drugs, you should not take this medication. Make sure your doctor is aware of any drug reactions you have experienced.

Unless directed to do so by your doctor, do not take this medication if you have coronary heart disease, circulatory problems, high blood pressure, impaired liver or kidney function, or an infection, or if you are pregnant.

Special warnings about this medication
It is extremely important that you do not exceed your recommended dosage, especially when Cafergot is used over long periods. There have been reports of psychological dependence in people who have abused this drug over long periods of time. Discontinuance of the drug may produce withdrawal symptoms such as sudden, severe headaches.

If you experience excessive nausea and vomiting during attacks, making it impossible for you to retain oral medication, your doctor will probably tell you to use rectal suppositories.

This drug is effective only for migraine and migraine-type headaches. Do not use it for any other kind of headache.

Possible food and drug interactions
when taking this medication

If Cafergot is taken with certain other drugs, the effects of either could be increased, decreased, or altered. It is especially important to check with your doctor before combining Cafergot with the following:

Beta-blocker drugs (blood pressure medications such as Inderal and Tenormin)

Drugs that constrict the blood vessels, such as EpiPen and the oral decongestant Sudafed

Macrolide antibiotics such as PCE, E.E.S., and Biaxin

Nicotine (Nicoderm, Habitrol, others)

Special information
if you are pregnant or breastfeeding

Do not take Cafergot if you are pregnant. Cafergot appears in breast milk and may have serious effects in your baby. If this medication is essential for your health, your doctor may advise you to discontinue breastfeeding.

Recommended dosage

Dosage should start at the first sign of an attack.

ADULTS

Orally

The total dose for any single attack should not exceed 6 tablets.

Rectally

The maximum dose for an individual attack is 2 suppositories.

The total weekly dosage should not exceed 10 tablets or 5 suppositories.

A preventive, short-term dose may be given at bedtime to certain people, but only as prescribed by a doctor.

Overdosage

If you suspect an overdose of Cafergot, seek emergency medical treatment immediately.

■ *Symptoms of Cafergot overdose include:*
Coma, convulsions, diminished or absent pulses, drowsiness, high or low blood pressure, numbness, shock, stupor, tingling, pain and bluish discoloration of the limbs, unresponsiveness, vomiting

Brand name:

CALAN

Pronounced: CAL-an
Generic name: Verapamil hydrochloride
Other brand names: Calan SR, Covera-HS, Isoptin, Isoptin SR, Verelan

Why is this drug prescribed?
Verapamil, the active ingredient in Calan, Covera-HS, Isoptin, and Verelan, is prescribed for the treatment of various types of angina (chest pain, caused by clogged arteries that reduce the heart muscle's oxygen supply). It is also used for irregular heartbeat and for high blood pressure.

The sustained release formulas (SR and Verelan) are used only for the treatment of high blood pressure; the extended-release tablets (Covera-HS) are used for high blood pressure and angina and are designed to release the drug 4 to 5 hours after they are taken.

Verapamil is a type of medication called a calcium channel blocker. It eases the heart's workload by slowing down the passage of nerve impulses through it, and hence the contractions of the heart muscle. This improves blood flow through the heart and throughout the body, reduces blood pressure, corrects irregular heartbeat, and helps prevent angina pain.

Some doctors also prescribe verapamil to prevent migraine headache and asthma and to treat manic depression and panic attacks.

Most important fact about this drug
If you have high blood pressure, you must take verapamil regularly for it to be effective. Since blood pressure declines gradually, it may be several weeks before you get the full benefit of verapamil; and you must continue taking it even if you are feeling well. Verapamil does not cure high blood pressure; it merely keeps it under control.

How should you take this medication?
Calan, Isoptin, and Verelan can be taken with or without food. Calan SR and Isoptin SR should be taken with food.

Covera-HS, Calan SR, Isoptin SR, and Verelan must be swallowed whole and should not be crushed, broken, or chewed.

You may open Verelan capsules and sprinkle the pellets on a spoonful of cool applesauce. Swallow all of the mixture immediately, and then drink a glass of cool water.

Take this medication exactly as prescribed, even if you are feeling well. Try not to miss any doses. If the drug is not taken regularly, your condition can get worse.

Check with your doctor before you stop taking this drug; a slow reduction in the dose may be required.

- *If you miss a dose...*
  Take it as soon as you remember. If it is almost time for your next dose, skip the one you missed and go back to your regular schedule. Never take 2 doses at the same time.

- *Storage instructions...*
  Store at room temperature away from heat, light, and moisture.

What side effects may occur?
Side effects cannot be anticipated. If any develop or change in intensity, inform your doctor as soon as possible. Only your doctor can determine if it is safe for you to continue taking verapamil.

- *More common side effects may include:*
  Congestive heart failure, constipation, dizziness, fatigue, fluid retention, headache, low blood pressure, nausea, rash, shortness of breath, slow heartbeat, upper respiratory infection

- *Less common or rare side effects may include:*
  Angina, blurred vision, breast development in males, bruising, chest pain, confusion, diarrhea, difficulty sleeping, drowsiness, dry mouth, excessive milk secretion, fainting, fatigue, fever and rash, flushing, hair loss, heart attack, hives, impotence, increased urination, indigestion, intestinal blockage, joint pain, light-headedness upon standing up, limping, loss of balance, muscle cramps, pounding heartbeat, rash, shakiness, skin peeling, sleepiness, spotty menstruation, sweating, tingling or pins and needles, upset stomach

Why should this drug not be prescribed?
If you have low blood pressure or certain types of heart disease or heartbeat irregularities, you should not take verapamil. Make sure the doctor is aware of any cardiac problems you may have.

If you are sensitive to or have ever had an allergic reaction to Calan or any other brands of verapamil, or other calcium channel blockers, do not take this medication.

Special warnings about this medication

Verapamil can reduce or eliminate angina pain caused by exertion or exercise. Be sure to discuss with your doctor how much exertion is safe for you.

Verapamil may cause your blood pressure to become too low. If you experience dizziness or light-headedness, notify your doctor.

Congestive heart failure and fluid in the lungs have occurred in people taking verapamil together with other heart drugs known as beta blockers. Make sure your doctor is aware of all medications you are taking.

If you have a heart condition, liver disease, kidney disease, or Duchenne's dystrophy (the most common type of muscular dystrophy), make certain your doctor knows about it. Verapamil should be used with caution.

If you are taking Covera-HS and you have a narrowing in your stomach or intestines, be sure your doctor was aware of it when the drug was prescribed.

The outer shell of Covera-HS does not dissolve; do not worry if you see it in your stool.

Possible food and drug interactions
when taking this medication

If verapamil is taken with certain other drugs, the effects of either could be increased, decreased, or altered. It is especially important to check with your doctor before combining verapamil with the following:

ACE inhibitor-type blood pressure drugs such as Capoten and Vasotec
Beta-blocker-type blood pressure drugs such as Lopressor, Tenormin, and Inderal
Vasodilator-type blood pressure drugs such as Loniten
Other high blood pressure drugs such as Minipress
Alcohol
Amiodarone (Cordarone)
Carbamazepine (Tegretol)
Chloroquine (Aralen)
Cimetidine (Tagamet)
Cyclosporine (Sandimmune, Neoral)
Dantrolene (Dantrium)
Digitalis (Lanoxin)
Disopyramide (Norpace)
Diuretics such as Lasix and HydroDIURIL
Flecainide (Tambocor)
Glipizide (Glucotrol)
Imipramine (Tofranil)
Lithium (Lithonate)

Nitrates such as Transderm Nitro and Isordil
Phenobarbital
Phenytoin (Dilantin)
Quinidine (Quinidex)
Rifampin (Rifadin)
Theophylline (Theo-Dur)

Special information
if you are pregnant or breastfeeding

The effects of verapamil during pregnancy have not been adequately studied. If you are pregnant or plan to become pregnant, inform your doctor immediately. The drug appears in breast milk and could affect a nursing infant. If this medication is essential to your health, your doctor may advise you to discontinue breastfeeding until your treatment is finished.

Recommended dosage

FOR CALAN AND ISOPTIN

Dosages of this medication must be adjusted to meet individual needs. In general, dosages of this medication should not exceed 480 milligrams per day. Your doctor will closely monitor your response to this drug, usually within 8 hours of the first dose.

Safety and effectiveness of this drug in children have not been established.

Angina

The usual initial dose is 80 to 120 milligrams, 3 times a day. Lower doses of 40 milligrams 3 times a day may be used by people who have a stronger response to this medication, such as the elderly or those with decreased liver function. The dosage may be increased by your doctor either daily or weekly until the desired response is seen.

Irregular Heartbeat

The usual dose in people who are also on digitalis ranges from 240 to 320 milligrams per day divided into 3 or 4 doses.

In those not on digitalis, doses range from a total of 240 to 480 milligrams per day divided into 3 or 4 doses.

Maximum effects of this drug should be seen in the first 48 hours of use.

High Blood Pressure

Effects of this drug on blood pressure should be seen within the first week of use. Any adjustment of this medication to a higher dose will be based on its effectiveness as determined by your doctor.

The usual dose of this drug, when used alone for high blood pressure, is 80 milligrams, 3 times per day. Total daily doses of 360 milligrams and 480 milligrams may be used. Smaller doses of 40 milligrams 3 times per day may be taken by smaller individuals and the elderly.

FOR CALAN SR, ISOPTIN SR, AND VERELAN

Dosages for high blood pressure should be adjusted to meet each individual's needs.

Adults

The usual starting dose of Calan SR and Isoptin SR is 180 milligrams taken in the morning. For Verelan, it is 240 milligrams. A lower starting dose of 120 milligrams may be taken if the person is smaller. Your doctor will monitor your response to this drug and may adjust it each week. In addition, your doctor may increase the dose and add evening doses to the morning dose, based on the effectiveness of the drug.

You should see results from the drug within a week.

Children

The safety and effectiveness of this drug in children under age 18 have not been established.

Older Adults

Your doctor may start you at a lower dose of 120 milligrams and then adjust it according to your response.

FOR COVERA-HS

Adults

The usual starting dose is 180 milligrams, taken at bedtime, for both angina and high blood pressure. Your doctor may raise the dose gradually if you need more.

Children

Safety and effectiveness in children under age 18 have not been established.

Older Adults

If you have poor kidneys, the dosage may need to be lowered.

Overdosage

Any medication taken in excess can have serious consequences. If you suspect an overdose, seek medical attention immediately.

An overdose of Calan can cause dangerously low blood pressure and life-threatening heart problems. After treatment for an overdose, you should remain under observation in the hospital for at least 48 hours, especially if you have taken the sustained-release form of the drug.

Brand name:

CALCIMAR

See Miacalcin, page 757.

Generic name:

CALCITONIN-SALMON

See Miacalcin, page 757.

Generic name:

CALCITRIOL

See Rocaltrol, page 1098.

Brand name:

CAPOTEN

Pronounced: KAP-o-ten
Generic name: Captopril

Why is this drug prescribed?

Capoten is used in the treatment of high blood pressure and congestive heart failure. When prescribed for high blood pressure, it is effective used alone or combined with diuretics. If it is prescribed for congestive heart failure, it is used in combination with digitalis and diuretics. Capoten is in a family of drugs known as "ACE (angiotensin converting enzyme) inhibitors." It works by preventing a chemical in your blood called angiotensin I from converting into a more potent form that increases salt and water retention in your body. Capoten also enhances blood flow throughout your blood vessels.

In addition, Capoten is used to improve survival in certain people who have suffered heart attacks and to treat kidney disease in diabetics.

Some doctors also prescribe Capoten for angina pectoris (crushing chest pain), Raynaud's phenomenon (a disorder of the blood vessels that causes the fingers to turn white when exposed to cold), and rheumatoid arthritis.

Most important fact about this drug
If you have high blood pressure, you must take Capoten regularly for it to be effective. Since blood pressure declines gradually, it may be several weeks before you get the full benefit of Capoten; you must continue taking it even if you are feeling well. Capoten does not cure high blood pressure; it merely keeps it under control.

How should you take this medication?
Capoten should be taken 1 hour before meals. If you are taking an antacid such as Mylanta, take it 2 hours prior to Capoten.

Take this medication exactly as prescribed. Stopping Capoten suddenly could cause your blood pressure to increase.

■ *If you miss a dose...*
Take it as soon as you remember. If it is almost time for your next dose, skip the one you missed and go back to your regular schedule. Never take 2 doses at the same time.

■ *Storage instructions...*
Store Capoten at room temperature, away from moisture, in a tightly closed container.

What side effects may occur?
Side effects cannot be anticipated. If any develop or change in intensity, inform your doctor as soon as possible. Only your doctor can determine if it is safe for you to continue taking Capoten.

■ *More common side effects may include:*
Itching, loss of taste, low blood pressure, rash

■ *Less common or rare side effects may include:*
Abdominal pain, anemia, angina pectoris (severe chest pain), blisters, blurred vision, breast development in males, cardiac arrest, changes in heart rhythm, chest pain, confusion, constipation, cough, depression, diarrhea, difficulty swallowing, dizziness, dry mouth, fatigue, fever and chills, flushing, general feeling of ill health, hair loss, headache, heart attack, heart failure, impotence, inability to sleep, indigestion, inflammation of the nose, inflammation of the tongue, labored breathing, lack of coordination, loss of appetite, lung inflammation, muscle pain and/or weakness, nausea, nervousness, pallor, palpitations, peptic ulcer, rapid heartbeat, sensitivity to light, skin inflammation, skin peeling, sleepiness,

sore throat, stomach irritation, stroke, sudden fainting or loss of strength, swelling of face, lips, tongue, throat, or arms and legs, tingling or pins and needles, vomiting, weakness, wheezing, yellow eyes and skin

Why should this drug not be prescribed?

If you are sensitive to or have ever had an allergic reaction to Capoten or similar drugs such as Vasotec, you should not take this medication. Make sure that your doctor is aware of any drug reactions that you have experienced.

Special warnings about this medication

If you develop swelling of the face around your lips, tongue or throat (or of your arms and legs) or have difficulty swallowing, you should stop taking Capoten and contact your doctor immediately. You may need emergency treatment.

If you are receiving bee or wasp venom to prevent an allergic reaction to stings, use of Capoten at the same time may cause a severe allergic reaction.

If you are taking Capoten, a complete assessment of your kidney function should be done; and your kidney function should continue to be monitored. If you have kidney disease, Capoten should be used only if you have taken other blood pressure medications and your doctor has determined that the results were unsatisfactory.

Some people taking Capoten have had a severe allergic reaction during kidney dialysis.

If you are taking Capoten for your heart, be careful not to increase physical activity too quickly. Check with your doctor as to how much exercise is safe for you.

If you are taking Capoten for congestive heart failure, your blood pressure may drop temporarily after the first few doses and you may feel light-headed for a time. Your doctor should monitor you closely when you start taking the medication or when your dosage is increased.

If you are taking high doses of diuretics and Capoten, you may develop excessively low blood pressure. Your doctor may reduce your diuretic dose so that your blood pressure doesn't drop too far.

If you notice a yellow coloring to your skin or the whites of your eyes, stop taking the drug and notify your doctor immediately. You could be developing a liver problem.

Capoten may cause you to become drowsy or less alert, especially if you are also taking a diuretic at the same time. If it has this effect on you, driving or participating in any potentially hazardous activity is not recommended.

Dehydration may cause a drop in blood pressure. If you experience symptoms such as excessive perspiration, vomiting, and/or diarrhea, notify your doctor immediately.

If you develop a sore throat or fever you should contact your doctor immediately. It could indicate a more serious illness.

If you develop a persistent, dry cough, tell your doctor. It may be due to the medication and, if so, will disappear if you stop taking Capoten.

Possible food and drug interactions
when taking this medication

If Capoten is taken with certain other drugs, the effects of either could be increased, decreased, or altered. It is especially important to check with your doctor before combining Capoten with the following:

Allopurinol (Zyloprim)
Aspirin
Blood pressure drugs known as beta blockers, such as Inderal and
    Tenormin
Cyclosporine (Sandimmune)
Digoxin (Lanoxin)
Diuretics such as HydroDIURIL
Lithium (Lithonate)
Nitroglycerin and similar heart medicines (Nitro-Dur, Transderm-Nitro,
    others)
Nonsteroidal anti-inflammatory drugs such as Indocin and Feldene
Potassium preparations such as Micro-K and Slow-K
Potassium-sparing diuretics such as Aldactone and Midamor

Do not use potassium-containing salt substitutes while taking Capoten.

Special information
if you are pregnant or breastfeeding

ACE inhibitors such as Capoten have been shown to cause injury and even death to the developing baby when used in pregnancy during the second and third trimesters. If you are pregnant or plan to become pregnant, contact your doctor immediately. Capoten appears in breast milk and could affect a nursing infant. If this medication is essential to your health, your doctor may advise you to discontinue breastfeeding until your treatment is finished.

Recommended dosage

ADULTS

High Blood Pressure

The usual starting dose is 25 milligrams taken 2 or 3 times a day. If you have any problems with your kidneys or suffer from other major health problems, your starting dose may be lower. Depending on how your blood pressure responds, your doctor may increase your dose later, up to a total of 150 milligrams 2 or 3 times a day. The maximum recommended daily dose is 450 milligrams.

Heart Failure

For most people, the usual dose is 25 milligrams taken 3 times a day. A daily dosage of 450 milligrams should not be exceeded.

After a Heart Attack

The usual starting dose is 6.25 milligrams, taken once, followed by 12.5 milligrams 3 times a day. Your doctor will increase the dose over the next several days to 25 milligrams taken 3 times a day and then, over the next several weeks, to 50 milligrams 3 times a day.

Kidney Disease in Diabetes

The usual dose is 25 milligrams taken 3 times a day.

CHILDREN

The safety and effectiveness of Capoten in children have not been established.

Overdosage

Any medication taken in excess can cause symptoms of overdose. If you suspect an overdose of Capoten, seek medical attention immediately.

Light-headedness or dizziness due to a sudden drop in blood pressure is the primary effect of a Capoten overdose.

Brand name:

CAPOZIDE

Pronounced: KAP-oh-zide
Generic ingredients: Captopril, Hydrochlorothiazide

Why is this drug prescribed?

Capozide is used in the treatment of high blood pressure. It combines an ACE inhibitor with a thiazide diuretic. Captopril, the ACE inhibitor, works by preventing a chemical in your blood called angiotensin I from converting into a more potent form that increases salt and water retention in your body. Captopril also enhances blood flow throughout your blood vessels. Hydrochlorothiazide, the diuretic, helps your body produce and eliminate more urine, which helps in lowering blood pressure.

Most important fact about this drug
You must take Capozide regularly for it to be effective. Since blood pressure declines gradually, it may be several weeks before you get the full benefit of Capozide; and you must continue taking it even if you are feeling well. Capozide does not cure high blood pressure; it merely keeps it under control.

How should you take this medication?
Capozide should be taken 1 hour before meals. Take it exactly as prescribed. Stopping Capozide suddenly could cause your blood pressure to increase.

■ *If you miss a dose...*
Take it as soon as you remember. If it is almost time for your next dose, skip the one you missed and go back to your regular schedule. Never take 2 doses at the same time.

■ *Storage instructions...*
Capozide should be stored at room temperature in a tightly closed container away from moisture.

What side effects may occur?
Side effects cannot be anticipated. If any develop or change in intensity, inform your doctor as soon as possible. Only your doctor can determine if it is safe for you to continue taking Capozide.

■ *More common side effects may include:*
Itching, loss of taste, low blood pressure, rash

■ *Less common or rare side effects may include:*
Abdominal pain, anemia, angina pectoris (severe chest pain), angioedema (swelling of the arms and legs, face, lips, tongue, or throat), blurred vision, breast development in males, bronchitis, bronchospasm, changes in heart rhythm, chest pain, confusion, constipation, cough, cramping, depression, diarrhea, dizziness, dizziness upon standing up, dry mouth, fainting, fatigue, fever, flushing, general feeling of ill health, hair loss,

headache, heart attack, heart failure, hepatitis, hives, inability to sleep, indigestion, impotence, inflammation of nose, inflammation of tongue, labored breathing, lack of coordination, loss of appetite, low potassium levels leading to symptoms such as dry mouth, excessive thirst, weak or irregular heartbeat, muscle pain or cramps, muscle weakness, muscle spasm, nausea, nervousness, pallor, peptic ulcer, rapid heartbeat, Raynaud's Syndrome (circulatory disorder), restlessness, sensitivity to light, severe allergic reactions, skin inflammation and/or peeling, sleepiness, stomach irritation, stroke, tingling or pins and needles, vomiting, vertigo, weakness, wheezing, yellow eyes and skin

Why should this drug not be prescribed?

If you are sensitive to or have ever had an allergic reaction to captopril, hydrochlorothiazide, other ACE inhibitors such as Vasotec, or other thiazide diuretics such as Diuril, or if you are sensitive to other sulfonamide-derived drugs, you should not take this medication. If you have a history of angioedema (swelling of face, extremities, and throat) or inability to urinate, you should not take this medication.

Special warnings about this medication

If you develop swelling of your face around your lips, tongue, or throat, or in your arms and legs, or if you begin to have difficulty swallowing, you should contact your doctor immediately. You may need emergency treatment.

If you develop a sore throat or fever you should contact your doctor immediately. It could indicate a more serious illness.

If you are taking Capozide, your doctor will make a complete assessment of your kidney function and will continue to monitor it.

If you have impaired kidney function, Capozide should be used only if you have taken other blood pressure medications and your doctor has determined that the results were unsatisfactory.

If you have liver disease or a disease of the connective tissue called lupus erythematosus, Capozide should be used with caution. Tell your doctor immediately if you notice a yellowish color in your skin or the whites of your eyes.

If you have congestive heart failure, you should be carefully watched for low blood pressure. You should not increase your physical activity too quickly.

Excessive sweating, dehydration, severe diarrhea, or vomiting could deplete your fluids and cause your blood pressure to become too low. Be careful when exercising and in hot weather.

This drug should be used with caution if you are on dialysis. There have been reports of extreme allergic reactions during dialysis in people taking ACE-inhibitor medications such as Capozide. Your odds of an allergic reaction also increase if you are being desensitized with bee venom while you are taking Capozide.

While taking Capozide, do not use potassium-sparing diuretics (such as Moduretic), potassium supplements, or salt substitutes containing potassium without talking to your doctor first.

Possible food and drug interactions when taking this medication

Capozide may intensify the effects of alcohol. Do not drink alcohol while taking this medication.

If Capozide is taken with certain other drugs, the effects of either could be increased, decreased, or altered. It is especially important to check with your doctor before combining Capozide with the following:

Antigout drugs such as Zyloprim
Barbiturates such as phenobarbital or Seconal
Calcium
Cardiac glycosides such as Lanoxin
Cholestyramine (Questran)
Colestipol (Colestid)
Corticosteroids such as prednisone (Deltasone)
Diabetes medications such as Micronase and Insulin
Diazoxide (Proglycem)
Heart medications such as Lanoxin
Lithium (Lithonate)
MAO inhibitors (antidepressants such as Nardil)
Methenamine (Mandelamine)
Narcotics such as Percocet
Nitroglycerin or other nitrates such as Transderm-Nitro
Nonsteroidal anti-inflammatory drugs such as Naprosyn
Norepinephrine (Levophed)
Oral blood thinners such as Coumadin
Other blood pressure drugs such as Hytrin and Minipress
Potassium-sparing diuretics such as Moduretic
Potassium supplements such as Slow K
Probenecid (Benemid)
Salt substitutes containing potassium
Sulfinpyrazone (Anturane)

Special information
if you are pregnant or breastfeeding

ACE inhibitors such as Capozide have been shown to cause injury and even death to the developing baby when used in pregnancy during the second or third trimesters. If you are pregnant your doctor should discontinue your use of this medication as soon as possible. If you plan to become pregnant and are taking Capozide, contact your doctor immediately to discuss the potential hazard to your unborn child. Capozide appears in breast milk and could affect a nursing infant. If this medication is essential to your health, your doctor may advise you to discontinue breastfeeding until your treatment is finished.

Recommended dosage

ADULTS

Dosages of this drug are always individualized, and your doctor will determine what combination works best for you. This medication can be used in conjunction with other blood pressure medications such as beta blockers. Dosages are also adjusted for people with decreased kidney function.

The initial dose is one 25 milligram/15 milligram tablet, once a day. If this is not effective, your doctor may adjust the dosage upward every 6 weeks. In general, the daily dose of captopril should not exceed 150 milligrams. The maximum recommended daily dose of hydrochlorothiazide is 50 milligrams.

CHILDREN

The safety and effectiveness of Capozide in children have not been established. Capozide should be used in children only if other measures for controlling blood pressure have not been effective.

OLDER ADULTS

Your doctor will determine the dosage according to your particular needs.

Overdosage

Any medication taken in excess can have serious consequences. If you suspect an overdose, seek medical attention immediately.

■ *The symptoms of Capozide overdose may include:*
Coma, lethargy, low blood pressure, sluggishness, stomach and intestinal irritation and hyperactivity

Generic name:

CAPTOPRIL

See Capoten, page 175.

Generic name:

CAPTOPRIL WITH HYDROCHLOROTHIAZIDE

See Capozide, page 179.

Brand name:

CARAFATE

Pronounced: CARE-uh-fate
Generic name: Sucralfate

Why is this drug prescribed?

Carafate Tablets and Suspension are used for the short-term treatment (up to 8 weeks) of an active duodenal ulcer; Carafate Tablets are also used for longer-term therapy at a reduced dosage after a duodenal ulcer has healed.

Carafate helps ulcers heal by forming a protective coating over them.

Some doctors also prescribe Carafate for ulcers in the mouth and esophagus that develop during cancer therapy, for digestive tract irritation caused by drugs, for long-term treatment of stomach ulcers, and to relieve pain following tonsil removal.

Most important fact about this drug

A duodenal ulcer is a recurring illness. While Carafate can cure an acute ulcer, it cannot prevent other ulcers from developing or lessen their severity.

How should you take this medication?

Carafate works best when taken on an empty stomach. If you take an antacid to relieve pain, avoid doing it within one-half hour before or after you take Carafate. Always take Carafate exactly as prescribed.

■ *If you miss a dose...*
  Take it as soon as you remember. If it is almost time for your next dose, skip the one you missed and go back to your regular schedule. Never take 2 doses at the same time.

■ *Storage instructions...*
Store at room temperature. Protect the suspension from freezing.

What side effects may occur?
Side effects cannot be anticipated. If any develop or change in intensity, inform your doctor as soon as possible. Only your doctor can determine if it is safe for you to continue taking Carafate.

■ *More common side effects may include:*
Constipation

■ *Less common or rare side effects may include:*
Back pain, diarrhea, dizziness, dry mouth, gas, headache, indigestion, insomnia, itching, nausea, possible allergic reactions, including hives and breathing difficulty, rash, sleepiness, stomach upset, vertigo, vomiting

Why should this drug not be prescribed?
There are no restrictions on the use of this drug.

Special warnings about this medication
If you have kidney failure or are on dialysis, the doctor will be cautious about prescribing this drug. Use of Carafate while taking aluminum-containing antacids may increase the possibility of aluminum poisoning in those with kidney failure.

Possible food and drug interactions when taking this medication
If Carafate is taken with certain other drugs, the effects of either could be increased, decreased, or altered. It is especially important to check with your doctor before combining Carafate with the following:

Antacids such as Mylanta and Maalox
Blood-thinning drugs such as Coumadin
Cimetidine (Tagamet)
Digoxin (Lanoxin)
Drugs for controlling spasms, such as Bentyl
Ketoconazole (Nizoral)
Levothyroxine (Synthroid)
Phenytoin (Dilantin)
Quinidine (Quinidex)
Quinolone antibiotics such as Cipro and Floxin
Ranitidine (Zantac)

Tetracycline (Sumycin)
Theophylline (Theo-Dur)

Special information
if you are pregnant or breastfeeding

The effects of Carafate during pregnancy have not been adequately studied. If you are pregnant or plan to become pregnant, inform your doctor immediately. Carafate may appear in breast milk and could affect a nursing infant. If this medication is essential to your health, your doctor may advise you to discontinue breastfeeding until your treatment with this medication is finished.

Recommended dosage

ADULTS

Active Duodenal Ulcer:
The usual dose is 1 gram (1 tablet or 2 teaspoonfuls of suspension) 4 times a day on an empty stomach. Although your ulcer may heal during the first 2 weeks of therapy, Carafate should be continued for 4 to 8 weeks.

Maintenance Therapy:
The usual dose is 1 gram (1 tablet) 2 times a day.

CHILDREN

The safety and effectiveness of Carafate in children have not been established.

Overdosage

Although the risk of overdose with Carafate is low, any medication taken in excess can have serious consequences. If you suspect an overdose, seek medical attention immediately.

■ *Symptoms of overdose may include:*
  Abdominal pain, indigestion, nausea, vomiting

Generic name:

CARBAMAZEPINE

See Tegretol, page 1199.

Generic name:

CARBIDOPA WITH LEVODOPA

See Sinemet CR, page 1138.

Brand name:

CARDENE

Pronounced: CAR-deen
Generic name: Nicardipine hydrochloride

Why is this drug prescribed?
Cardene, a type of medication called a calcium channel blocker, is prescribed for the treatment of chronic stable angina (chest pain usually caused by lack of oxygen to the heart resulting from clogged arteries, brought on by exertion) and for high blood pressure. When used to treat angina, Cardene is effective alone or in combination with beta-blocking medications such as Tenormin or Inderal. If it is used to treat high blood pressure, Cardene is effective alone or in combination with other high blood pressure medications. Calcium channel blockers ease the workload of the heart by slowing down its muscle contractions and the passage of nerve impulses through it. This improves blood flow through the heart and throughout the body, reducing blood pressure.

Cardene SR, a long-acting form of the drug, is prescribed only for high blood pressure.

Some doctors also prescribe Cardene to prevent migraine headache and to treat congestive heart failure. In combination with other drugs, such as Amicar, Cardene is also prescribed to manage neurological problems following certain kinds of stroke.

Most important fact about this drug
If you have high blood pressure, you must take Cardene regularly for it to be effective. Since blood pressure declines gradually, it may be several weeks before you get the full benefit of Cardene and you must continue taking it even if you are feeling well. Cardene does not cure high blood pressure; it merely keeps it under control.

How should you take this medication?
Take this medication exactly as prescribed, even if your symptoms have disappeared.

If you are taking Cardene SR, swallow the capsule whole; do not chew, crush, or divide it.

Try not to miss any doses. If Cardene is not taken regularly, your condition may worsen.

■ *If you miss a dose...*
Take it as soon as you remember. If it is almost time for the next dose, skip the one you missed and go back to your regular schedule. Do not take 2 doses at the same time.

■ *Storage instructions...*
Store at room temperature, away from light and moisture.

What side effects may occur?
Side effects cannot be anticipated. If any develop or change in intensity, inform your doctor as soon as possible. Only your doctor can determine if it is safe for you to continue taking Cardene.

■ *More common side effects may include:*
Dizziness, flushing, headache, increased chest pain (angina), indigestion, nausea, pounding or rapid heartbeat, sleepiness, swelling of feet, weakness

■ *Less common side effects may include:*
Abnormal dreaming, constipation, difficulty sleeping, drowsiness, dry mouth, excessive nighttime urination, fainting, fluid retention, muscle pain, nervousness, rash, shortness of breath, tingling or pins and needles, tremors, vomiting, vague feeling of bodily discomfort

■ *Rare side effects may include:*
Allergic reactions, anxiety, blurred vision, confusion, dizziness when standing, depression, hot flashes, increased movements, infection, inflammation of the nose, inflammation of the sinuses, impotence, joint pain, low blood pressure, more frequent urination, ringing in ears, sore throat, unusual chest pain, vertigo, vision changes

Why should this drug not be prescribed?
If you have advanced aortic stenosis (a narrowing of the aorta that causes obstruction of blood flow from the heart to the body), you should not take this medication.

If you are sensitive to or have ever had an allergic reaction to Cardene, you should not take this medication. Make sure your doctor is aware of any drug reactions you may have experienced.

Special warnings about this medication
Cardene can reduce or eliminate chest (angina) pain caused by exertion or exercise. Be sure to discuss with your doctor how much exercise or exertion is safe for you.

If you experience increased chest pain when you start taking Cardene or when your dosage is increased, contact your doctor immediately.

Your doctor will monitor your progress especially carefully if you have congestive heart failure, particularly if you are also taking a beta-blocking medication such as Tenormin or Inderal.

Cardene can cause your blood pressure to become too low, making you feel light-headed or faint. Your doctor should check your blood pressure when you start taking Cardene and continue to monitor it while your dosage is being adjusted.

If you have liver disease or decreased liver function, use this drug with caution.

Possible food and drug interactions
when taking this medication
If Cardene is taken with certain other drugs, the effects of either could be increased, decreased, or altered. It is especially important to check with your doctor before combining Cardene with the following:

Amiodarone (Cordarone)
Cimetidine (Tagamet)
Cyclosporine (Sandimmune)
Digoxin (Lanoxin)
Phenytoin (Dilantin)
Propranolol (Inderal)

Special information
if you are pregnant or breastfeeding
The effects of Cardene during pregnancy have not been adequately studied. If you are pregnant or plan to become pregnant, inform your doctor immediately. Cardene may appear in breast milk and could affect a nursing infant. If this medication is essential to your health, your doctor may advise you to discontinue breastfeeding until your treatment with Cardene is finished.

Recommended dosage

ADULTS

Angina

Your doctor will adjust the dosage according to your needs, usually beginning with 20 milligrams, 3 times a day. The usual regular dose is 20 to 40 milligrams, 3 times a day. Your physician may monitor your condition for at least 3 days before adjusting your dose.

High Blood Pressure

Your doctor will adjust the dosage to suit your needs. The starting dose of Cardene is usually 20 milligrams 3 times a day. The regular dose ranges from 20 to 40 milligrams 3 times a day.

The starting dose of Cardene SR is usually 30 milligrams 2 times a day. The regular dose ranges from 30 to 60 milligrams 2 times a day.

Your doctor may monitor your response to this medication for a few hours after the first dose, and will check your condition for at least 3 days before adjusting your dose.

CHILDREN

The safety and effectiveness of this drug in children under age 18 have not been established.

Overdosage

■ *Symptoms of Cardene overdose may include:*
Confusion, drowsiness, severe low blood pressure, slow heartbeat, slurred speech

If you suspect an overdose, seek medical attention immediately.

Brand name:

CARDIOQUIN

Pronounced: CAR-dee-o-kwin
Generic name: Quinidine polygalacturonate

Why is this drug prescribed?

Cardioquin corrects certain abnormal heart rhythms, including atrial fibrillation or flutter and life-threatening ventricular arrhythmias. It is usually prescribed only after other treatments have failed. If your condition does not improve after a reasonable period of time, your doctor may discontinue this medication and try other ways of restoring normal rhythm.

Most important fact about this drug
Before starting treatment with Cardioquin, your doctor will discuss with you the serious risks involved and weigh them against the good the drug may do. You should be closely monitored while on this medication.

How should you take this medication?
If you have certain types of high-risk heart problems, your doctor will start therapy with Cardioquin in a hospital setting where your response to the drug can be carefully monitored for the first 2 or 3 days.

Be careful to take Cardioquin exactly as directed. Never take more or less than prescribed, and try to remember every dose.

- *If you miss a dose...*
  If you remember it within 2 hours, take the missed dose immediately. If you do not remember until later, skip the dose and go back to your regular schedule. Never take a double dose.

- *Storage instructions...*
  Store at room temperature.

What side effects may occur?
Cardioquin can cause a variety of problems, including an increase in abnormal heart rhythms that could lead to death. Be certain to report any unusual symptoms to your doctor immediately. Only your doctor can determine whether it is safe for you to continue taking Cardioquin.

- *The most common side effects include...*
  Angina-like pain (chest pain), change in sleep habits, diarrhea, fatigue, headache, light-headedness, palpitations, rash, stomach and intestinal problems, vision problems, weakness

- *Other side effects may include:*
  Anemia, anxiety, depression, eye inflammation, fainting, fever, flushing, hives, inflammation of the connective tissue, itching, joint pain, lack of coordination, liver problems, lung inflammation and other conditions, muscle pain, nervousness, psychotic reaction, reddish or purplish spots below the skin, sensitivity to light, skin inflammation and peeling, swelling of the lips and tongue or throat, tremor, vomiting, wheezing

Another possible side effect is a sensitivity reaction called cinchonism. Symptoms include confusion, delirium, diarrhea, headache, hearing loss, intolerance to light, ringing in the ears, vertigo, vision disturbances, and vomiting.

Why should this drug not be prescribed?

Cardioquin should not be prescribed for the rhythm disturbance known as heart block, and you should not take this medication if your condition warrants a pacemaker. Cardioquin should be avoided if, like people with myasthenia gravis (abnormal muscle weakness), you might be affected by drugs that control muscle spasms, such as Anaspaz and Bentyl. You should also avoid Cardioquin if you have ever had an allergic reaction to quinidine or have ever developed reddish or purplish spots below the skin while taking quinidine or quinine.

Special warnings about this medication

Cardioquin has been known to cause life-threatening abnormal heart rhythms. If you have a history of congestive heart failure or any other heart problems, this medication should be used with caution, as it can cause low blood pressure, slowed heartbeat, or heart block.

If you have kidney or liver problems, your doctor may need to reduce your dosage. Be sure to tell your doctor about any medical conditions you have.

Possible food and drug interactions
when taking this medication

Concentrations of digoxin (Lanoxin) in your blood may increase or even double when this drug is taken with Cardioquin. Your doctor may need to reduce the amount of digoxin you take.

If Cardioquin is taken with certain other drugs, the effects of either could be increased, decreased, or altered. It is especially important to check with your doctor before combining Cardioquin with the following:

Amiodarone (Cordarone)
Antidepressants in the "polycyclic" category, including Desyrel, Elavil, Ludiomil, and Tofranil
Certain medications that make your urine less acid, such as Diamox, Diuril, Dyazide, Esidrix, Maxzide, Neptazane, and sodium bicarbonate
Cimetidine (Tagamet)
Felodipine (Plendil)
Haloperidol (Haldol)
Ketoconazole (Nizoral)
Major tranquilizers such as Mellaril and Thorazine
Mexiletine (Mexitil)

Nicardipine (Cardene)
Nifedipine (Procardia)
Nimodipine (Nimotop)
Phenobarbital
Phenytoin (Dilantin)
Procainamide (Procan SR)
Propranolol (Inderal)
Rifampin (Rifadin)
Verapamil (Calan)
Warfarin (Coumadin)

Special information
if you are pregnant or breastfeeding

The effects of Cardioquin during pregnancy have not been adequately studied. If you are pregnant or plan to become pregnant, tell your doctor immediately. Cardioquin does appear in breast milk and can affect a nursing infant. If this medication is essential to your health, your doctor may advise you to discontinue breastfeeding until your treatment is finished.

Recommended dosage

ADULTS

Your dose will be decided by your doctor, based on your particular heart problem and your general health. If you have a serious heart condition, your doctor will start therapy in the hospital, where you can be closely monitored. The usual starting dose is two 275-milligram tablets every 6 hours or one 275-milligram tablet every 6 to 8 hours, depending on the condition being treated. If you are able to tolerate this dosage and your condition warrants it, your doctor may increase the medication. After 2 or 3 days of close monitoring, you will be discharged and may be maintained on this dosage.

Your doctor may suggest using a Holter monitor (a device that records your heart rate 24 hours a day) to check your reaction to the drug.

CHILDREN

Quinidine has been used to treat malaria in children. However, the safety and effectiveness of this medication in children with abnormal heart rhythms has not been studied.

Overdosage

Any medication taken in excess can have serious consequences; and an overdose of Cardioquin can be fatal. If you suspect an overdose, seek medical treatment immediately.

■ *Symptoms of Cardioquin overdose may include:*
Abnormal heart rhythms, blurred and double vision, confusion, delirium, diarrhea, headache, hearing loss, intolerance to light, low blood pressure, ringing in ears, vertigo, vomiting

Brand name:

CARDIZEM

Pronounced: CAR-di-zem
Generic name: Diltiazem hydrochloride
Other brand name: Tiazac

Why is this drug prescribed?

Cardizem and Cardizem CD (a controlled release form of diltiazem) are used in the treatment of angina pectoris (chest pain usually caused by lack of oxygen to the heart due to clogged arteries) and chronic stable angina (caused by exertion). Cardizem CD is also used to treat high blood pressure. Another controlled release form, Cardizem SR, is used only in the treatment of high blood pressure. Cardizem, a calcium channel blocker, dilates blood vessels and slows the heart to reduce blood pressure and the pain of angina.

Doctors sometimes prescribe Cardizem for loss of circulation in the fingers and toes (Raynaud's Syndrome), for involuntary movements (tardive dyskinesia), and to prevent heart attack.

Tiazac is used only for high blood pressure. It may be taken alone or combined with other blood pressure medications.

Most important fact about this drug

If you are taking Cardizem for high blood pressure, remember that it does not cure the problem; it merely controls it. You may need to take a blood pressure medication for the rest of your life.

If you are taking Cardizem for angina, do not stop suddenly. This can lead to an increase in your attacks.

How should you take this medication?

Cardizem should be taken before meals and at bedtime. Cardizem CD and Cardizem SR should be swallowed whole; do not chew, crush, or divide.

Take this medication exactly as prescribed by your doctor, even if your symptoms have disappeared.

■ *If you miss a dose...*
If you forget to take a dose, take it as soon as you remember. If it's almost time for your next dose, skip the missed dose and go back to your regular schedule. Never take 2 doses at the same time.

■ *Storage instructions...*
Cardizem should be stored at room temperature; protect from moisture.

What side effects may occur?
Side effects cannot be anticipated. If any develop or change in intensity, inform your doctor as soon as possible. Only your doctor can determine if it is safe for you to continue taking Cardizem.

■ *More common side effects may include:*
Abnormally slow heartbeat (more common with Cardizem SR and Cardizem CD), dizziness, fluid retention, flushing (more common with Cardizem SR and Cardizem CD), headache, nausea, rash, weakness

■ *Less common or rare side effects may include:*
Abnormal dreams, allergic reaction, altered way of walking, amnesia, anemia, angina (severe chest pain), blood disorders, congestive heart failure, constipation, cough, depression, diarrhea, difficulty sleeping, drowsiness, dry mouth, excessive urination at night, eye irritation, fainting, flu symptoms, hair loss, hallucinations, heart attack, high blood sugar, hives, impotence, increased output of pale urine, indigestion, infection, irregular heartbeat, itching, joint pain, labored breathing, loss of appetite, low blood pressure, low blood sugar, muscle cramps, nasal congestion or inflammation, nervousness, nosebleed, pain, personality change, pounding heartbeat, rapid heartbeat, reddish or purplish spots on skin, ringing in ears, sexual difficulties, skin inflammation/flaking or peeling, sensitivity to light, sleepiness, sore throat, taste alteration, thirst, tingling or pins and needles, tremor, vision changes, vomiting, welts, weight increase

Why should this drug not be prescribed?
If you suffer from "sick sinus" syndrome or second- or third-degree heart block (various types of irregular heartbeat), you should not take this drug unless you have a ventricular pacemaker.

Do not take Cardizem if you have low blood pressure or an allergy to the drug.

Special warnings about this medication

If you have congestive heart failure or suffer from kidney or liver disease, use Cardizem with caution.

This medication may cause your heart rate to become too slow. You should check your pulse regularly.

Possible food and drug interactions
when taking this medication

If Cardizem is taken with certain other drugs, the effects of either could be increased, decreased, or altered. It is especially important to check with your doctor before combining Cardizem with the following:

Beta-blockers (heart and blood pressure drugs such as Tenormin and Inderal)
Carbamazepine (Tegretol)
Cimetidine (Tagamet)
Cyclosporine (Sandimmune, Neoral)
Digoxin (Lanoxin)

Special information
if you are pregnant or breastfeeding

The effects of Cardizem during pregnancy have not been adequately studied. If you are pregnant or plan to become pregnant, inform your doctor immediately. Cardizem appears in breast milk and could affect a nursing infant. If this medication is essential to your health, your doctor may advise you to discontinue breastfeeding until your treatment with this medication is finished.

Recommended dosage

ADULTS

Dosage levels are determined by each individual's needs.

Cardizem

The average daily dosage is between 180 milligrams and 360 milligrams, divided into 3 or 4 smaller doses.

Cardizem SR

The recommended starting dosage is 60 to 120 milligrams 2 times a day, to be increased to 240 to 360 milligrams a day.

Cardizem CD

This is a once-a-day form of this drug. For hypertension, starting doses range from 180 to 240 milligrams; for angina, 120 to 180 milligrams.

Tiazac

The usual starting dose is 120 to 240 milligrams once a day. After the drug has taken effect—in about 2 weeks—the dose can range from 120 to 540 milligrams.

CHILDREN

Safety and effectiveness in children have not been established.

Overdosage

Any medication taken in excess can have serious consequences. If you suspect an overdose of Cardizem, seek medical attention immediately.

■ *The symptoms of Cardizem overdose may include:*
Fainting, dizziness, and irregular pulse, heart failure, low blood pressure, very slow heartbeat

Brand name:

CARDURA

Pronounced: car-DUHR-uh
Generic name: Doxazosin mesylate

Why is this drug prescribed?

Cardura is used in the treatment of benign prostatic hyperplasia, a condition in which the prostate gland grows larger, pressing on the urethra and threatening to block the flow of urine from the bladder. The drug relieves symptoms such as a weak stream, dribbling, incomplete emptying of the bladder, frequent urination, and burning during urination.

Cardura is also used in the treatment of high blood pressure. It is effective when used alone or in combination with diuretics or beta-blocking medications.

Doctors also prescribe Cardura, along with other drugs such as digitalis and diuretics, for treatment of congestive heart failure.

Most important fact about this drug

If you have high blood pressure, you must take Cardura regularly for it to be effective. Since blood pressure declines gradually, it may be several weeks before you get the full benefit of Cardura; and you must continue taking it even if you are feeling well. Cardura does not cure high blood pressure; it merely keeps it under control.

How should you take this medication?
This medication can be taken with or without food.

Cardura should be taken exactly as prescribed, even if your symptoms have disappeared. Try not to miss any doses. If this medication is not taken regularly, your condition may worsen.

If you have benign prostatic hyperplasia, you should see improvement in a week. Blood pressure will fall in 2 to 6 hours.

■ *If you miss a dose...*
Take it as soon as you remember. If it is almost time for your next dose, skip the one you missed and go back to your regular schedule. Never take 2 doses at the same time.

■ *Storage instructions...*
Store at room temperature.

What side effects may occur?
Side effects cannot be anticipated. If any develop or change in intensity, inform your doctor as soon as possible. Only your doctor can determine if it is safe for you to continue taking Cardura.

■ *More common side effects may include:*
Dizziness, drowsiness, fatigue, headache

■ *Less common side effects may include:*
Arthritis, constipation, depression, difficulty sleeping, eye pain, flushing, gas, inability to hold urine or other urination problems, indigestion, inflammation of conjunctiva (pinkeye), itching, joint pain, lack of muscle coordination, low blood pressure, motion disorders, muscle cramps, muscle pain, muscle weakness, nausea, nervousness, nosebleeds, rash, ringing in ears, shortness of breath, tingling or pins and needles, weakness

■ *Rare side effects may include:*
Abnormal thinking, abnormal vision, agitation, altered sense of smell, amnesia, back pain, breast pain, changeable emotions, changes in taste, chest pain, confusion, coughing, decreased sense of touch, diarrhea, dizziness when standing up, dry mouth, dry skin, earache, excessive urination, fainting, fecal incontinence, fever, fluid retention, flu-like symptoms, gout, hair loss, heart attack, hot flushes, inability to concentrate, inability to tolerate light, increased appetite, increased sweating, increased thirst, infection, inflammation of the nose, loss of

appetite, loss of sense of personal identity, migraine headache, morbid dreams, nausea, nervousness, pain, pallor, rapid pounding heartbeat, sexual problems, sinus inflammation, slight or partial paralysis, sore throat, tremors, twitching, vertigo, weight gain, weight loss, wheezing

Why should this drug not be prescribed?

Cardura should not be taken if you are sensitive to or have ever had an allergic reaction to Cardura or such drugs as Minipress or Hytrin. Make sure your doctor is aware of any drug reactions you may have experienced.

Special warnings about this medication

Cardura can cause low blood pressure, especially when you first start taking the medication and when dosage is increased. This can cause you to become faint, dizzy, or light-headed, particularly when first standing up. You should avoid driving or any hazardous tasks where injury could occur for 24 hours after taking the first dose, after your dose has been increased, or if Cardura has been stopped and then restarted.

If you have liver disease or are taking other medications that alter liver function, your doctor will monitor you closely when you take Cardura.

Cardura may lower blood counts. Your doctor will most likely monitor your blood counts while you are taking this medication.

This medication may cause you to become drowsy or sleepy. For this reason, too, driving or operating dangerous machinery or participating in any hazardous activity that requires full mental alertness is not recommended.

Prostate cancer has some of the same symptoms as benign prostatic hyperplasia; your doctor will want to make sure you do not have cancer before starting you on Cardura.

Possible food and drug interactions
when taking this medication

No significant interactions have been reported.

Special information
if you are pregnant or breastfeeding

The effects of Cardura during pregnancy have not been adequately studied. If you are pregnant or plan to become pregnant, inform your doctor immediately. Cardura may appear in breast milk and could affect a nursing infant. If this medication is essential to your health, your doctor may advise you to discontinue breastfeeding until your treatment with this medication is finished.

Recommended dosage

ADULTS

Your doctor will adjust the dosage to fit your needs.

The usual starting dose is 1 milligram taken once a day. To minimize the potential for dizziness or fainting associated with Cardura, which may occur between 2 and 6 hours after a dose, your doctor will monitor your blood pressure during this period and afterwards.

After the effects of the starting dose are measured, your doctor may increase the daily dose to 2 milligrams and then, if necessary, to 4 milligrams, 8 milligrams, or, in people with high blood pressure only, up to 16 milligrams. As the dose increases, the potential for side effects such as dizziness, vertigo, light-headedness, and fainting also increases.

CHILDREN

The safety and effectiveness of this drug in children have not been established.

Overdosage

Any medication taken in excess can have serious consequences. Although no specific information is available, low blood pressure is the most likely symptom of an overdose of Cardura.

If you suspect an overdose, seek medical attention immediately.

Generic name:

CARISOPRODOL

See Soma, page 1149.

Generic name:

CARVEDILOL

See Coreg, page 269.

Brand name:

CATAFLAM

See Voltaren, page 1357.

Brand name:

CATAPRES

Pronounced: KAT-uh-press
Generic name: Clonidine hydrochloride

Why is this drug prescribed?
Catapres is prescribed for high blood pressure. It is effective when used alone or with other high blood pressure medications.

Doctors also prescribe Catapres for alcohol, nicotine, or benzodiazepine (tranquilizer) withdrawal; migraine headaches; smoking cessation programs; Tourette's syndrome (tics and uncontrollable utterances); narcotic/meth-adone detoxification; premenstrual tension; and diabetic diarrhea.

Most important fact about this drug
If you have high blood pressure, you must take Catapres regularly for it to be effective. Since blood pressure declines gradually, it may be several weeks before you get the full benefit of Catapres; and you must continue taking it even if you are feeling well. Catapres does not cure high blood pressure; it merely keeps it under control.

How should you take this medication?
Take this medication exactly as prescribed, even if you are feeling well. Try not to miss any doses. If Catapres is not taken regularly, your condition may get worse.

The Catapres-TTS patch should be put on a hairless, clean area of the upper outer arm or chest. Normally, a new one is applied every 7 days to a new area of the skin. If the patch becomes loose, use some adhesive tape or an adhesive bandage to keep it in place.

- *If you miss a dose...*
  Take it as soon as you remember, then go back to your regular schedule. If you forget to take the medication 2 or more times in a row, or if you forget to change the transdermal patch for 3 or more days, contact your doctor.

- *Storage instructions...*
  Store at room temperature in a tightly closed container away from light.

What side effects may occur?
Side effects cannot be anticipated. If any develop or change in intensity, inform your doctor as soon as possible. Only your doctor can determine if it is safe for you to continue taking Catapres.

- *More common side effects may include:*
  Agitation, constipation, dizziness, drowsiness, dry mouth, fatigue, impotence, loss of sex drive, nausea, nervousness, sedation (calm), vomiting, weakness

- *Less common side effects may include:*
  Changes in heartbeat, excessive nighttime urination, headache, loss of appetite, mental depression, pounding heartbeat, vague bodily discomfort, weight gain

- *Rare side effects may include:*
  Abdominal pain, anxiety, behavior changes, blurred vision, breast development in males, burning eyes, congestive heart failure, constipation, delirium, dry eyes, dry nasal passages, fainting, fever, greater sensitivity to alcohol, hallucinations, heart irregularities, hepatitis, hair loss, hives, insomnia, itching, joint pain, leg cramps, little or no urination, muscle pain, pallor, restlessness, vivid dreams or nightmares

- *Additional side effects of Catapres-TTS may include:*
  Abrasions, blisters, burning or reddened skin, discolored or whitened skin, pimples, throbbing skin

Why should this drug not be prescribed?
Do not take this medication if you have ever had an allergic reaction to Catapres or to any of the components of the transdermal patch.

Special warnings about this medication
Catapres should not be stopped suddenly. Headache, nervousness, agitation, tremor, confusion, and rapid rise in blood pressure can occur. Severe reactions such as disruption of brain functions, stroke, fluid in the lungs, and death have also been reported. Your doctor should gradually reduce your dosage over several days to avoid withdrawal symptoms.

If you see redness, blistering, or a rash near the transdermal patch, call your doctor. You may need to remove the patch. If you are troubled by mild irritation before completing 7 days of use, you may remove the patch and apply a new one at a different site.

If your doctor has switched you to oral Catapres (tablet) because you had an allergic reaction, such as a rash or hives, to the transdermal skin patch, be aware that you may have a similar reaction to the Catapres tablet.

If you have severe heart or kidney disease, are recovering from a heart attack, or have a disease of the blood vessels of the brain, your doctor will prescribe Catapres with caution.

If you are taking Catapres and a beta blocker such as Inderal or Tenormin, and your doctor wants to stop your medication, the beta blocker should be stopped several days before the gradual withdrawal of Catapres.

Catapres may cause drowsiness. If it has this effect on you, avoid driving, operating dangerous machinery, or participating in any hazardous activity that requires full mental alertness.

The used Catapres-TTS patch still contains enough drug to be harmful to children and pets. Fold the patch in half with the adhesive sides together and dispose of it out of the reach of children.

Possible food and drug interactions
when taking this medication

Catapres may increase the effects of alcohol. Do not drink alcohol while taking this medication.

If Catapres is taken with certain other drugs, the effects of either could be increased, decreased, or altered. It is especially important to check with your doctor before combining Catapres with the following:

Barbiturates such as Nembutal and Seconal
Beta-blocker drugs such as the blood pressure medications Inderal and Lopressor
Calcium blockers such as the heart medications Calan and Cardizem
Digitalis
Sedatives such as Valium, Xanax, and Halcion
Tricyclic antidepressants such as Elavil and Tofranil

Special information
if you are pregnant or breastfeeding

The effects of Catapres during pregnancy have not been adequately studied. If you are pregnant or plan to become pregnant, inform your doctor immediately. Catapres appears in breast milk and could affect a nursing infant. If this medication is essential to your health, your doctor may advise you to discontinue breastfeeding until your treatment with this medication is finished.

Recommended dosage

ADULTS

The dosage will be adjusted to your individual needs.

The usual starting dose is 0.1 milligram, twice a day (usually in the morning and at bedtime).

The regular dose of Catapres is determined by increasing the daily dose by 0.1 milligram at weekly intervals until the desired response is achieved. A larger portion of the increased dose can be taken at bedtime to reduce potential side effects of drowsiness and dry mouth that may appear when you begin taking this drug.

The most common effective dosages range from 0.2 milligram to 0.6 milligram per day divided into smaller doses. The maximum effective dose is 2.4 milligrams per day; however, this dose is not usually prescribed.

Transdermal Patch
The patch comes in different strengths, and your doctor will determine which is best for you based on your blood pressure response.

People who are using another high blood pressure medication should not stop taking it abruptly when they begin using the patch, because the medication in the patch may take a few days to begin working. The other medication should be discontinued slowly as the patch begins to take effect.

CHILDREN

Safety and effectiveness of the Catapres tablets and patch in children below the age of 12 have not been established.

OLDER ADULTS

Dosages are generally as above; however, the initial dosage for an older person may be lower than the regular starting dose.

Overdosage

■ *Symptoms of Catapres overdose may include:*
Constriction of pupils of the eye, drowsiness, high blood pressure followed by a drop in pressure, irritability, low body temperature, slowed breathing, slowed heartbeat, slowed reflexes, weakness

Large overdoses can cause changes in heart function or rhythm, coma, seizures, and temporary interruptions in breathing.

Getting a patch in the mouth or swallowing one can cause an overdose.

If you suspect symptoms of a Catapres overdose, seek medical attention immediately.

Brand name:

CAVERJECT

Pronounced: CA-vur-jekt
Generic name: Alprostadil
Other brand name: Edex

Why is this drug prescribed?

Caverject is used to treat male impotence. Your doctor also may use Caverject to help diagnose the exact nature of your impotence.

Most important fact about this drug

Caverject is known to have caused extremely long-lasting erections. Serious harm can occur from such a prolonged erection, so call your doctor or seek other professional help if an erection lasts more than 6 hours. Usually the erection should last about 1 hour.

How should you use this medication?

Caverject is injected into a specific area of the penis and produces an erection within 5 to 20 minutes. Do not use Caverject more than 3 times a week. Wait at least 24 hours between use.

The first injections are performed by your doctor in the doctor's office in order to determine the proper dosage. Afterwards, you can inject Caverject yourself as needed. Your doctor will train you in the proper technique for injecting Caverject and you'll be given complete printed instructions. Follow these directions exactly and do not change the dose your doctor has determined.

Do not use a Caverject solution that appears cloudy or colored or that contains particles. Do not shake the vial.

Wash your hands thoroughly and do not touch the needle. Carefully choose the injection site as instructed by your doctor, always avoiding visible veins. Cleanse the site with an alcohol swab. With each use, alternate the side of the penis and the site of the injection.

Use the needle/syringe and vial only once, then discard them properly. Do not share needles or allow anyone else to use your medication.

Caverject comes in both 10 microgram and 20 microgram strengths. Make sure you are using a vial with the correct strength.

After injecting Edex, put pressure on the injection site for 5 minutes, or until the bleeding stops.

■ *Storage instructions...*
Store unused packs of Caverject at room temperature for up to 3 months. Protect from freezing or from overheating.

Once the Caverject solution is mixed, you must use it immediately or discard it.

When traveling, take care to prevent exposing Caverject to freezing or excessive heat. Do not store Caverject in checked luggage or leave it in a closed car.

What side effects may occur?
Side effects cannot be anticipated. If any develop or change in intensity, inform your doctor as soon as possible. Only your doctor can determine if it is safe for you to continue using Caverject.

The most common side effect is mild to moderate pain in the penis during and/or after injection, reported by about one-third of users. A small amount of bleeding may occur at the injection site. Notify your doctor if you have a condition or are taking a medication that interferes with blood clotting. As with any injection, the site can become infected. Call your doctor if you notice any redness, lumps, swelling, tenderness, or curving of the erect penis.

Your doctor should examine your penis regularly if you use Caverject. Use of Caverject may result in formation of fibrous (hardened) tissue in the penis or erections at an unusual angle. If those side effects occur, inform your doctor and stop using Caverject.

■ *More common side effects may include:*
Blood-filled swelling at the site of injection, disorder of the penis (such as discoloration of the head, strange feeling, tearing of the skin), hardened tissue in the penis, pain in the penis, prolonged erection, upper respiratory infection

■ *Less common side effects may include:*
Abnormal vision, back pain, bruising at the injection site, cough, dizziness, flu symptoms, headache, heart attack, high blood pressure, infection, inflamed or enlarged prostate, injuries, fractures, abrasions, lacerations/ dislocations, leg pain, nasal congestion, pain, redness, sinus inflammation, skin disorders

■ *Rare side effects may include:*
Abnormal ejaculation, bleeding at the urethra, blood in the urine, dizziness, dry mouth, extreme dilation of the pupils, fainting, fluid retention at the injection site, frequent or urgent urination, hemorrhage at the injection

site, impaired urination, inflammation, irritation, itching, lack of sensation, leg cramps, low blood pressure, nausea, numbness, painful erection, pelvic pain, profuse sweating, rash on the penis, redness, sensitivity, swelling at the injection site, swelling of the head of the penis, swelling of the scrotum, testicular pain, tightness of the foreskin, warmth, weakness, yeast infection

Why should this drug not be prescribed?

Do not use Caverject if you have a condition that might result in long-lasting erections, such as sickle cell anemia, leukemia, and tumor of the bone marrow.

Men with penile implants or an unusually formed penis should not use Caverject. The drug is not for use in women, children, or men whose doctors have advised them not to have sex.

Do not use Caverject if it causes an allergic reaction or if you have ever had a reaction to any prostaglandin drugs.

Special warnings about this medication

Caverject offers no protection from the transmission of sexually transmitted diseases, such as HIV, the virus that causes AIDS. Small amounts of bleeding at the injection site can increase the risk of transmission of blood-borne diseases such as HIV.

Possible food and drug interactions
when using this medication

No interactions have been reported, but Caverject should not be used with other drugs that act on blood vessels.

You may have some bleeding at the site of injection. If you are taking anticoagulants such as heparin, you may bleed more after you inject this drug. Make sure that any doctor who prescribes heparin is aware that you are using this medication.

Recommended dosage

The correct dose of Caverject must be carefully determined by your doctor. Each man will need a different dose of Caverject, but the usual starting dosage is 1.25 or 2.5 micrograms, which is then increased gradually. Your doctor will adjust the dosage, particularly if it produces erections lasting longer than 1 hour.

The dosage range for Edex is 1 to 40 micrograms, given over 5 to 10 seconds.

Do not change your dosage without your doctor's approval. See your doctor every 3 months for a checkup.

Overdosage

No overdose of Caverject has been reported. However, any medication taken in excess can have serious consequences. The chief symptom of an overdose of this drug would be a prolonged erection. If you suspect an overdose, seek medical attention immediately.

Brand name:

CECLOR

Pronounced: SEE-klor
Generic name: Cefaclor

Why is this drug prescribed?

Ceclor, a cephalosporin antibiotic, is used in the treatment of ear, nose, throat, respiratory tract, urinary tract, and skin infections caused by specific bacteria, including staph, strep, and *E. coli.* Uses include treatment of sore or strep throat, pneumonia, and tonsillitis. Ceclor CD, an extended release form of the drug, is also used for flare-ups of chronic bronchitis.

Most important fact about this drug

If you are allergic to either penicillin or cephalosporin antibiotics in any form, consult your doctor *before taking* Ceclor. There is a possibility that you are allergic to both types of medication; and if a reaction occurs, it could be extremely severe. If you take the drug and feel signs of a reaction, seek medical attention immediately.

How should you take this medication?

Take this medication exactly as prescribed. It is important that you finish taking all of this medication to obtain the maximum benefit.

Ceclor works fastest when taken on an empty stomach. However, your doctor may ask you to take this drug with food to avoid stomach upset.

Ceclor CD should be taken with meals or at least within 1 hour of eating because it's better absorbed with food. Do not cut, crush, or chew the tablets.

Ceclor suspension should be shaken well before using.

■ *If you miss a dose...*
Take it as soon as you remember. If it is almost time for your next dose, skip the one you missed and go back to your regular schedule. Never take 2 doses at the same time.

■ *Storage instructions...*
Keep Ceclor capsules in the container they came in, tightly closed. Store at room temperature.

Refrigerate Ceclor suspension. Discard any unused portion after 14 days.

What side effects may occur?
Side effects cannot be anticipated. If any develop or change in intensity, inform your doctor as soon as possible. Only your doctor can determine if it is safe for you to continue taking Ceclor.

■ *More common side effects of Ceclor may include:*
Diarrhea, hives, itching

▨ *Less common or rare side effects of Ceclor may include:*
Blood disorders (an increase in certain types of white blood cells), liver disorders, nausea, severe allergic reactions (including swelling, weakness, breathing difficulty, or fainting), skin rashes accompanied by joint pain, vaginal inflammation, vomiting

■ *More common side effects of Ceclor CD may include:*
Diarrhea, headache, nasal inflammation, nausea

■ *Less common or rare side effects of Ceclor CD may include:*
Abdominal pain, accidental injury, anxiety, asthma, back pain, bronchitis, chest pain, chills, congestive heart failure, conjunctivitis (pinkeye), constipation, dizziness, ear pain or infection, fever, fluid retention with swelling, flu symptoms, gas, hives, increased cough, indigestion, infection, inflamed sinuses, insomnia, itching, joint pain, loss of appetite, lung problems, menstrual problems, muscle pain, nausea, neck pain, nervousness, rash, sleepiness, sore throat, sweating, throbbing heartbeat, tremor, urinary problems, vaginal inflammation or infection, vague feeling of illness, vomiting

Other problems have been reported in patients taking Ceclor, although it is not known whether the drug was the cause. Check with your doctor if you suspect a side effect.

Why should this drug not be prescribed?
If you are sensitive to or have ever had an allergic reaction to Ceclor or any other cephalosporin antibiotic, you should not take this medication. Make sure your doctor is aware of any drug reactions you have experienced.

Unless you are directed to do so by your doctor, do not take this medication if you have a history of gastrointestinal problems, particularly bowel inflammation (colitis). You may be at increased risk for side effects.

Special warnings about this medication

Ceclor may cause a false positive result with some urine sugar tests for diabetics. Your doctor can advise you of any adjustments you may need to make in your medication or diet.

Ceclor occasionally causes diarrhea. Some diarrhea medications can make this diarrhea worse. Check with your doctor before taking any diarrhea remedy.

Oral contraceptives may not work properly while you are taking Ceclor. For greater certainty, use other measures while taking Ceclor.

Possible food and drug interactions
when taking this medication

If Ceclor is taken with certain other drugs, the effects of either could be increased, decreased, or altered. It is especially important to check with your doctor before combining Ceclor with the following:

Antacids containing magnesium or aluminum, including Gelusil, Maalox,
    and Mylanta (interact with Ceclor CD only)
Certain antibiotics such as Amikin
Certain potent diuretics such as Edecrin and Lasix
Probenecid (Benemid)
Warfarin (Coumadin)

Special information
if you are pregnant or breastfeeding

The effects of Ceclor during pregnancy have not been adequately studied. If you are pregnant or plan to become pregnant, this drug should be used only when prescribed by your doctor. Ceclor appears in breast milk and could affect a nursing infant. If this medication is essential to your health, your doctor may advise you to stop nursing your baby until your treatment with Ceclor is finished.

Recommended dosage

CECLOR

Adults

The usual adult dose is 250 milligrams every 8 hours. For more severe infections (such as pneumonia), your doctor may increase the dosage.

Children

The usual daily dosage is 20 milligrams per 2.2 pounds of body weight per day divided into smaller doses and taken every 8 hours. In more serious infections, such as middle ear infection, the usual dose is 40 milligrams per 2.2 pounds of body weight per day divided into smaller doses. The total daily dose should not exceed 1 gram.

CECLOR CD

Adults: Bronchitis

The usual dose is 500 milligrams every 12 hours for 7 days.

Adults: Sore throat, Tonsillitis, and Skin Infections

The usual dose is 375 milligrams every 12 hours for 10 days (sore throat and tonsillitis) or 7 to 10 days (skin infections).

Children

Safety and effectiveness of Ceclor CD in children under age 16 have not been established.

Overdosage

■ *Symptoms of Ceclor overdose may include:*

Diarrhea, nausea, stomach upset, vomiting

If other symptoms are present, they may be related to an allergic reaction or other underlying disease. In any case, you should contact your doctor or an emergency room immediately.

Brand name:

CEDAX

Pronounced: SEE-daks
Generic name: Ceftibuten

Why is this drug prescribed?

Cedax cures mild-to-moderate bacterial infections of the throat, ear, and respiratory tract. Among these infections are strep throat, tonsillitis, and acute otitis media (middle ear infection) in children and adults. Cedax is also prescribed for acute flare-ups of chronic bronchitis in adults. Cedax is a cephalosporin antibiotic.

Most important fact about this drug
If you are allergic to either penicillin or cephalosporin antibiotics in any form, double-check with your doctor *before taking* Cedax. There is a possibility that you are allergic to both types of medication and if a reaction occurs, it could be extremely severe. (Symptoms include swelling of the face, lips, tongue, and throat, making it difficult to breathe.) If you take the drug and feel any signs of this reaction, seek medical attention immediately.

How should you take this medication?
To make certain your infection is fully cleared up, take all the Cedax your doctor prescribes, even if you begin to feel better after the first few days.

If you are using the oral suspension, it must be taken at least 2 hours before a meal or 1 hour after. Shake well before using.

- *If you miss a dose...*
  Take it as soon as you remember. If it is almost time for your next dose, skip the one you missed and go back to your regular schedule. Never take 2 doses at the same time.

- *Storage instructions...*
  Keep the oral suspension in the refrigerator, and discard any unused portion after 14 days. Capsules may be stored at room temperature.

What side effects may occur?
Side effects cannot be anticipated. If any develop or change in intensity, notify your doctor as soon as possible. Only your doctor can determine whether it is safe for you to continue taking Cedax.

ADULTS

- *More common side effects may include:*
  Diarrhea, headache, nausea

- *Less common or rare side effects in adults may include:*
  Abdominal pain, belching, breathing problems, constipation, dizziness, drowsiness, dry mouth, fatigue, gas, hives, indigestion, itching, loose stools, loss of appetite, painful urination, rash, stuffy nose, taste alteration, tingling, vaginal inflammation, vomiting, yeast infection

CHILDREN

■ *The most common side effect is:*
Diarrhea

■ *Less common or rare side effects may include:*
Abdominal pain, agitation, blood in urine, chills and fever, dehydration, diaper rash, dizziness, fever, gas, headache, hives, increased activity, insomnia, irritability, itching, loose stools, loss of appetite, nausea, rash, vomiting

Why should this drug not be prescribed?
If you are sensitive to or have ever had an allergic reaction to Cedax, other cephalosporins, such as Keflex, or any form of penicillin, do not take this medication. Make sure your doctor is aware of any drug reactions you have experienced.

Special warnings about this medication
If you have a history of gastrointestinal disease, particularly colitis, take Cedax with caution. If you develop diarrhea while taking Cedax, check with your doctor. The problem could be a sign of a serious condition.

Tell your doctor if you have kidney problems. Your dosage may have to be lowered. If you are diabetic, be sure to tell your doctor before starting therapy with Cedax; the oral suspension contains sugar.

If new infections (called superinfections) occur, talk to your doctor. You may need to be treated with a different antibiotic.

Do not give this medication to other people or use it for other infections before checking with your doctor. The drug is not effective against every type of germ.

Possible food and drug interactions
when taking this medication
Zantac may boost the level of Cedax in your system. Check with your doctor before combining these drugs.

Special information
if you are pregnant or breastfeeding
The effects of Cedax during pregnancy have not been adequately studied. If you are pregnant or plan to become pregnant, tell your doctor immediately.

Cedax may appear in breast milk and could affect a nursing infant. If this medication is essential to your health, your doctor may advise you to stop breastfeeding until your treatment is finished.

Recommended dosage

ADULTS

The usual dose is a single 400-milligram capsule once a day. People with serious kidney problems may need a smaller dose.

CHILDREN

The usual dose is 9 milligrams for each 2.2 pounds of body weight, once a day. Your doctor will specify the number of teaspoonfuls required. Children weighing more than 90 pounds should take 400 milligrams once a day.

Overdosage

Although no specific information is available, an overdose of cephalosporins has been known to cause convulsions. Any medication taken in excess can have serious consequences. If you suspect an overdose of Cedax, seek medical attention immediately.

Generic name:

CEFACLOR

See Ceclor, page 208.

Generic name:

CEFADROXIL

See Duricef, page 422.

Generic name:

CEFIXIME

See Suprax, page 1168.

Generic name:

CEFPROZIL

See Cefzil, page 218.

Generic name:

CEFTIBUTEN

See Cedax, page 211.

Brand name:

CEFTIN

Pronounced: SEF-tin
Generic name: Cefuroxime axetil

Why is this drug prescribed?
Ceftin, a cephalosporin antibiotic, is prescribed for mild to moderately severe bacterial infections of the throat, lungs, ears, skin, sinuses, and urinary tract, and for gonorrhea. Ceftin tablets are also prescribed in the early stages of Lyme disease.

Most important fact about this drug
If you are allergic to either penicillin or cephalosporin antibiotics such as Ceclor, Cefzil, or Keflex, consult your doctor *before taking* Ceftin. There is a possibility that you are allergic to both types of medication; if a reaction occurs, it could be extremely severe. If you take the drug and develop shortness of breath, a pounding heartbeat, a skin rash, or hives, seek medical attention immediately.

How should you take this medication?
Ceftin tablets can be taken on a full or empty stomach. However, this drug enters the bloodstream and works faster when taken after meals. Ceftin oral suspension must be taken with food. Shake the suspension well before each use.

Take this medication exactly as prescribed: It is important that you finish taking all of this medication to obtain the maximum benefit.

The crushed tablet has a strong, persistent, bitter taste. Children who cannot swallow the tablet whole should take the oral suspension. Shake the oral suspension well before each use.

■ *If you miss a dose...*
Take it as soon as you remember. If it is almost time for your next dose skip the one you missed and go back to the regular schedule. Do not take 2 doses at once.

■ *Storage instructions...*
Store tablets at room temperature in a tightly closed container. Protect from moisture. The oral suspension may be stored either in the refrigerator or at room temperature. Replace the cap securely after each use. Discard any unused suspension after 10 days.

What side effects may occur?
Side effects cannot be anticipated. If any develop or change in intensity, inform your doctor as soon as possible. Only your doctor can determine if it is safe for you to continue taking Ceftin.

■ *More common side effects may include:*
Diaper rash in infants, diarrhea, nausea, vomiting

■ *Rare side effects of the tablets include:*
Abdominal pain or cramps, chest pain, chills, gas, headache, hives, indigestion, itch, loss of appetite, mouth ulcers, rash, shortness of breath, sleepiness, swollen tongue, thirst, urinary problems, vaginitis

■ *Rare side effects of the oral suspension include:*
Abdominal pain, cough, drooling, fever, gas, gastrointestinal infection, hyperactivity, inflamed sinuses, irritability, joint pain and swelling, rash, upper respiratory infection, urinary infection, vaginal irritation, virus infection, yeast infection

Why should this drug not be prescribed?
Ceftin should not be prescribed if you have a known allergy to cephalosporin antibiotics.

Special warnings about this medication
Inflammation of the bowel (colitis) has been reported with the use of Ceftin; therefore, if you develop diarrhea while taking this medication, notify your doctor.

Continued or prolonged use of Ceftin may result in an overgrowth of bacteria that do not respond to this medication and can cause a second infection. You should take this drug only when it is prescribed by your doctor, even if you have symptoms like those of a previous infection. Tell your doctor if you have any kidney problems. Your dosage may need to be lowered.

If you are allergic to penicillin, you may also be allergic to Ceftin. Make sure your doctor is aware of any allergies you have.

Possible food and drug interactions
when taking this medication

It is important to consult your doctor before taking this drug with probenecid (Benemid), a gout medication.

If diarrhea occurs while taking Ceftin, consult your doctor before taking an antidiarrhea medication. Certain drugs, such as Lomotil, may cause your diarrhea to become worse.

Be cautious if you are taking potent water pills (diuretics) such as Lasix while on Ceftin. The combination could affect your kidneys.

Special information
if you are pregnant or breastfeeding

The effects of Ceftin during pregnancy have not been adequately studied. If you are pregnant or plan to become pregnant, inform your doctor immediately. Ceftin appears in breast milk and could affect a nursing infant. If this medication is essential to your health, your doctor may advise you to discontinue breastfeeding until your treatment with this medication is finished.

Recommended dosage

ADULTS

The usual dose for adults and children 13 years and older is 250 milligrams, 2 times a day for 10 days. For more severe infections the dose may be increased to 500 milligrams, 2 times a day.

Urinary Tract Infection

The usual dose is 125 milligrams, 2 times a day for 7 to 10 days. This dose may be increased to 250 milligrams 2 times a day for severe infection.

Gonorrhea

The usual treatment is a single dose of 1 gram.

Early Lyme Disease

The usual dosage is 500 milligrams taken twice a day for 20 days.

CHILDREN

Ceftin oral suspension may be given to children ranging in age from 3 months to 12 years.

Your doctor will determine the dosage based on your child's weight and the type of infection being treated. Ceftin oral suspension is given twice a day for 10 days. The maximum daily dose ranges from 500 to 1000 milligrams.

Overdosage

Any medication taken in excess can have serious consequences. Overdosage with cephalosporin antibiotics can cause brain irritation leading to convulsions. If you suspect an overdose, seek medical attention immediately.

Generic name:

CEFUROXIME

See Ceftin, page 215.

Brand name:

CEFZIL

Pronounced: SEFF-zil
Generic name: Cefprozil

Why is this drug prescribed?

Cefzil, a cephalosporin antibiotic, is prescribed for mild to moderately severe bacterial infections of the throat, ear, sinuses, respiratory tract, and skin. Among these infections are strep throat, tonsillitis, bronchitis, and pneumonia.

Most important fact about this drug

If you are allergic to penicillin or cephalosporin antibiotics in any form, consult your doctor *before taking* Cefzil. An allergy to either type of medication may signal an allergy to Cefzil; and if a reaction occurs, it could be extremely severe. If you take the drug and feel signs of a reaction, seek medical attention immediately.

How should you use this medication?

Take this medication exactly as prescribed. It is important that you finish all of the medication to obtain the maximum benefit.

Cefzil works fastest when taken on an empty stomach, but can be taken with food to avoid stomach upset.

Cefzil oral suspension should be shaken well before using.

■ *If you miss a dose...*
Take it as soon as you remember. If it is almost time for your next dose, skip the one you missed and go back to your regular schedule. Never take 2 doses at the same time.

■ *Storage instructions...*
Store Cefzil tablets at room temperature. Keep the oral suspension in the refrigerator; discard any unused portion after 14 days.

What side effects may occur?
Side effects cannot be anticipated. If any develop or change in intensity, notify your doctor as soon as possible. Only your doctor can determine whether it is safe for you to continue taking Cefzil.

The most common side effect is nausea.

■ *Less common or rare side effects may include:*
Abdominal pain, confusion, diaper rash, diarrhea, difficulty sleeping, dizziness, genital itching, headache, hives, hyperactivity, nervousness, rash, sleepiness, superinfection (additional infection), vaginal inflammation, vomiting, yellow eyes and skin

Although not reported for Cefzil, similar antibiotics have been known occasionally to have severe side effects such as anaphylaxis (a severe allergic reaction), skin rash with blisters, Stevens-Johnson syndrome (a rare skin condition characterized by severe blisters and bleeding in the lips, eyes, mouth, nose, and genitals), and "serum-sickness" (itchy rash, fever, and pain in the joints).

Why should this drug not be prescribed?
If you are sensitive to or have ever had an allergic reaction to Cefzil or other cephalosporin antibiotics, do not take this medication. Make sure your doctor is aware of any drug reactions you have experienced.

Special warnings about this medication
Cefzil occasionally causes colitis (inflammation of the bowel) leading to diarrhea. Some diarrhea medications can make this diarrhea worse. Check with your doctor before taking any diarrhea remedy.

Oral contraceptives may not work properly while you are taking Cefzil. For greater certainty, use other measures while taking Cefzil.

Your doctor will check your kidney function before and during your treatment with this medication.

Use Cefzil with caution if you are taking a strong diuretic, or if you have ever had stomach and intestinal disease, particularly colitis.

If new infections (called superinfections) occur, talk to your doctor. You may need to be treated with a different antibiotic.

Cefzil may alter the results of some urine sugar tests for diabetics. Your doctor can advise you of any adjustments you may need to make in your medication or diet.

Possible food and drug interactions
when taking this medication

When Cefzil is taken with certain other drugs, the effects of either could be increased, decreased, or altered. It is especially important to check with your doctor before combining Cefzil with the following:

   Certain other antibiotics such as Amikin
   Certain potent diuretics such as Edecrin and Lasix
   Oral contraceptives
   Probenecid (Benemid)
   Propantheline (Pro-Banthine)

Special information
if you are pregnant or breastfeeding

The effects of Cefzil during pregnancy have not been adequately studied. If you are pregnant or plan to become pregnant, inform your doctor immediately. Cefzil does appear in breast milk and could affect a nursing infant. If this medication is essential to your health, your doctor may advise you to stop breastfeeding until your treatment with this medication is finished.

Recommended dosage

ADULTS

Throat and Respiratory Tract Infections
The usual dose is 500 milligrams, taken once or twice a day for 10 days.

Sinus Infection
The usual dose is 250 milligrams every 12 hours for 10 days; for severe infections the dose is 500 milligrams.

Skin Infections
The dosage is usually either 250 milligrams taken 2 times a day, or 500 milligrams taken once or twice a day for 10 days.

CHILDREN 2 TO 12 YEARS OF AGE

Throat Infections and Tonsillitis
The usual dose is 7.5 milligrams for each 2.2 pounds of body weight, taken 2 times a day for 10 days.

Skin Infections
The usual dose is 20 milligrams for each 2.2 pounds of body weight, taken once a day for 10 days.

INFANTS AND CHILDREN 6 MONTHS TO 12 YEARS OF AGE

Ear Infections
The usual dose is 15 milligrams for each 2.2 pounds of body weight, taken 2 times a day for 10 days.

Sinus Infection
The usual dose is 7.5 milligrams for each 2.2 pounds of body weight every 12 hours for 10 days. For severe infections, the amount may be doubled.

Overdosage
Although no specific information is available, any medication taken in excess can have serious consequences. If you suspect an overdose of Cefzil, seek medical attention immediately.

Brand name:

CENTRUM

See Multivitamins, page 804.

Generic name:

CEPHALEXIN

See Keflex, page 627.

Generic name:

CERIVASTATIN

See Baycol, page 130.

Generic name:

CETIRIZINE

See Zyrtec, page 1426.

Generic name:

CHLORDIAZEPOXIDE

See Librium, page 667.

Generic name:

CHLORDIAZEPOXIDE WITH CLIDINIUM

See Librax, page 665.

Generic name:

CHLORHEXIDINE

See Peridex, page 945.

Generic name:

CHLOROTHIAZIDE

See Diuril, page 402.

Generic name:

CHLORPHENIRAMINE WITH PSEUDOEPHEDRINE

See Deconamine, page 331.

Generic name:

CHLORPROMAZINE

See Thorazine, page 1232.

Generic name:

CHLORPROPAMIDE

See Diabinese, page 363.

Generic name:

CHLORTHALIDONE

See Hygroton, page 576.

Generic name:

CHLORZOXAZONE

See Parafon Forte DSC, page 911.

Generic name:

CHOLESTYRAMINE

See Questran, page 1046.

Generic name:

CHOLINE MAGNESIUM TRISALICYLATE

See Trilisate, page 1281.

Brand name:

CHRONULAC SYRUP

Pronounced: KRON-yoo-lak
Generic name: Lactulose
Other brand name: Duphalac

Why is this drug prescribed?
Chronulac treats constipation. In people who are chronically constipated, Chronulac increases the number and frequency of bowel movements.

Most important fact about this drug
It may take 24 to 48 hours to produce a normal bowel movement.

How should you take this medication?
Take this medication exactly as prescribed. If you find the taste of Chronulac unpleasant, it can be mixed with water, fruit juice, or milk.

- *If you miss a dose...*
  Take the forgotten dose as soon as you remember; but do not try to "catch up" by taking a double dose.

■ *Storage instructions...*
Store at room temperature. Avoid excessive heat or direct light. The liquid may darken in color, which is normal. Do not freeze.

What side effects may occur?
Side effects cannot be anticipated. If any develop or change in intensity, inform your doctor as soon as possible. Only your doctor can determine if it is safe for you to continue taking Chronulac.

■ *Side effects may include:*
Diarrhea, gas (temporary, at the beginning of use), intestinal cramps (temporary, at the beginning of use), nausea, potassium and fluid loss, vomiting

Why should this drug not be prescribed?
Chronulac contains galactose, a simple sugar. If you are on a low-galactose diet, do not take this medication.

Special warnings about this medication
Because of its sugar content, this medication should be used with caution if you have diabetes.

If unusual diarrhea occurs, contact your doctor.

Possible food and drug interactions
when taking this medication
If Chronulac is taken with certain other drugs, the effects of either could be increased, decreased, or altered. It is especially important to check with your doctor before combining Chronulac with non-absorbable antacids such as Maalox and Mylanta.

Special information
if you are pregnant or breastfeeding
The effects of Chronulac during pregnancy have not been adequately studied. If you are pregnant or plan to become pregnant, inform your doctor immediately. Chronulac may appear in breast milk and could affect a nursing infant. If this medication is essential to your health, your doctor may advise you to stop breastfeeding until your treatment is finished.

Recommended dosage
The usual dose is 1 to 2 tablespoonfuls (15 to 30 milliliters) daily. Your doctor may increase the dose to 60 milliliters a day, if necessary.

Safety and effectiveness for children have not been established.

Overdosage

Any medication taken in excess can have serious consequences. If you suspect an overdose, seek medical treatment immediately.

- *Symptoms of Chronulac overdose may include:*
  Abdominal cramps, diarrhea

Brand name:

CIBALITH-S

See Lithonate, page 677.

Generic name:

CICLOPIROX

See Loprox, page 695.

Generic name:

CIMETIDINE

See Tagamet, page 1181.

Brand name:

CIPRO

Pronounced: SIP-roh
Generic name: Ciprofloxacin hydrochloride

Why is this drug prescribed?

Cipro is used to treat infections of the lower respiratory tract, the abdomen, the skin, the bones and joints, and the urinary tract, including cystitis (bladder inflammation) in women. It is also prescribed for severe sinus or bronchial infections, infectious diarrhea, typhoid fever, infections of the prostate gland, and some sexually transmitted diseases. Additionally, some doctors prescribe Cipro for certain serious ear infections, tuberculosis, and some of the infections common in people with AIDS.

Because Cipro is effective only for certain types of bacterial infections, before beginning treatment your doctor may perform tests to identify the specific organisms causing your infection.

Most important fact about this drug

Cipro kills a variety of bacteria, and is frequently used to treat infections in many parts of the body. However, be sure to notify your doctor immediately at the first sign of a skin rash or any other allergic reaction. Although quite rare, serious and occasionally fatal allergic reactions—some following the first dose—have been reported in people receiving this type of antibacterial drug. Some reactions have been accompanied by collapse of the circulatory system, loss of consciousness, swelling of the face and throat, shortness of breath, tingling, itching, and hives.

How should you take this medication?

Cipro may be taken with or without meals but is best tolerated when taken 2 hours after a meal.

Drink plenty of fluids while taking this medication.

Cipro, like other antibiotics, works best when there is a constant amount in the blood and urine. To help keep the level constant, try not to miss any doses, and take them at evenly spaced intervals around the clock.

■ *If you miss a dose...*
Take it as soon as you remember. If it is almost time for your next dose, skip the one you missed and go back to your regular schedule. Never take 2 doses at the same time.

■ *Storage instructions...*
Cipro should be stored at room temperature.

What side effects may occur?

Side effects cannot be anticipated. If any develop or change in intensity, inform your doctor as soon as possible. Only your doctor can determine if it is safe for you to continue taking Cipro.

■ *Most common side effect:*
Nausea

■ *Less common side effects may include:*
Abdominal pain/discomfort, diarrhea, headache, rash, restlessness, vomiting

■ *Rare side effects may include:*
Abnormal dread or fear, achiness, bleeding in the stomach and/or intestines, blood clots in the lungs, blurred vision, change in color perception, chills, confusion, constipation, convulsions, coughing up blood, decreased vision, depression, difficulty in swallowing, dizziness, double vision, drowsiness, eye pain, fainting, fever, flushing, gas, gout flare up,

hallucinations, hearing loss, heart attack, hiccups, high blood pressure, hives, inability to fall or stay asleep, inability to urinate, indigestion, intestinal inflammation, involuntary eye movement, irregular heartbeat, irritability, itching, joint or back pain, joint stiffness, kidney failure, labored breathing, lack of muscle coordination, lack or loss of appetite, large volumes of urine, light-headedness, loss of sense of identity, loss of sense of smell, mouth sores, neck pain, nightmares, nosebleed, pounding heartbeat, ringing in the ears, seizures, sensitivity to light, severe allergic reaction, skin peeling, redness, sluggishness, speech difficulties, swelling of the face, neck, lips, eyes, or hands, swelling of the throat, tender, red bumps on skin, tingling sensation, tremors, unpleasant taste, unusual darkening of the skin, vaginal inflammation, vague feeling of illness, weakness, yellowed eyes and skin

Why should this drug not be prescribed?

If you are sensitive to or have ever had an allergic reaction to Cipro or certain other antibiotics of this type, you should not take this medication. Make sure that your doctor is aware of any drug reactions that you have experienced.

Special warnings about this medication

Cipro may cause you to become dizzy or light-headed; therefore, you should not drive a car, operate dangerous machinery, or participate in any hazardous activity that requires full mental alertness until you know how the drug affects you.

Continued or prolonged use of this drug may result in a growth of bacteria that do not respond to this medication and can cause a secondary infection. Therefore, it is important that your doctor monitor your condition on a regular basis.

Convulsions have been reported in people receiving Cipro. If you experience a seizure or convulsion, notify your doctor immediately.

This medication may stimulate the central nervous system, which may lead to tremors, restlessness, light-headedness, confusion, and hallucinations. If these reactions occur, consult your doctor at once.

If you have a known or suspected central nervous system disorder such as epilepsy or hardening of the arteries in the brain, make sure your doctor knows about it when prescribing Cipro.

You may become more sensitive to light while taking this drug. Try to stay out of the sun as much as possible.

People taking Cipro have been known to suffer torn tendons. If you feel any pain or inflammation in a tendon area, stop taking the drug and call your doctor; you should rest and avoid exercise. You may need surgery to repair the tendon.

If you must take Cipro for an extended period of time, your doctor will probably order blood tests and tests for urine, kidney, and liver function.

Possible food and drug interactions
when taking this medication

Serious and fatal reactions have occurred when Cipro was taken in combination with theophylline (Theo-Dur). These reactions have included cardiac arrest, seizures, status epilepticus (continuous attacks of epilepsy with no periods of consciousness), and respiratory failure.

Products containing iron, multi-vitamins containing zinc, or antacids containing magnesium, aluminum, or calcium, when taken in combination with Cipro, may interfere with absorption of this medication.

Cipro may increase the effects of caffeine.

If Cipro is taken with certain other drugs, the effects of either could be increased, decreased, or altered. These drugs include:

  Cyclophosphamide (Cytoxan)
  Cyclosporine (Sandimmune, Neoral)
  Glyburide (DiaBeta, Glynase, Micronase)
  Metoprolol (Lopressor)
  Phenytoin (Dilantin)
  Probenecid (Benemid)
  Sucralfate (Carafate)
  Theophylline (Theo-Dur)
  Warfarin (Coumadin)

Special information
if you are pregnant or breastfeeding

The effects of Cipro during pregnancy have not been adequately studied. If you are pregnant or plan to become pregnant, notify your doctor immediately. Cipro does appear in breast milk and could affect a nursing infant. If this medication is essential to your health, your doctor may advise you to discontinue breastfeeding your baby until your treatment is finished.

Recommended dosage

ADULTS

The length of treatment with Cipro depends upon the severity of infection. Generally, Cipro should be continued for at least 2 days after the signs and symptoms of infection have disappeared. The usual length of time is 7 to 14 days; however, for severe and complicated infections, treatment may be prolonged.

Cystitis in women is treated for 3 days.

Bone and joint infections may require treatment for 4 to 6 weeks or longer.

Infectious diarrhea may be treated for 5 to 7 days.

Typhoid fever should be treated for 10 days.

Chronic prostate inflammation should be treated for 28 days.

Urinary Tract Infections
The usual adult dosage is 250 milligrams taken every 12 hours. Complicated infections, as determined by your doctor, may require 500 milligrams taken every 12 hours.

For cystitis in women, the usual dosage is 100 milligrams every 12 hours.

Lower Respiratory Tract, Skin, Bone, and Joint Infections
The usual recommended dosage is 500 milligrams taken every 12 hours. Complicated infections, as determined by your doctor, may require a dosage of 750 milligrams taken every 12 hours.

Infectious Diarrhea; Typhoid Fever; Sinus, Prostate, and Abdominal Infections
The recommended dosage is 500 milligrams taken every 12 hours.

Gonorrhea in the Urethra or Cervix
For these sexually transmitted diseases, a single 250-milligram dose is the usual treatment.

CHILDREN

Safety and effectiveness have not been established in children and adolescents under 18 years of age.

Overdosage
Any medication taken in excess can have serious consequences. If you suspect an overdose, seek medical attention immediately.

Generic name:

CIPROFLOXACIN

See Cipro, page 225.

Generic name:

CISAPRIDE

See Propulsid, page 1021.

Generic name:

CLARITHROMYCIN

See Biaxin, page 153.

Brand name:

CLARITIN

Pronounced: CLAR-i-tin
Generic name: Loratadine

Why is this drug prescribed?
Claritin is an antihistamine that relieves the sneezing, runny nose, stuffiness, itching, and tearing eyes caused by hay fever.

Most important fact about this drug
If you have liver or kidney disease, your doctor should prescribe a lower starting dose of Claritin.

How should you take this medication?
Take Claritin exactly as prescribed by your doctor.

- *If you miss a dose...*
  Take the forgotten dose as soon as you remember. If it is almost time for your next dose, skip the one you missed. Never take 2 doses at the same time.

- *Storage instructions...*
  Claritin can be stored at room temperature.

What side effects may occur?
Side effects cannot be anticipated. If any develop or change in intensity, inform your doctor as soon as possible. Only your doctor can determine if it is safe for you to continue taking Claritin.

■ *More common side effects may include:*
Dry mouth, fatigue, headache, sleepiness

■ *Less common or rare side effects may include:*
Abdominal discomfort or pain, abnormal dreams, agitation, anxiety, back pain, blurred vision, breast enlargement, breast pain, bronchitis, change in salivation, change in taste, chest pain, chills and fever, confusion, conjunctivitis (pinkeye), constipation, coughing up blood, coughing, decreased sensitivity to touch, decreased sex drive, depression, diarrhea, difficult or labored breathing, difficulty concentrating, difficulty speaking, discoloration of urine, dizziness, dry hair, dry skin, earache, eye pain, fainting, fever, flushing, gas, general feeling of illness, hair loss, hepatitis, high blood pressure, hives, hyperactivity, impotence, increased appetite, increased or decreased eye tearing, increased sweating, indigestion, inflammation of the mouth, insomnia, itching, joint pain, laryngitis, leg cramps, loss of appetite, low blood pressure, memory loss, menstrual changes, migraine, muscle pain, nasal congestion or dryness, nausea, nervousness, nosebleeds, palpitations, rapid heartbeat, rash, ringing in ears, seizures, sensitivity to light, sinus inflammation, skin inflammation, sneezing, sore throat, stomach inflammation, swelling, thirst, tingling, toothache, tremor, twitching of the eye, upper respiratory infection, urinary changes, vaginal inflammation, vertigo, vomiting, weakness, weight gain, wheezing, yellow eyes and skin

Why should this drug not be prescribed?
Do not take Claritin if you are sensitive to or have ever had an allergic reaction to it. Make sure your doctor is aware of any drug reactions that you have experienced.

Special warnings about this medication
This medication may cause excessive sleepiness in people with liver or kidney disease, or the elderly, and should be used with caution.

Possible food and drug interactions
when taking this medication
Although no harmful interactions with Claritin have been reported, there is a theoretical possibility of an interaction with the following drugs:

Antibiotics such as erythromycin and Biaxin
Cimetidine (Tagamet)
Ketoconazole (Nizoral)
Ranitidine (Zantac)
Theophylline (Theo-Dur)

**Special information
if you are pregnant or breastfeeding**

The effects of Claritin during pregnancy have not been adequately studied. If you are pregnant or plan to become pregnant, inform your doctor immediately. Claritin appears in breast milk and could affect a nursing infant. If this medication is essential to your health, your doctor may advise you to discontinue breastfeeding until your treatment with Claritin is finished.

Recommended dosage

ADULTS AND CHILDREN 12 YEARS OF AGE AND OVER

The usual dose is one 10-milligram tablet taken once a day. In people with liver or kidney disease, the usual dose is one 10-milligram tablet taken every other day.

Overdosage

Any medication taken in excess can have serious consequences. If you suspect an overdose, seek medical attention immediately.

■ *Symptoms of Claritin overdose may include:*
  Headache, rapid heartbeat, sleepiness

Brand name:

CLARITIN-D

Pronounced: CLAR-i-tin dee
Generic ingredients: Loratadine, Pseudoephedrine sulfate

Why is this drug prescribed?

Claritin-D is an antihistamine and decongestant that relieves the sneezing, runny nose, stuffiness, and itchy, tearing eyes caused by hay fever. Two versions are available: Claritin-D 12 Hour for twice-daily dosing and Claritin-D 24 Hour for once-a-day use.

Most important fact about this drug

If you have liver disease, make sure the doctor is aware of it. Claritin-D is not recommended in this situation.

How should you take this medication?

Take Claritin-D exactly as prescribed by your doctor. Do not break or chew the tablet. Take the 24-hour variety with a glass of water.

- *If you miss a dose...*
  Take it as soon as you remember. If it is almost time for your next dose, skip the one you missed. Never take 2 doses at the same time.

- *Storage instructions...*
  Store at room temperature.

What side effects may occur?
Side effects cannot be anticipated. If any develop or change in intensity, inform your doctor as soon as possible. Only your doctor can determine if it is safe for you to continue taking Claritin-D.

- *More common side effects may include:*
  Dry mouth, insomnia, sleepiness

- *Less common or rare side effects may include:*
  Dizziness, fatigue, headache, indigestion, nausea, nervousness, sore throat

Why should this drug not be prescribed?
Do not take Claritin-D if you have ever had an allergic reaction to any of its ingredients.

Avoid Claritin-D if you have the eye condition called narrow-angle glaucoma, very high blood pressure, or coronary artery disease; and do not take the drug if you have difficulty urinating. Also avoid taking Claritin-D within 14 days of taking any drug classified as an MAO inhibitor, including the antidepressants Nardil and Parnate.

Do not use Claritin-D 24 Hour if you have trouble swallowing or have been diagnosed with a narrowing of the food canal (esophagus) leading to your stomach.

Special warnings about this medication
If you are taking Claritin-D and experience insomnia, dizziness, weakness, tremor, or unusual heartbeats, tell your doctor; you may be having an allergic reaction.

You must be careful using Claritin-D if you have diabetes, heart disease, an overactive thyroid gland, kidney or liver problems, or an enlarged prostate gland.

Do not use Claritin-D with over-the-counter antihistamines and decongestants.

Possible food and drug interactions
when taking this medication

Check with your doctor before combining Claritin-D with any of the following:

Blood pressure medications classified as beta blockers, such as Inderal and Tenormin

Digoxin (Lanoxin)

MAO inhibitors, such as the antidepressants Nardil and Parnate

Mecamylamine (Inversine)

Methyldopa (Aldomet)

Reserpine

Special information
if you are pregnant or breastfeeding

The effects of Claritin-D during pregnancy have not been adequately studied. If you are pregnant or plan to become pregnant, inform your doctor immediately. Claritin-D may appear in breast milk. If this medication is essential to your health, your doctor may advise you not to breastfeed until your treatment is finished.

Recommended dosage

ADULTS AND CHILDREN 12 YEARS OF AGE AND OVER

The usual dose is 1 tablet every 12 hours for Claritin-D 12 Hour, 1 tablet a day for Claritin-D 24 Hour. If you have kidney trouble, your doctor will start you on 1 tablet a day (1 tablet every other day for Claritin-D 24 Hour).

Overdosage

Any medication taken in excess can have serious consequences. If you suspect an overdose, seek medical attention immediately.

■ *Symptoms of Claritin-D overdose may include:*
Anxiety, breathing difficulty, chest pain, coma, convulsions, delusions, difficulty urinating, fast, fluttery heartbeat, giddiness, hallucinations, headache, insomnia, irregular heartbeat, nausea, rapid heartbeat, restlessness, sleepiness, sweating, tension, thirst, vomiting, weakness

Generic name:

CLEMASTINE

See Tavist, page 1196.

Brand name:

CLEOCIN T

Pronounced: KLEE-oh-sin tee
Generic name: Clindamycin phosphate

Why is this drug prescribed?
Cleocin T is an antibiotic used to treat acne.

Most important fact about this drug
Although applied only to the skin, some of this medication could be absorbed into the bloodstream; and it has been known to cause severe—sometimes even fatal—colitis (an inflammation of the lower bowel) when taken internally. Symptoms, which can occur a few days, weeks, or months after beginning treatment with this drug, include severe diarrhea, severe abdominal cramps, and the possibility of the passage of blood.

How should you take this medication?
Use this medication exactly as prescribed. Excessive use of Cleocin T can cause your skin to become too dry or irritated.

- *If you miss a dose...*
  Apply it as soon as you remember. If it is almost time for your next dose, skip the one you missed and go back to your regular schedule.

- *Storage instructions...*
  Store at room temperature. Keep from freezing. Store liquids in tightly closed containers.

What side effects may occur?
Side effects cannot be anticipated. If any develop or change in intensity, inform your doctor as soon as possible. Only your doctor can determine if it is safe for you to continue taking Cleocin T.

- *More common side effects may include:*
  Burning, itching, peeling skin, reddened skin, skin dryness

- *Less common or rare side effects may include:*
  Abdominal pain, bloody diarrhea, colitis, diarrhea, oily skin, skin inflammation and irritation, stomach and intestinal disturbances

Why should this drug not be prescribed?

If you are sensitive to or have ever had an allergic reaction to Cleocin T or similar drugs, such as Lincocin, you should not use this medication. Make sure your doctor is aware of any drug reactions you have experienced.

Unless you are directed to do so by your doctor, do not take this medication if you have ever had an intestinal inflammation, ulcerative colitis, or antibiotic-associated colitis.

Special warnings about this medication

Cleocin T contains an alcohol base, which can cause burning and irritation of the eyes. It also has an unpleasant taste. Use caution when applying this medication so as not to get it in the eyes, nose, mouth, or skin abrasions. In the event of accidental contact, rinse the affected area with cool water.

Use with caution if you have hay fever, asthma, or eczema.

Possible food and drug interactions
when taking this medication

If you have diarrhea while taking Cleocin T, check with your doctor before taking an antidiarrhea medication, as certain drugs may cause your diarrhea to become worse.

The diarrhea should not be treated with the commonly used drugs that slow movement through the intestinal tract, such as Lomotil or products containing paregoric.

Special information
if you are pregnant or breastfeeding

The effects of Cleocin T during pregnancy have not been adequately studied. If you are pregnant or plan to become pregnant, inform your doctor immediately. Cleocin T may appear in breast milk and could affect a nursing infant. If this medication is essential to your health, your doctor may advise you to discontinue breastfeeding your baby until your treatment with this medication is finished.

Recommended dosage

ADULTS

Apply a thin film of gel, solution, or lotion to the affected area 2 times a day, or use a solution pledget (application pad). Discard a pledget after you have used it once; you may use more than 1 pledget for a treatment. Do not remove the pledget from its foil container until you are ready to use it.

If you are using the lotion, shake it well immediately before using.

CHILDREN

The safety and effectiveness of Cleocin T have not been established in children under 12 years of age.

Overdosage

Cleocin T can be absorbed through the skin and produce side effects in the body. If you suspect an overdose, seek medical attention immediately.

Brand name:

CLIMARA

See Estraderm, page 469.

Generic name:

CLINDAMYCIN

See Cleocin T, page 235.

Brand name:

CLINDEX

See Librax, page 665.

Brand name:

CLINORIL

Pronounced: CLIN-or-il
Generic name: Sulindac

Why is this drug prescribed?

Clinoril, a nonsteroidal anti-inflammatory drug, is used to relieve the inflammation, swelling, stiffness, and joint pain associated with rheumatoid arthritis, osteoarthritis (the most common form of arthritis), and ankylosing spondylitis (stiffness and progressive arthritis of the spine). It is also used to treat bursitis, tendinitis, acute gouty arthritis, and other types of pain.

The safety and effectiveness of this medication in the treatment of people with severe, incapacitating rheumatoid arthritis have not been established.

Most important fact about this drug

You should have frequent checkups with your doctor if you take Clinoril regularly. Ulcers or internal bleeding can occur without warning.

How should you take this medication?
Take this medication exactly as prescribed by your doctor.

If you are using Clinoril for arthritis, it should be taken regularly.

■ *If you miss a dose...*
Take it as soon as you remember. If it is almost time for your next dose, skip the one you missed and go back to your regular schedule. Never take 2 doses at the same time.

■ *Storage instructions...*
Do not store in damp places like the bathroom.

What side effects may occur?
Side effects cannot be anticipated. If any develop or change in intensity, inform your doctor as soon as possible. Only your doctor can determine if it is safe for you to continue taking Clinoril.

■ *More common side effects may include:*
Abdominal pain, constipation, diarrhea, dizziness, gas, headache, indigestion, itching, loss of appetite, nausea, nervousness, rash, ringing in ears, stomach cramps, swelling due to fluid retention, vomiting

■ *Less common or rare side effects may include:*
Abdominal bleeding, abdominal inflammation, anemia, appetite change, bloody diarrhea, blurred vision, change in color of urine, chest pain, colitis, congestive heart failure, depression, fever, hair loss, hearing loss, hepatitis, high blood pressure, inability to sleep, inflammation of lips and tongue, kidney failure, liver failure, loss of sense of taste, low blood pressure, muscle and joint pain, nosebleed, painful urination, pancreatitis, peptic ulcer, sensitivity to light, shortness of breath, skin eruptions, sleepiness, Stevens-Johnson syndrome (blisters in the mouth and eyes), vaginal bleeding, weakness, yellow eyes and skin

Why should this drug not be prescribed?
If you are sensitive to or have ever had an allergic reaction to Clinoril, aspirin, or similar drugs, or if you have had asthma attacks caused by aspirin or other drugs of this type, you should not take this medication. Make sure that your doctor is aware of any drug reactions that you have experienced.

Special warnings about this medication

Peptic ulcers and bleeding can occur without warning.

This drug should be used with caution if you have kidney or liver disease; it can cause liver inflammation in some people.

Do not take aspirin or any other anti-inflammatory medications while taking Clinoril, unless your doctor tells you to do so.

Nonsteroidal anti-inflammatory drugs such as Clinoril can hide the signs and symptoms of an infection. Be sure your doctor knows about any infection you may have.

Clinoril can cause vision problems. If you experience a change in your vision, inform your doctor.

If you have heart disease or high blood pressure, this drug can increase water retention. Use with caution.

If you develop pancreatitis (inflammation of the pancreas), Clinoril should be stopped immediately and not restarted.

Clinoril may cause you to become drowsy or less alert. If this happens, driving or operating dangerous machinery or participating in any hazardous activity that requires full mental alertness is not recommended.

Possible food and drug interactions
when taking this medication

If Clinoril is taken with certain other drugs, the effects of either could be increased, decreased, or altered. It is especially important to check with your doctor before combining Clinoril with the following:

Aspirin
Blood thinners such as Coumadin
Cyclosporine (Sandimmune)
Diflunisal (Dolobid)
Dimethyl sulfoxide (DMSO)
Lithium
Loop diuretics such as Lasix
Methotrexate
Oral diabetes medications
Other nonsteroidal anti-inflammatory drugs (Aleve, Motrin, others)
The antigout medication Benemid

Special information
if you are pregnant or breastfeeding

The effects of Clinoril during pregnancy have not been adequately studied; drugs of this class are known to cause birth defects. If you are pregnant or plan to become pregnant, inform your doctor immediately. Clinoril may appear in breast milk and could affect a nursing infant. If this medication is essential to your health, your doctor may advise you to discontinue breastfeeding until your treatment with Clinoril is finished.

Recommended dosage

ADULTS

Osteoarthritis, Rheumatoid Arthritis, Ankylosing Spondylitis
Starting dosage is 150 milligrams 2 times a day. Take with food. Doses should not exceed 400 milligrams per day.

Acute Gouty Arthritis or Arthritic Shoulder and Joint Condition
400 milligrams daily taken in doses of 200 milligrams 2 times a day.

For acute painful shoulder, therapy lasting 7 to 14 days is usually adequate.

For acute gouty arthritis, therapy lasting 7 days is usually adequate.

The lowest dose that proves beneficial should be used.

CHILDREN

The safety and effectiveness of Clinoril have not been established in children.

Overdosage

Any medication taken in excess can cause symptoms of overdose. If you suspect an overdose, seek medical attention immediately.

■ *Symptoms of Clinoril overdose may include:*
  Coma, low blood pressure, reduced output of urine, stupor

Generic name:

CLOBETASOL

See Temovate, page 1204.

Brand name:

CLOMID

See Clomiphene Citrate, page 241.

Generic name:

CLOMIPHENE CITRATE

Pronounced: KLAHM-if-een SIT-rate
Brand names: Clomid, Serophene

Why is this drug prescribed?
Clomiphene is prescribed for the treatment of ovulatory failure in women who wish to become pregnant and whose husbands are fertile and potent.

Most important fact about this drug
Properly timed sexual intercourse is very important to increase the chances of conception. The likelihood of conception diminishes with each succeeding course of treatment. Your doctor will determine the need for continuing therapy after the first course. If you do not ovulate after 3 courses or do not become pregnant after 3 ovulations, your doctor will stop the therapy.

How should you take this medication?
Take this medication exactly as prescribed by your doctor.

- *If you miss a dose...*
  Take it as soon as you remember. If it is time for your next dose, take the 2 doses together and go back to your regular schedule. If you miss more than 1 dose, contact your doctor.

- *Storage instructions...*
  Store at room temperature in a tightly closed container, away from light, moisture, and excessive heat.

What side effects may occur?
Side effects occur infrequently and generally do not interfere with treatment at the recommended dosage of clomiphene. They tend to occur more frequently at higher doses and during long-term treatment.

- *More common side effects include:*
  Abdominal discomfort, enlargement of the ovaries, hot flushes

■ *Less common side effects include:*
Abnormal uterine bleeding, breast tenderness, depression, dizziness, fatigue, hair loss, headache, hives, inability to fall or stay asleep, increased urination, inflammation of the skin, light-headedness, nausea, nervousness, ovarian cysts, visual disturbances, vomiting, weight gain

Why should this drug not be prescribed?
If you are pregnant or think you may be, do not take this drug.

Unless directed to do so by your doctor, do not use this medication if you have an uncontrolled thyroid or adrenal gland disorder, an abnormality of the brain such as a pituitary gland tumor, a liver disease or a history of liver problems, abnormal uterine bleeding of undetermined origin, ovarian cysts, or enlargement of the ovaries not caused by polycystic ovarian syndrome (a hormonal disorder causing lack of ovulation).

Special warnings about this medication
Your doctor will evaluate you for normal liver function and normal estrogen levels before considering you for treatment with clomiphene.

Your doctor will also examine you for pregnancy, ovarian enlargement, or cyst formation prior to treatment with this drug and between each treatment cycle. He or she will do a complete pelvic examination before each course of this medication.

Clomiphene treatment increases the possibility of multiple births; also, birth defects have been reported following treatment to induce ovulation with clomiphene, although no direct effects of the drug on the unborn child have been established.

Because blurring and other visual symptoms may occur occasionally with clomiphene treatment, you should be cautious about driving a car or operating dangerous machinery, especially under conditions of variable lighting.

If you experience visual disturbances, notify your doctor immediately. Symptoms of visual disturbance may include blurring, spots or flashes, double vision, intolerance to light, decreased visual sharpness, loss of peripheral vision, and distortion of space. Your doctor may recommend a complete evaluation by an eye specialist.

Ovarian hyperstimulation syndrome (or OHSS, enlargement of the ovary) has occurred in women receiving treatment with clomiphene. OHSS may progress rapidly and become serious. The early warning signs are severe pelvic pain, nausea, vomiting, and weight gain. Symptoms include abdominal pain, abdominal enlargement, nausea, vomiting, diarrhea, weight gain, difficult or labored breathing, and less urine production. If you experience any of these warning signs or symptoms, notify your doctor immediately.

To lessen the risks associated with abnormal ovarian enlargement during treatment with clomiphene, the lowest effective dose should be prescribed. Women with the hormonal disorder, polycystic ovarian syndrome, may be unusually sensitive to certain hormones and may respond abnormally to usual doses of this drug. If you experience pelvic pain, notify your doctor. He may discontinue your use of clomiphene until the ovaries return to pretreatment size.

Because the safety of long-term treatment with clomiphene has not been established, your doctor will not prescribe more than about 6 courses of therapy. Prolonged use may increase the risk of a tumor in the ovaries.

**Possible food and drug interactions
when taking this medication**
No food or drug interactions have been reported.

**Special information
if you are pregnant or breastfeeding**
If you become pregnant, notify your doctor immediately. You should not be taking this drug while you are pregnant.

Recommended dosage
The recommended dosage for the first course of treatment is 50 milligrams (1 tablet) daily for 5 days. If ovulation does not appear to have occurred, your doctor may try up to 2 more times.

Overdosage
Taking any medication in excess can have serious consequences. If you suspect an overdose of clomiphene, contact your doctor immediately.

Generic name:

CLOMIPRAMINE

See Anafranil, page 58.

Generic name:

CLONAZEPAM

See Klonopin, page 631.

Generic name:

CLONIDINE

See Catapres, page 201.

Generic name:

CLOPIDOGREL

See Plavix, page 972.

Generic name:

CLORAZEPATE

See Tranxene, page 1267.

Generic name:

CLOTRIMAZOLE

See Gyne-Lotrimin, page 549.

Generic name:

CLOTRIMAZOLE WITH BETAMETHASONE

See Lotrisone, page 708.

Generic name:

CLOZAPINE

See Clozaril, page 244.

Brand name:

CLOZARIL

Pronounced: KLOH-zah-ril
Generic name: Clozapine

Why is this drug prescribed?

Clozaril is given to help people with severe schizophrenia who have failed to respond to standard treatments. Clozaril is not a cure, but it can help some people return to more normal lives.

Most important fact about this drug
Even though it does not produce some of the disturbing side effects of other antipsychotic medications, Clozaril may cause agranulocytosis, a potentially lethal disorder of the white blood cells. Because of the risk of agranulocytosis, anyone who takes Clozaril is required to have a blood test once a week. The drug is carefully controlled so that those taking it must get their weekly blood test before receiving the following week's supply of medication. Anyone whose blood test results are abnormal will be taken off Clozaril either temporarily or permanently, depending on the results of an additional 4 weeks of testing.

How should you take this medication?
Take Clozaril exactly as directed by your doctor. Because of the significant risk of serious side effects associated with this drug, your doctor will periodically reassess the need for continued Clozaril therapy. Clozaril is distributed *only* through the Clozaril Patient Management System, which ensures weekly white blood cell testing, monitoring, and pharmacy services prior to delivery of the next week's supply.

Clozaril may be taken with or without food.

■ *If you miss a dose...*
Take it as soon as you remember. If it is almost time for your next dose, skip the one you missed and go back to your regular schedule. Do not take 2 doses at once.

If you stop taking Clozaril for more than 2 days, do not start taking it again without consulting your physician.

■ *Storage instructions...*
Store at room temperature.

What side effects may occur?
Side effects cannot be anticipated. If any develop or change in intensity, inform your doctor as soon as possible. Only your doctor can determine if it is safe for you to continue taking Clozaril.

The most feared side effect is agranulocytosis, a dangerous drop in the number of a certain kind of white blood cell. Symptoms include fever, lethargy, sore throat, and weakness. If not caught in time, agranulocytosis can be fatal. That is why all people who take Clozaril must have a blood test every week. About 1 percent develop agranulocytosis and must stop taking the drug.

Seizures are another potential side effect, occurring in some 5 percent of people who take Clozaril. The higher the dosage, the greater the risk of seizures.

■ *More common side effects may include:*
Abdominal discomfort, agitation, confusion, constipation, disturbed sleep, dizziness, drowsiness, dry mouth, fainting, fever, headache, heartburn, high blood pressure, inability to sit down, loss or slowness of muscle movement, low blood pressure, nausea, nightmares, rapid heartbeat and other heart conditions, restlessness, rigidity, salivation, sedation, sweating, tremors, vertigo, vision problems, vomiting, weight gain

■ *Less common side effects may include:*
Anemia, angina (severe, crushing chest pain), anxiety, appetite increase, blocked intestine, blood clots, bloodshot eyes, bluish tinge in the skin, breast pain or discomfort, bronchitis, bruising, chest pain, chills or chills and fever, constant involuntary eye movement, coughing, delusions, depression, diarrhea, difficult or labored breathing, difficulty swallowing, dilated pupils, disorientation, dry throat, ear disorders, ejaculation problems, excessive movement, eyelid disorder, fast, fluttery heartbeat, fatigue, fluid retention, frequent urination, hallucinations, heart problems, hives, hot flashes, impacted stool, impotence, inability to fall asleep or stay asleep, inability to hold urine, inability to urinate, increase or decrease in sex drive, involuntary movement, irritability, itching, jerky movements, joint pain, lack of coordination, laryngitis, lethargy, light-headedness (especially when rising quickly from a seated or lying position), loss of appetite, loss of speech, low body temperature, memory loss, muscle pain or ache, muscle spasm, muscle weakness, nosebleed, numbness, pain in back, neck, or legs, painful menstruation, pallor, paranoia, pneumonia or pneumonia-like symptoms, poor coordination, rapid breathing, rash, runny nose, shakiness, shortness of breath, skin inflammation, redness, scaling, slow heartbeat, slurred speech, sneezing, sore or numb tongue, speech difficulty, stomach pain, stuffy nose, stupor, stuttering, swollen salivary glands, thirst, throat discomfort, tics, twitching, urination problems, vaginal infection, vaginal itch, a vague feeling of being sick, weakness, wheezing, yellow skin and eyes

Why should this drug not be prescribed?
Clozaril is considered a somewhat risky medication because of its potential to cause agranulocytosis and seizures. It should be taken only by people whose condition is serious, and who have not been helped by more traditional antipsychotic medications such as Haldol or Mellaril.

You should not take Clozaril if:

- You have a bone marrow disease or disorder;
- You have epilepsy that is not controlled;
- You ever developed an abnormal white blood cell count while taking Clozaril;
- You are currently taking some other drug, such as Tegretol, that could cause a decrease in white blood cell count or a drug that could affect the bone marrow.

Special warnings about this medication

Clozaril can cause drowsiness, especially at the start of treatment. For this reason, and also because of the potential for seizures, you should not drive, swim, climb, or operate dangerous machinery while you are taking this medication, at least in the early stages of treatment.

Even though you will have weekly blood tests while taking Clozaril, you should stay alert for early symptoms of agranulocytosis: weakness, lethargy, fever, sore throat, a general feeling of illness, a flu-like feeling, or ulcers of the lips, mouth, or other mucous membranes. If any such symptoms develop, tell your doctor immediately.

Especially during the first 3 weeks of treatment, you may develop a fever. If you do, notify your doctor.

While taking Clozaril, do not drink alcohol or use drugs of any kind, including over-the-counter medicines, without first checking with your doctor.

If you take Clozaril, you must be monitored especially closely if you have either the eye condition called narrow-angle glaucoma or an enlarged prostate; Clozaril could make these conditions worse.

On rare occasions, Clozaril can cause intestinal problems—constipation, impaction, or blockage—that can, in extreme cases, be fatal.

Especially when you begin taking Clozaril, you may feel light-headed upon standing up, to the point where you pass out.

If you have kidney, liver, lung, or heart disease, or a history of seizures or prostate problems, you should discuss these with your doctor before taking Clozaril. Nausea, vomiting, loss of appetite, and a yellow tinge to your skin and eyes are signs of liver trouble; call your doctor immediately if you develop these symptoms.

Drugs such as Clozaril can sometimes cause a set of symptoms called Neuroleptic Malignant Syndrome. Symptoms include high fever, muscle rigidity, irregular pulse or blood pressure, rapid heartbeat, excessive perspiration, and changes in heart rhythm. Your doctor will have you stop taking Clozaril while this condition is being treated.

There is also a risk of developing tardive dyskinesia, a condition of involuntary, slow, rhythmical movements. It happens more often in older adults, especially older women.

Clozaril has been known to occasionally raise blood sugar levels, causing unusual hunger, thirst, and weakness, along with excessive urination. If you develop these symptoms, alert your doctor. You may have to switch to a different medication.

In very rare instances, Clozaril may also cause a blood clot in the lungs. If you develop severe breathing problems or chest pain, call your doctor immediately.

Possible food and drug interactions
when taking this medication
If Clozaril is taken with certain other drugs, the effects of either could be increased, decreased, or altered. It is especially important to check with your doctor before combining Clozaril with the following:

Alcohol
Antidepressants such as Prozac and Zoloft
Antipsychotic drugs such as Thorazine and Mellaril
Blood pressure medications such as Aldomet and Hytrin
Cimetidine (Tagamet)
Digitoxin (Crystodigin)
Digoxin (Lanoxin)
Drugs that depress the central nervous system such as phenobarbital and Seconal
Drugs that contain atropine such as Donnatal and Levsin
Epilepsy drugs such as Tegretol and Dilantin
Epinephrine (EpiPen)
Erythromycin (E-Mycin, ERYC, others)
Heart rhythm stabilizers such as Quinidex and Tambocor
Tranquilizers such as Valium and Xanax
Warfarin (Coumadin and Panwarfin)

Special information
if you are pregnant or breastfeeding
The effects of Clozaril during pregnancy have not been adequately studied. If you are pregnant or plan to become pregnant, inform your doctor immediately. Clozaril treatment should be continued during pregnancy only if absolutely

necessary. You should not breastfeed if you are taking Clozaril, since the drug may appear in breast milk.

Recommended dosage

ADULTS

Your doctor will carefully individualize your dosage and monitor your response weekly.

The usual recommended initial dose is half of a 25-milligram tablet (12.5 milligrams) 1 or 2 times daily. Your doctor may increase the dosage in increments of 25 to 50 milligrams a day to achieve a daily dose of 300 to 450 milligrams by the end of 2 weeks. Dosage increases after that will be only once or twice a week and will be no more than 100 milligrams each time. The most you can take is 900 milligrams a day divided into 2 or 3 doses.

Your doctor will determine long-term dosage depending upon your response and results of the weekly blood test.

CHILDREN

Safety and efficacy have not been established for children up to 16 years of age.

Overdosage

Any medication taken in excess can have serious consequences. If you suspect an overdose, seek emergency medical attention immediately.

- *Symptoms of overdose with Clozaril may include:*
  Coma, delirium, drowsiness, excess salivation, low blood pressure, faintness, pneumonia, rapid heartbeat, seizures, shallow breathing or absence of breathing

Brand name:

COGENTIN

Pronounced: co-JEN-tin
Generic name: Benztropine mesylate

Why is this drug prescribed?

Cogentin is given to help relieve the symptoms of "parkinsonism": the muscle rigidity, tremors, and difficulties with posture and balance that occur in Parkinson's disease and that sometimes develop as unwanted side effects of antipsychotic drugs such as Haldol and Thorazine.

Cogentin is an "anticholinergic" medication, a drug that controls spasms. It reduces the symptoms of parkinsonism, but it is not a cure.

Most important fact about this drug

When starting Cogentin, you may not feel its effect for 2 or 3 days. Symptoms caused by drugs such as Haldol and Thorazine are often temporary, so if drug-induced parkinsonism is your problem, you may need to take Cogentin for only a couple of weeks.

How should you take this medication?

Take Cogentin exactly as prescribed. Unlike some of the other antiparkinsonian medications, Cogentin acts over a long period of time. It is thus particularly suitable as a bedtime medication because it lasts through the night. Taken at bedtime, it may help a person regain enough muscle control to move and roll over during sleep and to arise unaided in the morning.

Cogentin causes dry mouth. Sucking on sugarless hard candy or sipping water can relieve this problem.

Cogentin can reduce the ability to sweat, one of the key ways your body prevents overheating. Avoid excess sun or exercise that may cause overheating.

■ *If you miss a dose...*
Take it as soon as you remember. If it is within 2 hours of your next dose, skip the one you missed and go back to your regular schedule. Do not take 2 doses at once.

■ *Storage instructions...*
Store away from heat, light, and moisture.

What side effects may occur?

Side effects cannot be anticipated. If any develop or change in intensity, inform your doctor as soon as possible. Only your doctor can determine if it is safe for you to continue taking Cogentin.

■ *Side effects may include:*
Blurred vision, bowel blockage, confusion, constipation, depression, dilated pupils, disorientation, dry mouth, fever, hallucinations, heat stroke, impaired memory, inability to urinate, listlessness, nausea, nervousness, numbness in fingers, painful urination, rapid heartbeat, rash, vomiting

Why should this drug not be prescribed?

Do not take Cogentin if you are sensitive to it or if you have ever had an allergic reaction to it or to any similar antispasmodic medication.

Do not take Cogentin if you have an eye condition called angle-closure glaucoma.

Some people who take certain antipsychotic medications develop tardive dyskinesia, a syndrome of involuntary movements of the mouth, jaw, arms, and legs. Cogentin should not be given to treat tardive dyskinesia; it will not help, and it may make the condition worse.

Cogentin should not be given to children under the age of 3; it should be used with caution in older children.

Special warnings about this medication

Do not drive or operate dangerous machinery while taking Cogentin, since the drug may impair your mental or physical abilities.

Be sure to tell your doctor if you have ever had tachycardia (excessively rapid heartbeats) or if you have an enlarged prostate; you will require especially close monitoring while taking Cogentin in these cases.

Tell your doctor if Cogentin produces weakness in particular muscle groups. For example, if you have been suffering from neck rigidity and Cogentin suddenly causes your neck to relax so much that it feels weak, you may be taking more Cogentin than you need.

If you have been taking another antiparkinsonism drug, do not stop taking it abruptly when you start taking Cogentin. If you are to stop taking the other drug, your doctor will have you taper off gradually.

Cogentin has a drying effect on the mouth and other moist tissues. If you take it along with another drug that also has a drying effect, you are at risk for anhidrosis (inability to sweat), heat stroke, and even death from hyperthermia (high fever). Chronic illness, alcoholism, central nervous system (brain and spinal cord) disease, or heavy manual labor in a hot environment can increase this risk. In hot weather, your doctor may lower your dosage of Cogentin.

Possible food and drug interactions when taking this medication

When taken simultaneously with an antipsychotic medication (Thorazine, Stelazine, Haldol, others) or a tricyclic antidepressant medication (Elavil, Norpramin, Tofranil, others), Cogentin has occasionally caused bowel blockage or heat stroke that proved dangerous or even fatal. If you are taking Cogentin along with an antipsychotic or with a tricyclic antidepressant, tell your doctor immediately if you begin to have any stomach or bowel complaint, fever, or heat intolerance.

Antacids, such as Tums, Maalox, and Mylanta, may decrease the effects of Cogentin. Do not take them within 1 hour of taking Cogentin.

Certain other drugs may also interact with Cogentin. Consult your doctor before combining Cogentin with any of the following:

Amantadine (Symmetrel)
Doxepin (Sinequan)
Antihistamines such as Benadryl and Tavist
Other anticholinergic agents such as Bentyl

Special information
if you are pregnant or breastfeeding

If you are pregnant or plan to become pregnant, inform your doctor immediately. No information is available about the safety of taking Cogentin during pregnancy or while you are breastfeeding.

Recommended dosage

Your doctor will individualize the dose of Cogentin, taking into consideration your age and weight, the condition being treated, the presence of other diseases, and any physical disorder.

In general, the usual oral dose is 1 to 2 milligrams a day, but it can range from 0.5 to 6 milligrams a day.

Overdosage

Any medication taken in excess can have serious consequences. If you suspect symptoms of an overdose of Cogentin, seek medical attention immediately. Symptoms of overdose may include any of those listed in the "side effects section" (see page 250) or any of the following:

Blurred vision, confusion, coma, constipation, convulsions, delirium, difficulty swallowing or breathing, dilated pupils, dizziness, dry mouth, flushed, dry skin, glaucoma, hallucinations, headache, high blood pressure, high body temperature, inability to sweat, listlessness, muscle weakness, nausea, nervousness, numb fingers, painful urination, palpitations, rapid heartbeat, rash, shock, uncoordinated movements, vomiting

Brand name:

CO-GESIC

See Vicodin, page 1337.

Brand name:

COGNEX

Pronounced: COG-necks
Generic name: Tacrine hydrochloride

Why is this drug prescribed?

Cognex is used for the treatment of mild to moderate Alzheimer's disease. This progressive, degenerative disorder causes physical changes in the brain that disrupt the flow of information and affect memory, thinking, and behavior. As someone caring for a person with Alzheimer's, you should be aware that Cognex is not a cure, but has helped some people.

Most important fact about this drug

Do not abruptly stop Cognex treatment, or reduce the dosage, without consulting the doctor. A sudden reduction can cause the person you are caring for to become more disturbed and forgetful. Taking more Cognex than the doctor advises can also cause serious problems. Do not change the dosage of Cognex unless instructed by the doctor.

How should you take this medication?

This medication will work better if taken at regular intervals, usually 4 times a day. Cognex is best taken between meals; however, if it is irritating to the stomach, the doctor may advise taking it with meals. If Cognex is not taken regularly, as the doctor directs, the condition may get worse.

- *If you miss a dose...*
  Give the forgotten dose as soon as possible. If it is within 2 hours of the next dose, skip the missed dose and go back to the regular schedule. Do not double the doses.

- *Storage instructions...*
  Store at room temperature away from moisture.

What side effects may occur?

Side effects cannot be anticipated. If any develop or change in intensity, tell the doctor as soon as possible. Only the doctor can determine if it is safe to continue giving Cognex.

- *More common side effects may include:*
  Abdominal pain, abnormal thinking, agitation, anxiety, chest pain, clumsiness or unsteadiness, confusion, constipation, coughing, depression, diarrhea, dizziness, fatigue, flushing, frequent urination, gas, headache, inflamed nasal passages, insomnia, indigestion, liver function disorders,

loss of appetite, muscle pain, nausea, rash, sleepiness, upper respiratory infection, urinary tract infection, vomiting, weight loss

■ *Less common side effects may include:*
Back pain, hallucinations, hostile attitude, purple or red spots on the skin, skin discoloration, tremor, weakness

Be sure to report any symptoms that develop while on Cognex therapy. You should alert the doctor if the person you are caring for develops nausea, vomiting, loose stools, or diarrhea at the start of therapy or when the dosage is increased. Later in therapy, be on the lookout for rash or fever, yellowing of the eyes and skin, or changes in the color of the stool.

Why should this drug not be prescribed?
People who are sensitive to or have ever had an allergic reaction to Cognex should not take this medication. Before starting treatment with Cognex, it is important to discuss any medical problems with the doctor. If during previous Cognex therapy the person you are caring for developed jaundice (yellow skin and eyes), which signals that something is wrong with the liver, Cognex should not be used again.

Special warnings about this medication
Use Cognex with caution if the person you are caring for has a history of liver disease, certain heart disorders, stomach ulcers, or asthma.

Because of the risk of liver problems when taking Cognex, the doctor will schedule blood tests every other week to monitor liver function for the first 16 weeks of treatment. After 16 weeks, blood tests will be given monthly for 2 months and every 3 months after that. If the person you are caring for develops any liver problems, the doctor may temporarily discontinue Cognex treatment until further testing shows that the liver has returned to normal. If the doctor resumes Cognex treatment, regular blood tests will be conducted again. Blood tests should be performed every other week for at least the first 16 weeks at the beginning of Cognex treatment in order to monitor liver function. If no significant changes in liver function have been observed, monitoring may be decreased to monthly for 2 months and every 3 months thereafter.

Before having any surgery, including dental surgery, tell the doctor that the person is being treated with Cognex.

Cognex can cause seizures, and may cause difficulty urinating.

Possible food and drug interactions when taking this medication
If Cognex is taken with certain other drugs, the effects of either could be

increased, decreased, or altered. It is especially important that you check with your doctor before combining Cognex with the following:

Antispasmodic drugs such as Bentyl and Cogentin
Bethanechol chloride (Urecholine)
Cimetidine (Tagamet)
Theophylline (Theo-Dur)

Special information
if you are pregnant or breastfeeding
The effects of Cognex during pregnancy have not been studied; and it is not known whether Cognex appears in breast milk.

Recommended dosage

ADULTS
The usual starting dose is 10 milligrams 4 times a day, for at least 6 weeks. Do not increase the dose during this 6-week period unless directed by your doctor. The doctor may then increase the dosage to 20 milligrams 4 times a day.

CHILDREN
The safety and effectiveness of Cognex have not been established in children.

Overdosage
Any medication taken in excess can have serious consequences. If you suspect an overdose, seek medical attention immediately.

- *Symptoms of Cognex overdose include:*
  Collapse, convulsions, extreme muscle weakness, possibly ending in death (if breathing muscles are affected), low blood pressure, nausea, salivation, slowed heart rate, sweating, vomiting.

Brand name:

COLACE

Pronounced: KOH-lace
Generic name: Docusate sodium
Other brand name: Sof-Lax

Why is this drug prescribed?
Colace, a stool softener, promotes easy bowel movements without straining. It softens the stool by mixing in fat and water.

Colace is helpful for people who have had recent rectal surgery, people with heart problems, high blood pressure, hemorrhoids, or hernias, and women who have just had babies.

Colace Microenema is used to relieve occasional constipation.

Most important fact about this drug
Colace is for short-term relief only, unless your doctor directs otherwise. It usually takes a day or two for the drug to achieve its laxative effect; some people may need to wait 4 or 5 days. Sof-Lax Overnight works in 6 to 12 hours. Colace Microenema works in 2 to 15 minutes.

How should you take this medication?
To conceal the drug's bitter taste, take Colace liquid in half a glass of milk or fruit juice; it can be given in infant formula. The proper dosage of this medication may also be added to a retention or flushing enema.

For Colace Microenema:
1. Lubricate the tip by pushing out a drop of the medication.
2. Slowly insert the full length of the nozzle into the rectum. (Stop halfway for children aged 3 to 12 years of age.)
3. Squeeze out the contents of the tube.
4. Remove the nozzle before you release your grip on the tube.

■ *If you miss a dose...*
Take this medication only as needed.

■ *Storage instructions...*
Store at room temperature. Keep from freezing.

What side effects may occur?
Side effects are unlikely. The main ones reported are bitter taste, throat irritation, and nausea (mainly associated with use of the syrup and liquid). Rash has occurred.

Why should this drug not be prescribed?
There are no known reasons this drug should not be prescribed.

Special warnings about this medication
Do not use this product if you have any abdominal pain, nausea, or vomiting, unless your doctor advises it. Do not take this product if you are taking

mineral oil. If you have noticed a change in your bowel habits that has lasted for 2 weeks, ask your doctor before you use this product. If you bleed from the rectum or you do not have a bowel movement after using this product, stop using it and call your doctor; you may have a more serious condition. Do not use any laxative for more than a week without your doctor's approval.

Possible food and drug interactions
when taking this medication
No interactions have been reported with Colace.

Special information
if you are pregnant or breastfeeding
If you are pregnant, plan to become pregnant, or are breastfeeding your baby, notify your doctor before using this medication.

Recommended dosage
Your doctor will adjust the dosage according to your needs.

You will be using higher doses at the start of treatment with Colace. You should see an effect on stools 1 to 3 days after the first dose.

Colace Microenema should produce a bowel movement in 2 to 15 minutes.

ADULTS AND CHILDREN 12 AND OLDER
The suggested daily dosage of Colace is 50 to 200 milligrams.

In enemas, add 50 to 100 milligrams of Colace or 5 to 10 milliliters of Colace liquid to a retention or flushing enema, as prescribed by your doctor.

For Colace Microenema, use the entire contents of the tube.

CHILDREN UNDER 12
The suggested daily dosage of Colace for children 6 to 12 years of age is 40 to 120 milligrams; for children 3 to 6, it is 20 to 60 milligrams; for children under 3, it is 10 to 40 milligrams.

Colace Microenema should not be given to children under 3.

Overdosage
Overdose is unlikely with normal use of Colace. If you or your child should accidentally take too much, call your doctor or a Poison Control Center.

Brand name:

COLESTID

Pronounced: Koh-LESS-tid
Generic name: Colestipol hydrochloride

Why is this drug prescribed?

Colestid, in conjunction with diet, is used to help lower high levels of cholesterol in the blood. It is available in plain and orange-flavored granules and in tablet form.

Most important fact about this drug

Accidentally inhaling Colestid granules may cause serious effects. To avoid this, NEVER take them in their dry form. Colestid granules should always be mixed with water or other liquids BEFORE you take them.

How should you take this medication?

Colestid granules should be mixed with liquids such as:
Carbonated beverages (may cause stomach or intestinal discomfort)
Flavored drinks
Milk
Orange juice
Pineapple juice
Tomato juice
Water

Colestid may also be mixed with:
Milk used on breakfast cereals
Pulpy fruit (such as crushed peaches, pears, or pineapple) or fruit
    cocktail
Soups with a high liquid content (such as chicken noodle or tomato)

To take Colestid granules with beverages:
1. Measure at least 3 ounces of liquid into a glass.
2. Add the prescribed dose of Colestid to the liquid.
3. Stir until Colestid is completely mixed (it will not dissolve) and then drink the mixture.
4. Pour a small amount of the beverage into the glass, swish it around, and drink it. This will help make sure you have taken all the medication.

Swallow Colestid tablets whole, one at a time. Do not cut, chew, or crush them. Take the tablets with plenty of water or other liquid.

■ *If you miss a dose...*
Take the forgotten dose as soon as you remember. If it is almost time for the next dose, skip the one you missed and go back to your regular schedule. Never try to "catch up" by doubling the dose.

■ *Storage instructions...*
Store Colestid granules and tablets at room temperature.

What side effects may occur?
Side effects cannot be anticipated. If any develop or change in intensity, inform your doctor as soon as possible. Only your doctor can determine if it is safe for you to continue taking Colestid.

■ *Most common side effects:*
Constipation, worsening of hemorrhoids

■ *Less common or rare side effects may include:*
Abdominal bloating or distention/cramping/pain, arthritis, diarrhea, dizziness, fatigue, gas, headache, hives, joint pain, loss of appetite, muscle pain, nausea, shortness of breath, skin inflammation, vomiting, weakness

■ *Additional side effects from regular Colestid granules may include:*
Anxiety, belching, drowsiness, vertigo

■ *Additional side effects from Flavored Colestid granules or Colestid tablets may include:*
Aches and pains in arms and legs, angina (crushing chest pain), backache, bleeding hemorrhoids, blood in the stool, bone pain, chest pain, heartburn, indigestion, insomnia, light-headedness, loose stools, migraine, rapid heartbeat, rash, sinus headache, swelling of hands or feet

Why should this drug not be prescribed?
You should not be using Colestid if you are allergic to it or any of its components.

Special warnings about this medication
Before starting treatment with Colestid, you should:

■ Be tested (and treated) for diseases that may contribute to increased blood cholesterol, such as an underactive thyroid gland, diabetes, nephrotic syndrome (a kidney disease), dysproteinemia (a blood disease), obstructive liver disease, and alcoholism.

- Be on a diet plan (approved by your doctor) that stresses low-cholesterol foods and weight loss (if necessary).

Because certain medications may increase cholesterol, you should tell your doctor all of the medications you use.

Colestid may prevent the absorption of vitamins such as A, D, and K. Long-term use of Colestid may be connected to increased bleeding from a lack of vitamin K. Taking vitamin K_1 will help relieve this condition and prevent it in the future.

Your cholesterol and triglyceride levels should be checked regularly while you are taking Colestid.

Colestid may cause or worsen constipation. Dosages should be adjusted by your doctor. You may need to increase your intake of fiber and fluid. A stool softener also may be needed occasionally. People with coronary artery disease should be especially careful to avoid constipation. Hemorrhoids may be worsened by constipation related to Colestid.

If you have phenylketonuria (a hereditary disease caused by your body's inability to handle the amino acid phenylalanine), be aware that Flavored Colestid granules contain phenylalanine.

Possible food and drug interactions when taking this medication

Colestid may delay or reduce the absorption of other drugs. Allow as much time as possible between taking Colestid and taking other medications. Other drugs should be taken at least 1 hour before or 4 hours after taking Colestid.

If Colestid is taken with certain other drugs, the effects of either could be increased, decreased, or altered. It is especially important to check with your doctor before combining Colestid with the following:

Chlorothiazide (Diuril)
Digitalis (Lanoxin)
Folic acid and vitamins such as A, D, and K
Furosemide (Lasix)
Gemfibrozil (Lopid)
Hydrochlorothiazide (HydroDIURIL)
Hydrocortisone (Anusol-HC, Cortisporin, others)
Penicillin G, including brands such as Pentids
Phosphate supplements
Propranolol (Inderal)
Tetracycline drugs such as Sumycin

Special information
if you are pregnant or breastfeeding

The effects of Colestid during pregnancy have not been adequately studied. If you are pregnant or planning to become pregnant, or plan to breastfeed, check with your doctor. Since Colestid interferes with the absorption of fat soluble vitamins A, D, and K it may affect both the mother and the nursing infant.

Recommended dosage

ADULTS

One packet or 1 level scoopful of Flavored Colestid granules contains 5 grams of Colestipol.

The usual starting dose is 1 packet or 1 level scoopful once or twice a day. Your doctor may increase this by 1 dose a day every month or every other month, up to 6 packets or 6 level scoopfuls taken once a day or divided into smaller doses.

If you are taking Colestid tablets, the usual starting dose is 2 grams (2 tablets) once or twice a day. Your doctor may increase the dose every month or every other month, to a maximum of 16 grams a day, taken once a day or divided into smaller doses.

CHILDREN

The safety and effectiveness of Colestid have not been established for children.

Overdosage

Overdoses of Colestid have not been reported. If an overdose occurred, the most likely harmful effect would be obstruction of the stomach and/or intestines. If you suspect an overdose, seek medical help immediately.

Generic name:

COLESTIPOL

See Colestid, page 258.

Generic name:

COLISTIN, NEOMYCIN, HYDROCORTISONE, AND THONZONIUM

See Coly-Mycin S Otic, page 262.

Brand name:

COLY-MYCIN S OTIC

Pronounced: KOH-lee-MY-sin ESS OH-tic
Generic ingredients: Colistin sulfate, Neomycin sulfate,
  Hydrocortisone acetate, Thonzonium bromide

Why is this drug prescribed?
Coly-Mycin S Otic is a liquid suspension used to treat ear infections. Colistin sulfate and neomycin sulfate are antibiotics used to treat the bacterial infection itself, while hydrocortisone acetate is a steroid that helps reduce the inflammation, swelling, itching, and other skin reactions associated with an ear infection; thonzonium bromide facilitates the drug's effects.

Most important fact about this drug
As with other antibiotics, long-term treatment may encourage other infections. Therefore, if your ear infection does not improve within a week, your physician may want to change your medication.

How should you use this medication?
Use Coly-Mycin S Otic for the full course of treatment (but no more than 10 days) even if you start to feel better in a few days.

Shake well before using.

The external ear canal should be thoroughly cleaned and dried with a sterile cotton swab (applicator). The person should lie with the infected ear facing up. Pull the earlobe down and back (for children) or up and back (for adults) to straighten the ear canal. Drop the suspension into the ear. The person should lie in this position for 5 minutes to help the drops penetrate into the ear. If necessary, this procedure should be repeated for the other ear. To keep the medicine from leaking out, you can gently insert a sterile cotton plug.

If you prefer, a sterile cotton wick or plug may be inserted into the ear canal and then soaked with the Coly-Mycin S Otic suspension. This cotton wick should be moistened every 4 hours with more suspension and replaced at least once every 24 hours.

Avoid touching the dropper to the ear or other surfaces.

■ *If you miss a dose...*
  Apply it as soon as you remember. If it is almost time for your next dose, skip the one you missed and go back to your regular schedule.

■ *Storage instructions...*
Store at room temperature; avoid prolonged exposure to high temperatures.

What side effects may occur?
No specific side effects have been reported; however, neomycin (an ingredient in Coly-Mycin S Otic) may be associated with an increased risk of allergic skin reaction.

Why should this drug not be prescribed?
You should not take this drug if you have had an allergic reaction to any of the ingredients, or if you suffer from herpes simplex, vaccinia (cowpox), or varicella (chickenpox).

Special warnings about this medication
Treatment should not continue for more than 10 days.

If you warm Coly-Mycin S Otic before applying, do not heat the suspension to above body temperature, since this will lessen its potency. Warm the drops by holding the bottle in your hand for a few minutes.

If an allergic reaction occurs, you should stop using Coly-Mycin S Otic immediately. Your doctor may also recommend that future treatment with kanamycin, paromomycin, streptomycin, and possibly gentamicin be avoided, since you may also be allergic to these medications.

Use Coly-Mycin S Otic with care if you have a perforated eardrum or chronic otitis media (inflammation of the middle ear).

Possible food and drug interactions
when using this medication
No interactions have been reported.

Special information
if you are pregnant or breastfeeding
The effects of Coly-Mycin S Otic during pregnancy have not been adequately studied. If you are pregnant or plan to become pregnant, inform your doctor immediately. Coly-Mycin S Otic may appear in breast milk and could affect a nursing infant. If this medication is essential to your health, your doctor may advise you to stop breastfeeding until your treatment is finished.

Recommended dosage

ADULTS

The usual dose is 5 drops (when using the supplied measured dropper) or 4 drops (when using the dropper-bottle container) in the affected ear, 3 or 4 times daily.

INFANTS AND CHILDREN

The usual dose is 4 drops (when using the supplied measured dropper) or 3 drops (when using the dropper-bottle container) in the affected ear 3 or 4 times daily.

Please see the "How should you use this medication?" section on page 262 for more information on applying Coly-Mycin S Otic.

Overdosage

Although no specific information is available, any medication taken in excess can have serious consequences. If you suspect an overdose of Coly-Mycin S Otic, seek medical treatment immediately.

Brand name:

COMPAZINE

Pronounced: KOMP-ah-zeen
Generic name: Prochlorperazine

Why is this drug prescribed?

Compazine is used to control severe nausea and vomiting. It is also used to treat symptoms of mental disorders such as schizophrenia, and is occasionally prescribed for anxiety.

Most important fact about this drug

Compazine may cause tardive dyskinesia—involuntary muscle spasms and twitches in the face and body. This condition may be permanent. It appears to be most common among the elderly, especially women. Ask your doctor for information about this possible risk.

How should you take this medication?

Never take more Compazine than prescribed. It can increase the risk of serious side effects.

If you are using the suppository form of Compazine and find it is too soft to insert, you can chill it in the refrigerator for about 30 minutes or run cold water over it before removing the wrapper.

To insert a suppository, first remove the wrapper and moisten the suppository with cold water. Then lie down on your side and use a finger to push the suppository well up into the rectum.

■ *If you miss a dose...*
Take the forgotten dose as soon as you remember. If it is almost time for the next dose, skip the one you missed and go back to your regular schedule. Never try to "catch up" by doubling the dose.

■ *Storage instructions...*
Store at room temperature. Protect from heat and light.

What side effects may occur?
Side effects cannot be anticipated. If any develop or change in intensity, inform your doctor as soon as possible. Only your doctor can determine if it is safe for you to continue taking Compazine.

■ *Side effects may include:*
Abnormal muscle rigidity, abnormal secretion of milk, abnormal sugar in urine, abnormalities of posture and movement, agitation, anemia, appetite changes, asthma, blurred vision, breast development in males, chewing movements, constipation, convulsions, difficulty swallowing, discolored skin tone, dizziness, drooling, drowsiness, dry mouth, ejaculation problems, exaggerated reflexes, fever, fluid retention, head arched backward, headache, heart attack, heels bent back on legs, high or low blood sugar, hives, impotence, inability to urinate, increased psychotic symptoms, increased weight, infection, insomnia, intestinal obstruction, involuntary movements of arms, hands, legs, and feet, involuntary movements of face, tongue, and jaw, irregular movements, jerky movements, jitteriness, light sensitivity, low blood pressure, mask-like face, menstrual irregularities, narrowed or dilated pupils, nasal congestion, nausea, pain in the shoulder and neck area, painful muscle spasm, parkinsonism-like symptoms, persistent, painful erections, pill-rolling motion, protruding tongue, puckering of the mouth, puffing of the cheeks, rigid arms, feet, head, and muscles, rotation of eyeballs or state of fixed gaze, shock, shuffling gait, skin peeling, rash and inflammation, sore throat, mouth, and gums, spasms in back, feet and ankles, jaw, and neck, swelling and itching skin, swelling in throat, tremors, yellowed eyes and skin

Why should this drug not be prescribed?
Do not take Compazine if you are sensitive to or have ever had an allergic reaction to prochlorperazine or other phenothiazine drugs such as Thorazine, Prolixin, Triavil, Mellaril, or Stelazine.

Special warnings about this medication

Never take large amounts of alcohol, barbiturates, or narcotics when taking Compazine. Serious problems can result.

If you suddenly stop taking Compazine, you may experience a change in appetite, dizziness, nausea, vomiting, and tremors. Follow your doctor's instructions closely when discontinuing this drug.

Make sure the doctor knows if you are being treated for a brain tumor, intestinal blockage, heart disease, glaucoma, or an abnormal blood condition such as leukemia, or if you are exposed to extreme heat or pesticides.

This drug may impair your ability to drive a car or operate potentially dangerous machinery. Do not participate in any activities that require full alertness if you are unsure about your ability.

While taking Compazine, try to stay out of the sun. Use sun block and wear protective clothing. Your eyes may become more sensitive to sunlight, too, so keep sunglasses handy.

Compazine interferes with your ability to shed extra heat. Be cautious in hot weather.

Compazine may cause false-positive pregnancy tests.

Possible food and drug interactions
when taking this medication

If Compazine is taken with certain other drugs, the effects of either could be increased, decreased, or altered. It is especially important to check with your doctor before combining Compazine with the following:

Antiseizure drugs such as Dilantin and Tegretol
Anticoagulants such as Coumadin
Guanethidine (Ismelin)
Lithium (Lithobid, Eskalith)
Narcotic painkillers such as Demerol and Tylenol with Codeine
Other central nervous system depressants such as Xanax, Valium,
    Seconal, Halcion
Propranolol (Inderal)
Thiazide diuretics such as Dyazide

Special information
if you are pregnant or breastfeeding

Compazine is not usually recommended for pregnant women. However, your doctor may prescribe it for severe nausea and vomiting if the potential benefits of the drug outweigh the potential risks. Compazine appears in breast milk and may affect a nursing infant. If this drug is essential to your health, your doctor may recommend that you stop breastfeeding until your treatment is finished.

Recommended dosage

ADULTS

To Control Severe Nausea and Vomiting
Tablets: The usual dosage is one 5-milligram or 10-milligram tablet 3 or 4 times a day.

"Spansule" Capsules: The usual starting dose is one 15-milligram capsule on getting out of bed or one 10-milligram capsule every 12 hours.

The usual rectal dosage (suppository) is 25 milligrams, taken 2 times a day.

For Non-psychotic Anxiety
Tablets: The usual dose is 5 milligrams, taken 3 or 4 times a day.

"Spansule" capsule: The usual starting dose is one 15-milligram capsule on getting up or one 10-milligram capsule every 12 hours.

Treatment should not continue for longer than 12 weeks, and daily doses should not exceed 20 milligrams.

Relatively Mild Psychotic Disorders
The usual dose is 5 or 10 milligrams, taken 3 or 4 times daily.

Moderate to Severe Psychotic Disorders
Dosages usually start at 10 milligrams, taken 3 or 4 times a day. If needed, dosage may be gradually increased; 50 to 75 milligrams daily has been helpful for some people.

More Severe Psychotic Disorders
Dosages may range from 100 to 150 milligrams per day.

CHILDREN

Children under 2 years of age or weighing less than 20 pounds should not be given Compazine. If a child becomes restless or excited after taking Compazine, do not give the child another dose.

For Severe Nausea and Vomiting
An oral or rectal dose of Compazine is usually not needed for more than 1 day.

Children 20 to 29 Pounds
The usual dose is 2½ milligrams 1 or 2 times daily. Total daily amount should not exceed 7.5 milligrams.

Children 30 to 39 Pounds
The usual dose is 2½ milligrams 2 or 3 times daily. Total daily amount should not exceed 10 milligrams.

Children 40 to 85 Pounds
The usual dose is 2½ milligrams 3 times daily, or 5 milligrams 2 times daily.

Total daily amount should not exceed 15 milligrams.

For Psychotic Disorders

Children 2 to 5 Years Old
The starting oral or rectal dose is 2½ milligrams 2 or 3 times daily. Do not exceed 10 milligrams the first day and 20 milligrams thereafter.

Children 6 to 12 Years Old
The starting oral or rectal dose is 2½ milligrams 2 or 3 times daily. Do not exceed 10 milligrams the first day and 25 milligrams thereafter.

OLDER ADULTS

In general, older people take lower dosages of Compazine. Because they may develop low blood pressure while taking the drug, the doctor should monitor them closely. Older people (especially women) may be more susceptible to tardive dyskinesia—a possibly permanent condition. Tardive dyskinesia causes involuntary muscle spasms and twitches in the face and body. Consult your doctor for more information about these potential risks.

Overdosage
An overdose of Compazine can be fatal. If you suspect an overdose, seek medical help immediately.

■ *Symptoms of Compazine overdose may include:*
  Agitation, coma, convulsions, dry mouth, extreme sleepiness, fever, intestinal blockage, irregular heart rate, restlessness

Generic name:

CONJUGATED ESTROGENS

See Premarin, page 995.

Brand name:

COREG

Pronounced: KOE-regg
Generic name: Carvedilol

Why is this drug prescribed?

Coreg lowers blood pressure and increases the output of the heart. It is prescribed for both congestive heart failure and high blood pressure. It is often used with other drugs.

Most important fact about this drug

In some people, Coreg causes a drop in blood pressure when they first stand up, resulting in dizziness or even fainting. If this happens, sit or lie down and notify your doctor. Taking the drug with food reduces the chance of this problem. Even so, during the first month of therapy, or after a change in your dose, be careful about driving and operation of dangerous machinery.

How should you take this medication?

Take Coreg twice a day with food. If you are taking the drug for high blood pressure, there should be improvement within 7 to 14 days.

■ *If you miss a dose...*
Take it as soon as you remember. If it is almost time for your next dose, skip the one you missed and go back to your regular schedule. Do not take 2 doses at once.

■ *Storage instructions...*
Coreg should be stored at room temperature, away from light and moisture. Keep the container tightly closed.

What side effects may occur?

Side effects cannot be anticipated. If any develop or change in intensity, inform your doctor as soon as possible. Only your doctor can determine if it is safe for you to continue taking Coreg.

■ *More common side effects may include:*
Abdominal pain, back pain, bronchitis, chest pain, diarrhea, dizziness, fainting, fatigue, fever, gout, headache, increased blood sugar levels, joint pain, low blood pressure, muscle aches, nausea, pain, respiratory infection, sinus problems, slow heartbeat, sore throat, swelling, urinary infection, vision changes, vomiting, weight gain

- *Less common side effects may include:*
  Allergy, blood in urine, dark stools, dehydration, feeling of illness, gum disease, high blood pressure, impotence, increased sweating, infection, lack of sensitivity to touch, reddish or purplish spots, runny nose, shortness of breath, sleepiness, tingling or numbness, trouble sleeping, vertigo

- *Rare side effects may include:*
  Abnormal thinking, anemia, asthma, changeable emotions, convulsions, decreased sex drive in males, diabetes, digestive bleeding, dry mouth, hair loss, hearing problems, heart problems, impaired concentration, increased urination, itching, memory loss, migraine, nervousness, paralysis, rapid heartbeat, rash, ringing in ears, sensitivity to light, skin flaking, slow movement, wheezing, worsening of depression

Why should this drug not be prescribed?
Avoid Coreg if you have asthma, certain serious heart conditions, or liver disease. Do not take the drug if it causes an allergic reaction.

Special warnings about this medication
Coreg sometimes aggravates chronic bronchitis and emphysema. If you have either condition, make sure the doctor is aware of it. You'll need to use the drug cautiously. Report any weight gain or shortness of breath to your doctor immediately.

Liver damage is a rare side effect of the drug. Notify your doctor immediately if you develop these signs of liver disorder: appetite loss, dark urine, flu-like symptoms, itching, pain in your side, or yellowing of the skin. You will need to be switched from Coreg.

Make sure your doctor knows if you have diabetes or low blood sugar. Coreg can interfere with the effectiveness of diabetes drugs and can cover up the symptoms of low blood sugar. Monitor your blood sugar regularly, and report any changes to your doctor.

When Coreg is taken for heart failure, there is a slight chance that it will interfere with the kidneys. If this reaction seems likely, the doctor will monitor your kidney function and, if necessary, change your dosage—or take you off the drug.

Under no circumstances should you abruptly stop taking this drug on your own. Your symptoms could return with a vengeance; and if you have an overactive thyroid, those symptoms could be aggravated as well. The doctor will taper you off the drug gradually, if need be. Notify the doctor if you miss even a few doses of Coreg.

If you wear contact lenses, you should know that Coreg can dry your eyes.

Possible food and drug interactions
when taking this medication

If Coreg is taken with certain other drugs, the effects of either could be increased, decreased, or altered. It is especially important to check with your doctor before combining Coreg with any of the following:

Calcium channel blockers (blood pressure and heart medications such as Calan, Cardizem, Isoptin, and Verelan)
Cimetidine (Tagamet)
Clonidine (Catapres)
Diabetes pills such as Diabinese, Glucophage, and Rezulin
Drugs classified as MAO inhibitors, including the antidepressants Nardil and Parnate
Digoxin (Lanoxin)
Fluoxetine (Prozac)
Insulin
Paroxetine (Paxil)
Propafenone (Rythmol)
Quinidine (Quinaglute)
Reserpine (Ser-Ap-Es)
Rifampin (Rifadin)

Special information
if you are pregnant or breastfeeding

Coreg has not been adequately studied in pregnant women; and it is not known whether the drug appears in breast milk. If you are pregnant or plan to become pregnant, check with your doctor immediately.

Recommended dosage

ADULTS

Hypertension

The starting dose is 6.25 milligrams twice a day with food. Your doctor may raise the dosage every 1 or 2 weeks to a maximum of 50 milligrams a day.

Congestive heart failure

The starting dose is 3.125 milligrams twice a day with food. Your doctor may increase the dosage every 2 weeks. The maximum dosage for people weighing under 187 pounds is 50 milligrams a day; for those over 187 pounds, the maximum is 100 milligrams a day.

CHILDREN

The safety and effectiveness of Coreg have not been studied in children under 18.

Overdosage

Any medication taken in excess can have serious consequences. If you suspect an overdose, seek medical treatment immediately.

■ *Symptoms of Coreg overdose may include:*
  Breathing difficulties, loss of consciousness, seizures, heart problems, slow heartbeat, very low blood pressure, vomiting

Brand name:

CORGARD

Pronounced: CORE-guard
Generic name: Nadolol

Why is this drug prescribed?

Corgard is used in the treatment of angina pectoris (chest pain, usually caused by lack of oxygen to the heart due to clogged arteries) and to reduce high blood pressure.

When prescribed for high blood pressure, it is effective when used alone or in combination with other high blood pressure medications. Corgard is a type of drug known as a beta blocker. It decreases the force and rate of heart contractions, reducing the heart's demand for oxygen and lowering blood pressure.

Most important fact about this drug

If you have high blood pressure, you must take Corgard regularly for it to be effective. Since blood pressure declines gradually, it may be several weeks before you get the full benefit of Corgard; and you must continue taking it even if you are feeling well. Corgard does not cure high blood pressure; it merely keeps it under control.

How should you take this medication?

Corgard can be taken with or without food. Take it exactly as prescribed even if your symptoms have disappeared.

Try not to miss any doses. Corgard is taken once a day. If it is not taken regularly, your condition may worsen.

■ *If you miss a dose...*
Take it as soon as you remember. If it is within 8 hours of your next scheduled dose, skip the one you missed and go back to your regular schedule. Never take 2 doses at the same time.

■ *Storage instructions...*
Store at room temperature, away from light and heat, in a tightly closed container.

What side effects may occur?
Side effects cannot be anticipated. If any develop or change in intensity, inform your doctor as soon as possible. Only your doctor can determine if it is safe for you to continue taking Corgard.

■ *More common side effects may include:*
Change in behavior, changes in heartbeat, dizziness or light-headedness, mild drowsiness, slow heartbeat, weakness or tiredness

■ *Less common or rare side effects may include:*
Abdominal discomfort, asthma-like symptoms, bloating, confusion, constipation, cough, decreased sex drive, diarrhea, dry eyes, dry mouth, dry skin, facial swelling, gas, headache, heart failure, impotence, indigestion, itching, loss of appetite, low blood pressure, nasal stuffiness, nausea, rash, ringing in ears, slurred speech, vision changes, vomiting, weight gain

Why should this drug not be prescribed?
If you have a slow heartbeat, bronchial asthma, certain types of heartbeat irregularity, cardiogenic shock (shock due to inadequate blood supply from the heart), or active heart failure, you should not take this medication.

Special warnings about this medication
If you have a history of congestive heart failure, your doctor will prescribe Corgard with caution.

Corgard should not be stopped suddenly. This can cause increased chest pain and even a heart attack. Dosage should be gradually reduced.

If you suffer from asthma, chronic bronchitis, emphysema, seasonal allergies or other bronchial conditions, or kidney or liver disease, this medication should be used with caution.

Ask your doctor if you should check your pulse while taking Corgard. It can cause your heartbeat to become too slow.

This medication may mask the symptoms of low blood sugar or alter blood sugar levels. If you are diabetic, discuss this with your doctor.

This medication may cause you to become drowsy or less alert; therefore, driving or operating dangerous machinery or participating in any hazardous activity that requires full mental alertness is not recommended until you know how you respond to this medication.

Notify your doctor or dentist that you are taking Corgard if you have a medical emergency or before you have surgery or dental treatment.

Possible food and drug interactions when taking this medication
If Corgard is taken with certain other drugs, the effects of either could be increased, decreased, or altered. It is especially important to check with your doctor before combining Corgard with the following:

> Antidiabetic drugs, including insulin and oral drugs such as Micronase
> Certain blood pressure drugs such as Diupres and Ser-Ap-Es
> Epinephrine (EpiPen)

Special information if you are pregnant or breastfeeding
The effects of Corgard during pregnancy have not been adequately studied. If you are pregnant or plan to become pregnant, inform your doctor immediately. Corgard appears in breast milk and could affect a nursing infant. If this medication is essential to your health, your doctor may advise you to discontinue breastfeeding until your treatment with this medication is finished.

Recommended dosage

ADULTS

Dosage is tailored to each individual's needs.

Angina Pectoris
The usual starting dose is 40 milligrams once daily. The usual long-term dose is 40 or 80 milligrams, once a day. Doses up to 160 or 240 milligrams, once a day, may be needed.

High Blood Pressure
The usual starting dose is 40 milligrams once daily.

The usual long-term dose is 40 or 80 milligrams, once a day. Doses up to 240 or 320 milligrams, once a day, may be needed.

CHILDREN
The safety and effectiveness of Corgard have not been established in children.

Overdosage
Any medication taken in excess can have serious consequences. If you suspect an overdose, seek medical attention immediately.

- *The symptoms of Corgard overdose may include:*
  Difficulty in breathing, heart failure, low blood pressure, slow heartbeat

Brand name:

CORMAX

See Temovate, page 1204.

Brand name:

CORTISPORIN OPHTHALMIC SUSPENSION

Pronounced: KORE-ti-SPORE-in
Generic ingredients: Polymyxin B sulfate, Neomycin
  sulfate, Hydrocortisone
Other brand name: Bacticort

Why is this drug prescribed?
Cortisporin Ophthalmic Suspension is a combination of the steroid drug, hydrocortisone, and two antibiotics. It is prescribed to relieve inflammatory conditions such as irritation, swelling, redness, and general eye discomfort, and to treat superficial bacterial infections of the eye.

Most important fact about this drug
Prolonged use of this medication may increase pressure within the eye, leading to potential damage to the optic nerve and visual problems. Prolonged use also may suppress your immune response and thus increase the hazard of secondary eye infections. Your doctor should measure your eye pressure periodically if you are using this product for 10 days or longer.

How should you use this medication?

To help clear up your infection completely, use this medication exactly as prescribed for the full time of treatment, even if your symptoms have disappeared.

Administer the eyedrops as follows:
1. Shake the dropper bottle well.
2. Wash your hands thoroughly.
3. Gently pull your lower eyelid down to form a pocket between your eye and eyelid.
4. Hold the bottle on the bridge of your nose or on your forehead.
5. Tilt your head back and squeeze the medication into your eye.
6. Do not touch the applicator tip to any surface, including your eye.
7. Close your eyes gently, and keep them closed for 1 to 2 minutes.
8. Do not rinse the dropper.
9. Wait 5 to 10 minutes before using any other eyedrops.

If you do not improve after 2 days, your doctor should re-evaluate your case.

Do not share this medication with anyone else; you may spread the infection.

▪ *If you miss a dose...*
   Apply it as soon as you remember. If it is almost time for your next dose, skip the one you missed and go back to your regular schedule.

▪ *Storage instructions...*
   Store at room temperature. Keep tightly closed and protect from freezing.

What side effects may occur?

Side effects cannot be anticipated. If any develop or change in intensity, inform your doctor as soon as possible. Only your doctor can determine if it is safe for you to continue using Cortisporin.

▪ *Side effects may include:*
   Cataract formation (results in blurred vision), delayed wound healing, increased eye pressure (with possible development of glaucoma and, infrequently, optic nerve damage), irritation when drops are instilled, local allergic reactions (itching, swelling, redness), other infections (particularly fungal infections of the cornea and bacterial eye infections), severe allergic reactions

Why should this drug not be prescribed?
Cortisporin should not be used if you have certain viral or fungal diseases of the eye, including inflammation of the cornea caused by herpes simplex, chickenpox, or cowpox, or if you are sensitive to or have ever had an allergic reaction to any of its ingredients.

Special warnings about this medication
Remember that steroids such as hydrocortisone may hide the existence of an infection or worsen an existing one.

If you are using this medication for more than 10 days, your doctor should routinely check your eye pressure. If you already have high pressure within the eye (glaucoma), use this medication cautiously.

Neomycin, one of the ingredients in Cortisporin, may cause an allergic reaction—usually itching, redness, and swelling—or failure to heal. If you develop any of these signs, stop using Cortisporin; the symptoms should quickly subside. If the condition persists or gets worse, or if a rash or allergic reaction develops, call your doctor immediately. You are more likely to be sensitive to neomycin if you are sensitive to the following antibiotics: kanamycin, paromomycin, streptomycin, and possibly gentamicin.

The use of steroids in the eye can prolong and worsen many viral infections of the eye, including herpes simplex. Use this medication with extreme caution if you have this infection.

If you develop a sensitivity to Cortisporin, avoid other topical medications that contain neomycin.

Eye products that are not handled properly can become contaminated with bacteria that cause eye infections. If you use a contaminated product, you can seriously damage your eyes, even to the point of blindness.

**Possible food and drug interactions
when taking this medication**
No interactions have been reported.

**Special information
if you are pregnant or breastfeeding**
Although the effects of Cortisporin during pregnancy have not been adequately studied, steroids should be used during pregnancy only if the benefits outweigh the dangers to the fetus. If you are pregnant or plan to become pregnant, inform your doctor immediately. Hydrocortisone, when taken orally, appears in breast milk. Since medication may be absorbed into

the bloodstream when it is applied to the eye, your doctor may advise you to stop breastfeeding until your treatment with Cortisporin is finished.

Recommended dosage

ADULTS

The usual recommended dose is 1 or 2 drops in the affected eye every 3 or 4 hours, depending on the severity of the condition. Cortisporin may be used more often if necessary.

Overdosage

Any medication used in excess can have serious consequences. If you suspect an overdose of Cortisporin Ophthalmic Suspension, seek medical treatment immediately.

Brand name:

CORZIDE

Pronounced: CORE-zide
Generic ingredients: Nadolol, Bendroflumethiazide

Why is this drug prescribed?

Corzide is a combination drug used in the treatment of high blood pressure. It combines a beta blocker and a thiazide diuretic. Nadolol, the beta blocker, decreases the force and rate of heart contractions thereby reducing blood pressure. Bendroflumethiazide, the diuretic, helps your body produce and eliminate more urine, which also helps in lowering blood pressure.

Most important fact about this drug

You must take Corzide regularly for it to be effective. Since blood pressure declines gradually, it may be several weeks before you get the full benefit of Corzide; and you must continue taking it even if you are feeling well. Corzide does not cure high blood pressure; it merely keeps it under control.

How should you take this medication?

Corzide may be taken with or without food. Take it exactly as prescribed, even if your symptoms have disappeared.

Try not to miss any doses. Corzide is taken once a day. If this medication is not taken regularly, your condition may worsen.

- *If you miss a dose...*
Take it as soon as you remember. If it's within 8 hours of your next scheduled dose, skip the one you missed and go back to your regular schedule. Never take 2 doses at the same time.

- *Storage instructions...*
Store at room temperature, away from heat, in a tightly closed container.

What side effects may occur?
Side effects cannot be anticipated. If any develop or change in intensity, inform your doctor as soon as possible. Only your doctor can determine if it is safe for you to continue taking Corzide.

- *More common side effects may include:*
Asthma-like symptoms, changes in heart rhythm, cold hands and feet, dizziness, fatigue, low blood pressure, low potassium levels (symptoms include dry mouth, excessive thirst, weak or irregular heartbeat, muscle pain or cramps), slow heartbeat

- *Less common or rare side effects may include:*
Abdominal discomfort, anemia, bloating, blurred vision, certain types of irregular heartbeat, change in behavior, constipation, cough, diarrhea, dry mouth, eyes, or skin, facial swelling, gas, headache, heart failure, hepatitis, impotence, indigestion, inflammation of the pancreas, itching, loss of appetite, lowered sex drive, muscle spasm, nasal stuffiness, nausea, rash, ringing in ears, sedation, sensitivity to light, slurred speech, sweating, tingling or pins and needles, vertigo, vomiting, weakness, weight gain, wheezing, yellowed eyes and skin

Why should this drug not be prescribed?
If you have bronchial asthma, slow heartbeat, certain heartbeat irregularities (heart block), inadequate blood supply to the circulatory system (cardiogenic shock), active congestive heart failure, inability to urinate, or if you are sensitive to or have ever had an allergic reaction to Corzide, its ingredients, or similar drugs, you should not take this medication.

Special warnings about this medication
If you have a history of congestive heart failure, your doctor will prescribe Corzide with caution.

Corzide should not be stopped suddenly. This can cause increased chest pain and even a heart attack. Dosage should be gradually reduced.

If you suffer from asthma, seasonal allergies, emphysema or other bronchial conditions, or kidney or liver disease, this medication should be used with caution.

Ask your doctor if you should check your pulse while taking Corzide. It can cause your heartbeat to become too slow.

Corzide may mask the symptoms of low blood sugar or alter blood sugar levels. If you are diabetic, discuss this with your doctor.

This medication can cause you to become drowsy or less alert; therefore, activity that requires full mental alertness is not recommended until you know how you respond to this medication.

Notify your doctor or dentist that you are taking Corzide if you have a medical emergency, or before you have surgery or dental treatment.

Possible food and drug interactions
when taking this medication
Corzide may intensify the effects of alcohol. Do not drink alcohol while taking this medication.

If Corzide is taken with any other drug, the effects of either could be increased, decreased, or altered. It is especially important to check with your doctor before combining Corzide with the following:

Amphotericin B
Antidepressant drugs known as MAO inhibitors, such as Nardil and
    Parnate
Antidiabetic drugs, including insulin and oral drugs such as Micronase
Antigout drugs such as Benemid
Barbiturates such as phenobarbital
Blood thinners such as Coumadin
Calcium salt
Certain blood pressure drugs such as Diupres and Ser-Ap-Es
Cholestyramine (Questran)
Colestipol (Colestid)
Diazoxide (Proglycem)
Digitalis medications such as Lanoxin
Lithium (Lithonate)
Methenamine (Mandelamine)
Narcotics such as Percocet
Nonsteroidal anti-inflammatory drugs, such as Motrin, Naprosyn, and
    Nuprin
Other antihypertensives such as Vasotec
Steroid medications such as prednisone
Sulfinpyrazone (Anturane)

Special information
if you are pregnant or breastfeeding

The effects of Corzide during pregnancy have not been adequately studied. If you are pregnant or plan to become pregnant, inform your doctor immediately. Corzide appears in breast milk and could affect a nursing infant. If this medication is essential to your health, your doctor may advise you to discontinue breastfeeding until your treatment with Corzide is finished.

Recommended dosage

ADULTS

Dosages of this drug are always tailored to the individual's needs.

The usual dose is 1 Corzide 40/5 milligram tablet per day or, if necessary, 1 Corzide 80/5 milligram tablet per day. Your doctor may gradually add another high blood pressure medication to this drug.

CHILDREN

The safety and effectiveness of Corzide have not been established in children.

Overdosage

Any medication taken in excess can have serious consequences. If you suspect an overdose, seek medical attention immediately.

▪ *The symptoms of Corzide overdose may include:*
Abdominal irritation, central nervous system depression, coma, extremely slow heartbeat, heart failure, lethargy, low blood pressure, wheezing

Brand name:

COTRIM

See Bactrim, page 124.

Brand name:

COUMADIN

Pronounced: COO-muh-din
Generic name: Warfarin sodium

Why is this drug prescribed?

Coumadin is an anticoagulant (blood thinner). It is prescribed to:

Prevent and/or treat a blood clot that has formed within a blood vessel or in the lungs.

Prevent and/or treat blood clots associated with certain heart conditions or replacement of a heart valve.

Aid in the prevention of blood clots that may form in blood vessels anywhere in the body after a heart attack.

Reduce the risk of death, another heart attack, or stroke after a heart attack.

Most important fact about this drug
The most serious risks associated with Coumadin treatment are hemorrhage (severe bleeding resulting in the loss of a large amount of blood) in any tissue or organ and, less frequently, the destruction of skin tissue cells (necrosis) or gangrene. The risk of hemorrhage usually depends on the dosage and length of treatment with this drug.

Hemorrhage and necrosis have been reported to result in death or permanent disability. Severe necrosis can lead to the removal of damaged tissue or amputation of a limb. Necrosis appears to be associated with blood clots located in the area of tissue damage and usually occurs within a few days of starting Coumadin treatment.

How should you take this medication?
The objective of treatment with a blood-thinner is to control the blood-clotting process without causing severe bleeding, so that a clot does not form and cut off the blood supply necessary for normal body function. Therefore, it is very important that you take this medication exactly as prescribed by your doctor and that your doctor monitor your condition on a regular basis. Be especially careful to stick to the exact dosage schedule your doctor prescribes.

Effective treatment with minimal complications depends on your cooperation and communication with the doctor.

Do not take or discontinue any other medication unless directed to do so by your doctor. Avoid alcohol, salicylates such as aspirin, larger than usual amounts of foods rich in vitamin K (including liver, vegetable oil, egg yolks, and green leafy vegetables), which can counteract the effect of Coumadin, or any other drastic change in diet.

Note that Coumadin often turns urine reddish-orange.

You should carry an identification card that indicates you are taking Coumadin.

■ *If you miss a dose...*
Take the forgotten dose as soon as you remember, then go back to your regular schedule. If you do not remember until the next day, skip the dose. Never try to "catch up" by doubling the dose. Keep a record for your doctor of any doses you miss.

■ *Storage instructions...*
Coumadin can be stored at room temperature. Close the container tightly and protect from light.

What side effects may occur?
Side effects cannot be anticipated. If any develop or change in intensity, inform your doctor as soon as possible. Only your doctor can determine if it is safe for you to continue taking Coumadin.

■ *More common side effects may include:*
Hemorrhage: Signs of severe bleeding resulting in the loss of large amounts of blood depend upon the location and extent of bleeding. Symptoms include: chest, abdomen, joint, muscle, or other pain; difficult breathing or swallowing; dizziness; headache; low blood pressure; numbness and tingling; paralysis; shortness of breath; unexplained shock; unexplained swelling; weakness

■ *Less common side effects may include:*
Abdominal pain and cramping, allergic reactions, diarrhea, fatigue, feeling cold and chills, feeling of illness, fever, fluid retention and swelling, gas and bloating, hepatitis, hives, intolerance to cold, itching, lethargy, liver damage, loss of hair, nausea, necrosis (gangrene), pain, purple toes, rash, severe or long-lasting inflammation of the skin, taste changes, vomiting, yellowed skin and eyes

Why should this drug not be prescribed?
This drug should not be used for any condition where the danger of hemorrhage may be greater than the potential benefits of treatment. Unless directed to do so by your doctor, do not take this medication if one of the following conditions or situations applies to you:

A tendency to hemorrhage
Alcoholism
An abnormal blood condition

Aneurysm (balloon-like swelling of a blood vessel) in the brain or heart

Bleeding tendencies associated with: ulceration or bleeding of the stomach, intestines, respiratory tract, or the genital or urinary system

Eclampsia (a rare and serious pregnancy disorder producing life-threatening convulsions), or preeclampsia (a toxic condition— including headache, high blood pressure, and swelling of the legs and feet—that can lead to eclampsia)

Excessive bleeding of brain blood vessels

Inflammation, due to bacterial infection, of the membrane that lines the inside of the heart

Inflammation of the sac that surrounds the heart or an escape of fluid from the heart sac

Malignant hypertension (extremely elevated blood pressure that damages the inner linings of blood vessels, the heart, spleen, kidneys, and brain)

Pregnancy

Recent or contemplated surgery of the central nervous system (brain and spinal cord) or eye

Spinal puncture or any procedure that can cause uncontrollable bleeding

Threatened miscarriage

Allergy to any of the drug's ingredients

Special warnings about this medication

Treatment with blood thinners may increase the risk that fatty plaque will break away from the wall of an artery and lodge at another point, causing the blockage of a blood vessel. If you notice any of the following symptoms, contact your doctor immediately:

Abdominal pain; abrupt and intense pain in the leg, foot, or toes; blood in the urine; bluish mottling of the skin of the legs and hands; foot ulcers; gangrene; high blood pressure; muscle pain; "purple toes syndrome" (see below); rash; or thigh or back pain.

If you have any of the following conditions, tell your doctor. He or she will have to consider the risks against the benefits before giving you Coumadin.

An infectious disease or intestinal disorder

A history of recurrent blood clot disorders in you or your family

An implanted catheter

Dental procedures

Inflammation of a blood vessel

Moderate to severe high blood pressure

Moderate to severe kidney or liver dysfunction

Polycythemia vera (blood disorder)
Severe diabetes
Surgery or injury that leaves large raw surfaces
Trauma or injury that may result in internal bleeding

Purple toes syndrome can occur when taking Coumadin, usually 3 to 10 weeks after the start of anticoagulation therapy. Symptoms include dark purplish or mottled color of the toes that turns white when pressure is applied and fades when you elevate your legs, pain and tenderness of the toes, and change in intensity of the color over a period of time. If any of these symptoms develop, notify your doctor immediately.

If you are taking Coumadin, your doctor should periodically check the time it takes for your blood to start the clotting process (prothrombin time). Numerous factors such as travel and changes in diet, environment, physical state, and medication may alter your response to treatment with an anticoagulant. Clotting time should also be monitored after your release from the hospital and whenever other medications are started, discontinued, or taken sporadically.

While taking Coumadin, avoid activities and sports that could cause an injury. Remain cautious after you stop taking Coumadin. It will continue to work for 2 to 5 days.

If you have congestive heart failure, you may become more sensitive to Coumadin and may need to have your dosage reduced. Your doctor will have you tested regularly.

Notify your doctor if any illness, such as diarrhea, infection, or fever develops; if any unusual symptoms, such as pain, swelling, or discomfort, appear; or if you see prolonged bleeding from cuts, increased menstrual flow, vaginal bleeding, nosebleeds, bleeding of gums from brushing, unusual bleeding or bruising, red or dark brown urine, red or tarry black stool, headache, dizziness, or weakness.

Possible food and drug interactions
when taking this medication
Coumadin can interact with a very wide variety of drugs, both prescription and over-the-counter. Check with your doctor before taking ANY other medication or vitamin product.

Special information
if you are pregnant or breastfeeding
Coumadin should not be taken by women who are or may become pregnant since the drug may cause fatal hemorrhage in the developing baby. There

have also been reports of birth malformations, low birth weight, and retarded growth in children born to mothers treated with Coumadin during pregnancy. Spontaneous abortions and stillbirths are also known to occur. If you become pregnant while taking this drug, inform your doctor immediately. Coumadin may appear in breast milk and could affect a nursing infant. If this medication is essential to your health, your doctor may advise you to stop nursing your baby until your treatment with this drug is finished.

Recommended dosage

ADULTS

The administration and dosage of Coumadin must be individualized by your doctor according to your sensitivity to the drug.

A common starting dosage of Coumadin tablets for adults is 2 to 5 milligrams per day. Individualized daily dosage adjustments are based on the results of tests that determine the amount of time it takes for the blood clotting process to begin.

A maintenance dose of 2 to 10 milligrams per day is satisfactory for most people. The duration of treatment will be determined by your physician.

CHILDREN

Although Coumadin has been widely used in children below the age of 18, its safety and effectiveness for this purpose have not been formally established.

Overdosage

Signs and symptoms of Coumadin overdose reflect abnormal bleeding.

■ *Symptoms of abnormal bleeding include:*
  Blood in stools or urine, excessive menstrual bleeding, black stools, reddish or purplish spots on skin, excessive bruising, persistent bleeding from superficial injuries

If you suspect an overdose, seek emergency medical treatment immediately.

Brand name:

COVERA-HS

See Calan, page 170.

Brand name:

COZAAR

Pronounced: CO-zahr
Generic name: Losartan potassium

Why is this drug prescribed?
Cozaar is used in the treatment of high blood pressure. It is effective when used alone or with other high blood pressure medications, such as diuretics that help the body get rid of water.

Cozaar is the first of a new class of blood pressure medications called angiotensin II receptor antagonists. Cozaar works, in part, by preventing the hormone angiotensin II from constricting the blood vessels, which tends to raise blood pressure.

Most important fact about this drug
You must take Cozaar regularly for it to be effective. Since blood pressure declines gradually, it may be several weeks before you get the full benefit of Cozaar, and you must continue taking it even if you are feeling well. Cozaar does not cure high blood pressure; it merely keeps it under control.

How should you take this medication?
Cozaar can be taken with or without food.

Take it at the same time each day. For example, if you take the medication every morning before or after breakfast, you will establish a regular routine and be less likely to forget your dose.

- *If you miss a dose...*
  Take it as soon as possible. If it is almost time for your next dose, skip the missed dose and go back to your regular schedule.

- *Storage instructions...*
  Store at room temperature. Keep in a tightly closed container, away from light.

What side effects may occur?
Side effects cannot be anticipated. If any develop or change in intensity, tell your doctor as soon as possible. Only your doctor can determine if it is safe for you to continue taking Cozaar.

- *More common side effects may include:*
  Cough, dizziness, upper respiratory infection

- *Less common and rare side effects may include:*
  Back and leg pain, diarrhea, indigestion, insomnia, muscle cramps or pain, nasal congestion, sinus problems, swelling of face, lips, throat, and tongue

Why should this drug not be prescribed?
Do not take Cozaar when you are pregnant. Avoid it if you have ever had an allergic reaction to it.

Special warnings about this medication
Cozaar can cause low blood pressure, especially if you are also taking a diuretic. You may feel light-headed or faint, especially during the first few days of therapy. If these symptoms occur, contact your doctor. Your dosage may need to be adjusted or discontinued. Be sure you know how you react to Cozaar before you drive or operate machinery.

Excessive sweating, dehydration, severe diarrhea, or vomiting could make you lose too much water, causing a severe drop in blood pressure. Call your doctor if you experience any of these symptoms. Be sure to tell your doctor about any medical conditions you have, especially liver or kidney disease.

Possible food and drug interactions
when taking this medication
If Cozaar is taken with certain other drugs, the effects of either could be increased, decreased, or altered. It is especially important to check with your doctor before taking Cozaar with the following:

  Ketoconazole (Nizoral)
  Troleandomycin (Tao)

Special information
if you are pregnant or breastfeeding
Drugs such as Cozaar can cause injury or even death to the unborn child when used in the second or third trimester of pregnancy. Stop taking Cozaar as soon as you know you are pregnant. If you are pregnant or plan to become pregnant, tell your doctor before taking Cozaar. Cozaar may appear in breast milk and could affect the nursing infant. If this medication is essential to your health, your doctor may advise you to stop breastfeeding while you are taking Cozaar.

Recommended dosage

ADULTS

The usual starting dose is 50 milligrams once daily. However, Cozaar can also be taken twice daily, with total daily doses ranging from 25 milligrams to 100 milligrams. If your blood pressure does not respond, your doctor may increase your dose or add a low-dose diuretic to your regimen.

People taking diuretics and people with liver problems
The usual starting dose is 25 milligrams daily. Your doctor may adjust your dosage according to your response.

CHILDREN

The safety and effectiveness of Cozaar in children have not been studied.

Overdosage

Any medication taken in excess can have serious consequences. If you suspect an overdose, seek medical attention immediately. Information concerning Cozaar overdosage is limited. However, hypotension (low blood pressure) and abnormally rapid or slow heartbeat may be signs of an overdose.

Brand name:

CREON

See Pancrease, page 908.

Brand name:

CRIXIVAN

Pronounced: CRIX-i-van
Generic name: Indinavir sulfate

Why is this drug prescribed?

Crixivan is used in the treatment of human immunodeficiency virus (HIV) infection. HIV causes the immune system to break down so that it can no longer fight off other infections. This leads to the fatal disease known as acquired immune deficiency syndrome (AIDS).

HIV thrives by taking over the immune system's vital CD4 cells (white blood cells) and using their inner workings to make additional copies of itself.

Crixivan belongs to a new class of HIV drugs called protease inhibitors, which work by interfering with an important step in the virus's reproductive cycle. Although Crixivan cannot eliminate HIV already present in the body, it can reduce the amount of virus available to infect other cells.

Crixivan can be taken alone or in combination with other HIV drugs such as Retrovir. Because Crixivan and Retrovir attack the virus in different ways, the combination is likely to be more effective than either drug alone.

Most important fact about this drug
It is important that you drink at least 48 ounces (4 soda-can sized glasses) of liquid daily while taking Crixivan. If you do not get enough liquid, you may develop kidney stones and have to temporarily stop taking Crixivan or even discontinue it altogether.

How should you take this medication?
Take this medication exactly as prescribed by your doctor. Do not share this medication with anyone and do not take more than your recommended dosage.

To ensure maximum absorption, do not take Crixivan with food. Instead, take it with water 1 hour before or 2 hours after a meal. (Crixivan may also be taken with liquids such as skim milk, juice, coffee, or tea, or even with a light meal such as dry toast with jelly, juice, and coffee with skim milk and sugar, or corn flakes with skim milk and sugar.)

■ *If you miss a dose...*
Skip it and take the next dose at the regularly scheduled time. Do not double the dose.

■ *Storage instructions...*
Crixivan capsules are sensitive to moisture. Store Crixivan at room temperature in the original container and leave the drying agent in the bottle to keep the medication dry. Keep the container tightly closed.

What side effects may occur?
Side effects cannot be anticipated. If any develop or change in intensity, inform your doctor as soon as possible. Only your doctor can determine if it is safe for you to continue taking Crixivan.

■ *Possible side effects may include:*
Abdominal pain, anemia, back pain, blood in the urine, changes in taste, diarrhea, discolored skin, dizziness, drowsiness, dry skin and mouth,

fatigue, general feeling of illness, headache, indigestion, insomnia, kidney stones, liver problems, loss of appetite, nausea, pain in the side, rash, sore throat, upper respiratory infection, vomiting, weakness, yellow skin or eyes

Why should this drug not be prescribed?
If you suffer a severe allergic reaction to Crixivan or any of its ingredients, you should not take this medication.

Special warnings about this medication
Although Crixivan reduces the amount of HIV in the blood and increases the white blood cell count, its long-term effect on survival is still unknown. The virus remains in the body, and you will continue to face the possibility of complications, including opportunistic infections (rare infections that develop when the immune system falters) such as certain types of pneumonia, tuberculosis, and fungal infection. Therefore, it is important that you remain under the care of a doctor and keep all your follow-up appointments.

Crixivan is not a cure for HIV infection, and it does not reduce the risk of transmission of HIV to others through sexual contact or blood contamination. Therefore, you should continue to avoid practices that could spread HIV.

Check with your doctor if you have liver disease, particularly cirrhosis of the liver, before using Crixivan. Because there is little information concerning the use of this drug in people with kidney disease or severe liver disease, be sure to tell your doctor if you have either condition.

Possible food and drug interactions
when taking this medication
Do not take Crixivan with the following medications. The combination may cause serious or life-threatening effects.

    Astemizole (Hismanal)
    Cisapride (Propulsid)
    Midazolam (Versed)
    Terfenadine (Seldane)
    Triazolam (Halcion)

Crixivan may also interact with certain other drugs, and the effects of either could be increased, decreased, or altered. It is especially important to check with your doctor before combining Crixivan with the following:

    Carbamazepine (Tegretol)
    Clarithromycin (Biaxin)

Dexamethasone (Decadron))
Didanosine (Videx)
Fluconazole (Diflucan)
Isoniazid (Nydrazid)
Ketoconazole (Nizoral)
Ortho-Novum
Phenytoin (Dilantin)
Quinidine (Quinidex)
Rifabutin (Mycobutin)
Rifampin (Rifadin)
Trimethoprim (Bactrim, Trimpex, Septra)

Avoid drinking grapefruit juice while taking Crixivan. This kind of juice can reduce the drug's effectiveness.

Be sure to tell your doctor and pharmacist about all medications you are taking, both prescription and over-the-counter. Alert them, too, when you *stop* taking a medication.

Special information
if you are pregnant or breastfeeding
The effects of Crixivan during pregnancy have not been adequately studied. If you are pregnant or plan to become pregnant, tell your doctor immediately. Do not breastfeed your baby. HIV appears in breast milk and can infect a nursing infant.

Recommended dosage

ADULTS

The recommended dose of Crixivan is 800 milligrams (two 400-milligram capsules) every 8 hours. Your doctor may lower the dose to 600 milligrams every 8 hours if you have mild-to-moderate liver problems due to cirrhosis. If you have been prescribed another HIV drug along with Crixivan, take it as directed.

CHILDREN

The safety and effectiveness of Crixivan for use in children have not been established.

Overdosage
There is no information presently available on Crixivan overdose. However, any medication taken in excess can have serious consequences. If you suspect an overdose, seek emergency medical treatment immediately.

Brand name:

CROLOM

Pronounced: CROW-lum
Generic name: Cromolyn sodium

Why is this drug prescribed?
Crolom is an eyedrop that relieves the itching, tearing, discharge, and redness caused by seasonal and chronic allergies. The drug works by preventing certain cells in the body from releasing histamine and other substances that can cause an allergic reaction.

Most important fact about this drug
In order for Crolom to work properly, you must continue to use it every day at regular intervals even if your symptoms have disappeared. It can take up to 6 weeks for your condition to clear up.

How should you use this medication?
Use Crolom exactly as directed by your doctor. Do not use more or less than required and apply it only when scheduled. To administer Crolom, follow these steps:

1. Wash your hands thoroughly.
2. Gently pull your lower eyelid down to form a pocket between your eye and the lid.
3. Drop the medicine into this pocket. Let go of the eyelid and gently close the eye. Do not blink. Keep your eyes closed for a minute or two.
4. Do not touch the applicator tip to your eye or any other surface. This could lead to infection.
5. Do not rinse the dropper.

■ *If you miss a dose...*
Use it as soon as possible. Then go back to your regular schedule.

■ *Storage instructions...*
Keep the container tightly closed and away from light. Store at room temperature.

What side effects may occur?
You may experience temporary burning or stinging in the eye after you apply Crolom.

- *Rare side effects may include:*
  Dryness around the eye, eye irritation, inflammation of the eyelids, itchy eyes, puffy eyes, styes, watery eyes

Why should this drug not be prescribed?
If you have ever had an allergic reaction to cromolyn sodium, avoid this medication.

Special warnings about this medication
Do not wear soft contact lenses while you are using Crolom.

If your symptoms do not begin to improve, alert your doctor.

Possible food and drug interactions with the medication
No interactions have been reported.

Special information if you are pregnant or breastfeeding
There are no studies on use of Crolom with pregnant women. If you are pregnant or plan to become pregnant, tell your doctor. Crolom should be used during pregnancy only if clearly needed. It is not known whether Crolom appears in human breast milk. If you are nursing and need to use Crolom, use it with caution.

Recommended dosage

ADULTS AND CHILDREN

Put 1 or 2 drops into each eye 4 to 6 times a day at evenly spaced intervals.

It is not known whether Crolom is safe and effective for children under 4 years.

Overdosage
Although there is no information on Crolom overdose, any medication taken in excess can have serious consequences. If you suspect an overdose, seek medical attention immediately.

Generic name:

CROMOLYN, INHALED

See Intal, page 616.

Generic name:

CROMOLYN, OCULAR

See Crolom, page 293.

Generic name:

CYCLOBENZAPRINE

See Flexeril, page 510.

Brand name:

CYCLOCORT

Pronounced: SIKE-low-court
Generic name: Amcinonide

Why is this drug prescribed?
Cyclocort is prescribed for the relief of the inflammatory and itchy symptoms of skin disorders that are responsive to corticosteroid treatment.

Most important fact about this drug
When you use Cyclocort, you inevitably absorb some of the medication through your skin and into the bloodstream. Too much absorption can lead to unwanted side effects elsewhere in the body. To keep this problem to a minimum, avoid using large amounts of Cyclocort over large areas, and do not cover it with airtight dressings such as plastic wrap or adhesive bandages unless specifically told to by your doctor.

How should you use this medication?
Use this medication exactly as prescribed by your doctor. It is for use only on the skin. Be careful to keep it out of your eyes.

Apply Cyclocort sparingly. Rub it in gently.

■ *If you miss a dose...*
Apply the forgotten dose as soon as you remember. Use the remaining doses for that day at evenly spaced intervals. Never try to "catch up" by doubling the amount applied.

■ *Storage instructions...*
Cyclocort can be stored at room temperature. Protect from freezing.

What side effects may occur?
Side effects cannot be anticipated. If any develop or change in intensity, inform your doctor as soon as possible. Only your doctor can determine if it is safe for you to continue taking Cyclocort.

■ *More common side effects may include:*
Burning, itching, soreness, stinging

■ *Less common or rare side effects may include:*
Dryness, excessive growth of hair, infection, inflammation of hair follicles, inflammation of the skin around the mouth, irritation, prickly heat, skin eruptions resembling acne, softening of the skin, stretch marks

Why should this drug not be prescribed?
If you are sensitive to or have ever had an allergic reaction to amcinonide or other steroid medications, you should not use Cyclocort. Make sure your doctor is aware of any drug reactions you have experienced.

Special warnings about this medication
Do not use this drug for any disorder other than the one for which it was prescribed.

The use of tight-fitting diapers or plastic pants is not recommended for a child being treated in the diaper area. These garments may act as airtight dressings or bandages.

The treated skin area should not be bandaged, covered, or wrapped unless you have been directed to do so by your doctor.

If an irritation or allergic reaction develops while you are using Cyclocort, notify your doctor.

Possible food and drug interactions
when taking this medication
No interactions with food or other drugs have been reported.

Special information
if you are pregnant or breastfeeding
The effects of Cyclocort during pregnancy have not been adequately studied. If you are pregnant or plan to become pregnant, inform your doctor immediately. It is not known whether this medication appears in breast milk. If this drug is essential to your health, your doctor may advise you to discontinue breastfeeding until your treatment is finished.

Recommended dosage

ADULTS

Apply a thin film of Cyclocort to the affected area 2 or 3 times a day, depending on the severity of the condition.

Cyclocort lotion may be applied to the affected areas, particularly hairy areas, 2 times per day. The lotion should be rubbed in completely, and the area should not be washed and should be protected from clothing until the lotion has dried.

Your doctor may recommend airtight bandages or dressings if you are being treated for psoriasis (a skin disorder characterized by patches of red, dry, scale-covered skin) or other stubborn skin conditions. If an infection develops, stop bandaging the area.

CHILDREN

Topical use of Cyclocort on children should be limited to the smallest amount that is effective. Long-term treatment may interfere with children's growth and development.

Overdosage

A severe overdosage is unlikely with the use of Cyclocort; however, long-term or prolonged use can produce side effects throughout the body (see "Most important fact about this drug" on page 295).

Generic name:

CYCLOPHOSPHAMIDE

See Cytoxan, page 306.

Generic name:

CYCLOSPORINE

See Sandimmune, page 1114.

Brand name:

CYCRIN

See Provera, page 1034.

Brand name:

CYLERT

Pronounced: SIGH-lert
Generic name: Pemoline

Why is this drug prescribed?
Cylert is used to help treat children who have attention deficit disorder with hyperactivity. However, this condition does not always require drug treatment. Drugs such as Cylert should be taken as part of a comprehensive treatment plan offering psychological and educational support to help the child become more stable.

Children who have attention deficit disorder with hyperactivity may show signs of:

Emotional mood swings
Hyperactivity
Impulsive actions
Moderate to severe distractibility
Short attention span

Most important fact about this drug
Because long-term use of drugs such as Cylert may affect a child's growth, your doctor will monitor your child carefully if he or she is taking this drug for an extended period.

How should you take this medication?
Cylert should be taken once a day, in the morning.

▪ *If you miss a dose...*
Have your child take it as soon as you remember, then go back to the regular schedule. If you do not remember it until the next day, skip the missed dose and go back to the regular schedule. Do not give 2 doses at once.

▪ *Storage instructions...*
Store at room temperature.

What side effects may occur?
Side effects cannot be anticipated. If any develop or change in intensity, inform your doctor as soon as possible. Only your doctor can determine if it is safe for your child to continue taking Cylert.

■ *More common side effects may include:*
Insomnia

■ *Less common side effects may include:*
Dizziness, drowsiness, hallucinations, headache, hepatitis and other liver problems, increased irritability, involuntary, fragmented movements of the face, eyes, lips, tongue, arms, and legs, loss of appetite, mild depression, nausea, seizures, skin rash, stomachache, suppressed growth, uncontrolled vocal outbursts (such as grunts, shouts, and obscene language), weight loss, yellowing of skin or eyes

■ *Rare side effects may include:*
A rare form of anemia with symptoms such as bleeding gums, bruising, chest pain, fatigue, headache, nosebleeds, and abnormal paleness

Why should this drug not be prescribed?
Your child should not be using Cylert if he or she is allergic to it or if he or she has liver problems.

Special warnings about this medication
Cylert may cause dizziness. Warn your child to be careful climbing stairs or participating in activities that require mental alertness.

Although there have been no reports that Cylert is physically addictive, it is chemically similar to a class of drugs that are potentially addictive. Make sure your child takes no more than the prescribed dosage.

Remember that children who take this drug on a long-term basis should be carefully monitored for signs of stunted growth.

Use Cylert cautiously if your child has kidney problems.

Psychotic children who take Cylert may experience increasingly disordered thoughts and behavioral disturbances.

**Possible food and drug interactions
when taking this medication**
If Cylert is taken with certain other drugs, the effects of either could be increased, decreased, or altered. It is especially important to check with your doctor before combining Cylert with the following:

Seizure medications such as Tegretol
Other drugs that affect the central nervous system (brain and spinal
    cord) such as Ritalin

Special information
if you are pregnant or breastfeeding

This drug is for use only in children, and its effects in pregnancy have not been adequately studied. Cylert should be used during pregnancy only if it is clearly necessary. The drug may appear in breast milk and affect the baby.

Recommended dosage

The recommended beginning dose is 37.5 milligrams daily. Dosages may be gradually increased if needed. Most children take doses ranging from 56.25 to 75 milligrams a day. The maximum recommended daily dose of Cylert is 112.5 milligrams. Significant improvement is gradual and may not be apparent until the third or fourth week of treatment with Cylert.

Your doctor may occasionally stop treatment with Cylert to see whether behavioral problems return and whether further treatment with Cylert is necessary.

Overdosage

Any medication taken in excess can have serious consequences. If you suspect an overdose, seek medical help immediately.

■ *Symptoms of Cylert overdose may include:*
Agitation, coma, confusion, convulsions, delirium, dilated pupils, exaggerated feeling of well-being, extremely high temperature, flushing, hallucinations, headache, high blood pressure, increased heart rate, increased reflex reactions, muscle twitches, sweating, tremors, vomiting

Generic name:

CYPROHEPTADINE

See Periactin, page 942.

Brand name:

CYSTADANE

Pronounced: SIST-uh-dane
Generic name: Betaine anhydrous

Why is this drug prescribed?

Cystadane is prescribed to reduce dangerously high blood levels of the naturally occurring amino acid homocysteine. Excessive levels of homocysteine can lead to formation of clots within your blood vessels, brittle bones (osteoporosis), other bone abnormalities, and dislocation of the lens of the eye. Homocysteine is also linked with an increased risk of heart disease and heart attack.

When homocysteine levels are so high that the substance appears in the urine, the condition is called homocystinuria. The problem is usually the result of an inherited lack of the enzymes needed to process homocysteine and generally shows up within the first months or years of life. Early signs of homocystinuria include delays in development, failure to thrive, seizures, and sluggishness.

Most important fact about this drug
The active ingredient in Cystadane (betaine) is found in our bodies and in foods such as beets, cereals, seafood, and spinach. Your doctor may prescribe Cystadane along with vitamin B_6 (pyridoxine), vitamin B_{12} (cobalamin), and folate. All of these dietary substances aid in the proper processing of homocysteine.

How should you take this medication?
Take Cystadane exactly as directed. To avoid forgetting a dose, try to get in the habit of taking it at the same time each day.

Cystadane will start to work within a week, and should have your condition completely under control within a month. You can continue therapy indefinitely; people have taken betaine for years without a problem.

■ *If you miss a dose...*
Take the forgotten dose as soon as you remember. If it is almost time for your next dose, skip the one you missed and go back to your regular schedule.

■ *Storage instructions...*
Store Cystadane at room temperature and protect from moisture. Keep the bottle tightly closed.

What side effects may occur?
Side effects of Cystadane are minimal. If any develop or change in intensity, inform your doctor as soon as possible. Only your doctor can determine whether it is safe for you to continue taking Cystadane.

■ *Side effects may include:*
Diarrhea, nausea, odor, stomach and intestinal problems, possible mental changes

Why should this drug not be prescribed?
There are no known reasons for avoiding Cystadane.

Special warnings about this medication
Do not use the powder if it does not completely dissolve in water, or if it makes a colored solution.

Possible food and drug interactions
when taking this medication
No interactions have been reported.

Special information
if you are pregnant or breastfeeding
The effects of Cystadane during pregnancy have not been studied. If you are pregnant or plan to become pregnant, check with your doctor immediately. It is not known whether Cystadane appears in breast milk. If this medication is essential to your health, your doctor may advise you to avoid breastfeeding.

Recommended dosage
Shake the bottle of Cystadane before removing the cap. Measure the number of scoops your doctor has prescribed by using the scoop provided.

ADULTS

The usual dosage is 3 scoops (3 grams) mixed with 4 to 6 ounces of water twice a day (6 grams daily). Make sure the powder is completely dissolved before drinking. Drink immediately after mixing.

The doctor will gradually increase your dosage until your homocysteine levels are under control. Dosages of up to 20 grams daily are sometimes necessary.

CHILDREN

In children less than 3 years old, the usual starting dose is 100 milligrams per 2.2 pounds of body weight per day. Each week, the doctor will increase the daily dose by 100 milligrams per 2.2 pounds until homocysteine levels are normal.

Overdosage
There have been no reported cases of overdose with Cystadane. However, a massive overdose could be dangerous. If you suspect an overdose, seek medical attention immediately.

Brand name:

CYTOTEC

Pronounced: SITE-oh-tek
Generic name: Misoprostol

Why is this drug prescribed?
Cytotec, a synthetic prostaglandin (hormone-like substance), reduces the production of stomach acid and protects the stomach lining. People who take nonsteroidal anti-inflammatory drugs (NSAIDs) may be given Cytotec tablets to help prevent stomach ulcers.

Aspirin and other NSAIDs such as Motrin, Naprosyn, Feldene, and others, which are widely used to control the pain and inflammation of arthritis, are generally hard on the stomach. If you must take an NSAID for a prolonged period of time, and if you are elderly or have ever had a stomach ulcer, your doctor may want you to take Cytotec for as long as you take the NSAID.

Most important fact about this drug
You must not become pregnant while using Cytotec. This drug causes uterine contractions that could lead to a miscarriage. If you do have a miscarriage, there is a risk that it might be incomplete. This could lead to bleeding, hospitalization, surgery, infertility, or even death. It is vitally important to use reliable contraception while taking Cytotec.

How should you take this medication?
Take Cytotec with meals, exactly as prescribed.

Take Cytotec for the full course of NSAID treatment, even if you notice no stomach problems.

Take the final dosage at bedtime.

▪ *If you miss a dose...*
Take it as soon as you remember. If it is almost time for your next dose, skip the one you missed and go back to your regular schedule. Do not take 2 doses at once.

▪ *Storage instructions...*
Store at room temperature in a dry place.

What side effects may occur?
Cytotec may cause abdominal cramps, diarrhea, and/or nausea, especially during the first few weeks of treatment. These symptoms may disappear as

your body gets used to the drug. Taking Cytotec with food can help minimize diarrhea. If you have prolonged difficulty (more than 8 days), or if you have severe diarrhea, cramping, or nausea, call your doctor.

■ *Other side effects may include:*
Constipation, gas, indigestion, headache, heavy menstrual bleeding, menstrual disorder, menstrual pain or cramps, paleness, spotting (light bleeding between menstrual periods), stomach or intestinal bleeding, vomiting

Cytotec may cause uterine bleeding even if you have gone through menopause. However, postmenopausal bleeding could be a sign of some other gynecological problem. If you experience any such bleeding while taking Cytotec, notify your doctor at once.

Why should this drug not be prescribed?
Do not take Cytotec if you are sensitive to or have ever had an allergic reaction to it or to another prostaglandin medication.

Do not take Cytotec if you are pregnant or might become pregnant while taking it.

Special warnings about this medication
Since Cytotec may cause diarrhea, you should use this drug very cautiously if you have inflammatory bowel disease or any other condition in which the loss of fluid caused by diarrhea would be particularly dangerous.

To reduce the risk of diarrhea, take Cytotec with food and avoid taking it with a magnesium-containing antacid, such as Di-Gel, Gelusil, Maalox, Mylanta, and others. Have frequent medical checkups.

Never give Cytotec to anyone else; the dosage might be wrong, and if the other person is pregnant, the drug might harm the unborn baby or cause a miscarriage.

Possible food and drug interactions
when taking this medication
Cytotec does not interfere with arthritis medications such as aspirin and ibuprofen.

Special information
if you are pregnant or breastfeeding
If you are pregnant or plan to become pregnant, inform your doctor immediately. Because Cytotec can cause miscarriage, it should not be taken

during pregnancy. If you are a woman of childbearing age, you should not take Cytotec unless you have thoroughly discussed the risks with your doctor and believe you are able to take effective contraceptive measures.

You will need to take a pregnancy test about 2 weeks before starting to take Cytotec. To be sure you are not pregnant at the start of Cytotec treatment, your doctor will have you take your first dose on the second or third day of your menstrual period.

Even the most scrupulous contraceptive measures sometimes fail. If you believe you may have become pregnant while taking Cytotec, stop taking the drug and contact your doctor immediately.

It is not known if Cytotec appears in breast milk. Because of the potential for severe diarrhea in a nursing infant, your doctor may have you stop breastfeeding until your treatment is finished.

Recommended dosage

ADULTS

The recommended oral dose of Cytotec for the prevention of NSAID-induced stomach ulcers is 200 micrograms 4 times daily with food. Take the last dose of the day at bedtime.

If you cannot tolerate this dosage, your doctor can prescribe a dose of 100 micrograms.

Your should take Cytotec for the duration of NSAID therapy, as prescribed by your doctor.

For People with Kidney Impairment

You will not normally need an adjustment in the dosing schedule, but your doctor can reduce the dosage if you have trouble handling the usual dose.

Overdosage

Any medication taken in excess can have serious consequences. If you suspect symptoms of an overdose of Cytotec, seek medical attention immediately.

- *Symptoms of Cytotec overdose may include:*
  Abdominal pain, breathing difficulty, convulsions, diarrhea, fever, heart palpitations, low blood pressure, sedation (extreme drowsiness), slowed heartbeat, stomach or intestinal discomfort, tremors

Brand name:

CYTOXAN

Pronounced: sigh-TOKS-an
Generic name: Cyclophosphamide

Why is this drug prescribed?

Cytoxan, an anticancer drug, works by interfering with the growth of malignant cells. It may be used alone but is often given with other anticancer medications.

Cytoxan is used in the treatment of the following types of cancer:

Breast cancer
Leukemias (cancers affecting the white blood cells)
Malignant lymphomas (Hodgkin's disease or cancer of the lymph nodes)
Multiple myeloma (a malignant condition or cancer of the plasma cells)
Advanced mycosis fungoides (cancer of the skin and lymph nodes)
Neuroblastoma (a malignant tumor of the adrenal gland or sympathetic nervous system)
Ovarian cancer (adenocarcinoma)
Retinoblastoma (a malignant tumor of the retina)

In addition, Cytoxan may sometimes be given to children who have "minimal change" nephrotic syndrome (kidney damage resulting in loss of protein in the urine) and who have not responded well to treatment with steroid medications.

Most important fact about this drug

Cytoxan may cause bladder damage, probably from toxic byproducts of the drug that are excreted in the urine. Potential problems include bladder infection with bleeding and fibrosis of the bladder.

While you are being treated with Cytoxan, drink 3 or 4 liters of fluid a day to help prevent bladder problems. The extra fluid will dilute your urine and make you urinate frequently, thus minimizing the Cytoxan byproducts' contact with your bladder.

How should you take this medication?

Take Cytoxan exactly as prescribed. You will undergo frequent blood tests, and the doctor will adjust your dosage depending on the evolution of your white blood cell count; a dosage reduction is necessary if the count drops below a certain level. You will also have frequent urine tests to check for blood in the urine, a sign of bladder damage.

Take Cytoxan on an empty stomach. If you have severe stomach upset, then you may take it with food.

If you are unable to swallow the tablet form, you may be given an oral solution made from the injectable form of Cytoxan and Aromatic Elixir. This solution should be used within 14 days.

■ *If you miss a dose...*
Do not take the dose you missed. Go back to your regular schedule and contact your doctor. Do not take 2 doses at once.

■ *Storage instructions...*
Store tablets at room temperature. Store the oral solution in the refrigerator.

What side effects may occur?
Side effects cannot be anticipated. If any develop or change in intensity, inform your doctor immediately. Only your doctor can determine if it is safe for you to continue using Cytoxan.

One possible Cytoxan side effect is the development of a secondary cancer, typically of the bladder, lymph nodes, or bone marrow. A secondary cancer may occur up to several years after the drug is given.

Cytoxan can lower the activity of your immune system, making you more vulnerable to infection.

Noncancerous bladder problems may occur during Cytoxan therapy (see "Most important fact about this drug" section, page 306).

■ *More common side effects may include:*
Loss of appetite, nausea and vomiting, temporary hair loss

■ *Less common or rare side effects may include:*
Abdominal pain, anemia, bleeding, inflamed colon, darkening of skin and changes in fingernails, decreased sperm count, diarrhea, fever, impaired wound healing, mouth sores, new tumor growth, prolonged impairment of fertility or temporary sterility in men, rash, severe allergic reaction, temporary failure to menstruate, yellowing of eyes and skin

Why should this drug not be prescribed?
Do not take this medication if you have ever had an allergic reaction to it.

Also, tell your doctor if you have ever had an allergic reaction to another alkylating anticancer drug such as Alkeran, CeeNU, Emcyt, Leukeran, Myleran, or Zanosar.

In adults, Cytoxan should not be given for "minimal change" nephrotic syndrome or any other kidney disease.

Also, Cytoxan should not be given to anyone who is unable to produce normal blood cells because the bone marrow—where blood cells are made—is not functioning well.

Special warnings about this medication
You are at increased risk for toxic side effects from Cytoxan if you have any of the following conditions:

Blood disorder (low white blood cell or platelet count)
Bone marrow tumors
Kidney disorder
Liver disorder
Past anticancer therapy
Past X-ray therapy

Possible food and drug interactions
when taking this medication
If Cytoxan is taken with certain other drugs, the effects of either could be increased, decreased, or altered. It is especially important to check with your doctor before combining Cytoxan with the following:

Anticancer drugs such as Adriamycin
Allopurinol (the gout medicine Zyloprim)
Phenobarbital

If you take adrenal steroid hormones because you have had your adrenal glands removed, you are at increased risk for toxic effects from Cytoxan; your dosage of both steroids and Cytoxan may need to be modified.

Special information
if you are pregnant or breastfeeding
If you are pregnant or plan to become pregnant, inform your doctor immediately. When taken during pregnancy, Cytoxan can cause defects in the unborn baby. Women taking Cytoxan should use effective contraception. Cytoxan does appear in breast milk. A new mother will need to choose between taking this drug and nursing her baby.

Recommended dosage

ADULTS AND CHILDREN

Malignant Diseases
Your doctor will tailor your dosage according to your condition and other drugs taken with Cytoxan.

The recommended oral dosage range is 1 to 5 milligrams per 2.2 pounds of body weight per day.

CHILDREN

"Minimal Change" Nephrotic Syndrome
The recommended oral dosage is 2.5 to 3 milligrams per 2.2 pounds of body weight per day for a period of 60 to 90 days.

Overdosage
Although there is no specific information on Cytoxan overdose, any medication taken in excess can have serious consequences. If you suspect an overdose of Cytoxan, seek medical attention immediately.

Brand name:

DALMANE

Pronounced: DAL-main
Generic name: Flurazepam hydrochloride

Why is this drug prescribed?
Dalmane is used for the relief of insomnia, defined as difficulty falling asleep, waking up frequently at night, or waking up early in the morning. It can be used by people whose insomnia keeps coming back and in those who have poor sleeping habits. It belongs to a class of drugs known as benzodiazepines.

Most important fact about this drug
Tolerance and dependence can occur with the use of Dalmane. You may experience withdrawal symptoms if you stop using this drug abruptly. Discontinue or change your dose only in consultation with your doctor.

How should you take this medication?
Take this medication exactly as prescribed.

■ *If you miss a dose...*
Take the dose you missed as soon as you remember, if it is within an hour or so of the scheduled time. If you do not remember it until later, skip the dose you missed and go back to your regular schedule. Do not take 2 doses at once.

■ *Storage instructions...*
Store away from heat, light, and moisture.

What side effects may occur?
Side effects cannot be anticipated. If any develop or change in intensity, inform your doctor as soon as possible. Only your doctor can determine if it is safe for you to continue taking Dalmane.

■ *More common side effects may include:*
Dizziness, drowsiness, falling, lack of muscular coordination, light-headedness, staggering

■ *Less common or rare side effects may include:*
Apprehension, bitter taste, blurred vision, body and joint pain, burning eyes, chest pains, confusion, constipation, depression, diarrhea, difficulty in focusing, dry mouth, exaggerated feeling of well-being, excessive salivation, excitement, faintness, flushes, genital and urinary tract disorders, hallucinations, headache, heartburn, hyperactivity, irritability, itching, loss of appetite, low blood pressure, nausea, nervousness, rapid, fluttery heartbeat, restlessness, shortness of breath, skin rash, slurred speech, stimulation, stomach and intestinal pain, stomach upset, sweating, talkativeness, vomiting, weakness

■ *Side effects due to rapid decrease or abrupt withdrawal from Dalmane:*
Abdominal and muscle cramps, convulsions, depressed mood, inability to fall asleep or stay asleep, sweating, tremors, vomiting

Why should this drug not be prescribed?
If you are sensitive to or have had an allergic reaction to Dalmane or similar drugs such as Valium, you should not take this medication. Make sure your doctor is aware of any drug reactions you have experienced.

Special warnings about this medication
Dalmane will cause you to become drowsy or less alert; therefore, you should not drive or operate dangerous machinery or participate in any hazardous activity that requires full mental alertness after taking Dalmane.

If you are severely depressed or have suffered from severe depression, consult with your doctor before taking this medication.

If you have decreased kidney or liver function or chronic respiratory or lung disease, discuss use of this drug with your doctor.

Possible food and drug interactions
when taking this medication

Alcohol intensifies the effects of Dalmane. Do not drink alcohol while taking this medication.

If Dalmane is taken with certain other drugs, the effects of either could be increased, decreased, or altered. It is especially important to check with your doctor before combining Dalmane with the following:

Antidepressants such as Elavil and Tofranil
Antihistamines such as Benadryl and Tavist
Barbiturates such as Seconal and phenobarbital
Major tranquilizers such as Mellaril and Thorazine
Narcotic painkillers such as Demerol and Tylenol with Codeine
Sedatives such as Xanax and Halcion
Tranquilizers such as Librium and Valium

Special information
if you are pregnant or breastfeeding

Do not take Dalmane if you are pregnant or planning to become pregnant. There is an increased risk of birth defects. This drug may appear in breast milk and could affect a nursing infant. If this medication is essential to your health, your doctor may advise you to discontinue breastfeeding until your treatment with Dalmane is finished.

Recommended dosage

ADULTS

The usual recommended dose is 30 milligrams at bedtime; however, 15 milligrams may be all that is necessary. Your doctor will adjust the dose to your needs.

CHILDREN

Safety and effectiveness of Dalmane have not been established in children under 15 years of age.

OLDER ADULTS

Your doctor will limit the dosage to the smallest effective amount to avoid oversedation, dizziness, confusion, or lack of muscle coordination. The usual starting dose is 15 milligrams.

Overdosage

Any medication taken in excess can cause symptoms of overdose. If you suspect an overdose of Dalmane, seek medical attention immediately.

- *The symptoms of Dalmane overdose may include:*
  Coma, confusion, low blood pressure, sleepiness

Brand name:

DARVOCET-N

Pronounced: DAR-voe-set en
Generic ingredients: Propoxyphene napsylate,
  Acetaminophen
Other brand names: Darvon-N (propoxyphene napsylate),
  Darvon (propoxyphene hydrochloride), Darvon
  Compound-65 (propoxyphene hydrochloride, aspirin, and
  caffeine)

Why is this drug prescribed?

Darvocet-N and Darvon Compound-65 are mild narcotic analgesics prescribed for the relief of mild to moderate pain, with or without fever.

Darvon-N and Darvon are prescribed for the relief of mild to moderate pain.

Most important fact about this drug

You can build up tolerance to, and become dependent on, these drugs if you take them in higher than recommended doses over long periods of time.

How should you take this medication?

Take these drugs exactly as prescribed. Do not increase the amount you take without your doctor's approval. Do not take them for any reason other than those for which they are prescribed. Do not give them to others who may have similar symptoms.

■ *If you miss a dose...*
Take it as soon as you remember. If it is almost time for your next dose, skip the one you missed and go back to your regular schedule. Do not take 2 doses at once.

■ *Storage instructions...*
Store at room temperature.

What side effects may occur?
Side effects cannot be anticipated. If any develop or change in intensity, inform your doctor as soon as possible. Only your doctor can determine if it is safe for you to continue taking one of these medications.

■ *More common side effects may include:*
Drowsiness, dizziness, nausea, sedation, vomiting

If these side effects occur, it may help if you lie down after taking the medication.

■ *Less common side effects may include:*
Abdominal pain, constipation, feelings of elation or depression, hallucinations, headache, kidney problems, light-headedness, liver problems, minor visual disturbances, skin rashes, weakness, yellowed eyes and skin

Why should this drug not be prescribed?
If you are sensitive to or have ever had an allergic reaction to propoxyphene, any of the other ingredients in these drugs, or other pain relievers of this type, you should not take this medication. Make sure your doctor is aware of any drug reactions you have experienced.

Special warnings about this medication
These medicines may cause you to become drowsy or less alert; therefore, you should not drive or operate dangerous machinery or participate in any hazardous activity that requires full mental alertness until you know how the drug affects you.

If you have a kidney or liver disorder, consult your doctor before taking Darvocet-N.

Darvon Compound-65 contains aspirin and caffeine. If you have an ulcer or a blood clotting problem, consult your doctor before taking this medication. Aspirin may irritate the stomach lining and could cause bleeding.

Because there is a possible association between aspirin and the severe neurological disorder known as Reye's syndrome, children and teenagers with chickenpox or flu should not take Darvon Compound-65 unless prescribed by a doctor.

Aspirin may cause asthma attacks. If you have had an asthma attack while taking aspirin, consult your doctor before you take Darvon Compound-65.

Possible food and drug interactions
when taking this medication

The propoxyphene in these drugs slows down the central nervous system and intensifies the effects of alcohol. Heavy use of alcohol with this drug may cause overdose symptoms. Therefore, limit or avoid use of alcohol while you are taking this medication.

If these medications are taken with certain other drugs, the effects of either could be increased, decreased, or altered. It is especially important to check with your doctor before combining them with the following:

Antiseizure medications such as Tegretol
Antidepressant drugs such as Elavil
Antihistamines such as Benadryl
Muscle relaxants such as Flexeril
Narcotic pain relievers such as Demerol
Sleep aids such as Halcion
Tranquilizers such as Xanax and Valium
Warfarin-like drugs such as Coumadin

The use of these drugs with propoxyphene can lead to potentially fatal overdose symptoms.

Severe neurologic disorders, including coma, have occurred with the use of propoxyphene in combination with Tegretol.

The use of anticoagulants (blood thinners such as Coumadin) in combination with Darvon Compound-65 may cause bleeding. If you are taking an anticoagulant, consult your doctor before taking this drug.

The use of aspirin with drugs for gout may alter the effects of the antigout medication. Consult your doctor before taking Darvon Compound-65.

Special information
if you are pregnant or breastfeeding

Do not take these medications if you are pregnant or planning to become pregnant unless you are directed to do so by your doctor. Temporary drug dependence may occur in newborns when the mother has taken this drug consistently in the weeks before delivery. The use of Darvon Compound-65 (which contains aspirin) during pregnancy may cause problems in the developing baby or complications during delivery. Do not take it during the last 3 months of pregnancy. Darvocet-N does appear in breast milk. However, no adverse effects have been found in nursing infants.

Recommended dosage

ADULTS

These medicines may be taken every 4 hours as needed for pain. The usual doses are:

Darvocet-N 50: 2 tablets

Darvocet-N 100: 1 tablet

Darvon: 1 capsule

Darvon Compound-65: 1 capsule

Your doctor may lower the total daily dosage if you have kidney or liver problems.

The most you should take of Darvon or Darvon Compound-65 is 6 capsules a day.

CHILDREN

The safety and effectiveness of Darvocet-N have not been established in children.

OLDER ADULTS

Your doctor may lengthen the time between doses.

Overdosage

Any medication taken in excess can have serious consequences. If you suspect an overdose, seek medical attention immediately.

- *Symptoms of a propoxyphene overdose may include:*
  Bluish tinge to the skin, coma, convulsions, decreased or difficult breathing to the point of temporary stoppage, decreased heart function, extreme sleepiness, irregular heartbeat, low blood pressure, pinpoint pupils becoming dilated later, stupor

- *Additional symptoms of overdose with Darvocet-N:*
  Abdominal pain, excessive sweating, general feeling of illness, kidney failure, liver problems, loss of appetite, nausea, vomiting

■ *Additional symptoms of overdose with Darvon Compound-65:*
Confusion, deafness, excessive perspiration, headache, mental dullness, nausea, rapid breathing, rapid pulse, ringing in the ears, vertigo, vomiting

Extreme overdosage may lead to unconsciousness and death.

Brand name:

DARVON

See Darvocet-N, page 312.

Brand name:

DARVON COMPOUND-65

See Darvocet-N, page 312.

Brand name:

DARVON-N

See Darvocet-N, page 312.

Brand name:

DAYPRO

Pronounced: DAY-pro
Generic name: Oxaprozin

Why is this drug prescribed?
Daypro is a nonsteroidal anti-inflammatory drug used to relieve the inflammation, swelling, stiffness, and joint pain associated with rheumatoid arthritis and osteoarthritis (the most common kind of arthritis).

Most important fact about this drug
You should have frequent check-ups with your doctor if you take Daypro regularly. Ulcers and internal bleeding can occur without warning.

How should you take this medication?
Take Daypro with a full glass of water. If the drug upsets your stomach, your doctor may recommend taking Daypro with food, milk, or an antacid, even though food may delay onset of relief.

It will also help to prevent irritation in your upper digestive tract if you avoid lying down for about 20 minutes after taking Daypro.

Take this medication exactly as prescribed.

■ *If you miss a dose...*
Try to take Daypro at the same time each day—for example, after breakfast. If you forget to take a dose and remember later in the day, you can still take it. If you completely forget to take your medication, do *not* double the dose the next day to make up for the missed dose. You should get back on your normal schedule as soon as possible.

■ *Storage instructions...*
Store at room temperature in a tightly closed container, away from light.

What side effects may occur?
Side effects cannot be anticipated. If any develop or change in intensity, tell your doctor as soon as possible. Only your doctor can decide if it is safe for you to continue taking Daypro.

■ *More common side effects may include:*
Constipation, diarrhea, indigestion, nausea, rash

■ *Less common side effects may include:*
Abdominal pain, confusion, depression, frequent or painful urination, gas, loss of appetite, ringing in the ears, sleep disturbances, sleepiness, vomiting

■ *Rare side effects may include:*
Anaphylaxis (a severe allergic reaction), anemia, blood in the urine, blood pressure changes, blurred vision, bruising, changes in kidney and liver function, decreased menstrual flow, fluid retention, general feeling of illness, hemorrhoidal or rectal bleeding, hepatitis, hives, inflammation of the mouth, inflammation of the pancreas, irritated eyes, itching, peptic ulcerations, respiratory infection, sensitivity to light, stomach and intestinal bleeding, weight gain or loss, weakness

Why should this drug not be prescribed?
If you are sensitive to or have ever had an allergic reaction to Daypro, or if you have ever developed asthma, nasal tumors, or other allergic reactions due to aspirin or other nonsteroidal anti-inflammatory drugs, you should not take this medication. Make sure your doctor is aware of any drug reactions you have experienced.

Special warnings about this medication
Use Daypro with caution if you have kidney or liver disease.

Do not take aspirin or any other anti-inflammatory medications while taking Daypro, unless your doctor tells you to do so.

Daypro can increase water retention. Use with caution if you have heart disease or high blood pressure.

If you are taking Daypro for an extended period, your doctor should check your blood for anemia.

Daypro can prolong bleeding time. If you are taking a blood-thinning medication, use Daypro with caution.

Daypro may cause sensitivity to sunlight. Avoid prolonged exposure to the sun. Use sunscreens and wear protective clothing.

Do not use Daypro if you are planning to have surgery in the immediate future.

**Possible food and drug interactions
when taking this medication**
If you take Daypro with certain other drugs, the effects of either medication could be increased, decreased, or altered. It is especially important to check with your doctor before combining Daypro with the following medications:

Aspirin
Beta-blocking blood pressure medications such as Inderal and Tenormin
Blood thinners such as Coumadin
Digitalis and digoxin (Lanoxin)
Diuretics such as Lasix and Midamor
Lithium (Lithonate)
Ulcer drugs such as Tagamet and Zantac

Avoid alcoholic beverages while taking Daypro.

**Special information
if you are pregnant or breastfeeding**
The effects of Daypro during pregnancy have not been adequately studied. If you are pregnant or plan to become pregnant, tell your doctor immediately. Since the effects of Daypro on nursing infants are not known, tell your doctor if you are nursing or plan to nurse. If Daypro treatment is necessary for your health, your doctor may tell you to discontinue nursing until your treatment is finished.

Recommended dosage

ADULTS

Your doctor will adjust the dose based on your needs.

Rheumatoid Arthritis

The usual daily dose is 1200 milligrams (two 600-milligram caplets) once a day.

Osteoarthritis

The usual starting dose for moderate to severe osteoarthritis is 1200 milligrams (two 600-milligram caplets) once a day.

The most you should take in a day is 1800 milligrams divided into smaller doses, or 26 milligrams per 2.2 pounds of body weight, whichever is lower.

CHILDREN

The safety and efficacy of Daypro in children have not been determined.

Overdosage

If you take too much of any medication, it can have serious consequences. If you suspect an overdose, seek medical attention immediately.

■ *Symptoms of Daypro overdose may include:*
Coma, drowsiness, fatigue, nausea, pain in the stomach, stomach and intestinal bleeding, vomiting

Acute kidney failure, high blood pressure, and a slowdown in breathing have occurred rarely.

Brand name:

DDAVP

Pronounced: dee-dee-ai-vee-pee
Generic name: Desmopressin acetate
Other brand name: Stimate

Why is this drug prescribed?

DDAVP nasal spray, nose drops, and tablets are given to prevent or control the frequent urination and loss of water associated with diabetes insipidus (a rare condition characterized by very large quantities of diluted urine and excessive thirst). They are also used to treat frequent passage of urine and increased thirst in people with certain brain injuries, and those who have undergone surgery in the pituitary region of the brain. DDAVP nasal spray and nose drops are also prescribed to help stop some types of bed-wetting.

Stimate nasal spray is used to stop bleeding in certain types of hemophilia (failure of the blood to clot).

Most important fact about this drug

When taking DDAVP, elderly and young people in particular should limit their fluid intake to no more than what satisfies thirst. Although extremely rare, there is a possibility of water intoxication, in which reduced sodium levels in the blood can lead to seizures.

How should you use this medication?

Use DDAVP exactly as prescribed. The spray and drops are for nasal use only; never swallow the medication or allow the liquid to run into your mouth.

Your doctor may increase or decrease your dosage, depending on how you respond to DDAVP. Your response will be judged by how long you are able to sleep without having to get up to urinate and how much urine your kidneys produce.

The DDAVP nasal spray pump bottle accurately delivers 50 doses of the medication. After the 50th dose, the amount of medication that comes out with each spray will no longer be a full dose. When this happens, throw the bottle away even if it is not completely empty.

Stimate nasal spray delivers 25 doses; the same instructions apply. The Stimate nasal spray pump must be primed before you use it for the first time: Press down 4 times.

Since the DDAVP spray bottle delivers only a standard-sized dose, those who need more or less medication should use the nose drops instead of the spray.

If nasal congestion, scars, or swelling inside the nose make it difficult to absorb DDAVP, your doctor may temporarily stop the drug or give you tablets or an injectable form. If you are switched to tablets, you should start taking them 12 hours after you last used the nasal spray or nose drops.

■ *If you miss a dose...*
Take the forgotten dose as soon as you remember. If you take 1 dose a day and don't remember until the next day, skip the dose. If you take DDAVP more than once a day and it is almost time for the next dose, skip the one

you missed and go back to your regular schedule. Never try to "catch up" by doubling the dose.

■ *Storage instructions...*
The drops should be stored in the refrigerator. If you are traveling, they will stay fresh at room temperature for up to 3 weeks.

The tablets and nasal spray can be kept at room temperature. Protect the tablets from heat and light.

What side effects may occur?
Too high a dosage of DDAVP nasal spray or drops may produce headache, nausea, mild abdominal cramps, stuffy nose, irritation of the nose, or flushing. These symptoms will probably disappear when the dosage is reduced. Some people have complained of nosebleed, sore throat, cough, or a cold or other upper respiratory infections after taking DDAVP nasal spray or drops.

■ *Other potential side effects include:*
Abdominal pain, chills, conjunctivitis (pinkeye), depression, dizziness, inability to produce tears, leg rash, nostril pain, rash, stomach or intestinal upset, swelling around the eyes, weakness

■ *Side effects of Stimate nasal spray may include:*
Agitation, chest pain, chills, dizziness, fluid retention and swelling, indigestion, inflammation of the penis, insomnia, itchy or light-sensitive eyes, pain, pounding heartbeat, rapid heartbeat, sleepiness, vomiting, warm feeling

Why should this drug not be prescribed?
Do not use DDAVP if you are sensitive to or have ever had an allergic reaction to any of its ingredients.

Special warnings about this medication
If you have cystic fibrosis or any other condition in which there is fluid and electrolyte imbalance, you should use DDAVP with extreme caution.

Because DDAVP may cause a rise in blood pressure, use this medication cautiously if you have high blood pressure and/or coronary artery disease. Your blood pressure could also fall temporarily. If you continue to experience bleeding after using Stimate nasal spray, contact your doctor.

**Possible food and drug interactions
when taking this medication**

If DDAVP is taken with certain other drugs, the effects of either could be increased, decreased, or altered. It is especially important to check with your doctor before combining DDAVP with the following:

Any drug used to increase blood pressure
Clofibrate (Atromid-S)
Glyburide (Micronase)
Epinephrine (EpiPen)

**Special information
if you are pregnant or breastfeeding**

If you are pregnant or plan to become pregnant, inform your doctor immediately. Although DDAVP is not known to cause birth defects, it should be used with caution. DDAVP should be taken during pregnancy only if clearly needed. DDAVP is not believed to appear in breast milk. However, check with your doctor before using the drug while breastfeeding.

Recommended dosage

Your doctor will carefully tailor your dosage to meet your individual needs.

CENTRAL CRANIAL DIABETES INSIPIDUS

DDAVP Nasal Spray and Nose Drops

Adults: The usual recommended dosage range is 0.1 to 0.4 milliliter daily, either as a single dose or divided into 2 or 3 doses. Most adults require 0.2 milliliter per day divided into 2 doses.

Children: The usual dosage range for children aged 3 months to 12 years is 0.05 to 0.3 milliliter daily, either as a single dose or divided into 2 doses.

DDAVP Tablets

Adults and Children Aged 4 and Over: The usual starting dose is half of a 0.1-milligram tablet twice a day. Your doctor will adjust the dose to suit you. You will eventually take 0.1 to 1.2 milligrams a day, divided into smaller doses.

PRIMARY NOCTURNAL ENURESIS (BEDWETTING)

DDAVP Nasal Spray/Nose Drops

Children 6 Years of Age and Older: The usual recommended dose is 20 micrograms or 0.2 milliliter at bedtime. Dosage requirements range from 10 to 40 micrograms. One-half the dose should be taken in each nostril.

HEMOPHILIA

Stimate Nasal Spray

To stop bleeding, the usual dose is one 150-microgram spray in each nostril. If you use the spray more frequently than every 48 hours, you may find you are not responding as well as you should to the drug.

Overdosage

An overdose of DDAVP may cause abdominal cramps, flushing, headache, or nausea. If you suspect an overdose of DDAVP, seek medical attention immediately.

Brand name:

DECADRON TABLETS

Pronounced: DECK-uh-drohn
Generic name: Dexamethasone

Why is this drug prescribed?

Decadron, a corticosteroid drug, is used to reduce inflammation and relieve symptoms in a variety of disorders, including rheumatoid arthritis and severe cases of asthma. It may be given to people to treat primary or secondary adrenal cortex insufficiency (lack of sufficient adrenal hormone). It is also given to help treat the following disorders:

Severe allergic conditions such as drug-induced allergies
Blood disorders such as various anemias
Certain cancers (along with other drugs)
Skin diseases such as severe psoriasis
Collagen (connective tissue) diseases such as systemic lupus
    erythematosus
Digestive tract disease such as ulcerative colitis
High serum levels of calcium associated with cancer
Fluid retention due to nephrotic syndrome (a condition in which damage
    to the kidneys causes the body to lose protein in the urine)
Eye diseases such as allergic conjunctivitis
Lung diseases such as tuberculosis (along with other drugs)

Most important fact about this drug

Decadron lowers your resistance to infections and can make them harder to treat. Decadron may also mask some of the signs of an infection, making it difficult for your doctor to diagnose the actual problem.

How should you take this medication?
Decadron should be taken exactly as prescribed by your doctor.

If you are taking large doses, your doctor may advise you to take Decadron with meals and to take antacids between meals, to prevent a peptic ulcer from developing.

Check with your doctor before stopping Decadron abruptly. If you have been taking the drug for a long time, you may need to reduce your dose gradually over a period of days or weeks.

The lowest possible dose should always be used, and as symptoms subside, dosage should be reduced gradually.

■ *If you miss a dose...*
Take the forgotten dose as soon as you remember. If it is almost time for the next dose, skip the one you missed and go back to your regular schedule. Never try to "catch up" by doubling the dose.

■ *Storage instructions...*
There are no special storage requirements.

What side effects may occur?
Side effects cannot be anticipated. If any develop or change in intensity, inform your doctor as soon as possible. Only your doctor can determine if it is safe for you to continue taking Decadron.

■ *Side effects may include:*
Abdominal distention, allergic reactions, blood clots, bone fractures and degeneration, bruises, cataracts, congestive heart failure, convulsions, "cushingoid" symptoms (moon face, weight gain, high blood pressure, emotional disturbances, growth of facial hair in women), excessive hairiness, fluid and salt retention, general feeling of illness, glaucoma, headache, hiccups, high blood pressure, hives, increased appetite, increased eye pressure, increased pressure in head, increased sweating, increases in amounts of insulin or hypoglycemic medications needed in diabetes, inflammation of the esophagus, inflammation of the pancreas, irregular menstruation, loss of muscle mass, low potassium levels in blood (leading to symptoms such as dry mouth, excessive thirst, weak or irregular heartbeat, and muscle pain or cramps), muscle weakness, nausea, osteoporosis, peptic ulcer, perforated small and large bowel, poor healing of wounds, protruding eyeballs, suppression of growth in children, thin skin, tiny red or purplish spots on the skin, torn tendons, vertigo, weight gain

Why should this drug not be prescribed?
Decadron should not be used if you have a fungal infection, or if you are sensitive or allergic to any of its ingredients.

Special warnings about this medication
Decadron can alter the way your body responds to unusual stress. If you are injured, need surgery, or develop an acute illness, inform your doctor. Your dosage may need to be increased.

Corticosteroids such as Decadron can lower your resistance to infection. Diseases such as measles and chickenpox can be serious and even fatal in adults. Likewise, a simple case of threadworm can run rampant, producing life-threatening complications. If you are taking Decadron and are exposed to chickenpox or measles—or suspect a case of threadworm—notify your doctor immediately. Symptoms of threadworm include stomach pain, vomiting, and diarrhea.

Do not get a smallpox vaccination or any other immunizations while taking Decadron, especially in high doses. The vaccination might not take, and could do harm to the nervous system.

Decadron may reactivate a dormant case of tuberculosis. If you have inactive tuberculosis and must take Decadron for an extended period, your doctor will prescribe anti-TB medication as well.

When you stop taking Decadron after long-term therapy, you may develop withdrawal symptoms such as fever, muscle or joint pain, and a feeling of illness.

Long-term use of Decadron may cause cataracts, glaucoma, and eye infections.

If you have any of the following conditions, make sure your doctor knows about it:

Allergy to any cortisone-like drug
Cirrhosis
Diabetes
Diverticulitis
Eye infection (herpes simplex)
Glaucoma
High blood pressure
Impaired thyroid function
Kidney disease
Myasthenia gravis (a muscle disorder)

Osteoporosis (brittle bones)
Peptic ulcer
Recent heart attack
Tuberculosis
Ulcerative colitis

Steroids may alter male fertility.

This medication can aggravate existing emotional problems or cause emotional disturbances. Symptoms range from an exaggerated sense of well-being and difficulty sleeping to mood swings and psychotic episodes. If you experience any changes in mood, contact your doctor.

If you have recently been to the tropics or are suffering from diarrhea with no apparent cause, inform your doctor before taking Decadron.

Possible food and drug interactions
when taking this medication

If Decadron is taken with certain other drugs, the effects of either could be increased, decreased, or altered. It is especially important to check with your doctor before combining Decadron with the following:

Aspirin
Blood-thinning medications such as Coumadin
Ephedrine (a decongestant in drugs such as Marax and Rynatuss)
Indomethacin (Indocin)
Phenobarbital
Phenytoin (Dilantin)
Rifampin (Rifadin, Rimactane)
Water pills that pull potassium out of the system, such as HydroDIURIL

Special information
if you are pregnant or breastfeeding

The effects of Decadron during pregnancy have not been adequately studied. If you are pregnant or plan to become pregnant, inform your doctor immediately. Infants born to mothers who have taken substantial doses of corticosteroids during pregnancy should be carefully watched for adrenal problems. Corticosteroids appear in breast milk and can suppress growth in infants. If Decadron is essential to your health, your doctor may advise you to stop breastfeeding until your treatment with Decadron is finished.

Recommended dosage

ADULTS

Your doctor will tailor your individual dose to the condition being treated. Initial doses range from 0.75 milligram to 9 milligrams a day.

After the drug produces a satisfactory response, your doctor will gradually lower the dose to the minimum effective level.

Overdosage

Reports of overdose with this medication are rare. However, if you suspect an overdose, seek medical treatment immediately.

Brand name:

DECADRON TURBINAIRE AND RESPIHALER

Pronounced: DECK-ah-drahn tur-bin-AIR and RESS-pi-hail-er
Generic name: Dexamethasone sodium phosphate
Other brand name: Dexacort

Why is this drug prescribed?

Decadron is a synthetic adrenocortical steroid (a hormone created in the laboratory). Decadron Turbinaire is used to treat hay fever and other nasal allergies, and to assist in the treatment of nasal polyps. Decadron Respihaler is prescribed for bronchial asthma in people who need sustained treatment.

Most important fact about this drug

Decadron lowers your resistance to infections and can make them harder to treat. Decadron may also mask some of the signs of an infection, making it difficult for your doctor to diagnose the actual problem.

How should you take this medication?

These medications come with directions. Read them carefully before using the medicine. To work, the medications must be used exactly as directed.

If you are using the Decadron Respihaler, gargling and rinsing your mouth with water after each dose may help prevent hoarseness and throat irritation. Do not swallow the water after you rinse.

■ *If you miss a dose...*
Take the forgotten dose as soon as possible and take the remaining doses for that day at evenly spaced intervals. If it is time for your next dose, skip the one you missed. Never take a double dose.

■ *Storage instructions...*
Store Decadron at room temperature. Since the contents are under pressure, keep the container away from fire or extreme heat.

What side effects may occur?
Side effects cannot be anticipated. If any develop or change in intensity, inform your doctor as soon as possible. Only your doctor can determine whether it is safe to continue using Decadron.

■ *More common side effects of Decadron Turbinaire may include:*
Nasal dryness and irritation

■ *Less common side effects of Decadron Turbinaire may include:*
Bronchial asthma, headache, hives, light-headedness, loss of smell, nausea, nosebleeds, perforated nasal septum (dividing wall of the nose), rebound nasal congestion

■ *Side effects of Decadron Respihaler may include:*
Coughing, fungal infections in the throat, hoarseness, throat irritation

■ *Side effects that may occur when Decadron is absorbed into the bloodstream:*
Abdominal distention, abnormal skin redness, allergic reactions, blood clots, bruising, cataracts, congestive heart failure, convulsions, development of Cushing's syndrome (moon face, emotional disturbances, high blood pressure, weight gain, and growth of facial and body hair in women), diabetes, emotional disturbances, excessive hairiness, fractures of the long bones, fractures of the vertebrae, fragile skin, glaucoma, headache, hiccups, high blood pressure, hives, increased appetite, increased eye pressure, increased pressure in head), increased sweating, loss of muscle mass, menstrual irregularities, muscle weakness, nausea, osteoporosis, perforated small or large bowel, poor wound healing, potassium loss, protruding eyeballs, reddish or purplish spots on the skin, ruptured tendons, salt and fluid retention, stomach ulcer, ulcer of the esophagus, vague feeling of weakness, vertigo, weight gain

Why should this drug not be prescribed?

Do not use Decadron if you have a fungal infection or if you have ever had an allergic reaction or are sensitive to any cortisone-like medication such as Beclovent. Decadron Turbinaire should not be used if you have tuberculosis or a nasal condition caused by a virus or a fungus, or if you have herpes simplex infection of the eye. Decadron Respihaler should not be used if tests show that you have a yeast infection (*Candida albicans*).

Special warnings about this medication

Decadron does not expand the bronchial passages, and should be used for asthma only if bronchodilators and other asthma medications are not effective. Decadron does not provide rapid relief of symptoms, but does help to control asthma when taken routinely.

Decadron can alter the way your body responds to unusual stress. If you are injured, need surgery, or develop an acute illness, tell your doctor. Your dosage may need to be increased.

If you develop an infection of the throat or voice box while using the Decadron Respihaler, stop using the Respihaler and notify your doctor. You will need medication.

Corticosteroids such as Decadron may mask the symptoms of infection and make you more susceptible to infections. Diseases such as chickenpox and measles can be serious and even fatal in adults who have never had these illnesses. If you are using Decadron Turbinaire or Respihaler and are exposed to chickenpox or measles, notify your doctor immediately. Do not get a smallpox vaccination or any other immunizations while taking Decadron, especially in high doses. The vaccination might not take, and could do harm to the nervous system.

Using Decadron for a long time may cause cataracts, glaucoma, and eye infections.

Large doses of Decadron may raise blood pressure and increase salt and water retention. If this happens, your doctor may tell you to restrict salt in your diet.

Decadron should be used with extreme caution if you have dormant tuberculosis or test positive for tuberculosis. Decadron may reactivate the disease.

When you stop taking Decadron after long-term therapy, you may develop withdrawal symptoms such as fever, muscle or joint pain, and weakness.

Decadron should be used with care if you have an underactive thyroid or cirrhosis.

Your doctor will prescribe the lowest possible dose to control your condition, and reduce your dosage of Decadron gradually. Do not suddenly stop taking it.

Decadron may aggravate existing emotional problems or cause emotional disturbances. Symptoms range from euphoria (an exaggerated sense of well-being) and difficulty sleeping to mood swings, personality changes, severe depression, and psychotic episodes. If you experience any changes in mood, call your doctor.

Decadron should be used with care if you have ulcerative colitis, diverticulitis (an inflammation of the digestive tract), peptic ulcer, kidney disease, high blood pressure, osteoporosis, or myasthenia gravis (muscle weakness, especially in the face and neck), or if you have recently had a heart attack.

Long-term therapy with Decadron may affect the growth and development of children and should be carefully checked by your doctor. Decadron Turbinaire is not recommended for children under 6 years of age.

If you have recently been to the tropics or are suffering from diarrhea with no apparent cause, inform your doctor before using Decadron.

Possible food and drug interactions
when taking this medication

If Decadron is taken with certain other drugs, the effects of either could be increased, decreased, or altered. It is especially important to check with your doctor before combining Decadron with the following:

Aspirin
Blood thinners such as Coumadin
Ephedrine
Phenytoin (Dilantin)
Phenobarbital (Bellergal-S, Donnatal, others)
Potassium-depleting diuretics such as Dyazide and Esidrix
Rifampin (Rifadin, Rimactane)

Special information
if you are pregnant or breastfeeding

The effects of Decadron during pregnancy have not been adequately studied. If you are pregnant or plan to become pregnant, inform your doctor immediately. Infants born to mothers who have taken substantial doses of steroids during pregnancy may have problems with their adrenal glands. Corticosteroids appear in breast milk and could affect infant growth or cause other damaging effects. Decadron is not recommended for nursing mothers. If Decadron is essential to your health, your doctor may advise you to stop breastfeeding until your treatment with Decadron is finished.

Recommended dosage

TURBINAIRE

Adults

The usual initial dosage is 2 sprays in each nostril, 2 or 3 times a day.

Children (6 to 12 Years of Age)

The usual initial dosage is 1 or 2 sprays in each nostril 2 times a day, depending on age.

Dosage should be gradually reduced when improvement occurs. The maximum daily dosage for adults is 12 sprays and for children, 8 sprays. Therapy should be stopped as soon as possible. If symptoms return, your doctor may start the medication again.

RESPIHALER

Adults

The recommended initial dose is 3 inhalations, 3 or 4 times a day.

Children

The recommended initial dose is 2 inhalations, 3 or 4 times a day.

Dosage should be gradually reduced when improvement occurs. The maximum daily dosage for adults is 3 inhalations per dose, 12 inhalations per day; and for children, 2 inhalations per dose, 8 inhalations per day.

Overdosage

There have been rare reports of toxicity (poisoning) and death following steroid overdose. If you suspect Decadron overdose, seek medical treatment immediately.

Brand name:

DECONAMINE

Pronounced: dee-CON-uh-meen
Generic ingredients: Chlorpheniramine maleate,
d-Pseudoephedrine hydrochloride

Why is this drug prescribed?

Deconamine is an antihistamine and decongestant used for the temporary relief of persistent runny nose, sneezing, and nasal congestion caused by upper respiratory infections (the common cold), sinus inflammation, or hay fever. It is also used to help clear nasal passages and shrink swollen membranes and to drain the sinuses and relieve sinus pressure.

Most important fact about this drug
Deconamine may cause you to become drowsy or less alert. You should not drive or operate machinery or participate in any activity that requires full mental alertness until you know how you react to Deconamine.

How should you take this medication?
If Deconamine makes you nervous or restless, or you have trouble sleeping, take the last dose of the day a few hours before you go to bed. Take Deconamine exactly as prescribed.

Antihistamines can make your mouth and throat dry. It may help to suck on hard candy, chew gum, or melt bits of ice in your mouth.

- *If you miss a dose...*
  Take it as soon as you remember. If it is almost time for your next dose, skip the one you missed and go back to your regular schedule. Never take 2 doses at once.

- *Storage instructions...*
  Store at room temperature.

What side effects may occur?
Side effects cannot be anticipated. If any develop or change in intensity, inform your doctor as soon as possible. Only your doctor can determine if it is safe for you to continue taking Deconamine.

The most common side effect is mild to moderate drowsiness.

- *Less common or rare side effects may include:*
  Anaphylactic shock (extreme allergic reaction), anemia, anxiety, blurred vision, breathing difficulty, chills, confusion, constipation, convulsion, diarrhea, difficulty sleeping, difficulty in carrying out movements, disturbed coordination, dizziness, double vision, dry mouth, nose, and throat, early menstruation, exaggerated sense of well being, excessive perspiration, excitation, fatigue, extreme calm (sedation), fear, frequent or difficult urination, hallucinations, headache, hives, hysteria, increased chest congestion, irregular heartbeat, irritability, light-headedness, loss of appetite, low blood pressure, nausea, nervousness, painful urination, pallor, pounding heartbeat, rapid heartbeat, restlessness, ringing in ears, sensitivity to light, skin rash, stomach upset or pain, stuffy nose,

tenseness, tightness of chest, tingling or numbness, tremor, unusual bleeding or bruising, vertigo, vomiting, weakness, wheezing

Why should this drug not be prescribed?
Do not use Deconamine if you have severe high blood pressure or severe heart disease, are taking an antidepressant drug known as an MAO inhibitor (Nardil, Parnate, others), or are sensitive to or have ever had an allergic reaction to antihistamines or decongestants.

Special warnings about this medication
Use Deconamine with extreme caution if you have the eye condition called glaucoma, peptic ulcer or stomach obstructions, an enlarged prostate, or difficulty urinating.

Also use caution if you have bronchial asthma, emphysema, chronic lung disease, high blood pressure, heart disease, diabetes, or an overactive thyroid.

Deconamine may cause excitability, especially in children.

Possible food and drug interactions
when taking this medication
Alcohol increases the sedative effect of Deconamine. Avoid it while taking this medication.

If Deconamine is taken with certain other drugs, the effects of either may be increased, decreased, or altered. It is especially important to check with your doctor before combining Deconamine with the following:

Antidepressant drugs such as the MAO inhibitors Nardil and Parnate
Asthma medications such as Ventolin and Proventil
Bromocriptine (Parlodel)
Mecamylamine (Inversine)
Methyldopa (Aldomet)
Narcotic pain killers such as Demerol and Percocet
Phenytoin (Dilantin)
Reserpine (Ser-Ap-Es, others)
Sleep aids such as Halcion and Seconal
Tranquilizers such as Valium and Xanax

Special information
if you are pregnant or breastfeeding
The effects of Deconamine during pregnancy have not been adequately studied. If you are pregnant or plan to become pregnant, notify your doctor immediately. Deconamine appears in breast milk and could affect a nursing

infant. If this medication is essential to your health, your doctor may advise you to discontinue breastfeeding until your treatment with Deconamine is finished.

Recommended dosage

DECONAMINE TABLETS

Adults and Children over 12 Years
The usual dosage is 1 tablet 3 or 4 times daily.

Children under 12 Years
Use Deconamine Syrup or Chewable Tablets instead of the tablets.

DECONAMINE SYRUP

Adults and Children over 12 Years
The usual dose is 1 to 2 teaspoonfuls (5 to 10 milliliters) 3 or 4 times daily.

Children 6 to 12 Years
The usual dose is ½ to 1 teaspoonful (2.5 to 5 milliliters) 3 or 4 times daily, not to exceed 4 teaspoonfuls in 24 hours.

Children 2 to 6 Years
The usual dose is ½ teaspoonful (2.5 milliliters) 3 or 4 times daily, not to exceed 2 teaspoonfuls in 24 hours.

Children under 2 Years
Use as directed by your doctor.

DECONAMINE SR CAPSULES

Adults and Children over 12 Years
The usual dose is 1 capsule every 12 hours.

Children under 12 Years
Use Deconamine Syrup or Chewable Tablets instead of the capsules.

DECONAMINE CHEWABLE TABLETS

Adults
The usual dose is 2 tablets 3 or 4 times a day.

Children 6 to 12 Years
The usual dose is 1 tablet 3 or 4 times a day.

Children 2 to 6 Years
The usual dose is ½ tablet 3 or 4 times a day.

Overdosage
Any medication taken in excess can have serious consequences. If you suspect an overdose, seek medical attention immediately.

■ *Symptoms of Deconamine overdose include:*
Convulsions, diminished alertness, hallucinations, severe drowsiness, severe dryness of mouth, nose, and throat, shortness of breath/difficulty breathing, sleep problems, slow or rapid heartbeat, tremors

Brand name:

DELTASONE

Pronounced: DELL-tuh-zone
Generic name: Prednisone
Other brand name: Orasone

Why is this drug prescribed?
Deltasone, a steroid drug, is used to reduce inflammation and alleviate symptoms in a variety of disorders, including rheumatoid arthritis and severe cases of asthma. It may be given to treat primary or secondary adrenal cortex insufficiency (lack of sufficient adrenal hormone in the body). It is used in treating all of the following:

Abnormal adrenal gland development
Allergic conditions (severe)
Blood disorders
Certain cancers (along with other drugs)
Diseases of the connective tissue including systemic lupus
    erythematosus
Eye diseases of various kinds
Flare-ups of multiple sclerosis
Fluid retention due to "nephrotic syndrome" (a condition in which
    damage to the kidneys causes protein to be lost in the urine)
Lung diseases, including tuberculosis

Meningitis (inflamed membranes around the brain)
Prevention of organ rejection
Rheumatoid arthritis and related disorders
Severe flare-ups of ulcerative colitis or enteritis (inflammation of the intestines)
Skin diseases
Thyroid gland inflammation
Trichinosis (with complications)

Most important fact about this drug
Deltasone lowers your resistance to infections and can make them harder to treat. Deltasone may also mask some of the signs of an infection, making it difficult for your doctor to diagnose the actual problem.

How should you take this medication?
Take Deltasone exactly as prescribed. Dosages are kept to an absolute minimum.

If you need long-term Deltasone treatment, your doctor may prescribe alternate-day therapy, in which you take the medication only every other morning. The "resting day" gives your adrenal glands a chance to produce some hormone naturally so they will not lose the ability.

If you have been taking Deltasone for a period of time, you will probably need an increased dosage of the medication before, during, and after any stressful situation. Always consult your doctor if you are anticipating stress and think you may need a temporary dosage increase.

When stopping Deltasone treatment, tapering off is better than quitting abruptly. Your doctor will probably have you decrease the dosage very gradually over a period of days or weeks.

You should take Deltasone with food to avoid stomach upset.

If you are on alternate-day therapy or have been prescribed a single daily dose, take Deltasone in the morning with breakfast (about 8 AM). If you have been prescribed several doses per day, take them at evenly spaced intervals around the clock.

Patients on long-term Deltasone therapy should wear or carry identification.

■ *If you miss a dose...*
   If you take your dose once a day, take it as soon as you remember. If you don't remember until the next day, skip the one you missed.

If you take several doses a day, take the forgotten dose as soon as you remember and then go back to your regular schedule. If you don't remember until your next dose, double the dose you take.

If you take your dose every other day, and you remember it the same morning, take it as soon as you remember, then go back to your regular schedule. If you don't remember until the afternoon, do not take a dose until the following morning, then skip a day.

■ *Storage instructions...*
Store at room temperature.

What side effects may occur?
Side effects cannot be anticipated. If any develop or change in intensity, inform your doctor as soon as possible. Only your doctor can determine if it is safe for you to continue taking Deltasone.

Deltasone may cause euphoria, insomnia, mood changes, personality changes, psychotic behavior, or severe depression. It may worsen any existing emotional instability.

At a high dosage, Deltasone may cause fluid retention and high blood pressure. If this happens, you may need a low-salt diet and a potassium supplement.

With prolonged Deltasone treatment, eye problems may develop (e.g., a viral or fungal eye infection, cataracts, or glaucoma).

If you take Deltasone over the long term, the buildup of adrenal hormones in your body may cause a condition called Cushing's syndrome, marked by weight gain, a "moon-faced" appearance, thin, fragile skin, muscle weakness, brittle bones, and purplish stripe marks on the skin. Women are more vulnerable to this problem than men. Alternate-day therapy may help prevent its development.

■ *Other potential side effects from Deltasone include:*
Bone fractures, bruising, bulging eyes, congestive heart failure, convulsions, distended abdomen, face redness, glaucoma, headache, hives and other allergic-type reactions, increased pressure inside eyes or skull, inflamed esophagus or pancreas, irregular menstrual periods, muscle weakness or disease, osteoporosis, peptic ulcer, poor healing of wounds, stunted growth (in children), sweating, thin, fragile skin, vertigo

Why should this drug not be prescribed?
Do not take Deltasone if you have ever had an allergic reaction to it.

You should not be treated with Deltasone if you have a body-wide fungus infection, such as candidiasis or cryptococcosis.

Special warnings about this medication

Do not get a smallpox vaccination or any other immunization while you are taking Deltasone. The vaccination might not "take," and could do harm to the nervous system.

Deltasone may reactivate a dormant case of tuberculosis. If you have inactive TB and must take Deltasone for an extended time, you should be given anti-TB medication as well.

If you have an underactive thyroid gland or cirrhosis of the liver, your doctor will probably need to prescribe Deltasone for you at a lower-than-average dosage.

If you have an eye infection caused by the herpes simplex virus, Deltasone should be used with great caution; there is a potential danger that the cornea will become perforated.

A few people taking Deltasone develop Kaposi's sarcoma, a form of cancer; it may disappear when the drug is stopped.

Deltasone should also be taken with caution if you have any of the following conditions:

  Diverticulitis or other disorder of the intestine
  High blood pressure
  Kidney disorder
  Myasthenia gravis (a muscle-weakness disorder)
  Osteoporosis (brittle bones)
  Peptic ulcer
  Ulcerative colitis (inflammation of the bowel)

Long-term treatment with Deltasone may stunt growth. If this medication is given to a child, the youngster's growth should be monitored carefully.

Diseases such as chickenpox or measles can be very serious or even fatal in both children and adults who are taking this drug. Try to avoid exposure to these diseases.

Possible food and drug interactions
when taking this medication

Deltasone may decrease your carbohydrate tolerance or activate a latent case of diabetes. If you are already taking insulin or oral medication for diabetes, make sure your doctor knows this; you may need an increased dosage while you are being treated with Deltasone.

If you have a blood-clotting disorder caused by a vitamin K deficiency and are taking Deltasone, check with your doctor before you use aspirin.

You may be at risk of convulsions if you take the immunosuppressant drug cyclosporine (Sandimmune) while being treated with Deltasone.

If Deltasone is taken with certain other drugs, the effects of either could be increased, decreased, or altered. Check with your doctor before combining Deltasone with any of the following:

Amphotericin B (Fungizone)
Blood thinners such as Coumadin
Carbamazepine (Tegretol)
Estrogen drugs such as Premarin
Ketoconazole (Nizoral)
Oral contraceptives
Phenobarbital (Donnatal, others)
Phenytoin (Dilantin)
Potent diuretics such as Lasix
Rifampin (Rifadin)
Troleandomycin (Tao)

Special information
if you are pregnant or breastfeeding

If you are pregnant or plan to become pregnant, inform your doctor immediately. Deltasone should be taken during pregnancy or while breast-feeding only if clearly needed and only if the benefit outweighs the potential risks to the child.

Recommended dosage

Dosage is determined by the condition being treated and your response to the drug. Typical starting doses can range from 5 milligrams to 60 milligrams a day. Once you respond to the drug, your doctor will lower the dose gradually to the minimum effective amount. For treatment of acute attacks of multiple sclerosis, doses of as much as 200 milligrams per day may be given for a week, followed by 80 mg every other day for a month.

Overdosage

Long-term high doses of Deltasone may produce Cushing's syndrome (see "side effects" section). Although no specific information is available regarding short-term overdosage, any medication taken in excess can have serious consequences. If you suspect an overdose of Deltasone, seek medical attention immediately.

...IOL

Pronounced: DEM-er-awl
Generic name: Meperidine hydrochloride

Why is this drug prescribed?
Demerol, a narcotic analgesic, is prescribed for the relief of moderate to severe pain.

Most important fact about this drug
Do not take Demerol if you are currently taking drugs known as MAO inhibitors or have used them in the previous 2 weeks. Drugs in this category include the antidepressants Nardil and Parnate. When taken with Demerol, they can cause unpredictable, severe, and occasionally fatal reactions.

How should you take this medication?
Take Demerol exactly as prescribed. Do not increase the amount or length of time you take this drug without your doctor's approval.

If you are using Demerol in syrup form, take each dose in a half glass of water.

■ *If you miss a dose...*
   Take it as soon as you remember. If it is almost time for your next dose, skip the one you missed and go back to your regular schedule. Never take 2 doses at once.

■ *Storage instructions...*
   Store at room temperature. Protect from heat.

What side effects may occur?
Side effects cannot be anticipated. If any develop or change in intensity, inform your doctor as soon as possible. Only your doctor can determine if it is safe for you to continue taking Demerol.

■ *More common side effects may include:*
   Dizziness, light-headedness, nausea, sedation, sweating, vomiting

If any of these side effects occur, it may help if you lie down after taking the medication.

■ *Less common or rare side effects may include:*
Agitation, constipation, difficulty urinating, disorientation, dry mouth, fainting, fast heartbeat, feeling of elation or depression, flushing of the face, hallucinations, headache, hives, impairment of physical performance, itching, low blood pressure, mental sluggishness or clouding, palpitations, rashes, restlessness, severe convulsions, slow heartbeat, tremors, troubled and slowed breathing, uncoordinated muscle movements, visual disturbances, weakness

Why should this drug not be prescribed?
If you are sensitive to or have ever had an allergic reaction to Demerol or other narcotic painkillers, you should not use this medication. Make sure your doctor is aware of any drug reactions you have experienced.

Do not take Demerol with MAO inhibitors such as Nardil and Parnate.

Special warnings about this medication
Demerol may affect you both mentally and physically. You should not drive a car, operate machinery, or perform any other potentially hazardous activities until you know how the drug affects you.

You can build up tolerance to, and both mental and physical dependence on, Demerol if you take it repeatedly. If you have ever had a problem with drug abuse, consult with your doctor before taking this drug.

Use Demerol with caution if you have a severe liver or kidney disorder, hypothyroidism (underactive thyroid gland), Addison's disease (adrenal gland failure), an enlarged prostate, a urethral stricture (narrowing of the tube leading from the bladder), a head injury, a severe abdominal condition, or an irregular heartbeat, or if you have ever had convulsions.

Be very careful taking this drug if you are having a severe asthma attack, if you have frequently recurring lung disease, if you are unable to inhale or exhale extra air when needed, or if you have any pre-existing breathing difficulties.

Because Demerol may cause unusually slow or troubled breathing and may increase the pressure from fluid surrounding the brain and spinal cord, this drug should be used by people with head injury only if the doctor considers it absolutely necessary.

Demerol may make you feel light-headed or dizzy when you get up from lying down.

Before having surgery, make sure the doctor knows you are taking Demerol.

Possible food and drug interactions
when taking this medication

Demerol slows brain activity and intensifies the effects of alcohol. Do not drink alcohol while taking this medication.

If Demerol is taken with certain other drugs, the effects of either could be increased, decreased, or altered. It is especially important to check with your doctor before combining Demerol with the following:

Antidepressant drugs such as Elavil, Tofranil
Antihistamines such as Benadryl
Cimetidine (Tagamet)
Major tranquilizers such as Mellaril and Thorazine
MAO inhibitors such as the antidepressant drugs Nardil and Parnate
Other narcotic painkillers such as Percocet and Tylenol with Codeine
Phenytoin (Dilantin)
Sedatives such as Halcion and Restoril
Tranquilizers such as Xanax and Valium

Special information
if you are pregnant or breastfeeding

Do not take Demerol if you are pregnant or planning to become pregnant unless you are directed to do so by your doctor. Demerol appears in breast milk and could affect a nursing infant. If this medication is essential to your health, your doctor may advise you to discontinue breastfeeding your baby until your treatment is finished.

Recommended dosage

ADULTS

The usual dosage of Demerol is 50 milligrams to 150 milligrams every 3 or 4 hours, determined according to your response and the severity of the pain.

CHILDREN

The usual dosage is 0.5 milligram to 0.8 milligram per pound of body weight, taken every 3 or 4 hours, as determined by your doctor.

OLDER ADULTS

Your doctor may reduce the dosage.

Overdosage

■ *Symptoms of Demerol overdose include:*
Bluish discoloration of the skin, cold and clammy skin, coma or extreme sleepiness, limp, weak muscles, low blood pressure, slow heartbeat, troubled or slowed breathing

With severe overdose, a person may stop breathing, have a heart attack, and even die.

If you suspect an overdose, seek emergency medical treatment immediately.

Brand name:

DEMULEN

See Oral Contraceptives, page 887.

Brand name:

DENAVIR

Pronounced: DEN-a-veer
Generic name: Penciclovir

Why is this drug prescribed?
Denavir cream is used to treat recurrent cold sores on the lips and face. It works by interfering with the growth of the herpesvirus responsible for the sores.

Most important fact about this drug
You should begin applying Denavir at the first hint of a developing cold sore. The drug will not cure herpes, but it will reduce pain and may speed healing.

How should you use this medication?
Avoid using Denavir cream in or near the eyes; it can irritate them. Apply it only to sores on the lips and face.

■ *If you miss a dose...*
Apply it as soon as you remember. If it is almost time for your next dose, skip the one you missed and go back to your regular schedule.

■ *Storage instructions...*
Store at room temperature; avoid freezing.

What side effects may occur?

Reactions to Denavir are quite rare. If any develop or change in intensity, inform your doctor as soon as possible. Only your doctor can determine if it is safe for you to continue using this medication.

■ *Side effects may include:*
Headache, numbing of the skin, rash, skin reaction where the cream was applied, taste alteration

Why should this drug not be prescribed?

If you have ever had an allergic reaction to any of the ingredients in Denavir, you should not use this medication.

Special warnings about this medication

It is not known whether Denavir is effective for people with weak immune systems.

Possible food and drug interactions
when using this medication

No interactions with Denavir cream have been reported.

Special information
if you are pregnant or breastfeeding

The effects of Denavir during pregnancy have not been adequately studied. If you are pregnant or plan to become pregnant, inform your doctor immediately. Researchers do not know whether this drug will appear in breast milk after external application. For safety's sake, your doctor may advise you to discontinue breastfeeding your baby until your treatment with Denavir is finished.

Recommended dosage

ADULTS

Apply cream every 2 hours, while awake, for 4 days.

CHILDREN

The safety and effectiveness of this drug in children have not been established.

Overdosage

There have been no reported overdoses of this medication. Even if the cream is accidentally swallowed, it is unlikely to cause a harmful reaction.

Brand name:

DEPAKENE

Pronounced: DEP-uh-keen
Generic name: Valproic acid

Why is this drug prescribed?

Depakene, an epilepsy medicine, is used to treat certain types of seizures and convulsions. It may be prescribed alone or with other anticonvulsant medications.

Most important fact about this drug

Depakene can cause serious liver damage, especially during the first 6 months of treatment. Children under 2 years of age are the most vulnerable, especially if they are also taking other anticonvulsant medicines and have certain other disorders such as mental retardation. The risk of liver damage decreases with age; but you should always be alert for the following symptoms: loss of seizure control, weakness, dizziness, drowsiness, a general feeling of ill health, facial swelling, loss of appetite, vomiting, and yellowing of the skin and eyes. If you suspect a liver problem, call your doctor immediately.

How should you take this medication?

If Depakene irritates your digestive system, take it with food. To avoid irritating your mouth and throat, swallow Depakene capsules whole; do not chew them.

■ *If you miss a dose...*
If you take 1 dose a day, take the dose you missed as soon as you remember. If you do not remember until the next day, skip the dose you missed and go back to your regular schedule.

If you take more than 1 dose a day and you remember the missed dose within 6 hours of the scheduled time, take it immediately. Take the rest of the doses for that day at equally spaced intervals. Never take 2 doses at once.

■ *Storage instructions...*
Store at room temperature.

What side effects may occur?

Side effects cannot be anticipated. If any develop or change in intensity, inform your doctor as soon as possible. Only your doctor can determine if it is safe for you to continue taking Depakene.

■ *More common side effects may include:*
Indigestion, nausea, vomiting

■ *Less common or rare side effects may include:*
Abdominal cramps, aggression, anemia, bleeding, blood disorders, breast enlargement, breast milk not associated with pregnancy or nursing, bruising, changes in behavior, coma, constipation, depression, diarrhea, difficulty in speaking, dizziness, double vision, drowsiness, emotional upset, excessive urination (mainly children), fever, growth failure in children, hair loss (temporary), hallucinations, headache, involuntary eye movements, involuntary jerking or tremors, irregular menstrual periods, itching, lack of coordination, liver disease, loss of bladder control, loss of or increased appetite, overactivity, rash, rickets (mainly children), sedation, sensitivity to light, skin eruptions or peeling, spots before the eyes, swelling of the arms and legs due to fluid retention, swollen glands, weakness, weight loss or gain

Why should this drug not be prescribed?
You should not take this drug if you have liver disease or your liver is not functioning properly, or if you have had an allergic reaction to it.

Special warnings about this medication
Remember that liver failure is possible when taking Depakene (see "Most important fact about this drug"). Your doctor should test your liver function at regular intervals.

Because of the potential for side effects involving blood disorders, your doctor will probably test your blood before prescribing Depakene and at regular intervals while you are taking it. Bruising, hemorrhaging, or clotting disorders usually mean the dosage should be reduced or the drug should be stopped altogether.

Since Depakene may cause drowsiness, you should not drive a car, operate heavy machinery, or engage in hazardous activity until you know how you react to the drug.

Do not abruptly stop taking this medicine without first consulting your doctor. A gradual reduction in dosage is usually required.

This drug can also increase the effect of painkillers and anesthetics. Before any surgery or dental procedure, make sure the doctor knows you are taking Depakene.

Possible food and drug interactions
when taking this medication

If Depakene is taken with certain other drugs, the effects of either could be increased, decreased, or altered. It is especially important to check with your doctor before combining Depakene with the following:

Aspirin
Barbiturates such as phenobarbital and Seconal
Blood-thinning drugs such as Coumadin and Dicumarol
Carbamazepine (Tegretol)
Clonazepam (Klonopin)
Felbamate (Felbatol)
Oral contraceptives
Phenytoin (Dilantin)
Primidone (Mysoline)

Extreme drowsiness and other serious effects may occur if Depakene is taken with alcohol or other central nervous system depressants such as Halcion, Restoril, or Xanax.

Special information
if you are pregnant or breastfeeding

If taken during pregnancy, Depakene may harm the baby. The drug is not recommended for pregnant women unless the benefits of therapy clearly outweigh the risks. In fact, women in their childbearing years should take Depakene only if it has been shown to be essential in the control of seizures. Since Depakene appears in breast milk, nursing mothers should use it only with caution.

Recommended dosage

The usual starting dose is 15 milligrams per 2.2 pounds of body weight per day. Your doctor may increase the dose at weekly intervals by 5 to 10 milligrams per 2.2 pounds per day until seizures are controlled or side effects become too severe. The daily dose should not exceed 60 milligrams per 2.2 pounds per day.

Overdosage

Any medication taken in excess can have serious consequences. An overdose of Depakene can be fatal. If you suspect an overdose, seek medical help immediately.

- *Symptoms of Depakene overdose may include:*
  Coma, extreme drowsiness, heart problems

Brand name:

DEPAKOTE

Pronounced: DEP-uh-coat
Generic name: Divalproex sodium (Valproic acid)

Why is this drug prescribed?
Depakote, in both tablet and capsule form, is used to treat certain types of seizures and convulsions. It may be prescribed alone or with other epilepsy medications.

The tablets are also used to control the manic episodes—periods of abnormally high spirits and energy—that occur in bipolar disorder (manic depression).

The tablet form is also prescribed to prevent migraine headaches.

Most important fact about this drug
Depakote can cause serious liver damage, especially during the first 6 months of treatment. Children under 2 years of age are the most vulnerable, especially if they are also taking other anticonvulsant medicines and have certain other disorders such as mental retardation. The risk of liver damage decreases with age; but you should always be alert for the following symptoms: loss of seizure control, weakness, dizziness, drowsiness, a general feeling of ill health, facial swelling, loss of appetite, vomiting, and yellowing of the skin and eyes. If you suspect a liver problem, call your doctor immediately.

How should you take this medication?
Take the tablet with water and swallow it whole (don't chew it or crush it). It has a special coating to avoid upsetting your stomach.

If you are taking the sprinkle capsule, you can swallow it whole or open it and sprinkle the contents on a teaspoon of soft food such as applesauce or pudding. Swallow it immediately, without chewing. The sprinkle capsules are large enough to be opened easily.

Depakote can be taken with meals or snacks to avoid stomach upset. Take it exactly as prescribed.

■ *If you miss a dose...*
If you take Depakote once a day, take your dose as soon as you remember. If you don't remember until the next day, skip the missed dose and return to your regular schedule. Never take 2 doses at the same time.

If you take more than one dose a day, take your dose right away if it's within 6 hours of the scheduled time, and take the rest of the day's doses at equal intervals during the day. Never take 2 doses at the same time.

■ *Storage instructions...*
Store at room temperature.

What side effects may occur?
Side effects cannot be anticipated. If any develop or change in intensity, inform your doctor as soon as possible. Because Depakote is often used with other antiseizure drugs, it may not be possible to determine whether a side effect is due to Depakote alone. Only your doctor can determine if it is safe• for you to continue taking Depakote.

■ *More common side effects may include:*
Abdominal pain, abnormal thinking, breathing difficulty, bronchitis, bruising, constipation, depression, diarrhea, dizziness, emotional changeability, fever, flu symptoms, hair loss, headache, incoordination, indigestion, infection, insomnia, loss of appetite, memory loss, nasal inflammation, nausea, nervousness, ringing in the ears, sleepiness, sore throat, tremor, vision problems, vomiting, weakness, weight loss or gain

■ *Less common or rare side effects may include:*
Abnormal dreams, abnormal milk secretion, abnormal walk, aggression, anemia, anxiety, back pain, behavior problems, belching, bleeding, blood disorders, bone pain, breast enlargement, chest pain, chills, coma, confusion, coughing up blood, dental abscess, drowsiness, dry skin, ear or hearing problems, excessive urination (mainly children) or other urination problems, eye problems, feeling of illness, gas, growth failure in children, hallucinations, heart palpitations, high blood pressure, hostility, increased appetite, increased cough, involuntary rapid movement of eyeball, irregular or painful menstruation, itching, jerky movements, lack of muscular coordination, leg cramps, liver problems, loss of bladder or bowel control, muscle or joint pain, muscle weakness, neck pain, nosebleed, overactivity, pneumonia, rickets (mainly children), sedation, seeing "spots before your eyes", sensitivity to light, sinus inflammation, skin eruptions or peeling,

skin rash, speech difficulties, stomach and intestinal disorders, swelling of arms and legs due to fluid retention, swollen glands, taste changes, tingling or pins and needles, twitching, urinary problems, vertigo

Why should this drug not be prescribed?
You should not take this medication if you have liver disease or your liver is not functioning well.

If you are sensitive to or have ever had an allergic reaction to Depakote, you should not take this medication.

Special warnings about this medication
This medication can severely damage the liver (see "Most important fact about this drug").

Depakote causes some people to become drowsy or less alert. You should not drive or operate dangerous machinery or participate in any hazardous activity that requires full mental alertness until you are certain the drug does not have this effect on you.

Do not abruptly stop taking this medicine without first consulting your doctor. A gradual reduction in dosage is usually required.

Depakote prolongs the time it takes blood to clot, which increases your chances of serious bleeding.

This drug can also increase the effect of painkillers and anesthetics. Before any surgery or dental procedure, make sure the doctor knows you are taking Depakote.

If you are taking Depakote to prevent migraine, remember that it will not cure a headache once it has started.

Some coated particles from the capsules may appear in your stool. This is to be expected, and need not worry you.

Possible food and drug interactions
when taking this medication
Depakote depresses activity of the central nervous system, and may increase the effects of alcohol. Do not drink alcohol while taking this medication.

If Depakote is taken with certain other drugs, the effects of either could be increased, decreased, or altered. It is especially important to check with your doctor before combining Depakote with the following:

Aspirin
Barbiturates such as phenobarbital and Seconal
Blood thinners such as Coumadin
Cyclosporine (Sandimmune, Neoral)
Oral contraceptives
Other seizure medications, including carbamazepine (Tegretol),
    clonazepam (Klonopin), ethosuximide (Zarontin), felbamate (Felbatol),
    phenytoin (Dilantin), and Primidone (Mysoline)
Sleep aids such as Halcion
Tranquilizers such as Valium and Xanax

Special information
if you are pregnant or breastfeeding
Depakote may produce birth defects if it is taken during pregnancy. If you are
pregnant or plan to become pregnant, inform your doctor immediately.
Depakote appears in breast milk and could affect a nursing infant. If
Depakote is essential to your health, your doctor may advise you to
discontinue breastfeeding until your treatment with this medication is
finished.

Recommended dosage

EPILEPSY

Dosage for adults and children is determined by body weight. The usual
recommended starting dose is 10 to 15 milligrams per 2.2 pounds per day,
depending on the type of seizure. Your doctor may increase the dose at 1-
week intervals by 5 to 10 milligrams per 2.2 pounds per day until your
seizures are controlled or the side effects become too severe. The most you
should take is 60 milligrams per 2.2 pounds per day. If your total dosage is
more than 250 milligrams a day, your doctor will divide it into smaller
individual doses.

MANIC EPISODES

The usual starting dose for those aged 18 and over is 750 milligrams a day,
divided into smaller doses. Your doctor will adjust the dose for best results.

MIGRAINE PREVENTION

The usual starting dose for those aged 16 and over is 250 milligrams twice a
day. Your doctor will adjust the dose, up to a maximum of 1,000 milligrams
a day. The drug has not been tested for migraine in adults over age 65.

Overdosage
Any medication taken in excess can have serious consequences. An overdose of Depakote can be fatal. If you suspect an overdose, seek medical attention immediately.

■ *Symptoms of Depakote overdose may include:*
Coma, extreme sleepiness, heart problems

Brand name:

DERMACIN

See Lidex, page 671.

Generic name:

DESIPRAMINE

See Norpramin, page 868.

Generic name:

DESMOPRESSIN

See DDAVP, page 319.

Brand name:

DESOGEN

See Oral Contraceptives, page 887.

Generic name:

DESONIDE

See Tridesilon, page 1278.

Brand name:

DESOWEN

See Tridesilon, page 1278.

Generic name:

DESOXIMETASONE

See Topicort, page 1260.

Brand name:

DESQUAM-E

Pronounced: DES-kwam ee
Generic name: Benzoyl peroxide
Other brand names: Benzac W, Benzagel, BenzaShave,
Theroxide, Triaz

Why is this drug prescribed?

Desquam-E gel is used to treat various types of acne. It can be used alone or with other treatments, including antibiotics and products that contain retinoic acid, sulfur, or salicylic acid.

Most important fact about this drug

Significant clearing of the skin should occur after 2 to 3 weeks of treatment with Desquam-E.

How should you use this medication?

Cleanse the affected area thoroughly before applying the medication. Desquam-E should then be gently rubbed in.

■ *If you miss a dose...*
Apply it as soon as you remember. Then go back to your regular schedule.

■ *Storage instructions...*
Store at room temperature.

What side effects may occur?

Side effects cannot be anticipated. If any develop or change in intensity, notify your doctor as soon as possible. Only your doctor can determine whether it is safe for you to continue using Desquam-E.

■ *Side effects may include:*
Allergic reaction (itching, rash in area where the medication was applied), excessive drying (red and peeling skin and possible swelling)

Why should this drug not be prescribed?
Do not use Desquam-E if you are sensitive to or allergic to benzoyl peroxide or any other components of the drug.

Special warnings about this medication
Desquam-E is for external use only. Avoid contact with your eyes, nose, lips, or throat. If the drug does touch these areas accidentally, rinse with water.

If you are sensitive to medications derived from benzoic acid (including certain topical anesthetics) or to cinnamon, you may also be sensitive to Desquam-E.

If your skin becomes severely irritated, stop using the drug and call your doctor.

Desquam-E can bleach or discolor hair or colored fabric.

Stay out of the sun as much as possible, and use a sunscreen.

Possible food and drug interactions
when using this medication
When used with sunscreens containing PABA (para-aminobenzoic acid), Desquam-E may cause temporary skin discoloration.

Special information
if you are pregnant or breastfeeding
The effects of Desquam-E during pregnancy have not been adequately studied. It should be used only if clearly needed. If you are pregnant or plan to become pregnant, inform your doctor immediately. This medication may appear in breast milk and could affect a nursing infant. If this medication is essential to your health, your doctor may advise you to stop breastfeeding until your treatment with Desquam-E is finished.

Recommended dosage

ADULTS AND CHILDREN 12 YEARS AND OVER

Gently rub Desquam-E gel into all affected areas once or twice a day. If you are fair-skinned or live in an excessively dry climate, you should probably start with one application a day. You can continue to use Desquam-E for as long as your doctor thinks it is necessary.

Overdosage
Overdosage of Desquam-E can result in excessive scaling of the skin, reddening skin, or swelling due to fluid retention. Any medication taken in excess can have serious consequences. If you suspect an overdose, seek medical attention.

Brand name:

DESYREL

Pronounced: DES-ee-rel
Generic name: Trazodone hydrochloride

Why is this drug prescribed?
Desyrel is prescribed for the treatment of depression.

Most important fact about this drug
Desyrel does not provide immediate relief. It may take up to 4 weeks before you begin to feel better, although most patients notice improvement within 2 weeks.

How should you take this medication?
Take Desyrel shortly after a meal or light snack. You may be more apt to feel dizzy or light-headed if you take the drug before you have eaten.

Desyrel may cause dry mouth. Sucking on a hard candy, chewing gum, or melting bits of ice in your mouth can relieve the problem.

■ *If you miss a dose...*
Take it as soon as you remember. If it is within 4 hours of your next dose, skip the one you missed and go back to your regular schedule. Never take 2 doses at once.

■ *Storage instructions...*
Store at room temperature in a tightly closed container away from light and excessive heat.

What side effects may occur?
Side effects cannot be anticipated. If any develop or change in intensity, inform your doctor as soon as possible. Only your doctor can determine if it is safe for you to continue taking Desyrel.

■ *More common side effects may include:*
Abdominal or stomach disorder, aches or pains in muscles and bones, anger or hostility, blurred vision, brief loss of consciousness, confusion, constipation, decreased appetite, diarrhea, dizziness or light-headedness, drowsiness, dry mouth, excitement, fainting, fast or fluttery heartbeat, fatigue, fluid retention and swelling, headache, inability to fall or stay asleep, low blood pressure, nasal or sinus congestion, nausea, nervous-

ness, nightmares or vivid dreams, tremors, uncoordinated movements, vomiting, weight gain or loss

■ *Less common or rare side effects may include:*
Allergic reactions, anemia, bad taste in mouth, blood in the urine, chest pain, delayed urine flow, decreased concentration, decreased sex drive, disorientation, ejaculation problems, excess salivation, gas, general feeling of illness, hallucinations or delusions, high blood pressure, impaired memory, impaired speech, impotence, increased appetite, increased sex drive, menstrual problems, more frequent urination, muscle twitches, numbness, prolonged erections, red, tired, itchy eyes, restlessness, ringing in the ears, shortness of breath, sweating or clammy skin, tingling or pins and needles

Why should this drug not be prescribed?
If you are sensitive to or have ever had an allergic reaction to Desyrel or similar drugs, you should not take this medication. Make sure your doctor is aware of any drug reactions you have experienced.

Special warnings about this medication
Desyrel may cause you to become drowsy or less alert and may affect your judgment. Therefore, you should not drive or operate dangerous machinery or participate in any hazardous activity that requires full mental alertness until you know how this drug affects you.

Desyrel has been associated with priapism, a persistent, painful erection of the penis. Men who experience prolonged or inappropriate erections should stop taking this drug and consult their doctor.

Notify your doctor or dentist that you are taking this drug if you have a medical emergency, and before you have surgery or dental treatment. Your doctor will ask you to stop using the drug if you are going to have elective surgery.

Be careful taking this drug if you have heart disease. Desyrel can cause irregular heartbeats.

Possible food and drug interactions
when taking this medication
Desyrel may intensify the effects of alcohol. Do not drink alcohol while taking this medication.

If Desyrel is taken with certain other drugs, the effects of either could be increased, decreased, or altered. It is especially important to check with your doctor before combining Desyrel with the following:

Antidepressant drugs known as MAO inhibitors, including Nardil and
  Parnate
Barbiturates such as Seconal
Central nervous system depressants such as Demerol and Halcion
Chlorpromazine (Thorazine)
Digoxin (Lanoxin)
Drugs for high blood pressure such as Catapres and Wytensin
Other antidepressants such as Prozac and Norpramin
Phenytoin (Dilantin)
Warfarin (Coumadin)

Special information
if you are pregnant or breastfeeding

The effects of Desyrel during pregnancy have not been adequately studied. If
you are pregnant or planning to become pregnant, inform your doctor
immediately. This medication may appear in breast milk. If treatment with
this drug is essential to your health, your doctor may advise you to
discontinue breastfeeding your baby until your treatment is finished.

Recommended dosage

ADULTS

The usual starting dosage is a total of 150 milligrams per day, divided into 2
or more smaller doses. Your doctor may increase your dose by 50 milligrams
per day every 3 or 4 days. Total dosage should not exceed 400 milligrams per
day, divided into smaller doses. Once you have responded well to the drug,
your doctor may gradually reduce your dose. Because this medication makes
you drowsy, your doctor may tell you to take the largest dose at bedtime.

CHILDREN

The safety and effectiveness of Desyrel have not been established in children
below 18 years of age.

Overdosage

Any medication taken in excess can have serious consequences. An overdose
of Desyrel in combination with other drugs can be fatal.

- *Symptoms of a Desyrel overdose may include:*
  Breathing failure, drowsiness, irregular heartbeat, prolonged, painful
  erection, seizures, vomiting

If you suspect an overdose, seek medical attention immediately.

Brand name:

DEXACORT

See Decadron Turbinaire and Respihaler, page 327.

Generic name:

DEXAMETHASONE

See Decadron Tablets, page 323.

Generic name:

DEXAMETHASONE SODIUM PHOSPHATE

See Decadron Turbinaire and Respihaler, page 327.

Generic name:

DEXAMETHASONE WITH NEOMYCIN

See Neodecadron Ophthalmic Ointment and Solution, page 827.

Brand name:

DEXEDRINE

Pronounced: DEX-eh-dreen
Generic name: Dextroamphetamine sulfate

Why is this drug prescribed?
Dexedrine, a stimulant drug available in tablet or sustained-release capsule form, is prescribed to help treat the following conditions:

1. Narcolepsy (recurrent "sleep attacks")
2. Attention deficit disorder with hyperactivity. (The total treatment program should include social, psychological, and educational guidance along with Dexedrine.)

Most important fact about this drug
Because it is a stimulant, this drug has high abuse potential. The stimulant effect may give way to a letdown period of depression and fatigue. Although the letdown can be relieved by taking another dose, this soon becomes a vicious circle.

If you habitually take Dexedrine in doses higher than recommended, or if you take it over a long period of time, you may eventually become dependent on the drug and suffer from withdrawal symptoms when it is unavailable.

How should you take this medication?

Take Dexedrine exactly as prescribed. If it is prescribed in tablet form, you may need up to 3 doses a day. Take the first dose when you wake up; take the next 1 or 2 doses at intervals of 4 to 6 hours. You can take the sustained-release capsules only once a day.

Do not take Dexedrine late in the day, since this could cause insomnia. If you experience insomnia or loss of appetite while taking this drug, notify your doctor; you may need a lower dosage.

It is likely that your doctor will periodically take you off Dexedrine to determine whether you still need it.

Do not chew or crush the sustained-release form, Dexedrine Spansules.

Do not increase the dosage, except on your doctor's advice.

Do not use Dexedrine to improve mental alertness or stay awake. Do not share it with others.

■ *If you miss a dose...*
   If you take 1 dose a day, take it as soon as you remember, but not within 6 hours of going to bed. If you do not remember until the next day, skip the dose you missed and go back to your regular schedule.

   If you take 2 or 3 doses a day, take the dose you missed if it is within an hour or so of the scheduled time. Otherwise, skip the dose and go back to your regular schedule. Never take 2 doses at once.

■ *Storage instructions...*
   Store at room temperature in a tightly closed container, away from light.

What side effects may occur?

Side effects cannot be anticipated. If any develop or change in intensity, inform your doctor as soon as possible. Only your doctor can determine if it is safe for you to continue taking Dexedrine.

■ *More common side effects may include:*
   Excessive restlessness, overstimulation

■ *Other side effects may include:*
Changes in sex drive, constipation, diarrhea, dizziness, dry mouth, exaggerated feeling of well-being or depression, headache, heart palpitations, high blood pressure, hives, impotence, loss of appetite, rapid heartbeat, sleeplessness, stomach and intestinal disturbances, tremors, uncontrollable twitching or jerking, unpleasant taste in the mouth, weight loss

■ *Effects of chronic heavy abuse of Dexedrine may include:*
Hyperactivity, irritability, personality changes, schizophrenia-like thoughts and behavior, severe insomnia, severe skin disease

Why should this drug not be prescribed?
Do not take Dexedrine if you are sensitive to or have ever had an allergic reaction to it.

Do not take Dexedrine for at least 14 days after taking a monoamine oxidase inhibitor (MAO inhibitor) such as the antidepressants Nardil and Parnate. Dexedrine and MAO inhibitors may interact to cause a sharp, potentially life-threatening rise in blood pressure.

Your doctor will not prescribe Dexedrine for you if you suffer from any of the following conditions:

Agitation
Cardiovascular disease
Glaucoma
Hardening of the arteries
High blood pressure
Overactive thyroid gland
Substance abuse

Special warnings about this medication
Be aware that one of the inactive ingredients in Dexedrine is a yellow food coloring called tartrazine (Yellow No. 5). In a few people, particularly those who are allergic to aspirin, tartrazine can cause a severe allergic reaction.

Dexedrine may impair judgment or coordination. Do not drive or operate dangerous machinery until you know how you react to the medication.

There is some concern that Dexedrine may stunt a child's growth. For the sake of safety, any child who takes Dexedrine should have his or her growth monitored.

Possible food and drug interactions
when taking this medication

If Dexedrine is taken with certain foods or drugs, the effects of either could be increased, decreased, or altered. It is especially important to check with your doctor before combining Dexedrine with the following:

- *Substances that dampen the effects of Dexedrine:*
  Ammonium chloride
  Chlorpromazine (Thorazine)
  Fruit juices
  Glutamic acid hydrochloride
  Guanethidine (Ismelin)
  Haloperidol (Haldol)
  Lithium carbonate (Lithonate)
  Methenamine (Urised)
  Reserpine (Diupres)
  Sodium acid phosphate
  Vitamin C (as ascorbic acid)

- *Substances that boost the effects of Dexedrine:*
  Acetazolamide (Diamox)
  MAO inhibitors such as Nardil and Parnate
  Propoxyphene (Darvon)
  Sodium bicarbonate (baking soda)
  Thiazide diuretics such as Diuril

- *Substances that have decreased effect when taken with Dexedrine:*
  Antihistamines such as Benadryl
  Blood pressure medications such as Catapres, Hytrin, and Minipress
  Ethosuximide (Zarontin)
  Veratrum alkaloids (found in certain blood pressure drugs)

- *Substances that have increased effect when taken with Dexedrine:*
  Antidepressants such as Norpramin and Vivactil
  Meperidine (Demerol)
  Norepinephrine (Levophed)
  Phenobarbital
  Phenytoin (Dilantin)

Special information
if you are pregnant or breastfeeding

The effects of Dexedrine during pregnancy have not been adequately studied. If you are pregnant or plan to become pregnant, inform your doctor immediately. Babies born to women taking Dexedrine may be premature or have low birth weight. They may also be depressed, agitated, or apathetic due to withdrawal symptoms. Since Dexedrine appears in breast milk, it should not be taken by a nursing mother.

Recommended dosage

Take no more Dexedrine than your doctor prescribes. Intake should be kept to the lowest level that proves effective.

NARCOLEPSY

Adults

The usual dose is 5 to 60 milligrams per day, divided into smaller, equal doses.

Children

Narcolepsy seldom occurs in children under 12 years of age; however, when it does, Dexedrine may be used.

The suggested initial dose for children between 6 and 12 years of age is 5 milligrams per day. Your doctor may increase the daily dose in increments of 5 milligrams at weekly intervals until it becomes effective.

Children 12 years of age and older will be started with 10 milligrams daily. The daily dosage may be raised in increments of 10 milligrams at weekly intervals until effective. If side effects such as insomnia or loss of appetite appear, the dosage will probably be reduced.

ATTENTION DEFICIT DISORDER WITH HYPERACTIVITY

This drug is not recommended for children under 3 years of age.

Children from 3 to 5 Years of Age

The usual starting dose is 2.5 milligrams daily, in tablet form. Your doctor may raise the daily dosage by 2.5 milligrams at weekly intervals until the drug becomes effective.

Children 6 Years of Age and Older

The usual starting dose is 5 milligrams once or twice a day. Your doctor may raise the dose by 5 milligrams at weekly intervals until he or she is satisfied with the response. Only in rare cases will the child take more than 40 milligrams per day.

The doctor may prescribe "Spansule" capsules for your child. They are taken once a day.

Your child should take the first dose when he or she wakes up; the remaining 1 or 2 doses are taken at intervals of 4 to 6 hours. Your doctor may interrupt the schedule occasionally to see if behavioral symptoms come back enough to require continued therapy.

Overdosage

An overdose of Dexedrine can be fatal. If you suspect an overdose, seek medical attention immediately.

■ *Symptoms of an acute Dexedrine overdose may include:*
Abdominal cramps, assaultiveness, coma, confusion, convulsions, depression, diarrhea, fatigue, hallucinations, high fever, heightened reflexes, high or low blood pressure, irregular heartbeat, nausea, panic, rapid breathing, restlessness, tremor, vomiting

Generic name:

DEXTROAMPHETAMINE

See Dexedrine, page 358.

Brand name:

DIABETA

See Micronase, page 763.

Brand name:

DIABINESE

Pronounced: dye-AB-in-eez
Generic name: Chlorpropamide

Why is this drug prescribed?

Diabinese is an oral antidiabetic medication used to treat Type II (non-insulin-dependent) diabetes. Diabetes occurs when the body fails to produce enough insulin or is unable to use it properly. Insulin is believed to work by helping sugar penetrate the cell wall so it can be used by the cell.

There are two forms of diabetes: Type I insulin-dependent and Type II non-insulin-dependent. Type I usually requires insulin injection for life, while Type II diabetes can usually be treated by dietary changes and oral antidiabetic medications such as Diabinese. Apparently, Diabinese controls diabetes by stimulating the pancreas to secrete more insulin. Occasionally, Type II diabetics must take insulin injections on a temporary basis, especially during stressful periods or times of illness.

Most important fact about this drug
Always remember that Diabinese is an aid to, not a substitute for, good diet and exercise. Failure to follow a sound diet and exercise plan can lead to serious complications, such as dangerously high or low blood sugar levels. Remember, too, that Diabinese is *not* an oral form of insulin, and cannot be used in place of insulin.

How should you take this medication?
Ordinarily, your doctor will ask you to take a single daily dose of Diabinese each morning with breakfast. However, if this upsets your stomach, he or she may ask you to take Diabinese in smaller doses throughout the day.

To prevent low blood sugar levels (hypoglycemia):

- You should understand the symptoms of hypoglycemia
- Know how exercise affects your blood sugar levels
- Maintain an adequate diet
- Keep a source of quick-acting sugar with you all the time

- *If you miss a dose...*
  Take it as soon as you remember. If it is almost time for the next dose, skip the one you missed and go back to your regular schedule. Do not take 2 doses at the same time.

- *Storage instructions...*
  Store at room temperature.

What side effects may occur?
Side effects cannot be anticipated. If any develop or change in intensity, inform your doctor as soon as possible. Only your doctor can determine if it is safe for you to continue taking Diabinese.

Side effects from Diabinese are rare and seldom require discontinuation of the medication.

- *More common side effects include:*
  Diarrhea, hunger, itching, loss of appetite, nausea, stomach upset, vomiting

- *Less common or rare side effects may include:*
  Anemia and other blood disorders, hives, inflammation of the rectum and colon, sensitivity to light, yellowing of the skin and eyes

Diabinese, like all oral antidiabetics, can cause hypoglycemia (low blood sugar). The risk of hypoglycemia is increased by missed meals, alcohol, other medications, and excessive exercise. To avoid hypoglycemia, closely follow the dietary and exercise regimen suggested by your physician.

- *Symptoms of mild hypoglycemia may include:*
  Cold sweat, drowsiness, fast heartbeat, headache, nausea, nervousness

- *Symptoms of more severe hypoglycemia may include:*
  Coma, pale skin, seizures, shallow breathing

Contact your doctor immediately if these symptoms of severe low blood sugar occur.

Why should this drug not be prescribed?
You should not take Diabinese if you have ever had an allergic reaction to it.

Do not take Diabinese if you are suffering from diabetic ketoacidosis (a life-threatening medical emergency caused by insufficient insulin and marked by excessive thirst, nausea, fatigue, pain below the breastbone, and a fruity breath).

Special warnings about this medication
It's possible that drugs such as Diabinese may lead to more heart problems than diet treatment alone, or diet plus insulin. If you have a heart condition, you may want to discuss this with your doctor.

If you are taking Diabinese, you should check your blood and urine periodically for the presence of abnormal sugar levels.

Remember that it is important that you closely follow the diet and exercise regimen established by your doctor.

Even people with well-controlled diabetes may find that stress, illness, surgery, or fever results in a loss of control. If this happens, your doctor may recommend that Diabinese be discontinued temporarily and insulin used instead.

In addition, the effectiveness of any oral antidiabetic, including Diabinese, may decrease with time. This may occur because of either a diminished responsiveness to the medication or a worsening of the diabetes.

Possible food and drug interactions
when taking this medication

When you take Diabinese with certain other drugs, the effects of either could be increased, decreased, or altered. It is important that you consult with your doctor before taking Diabinese with the following:

Anabolic steroids
Aspirin in large doses
Barbiturates such as Seconal
Beta-blocking blood pressure medications such as Inderal and Tenormin
Calcium-blocking blood pressure medications such as Cardizem and Procardia
Chloramphenicol (Chloromycetin)
Coumarin (Coumadin)
Diuretics such as Diuril and HydroDIURIL
Epinephrine (EpiPen)
Estrogen medications such as Premarin
Isoniazid (Nydrazid)
Major tranquilizers such as Mellaril and Thorazine
MAO inhibitor-type antidepressants such as Nardil and Parnate
Nicotinic acid (Nicobid, Nicolar)
Nonsteroidal anti-inflammatory agents such as Advil, Motrin, Naprosyn, and Nuprin
Oral contraceptives
Phenothiazines
Phenylbutazone
Phenytoin (Dilantin)
Probenecid (Benemid, ColBENEMID)
Steroids such as prednisone
Sulfa drugs such as Bactrim and Septra
Thyroid medications such as Synthroid

Avoid alcohol since excessive alcohol consumption can cause low blood sugar, breathlessness, and facial flushing.

Special information
if you are pregnant or breastfeeding

The effects of Diabinese during pregnancy have not been adequately established. If you are pregnant or plan to become pregnant you should inform your doctor immediately. Since studies suggest the importance of maintaining normal blood sugar (glucose) levels during pregnancy, your physician may prescribe injected insulin.

To minimize the risk of low blood sugar (hypoglycemia) in newborn babies, Diabinese, if prescribed during pregnancy, should be discontinued at least 1 month before the expected delivery date.

Since Diabinese appears in breast milk, it is not recommended for nursing mothers. If diet alone does not control glucose levels, then insulin should be considered.

Recommended dosage

Dosage levels are determined by each individual's needs.

ADULTS

Usually, an initial daily dose of 250 milligrams is recommended for stable, middle-aged, non-insulin-dependent diabetics. After 5 to 7 days, your doctor may adjust this dosage in increments of 50 to 125 milligrams every 3 to 5 days to achieve the best benefit. People with mild diabetes may respond well to daily doses of 100 milligrams or less of Diabinese, while those with severe diabetes may require 500 milligrams daily. Maintenance doses above 750 milligrams are not recommended.

OLDER ADULTS

People who are old, malnourished, or debilitated and those with impaired kidney and liver function usually take an initial dose of 100 to 125 milligrams.

CHILDREN

Safety and effectiveness have not been established.

Overdosage

An overdose of Diabinese can cause low blood sugar (see "What side effects may occur?" for symptoms).

Eating sugar or a sugar-based product will often correct the condition. If you suspect an overdose, seek medical attention immediately.

Brand name:

DIAMOX

Pronounced: DYE-uh-mocks
Generic name: Acetazolamide

Why is this drug prescribed?

Diamox controls fluid secretion. It is used in the treatment of glaucoma (excessive pressure in the eyes), epilepsy (for both brief and unlocalized seizures), and fluid retention due to congestive heart failure or drugs. It is also used to prevent or relieve the symptoms of acute mountain sickness in climbers attempting a rapid climb and those who feel sick even though they are making a gradual climb.

Most important fact about this drug

This drug is considered to be a sulfa drug because of its chemical properties. Although rare, severe reactions have been reported with sulfa drugs. If you develop a rash, bruises, sore throat, or fever contact your doctor immediately.

How should you take this medication?

Take this medication exactly as prescribed by your doctor.

- *If you miss a dose...*
  Take it as soon as you remember. If it is almost time for your next dose, skip the one you missed and go back to your regular schedule. Never take 2 doses at the same time.

- *Storage instructions...*
  Store at room temperature.

What side effects may occur?

Side effects cannot be anticipated. If any develop or change in intensity, inform your doctor as soon as possible. Only your doctor can determine if it is safe for you to continue taking Diamox.

- *More common side effects may include:*
  Change in taste, diarrhea, increase in amount or frequency of urination, loss of appetite, nausea, ringing in the ears, tingling or pins and needles in hands or feet, vomiting

■ *Less common or rare side effects may include:*
Anemia, black or bloody stools, blood in urine, confusion, convulsions, drowsiness, fever, hives, liver dysfunction, nearsightedness, paralysis, rash, sensitivity to light, severe allergic reaction, skin peeling

Why should this drug not be prescribed?
Your doctor will not prescribe this medication for you if your sodium or potassium levels are low, or if you have kidney or liver disease, including cirrhosis.

Diamox should not be used as a long-term treatment for the type of glaucoma called chronic noncongestive angle-closure glaucoma.

Special warnings about this medication
Be very careful about taking high doses of aspirin if you are also taking Diamox. Effects of this combination can range from loss of appetite, sluggishness, and rapid breathing to unresponsiveness; the combination can be fatal.

If you have emphysema or other breathing disorders, use this drug with caution.

If you are taking Diamox to help in rapid ascent of a mountain, you must still come down promptly if you show signs of severe mountain sickness.

Possible food and drug interactions
when taking this medication
If Diamox is taken with certain other drugs, the effects of either could be increased, decreased, or altered. It is especially important to check with your doctor before combining Diamox with the following:

Amitriptyline (Elavil)
Amphetamines such as Dexedrine
Aspirin
Cyclosporine (Sandimmune)
Lithium (Lithonate)
Methenamine (Urex)
Oral diabetes drugs such as Micronase
Quinidine (Quinidex)

Special information
if you are pregnant or breastfeeding

The effects of Diamox during pregnancy have not been adequately studied. If you are pregnant or plan to become pregnant, inform your doctor immediately. Diamox may appear in breast milk and could affect a nursing infant. If this medication is essential to your health, your doctor may advise you to discontinue breastfeeding until your treatment with Diamox is finished.

Recommended dosage

ADULTS

This medication is available in both oral and injectable form. Dosages are for the oral form only.

Glaucoma

This medication is used as an addition to regular glaucoma treatment. Dosages for open-angle glaucoma range from 250 milligrams to 1 gram per 24 hours in 2 or more smaller doses. Your doctor will supervise your dosage and watch the effect of this medication carefully if you are using it for glaucoma. In secondary glaucoma and before surgery in acute congestive (closed-angle) glaucoma, the usual dosage is 250 milligrams every 4 hours or, in some cases, 250 milligrams twice a day. Some people may take 500 milligrams to start, and then 125 or 250 milligrams every 4 hours. The injectable form of this drug is occasionally used in acute cases.

The usual dosage of Diamox Sequels (sustained-release capsules) is 1 capsule (500 milligrams) twice a day, usually in the morning and evening.

Your doctor may adjust the dosage, as needed.

Epilepsy

The daily dosage is 8 to 30 milligrams per 2.2 pounds of body weight in 2 or more doses. Typical dosage may range from 375 to 1,000 milligrams per day. Your doctor will adjust the dosage to suit your needs; Diamox can be used with other anticonvulsant medication.

Congestive Heart Failure

The usual starting dosage to reduce fluid retention in people with congestive heart failure is 250 milligrams to 375 milligrams per day or 5 milligrams per 2.2 pounds of body weight, taken in the morning. Diamox works best when it is taken every other day—or 2 days on, 1 day off—for this condition.

Edema Due to Medication
The usual dose is 250 milligrams to 375 milligrams daily for 1 or 2 days, alternating with a day of rest.

Acute Mountain Sickness
The usual dose is 500 milligrams to 1,000 milligrams a day in 2 or more doses, using either tablets or sustained-release capsules. Doses of this medication are often begun 1 or 2 days before attempting to reach high altitudes.

CHILDREN

The safety and effectiveness of Diamox in children have not been established. However, doses of 8 milligrams to 30 milligrams per 2.2 pounds of body weight have been used in children with various forms of epilepsy.

Overdosage
There is no specific information available on Diamox overdose, but any medication taken in excess can have serious consequences. If you suspect an overdose, seek medical attention immediately.

Generic name:

DIAZEPAM

See Valium, page 1319.

Generic name:

DICLOFENAC

See Voltaren, page 1357.

Generic name:

DICYCLOMINE

See Bentyl, page 141.

Generic name:

DIDANOSINE

See Videx, page 1344.

Generic name:

DIETHYLPROPION

See Tenuate, page 1216.

Brand name:

DIFFERIN

Pronounced: DIFF-er-in
Generic name: Adapalene

Why is this drug prescribed?
Differin is prescribed for the treatment of acne.

Most important fact about this drug
Differin makes your skin more sensitive to sunlight. While using this product, keep your exposure to the sun at a minimum, and protect yourself with sunscreen and clothing. Never apply Differin to sunburned skin.

How should you use this medication?
Differin should be applied once a day at bedtime. Wash the affected areas, then apply a thin layer of the gel. Avoid eyes, lips, and nostrils.

Use Differin exactly as prescribed. Applying excessive amounts or using the gel more than once a day will not produce better results and may cause severe redness, peeling, and discomfort.

- *If you miss a dose...*
  Don't try to make it up. Simply return to your regular schedule on the following day.

- *Storage instructions...*
  Store at room temperature.

What side effects may occur?
Side effects cannot be anticipated. If any develop or change in intensity, inform your doctor as soon as possible. Only your doctor can determine if it is safe for you to continue using Differin.

Side effects are most likely to occur during the first 2 to 4 weeks and usually diminish with continued treatment. If side effects are severe, your doctor may advise you to reduce the frequency of use or discontinue the drug entirely. Side effects disappear when the drug is stopped.

■ *Side effects may include...*
Acne flare-ups, burning, dryness, irritation, itching, redness, scaling, stinging, sunburn

Why should this drug not be prescribed?
Do not use Differin if you are sensitive to adapalene or any other components of the gel.

Special warnings about this medication
If you have an allergic reaction or severe irritation, stop using the medication and call your doctor.

Remember that Differin increases sensitivity to sunlight. Take measures to protect yourself from overexposure. Wind and cold weather may also be irritating.

Do not apply Differin to cuts, abrasions, eczema, or sunburned skin.

In the first few weeks of treatment, your acne may actually seem to get worse. This just means the medication is working on hidden acne sores. Continue using the product. It can take as much as 8 to 12 weeks before you start to see improvement in your condition.

Differin has not been tested for children under 12 years old.

Possible food and drug interactions
when using this medication
Avoid using Differin with any other product that can irritate the skin, such as medicated soaps and cleansers, soaps and cosmetics that have a strong drying effect, and products with high concentrations of alcohol, astringents, spices, and lime.

Special caution is necessary if you have used, or are currently using, any skin product containing sulfur, resorcinol, or salicylic acid. Do not use such a product with Differin. If you have used one of these products recently, do not begin Differin treatment until the effects of the other product have subsided.

Special information
if you are pregnant or breastfeeding
The effects of Differin during pregnancy and breastfeeding have not been adequately studied. If you are pregnant or plan to become pregnant, notify your doctor immediately. It is not known whether Differin appears in breast milk. If you are nursing and need to use Differin, your doctor may advise you to discontinue breastfeeding while using the medication.

Recommended dosage

The usual dose is a thin film applied over the acne-affected area just before bedtime.

Overdosage

Any medication taken in excess can have serious consequences. Overuse of Differin can cause redness, peeling, and discomfort. If you suspect an overdose, check with your doctor immediately.

Generic name:

DIFLORASONE

See Psorcon, page 1042.

Brand name:

DIFLUCAN

Pronounced: Dye-FLEW-can
Generic name: Fluconazole

Why is this drug prescribed?

Diflucan is used to treat fungal infections called candidiasis (also known as thrush or yeast infections). These include vaginal infections, throat infections, and fungal infections elsewhere in the body, such as infections of the urinary tract, peritonitis (inflammation of the lining of the abdomen), and pneumonia. Diflucan is also prescribed to guard against candidiasis in some people receiving bone marrow transplants, and is used to treat meningitis (brain or spinal cord inflammation) caused by another type of fungus.

In addition, Diflucan is now being prescribed for fungal infections in kidney and liver transplant patients, and fungal infections in patients with AIDS.

Most important fact about this drug

Strong allergic reactions to Diflucan, although rare, have been reported. Symptoms may include hives, itching, swelling, sudden drop in blood pressure, difficulty breathing or swallowing, diarrhea, or abdominal pain. If you experience any of these symptoms, notify your doctor immediately.

How should you take this medication?

You can take Diflucan with or without meals.

Take this medication exactly as prescribed, and continue taking it for as long as your doctor instructs. You may begin to feel better after the first few days; but it takes weeks or even months of treatment to completely cure certain fungal infections.

■ *If you miss a dose...*
Take the forgotten dose as soon as you remember. However, if it is almost time for your next dose, skip the one you missed and return to your regular schedule. Do not take double doses.

■ *Storage instructions...*
Diflucan tablets should be stored at normal room temperature. Avoid exposing them to temperatures above 86°F.

What side effects may occur?
Side effects cannot be anticipated. If any develop or change in intensity, inform your doctor as soon as possible. Only your doctor can determine if it is safe for you to continue taking Diflucan.

The most common side effect for people taking more than one dose is nausea.

For women taking a single dose to treat vaginal infection, the most common side effects are abdominal pain, diarrhea, headache, and nausea; changes in taste, dizziness, and indigestion may occur less often.

■ *Less common side effects may include:*
Abdominal pain, diarrhea, headache, skin rash, vomiting

Why should this drug not be prescribed?
Do not take Diflucan if you are sensitive to any of its ingredients or have ever had an allergic reaction to similar drugs, such as Nizoral. Make sure your doctor is aware of any drug reactions you have experienced.

Special warnings about this medication
Your doctor will watch your liver function carefully while you are taking Diflucan.

If your immunity is low and you develop a rash, your doctor should monitor your condition closely. You may have to stop taking Diflucan if the rash gets worse.

**Possible food and drug interactions
when taking this medication**
If Diflucan is taken with certain other drugs, the effects of either could be increased, decreased, or altered. It is especially important to check with your doctor before combining Diflucan with the following:

Blood-thinning drugs such as Coumadin
Antidiabetic drugs such as Orinase, DiaBeta, and Glucotrol
Astemizole (Hismanal)
Cisapride (Propulsid)
Cyclosporine (Sandimmune, Neoral)
Hydrochlorothiazide (HydroDIURIL)
Phenytoin (Dilantin)
Rifampin (Rifadin)
Terfenadine (Seldane)
Ulcer medications such as Tagamet

**Special information
if you are pregnant or breastfeeding**
The effects of Diflucan during pregnancy have not been adequately studied. If you are pregnant or plan to become pregnant, inform your doctor immediately. Diflucan appears in breast milk and could affect a nursing infant. If this medication is essential to your health, your doctor may advise you to stop breastfeeding until your treatment with Diflucan is finished.

Recommended dosage

ADULTS

For vaginal infections
The usual treatment is a single 150-milligram dose.

For throat infections
The usual dose for candidiasis of the mouth and throat is 200 milligrams on the first day, followed by 100 milligrams once a day. You should see results in a few days, but treatment should continue for at least 2 weeks to avoid a relapse. For candidiasis of the esophagus (gullet) the usual dose is 200 milligrams on the first day, followed by 100 milligrams once a day. Treatment should continue for a minimum of 3 weeks and for at least 2 weeks after symptoms have stopped.

For systemic (bodywide) infections
Doses of up to 400 milligrams per day are sometimes prescribed.

For cryptococcal meningitis

The usual dose is 400 milligrams on the first day, followed by 200 milligrams once a day. Treatment should continue for 10 to 12 weeks once tests of spinal fluid come back negative. For AIDS patients, a 200-milligram dose taken once a day is recommended to prevent relapse.

Prevention of candidiasis during bone marrow transplantation

The usual dose is 400 milligrams once a day.

If you have kidney disease, your doctor may have to reduce your dosage.

CHILDREN

For throat infections

The usual dose for candidiasis of the mouth and throat is 6 milligrams for each 2.2 pounds of the child's weight on the first day, and 3 milligrams per 2.2 pounds once a day after that.

The duration of treatment is the same as that for adults.

For systemic (bodywide) infections

The drug has been given at 6 to 12 milligrams per 2.2 pounds of weight per day.

For cryptococcal meningitis

The usual dose is 12 milligrams per 2.2 pounds of body weight per day on the first day, and 6 milligrams per 2.2 pounds per day after that. Treatment will last 10 to 12 weeks after the fungus disappears.

Overdosage

Any medication taken in excess can have serious consequences. If you suspect an overdose, seek medical treatment immediately.

- ■ *Symptoms of Diflucan overdose may include:*
  Hallucinations, paranoia

Generic name:

DIFLUNISAL

See Dolobid, page 405.

Generic name:

DIGOXIN

See Lanoxin, page 642.

Generic name:

DIHYDROCODEINE, ASPIRIN, AND CAFFEINE

See Synalgos-DC, page 1175.

Brand name:

DILANTIN

Pronounced: dye-LAN-tin
Generic name: Phenytoin sodium

Why is this drug prescribed?

Dilantin is an antiepileptic drug, prescribed to control grand mal seizures (a type of seizure in which the individual experiences a sudden loss of consciousness immediately followed by generalized convulsions) and temporal lobe seizures (a type of seizure caused by disease in the cortex of the temporal [side] lobe of the brain affecting smell, taste, sight, hearing, memory, and movement).

Dilantin may also be used to prevent and treat seizures occurring during and after neurosurgery (surgery of the brain and spinal cord).

Most important fact about this drug

If you have been taking Dilantin regularly, do not stop abruptly. This may precipitate prolonged or repeated epileptic seizures without any recovery of consciousness between attacks—a condition called status epilepticus that can be fatal if not treated promptly.

How should you take this medication?

It is important that you strictly follow the prescribed dosage regimen and tell your doctor about any condition that makes it impossible for you to take Dilantin as prescribed.

If you are given Dilantin Oral Suspension, shake it well before using. Use the specially marked measuring spoon, a plastic syringe, or a small measuring cup to measure each dose accurately.

Swallow Dilantin Kapseals whole. Dilantin Infatabs can be either chewed thoroughly and then swallowed, or swallowed whole. The Infatabs are not to be used for once-a-day dosing.

Do not change from one form of Dilantin to another without consulting your doctor. Different products may not work the same way.

Depending on the type of seizure disorder, your doctor may give you another drug with Dilantin.

■ *If you miss a dose...*
If you take one dose a day, take the dose you missed as soon as you remember. If you do not remember until the next day, skip the missed dose and go back to your regular schedule. Do not take 2 doses at once.

If you take more than 1 dose a day, take the missed dose as soon as possible. If it is within 4 hours of your next dose, skip the one you missed and go back to your regular schedule. Do not take 2 doses at once.

If you forget to take your medication 2 or more days in a row, check with your doctor.

■ *Storage instructions...*
Store at room temperature away from light and moisture.

What side effects may occur?
Side effects cannot be anticipated. If any develop or change in intensity, inform your doctor as soon as possible. Only your doctor can determine whether it is safe for you to continue taking Dilantin.

■ *More common side effects may include:*
Decreased coordination, involuntary eye movement, mental confusion, slurred speech

■ *Other side effects may include:*
Abnormal hair growth, abnormal muscle tone, blood disorders, coarsening of facial features, constipation, dizziness, enlargement of lips, fever, headache, inability to fall asleep or stay asleep, joint pain, nausea, nervousness, overgrowth of gum tissue, Peyronie's disease (a disorder of the penis that causes the penis to bend on an angle during erection, often making intercourse painful or difficult), rapid and spastic involuntary movement, skin peeling or scaling, skin rash, tremors, twitching, vomiting, yellowing of skin and eyes

Why should this drug not be prescribed?

If you have ever had an allergic reaction to or are sensitive to phenytoin or similar epilepsy medications such as Peganone or Mesantoin, do not take Dilantin. Make sure your doctor is aware of any drug reactions you have experienced.

Special warnings about this medication

Tell your doctor if you develop a skin rash. If the rash is scale-like, characterized by reddish or purplish spots, or consists of (fluid-filled) blisters, your doctor may stop Dilantin and prescribe an alternative treatment. If the rash is more like measles, your doctor may have you stop taking Dilantin until the rash is completely gone.

Because Dilantin is processed by the liver, people with impaired liver function, older adults, and those who are seriously ill may show early signs of drug poisoning.

Practicing good dental hygiene minimizes the development of gingival hyperplasia (excessive formation of the gums over the teeth) and its complications.

Avoid drinking alcoholic beverages while taking Dilantin.

Possible food and drug interactions
when taking this medication

If Dilantin is taken with certain other drugs, the effects of either could be increased, decreased, or altered. It is especially important to check with your doctor before combining Dilantin with the following:

Alcohol
Amiodarone (Cordarone)
Antacids containing calcium
Blood-thinning drugs such as Coumadin
Chloramphenicol (Chloromycetin)
Chlordiazepoxide (Librium)
Diazepam (Valium)
Dicumarol
Digitoxin (Crystodigin)
Disulfiram (Antabuse)
Doxycycline (Vibramycin)
Estrogens such as Premarin
Felbamate (Felbatol)
Fluoxetine (Prozac)
Furosemide (Lasix)

Isoniazid (Nydrazid)
Major tranquilizers such as Mellaril and Thorazine
Methylphenidate (Ritalin)
Molindone hydrochloride (Moban)
Oral contraceptives
Phenobarbital
Quinidine (Quinidex)
Reserpine (Diupres)
Rifampin (Rifadin)
Salicylates such as aspirin
Seizure medications such as Depakene, Depakote, Tegretol, and
  Zarontin
Steroid drugs such as prednisone (Deltasone)
Sucralfate (Carafate)
Sulfa drugs such as Gantrisin
Theophylline (Theo-Dur, others)
Tolbutamide (Orinase)
Trazodone (Desyrel)
Ulcer medications such as Tagamet and Zantac

Tricyclic antidepressants (such as Elavil, Norpramin, and others) may cause seizures in susceptible people, making a dosage adjustment of Dilantin necessary.

Hyperglycemia (high blood sugar) may occur in people taking Dilantin, which blocks the release of insulin. People with diabetes may experience increased blood sugar levels due to Dilantin.

Abnormal softening of the bones may occur in people taking Dilantin because of Dilantin's interference with vitamin D metabolism.

Special information
if you are pregnant or breastfeeding
If you are pregnant or plan to become pregnant, inform your doctor immediately. Because of the possibility of birth defects with antiepileptic drugs such as Dilantin, you may need to discontinue the drug. Do not, however, stop taking it without first consulting your doctor. Dilantin appears in breast milk; breastfeeding is not recommended during treatment with this drug.

Recommended dosage
Dosage is tailored to each individual's needs. Your doctor will monitor blood levels of the drug closely, particularly when switching you from one drug to another.

ADULTS

Standard Daily Dosage
If you have not had any previous treatment, your doctor will have you take one 100-milligram Dilantin capsule 3 times daily to start.

On a continuing basis, most adults need 1 capsule 3 to 4 times a day. Your doctor may increase that dosage to 2 capsules 3 times a day, if necessary.

Once-A-Day Dosage
If your seizures are controlled on 100-milligram Dilantin capsules 3 times daily, your doctor may allow you to take the entire 300 milligrams as a single dose once daily.

CHILDREN
The starting dose is 5 milligrams per 2.2 pounds of body weight per day, divided into 2 or 3 equal doses; the most a child should take is 300 milligrams a day. The regular daily dosage is usually 4 to 8 milligrams per 2.2 pounds. Children over 6 years of age and adolescents may need the minimum adult dose (300 milligrams per day).

Overdosage
An overdose of Dilantin can be fatal. If you suspect an overdose, seek medical attention immediately.

■ *Symptoms of Dilantin overdose may include:*
Coma, difficulty in pronouncing words correctly, involuntary eye movement, lack of muscle coordination, low blood pressure, nausea, sluggishness, slurred speech, tremors, vomiting

Brand name:

DILAUDID

Pronounced: Dye-LAW-did
Generic name: Hydromorphone hydrochloride

Why is this drug prescribed?
Dilaudid, a narcotic analgesic, is prescribed for the relief of moderate to severe pain such as that due to:

Biliary colic (pain caused by an obstruction in the gallbladder or bile duct)

Burns
Cancer
Heart attack
Injury (soft tissue and bone)
Renal colic (sharp lower back and groin pain usually caused by the
   passage of a stone through the ureter)
Surgery

Most important fact about this drug

High dose tolerance leading to mental and physical dependence can occur
with the use of Dilaudid when it is taken repeatedly. Physical dependence
(need for continual doses to prevent withdrawal symptoms) can occur after
only a few days of narcotic use, although it usually takes several weeks.

How should you take this medication?

Take Dilaudid exactly as prescribed by your doctor. Never increase the
amount you take without your doctor's approval.

■ *If you miss a dose...*
   Take the forgotten dose as soon as you remember. If it is almost time for
   the next dose, skip the one you missed and go back to your regular
   schedule. Never try to "catch up" by doubling the dose.

■ *Storage instructions...*
   Tablets and liquid should be stored at room temperature. Protect from light
   and extreme cold or heat. Suppositories should be stored in the
   refrigerator.

What side effects may occur?

Side effects cannot be anticipated. If any develop or change in intensity,
inform your doctor as soon as possible. Only your doctor can determine if it
is safe for you to continue taking Dilaudid.

■ *More common side effects may include:*
   Anxiety, constipation, dizziness, drowsiness, fear, impairment of mental
   and physical performance, inability to urinate, mental clouding, mood
   changes, nausea, restlessness, sedation, sluggishness, troubled and
   slowed breathing, vomiting

■ *Less common side effects may include:*
   Agitation, blurred vision, chills, cramps, diarrhea, difficulty urinating,
   disorientation, double vision, dry mouth, exaggerated feelings of depres-

sion or well-being, failure of breathing or heartbeat, faintness/fainting, flushing, hallucinations, headache, increased pressure in the head, insomnia, involuntary eye movements, itching, light-headedness, loss of appetite, low or high blood pressure, muscle rigidity or tremor, muscle spasms of the throat or air passages, palpitations, rashes, shock, slow or rapid heartbeat, small pupils, sudden dizziness on standing, sweating, taste changes, tingling and/or numbness, tremor, uncoordinated muscle movements, visual disturbances, weakness

Why should this drug not be prescribed?

If you are sensitive to or have ever had an allergic reaction to Dilaudid or narcotic pain killers you should not take this medication. Make sure that your doctor is aware of any drug reactions that you have experienced.

Special warnings about this medication

Dilaudid may impair the mental and/or physical abilities required for the performance of potentially hazardous tasks such as driving a car or operating machinery.

Dilaudid should be used with caution if you are in a weakened condition or if you have a severe liver or kidney disorder, hypothyroidism (underactive thyroid gland), Addison's disease (adrenal gland failure), an enlarged prostate, a urethral stricture (narrowing of the urethra), low blood pressure or a head injury.

Dilaudid suppresses the cough reflex; therefore, the doctor will be cautious about prescribing Dilaudid after an operation or for patients with a lung disease.

High doses of Dilaudid may produce labored or slowed breathing. This drug also affects centers that control breathing rhythm and may produce irregular breathing. People who already have breathing difficulties should be very careful about taking Dilaudid.

Narcotics such as Dilaudid may mask or hide the symptoms of sudden or severe abdominal conditions, making diagnosis and treatment difficult.

If you are prone to convulsions, your doctor may not prescribe Dilaudid. It can make seizures worse.

Possible food and drug interactions
when taking this medication

Dilaudid is a central nervous system depressant and intensifies the effects of alcohol. Do not drink alcohol while taking this medication.

If Dilaudid is taken with certain other drugs, the effects of either could be increased, decreased, or altered. It is especially important to check with your doctor before combining Dilaudid with the following:

Antiemetics (drugs that prevent or lessen nausea and vomiting such as Compazine and Phenergan)
Antihistamines such as Benadryl
General anesthetics
Other central nervous system depressants such as Nembutal, Restoril
Other narcotic analgesics such as Demerol and Percocet
Phenothiazines such as Thorazine
Sedative/hypnotics such as Valium, Halcion
Tranquilizers such as Xanax
Tricyclic antidepressants such as Elavil and Tofranil

Special information
if you are pregnant or breastfeeding

Do not take Dilaudid if you are pregnant or plan to become pregnant unless you are directed to do so by your doctor. Drug dependence occurs in newborns when the mother has taken narcotic drugs regularly during pregnancy. Withdrawal signs include irritability and excessive crying, tremors, overactive reflexes, increased breathing rate, increased stools, sneezing, yawning, vomiting, and fever. Dilaudid may appear in breast milk and could affect a nursing infant. If this medication is essential to your health, your doctor may advise you to discontinue breastfeeding your baby until your treatment is finished.

Recommended dosage

ADULTS

Tablets

The usual starting dose of Dilaudid tablets is 2 to 4 milligrams every 4 to 6 hours as determined by your doctor. Severity of pain, your individual response, and your size are used to determine your exact dosage.

Liquid

The usual dose of Dilaudid liquid is ½ to 2 teaspoonfuls every 3 to 6 hours. In some cases, the dosage may be higher.

Suppositories

Dilaudid suppositories (3 milligrams) may provide relief for a longer period of time. The usual adult dose is 1 suppository inserted rectally every 6 to 8 hours or as directed by your doctor.

CHILDREN

The safety and effectiveness of Dilaudid have not been established in children.

OLDER ADULTS

Be very careful when using Dilaudid. Your doctor will prescribe a dose individualized to suit your needs.

Overdosage

▪ *Symptoms of Dilaudid overdose include:*
Bluish tinge to skin, cold and clammy skin, constricted pupils, coma, extreme sleepiness progressing to a state of unresponsiveness, labored or slowed breathing, limp, weak muscles, low blood pressure, slow heart rate

In severe overdosage, the patient may stop breathing. Shock, heart attack, and death can occur.

If you suspect an overdose, seek emergency medical treatment immediately.

Generic name:

DILTIAZEM

See Cardizem, page 194.

Brand name:

DIMETANE-DC

Pronounced: DYE-meh-tayne DEE SEE
Generic ingredients: Brompheniramine maleate,
Phenylpropanolamine hydrochloride, Codeine phosphate

Why is this drug prescribed?

Dimetane-DC cough syrup is an antihistamine/decongestant/cough suppressant combination that relieves coughs and nasal congestion caused by allergies and the common cold. Brompheniramine, the antihistamine, reduces itching and dries up secretions from the nose, eyes, and throat. Phenylpropanolamine, the decongestant, clears nasal stuffiness and makes breathing easier. Codeine calms a cough.

Most important fact about this drug
Dimetane-DC may cause you to become drowsy or less alert. You should not drive or operate dangerous machinery or participate in any hazardous activity that requires full mental alertness until you know how you react to Dimetane-DC.

How should you take this medication?
Take this medication exactly as prescribed.

Do not exceed the directed dosage.

■ *If you miss a dose...*
Take it as soon as you remember. If it is almost time for your next dose, skip the one you missed and go back to your regular schedule. Do not take 2 doses at once.

■ *Storage instructions...*
Store at room temperature in a tightly closed container, away from light.

What side effects may occur?
Side effects cannot be anticipated. If any side effects develop or change in intensity, tell your doctor as soon as possible. Only your doctor can determine whether it is safe for you to continue taking Dimetane-DC.

■ *More common side effects may include:*
Dizziness/light-headedness, drowsiness, dry mouth, nose, and throat, sedation, thickening of phlegm

■ *Less common or rare side effects may include:*
Anemia, constipation, convulsions, diarrhea, difficulty sleeping, difficulty urinating, disturbed coordination, exaggerated sense of well-being or depression, frequent urination, headache, high blood pressure, hives, increased sensitivity to light, irregular heartbeat, irritability, itching, loss of appetite, low blood pressure, nausea, nervousness, rash, shortness of breath, stomach upset, tightness in chest, tremor, vision changes, vomiting, weakness, wheezing

Why should this drug not be prescribed?
This medication should not be given to children under 2 years of age or used by nursing mothers.

Do not take Dimetane-DC if you have severe high blood pressure or heart disease, or if you are taking antidepressant drugs known as MAO inhibitors (Nardil, Parnate). Dimetane-DC is not for treatment of asthma or other breathing disorders. Avoid Dimetane-DC if you have ever had an allergic reaction to it or are sensitive to any of its ingredients.

Special warnings about this medication

Use Dimetane-DC cautiously if you have, or have ever had, bronchial asthma, the eye condition called narrow-angle glaucoma, stomach, intestinal, or bladder obstruction, diabetes, high blood pressure, heart disease, or thyroid disease.

Codeine can cause drug dependence and tolerance with continued use; your doctor will monitor your use of this drug carefully.

Antihistamines can make young children excited.

Possible food and drug interactions
when taking this medication

Dimetane-DC may increase the effects of alcohol. Do not drink alcohol while taking this medication.

If Dimetane-DC is taken with certain other drugs, the effects of either drug could be increased, decreased, or altered. It is especially important to check with your doctor before combining Dimetane-DC with the following:

MAO inhibitor-type antidepressant drugs such as Nardil and Parnate
Medications for high blood pressure such as Aldomet
Sedatives/hypnotics such as phenobarbital, Halcion, and Seconal
Tranquilizers such as Xanax, BuSpar, Librium, and Valium

Special information
if you are pregnant or breastfeeding

No information is available about the safety of Dimetane-DC during pregnancy. If you are pregnant or plan to become pregnant, inform your doctor immediately.

Dimetane-DC should not be taken if you are breastfeeding. If Dimetane-DC is essential to your health, your doctor may advise you to stop breastfeeding until your treatment is finished.

Recommended dosage

Do not take more than 6 doses in 24 hours.

ADULTS AND CHILDREN 12 YEARS OLD AND OVER

The recommended dosage is 2 teaspoonfuls every 4 hours.

CHILDREN 6 TO UNDER 12 YEARS OLD

The usual dosage is 1 teaspoonful every 4 hours.

CHILDREN 2 TO UNDER 6 YEARS OLD

The dosage is one-half teaspoonful every 4 hours.

Overdosage

An overdose of antihistamines may cause hallucinations, convulsions, and death, especially in infants and small children. If you suspect an overdose, seek medical treatment immediately.

- *Symptoms of Dimetane-DC overdose may include:*
  Anxiety, breathing difficulty, convulsions, delirium, depression, dilated pupils, excessive excitement or stimulation, extreme sleepiness leading to loss of consciousness, hallucinations, heart attack, high blood pressure, irregular heartbeat, rapid heartbeat, restlessness, tremors

Brand name:

DIOVAN

Pronounced: DYE-oh-van
Generic name: Valsartan

Why is this drug prescribed?

Diovan is one of a new class of blood pressure medications called angiotensin II receptor antagonists. Diovan works by preventing the hormone angiotensin II from narrowing the blood vessels, which tends to raise blood pressure. Diovan may be prescribed alone or with other blood pressure medications, such as diuretics that help the body get rid of excess water.

Most important fact about this drug

You must take Diovan regularly for it to be effective. Since blood pressure declines gradually, it may be several weeks before you get the full benefit of Diovan, and you must continue taking it even if you are feeling well. Diovan does not cure high blood pressure; it merely keeps it under control.

How should you take this medication?

Diovan can be taken with or without food. Try to get in the habit of taking it at the same time each day—for example, before or after breakfast. You'll be less likely to forget your dose.

■ *If you miss a dose...*
Take it as soon as possible. If it is almost time for your next dose, skip the one you missed and go back to your regular schedule. Never take 2 doses at the same time.

■ *Storage instructions...*
Store at room temperature. Keep in a tightly closed container, away from moisture.

What side effects may occur?
Side effects cannot be anticipated. If any develop or change in intensity, tell your doctor as soon as possible. Only your doctor can determine if it is safe for you to continue taking Diovan.

■ *More common side effects may include:*
Cold or flu, dizziness, headache

■ *Less common side effects may include:*
Abdominal pain, fatigue

Why should this drug not be prescribed?
Do not take Diovan while pregnant. Avoid it if it causes an allergic reaction.

Special warnings about this medication
In rare cases, Diovan can cause a severe drop in blood pressure. The problem is more likely if your body's supply of water has been depleted by high doses of diuretics. Symptoms include light-headedness or faintness, and are more likely when you first start taking the drug. Call your doctor if they occur. You may need to have your dosage adjusted.

If you have liver or kidney disease, Diovan must be used with caution. Be sure the doctor is aware of either problem.

Possible food and drug interactions
when taking this medication
No significant interactions have been reported.

Special information
if you are pregnant or breastfeeding
Drugs such as Diovan can cause injury or even death to the unborn child when used during the last 6 months of pregnancy. As soon as you find out that you're pregnant, stop taking Diovan and call your doctor. Diovan may

also appear in breast milk and could affect the nursing infant. If this medication is essential to your health, your doctor may advise you to avoid breastfeeding while you are taking Diovan.

Recommended dosage

ADULTS

The usual starting dose is 80 milligrams once a day. If your blood pressure does not go down, your doctor may increase the dose or add a diuretic to your regimen. The maximum recommended dose is 320 milligrams a day.

CHILDREN

The safety and effectiveness of Diovan in children have not been studied.

Overdosage

Because Diovan is a relatively new drug, there has been little experience with overdosage. However, the most likely results would be extremely low blood pressure and an abnormally slow or rapid heartbeat. If you suspect an overdose, seek medical attention immediately.

Brand name:

DIPENTUM

Pronounced: dye-PENT-um
Generic name: Olsalazine sodium

Why is this drug prescribed?

Dipentum is an anti-inflammatory drug used to maintain long-term freedom from symptoms of ulcerative colitis (chronic inflammation and ulceration of the large intestine and rectum). It is prescribed for people who cannot take sulfasalazine (Azulfidine).

Most important fact about this drug

If you have kidney disease, Dipentum could cause further damage. You'll need regular checks on your kidney function, so be sure to keep all regular appointments with your doctor.

How should you take this medication?

Take Dipentum for as long as your doctor has directed, even if you feel better.

Take Dipentum with food.

■ *If you miss a dose...*
Take it as soon as you remember. If it is almost time for your next dose, skip the one you missed and go back to your regular schedule. Do not take 2 doses at once.

■ *Storage instructions...*
Store at room temperature.

What side effects may occur?
Side effects cannot be anticipated. If any develop or change in intensity, inform your doctor as soon as possible. Only your doctor can determine if it is safe for you to continue taking Dipentum.

Diarrhea or loose stools are the most common side effects.

■ *Other side effects may include:*
Abdominal pain/cramping, bloating, depression, dizziness, drowsiness, headache, heartburn, indigestion, inflammation of the mouth, insomnia, joint pain, light-headedness, loss of appetite, nausea, rectal bleeding, skin itching, skin rash, sluggishness, upper respiratory infection, vertigo, vomiting

Rare cases of hepatitis have been reported in people taking Dipentum. Symptoms may include aching muscles, chills, fever, headache, joint pain, loss of appetite, vomiting, and yellowish skin.

Why should this drug not be prescribed?
You should not be using Dipentum if you are allergic to salicylates such as aspirin.

Special warnings about this medication
If diarrhea occurs, contact your doctor.

Possible food and drug interactions
when taking this medication
If Dipentum is taken with certain other drugs, the effects of either could be increased, decreased, or altered. It is especially important to check with your doctor before combining Dipentum with warfarin (Coumadin).

Special information
if you are pregnant or breastfeeding
The effects of Dipentum in pregnancy have not been adequately studied. Pregnant women should use Dipentum only if the possible gains warrant the possible risks to the unborn child. Women who breastfeed an infant should

use Dipentum cautiously, because it is not known whether this drug appears in breast milk and what effect it might have on a nursing infant.

Recommended dosage

ADULTS

The usual dose is a total of 1 gram per day, divided into 2 equal doses.

CHILDREN

Safety and effectiveness have not been established in children.

Overdosage

There have been no reports of Dipentum overdose. However, should you suspect one, seek medical help immediately.

Generic name:

DIPHENHYDRAMINE

See Benadryl, page 137.

Generic name:

DIPHENOXYLATE WITH ATROPINE

See Lomotil, page 685.

Generic name:

DIPIVEFRIN

See Propine, page 1018.

Brand name:

DIPROLENE

Pronounced: dye-PROH-leen
Generic name: Betamethasone dipropionate

Why is this drug prescribed?

Diprolene, a synthetic cortisone-like steroid available in cream, gel, lotion, or ointment form, is used to treat certain itchy rashes and other inflammatory skin conditions.

Most important fact about this drug

When you use Diprolene, you inevitably absorb some of the medication through your skin and into the bloodstream. Too much absorption can lead to unwanted side effects elsewhere in the body. To keep this problem to a minimum, avoid using large amounts of Diprolene over large areas, and do not cover it with airtight dressings such as plastic wrap or adhesive bandages.

How should you use this medication?

Apply Diprolene in a thin film, exactly as prescribed by your doctor. A typical regimen is 1 or 2 applications per day. Do not use the medication for longer than prescribed.

Diprolene is for use only on the skin. Be careful to keep it out of your eyes.

Once you have applied Diprolene, never cover the skin with an airtight bandage or other tight dressing.

For a fungal or bacterial skin infection, you will need antifungal or antibacterial medication in addition to Diprolene. If improvement is not prompt, you should stop using Diprolene until the infection is visibly clearing.

■ *If you miss a dose...*
Apply it as soon as you remember. If it is almost time for the next dose, skip the one you missed and go back to your regular schedule.

■ *Storage instructions...*
Store at room temperature.

What side effects may occur?

Side effects cannot be anticipated. A possible side effect of Diprolene is stinging or burning of the skin where the medication is applied.

■ *Other side effects on the skin may include:*
Acne-like eruptions, atrophy, "broken" capillaries (fine reddish lines), cracking or tightening, dryness, infected hair follicles, irritation, itching, prickly heat, rash, redness, sensitivity

Diprolene can be absorbed and produce side effects elsewhere in the body; see the "Overdosage" section on page 396.

Why should this drug not be prescribed?

Do not use Diprolene if you are sensitive to it or have ever had an allergic reaction to it.

Special warnings about this medication
Do not use Diprolene to treat any condition other than the one for which it was prescribed.

**Possible food and drug interactions
when using this medication**
No interactions have been reported.

**Special information
if you are pregnant or breastfeeding**
It is not known whether Diprolene, when applied to skin, causes any problem during pregnancy or while breastfeeding. Nevertheless, let your doctor know if you are pregnant or are planning to become pregnant.

Recommended dosage

ADULTS

Diprolene products are not to be used with airtight dressings.

Cream or ointment
Apply a thin film to the affected skin areas once or twice daily. Treatment should be limited to 45 grams per week.

Lotion
Apply a few drops of Diprolene Lotion to the affected area once or twice daily and massage lightly until the lotion disappears.

Treatment must be limited to 14 days; do not use any more than 50 milliliters per week.

Gel
Apply a thin layer of Diprolene Gel to the affected area once or twice daily and rub in gently and completely.

Treatment must be limited to 14 days; do not use any more than 50 grams per week.

CHILDREN

Use of Diprolene Gel, Lotion, Ointment, and AF Cream is not recommended for children under 12 years of age. For those 12 and over, use no more than necessary to obtain results.

Overdosage

With copious or prolonged use of Diprolene, hormone absorbed into the bloodstream may cause high blood sugar, sugar in the urine, and a group of symptoms called Cushing's syndrome.

■ *Symptoms of Cushing's syndrome may include:*
Acne, depression, high blood pressure, humped upper back, insomnia, moon-faced appearance, muscle weakness, obese trunk, paranoia, stretch marks, susceptibility to bruising, fractures, infections, retardation of growth, delayed weight gain, wasted limbs

Cushing's syndrome may also trigger the development of diabetes mellitus. Left uncorrected, the syndrome may become serious. If you suspect your use of Diprolene has led to this problem, seek medical attention immediately.

Generic name:

DIPYRIDAMOLE

See Persantine, page 947.

Generic name:

DIRITHROMYCIN

See Dynabac, page 428.

Brand name:

DISALCID

Pronounced: dye-SAL-sid
Generic name: Salsalate

Why is this drug prescribed?

Disalcid, a nonsteroidal anti-inflammatory drug, is used to relieve the symptoms of rheumatoid arthritis, osteoarthritis (the most common form of arthritis), and other rheumatic disorders (conditions that involve pain and inflammation in joints and the tissues around them).

Most important fact about this drug

Disalcid contains salicylate, an ingredient that may be associated with the development of Reye's syndrome (a disorder that causes abnormal brain and liver function). It occurs mostly in children who have taken aspirin or other medications containing salicylate to relieve symptoms of the flu or chickenpox. Do not take Disalcid if you have flu symptoms or chickenpox.

How should you take this medication?
Take Disalcid exactly as prescribed. Food may slow its absorption. However, your doctor may ask you to take Disalcid with food in order to avoid stomach upset.

■ *If you miss a dose...*
Take it as soon as you remember. If it is almost time for your next dose, skip the one you missed and go back to your regular schedule. Never take 2 doses at once.

■ *Storage instructions...*
Store at room temperature. Keep out of the reach of children.

What side effects may occur?
Side effects cannot be anticipated. If any develop or change in intensity, inform your doctor as soon as possible. Only your doctor can determine if it is safe for you to continue taking Disalcid.

■ *Side effects may include:*
Hearing impairment, nausea, rash, ringing in the ears, vertigo

Why should this drug not be prescribed?
Disalcid should not be taken if you are sensitive to or have ever had an allergic reaction to salsalate.

Special warnings about this medication
Use Disalcid with extreme caution if you have chronic kidney disease or a peptic ulcer.

Salicylates occasionally cause asthma in people who are sensitive to aspirin. Although Disalcid contains a salicylate, it is less likely than aspirin to cause this reaction.

Possible food and drug interactions
when taking this medication
If Disalcid is taken with certain other drugs, the effects of either could be increased, decreased, or altered. It is especially important to check with your doctor before combining Disalcid with the following:

ACE inhibitor-type blood pressure drugs such as Capoten and Vasotec

Acetazolamide (Diamox)

Aspirin and other drugs containing salicylates such as Bufferin and
    Empirin

Blood-thinning medications such as Coumadin

Medications for gout such as Zyloprim and Benemid

Methotrexate (Rheumatrex)

Naproxen (Anaprox, Naprosyn)

Oral diabetes drugs such as Glucotrol and Tolinase

Penicillin (Pen-Vee K)

Phenytoin (Dilantin)

Steroids such as Deltasone and Decadron

Sulfinpyrazone (Anturane)

Thyroid medications such as Synthroid

Special information
if you are pregnant or breastfeeding

The effects of Disalcid during pregnancy have not been adequately studied. If
you are pregnant or plan to become pregnant, inform your doctor immediately. Disalcid may appear in breast milk and could affect a nursing infant. If this
medication is essential to your health, your doctor may advise you to stop
breastfeeding until your treatment with Disalcid is finished.

Recommended dosage

You may not feel the full benefit of this medication for 3 to 4 days.

ADULTS

The usual dosage is 3,000 milligrams daily, divided into smaller doses as
follows:

(1) 2 doses of two 750-milligram tablets

(2) 2 doses of three 500-milligram tablets or capsules

(3) 3 doses of two 500-milligram tablets or capsules

CHILDREN

Safety and effectiveness of Disalcid use in children have not been
established.

OLDER ADULTS

A lower dosage may be sufficient to achieve desired blood levels without the
more common side effects.

Overdosage

Any medication taken in excess can have serious consequences. Deaths have occurred from salicylate overdose. If you suspect an overdose, seek medical treatment immediately.

■ *Symptoms of Disalcid overdose may include:*
Confusion, dehydration, diarrhea, drowsiness, headache, high body temperature, hyperventilation, ringing in the ears, sweating, vertigo, vomiting

Generic name:

DISOPYRAMIDE

See Norpace, page 864.

Brand name:

DITROPAN

Pronounced: DYE-tro-pan
Generic name: Oxybutynin chloride

Why is this drug prescribed?

Ditropan relaxes the bladder muscle and reduces spasms. It is used to treat the urgency, frequency, leakage, incontinence, and painful or difficult urination caused by a neurogenic bladder (altered bladder function due to a nervous system abnormality).

Most important fact about this drug

Ditropan can cause heat prostration (fever and heat stroke due to decreased sweating) in high temperatures. If you live in a hot climate or will be exposed to high temperatures, take appropriate precautions.

How should you take this medication?

Take this medication exactly as prescribed.

Ditropan can make your mouth dry. Sucking hard candies or melting bits of ice in your mouth can remedy the problem.

■ *If you miss a dose...*
Take the forgotten dose as soon as you remember. If it is almost time for your next dose, skip the one you missed and go back to your regular schedule. Never take 2 doses at once.

■ *Storage instructions...*
Keep this medication in a tightly closed container and store it at room temperature. Protect the syrup from direct light.

What side effects may occur?
Side effects cannot be anticipated. If any develop or change in intensity, inform your doctor as soon as possible. Only your doctor can determine if it is safe for you to continue taking Ditropan.

■ *Side effects may include:*
Constipation, decreased production of tears, decreased sweating, difficulty falling or staying asleep, dilation of the pupil of the eye, dim vision, dizziness, drowsiness, dry mouth, eye paralysis, hallucinations, impotence, inability to urinate, nausea, palpitations, rapid heartbeat, rash, restlessness, suppression of milk production, weakness

Why should this drug not be prescribed?
You should not take Ditropan if you have certain types of untreated glaucoma (excessive pressure in the eye), partial or complete blockage of the gastrointestinal tract, or paralytic ileus (obstructed bowel). Ditropan should also be avoided if you have severe colitis (inflamed colon), myasthenia gravis (abnormal muscle weakness), or urinary tract obstruction. This drug is usually not prescribed for the elderly or debilitated.

Do not take this medication if you are sensitive or have ever had an allergic reaction to it. Make sure your doctor is aware of any allergic reactions you have experienced.

Special warnings about this medication
If you have an ileostomy or colostomy (an artificial opening to the bowel) and develop diarrhea while taking Ditropan, inform your doctor immediately.

Ditropan may cause drowsiness or blurred vision. Driving or operating dangerous machinery or participating in any hazardous activity that requires full mental alertness is not recommended until you know how this medication affects you.

Your doctor will prescribe Ditropan with caution if you have liver disease, kidney disease, or a nervous system disorder.

Ditropan may aggravate the symptoms of overactive thyroid, heart disease or congestive heart failure, irregular or rapid heartbeat, high blood pressure, or enlarged prostate.

Possible food and drug interactions
when taking this medication

If Ditropan is taken with certain other drugs, the effects of either may be increased, decreased or altered. It is especially important to check with your doctor before combining Ditropan with alcohol or sedatives such as Halcion or Restoril because increased drowsiness may occur.

Special information
if you are pregnant or breastfeeding

The effects of Ditropan during pregnancy have not been adequately studied. If you are pregnant or plan to become pregnant, inform your doctor immediately. Ditropan may appear in breast milk and could affect a nursing infant. If this medication is essential to your health, your doctor may advise you to stop breastfeeding until your treatment is finished.

Recommended dosage

ADULTS

Tablets

The usual dose is one 5 milligram tablet taken 2 to 3 times a day. You should not take more than 4 tablets a day.

Syrup

The usual dose is one teaspoonful 2 to 3 times a day, but not more than 4 times a day.

CHILDREN OVER 5 YEARS OF AGE

Tablets

The usual dose is one 5 milligram tablet taken twice a day. The most a child should take is 3 tablets a day.

Syrup

The usual dose is one teaspoonful 2 times a day, but not more than 3 times a day.

Ditropan is not recommended for children under 5 years of age.

Overdosage

Any medication taken in excess can have serious consequences. If you suspect an overdose, seek medical attention immediately.

- *Symptoms of Ditropan overdose may include:*
  Coma, convulsions, delirium, difficulty breathing, fever, flushing, hallucinations, irritability, low or high blood pressure, nausea, paralysis, rapid heartbeat, restlessness, tremor, vomiting

Brand name:

DIURIL

Pronounced: DYE-your-il
Generic name: Chlorothiazide

Why is this drug prescribed?
Diuril is used in the treatment of high blood pressure and other conditions that require the elimination of excess fluid (water) from the body. These conditions include congestive heart failure, cirrhosis of the liver, corticosteroid and estrogen therapy, and kidney disease. When used for high blood pressure, Diuril can be used alone or with other high blood pressure medications. Diuril contains a form of thiazide, a diuretic that prompts your body to eliminate more fluid, which helps lower blood pressure.

Most important fact about this drug
If you have high blood pressure, you must take Diuril regularly for it to be effective. Since blood pressure declines gradually, it may be several weeks before you get the full benefit of Diuril; and you must continue taking it even if you are feeling well. Diuril does not cure high blood pressure; it merely keeps it under control.

How should you take this medication?
Take Diuril exactly as prescribed. Stopping Diuril suddenly could cause your condition to worsen.

- *If you miss a dose...*
  Take it as soon as you remember. If it is almost time for your next dose, skip the one you missed and go back to your regular schedule. Never take 2 doses at the same time.

- *Storage instructions...*
  Store at room temperature in a tightly closed container. Protect from moisture and freezing.

What side effects may occur?
Side effects cannot be anticipated. If any develop or change in intensity, inform your doctor as soon as possible. Only your doctor can determine if it is safe for you to continue taking Diuril.

■ *Side effects may include:*
Abdominal cramps, anemia, changes in blood sugar, constipation, diarrhea, difficulty breathing, dizziness, dizziness on standing up, fever, fluid in lungs, hair loss, headache, high levels of sugar in urine, hives, hypersensitivity reactions, impotence, inflammation of the pancreas, inflammation of the salivary glands, light-headedness, loss of appetite, low blood pressure, low potassium (leading to symptoms such as dry mouth, excessive thirst, weak or irregular heartbeat, muscle pain or cramps), lung inflammation, muscle spasms, nausea, rash, reddish or purplish spots on skin, restlessness, sensitivity to light, Stevens-Johnson syndrome, stomach irritation, stomach upset, tingling or pins and needles, vertigo, vision changes, vomiting, weakness, yellow eyes and skin

Why should this drug not be prescribed?
If you are unable to urinate, you should not take this medication. If you are sensitive to or have ever had an allergic reaction to Diuril or other thiazide-type diuretics, or if you are sensitive to sulfa drugs, you should not take this medication.

Special warnings about this medication
Diuretics can cause your body to lose too much potassium. Signs of an excessively low potassium level include muscle weakness and rapid or irregular heartbeat. To boost your potassium level, your doctor may recommend eating potassium-rich foods or taking a potassium supplement.

If you are taking Diuril, your doctor will do a complete assessment of your kidney function and continue to monitor it. Use with caution if you have severe kidney disease.

If you have liver disease, diabetes, gout, or the connective tissue disease lupus erythematosus, your doctor will prescribe Diuril cautiously.

If you have bronchial asthma or a history of allergies you may be at greater risk for an allergic reaction to this medication.

Dehydration, excessive sweating, severe diarrhea, or vomiting could deplete your body's fluids and lower your blood pressure too much. Be careful when exercising and in hot weather.

Notify your doctor or dentist that you are taking Diuril if you have a medical emergency, and before you have surgery or dental treatment.

Possible food and drug interactions
when taking this medication
Diuril may increase the effects of alcohol. Do not drink alcohol while taking this medication.

If Diuril is taken with certain other drugs, the effects of either may be increased, decreased, or altered. It is especially important to check with your doctor before combining Diuril with the following:

Barbiturates such as phenobarbital and Seconal
Cholesterol-lowering drugs such as Questran and Colestid
Drugs to treat diabetes such as insulin and Micronase
Lithium (Lithonate)
Narcotic painkillers such as Percocet
Nonsteroidal anti-inflammatory drugs such as Naprosyn and Motrin
Norepinephrine (Levophed)
Other drugs for high blood pressure such as Capoten and Procardia XL
Steroids such as prednisone

Special information
if you are pregnant or breastfeeding

The effects of Diuril during pregnancy have not been adequately studied. If you are pregnant or plan to become pregnant, inform your doctor immediately. Diuril appears in breast milk and could affect a nursing infant. If this medication is essential to your health, your doctor may advise you to discontinue breastfeeding until your treatment is finished.

Recommended dosage

ADULTS

Diuril comes in tablets, an oral suspension, and an intravenous preparation, reserved for emergencies. Dosages below are for the oral preparations.

Swelling due to excess water

The usual dose is 0.5 gram to 1 gram 1 or 2 times per day. Your doctor may have you take this medication on alternate days or on some other on-off schedule.

High Blood Pressure

The starting dose is 0.5 gram to 1 gram per day, taken as one dose or two or more smaller doses. Your doctor will adjust the dosage to suit your needs.

CHILDREN

Dosages for children are adjusted according to weight, generally 10 milligrams per pound of body weight daily in 2 doses.

Under 6 months
Dosage may be up to 15 milligrams per pound of body weight per day in 2 doses.

Under 2 years
The usual dosage is 125 milligrams to 375 milligrams per day in 2 doses. The liquid form of this drug may be used in children under 2 years of age at ½ to 1½ teaspoons (2.5 to 7.5 milliliters) per day.

2 to 12 years
The usual dosage is 375 milligrams to 1 gram daily in 2 doses. The liquid form of this medication may be used in children 2 to 12 years at 1½ to 4 teaspoons (7.5 milliliters to 20 milliliters) per day.

Overdosage
Any medication taken in excess can have serious consequences. If you suspect an overdose, seek medical attention immediately.

- *Signs of Diuril overdose may include:*
  Dehydration and symptoms of low potassium (dry mouth, excessive thirst, weak or irregular heartbeat, muscle pain or cramps)

Generic name:

DIVALPROEX SODIUM

See Depakote, page 348.

Generic name:

DOCUSATE

See Colace, page 255.

Brand name:

DOLOBID

Pronounced: DOLL-oh-bid
Generic name: Diflunisal

Why is this drug prescribed?
Dolobid, a nonsteroidal anti-inflammatory drug, is used to treat mild to moderate pain and relieve the inflammation, swelling, stiffness, and joint

pain associated with rheumatoid arthritis and osteoarthritis (the most common form of arthritis).

Most important fact about this drug
You should have frequent checkups with your doctor if you take Dolobid regularly. Ulcers or internal bleeding can occur without warning.

How should you take this medication?
Dolobid should be taken with food or food together with an antacid, and with a full glass of water or milk. Never take it on an empty stomach.

Tablets should be swallowed whole, not chewed or crushed.

Take this medication exactly as prescribed by your doctor. If you are using Dolobid for arthritis, it should be taken regularly.

■ *If you miss a dose...*
   Take it as soon as you remember. If it is almost time for your next dose, skip the one you missed and go back to your regular schedule. Never take 2 doses at the same time.

■ *Storage instructions...*
   Do not store in damp places like the bathroom.

What side effects may occur?
Side effects cannot be anticipated. If any develop or change in intensity, inform your doctor as soon as possible. Only your doctor can determine if it is safe for you to continue taking Dolobid.

■ *More common side effects may include:*
   Abdominal pain, constipation, diarrhea, dizziness, fatigue, gas, headache, inability to sleep, indigestion, nausea, rash, ringing in ears, sleepiness, vomiting

■ *Less common or rare side effects may include:*
   Abdominal bleeding, anemia, blurred vision, confusion, depression, disorientation, dry mouth and nose, fluid retention, flushing, hepatitis, hives, inflammation of lips and tongue, itching, kidney failure, light-headedness, loss of appetite, nervousness, painful urination, peptic ulcer, pins and needles, protein or blood in urine, rash, sensitivity to light, skin eruptions, Stevens-Johnson syndrome, vertigo, weakness, yellow eyes and skin

Why should this drug not be prescribed?
If you are sensitive to or have had an allergic reaction to Dolobid, aspirin, or similar drugs, or if you have had asthma attacks caused by aspirin or other

drugs of this type, you should not take this medication. Make sure that your doctor is aware of any drug reactions that you have experienced.

Special warnings about this medication
Peptic ulcers and bleeding can occur without warning.

This drug should be used with caution if you have kidney or liver disease; and it can cause liver inflammation in some people.

Do not take aspirin or any other anti-inflammatory medications while taking Dolobid, unless your doctor tells you to do so.

Nonsteroidal anti-inflammatory drugs such as Dolobid can hide the signs and symptoms of infection. Be sure your doctor knows about any infection you may have.

Dolobid can cause vision problems. If you experience any changes in your vision, inform your doctor.

Dolobid may prolong bleeding time. If you are taking blood-thinning medication, take Dolobid with caution.

If you have heart disease or high blood pressure, use Dolobid with caution. It can increase water retention.

Dolobid may cause you to become drowsy or less alert; therefore, driving or operating dangerous machinery or participating in any hazardous activity that requires full mental alertness is not recommended.

Possible food and drug interactions
when taking this medication
If Dolobid is taken with certain other drugs, the effects of either could be increased, decreased, or altered. It is especially important to check with your doctor before combining Dolobid with the following:

Acetaminophen (Tylenol)
Antacids taken regularly
Aspirin
Cyclosporine (Sandimmune)
Methotrexate (Rheumatrex)
Oral anticoagulants (blood thinners)
Other nonsteroidal anti-inflammatory drugs (Advil, Motrin, Naprosyn, others)
The arthritis medication sulindac (Clinoril)
The diuretic hydrochlorothiazide

**Special information
if you are pregnant or breastfeeding**
The effects of Dolobid during pregnancy have not been adequately studied. If you are pregnant or plan to become pregnant, inform your doctor immediately. Dolobid appears in breast milk and could affect a nursing infant. If this medication is essential to your health, your doctor may advise you to discontinue breastfeeding until your treatment with Dolobid is finished.

Recommended dosage

ADULTS

Mild to Moderate Pain
Starting dose is 1,000 milligrams, followed by 500 milligrams every 8 to 12 hours, depending on the individual. Your physician may adjust your dosage according to your age and weight, and the severity of your symptoms.

Osteoarthritis and Rheumatoid Arthritis
The usual dose is 500 to 1,000 milligrams per day in 2 doses of 250 milligrams or 500 milligrams. Use no more than necessary to relieve the pain.

The maximum recommended dosage is 1,500 milligrams per day.

CHILDREN

Safety and effectiveness of Dolobid have not been established in children under 12 years of age. The drug is not recommended for this age group.

Overdosage
Any medication taken in excess can cause symptoms of overdose. If you suspect an overdose, seek medical attention immediately.

■ *Symptoms of Dolobid overdose may include:*
Abnormally rapid heartbeat, coma, diarrhea, disorientation, drowsiness, hyperventilation, nausea, ringing in the ears, stupor, sweating, vomiting

Generic name:

DONEPEZIL

See Aricept, page 80.

Brand name:

DONNATAL

Pronounced: DON-nuh-tal
Generic ingredients: Phenobarbital, Hyoscyamine sulfate,
* Atropine sulfate, Scopolamine hydrobromide*
Other brand name: Bellatal

Why is this drug prescribed?

Donnatal is a mild antispasmodic medication; it has been used with other drugs for relief of cramps and pain associated with various stomach, intestinal, and bowel disorders, including irritable bowel syndrome, acute colitis, and duodenal ulcer.

One of its ingredients, phenobarbital, is a mild sedative.

Most important fact about this drug

Phenobarbital, one of the ingredients of Donnatal, can be habit-forming. If you have ever been dependent on drugs, do not take Donnatal.

How should you take this medication?

Take Donnatal one-half hour to 1 hour before meals. Use it exactly as prescribed.

■ *If you miss a dose...*
  Take it as soon as you remember. If it is almost time for your next dose, skip the one you missed and go back to your regular schedule. Never take 2 doses at the same time.

■ *Storage instructions...*
  Store at room temperature in a tightly closed container. Protect from light.

What side effects may occur?

Side effects cannot be anticipated. If any develop or change in intensity, inform your doctor as soon as possible. Only your doctor can determine if it is safe for you to continue taking Donnatal.

■ *Side effects may include:*
  Agitation, allergic reaction, bloated feeling, blurred vision, constipation, decreased sweating, difficulty sleeping, difficulty urinating, dilation of the pupil of the eye, dizziness, drowsiness, dry mouth, excitement, fast or

fluttery heartbeat, headache, hives, impotence, muscular and bone pain, nausea, nervousness, rash, reduced sense of taste, suppression of lactation, vomiting, weakness

Why should this drug not be prescribed?
Do not take Donnatal if you suffer from the eye condition called glaucoma, diseases that block the urinary or gastrointestinal tracts, or myasthenia gravis, a condition in which the muscles become progressively paralyzed. Also, you should not use Donnatal if you have intestinal atony (loss of strength in the intestinal muscles), unstable cardiovascular status, severe ulcerative colitis (chronic inflammation and ulceration of the bowel), or hiatal hernia (a rupture in the diaphragm above the stomach). You should also avoid Donnatal if you have acute intermittent porphyria—a disorder of the metabolism in which there is severe abdominal pain and sensitivity to light.

If you are sensitive to or have ever had an allergic reaction to Donnatal, its ingredients, or similar drugs, you should not take this medication. Also avoid Donnatal if phenobarbital makes you excited or restless, instead of calming you down. Make sure your doctor is aware of any drug reactions you have experienced.

Special warnings about this medication
Be cautious in using Donnatal if you suffer from high blood pressure, overactive thyroid (hyperthyroidism), irregular or rapid heartbeat, or heart, kidney, or liver disease.

Donnatal can decrease sweating. If you are exercising or are subjected to high temperatures, be alert for heat prostration.

If you develop diarrhea, especially if you have an ileostomy or colostomy (artificial openings to the bowel), check with your doctor.

If you have a gastric ulcer, use this medication with caution.

Donnatal may cause you to become drowsy or less alert. You should not drive or operate dangerous machinery or participate in any hazardous activity that requires full mental alertness until you know how this drug affects you.

Possible food and drug interactions
when taking this medication
Donnatal may intensify the effects of alcohol. Check with your doctor before using alcohol with this medication.

Avoid taking antacids within 1 hour of a dose of Donnatal; they may reduce its effectiveness.

If Donnatal is taken with certain other drugs, the effects of either could be increased, decreased, or altered. It is especially important to check with your doctor before combining Donnatal with the following:

Antidepressants such as Elavil and Tofranil
Antidepressants known as MAO inhibitors, including Nardil and Parnate
Antihistamines such as Benadryl
Antispasmodic drugs such as Bentyl and Cogentin
Barbiturates such as Seconal
Blood-thinning drugs such as Coumadin
Diarrhea medications containing Kaolin or attapulgite
Digitalis (Lanoxin)
Narcotics such as Percocet
Potassium (Slow-K, K-Dur, others)
Steroids such as Medrol and Deltasone
Tranquilizers such as Valium

Special information
if you are pregnant or breastfeeding

The effects of Donnatal during pregnancy have not been adequately studied. If you are pregnant or plan to become pregnant, this drug should be used only when prescribed by your doctor. It is not known whether Donnatal appears in breast milk. If this medication is essential to your health, your doctor may advise you to discontinue breastfeeding until your treatment is finished.

Recommended dosage

ADULTS

Your doctor will adjust the dosage to your needs.

Tablets or Capsules
The usual dosage is 1 or 2 tablets or capsules, 3 or 4 times a day.

Liquid
The usual dosage is 1 or 2 teaspoonfuls, 3 or 4 times a day.

Donnatal Extentabs
The usual dosage is 1 tablet every 12 hours. Your doctor may tell you to take 1 tablet every 8 hours, if necessary.

CHILDREN

Dosage of the elixir is determined by body weight; it can be given every 4 to 6 hours. Follow your doctor's instructions carefully when giving this medication to a child.

Overdosage
Any medication taken in excess can cause symptoms of overdose. If you suspect an overdose, seek medical attention immediately.

- *The symptoms of Donnatal overdose may include:*
  Blurred vision, central nervous system stimulation, difficulty swallowing, dilated pupils, dizziness, dry mouth, headache, hot and dry skin, nausea, vomiting

Brand name:

DORAL

Pronounced: DOHR-al
Generic name: Quazepam

Why is this drug prescribed?
Doral, a sleeping medication available in tablet form, is taken as short-term treatment for insomnia. Symptoms of insomnia may include difficulty falling asleep, frequent awakenings throughout the night, or very early morning awakening.

Most important fact about this drug
Doral is a chemical cousin of Valium and is potentially addictive. Over time, your body will get used to the prescribed dosage of Doral, and you will no longer derive any benefit from it. If you were to increase the dosage against medical advice, the drug would again work as a sleeping pill—but only until your body adjusted to the higher dosage. This is a vicious circle that can lead to addiction. To avoid this danger, use Doral only as prescribed.

How should you take this medication?
Take Doral exactly as prescribed by your doctor—one dose per day, at bedtime. Keep in touch with your doctor; if you respond very well, it may be possible to cut your dosage in half after the first few nights. The older or more run-down you are, the more desirable it is to try for this early dosage reduction.

If you have been taking Doral regularly for 6 weeks or so, you may experience withdrawal symptoms if you stop suddenly, or even if you reduce the dosage without specific instructions on how to do it. Always follow your doctor's advice for tapering off gradually from Doral.

- *If you miss a dose...*
  Take this medication only if needed.

- *Storage instructions...*
  Store at room temperature, away from moisture.

What side effects may occur?
Side effects cannot be anticipated. If any develop or change in intensity, inform your doctor as soon as possible. Only your doctor can determine if it is safe for you to continue taking Doral.

- *More common side effects may include:*
  Drowsiness during the day, headache

- *Less common side effects may include:*
  Changes in sex drive, dizziness, dry mouth, fatigue, inability to urinate, incontinence, indigestion, irregular menstrual periods, irritability, muscle spasms, slurred or otherwise abnormal speech, yellowed eyes and skin

In rare instances, Doral produces agitation, sleep disturbances, hallucinations, or stimulation—exactly the opposite of the desired effect. If this should happen to you, tell your doctor; he or she will take you off the medication.

Why should this drug not be prescribed?
Do not take Doral if you are sensitive to it, or if you have ever had an allergic reaction to it or to another Valium-type medication.

You should not take Doral if you know or suspect that you have sleep apnea (short periods of interrupted breathing that occur during sleep).

You should not take Doral if you are pregnant.

Special warnings about this medication
Because Doral may decrease your daytime alertness, do not drive, climb, or operate dangerous machinery until you find out how the drug affects you. In some cases, Doral's sedative effect may last for several days after the last dose.

If you are suffering from depression, Doral may make your depression worse.

If you have ever abused alcohol or drugs, you are at special risk for addiction to Doral.

Never increase the dosage of Doral on your own. Tell your doctor right away if the medication no longer seems to be working.

Possible food and drug interactions
when taking this medication

If Doral is taken with certain other drugs, the effects of either could be increased, decreased, or altered. It is especially important to check with your doctor before combining Doral with the following:

Antihistamines such as Benadryl
Antiseizure medications such as Dilantin and Tegretol
Mood-altering medications such as Thorazine and Clozaril
Other central nervous system depressants such as Xanax and Valium

Do not drink alcohol while taking Doral; it can increase the drug's effects.

Special information
if you are pregnant or breastfeeding

Because Doral may cause harm to the unborn child, it should not be taken during pregnancy. If you want to have a baby, tell your doctor, and plan to discontinue taking Doral before getting pregnant.

Babies whose mothers are taking Doral at the time of birth may experience withdrawal symptoms from the drug. Such babies may be "floppy" (flaccid) instead of having normal muscle tone.

Since Doral does appear in breast milk, you should not take this medication if you are nursing a baby.

Recommended dosage

ADULTS

The recommended initial dose is 15 milligrams daily. Your doctor may later reduce this dosage to 7.5 milligrams.

CHILDREN

Safety and efficacy of Doral in children under 18 years old have not been established.

OLDER ADULTS

You may be more sensitive to this drug, and the doctor may reduce the dosage after only 1 or 2 nights.

Overdosage

Any medication taken in excess can have serious consequences. If you suspect an overdose of Doral, seek medical attention immediately.

■ *Symptoms of an overdose of Doral may include:*
Coma, confusion, extreme sleepiness

Brand name:

DORYX

Pronounced: DORE-icks
Generic name: Doxycycline hyclate
Other brand names: Vibramycin, Vibra-Tabs

Why is this drug prescribed?

Doxycycline is a broad-spectrum tetracycline antibiotic used against a wide variety of bacterial infections, including Rocky Mountain spotted fever and other fevers caused by ticks, fleas, and lice; urinary tract infections; trachoma (chronic infections of the eye); and some gonococcal infections in adults. It is also used with other medications to treat severe acne and amoebic dysentery (diarrhea caused by severe parasitic infection of the intestines).

Doxycycline may also be taken for the prevention of malaria on foreign trips of less than 4 months' duration.

Occasionally doctors prescribe doxycycline to treat early Lyme disease and to prevent "traveler's diarrhea." These are not yet officially approved uses for this drug.

Most important fact about this drug

Children under 8 years old and women in the last half of pregnancy should not take this medication. It may cause developing teeth to become permanently discolored (yellow-gray-brown).

How should you take this medication?

Take doxycycline with a full glass of water or other liquid to avoid irritating your throat or stomach. Doxycycline can be taken with or without food. However, if the medicine does upset your stomach, you may wish to take it with a glass of milk or after you have eaten. Doxycycline tablets should be swallowed whole.

Take this medication exactly as prescribed by your doctor, even if your symptoms have disappeared.

If you are taking an oral suspension form of doxycycline, shake the bottle well before using. Do not use outdated doxycycline.

■ *If you miss a dose...*

Take the forgotten dose as soon as you remember. If it is almost time for the next dose, put it off for several hours after taking the missed dose. Specifically, if you are taking one dose a day, take the next one 10 to 12 hours after the missed dose. If you are taking two doses a day, take the next one 5 to 6 hours after the missed dose. If you are taking three doses a day, take the next one 2 to 4 hours after the missed dose. Then return to your regular schedule.

■ *Storage instructions...*

Doxycycline can be stored at room temperature. Protect from light and excessive heat.

What side effects may occur?

Side effects cannot be anticipated. If any develop or change in intensity, inform your doctor as soon as possible. Only your doctor can determine if it is safe for you to continue taking doxycycline.

■ *More common side effects may include:*

Angioedema (chest pain; swelling of face, around lips, tongue and throat, arms and legs; difficulty swallowing), bulging foreheads in infants, diarrhea, difficulty swallowing, discolored teeth in infants and children (more common during long-term use of tetracycline), inflammation of the tongue, loss of appetite, nausea, rash, rectal or genital itching, severe allergic reaction (hives, itching, and swelling), skin sensitivity to light, vomiting

■ *Less common or rare side effects may include:*

Aggravation of lupus erythematosus (disease of the connective tissue), skin inflammation and peeling, throat inflammation and ulcerations

Why should this drug not be prescribed?

If you are sensitive to or have ever had an allergic reaction to doxycycline or drugs of this type, you should not take this medication. Make sure your doctor is aware of any drug reactions that you have experienced.

Special warnings about this medication

As with other antibiotics, treatment with doxycycline may result in a growth of bacteria that do not respond to this medication and can cause a secondary infection.

Bulging foreheads in infants and headaches in adults have occurred. These symptoms disappeared when doxycycline was discontinued.

You may become more sensitive to sunlight while taking doxycycline. Be careful if you are going out in the sun or using a sunlamp. If you develop a skin rash, notify your doctor immediately.

Birth control pills that contain estrogen may not be as effective while you are taking tetracycline drugs. Ask your doctor or pharmacist if you should use another form of birth control while taking doxycycline.

Doxycycline syrup (Vibramycin) contains a sulfite that may cause allergic reactions in certain people. This reaction happens more frequently to people with asthma.

Possible food and drug interactions
when taking this medication

If doxycycline is taken with certain other drugs, the effects of either could be increased, decreased, or altered. It is especially important to check with your doctor before combining doxycycline with the following:

Antacids containing aluminum, calcium, or magnesium, and iron-
    containing preparations such as Maalox, Mylanta, and others
Barbiturates such as phenobarbital
Bismuth subsalicylate (Pepto-Bismol)
Blood-thinning medications such as Coumadin
Carbamazepine (Tegretol)
Oral contraceptives
Penicillin (V-Cillin K, Pen-Vee K, others)
Phenytoin (Dilantin)
Sodium bicarbonate

Special information
if you are pregnant or breastfeeding

Doxycycline should not be used during pregnancy. Tetracycline can damage developing teeth during the last half of pregnancy. If you are pregnant or plan to become pregnant, inform your doctor immediately. Tetracyclines such as doxycycline appear in breast milk and can affect a nursing infant. If this medication is essential to your health, your doctor may advise you to discontinue breastfeeding until your treatment is finished.

Recommended dosage

ADULTS

The usual dose of oral doxycycline is 200 milligrams on the first day of treatment (100 milligrams every 12 hours) followed by a maintenance dose of 100 milligrams per day. The maintenance dose may be taken as a single dose or as 50 milligrams every 12 hours.

Your doctor may prescribe 100 milligrams every 12 hours for severe infections such as chronic urinary tract infection.

For Uncomplicated Gonorrhea (Except Anorectal Infections in Men)

The usual dose is 100 milligrams by mouth, twice a day for 7 days. An alternate, single-day treatment is 300 milligrams, followed in 1 hour by a second 300-milligram dose.

For Primary and Secondary Syphilis

The usual dose is 200 milligrams a day, divided into smaller, equal doses for 14 days.

For Prevention of Malaria

The usual dose is 100 milligrams a day. Treatment should begin 1 to 2 days before travel to the area where malaria is found, then continue daily during travel in the area and 4 weeks after leaving.

CHILDREN

For children above 8 years of age, the recommended dosage schedule for those weighing 100 pounds or less is 2 milligrams per pound of body weight, divided into 2 doses, on the first day of treatment, followed by 1 milligram per pound of body weight given as a single daily dose or divided into 2 doses on subsequent days.

For more severe infections, up to 2 milligrams per pound of body weight may be used.

For prevention of malaria, the recommended dose is 2 milligrams per 2.2 pounds of body weight up to 100 milligrams.

For children over 100 pounds, the usual adult dose should be used.

Overdosage

Any medication taken in excess can have serious consequences. If you suspect an overdose, seek medical treatment immediately.

Generic name:

DOXAZOSIN

See Cardura, page 197.

Generic name:

DOXEPIN

See Sinequan, page 1143.

Generic name:

DOXYCYCLINE

See Doryx, page 415.

Brand name:

DUPHALAC

See Chronulac Syrup, page 223.

Brand name:

DURACT

Pronounced: DOOR-act
Generic name: Bromfenac sodium

Why is this drug prescribed?

Duract, a new drug for short-term pain relief, was pulled off the market when several people died of liver failure after using it (see "Special warnings about this medication" on page 421).

If you have any Duract in your medicine cabinet, discard it immediately and see your doctor for other, safer forms of pain relief. For your information, a complete summary of the drug's hazards and side effects follows.

Most important fact about this drug

Duract can cause serious problems in the digestive system, including ulcers or internal bleeding. If you notice any acid back-up, stomach irritation, unusual bleeding, or black, tarry stools, alert your doctor immediately. To reduce the possibility of such problems, Duract is limited to short-term use at the lowest effective dose.

How should you take this medication?

It is best to avoid high-fat meals when taking Duract; they are likely to reduce the drug's effectiveness. Never take more than the prescribed dose.

- *If you miss a dose...*
  Take it as soon as you remember. If it is almost time for your next dose, skip the one you missed and go back to your regular schedule. Never take 2 doses at the same time.

- *Storage information...*
  Store at room temperature in a tight, light-resistant container away from moisture and light.

What side effects may occur?
Side effects cannot be anticipated. If any develop or change in intensity, inform your doctor as soon as possible. Only your doctor can determine if it is safe for you to continue taking Duract.

- *More common side effects may include:*
  Abdominal pain, dizziness, drowsiness, headache, indigestion, nausea

- *Less common side effects may include:*
  Belching, constipation, diarrhea, stomach gas, vomiting, weakness

- *Rare side effects may include:*
  Abnormal dreams, abnormal vision, amnesia, anemia, anxiety, appetite changes, asthma, back pain, bleeding, blood in the stool, blood in the urine, breast pain, bruising, cataract, chest pain, chills, confusion, dental problems, depression, difficulty breathing, dry eyes, dry mouth, ear problems, exaggerated feeling of well-being, face swelling, fainting, fever, flu-like symptoms, general feeling of illness, hair loss, hallucination, heart attack, hiccups, high blood pressure, hives, hyperventilation, impotence, incoordination, increased cough, increased sex drive, infection, inflamed eyelids, inflamed mouth, inflamed sinuses, inflammation of the digestive tract, internal stomach bleeding, irregular heartbeat, itching, leg cramps, light sensitivity, menstrual disorders, migraine headache, muscle aches, nervousness, nosebleed, oily skin, painful urination, pinkeye, rectal problems, ringing in the ears, skin disorders, stomach ulcer, sore throat, sugar in the urine, sweating, swelling, taste disturbances, tearing of the eyes, thirst, tingling sensation of the skin, tiredness, tremor, twitching, unstable emotions, urge to empty the rectum or bladder, urinary problems, uterine problems, weight changes

Why should this drug not be prescribed?
If Duract or similar drugs such as Advil, Aleve, aspirin, Motrin, and Naprosyn have ever given you an allergic reaction (asthma, swelling, or inflammation), do not take this medication. Also avoid Duract if you have hepatitis or any other type of severe liver disease.

Special warnings about this medication

If you have even minor liver problems, use Duract with caution. It has been known to cause liver damage in some people. Report any flu-like symptoms (a sign of possible liver damage) to your doctor immediately.

Remember that it's possible to develop ulcers and digestive-tract bleeding without warning. The danger is greater if you've had such problems in the past, and if you smoke, abuse alcohol, take steroid medications, or use drugs that affect blood clotting. Digestive problems are also more likely in people who are in poor health or over 75 years of age.

Because Duract can cause breathing problems, use it with caution if you have asthma. If you start to have a reaction, seek medical help immediately.

If you have kidney disease, heart disease, or severe dehydration—or are taking a water-pill (diuretic)—Duract could harm your kidneys; use it cautiously. Also use caution if you have high blood pressure, a weak heart, or swelling; Duract can cause water retention and extra swelling.

Because Duract may make clotting more difficult, use it cautiously if you are taking blood-thinning medications or have a bleeding disorder.

Possible food and drug interactions
when taking this medication

If Duract is taken with certain other drugs, the effects of either could be increased, decreased, or altered. It is especially important to check with your doctor before combining Duract with the following:

Antacids such as Maalox and Mylanta
Blood-thinning drugs such as Coumadin
Cimetidine (Tagamet)
Diuretics such as hydrochlorothiazide and Lasix
Lithium (Lithobid, Lithonate)
Phenytoin (Dilantin)
Steroids such as prednisone and hydrocortisone

Remember that combining Duract with a high-fat meal can interfere with its effect.

Special information
if you are pregnant or breastfeeding

Although the effects of Duract during pregnancy have not been adequately studied, similar drugs are known to cause abnormalities in developing babies. Avoid Duract late in your pregnancy, and inform your doctor immediately if you become pregnant or are planning a pregnancy.

It is not known whether Duract appears in breast milk, but because many drugs do, your doctor may advise you to discontinue breastfeeding until your treatment with Duract is finished.

Recommended dosage

ADULTS

The recommended dose is 25 milligrams every 6 to 8 hours as needed for pain.

Do not take more than 150 milligrams a day, or continue the drug for more than 10 days.

OLDER ADULTS

If you are over 75, your doctor may increase the time between doses.

CHILDREN

The safety and effectiveness of Duract have not been established in children.

Overdosage

No cases of Duract overdose have been reported. However, experience with similar drugs suggests the following.

■ *Symptoms of nonsteroidal anti-inflammatory drug overdose may include:*
Coma, bleeding in the digestive tract, decreased breathing, drowsiness, high blood pressure, kidney failure, nausea, sluggishness, upper abdominal pain, vomiting

If you suspect an overdose, seek medical attention immediately.

Brand name:

DURICEF

Pronounced: DUHR-i-sef
Generic name: Cefadroxil monohydrate
Other brand name: Ultracef

Why is this drug prescribed?

Duricef, a cephalosporin antibiotic, is used in the treatment of nose, throat, urinary tract, and skin infections that are caused by specific bacteria, including staph, strep, and *E. coli.*

Most important fact about this drug

If you are allergic to either penicillin or cephalosporin antibiotics in any form, consult your doctor *before taking* Duricef. An allergy to either type of medication may signal an allergy to Duricef; and if a reaction occurs, it could be extremely severe. If you take the drug and feel signs of a reaction, seek medical attention immediately.

How should you take this medication?

Take this medication exactly as prescribed. It is important that you finish all of it to obtain the maximum benefit.

- *If you miss a dose...*
  Take it as soon as you remember. If it is almost time for the next dose, and you take it once a day, take the one you missed and the next dose 10 to 12 hours later. If you take 2 doses a day, take the one you missed and the next dose 5 to 6 hours later. If you take it 3 or more times a day, take the one you missed and the next dose 2 to 4 hours later. Then go back to your regular schedule.

- *Storage information...*
  Store at room temperature.

What side effects may occur?

Side effects cannot be anticipated. If any develop or change in intensity, inform your doctor as soon as possible. Only your doctor can determine if it is safe for you to continue taking Duricef.

- *More common side effects may include:*
  Diarrhea

- *Less common or rare side effects may include:*
  Inflammation of the bowel (colitis), nausea, redness and swelling of skin, skin rash and itching, vaginal inflammation, vomiting

Why should this drug not be prescribed?

If you are sensitive to or have ever had an allergic reaction to a cephalosporin antibiotic, you should not take Duricef.

Special warnings about this medication

If you have allergies, particularly to drugs, or often develop diarrhea when taking other antibiotics, you should tell your doctor before taking Duricef.

Use with caution if you have a history of gastrointestinal disease, particularly inflammation of the bowel (colitis).

Continued or prolonged use of Duricef may result in a growth of bacteria that do not respond to this medication and can cause a second infection.

**Possible food and drug interactions
when taking this medication**
No significant interactions have been reported.

**Special information
if you are pregnant or breastfeeding**
The effects of Duricef during pregnancy have not been adequately studied. If you are pregnant or plan to become pregnant, inform your doctor immediately. Duricef may appear in breast milk and could affect a nursing infant. If this medication is essential to your health, your doctor may advise you to stop nursing your baby until your treatment time with Duricef is finished.

Recommended dosage

ADULTS

Urinary Tract Infections
The usual dosage for uncomplicated infections is a total of 1 to 2 grams per day in a single dose or 2 smaller doses. For all other urinary tract infections, the usual dosage is a total of 2 grams per day taken in 2 doses.

Skin and Skin Structure Infections
The usual dose is a total of 1 gram per day in a single dose or 2 smaller doses.

Throat Infections—Strep Throat and Tonsillitis:
The usual dosage is a total of 1 gram per day in a single dose or 2 smaller doses for 10 days.

CHILDREN

For urinary tract and skin infections, the usual dose is 30 milligrams per 2.2 pounds of body weight per day, divided into 2 doses and taken every 12 hours. For throat infections, the recommended dose per day is 30 milligrams per 2.2 pounds of body weight in a single dose or 2 smaller doses. In the treatment of strep throat, the dose should be taken for at least 10 days.

OLDER ADULTS

Your dose may be reduced by your doctor.

Overdosage

Duricef is generally safe. However, large amounts may cause seizures or the side effects listed above. If you suspect an overdose of Duricef, seek medical attention immediately.

Brand name:

DYAZIDE

Pronounced: DYE-uh-zide
Generic ingredients: Hydrochlorothiazide, Triamterene

Why is this drug prescribed?

Dyazide is a combination of diuretic drugs used in the treatment of high blood pressure and other conditions that require the elimination of excess fluid from the body. When used for high blood pressure, Dyazide can be taken alone or with other high blood pressure medications. Diuretics help your body produce and eliminate more urine, which helps lower blood pressure. Triamterene, one of the ingredients of Dyazide, helps to minimize the potassium loss that can be caused by the other component, hydrochlorothiazide.

Most important fact about this drug

If you have high blood pressure, you must take Dyazide regularly for it to be effective. Since blood pressure declines gradually, it may be several weeks before you get the full benefit of Dyazide; and you must continue taking it even if you are feeling well. Dyazide does not cure high blood pressure; it merely keeps it under control.

How should you take this medication?

Dyazide should be taken early in the day. To avoid stomach upset, take it with food.

■ *If you miss a dose...*
Take it as soon as you remember. If it is almost time for the next dose, skip the one you missed and go back to your regular schedule. Do not take 2 doses at the same time.

■ *Storage instructions...*
Store at room temperature, away from light.

What side effects may occur?
Side effects cannot be anticipated. If any occur or change in intensity, inform your doctor as soon as possible. Only your doctor can determine if it is safe for you to continue taking Dyazide.

■ *Side effects may include:*
Abdominal pain, anemia, breathing difficulty, change in potassium level (causing symptoms such as numbness, tingling, muscle weakness, slow heart rate, shock), constipation, diabetes, diarrhea, dizziness, dizziness when standing up, dry mouth, fatigue, headache, hives, impotence, irregular heartbeat, kidney stones, muscle cramps, nausea, rash, sensitivity to light, strong allergic reaction (localized hives, itching, and swelling or, in severe cases, shock), vomiting, weakness, yellow eyes and skin

Why should this drug not be prescribed?
If you are unable to urinate or have any serious kidney disease, if you have high potassium levels in your blood, or if you are taking other drugs that prevent loss of potassium, you should not take Dyazide.

If you are sensitive to or have ever had an allergic reaction to triamterene (Dyrenium), hydrochlorothiazide (Oretic), or sulfa drugs such as Gantrisin you should not take this medication.

Special warnings about this medication
When taking Dyazide, do not use potassium-containing salt substitutes. Take potassium supplements only if specifically directed to by your doctor. Your potassium level should be checked frequently.

If you are taking Dyazide and have kidney disease, your doctor should monitor your kidney function closely.

If you have liver disease, diabetes, cirrhosis of the liver, heart failure, or kidney stones, this medication should be used with care.

Possible food and drug interactions
when taking this medication
Dyazide should be used with caution if you are taking a type of blood pressure medication called an ACE inhibitor, such as Vasotec or Capoten.

If Dyazide is taken with certain other drugs, the effects of either could be increased, decreased, or altered. It is especially important to check with your doctor before combining Dyazide with the following:

Blood-thinning medications such as Coumadin
Corticosteroids such as Deltasone
Drugs for diabetes such as Micronase
Gout medications such as Zyloprim
Laxatives
Lithium (Lithonate)
Methenamine (Urised)
Nonsteroidal anti-inflammatory drugs such as Indocin and Dolobid
Other drugs that minimize potassium loss or contain potassium
Other high blood pressure medications such as Minipress
Salt substitutes containing potassium
Sodium polystyrene sulfonate (Kayexalate)

Special information
if you are pregnant or breastfeeding

The effects of Dyazide during pregnancy have not been adequately studied. If you are pregnant or plan to become pregnant, inform your doctor immediately. Dyazide appears in breast milk and could affect a nursing infant. If this medication is essential to your health, your doctor may advise you to discontinue breastfeeding until your treatment is finished.

Recommended dosage

ADULTS

The usual dose of Dyazide is 1 or 2 capsules once daily, with appropriate monitoring of blood potassium levels by your doctor.

CHILDREN

Safety and effectiveness in children have not been established.

Overdosage

Any medication taken in excess can have serious consequences. If you suspect an overdose, seek medical treatment immediately.

■ *Symptoms of Dyazide overdose may include:*
Fever, flushed face, nausea, production of large amounts of pale urine, vomiting, weakness, weariness

Brand name:

DYNABAC

Pronounced: DYE-na-bak
Generic name: Dirithromycin

Why is this drug prescribed?

Dynabac cures certain mild-to-moderate skin infections and respiratory infections such as strep throat, tonsillitis, pneumonia, and flare-ups of chronic bronchitis. Dynabac is part of the same family of drugs as the commonly prescribed antibiotic erythromycin.

Most important fact about this drug

Serious and sometimes fatal reactions have occurred in people who combined other erythromycin-type antibiotics with Seldane or Hismanal. If you are taking either of these drugs and have a heart condition, particularly irregular heart rhythms, do not take Dynabac.

How should you take this medication?

Take Dynabac with food or within 1 hour after a meal. Swallow the tablet whole; do not crush, chew, or break it.

To make sure your infection is completely cured, it's important to finish your entire prescription, even if you begin to feel better after the first few days. If you stop taking this medicine too soon, your symptoms may return.

- *If you miss a dose...*
  Take it as soon as you remember. If you don't remember until the next day, skip the forgotten dose and go back to your regular schedule. Never try to "catch up" by doubling the dose.

- *Storage instructions...*
  Store Dynabac at room temperature.

What side effects may occur?

Side effects cannot be anticipated. If any develop or change in intensity, tell your doctor as soon as possible. Only your doctor can determine if it is safe for you to continue taking Dynabac.

- *More common side effects may include:*
  Abdominal pain, diarrhea, headache, nausea, vomiting

- *Less common side effects may include:*
  Dizziness/vertigo, gas, hives, increased cough, insomnia, itching, pain, rash, shortness of breath, stomach and intestinal disturbances, weakness

- *Rare side effects may include:*
  Abnormal stools, allergic reaction, anxiety, constipation, coughing up blood, dehydration, depression, dry mouth, fainting, fever, fluid retention, flu-like symptoms, frequent urination, inflammation of the stomach and intestines, loss of appetite, mouth sores, muscle pain, neck pain, nervousness, nosebleeds, painful menstruation, "pins and needles," pounding heartbeat, rapid breathing, reduced vision or other eye problems, ringing in ears, sleepiness, sweating, swelling of hands and feet, taste alteration, thirst, tremor, vaginal fungus, vaginal inflammation

Why should this drug not be prescribed?
If you have ever had an allergic reaction to Dynabac or to similar antibiotics such as erythromycin (E.E.S., PCE, and others), do not take this medication.

Special warnings about this medication
Dynabac, like certain other antibiotics, may cause a potentially life-threatening form of diarrhea called pseudomembranous colitis. A mild case may clear up on its own when the drug is stopped. For a more severe case, your doctor may need to prescribe fluids, electrolytes, and another antibiotic.

**Possible food and drug interactions
when taking this medication**
If Dynabac is taken with certain other drugs, the effects of either could be increased, decreased, or altered. It is especially important to check with your doctor before combining Dynabac with the following:

Antacids (Maalox, Mylanta)
Cimetidine (Tagamet)
Ranitidine (Zantac)
Terfenadine (Seldane)
Theophylline drugs such as Bronkodyl, Slo-Phyllin, Theo-Dur, and others

The following medications can interact with the related drug erythromycin:

Astemizole (Hismanal)
Blood-thinning drugs such as Coumadin
Bromocriptine (Parlodel)
Carbamazepine (Tegretol)
Cyclosporine (Sandimmune)
Digoxin (Lanoxin)

Disopyramide (Norpace)
Ergot-containing drugs such as Cafergot and D.H.E.
Lovastatin (Mevacor)
Phenytoin (Dilantin)
Triazolam (Halcion)
Valproate (Depakene, Depakote)

Special information
if you are pregnant or breastfeeding

If you are pregnant or plan to become pregnant, tell your doctor immediately. You should take Dynabac during pregnancy only if it is clearly needed. It is not known whether Dynabac appears in breast milk. If this medication is essential to your health, your doctor may advise you to stop breastfeeding until your treatment is finished.

Recommended dosage

ADULTS AND CHILDREN 12 AND OVER

Bronchitis and Skin Infections
The usual dose is 500 milligrams (2 tablets) once a day for 7 days.

Pneumonia
The usual dose is 500 milligrams (2 tablets) once a day for 14 days.

Strep Throat and Tonsillitis
The usual dose is 500 milligrams (2 tablets) once a day for 10 days.

CHILDREN UNDER 12 YEARS OF AGE

The safety and effectiveness of Dynabac in children under the age of 12 have not been established.

Overdosage

Any medication taken in excess can have serious consequences. If you suspect an overdose, seek medical attention immediately.

■ *Symptoms of Dynabac overdose may include...*
Diarrhea, nausea, stomach problems, vomiting

Brand name:

DYNACIN

See Minocin, page 775.

Brand name:

DYNACIRC

Pronounced: DYE-na-serk
Generic name: Isradipine

Why is this drug prescribed?
DynaCirc, a type of medication called a calcium channel blocker, is prescribed for the treatment of high blood pressure. It is effective when used alone or with a thiazide-type diuretic. Calcium channel blockers ease the workload of the heart by slowing down the passage of nerve impulses through the heart muscle, thereby slowing the beat. This improves blood flow through the heart and throughout the body and reduces blood pressure.

Most important fact about this drug
You must take DynaCirc regularly for it to be effective. Since blood pressure declines gradually, it may be several weeks before you get the full benefit of DynaCirc; and you must continue taking it even if you are feeling well. DynaCirc does not cure high blood pressure; it merely keeps it under control.

How should you take this medication?
Take this medication exactly as prescribed, even if your symptoms have disappeared. Try not to miss any doses. If DynaCirc is not taken regularly, your condition may worsen.

Swallow the capsule whole, without crushing or chewing it.

■ *If you miss a dose...*
  Take it as soon as you remember. If it is almost time for your next dose, skip the one you missed and go back to your regular schedule. Never take 2 doses at the same time.

■ *Storage instructions...*
  Store at room temperature, away from light, in a tightly closed container.

What side effects may occur?
Side effects cannot be anticipated. If any develop or change in intensity, inform your doctor as soon as possible. Only your doctor can determine if it is safe for you to continue taking DynaCirc.

■ *More common side effects may include:*
Dizziness, fluid retention, flushing, headache, pounding heartbeat

■ *Less common side effects may include:*
Chest pain, diarrhea, fatigue, nausea, rapid heartbeat, rash, shortness of breath, stomach upset, unusually frequent urination, vomiting, weakness

■ *Rare side effects may include:*
Constipation, cough, decreased sex drive, depression, difficulty sleeping, drowsiness, dry mouth, excessive sweating, fainting, changes in heartbeat, heart attack, heart failure, hives, impotence, itching, leg and foot cramps, low blood pressure, nervousness, numbness, severe dizziness, sluggishness, stroke, throat discomfort, tingling or pins and needles, vision changes

Why should this drug not be prescribed?
If you are sensitive to or have ever had an allergic reaction to DynaCirc or other calcium channel blockers such as Vascor and Procardia, you should not take this medication. Tell your doctor about any drug reactions you have experienced.

Special warnings about this medication
DynaCirc can cause your blood pressure to become too low. If you feel lightheaded or faint, contact your doctor.

This medication should be carefully monitored if you have congestive heart failure, especially if you are also taking a beta-blocking medication such as Tenormin or Inderal.

Before having surgery, including dental surgery, tell the doctor that you are taking DynaCirc.

Possible food and drug interactions
when taking this medication
If DynaCirc is taken with certain other drugs, the effects of either could be increased, decreased, or altered. It is especially important to check with your doctor before combining DynaCirc with the following:

Beta-blocking blood pressure drugs such as Tenormin, Inderal, and Lopressor
Cimetidine (Tagamet)
Rifampin (Rifadin)

Special information
if you are pregnant or breastfeeding
The effects of DynaCirc during pregnancy have not been adequately studied. If you are pregnant or plan to become pregnant, consult your doctor immediately. DynaCirc may appear in breast milk and could affect a nursing infant. If this medication is essential to your health, your doctor may advise you to discontinue breastfeeding until your treatment with DynaCirc is finished.

Recommended dosage

ADULTS

Your dosage will be adjusted to meet your individual needs.

The usual starting dose is 2.5 milligrams, 2 times a day, either alone or in combination with a thiazide diuretic drug. DynaCirc may lower blood pressure 2 to 3 hours after taking the first dose, but the full effect of the drug may not take place for 2 to 4 weeks.

After a 2- to 4-week trial, your doctor may increase the dosage by 5 milligrams per day every 2 to 4 weeks until a maximum dose of 20 milligrams per day is reached. Side effects may increase or become more common after a 10-milligram dose.

If you have kidney or liver disease, you should still begin treatment with a 2.5-milligram dose 2 times per day; however, your doctor will monitor you closely, since your condition may alter the effects of this drug.

OLDER ADULTS

This drug's effects may be stronger in older people. The usual starting dose should still be 2.5 milligrams 2 times per day.

Overdosage
Although there is little information on DynaCirc, overdose has resulted in sluggishness, low blood pressure, and rapid heartbeat. The symptoms of overdose with other calcium channel blockers include drowsiness, severe low blood pressure, and rapid heartbeat.

If you suspect a DynaCirc overdose, seek medical attention immediately.

Generic name:

ECHOTHIOPHATE

See Phospholine Iodide, page 961.

Brand name:

EC-NAPROSYN

See Naprosyn, page 815.

Generic name:

ECONAZOLE

See Spectazole Cream, page 1152.

Brand name:

ECOTRIN

See Aspirin, page 90.

Brand name:

EDEX

See Caverject, page 205.

Brand name:

E.E.S.

See Erythromycin, Oral, page 461.

Brand name:

EFFEXOR

Pronounced: ef-ecks-OR
Generic name: Venlafaxine hydrochloride

Why is this drug prescribed?
Effexor is prescribed for the treatment of depression—that is, a continuing depression that interferes with daily functioning. The symptoms usually include changes in appetite, sleep habits, and mind/body coordination, decreased sex drive, increased fatigue, feelings of guilt or worthlessness, difficulty concentrating, slowed thinking, and suicidal thoughts.

Most important fact about this drug
Serious, sometimes fatal reactions have occurred when Effexor is used in

combination with other drugs known as MAO inhibitors, including the antidepressants Nardil and Parnate. Never take Effexor with one of these drugs; and do not begin therapy with Effexor within 14 days of discontinuing treatment with one of them. Also, allow at least 7 days between the last dose of Effexor and the first dose of an MAO inhibitor.

How should you take this medication?
Take Effexor with food, exactly as prescribed. It may take several weeks before you begin to feel better. Your doctor should check your progress periodically.

■ *If you miss a dose...*
It is not necessary to make it up. Skip the missed dose and continue with your next scheduled dose. Do not take 2 doses at once.

■ *Storage instructions...*
Store in a tightly closed container at room temperature. Protect from excessive heat and moisture.

What side effects may occur?
Side effects cannot be anticipated. If any develop or change in intensity, tell your doctor as soon as possible. Only your doctor can determine if it is safe for you to continue taking Effexor.

■ *More common side effects may include:*
Abnormal dreams, abnormal ejaculation/orgasm, anxiety, blurred vision, chills, constipation, diarrhea, dizziness, dry mouth, extreme muscle tension, flushing, frequent urination, gas, headache, impotence, inability to sleep, indigestion, loss of appetite, nausea, nervousness, prickling or burning sensation, rash, sleepiness, sweating, tremor, vomiting, weakness, yawning

■ *Less common side effects may include:*
Abnormal thinking, abnormal vision, accidental injury, agitation, belching, blood in the urine, bronchitis, bruising, changeable emotions, chest pain, confusion, decreased sex drive, depression, difficult or painful urination, difficulty in breathing, difficulty swallowing, dilated pupils, ear pain, high or low blood pressure, inflammation of the vagina, injury, itching, lack of orgasm, light-headedness on standing up, lockjaw, loss of touch with reality, menstrual problems, migraine headache, neck pain, orgasm disturbance, rapid heartbeat, ringing in the ears, taste changes, twitching, vague feeling of illness, vertigo, weight loss or gain

■ *Rare side effects may include:*
Abnormally slow movements, abnormal movements, abnormal sensitivity to sound, abnormal speech, abortion, abuse of alcohol, acne, alcohol intolerance, allergic reaction, anemia, angina pectoris (crushing chest pain), apathy, appendicitis, arthritis, asthma, bad breath, black stools, bleeding gums, blocked intestine, blood clots, blood clots in the lungs, blood disorders, bluish color to the skin, body odor, bone disease and/or pain (including osteoporosis), breast enlargement or swelling, breast pain, brittle nails, bulging eyes, cancerous growth, cataracts, changed sense of smell, chest congestion, cold hands and feet, colitis (inflamed bowel), confusion, conjunctivitis ("pinkeye"), coughing up blood, deafness, delusions, depression, diabetes, double vision, drug withdrawal symptoms, dry eyes, dry skin, ear infection, eczema, enlarged abdomen, enlarged thyroid gland, exaggerated feeling of well-being, excessive hair growth, excessive menstrual flow, eye disorders, eye pain, fainting, fungus infection, gallstones, glaucoma, gout, hair discoloration, hair loss, hallucinations, hangover effect, heart disorders, hemorrhoids, hepatitis, herpes infections, high cholesterol, hives, hostility, hyperventilation (fast, deep breathing), inability to communicate, increased mucus, increased physical activity, increased salivation, increased sensitivity to touch, increased sex drive, inflammation of the stomach, intestines, anus and rectum, gums, tongue, eyelid, or inner ear, intolerance to light, involuntary eye movements, irregular or slow heartbeat, kidney disorders, lack of menstruation, large amounts of urine, laryngitis, loss of consciousness, loss of muscle movement, low or high blood sugar, menstrual problems, middle ear infection, mouth fungus, mouth sores, muscle spasms, muscle weakness, nosebleeds, over- and underactive thyroid gland, overdose, paranoia, pelvic pain, pinpoint pupils, "pins and needles" around the mouth, pneumonia, prolonged erection, psoriasis, rectal hemorrhage, reduced menstrual flow, restlessness, secretion of milk, seizures, sensitivity to light, skin disorders, skin eruptions or hemorrhage, skin inflammation, sleep disturbance, soft stools, stiff neck, stomach or peptic ulcer, stroke, stupor, sugar in the urine, swelling due to fluid retention, swollen or discolored tongue, taste loss, temporary failure to breathe, thirst, twisted neck, ulcer, unconsciousness, uncoordinated movements, urgent need to urinate, urination at night, uterine and vaginal hemorrhage, varicose veins, voice changes, vomiting blood, yellowed eyes and skin

Why should this drug not be prescribed?
Never take Effexor while taking other drugs known as MAO inhibitors. (See "Most important fact about this drug.") Also avoid this drug if it has ever given you an allergic reaction.

Special warnings about this medication

Your doctor will prescribe Effexor with caution if you have high blood pressure, heart, liver, or kidney disease or a history of seizures or mania (extreme agitation or excitability). You should discuss all of your medical problems with your doctor before taking Effexor.

Effexor may cause you to feel drowsy or less alert and may affect your judgment. Therefore, avoid driving or operating dangerous machinery or participating in any hazardous activity that requires full mental alertness until you know how this drug affects you.

If you have ever been addicted to drugs, tell your doctor before you start taking Effexor.

If you develop a skin rash or hives while taking Effexor, notify your doctor.

Do not stop taking the drug without consulting your doctor. If you stop suddenly, you may have withdrawal symptoms, even though this drug does not seem to be habit-forming. Your doctor will have you taper off gradually.

Possible food and drug interactions
when taking this medication

Combining Effexor with MAO inhibitors could cause a fatal reaction. (See "Most important fact about this drug.")

Although Effexor does not interact with alcohol, the manufacturer recommends avoiding alcohol while taking this medication.

If you have high blood pressure or liver disease, or are elderly, check with your doctor before combining Effexor with cimetidine (Tagamet).

Effexor does not interact with Lithium or Valium. However, you should consult your doctor before combining Effexor with other drugs that affect the central nervous system, including narcotic painkillers, sleep aids, tranquilizers, antipsychotic medicines such as Haldol, and other antidepressants such as Tofranil.

Special information
if you are pregnant or breastfeeding

The effects of Effexor during pregnancy have not been adequately studied. If you are pregnant or are planning to become pregnant, tell your doctor immediately. Effexor should be used during pregnancy only if clearly needed. Effexor may appear in breast milk. If this medication is essential to your health, your doctor may tell you to discontinue breastfeeding your baby until your treatment with Effexor is finished.

Recommended dosage

ADULTS

The usual starting dose is 75 milligrams a day, divided into 2 or 3 smaller doses, and taken with food. If needed, your doctor may gradually increase your daily dose in steps of no more than 75 milligrams at a time up to a maximum of 375 milligrams per day.

If you have kidney or liver disease or are taking other medications, your doctor will adjust your dosage accordingly.

CHILDREN

The safety and effectiveness of Effexor have not been established in children under 18 years of age.

Overdosage

An overdose of Effexor, combined with other drugs or alcohol, can be fatal. If you suspect an overdose, seek medical attention immediately.

■ *Symptoms of Effexor overdose include:*
Convulsions, rapid heartbeat, sleepiness

Brand name:

EFUDEX

Pronounced: EFF-you-decks
Generic name: Fluorouracil

Why is this drug prescribed?

Efudex is prescribed for the treatment of actinic or solar keratoses (small red horny growths or flesh-colored wartlike growths caused by overexposure to ultraviolet radiation or the sun). Such growths may develop into skin cancer. When conventional methods are impractical—as when the affected sites are hard to get at—Efudex is useful in the treatment of superficial basal cell carcinomas, or slow-growing malignant tumors of the face usually found at the edge of the nostrils, eyelids, or lips. Efudex is available in cream and solution forms.

Most important fact about this drug

If you use an airtight dressing to cover the skin being treated, there may be inflammatory reactions in the normal skin around the treated area. If it is necessary to cover the treated area, use a porous gauze dressing to avoid skin reactions.

How should you take this medication?
Use care when applying Efudex around the eyes, nose, and mouth. Wash your hands immediately after applying this medication.

■ *If you miss a dose...*
Apply it as soon as you remember. If more than a few hours have passed, skip the dose you missed and go back to your regular schedule. If you miss more than 1 dose, contact your doctor.

■ *Storage instructions...*
Store away from heat, light, and moisture.

What side effects may occur?
Side effects cannot be anticipated. If any develop or change in intensity, inform your doctor as soon as possible. Only your doctor can determine if it is safe for you to continue using Efudex.

■ *More common side effects may include:*
Burning, discoloration of the skin, itching, pain

■ *Less common side effects may include:*
Allergic skin inflammation, pus, scaling, scarring, soreness, swelling, tenderness

Why should this drug not be prescribed?
If you are sensitive to or have ever had an allergic reaction to Efudex or similar drugs, you should not take this medication. Make sure your doctor is aware of any drug reactions you have experienced.

Special warnings about this medication
Avoid prolonged exposure to ultraviolet rays while you are under treatment with Efudex.

Skin may be unsightly during treatment with this drug and, in some cases, for several weeks after treatment has ended.

If your solar keratoses do not clear up with use of this drug, your doctor will probably order a biopsy (removal of a small amount of tissue to be examined under a microscope) to confirm the skin disease.

Your doctor will perform follow-up biopsies if you are being treated for superficial basal cell carcinoma.

**Possible food and drug interactions
when taking this medication**
There are no reported food or drug interactions.

**Special information
if you are pregnant or breastfeeding**
The effects of Efudex during pregnancy have not been adequately studied. If you are pregnant, plan to become pregnant, or are breastfeeding your baby, consult your doctor immediately.

Recommended dosage
When Efudex is applied to affected skin, the skin becomes abnormally red, blisters form, and the surface skin wears away. A lesion or sore forms at the affected site, and the diseased or cancerous skin cells die before a new layer of skin forms.

ADULTS

Actinic or Solar Keratosis
Apply cream or solution 2 times a day in an amount sufficient to cover the affected area. Continue using the medication until the inflammatory response reaches the stage where the skin wears away, a sore or lesion forms, and the skin cells die; your doctor will then have you stop using the medication. The usual length of treatment is from 2 to 4 weeks. You may not see complete healing of the affected area for 1 to 2 months after ending the treatment.

Superficial Basal Cell Carcinoma
You should use only the 5% strength of this medication. Twice a day, apply enough cream or solution to cover the affected area. Continue the treatment for at least 3 to 6 weeks; it may take 10 to 12 weeks of application before the lesions are gone.

Your doctor will want to monitor your condition to make sure it has been cured.

Overdosage
Although no specific information is available on Efudex overdosage, any medication used in excess can have serious consequences. If you suspect an overdosage, seek medical attention immediately.

Brand name:

ELAVIL

Pronounced: ELL-uh-vil
Generic name: Amitriptyline hydrochloride
Other brand name: Endep

Why is this drug prescribed?
Elavil is prescribed for the relief of symptoms of mental depression. It is a member of the group of drugs called tricyclic antidepressants. Some doctors also prescribe Elavil to treat bulimia (an eating disorder), to control chronic pain, to prevent migraine headaches, and to treat a pathological weeping and laughing syndrome associated with multiple sclerosis.

Most important fact about this drug
You may need to take Elavil regularly for several weeks before it becomes fully effective. Do not skip doses, even if they seem to make no difference or you feel you don't need them.

How should you take this medication?
Take Elavil exactly as prescribed. You may experience side effects, such as mild drowsiness, early in therapy. However, they usually disappear after a few days. Beneficial effects may take as long as 30 days to appear.

Elavil may cause dry mouth. Sucking a hard candy, chewing gum, or melting bits of ice in your mouth can provide relief.

■ *If you miss a dose...*
Take it as soon as you remember. If it is almost time for your next dose, skip the one you missed and go back to your regular schedule. Never take 2 doses at the same time.

If you take a single daily dose at bedtime, do not make up for it in the morning. It may cause side effects during the day.

■ *Storage instructions...*
Keep Elavil in a tightly closed container. Store at room temperature. Protect from light and excessive heat.

What side effects may occur?
Side effects cannot be anticipated. If any develop or change in intensity, inform your doctor as soon as possible. Only your doctor can determine if it is safe for you to continue taking Elavil.

■ *Side effects may include:*
Abnormal movements, anxiety, black tongue, blurred vision, breast development in males, breast enlargement, coma, confusion, constipation, delusions, diarrhea, difficult or frequent urination, difficulty in speech, dilation of pupils, disorientation, disturbed concentration, dizziness on getting up, dizziness or light-headedness, drowsiness, dry mouth, excessive or spontaneous flow of milk, excitement, fatigue, fluid retention, hair loss, hallucinations, headache, heart attack, hepatitis, high blood pressure, high fever, high or low blood sugar, hives, impotence, inability to sleep, increased or decreased sex drive, increased perspiration, increased pressure within the eye, inflammation of the mouth, intestinal obstruction, irregular heartbeat, lack or loss of coordination, loss of appetite, low blood pressure, nausea, nightmares, numbness, rapid and/or fast, fluttery heartbeat, rash, red or purple spots on skin, restlessness, ringing in the ears, seizures, sensitivity to light, stomach upset, strange taste, stroke, swelling due to fluid retention in the face and tongue, swelling of testicles, swollen glands, tingling and pins and needles in the arms and legs, tremors, vomiting, weakness, weight gain or loss, yellowed eyes and skin

■ *Side effects due to rapid decrease or abrupt withdrawal from Elavil include:*
Headache, nausea, vague feeling of bodily discomfort

■ *Side effects due to gradual dosage reduction may include:*
Dream and sleep disturbances, irritability, restlessness

These side effects do not signify an addiction to the drug.

Why should this drug not be prescribed?
If you are sensitive to or have ever had an allergic reaction to Elavil or similar drugs such as Norpramin and Tofranil, you should not take this medication. Make sure your doctor is aware of any drug reactions you have experienced.

Do not take Elavil while taking other drugs known as MAO inhibitors. Drugs in this category include the antidepressants Nardil and Parnate.

Unless you are directed to do so by your doctor, do not take this medication if you are recovering from a heart attack.

Special warnings about this medication
Do not stop taking Elavil abruptly, especially if you have been taking large doses for a long time. Your doctor probably will want to decrease your dosage gradually. This will help prevent a possible relapse and will reduce the possibility of withdrawal symptoms.

Elavil may make your skin more sensitive to sunlight. Try to stay out of the sun, wear protective clothing, and apply a sun block.

Elavil may cause you to become drowsy or less alert; therefore, you should not drive or operate dangerous machinery or participate in any hazardous activity that requires full mental alertness until you know how this drug affects you.

While taking this medication, you may feel dizzy or light-headed or actually faint when getting up from a lying or sitting position. If getting up slowly doesn't help or if this problem continues, notify your doctor.

Use Elavil with caution if you have ever had seizures, urinary retention, glaucoma or other chronic eye conditions, a heart or circulatory system disorder, or liver problems. Be cautious, too, if you are receiving thyroid medication. You should discuss all of your medical problems with your doctor before starting Elavil therapy.

Before having surgery, dental treatment, or any diagnostic procedure, tell the doctor that you are taking Elavil. Certain drugs used during surgery, such as anesthetics and muscle relaxants, and drugs used in certain diagnostic procedures may react badly with Elavil.

Possible food and drug interactions when taking this medication

Elavil may intensify the effects of alcohol. Do not drink alcohol while taking this medication.

If Elavil is taken with certain other drugs, the effects of either could be increased, decreased, or altered. It is especially important that you consult with your doctor before taking Elavil in combination with the following:

Airway-opening drugs such as Sudafed and Proventil
Antidepressants that raise serotonin levels, such as Paxil, Prozac, and Zoloft
Other antidepressants, such as Asendin
Antihistamines such as Benadryl and Tavist
Barbiturates such as phenobarbital
Certain blood pressure medicines such as Catapres and Ismelin
Cimetidine (Tagamet)
Disulfiram (Antabuse)
Drugs that control spasms, such as Bentyl and Donnatal
Estrogen drugs such as Premarin and oral contraceptives
Ethchlorvynol (Placidyl)
Major tranquilizers such as Mellaril and Thorazine

MAO inhibitors, such as Nardil and Parnate

Medications for irregular heartbeat, such as Tambocor and Rythmol

Painkillers such as Demerol and Percocet

Parkinsonism drugs such as Cogentin and Larodopa

Quinidine (Quinidex)

Seizure medications such as Tegretol and Dilantin

Sleep medicines such as Halcion and Dalmane

Thyroid hormones (Synthroid)

Tranquilizers such as Librium and Xanax

Warfarin (Coumadin)

Special information
if you are pregnant or breastfeeding

The effects of Elavil during pregnancy have not been adequately studied. If you are pregnant or planning to become pregnant, inform your doctor immediately. This medication appears in breast milk. If Elavil is essential to your health, your doctor may advise you to discontinue breastfeeding until your treatment is finished.

Recommended dosage

ADULTS

The usual starting dosage is 75 milligrams per day divided into 2 or more smaller doses. Your doctor may gradually increase this dose to 150 milligrams per day. The total daily dose is generally never higher than 200 milligrams.

Alternatively, your doctor may want you to start with 50 milligrams to 100 milligrams at bedtime. He or she may increase this bedtime dose by 25 or 50 milligrams up to a total of 150 milligrams a day.

For long-term use, the usual dose ranges from 40 to 100 milligrams taken once daily, usually at bedtime.

CHILDREN

Use of Elavil is not recommended for children under 12 years of age.

The usual dose for adolescents 12 years of age and over is 10 milligrams, 3 times a day, with 20 milligrams taken at bedtime.

OLDER ADULTS

The usual dose is 10 milligrams taken 3 times a day, with 20 milligrams taken at bedtime.

Overdosage
An overdose of Elavil can prove fatal.

- *Symptoms of Elavil overdose may include:*
  Abnormally low blood pressure, confusion, convulsions, dilated pupils and other eye problems, disturbed concentration, drowsiness, hallucinations, impaired heart function, rapid or irregular heartbeat, reduced body temperature, stupor, unresponsiveness or coma

- *Symptoms contrary to the effect of this medication are:*
  Agitation, extremely high body temperature, overactive reflexes, rigid muscles, vomiting

If you suspect an overdose, seek medical attention immediately.

Brand name:

ELDEPRYL

Pronounced: ELL-dep-rill
Generic name: Selegiline hydrochloride

Why is this drug prescribed?
Eldepryl is prescribed along with Sinemet (levodopa/carbidopa) for people with Parkinson's disease. It is used when Sinemet no longer seems to be working well. Eldepryl has no effect when taken by itself; it works only in combination with Larodopa (levodopa) or Sinemet.

Parkinson's disease, which causes muscle rigidity and difficulty with walking and talking, involves the progressive degeneration of a particular type of nerve cell. Early on, Larodopa or Sinemet alone may alleviate the symptoms of the disease. In time, however, these medications work less well; their effectiveness seems to switch on and off at random, and the individual may begin to experience side effects such as involuntary movements and "freezing" in mid-motion.

Eldepryl may be prescribed at this stage of the disease to help restore the effectiveness of Larodopa or Sinemet. When you begin to take Eldepryl, you may need a reduced dosage of the other medication.

Most important fact about this drug
Eldepryl belongs to a class of drugs known as MAO inhibitors. These drugs can interact with certain foods—including aged cheeses and meats, pickled

herring, beer, and wine—to cause a life-threatening surge in blood pressure. At the dose recommended for Eldepryl, this interaction is not a problem. But for safety's sake, you may want to watch your diet; and you should never take more Eldepryl than the doctor prescribed.

How should you take this medication?
Take Eldepryl and your other Parkinson's medication exactly as prescribed.

- ■ *If you miss a dose...*
  Take it as soon as you remember. If you do not remember until late afternoon or evening, skip the dose you missed and go back to your regular schedule. Never take 2 doses at once.

- ■ *Storage instructions...*
  Store at room temperature.

What side effects may occur?
Side effects cannot be anticipated. If any develop or change in intensity, inform your doctor as soon as possible. Only your doctor can determine if it is safe for you to continue taking Eldepryl.

- ■ *Side effects may include:*
  Abdominal pain, abnormal movements, abnormally fast walking, aches, agitation, angina (crushing chest pain), anxiety, apathy, asthma, back pain, behavior or mood changes, bleeding from the rectum, blurred vision, burning lips and mouth or throat, chills, confusion, constipation, delusions, depression, diarrhea, difficulty swallowing, disorientation, dizziness, double vision, drowsiness, dry mouth, excessive urination at night, eyelid spasm, facial grimace, facial hair, fainting, falling down, freezing, frequent urination, general feeling of illness, hair loss, hallucinations, headache, heartburn, heart palpitations, heart rhythm abnormalities, "heavy leg," high blood pressure, hollow feeling, inability to carry out purposeful movements, inability to urinate, increased or excessive sweating, increased tremor, insomnia, involuntary movements, irritability, lack of appetite, leg pain, lethargy, light-headedness upon standing up, loss of balance, low blood pressure, lower back pain, migraine, muscle cramps, nausea, nervousness, numbness in toes/fingers, overstimulation, pain over the eyes, personality change, poor appetite, rapid heartbeat, rash, restlessness (desire to keep moving), ringing in the ears, sensitivity to light, sexual problems, shortness of breath, sleep disturbance, slow heartbeat, slow urination, slowed body movements, speech problems, stiff neck, stomach and intestinal bleeding, swelling of the ankles or arms and

legs, taste disturbance, tension, tiredness, twitching, urinary problems, vertigo, vivid dreams or nightmares, vomiting, weakness, weight loss

Why should this drug not be prescribed?
Do not take Eldepryl if you are sensitive to or have ever had an allergic reaction to it. Do not take narcotic painkillers such as Demerol while you are taking Eldepryl.

Special warnings about this medication
Never take Eldepryl at a higher dosage than prescribed; doing so could put you at risk for a dangerous rise in blood pressure. If you develop a severe headache or any other unusual symptoms, contact your doctor immediately.

You may suffer a severe reaction if you combine Eldepryl with tricyclic antidepressants such as Elavil and Tofranil, or with antidepressants that affect serotonin levels, such as Prozac and Paxil. Wait at least 14 days after taking Eldepryl before beginning therapy with any of these drugs. If you have been taking antidepressants such as Prozac and Paxil, you should wait at least 5 *weeks* before taking Eldepryl. This much time is needed to clear the antidepressant completely from your system.

Possible food and drug interactions
when taking this medication
If Eldepryl is taken with certain other drugs, the effects of either could be increased, decreased, or altered. It is especially important to check with your doctor before combining Eldepryl with the following:

Antidepressant medications that raise serotonin levels, such as Paxil, Prozac, and Zoloft
Antidepressant medications classified as tricyclics, such as Elavil and Tofranil
Narcotic painkillers such as Demerol, Percocet, and Tylenol with Codeine

Eldepryl may worsen side effects caused by your usual dosage of levodopa.

Special information
if you are pregnant or breastfeeding
The effects of Eldepryl during pregnancy have not been adequately studied. If you are pregnant or plan to become pregnant, inform your doctor immediately. Although Eldepryl is not known to cause specific birth defects, it should not be taken during pregnancy unless it is clearly needed. It is not known whether Eldepryl appears in breast milk. As a general rule, a nursing mother should not take any drug unless it is clearly necessary.

Recommended dosage

ADULTS

The recommended dose of Eldepryl is 10 milligrams per day divided into 2 smaller doses of 5 milligrams each, taken at breakfast and lunch. There is no evidence of additional benefit from higher doses, and they increase the risk of side effects.

CHILDREN

The use of Eldepryl in children has not been evaluated.

Overdosage

Although no specific information is available about Eldepryl overdosage, it is assumed, because of chemical similarities, that the symptoms would resemble those of overdose with an MAO inhibitor antidepressant.

▪ *Symptoms of MAO inhibitor overdose may include:*
Agitation, chest pain, clammy skin, coma, convulsions, dizziness, drowsiness, extremely high fever, faintness, fast and irregular pulse, hallucinations, headache (severe), high blood pressure, hyperactivity, inability to breathe, irritability, lockjaw, low blood pressure (severe), shallow breathing, spasm of the entire body, sweating

It is important to note that after a large overdose, symptoms may not appear for up to 12 hours and may not reach their full force for 24 hours or more. An overdose can be fatal. If you suspect an Eldepryl overdose, seek medical attention immediately. Hospitalization is recommended, with continuous observation and monitoring for at least 2 days.

Brand name:

ELOCON

Pronounced: ELL-oh-con
Generic name: Mometasone furoate

Why is this drug prescribed?

Elocon is a cortisone-like steroid available in cream, ointment, and lotion form. It is used to treat certain itchy rashes and other inflammatory skin conditions.

Most important fact about this drug

When you use Elocon, you inevitably absorb some of the medication through your skin and into the bloodstream. Too much absorption can lead to unwanted side effects elsewhere in the body. To keep this problem to a minimum, avoid using large amounts of Elocon over large areas, and do not cover it with airtight dressings such as plastic wrap or adhesive bandages unless specifically told to by your doctor.

How should you use this medication?

Apply a thin film of the cream or ointment or a few drops of the lotion to the affected skin once a day. Massage it in until it disappears.

Elocon is for use only on the skin. Be careful to keep it out of your eyes.

For the most effective and economical use of Elocon lotion, hold the tip of the bottle very close to (but not touching) the affected skin and squeeze the bottle gently.

Once you have applied Elocon, never cover the skin with an airtight bandage, a tight diaper, plastic pants, or any other airtight dressing. This could encourage excessive absorption of the medication into your bloodstream.

Be careful not to use Elocon for a longer time than prescribed. If you do, you may disrupt your ability to make your own natural adrenal corticoid hormones (hormones secreted by the outer layer of the adrenal gland).

■ *If you miss a dose...*
  Apply it as soon as you remember. If it is almost time for your next dose, skip the one you missed and go back to your regular schedule.

■ *Storage instructions...*
  Store at room temperature.

What side effects may occur?

Side effects cannot be anticipated. If any develop or change in intensity, notify your doctor as soon as possible. Only your doctor can determine if it is safe for you to continue using Elocon.

■ *Side effects may include:*
  Acne-like pimples, allergic skin rash, boils, burning, damaged skin, dryness, excessive hairiness, infected hair follicles, infection of the skin, irritation, itching, light colored patches on skin, prickly heat, rash around the mouth, skin atrophy and wasting, softening of the skin, stretch marks, tingling or stinging

Why should this drug not be prescribed?

Do not use Elocon if you have ever had an allergic reaction to it or any other steroid medication.

Special warnings about this medication

Remember, Elocon is for external use only. Avoid getting it into your eyes. Do not use it to treat anything other than the condition for which it was prescribed.

If your skin becomes irritated, call your doctor.

If you have any kind of skin infection, tell your doctor before you start using Elocon.

Do not use Elocon on your face, underarms, or groin area unless your doctor tells you to.

If your condition doesn't improve in 2 weeks, call your doctor.

**Possible food and drug interactions
when using this medication**

No interactions have been noted.

**Special information
if you are pregnant or breastfeeding**

If you are pregnant or plan to become pregnant, inform your doctor immediately. Elocon should not be used during pregnancy unless the benefit outweighs the potential risk to the unborn child.

You should not use Elocon while breastfeeding, since absorbed hormone could make its way into the breast milk and perhaps harm the nursing baby. If you are a new mother, you should contact your doctor, who will help you decide between breastfeeding and using Elocon.

Recommended dosage

ADULTS

Apply once daily.

CHILDREN

Use should be limited to the least amount necessary. Use of steroids over a long period of time may interfere with growth and development.

Elocon cream and ointment may be used for children aged 2 and older, but not for more than 3 weeks.

Overdosage

With extensive or long-term use of Elocon, hormone absorbed into the bloodstream may cause a group of symptoms called Cushing's syndrome.

■ *Symptoms of Cushing's syndrome may include:*
Acne, depression, excessive hair growth, high blood pressure, humped upper back, insomnia, moon-faced appearance, obese trunk, paranoia, stretch marks, wasted limbs, stunted growth (in children), susceptibility to bruising, fractures, and infections

Cushing's syndrome may also trigger diabetes mellitus.

If it is left uncorrected, Cushing's syndrome may become serious. If you suspect your long-term use of Elocon has led to this problem, seek medical attention immediately.

Brand name:

ELTROXIN

See Synthroid, page 1178.

Brand name:

EMPIRIN

See Aspirin, page 90.

Brand name:

EMPIRIN WITH CODEINE

Pronounced: EM-pir-in with KOE-deen
Generic ingredients: Aspirin, Codeine phosphate

Why is this drug prescribed?
Empirin with Codeine is a narcotic pain reliever and anti-inflammatory medication. It is prescribed for mild, moderate, and moderate to severe pain.

Most important fact about this drug
Codeine can be habit-forming when taken over a long period of time or in high doses. Do not take more of the drug, or use it for a longer period of time than your doctor has indicated.

How should you take this medication?
Take Empirin with Codeine with food or a full glass of milk or water to reduce stomach irritation. Take it exactly as prescribed.

■ *If you miss a dose...*
Take it as soon as you remember. If it is almost time for your next dose,

skip the one you missed and go back to your regular schedule. Never take 2 doses at once.

■ *Storage instructions...*
Store at room temperature in a dry place; protect from light.

What side effects may occur?
Side effects cannot be anticipated. If any develop or change in intensity, inform your doctor as soon as possible. Only your doctor can determine if it is safe for you to continue using Empirin with Codeine.

■ *More common side effects may include:*
Constipation, dizziness, drowsiness, light-headedness, nausea, shallow breathing, vomiting

■ *Less common side effects may include:*
Abdominal pain, aggravation of peptic ulcer, anaphylactic shock (severe allergic reaction), asthma, bruising or bleeding, confusion, dizziness, drowsiness, exaggerated sense of well-being or depression, excessive bleeding following injury or surgery, fatigue, headache, hearing problems, heartburn, hives, indigestion, itching, nausea, rapid heartbeat, ringing in ears, runny nose, skin rashes, sweating, thirst, vision problems, vomiting, weakness

Why should this drug not be prescribed?
Empirin with Codeine should not be used if you: are sensitive or allergic to aspirin or codeine, experience severe bleeding, have a blood clotting disorder or severe vitamin K deficiency, are taking blood-thinning medications, have a peptic ulcer or have liver damage. Children or teenagers with symptoms of chickenpox or the flu should not take Empirin with Codeine because of the danger of contracting Reye's syndrome, a condition characterized by nausea, vomiting, and lethargy and disorientation deepening to coma.

Special warnings about this medication
Aspirin can cause severe allergic reactions including anaphylactic shock (difficulty breathing, bluish skin color caused by lack of oxygen, fever, rash or hives, irregular pulse, convulsions, or collapse).

Aspirin can cause bleeding if you have a peptic ulcer, open sores in the stomach or intestines, or a bleeding disorder. It may also prolong bleeding time after an injury or surgery.

Codeine can hide symptoms of serious abdominal conditions.

Use codeine with care if you have a head or brain injury. It can slow your breathing, make you drowsy, and increase pressure in your head.

Be careful taking Empirin with Codeine if you are elderly or in a weakened condition or have severe kidney or liver disease, gallstones or gallbladder disease, a breathing disorder, an irregular heartbeat, an inflamed stomach or intestines, an underactive thyroid gland, Addison's disease (a disorder of the adrenal glands), or an enlarged prostate or narrowing of the urethra.

Use aspirin with care if you have ever had any allergies. Sensitivity reactions are relatively common in people with asthma and nasal polyps (swollen growths in the nose).

Empirin with Codeine may make you drowsy or less alert. Be careful driving, operating machinery, or using appliances that require full mental alertness until you know how you react to this medication.

Remember, this medication can be habit-forming and should be taken exactly as prescribed. Do not take more of the medication, or use it more often, than your doctor has indicated.

Possible food and drug interactions when taking this medication

The effects of alcohol may be increased if taken with Empirin with Codeine. Avoid using alcohol while taking this medication.

If Empirin with Codeine is taken with certain other drugs, the effects of either could be increased, decreased, or altered. It is especially important to check with your doctor before combining Empirin with Codeine with the following:

Blood thinners such as Coumadin
Furosemide (Lasix)
Insulin
MAO inhibitors such as the antidepressants Parnate and Nardil
Mercaptopurine
Methotrexate (Rheumatrex)
Nonsteroidal anti-inflammatory drugs such as Advil, Motrin, and Indocin
Oral diabetes medications such as Diabinese and Tolinase
Other narcotic analgesics such as Percodan and Tylox
Para-amino salicylic acid
Penicillin
Probenecid (Benemid)
Sedatives such as phenobarbital and Nembutal
Steroids such as Medrol and prednisone
Sulfa drugs such as Azo Gantrisin and Septra
Sulfinpyrazone (Anturane)

Tranquilizers such as Xanax and Valium
Vitamin C

Special information
if you are pregnant or breastfeeding

The effects of Empirin with Codeine during pregnancy have not been adequately studied. If you are pregnant or plan to become pregnant, inform your doctor immediately. Aspirin and codeine appear in small amounts in breast milk and may affect a nursing infant. If this medication is essential to your health, your doctor may advise you to stop breastfeeding until your treatment with this medication is finished.

Recommended dosage

Dosage is determined by the severity of your pain and your response to this medication. Your doctor may prescribe more than the usual recommended dose if your pain is severe or if you are no longer getting enough pain relief from the dose you have been taking.

The usual adult dose for Empirin with Codeine No. 3 is 1 or 2 tablets every 4 hours as needed. The usual adult dose for Empirin with Codeine No. 4 is 1 tablet every 4 hours as required.

Overdosage

- *In adults, symptoms of Empirin with Codeine overdose may include:*
  Bluish skin color due to lack of oxygen, circulatory collapse, clammy skin, coma, constricted pupils, delirium, delusions, difficult or labored breathing, double vision, excitability, flabby muscles, garbled speech, hallucinations, restlessness, skin eruptions, slow and shallow breathing, stupor, vertigo

- *In children, symptoms of Empirin with Codeine overdose may include:*
  Confusion, convulsions, dehydration, difficulty hearing, dim vision, dizziness, drowsiness, extremely high body temperature, headache, nausea, rapid breathing, ringing in ears, sweating, thirst, vomiting

If you suspect an overdose, seek medical treatment immediately.

Brand name:

E-MYCIN

See Erythromycin, Oral, page 461.

Generic name:

ENALAPRIL

See Vasotec, page 1329.

Generic name:

ENALAPRIL WITH FELODIPINE

See Lexxel, page 661.

Generic name:

ENALAPRIL WITH HYDROCHLOROTHIAZIDE

See Vaseretic, page 1325.

Brand name:

ENDEP

See Elavil, page 441.

Generic name:

ENOXACIN

See Penetrex, page 929.

Brand name:

ENTEX LA

Pronounced: ENN-teks ELL AI
Generic ingredients: Guaifenesin, Phenylpropanolamine
   hydrochloride
Other brand name: Exgest LA

Why is this drug prescribed?
Entex LA is used to treat bronchitis, the common cold, sinus inflammation, nasal congestion, and sore throat.

Entex LA is a combination of two medications, phenylpropanolamine (a decongestant) and guaifenesin (an expectorant), specially formulated to deliver prolonged action. Phenylpropanolamine helps reduce congestion in the nasal passages, while guaifenesin breaks up mucus in the lower respiratory tract, making it easier to clear the passages.

Most important fact about this drug

Certain medical conditions can affect your use of Entex LA. If you have heart disease, high blood pressure, or diabetes, make sure the doctor knows about it. The phenylpropanolamine in Entex LA can raise blood pressure and speed up the heart, and can put you at a greater risk of heart or blood-vessel disease if you are diabetic.

How should you take this medication?

You may break Entex LA tablets in half to make them easier to swallow, but you must not chew or crush them.

■ *If you miss a dose...*
Take it as soon as you remember. If it is almost time for your next dose, skip the one you missed and go back to your regular schedule. Never take 2 doses at once.

■ *Storage instructions...*
Store at room temperature in a tightly closed container, away from light.

What side effects may occur?

Side effects cannot be anticipated. If any develop or change in intensity, inform your doctor as soon as possible. Only your doctor can determine if it is safe for you to continue taking Entex LA.

■ *Side effects may include:*
Difficulty urinating (in men with an enlarged prostate), headache, inability to sleep or difficulty sleeping, irritated stomach, nausea, nervousness, restlessness

Why should this drug not be prescribed?

You should not use Entex LA if you have severe high blood pressure, are sensitive to other stimulating drugs such as Dristan Decongestant, or take antidepressant medications known as MAO inhibitors, including Nardil and Parnate.

Special warnings about this medication

Use Entex LA cautiously if you have any of the following conditions:

Diabetes
Glaucoma (excessive pressure in the eyes)
Heart disease

High blood pressure
Hyperthyroidism (excessive thyroid gland activity)
Prostate enlargement

Possible food and drug interactions
when taking this medication

Do not take Entex LA if you are taking a medication classified as an MAO inhibitor, including the antidepressants Nardil and Parnate. Avoid other stimulating drugs such as Proventil, Ventolin, and many decongestants. Interactions can also occur with the following:

Bromocriptine (Parlodel)
Methyldopa (Aldomet)

Special information
if you are pregnant or breastfeeding

The effects of Entex LA during pregnancy have not been adequately studied. If you are pregnant or plan to become pregnant, notify your doctor immediately. It is not known whether Entex LA appears in breast milk. If this medication is essential to your health, your doctor may advise you to discontinue breastfeeding until treatment with this drug is finished.

Recommended dosage

ADULTS AND CHILDREN 12 YEARS AND OLDER

The usual dosage is 1 tablet every 12 hours.

CHILDREN 6 TO 12 YEARS OLD

The usual dosage is one-half tablet every 12 hours.

The safety and effectiveness of Entex LA have not been established in children under the age of 6.

Overdosage

Any medication taken in excess can have serious consequences. If you suspect an overdose, seek medical help immediately.

■ *Symptoms of Entex LA overdose may include:*
Coma, convulsions, high blood pressure

Brand name:

EPITOL

See Tegretol, page 1199.

Brand name:

EPIVIR

Pronounced: EPP-ih-veer
Generic name: Lamivudine

Why is this drug prescribed?
Epivir is one of the drugs used to fight infection with the human immunodeficiency virus (HIV), the deadly cause of AIDS. Doctors turn to Epivir as the infection gets worse. The drug is taken along with Retrovir, another HIV medication.

HIV does its damage by slowly destroying the immune system, eventually leaving the body defenseless against infections. Like other drugs for HIV, Epivir interferes with the virus's ability to reproduce. This staves off the collapse of the immune system.

Most important fact about this drug
The Epivir/Retrovir combination does not completely eliminate HIV or totally restore the immune system. There is still a danger of serious infections, so you should be sure to see your doctor regularly for monitoring and tests.

How should you take this medication?
It's important to keep adequate levels of Epivir in your bloodstream at all times, so you need to keep taking this medication regularly, just as prescribed, even when you're feeling better.

- *If you miss a dose...*
  Take it as soon as you remember. If it is almost time for the next dose, skip the one you missed and go back to your regular schedule. Do not take 2 doses at once.

- *Storage instructions...*
  Store at room temperature. Keep the bottle tightly closed.

What side effects may occur?
Side effects cannot be anticipated. If any develop or change in intensity, inform your doctor as soon as possible. Only your doctor can determine if it is safe for you to continue taking Epivir.

- *Side effects may include:*
  Abdominal cramps and pains, chills, cough, depression, diarrhea, dizziness, fatigue, fever, general feeling of illness, hair loss, headache, hives,

insomnia and other sleep problems, itching, joint pain, lost appetite, muscle and bone pain, nasal problems, nausea, skin rashes, stomach upset, vomiting, weakness

Why should this drug not be prescribed?
If Epivir gives you an allergic reaction, you cannot take this drug.

Special warnings about this medication
Remember that Epivir does not eliminate HIV from the body. The infection can still be passed to others through sexual contact or blood contamination.

The Epivir/Retrovir combination should be given to a child with a history of pancreatitis (inflammation of the pancreas) only when there is no alternative. If any signs of a pancreas problem develop while the child is taking this combination, treatment should be stopped immediately. The chief signs of pancreatitis are bouts of severe abdominal pain—usually lasting for days—accompanied by nausea and vomiting.

If you have the chronic liver disease hepatitis B, as well as HIV infection, the hepatitis B may come back when you stop taking Epivir.

Possible food and drug interactions
when taking this medication
Check with your doctor before combining Epivir with Bactrim or Septra.

While no other interactions with Epivir have been reported, its companion drug, Retrovir, can interact with a number of medications.

Special information
if you are pregnant or breastfeeding
The effects of Epivir during pregnancy have not been adequately studied, but there is reason to suspect some risk. If you are pregnant or plan to become pregnant, notify your doctor immediately.

Since HIV can be passed to your baby through breast milk, you should not plan on breastfeeding.

Recommended dosage

ADULTS

The usual dose (either tablets or liquid) is 150 milligrams twice daily. Your doctor may adjust the dosage if you have kidney problems or weigh less than 110 pounds.

CHILDREN UNDER 12 YEARS OF AGE

The usual dose is 4 milligrams per 2.2 pounds of body weight twice a day, up to a maximum of 150 milligrams twice daily.

Overdosage

The symptoms of Epivir overdose are unknown at this time. However, any medication taken in excess can have serious consequences. If you suspect an overdose, seek medical attention immediately.

Brand name:

EQUANIL

See Miltown, page 769.

Generic name:

ERGOLOID MESYLATES

See Hydergine, page 570.

Generic name:

ERGOTAMINE WITH CAFFEINE

See Cafergot, page 167.

Brand name:

ERYC

See Erythromycin, Oral, page 461.

Brand name:

ERYCETTE

See Erythromycin, Topical, page 465.

Brand name:

ERY-TAB

See Erythromycin, Oral, page 461.

Brand name:

ERYTHROCIN

See Erythromycin, Oral, page 461.

Generic name:

ERYTHROMYCIN, ORAL

Pronounced: *er-ITH-row MY-sin*
Brand names: *E.E.S., E-Mycin, ERYC, Ery-Tab,*
  Erythrocin, Ilosone, PCE

Why is this drug prescribed?

Erythromycin is an antibiotic used to treat many kinds of infections, including:

Acute pelvic inflammatory disease
Gonorrhea
Intestinal parasitic infections
Legionnaires' disease
Pinkeye
Skin infections
Syphilis
Upper and lower respiratory tract infections
Urinary tract infections
Whooping cough

Erythromycin is also prescribed to prevent infections of the heart (rheumatic fever and bacterial endocarditis) in people who are allergic to penicillin and who have congenital or rheumatic heart disease.

Most important fact about this drug

Erythromycin, like any other antibiotic, works best when there is a constant amount of drug in the blood. To help keep the drug amount constant, it is important not to miss any doses. Also, it is advisable to take the doses at evenly spaced times around the clock.

How should you take this medication?

Your doctor may advise you to take erythromycin at least 1 hour before or 2 hours after meals. If the drug upsets your stomach, taking it with meals may help. Ask your doctor whether this is advisable for you.

Chewable forms of erythromycin should be crushed or chewed before being swallowed.

Delayed-release brands and tablets and capsules that are coated to slow their breakdown should be swallowed whole. Do not crush or break. If you are not sure about the form of erythromycin you are taking, ask your pharmacist.

The liquid should be shaken well before each use.

■ *If you miss a dose...*
Take it as soon as you remember. If it is almost time for your next dose, and you take 2 doses a day, space the missed dose and the next dose 5 to 6 hours apart; if you take 3 or more doses a day, space the missed dose and the next one 2 to 4 hours apart. Never take 2 doses at the same time.

■ *Storage instructions...*
The liquid form of erythromycin should be kept in the refrigerator; use E.E.S. within 10 days. Do not freeze. Store tablets and capsules at room temperature.

What side effects may occur?
Side effects cannot be anticipated. If any develop or change in intensity, inform your doctor as soon as possible. Only your doctor can determine whether it is safe to continue taking this medication.

■ *More common side effects may include:*
Abdominal pain, diarrhea, loss of appetite, nausea, vomiting

■ *Less common side effects may include:*
Hives, rash, skin eruptions, yellow eyes and skin

■ *Rare side effects may include:*
Hearing loss (temporary), inflammation of the large intestine, irregular heartbeat, severe allergic reaction, skin reddening

Why should this drug not be prescribed?
You should not use erythromycin if you have ever had an allergic reaction to it or are sensitive to it. Erythromycin should not be used with Seldane, Hismanal, or Propulsid.

Special warnings about this medication
If you have ever had liver disease, consult your doctor before taking erythromycin.

If a new infection (called superinfection) develops, talk to your doctor. You may need to be treated with a different antibiotic.

This drug may cause a severe form of intestinal inflammation. If you develop diarrhea, contact your doctor immediately. If you have myasthenia gravis (muscle weakness), it can be aggravated by erythromycin.

Possible food and drug interactions
when taking this medication

If erythromycin is taken with certain other drugs, the effects of either could be increased, decreased, or altered. It is especially important to check with your doctor before combining erythromycin with the following:

Astemizole (Hismanal)
Blood-thinning drugs such as Coumadin
Bromocriptine (Parlodel)
Carbamazepine (Tegretol)
Cisapride (Propulsid)
Cyclosporine (Sandimmune, Neoral)
Digoxin (Lanoxin)
Dihydroergotamine (D.H.E. 45)
Disopyramide (Norpace)
Ergotamine (Cafergot)
Hexobarbital
Lovastatin (Mevacor)
Seizure medications such as Depakane, Depakote, and Dilantin
Tacrolimus (Prograf)
Terfenadine (Seldane)
Theophylline (Theo-Dur)
Triazolam (Halcion)

Special information
if you are pregnant or breastfeeding

If you are pregnant or plan to become pregnant, inform your doctor immediately. Erythromycin appears in breast milk and could affect a nursing infant. If this medication is essential to your health, your doctor may advise you to discontinue breastfeeding until your treatment is finished.

Recommended dosage

Dosage instructions are determined by the type (and severity) of infection being treated and may vary slightly for different brands of erythromycin. The following are recommended dosages for PCE, one of the most commonly prescribed brands.

ADULTS

Streptococcal Infections

The usual dose is 333 milligrams every 8 hours, or 500 milligrams every 12 hours. Depending on the severity of the infection, the dose may be increased to a total of 4 grams a day. However, when the daily dosage is larger than 1 gram, twice-a-day doses are not recommended, and the drug should be taken more often in smaller doses.

To treat streptococcal infections of the upper respiratory tract (tonsillitis or strep throat), erythromycin should be taken for at least 10 days.

To Prevent Bacterial Endocarditis (Inflammation and Infection of the Heart Lining and Valves) in Those Allergic to Penicillin

The oral regimen is 800 milligrams to 1 gram of erythromycin taken 1 to 2 hours before dental surgery or surgical procedures of the upper respiratory tract, followed by 400 to 500 milligrams 6 hours later.

Urinary Tract Infections Due to Chlamydia Trachomatis During Pregnancy

The usual dosage is 500 milligrams of erythromycin orally 4 times a day or 666 milligrams every 8 hours on an empty stomach for at least 7 days. For women who cannot tolerate this regimen, a decreased dose of 500 milligrams every 12 hours or 333 milligrams every 8 hours a day should be used for at least 14 days.

For Those with Uncomplicated Urinary, Reproductive Tract, or Rectal Infections Caused by Chlamydia Trachomatis When Tetracycline Cannot Be Taken

The usual oral dosage is 500 milligrams of erythromycin 4 times a day or 666 milligrams every 8 hours for at least 7 days.

For Those with Nongonococcal Urethral Infections When Tetracycline Cannot Be Taken

The usual dosage is 500 milligrams of erythromycin by mouth 4 times a day or 666 milligrams orally every 8 hours for at least 7 days.

Acute Pelvic Inflammatory Disease Caused by Neisseria Gonorrhoeae

The usual treatment is three days of intravenous erythromycin followed by 500 milligrams orally every 12 hours or 333 milligrams orally every 8 hours for 7 days.

Syphilis

The usual dosage is 30 to 40 grams divided into smaller doses over a period of 10 to 15 days.

Intestinal Infections

The usual dosage is 500 milligrams every 12 hours, or 333 milligrams every 8 hours, for 10 to 14 days.

Legionnaires' Disease

The usual dosage ranges from 1 to 4 grams daily, divided into smaller doses.

CHILDREN

Age, weight, and severity of the infection determine the correct dosage.

The usual dosage is from 30 to 50 milligrams daily for each 2.2 pounds of body weight, divided into equal doses for 10 to 14 days.

For more severe infections, this dosage may be doubled, but it should not exceed 4 grams per day.

Children weighing over 44 pounds should follow the recommended adult dose schedule.

For prevention of bacterial endocarditis, the children's dosage is 10 milligrams per 2.2 pounds of body weight 2 hours before dental work or surgery, followed by 5 milligrams per 2.2 pounds 6 hours later.

Overdosage

Any medication taken in excess can have serious consequences. If you suspect an overdose, seek medical help immediately.

- ■ *Symptoms of erythromycin overdose may include:*
  Diarrhea, nausea, stomach cramps, vomiting

Generic name:

ERYTHROMYCIN, TOPICAL

Pronounced: err-rith-ro-MY-sin
Brand names: A/T/S, Erycette, T-Stat

Why is this drug prescribed?

Topical erythromycin (applied directly to the skin) is used for the treatment of acne.

Most important fact about this drug
For best results, you should continue the treatment for as long as prescribed, even if your acne begins to clear up. This medicine is not an instant cure.

How should you use this medication?
Use exactly as prescribed by your doctor.

Thoroughly wash the affected area with soap and water and pat dry before applying medication.

Moisten the applicator or pad with the medication and lightly spread it over the affected area. A/T/S Topical Gel should not be rubbed in.

■ *If you miss a dose...*
Apply the forgotten dose as soon as you remember. If it is almost time for the next application, skip the one you missed and go back to your regular schedule.

■ *Storage instructions...*
This medicine can be stored at room temperature.

What side effects may occur?
Side effects cannot be anticipated. If any develop or change in intensity, inform your doctor as soon as possible. Only your doctor can determine if it is safe for you to continue using topical erythromycin.

■ *Side effects may include:*
Burning sensation, dryness, hives, irritation of the eyes, itching, oiliness, peeling, scaling, tenderness, unusual redness of the skin

Why should this drug not be prescribed?
Erythromycin should not be used if you are sensitive to or have ever had an allergic reaction to any of the ingredients.

Special warnings about this medication
This type of erythromycin is for external use only. Do not use it in the eyes, nose, or mouth.

If the acne does not improve after 6 to 8 weeks of treatment, or if it gets worse, stop using the topical erythromycin preparation and call your doctor.

The use of antibiotics can stimulate the growth of other bacteria that are resistant to the antibiotic you are taking. If new infections (called superinfections) occur, talk to your doctor. You may need to be treated with a different antibiotic drug.

If you develop diarrhea, let your doctor know right away. Drugs such as erythromycin can cause a potentially serious intestinal inflammation.

The use of other topical acne medications in combination with topical erythromycin may cause irritation, especially with the use of peeling, scaling, or abrasive medications.

The safety and effectiveness of A/T/S and Erycette have not been established in children.

Possible food and drug interactions
when using this medication
If topical erythromycin is used with certain other drugs, the effects of either could be increased, decreased, or altered. It is especially important to check with your doctor before combining topical erythromycin with other topical acne medications.

Special information
if you are pregnant or breastfeeding
The effects of topical erythromycin during pregnancy have not been adequately studied. If you are pregnant or plan to become pregnant, inform your doctor immediately. Erythromycin may appear in breast milk and could affect a nursing infant. If this medication is essential to your health, your doctor may advise you to stop breastfeeding until your treatment with erythromycin is finished.

Recommended dosage
Apply solution to the affected area 2 times a day. Moisten the applicator or a pad, then spread over the affected area. Use additional pads as needed. Apply gel products as a thin film over the affected area once or twice a day.

Make sure the area is thoroughly washed with soap and water and patted dry before applying medication. Thoroughly wash your hands after application of the medication.

Reducing the frequency of applications may reduce peeling and drying.

Overdosage
Although overdosage is unlikely, any medication used in excess can have serious consequences. If you suspect an overdose, seek medical treatment immediately.

Generic name:

ERYTHROMYCIN WITH BENZOYL PEROXIDE

See Benzamycin, page 144.

Generic name:

ERYTHROMYCIN WITH SULFISOXAZOLE

See Pediazole, page 925.

Brand name:

ESGIC

See Fioricet, page 496.

Brand name:

ESIDRIX

See HydroDIURIL, page 572.

Brand name:

ESKALITH

See Lithonate, page 677.

Generic name:

ESTAZOLAM

See ProSom, page 1025.

Brand name:

ESTRACE

See Estraderm, page 469.

Brand name:

ESTRADERM

Pronounced: ESS-tra-derm
Generic name: Estradiol
Other brand names: Alora, Climara, Estrace, Vivelle

Why is this drug prescribed?

Estraderm and other estrogen patches such as Alora, Climara, and Vivelle are used to reduce symptoms of menopause, including feelings of warmth in face, neck, and chest, and the sudden intense episodes of heat and sweating known as "hot flashes." Estrace tablets are also prescribed for this purpose, and another form of estrogen—Estrace vaginal cream—is prescribed to relieve dry, itchy external genitals and vaginal irritation. And some doctors prescribe estrogen for teenagers who fail to mature at the usual rate.

Along with diet, calcium supplements, and exercise, Estraderm patches are also prescribed to prevent osteoporosis, a condition in which the bones become brittle and easily broken. Estrace tablets are also used for this purpose.

All forms of this drug are used to treat low levels of estrogen in certain people. In addition, Climara patches are used to treat abnormal bleeding from the uterus in some cases, and Estrace tablets are used to provide relief in breast or prostate cancer.

Most important fact about this drug

Because estrogens have been linked with increased risk of endometrial cancer (cancer in the lining of the uterus), it is essential to have regular checkups and to report any unusual vaginal bleeding to your doctor immediately.

How should you take this medication?

ESTRADERM, ALORA, CLIMARA, AND VIVELLE

Each patch is individually sealed in a protective pouch and is applied directly to the skin.

A stiff protective liner covers the adhesive side of the patch. Remove the liner by sliding it sideways between your thumb and index finger. Holding the patch at one edge, remove the protective liner and discard it. Try to avoid touching the adhesive. Use immediately after removing the liner. If you are using Alora or Vivelle, peel off one side of the protective liner and discard it. Use the other half of the liner as a handle until you have applied the sticky area, then fold back the remaining side of the patch, pull off the rest of the liner, and smooth the second half of the patch onto your skin.

Apply the adhesive side to a clean, dry area of your skin on the trunk of your body (including the buttocks and abdomen). Do not apply to your breasts or waist. Firmly press the patch in place with the palm of your hand for about 10 seconds, to make sure the edges are flat against your skin. When first using Alora, start on the lower abdomen. Climara is applied only to the abdomen and is pressed in place with the fingers.

Contact with water during bathing, swimming, or showering will not affect the patch.

The application site must be rotated. Allow an interval of at least 1 week between applications to a particular site.

Alora, Estraderm, and Vivelle patches should be replaced twice a week.

ESTRACE

Estrace Tablets are taken orally.

If you are using Estrace vaginal cream, follow these steps to apply:

1. Load the supplied applicator to the fill line.
2. Lie on your back with your knees drawn up.
3. Gently insert the applicator high into the vagina. Release the medicine by pushing the plunger.
4. Withdraw the applicator.
5. Wash the applicator with soap and water.

■ *If you miss a dose...*
   If you forget to apply a new patch when you are supposed to, do it as soon as you remember. If it is almost time to change patches anyway, skip the one you missed and go back to your regular schedule. Do not apply more than one patch at a time.

   If you miss a dose of the tablets, take it as soon as you remember. If it is almost time for your next dose, skip the one you missed and go back to your regular schedule. Do not take 2 doses at once.

■ *Storage instructions...*
   Store patches at room temperature, in their sealed pouches. Store Estrace at room temperature in a tightly closed container; keep away from light.

What side effects may occur?

Side effects cannot be anticipated: If any develop or change in intensity, notify your doctor as soon as possible. Only your doctor can determine if it is safe for you to continue taking Estraderm.

■ *The most common side effect is:*
Skin redness and irritation at the site of the patch.

■ *Less common or rare side effects may include:*
Abdominal cramps, bloating, breakthrough bleeding, breast enlargement, breast tenderness, change in cervical secretions, change in menstrual flow, change in sex drive, change in weight, darkening of skin, dizziness, fluid retention, growth of benign fibroid tumors in the uterus, headache, intolerance to contact lenses, migraine, nausea, rash, severe allergic reaction, vaginal bleeding (more common at higher doses), vomiting, yellowing of eyes and skin

■ *Other side effects reported with estradiol include:*
Abnormal withdrawal bleeding, certain cancers, cardiovascular disease, depression, excessive growth of hair, gallbladder disease, hair loss, high blood pressure, reddened skin, twitching, vaginal yeast infection

Why should this drug not be prescribed?

Estraderm should not be used if you are sensitive to or have ever had an allergic reaction to any of its components.

Estrogens should not be used if you have ever had breast or uterine cancer or a tumor promoted by estrogen. Also avoid estrogens if you are pregnant or think you are pregnant, if you have abnormal, undiagnosed genital bleeding, or if you have blood clots or a blood clotting disorder.

Special warnings about this medication

The risk of cancer of the uterus increases when estrogen is used for a long time or taken in large doses. There also may be increased risk of breast cancer in women who take estrogen for an extended period of time or in high doses.

Women who take estrogen after menopause are more likely to develop gallbladder disease.

Tell your doctor if you have any problems with your circulation.

Estrogen also increases the risk of blood clots. These blood clots can cause stroke, heart attack, or other serious disorders.

While taking Estraderm, get in touch with your doctor right away if you notice any of the following:

Abdominal pain, tenderness, or swelling
Abnormal bleeding of the vagina
Breast lumps
Coughing up blood
Pain in your chest or calves
Severe headache, dizziness, or faintness
Skin irritation, redness, or rash
Sudden shortness of breath
Vision changes
Yellowing of the skin or eyes

A complete medical and family history should be taken by your doctor before starting any estrogen therapy.

In general, you should not take estrogen for more than 1 year without another physical examination by your doctor.

Estraderm may cause fluid retention in some people. If you have asthma, epilepsy, migraine, or heart or kidney disease, use this medication cautiously.

Estrogen therapy may cause uterine bleeding or breast pain.

Possible food and drug interactions
when taking this medication
If you take certain other drugs while using Estraderm, the effects of either could be increased, decreased, or altered. It is especially important to check with your doctor before taking the following:

Barbiturates such as phenobarbital and Seconal
Blood thinners such as Coumadin
Dantrolene (Dantrium)
Epilepsy drugs such as Tegretol and Dilantin
Rifampin (Rifadin)
Steroids such as Deltasone
Tricyclic antidepressants such as Elavil and Tofranil

Special information
if you are pregnant or breastfeeding
Estrogens should not be used during pregnancy or immediately after childbirth. Use of estrogens during pregnancy has been linked to reproductive tract problems in the children. If you are pregnant or plan to become pregnant, notify your doctor immediately. Estraderm may appear in breast milk and could affect a nursing infant. Estrogens decrease the quantity and

quality of breast milk. If this medication is essential to your health, your doctor may advise you to discontinue breastfeeding until your treatment is finished.

Recommended dosage

SYMPTOMS OF MENOPAUSE

After starting your therapy, the doctor will prescribe a higher dose if necessary, but should try decreasing the dose or discontinuing the medication every 3 to 6 months.

Estraderm, Alora, and Vivelle

The usual starting dose is one 0.05 milligram patch applied to the skin 2 times a week.

Estrace

The usual starting dose is 1 or 2 milligrams a day; you will take the tablets for 3 weeks and then have 1 week off for each cycle.

Climara

The usual starting dose for all uses is one 0.5 milligram patch applied to the skin once a week. You will use the patch for 3 weeks, then have 1 week off.

PREVENTION OF OSTEOPOROSIS

Estraderm

The usual starting dose is 0.05 milligram per day.

Estrace

The usual dose is 0.5 milligram taken every day for 23 days, followed by 5 days off.

LOW ESTROGEN LEVELS

Estrace

The usual starting dose is 1 or 2 milligrams a day.

Alora

The usual starting dose is one 0.05 milligram patch applied twice a week.

RELIEF IN BREAST CANCER

Estrace

The usual dose is 10 milligrams 3 times a day for at least 3 months.

RELIEF IN PROSTATE CANCER

Estrace
The usual dose is 1 to 2 milligrams 3 times a day.

VAGINAL ITCHING AND DRYNESS

Estrace Vaginal Cream
The usual dosage is 2 to 4 grams (marked on the applicator) inserted into the vagina once a day, for 1 to 2 weeks. The dosage and frequency may be reduced after your condition improves.

To prevent recurrence, a dosage of 1 gram 1 to 3 times a week is recommended.

Overdosage
Any medication taken in excess can have serious consequences. If you suspect an overdose, seek medical attention immediately.

■ *Symptoms of Estraderm overdose may include:*
  Nausea, vomiting, withdrawal bleeding

Generic name:

ESTRADIOL

See Estraderm, page 469.

Generic name:

ESTRADIOL VAGINAL RING

See Estring, page 474.

Brand name:

ESTRING

Pronounced: ESST-ring
Generic name: Estradiol vaginal ring

Why is this drug prescribed?
Estring is an estrogen replacement system for relief of the vaginal problems that often occur after menopause, including vaginal dryness, burning, and itching, and difficult or painful intercourse. Estring is also prescribed for

postmenopausal urinary problems such as difficulty urinating or urinary urgency.

Most important fact about this drug
Because estrogen replacement therapy is not advisable if you are in any danger of developing cancer, your doctor should take a complete medical and family history—and do a complete physical exam—before prescribing Estring. As a general rule, you should have an examination at least once a year while using Estring.

How should you use this medication?
Each Estring is left in place for 3 months. Press the Estring into an oval and insert it as deeply as possible into the upper third of the vagina. The exact position is unimportant as long as you don't feel the ring. If the ring causes discomfort, it is probably not far enough inside.

If the ring slips down into the lower part of the vagina, push it back up with your finger. If it falls out, rinse it in warm water and reinsert it. When replacing the ring, simply hook a finger through it and pull it out.

■ *If you miss a dose...*
If the ring is not replaced after 90 days, the dose of estrogen will gradually decline and your symptoms will return.

■ *Storage instructions...*
Store at room temperature.

What side effects may occur?
Side effects cannot be anticipated. If any develop or change in intensity, tell your doctor as soon as possible. Only your doctor can determine if it is safe for you to continue using Estring.

■ *More common side effects may include:*
Abdominal pain, arthritis, back pain, flu-like symptoms, headaches, insomnia, joint pain, nausea, sinus inflammation, upper respiratory tract infections, vaginal discharge, vaginal discomfort or pain, vaginal inflammation or bleeding, yeast infection

■ *Less common side effects may include:*
Abnormal bleeding from the uterus, allergic reaction, bone pain, breast pain, bronchitis, chest pain, diarrhea, fainting, family stress, gas, genital itching or eruptions, hemorrhoids, hot flashes, inability to hold urine, indigestion, middle ear infection, migraine, painful urination, skin inflam-

mation, sore throat, stomach inflammation, swelling of legs, toothache, urinary tract infection

Why should this drug not be prescribed?
Do not use Estring if there is any chance that you have breast cancer or any other cancer stimulated by estrogen. Also avoid Estring if there is a possibility that you are pregnant. Do not use Estring if you have unexplained genital bleeding, and avoid it in the event of an allergic reaction.

Special warnings about this medication
Estrogen replacement therapy is associated with a slight increase in the chances of heart disease, high blood pressure, gallbladder disease, certain forms of cancer, and excessive calcium levels. Estrogen is also suspected of increasing the risk of breast cancer, although this remains controversial.

Any vaginal infection should be cleared up before you begin Estring therapy. If an infection develops after you begin, you'll need to remove the ring during treatment.

If you have a liver problem, Estring should be used with caution. Make sure your doctor is aware of the situation.

Possible food and drug interactions
when using this medication
No interactions have been reported, but Estring should be removed during treatment with other vaginally administered drugs.

Special information
if you are pregnant or breastfeeding
Estring must not be used during pregnancy and is not intended for nursing mothers.

Recommended dosage
Insert a new ring every 3 months.

Overdosage
An overdose from Estring is unlikely. An oral overdose of estrogen could be expected to cause the symptoms listed below.

■ *Symptoms of estrogen overdose may include:*
  Nausea, vomiting, vaginal bleeding

Generic name:

ESTROPIPATE

See Ogen, page 878.

Generic name:

ETODOLAC

See Lodine, page 681.

Brand name:

EULEXIN

Pronounced: you-LEKS-in
Generic name: Flutamide

Why is this drug prescribed?

Eulexin is used along with drugs such as Lupron to treat prostate cancer. Eulexin belongs to a class of drugs known as antiandrogens. It blocks the effect of the male hormone testosterone. Giving Eulexin with Lupron, which reduces the body's testosterone levels, is one way of treating prostate cancer. For some forms of prostate cancer, radiation therapy is given along with the drugs.

Most important fact about this drug

Taking Eulexin and Lupron together is essential in this form of treatment. You should not interrupt their doses or stop taking either of these medications without consulting your doctor.

How should you take this medication?

Take Eulexin exactly as prescribed. Do not use more or less, and do not take it more often than instructed.

■ *If you miss a dose...*
Take it as soon as you remember. If it is almost time for your next dose, skip the one you missed and go back to your regular schedule. Never take 2 doses at once.

■ *Storage instructions...*
Store at room temperature.

What side effects may occur?

Side effects cannot be anticipated. If any develop or change in intensity, inform your doctor immediately. Since Eulexin is always given with another antiandrogen drug, when a side effect develops, it is difficult to know which drug is responsible. Only your doctor can determine if it is safe for you to continue taking Eulexin.

■ *More common side effects may include:*
   Breast tissue swelling and tenderness, diarrhea, hot flashes, impotence, loss of sex drive, nausea, vomiting

■ *Less common side effects may include:*
   Confusion, decreased sexual ability, jaundice and liver damage, rash, sun sensitivity (rashes, blisters upon exposure to sun), urine discoloration (amber or yellow-green)

When the drugs are used along with radiation therapy, additional side effects may include bladder inflammation, bleeding from the rectum, blood in the urine, and intestinal problems.

Why should this drug not be prescribed?

Do not take Eulexin if you have ever had an allergic reaction to it or are sensitive to it or to any of the colorings or other inactive ingredients in the capsules.

Special warnings about this medication

Eulexin may cause liver damage in some people. Your doctor will do blood tests to check your liver function before you start treatment with Eulexin, and at regular intervals thereafter. If a liver problem does develop, you may need to take less Eulexin or stop taking the drug altogether. Report any signs or symptoms that might suggest liver damage to your doctor right away. Warning signs include dark urine, itching, flu-like symptoms, jaundice (a yellowing of the skin and eyes), persistent appetite loss, and persistent tenderness on the right side of the upper abdomen.

Possible food and drug interactions
when taking this medication

If you are already taking the anticoagulant drug warfarin (Coumadin), you will need to be monitored especially closely after treatment with Eulexin begins. Your doctor may need to lower your dosage of warfarin.

Recommended dosage

The recommended adult Eulexin dosage is 2 capsules 3 times a day at 8-hour intervals for a total daily dosage of 750 milligrams.

Overdosage

You may notice breast development or tenderness with an overdose of Eulexin. Any medication taken in excess can have serious consequences. If you suspect an overdose, seek medical attention immediately.

Brand name:

EVISTA

Pronounced: Eve-IST-ah
Generic name: Raloxifene hydrochloride

Why is this drug prescribed?

Evista is prescribed to prevent osteoporosis, the brittle-bone disease that strikes some women after menopause. A variety of factors promote osteoporosis. The more factors that apply to you, the greater your chances of developing the disease. These factors include:

Caucasian or Asian descent
Slender build
Early menopause
Smoking
Drinking
A diet low in calcium
An inactive lifestyle
Osteoporosis in the family

Most important fact about this drug

Like estrogen, Evista reduces bone loss and increases bone density. However, Evista does not have estrogen-like effects on the uterus and breasts, and therefore is unlikely to increase the risk of cancer, as estrogen therapy sometimes can do.

Although Evista has been shown to increase bone density over the course of a two-year study, its longer-term ability to prevent bone fractures has not yet been proven.

How should you use this medication?

Take Evista once daily, at any time, with or without food. Take calcium and vitamin D supplements as well, if you do not get enough in your diet. Avoid alcohol and tobacco. Do weight-bearing exercises to strengthen your bones.

■ *If you miss a dose...*
Take it as soon as you remember. If it is almost time for your next dose, skip the one you missed and go back to your regular schedule. Never take a double dose.

■ *Storage instructions...*
Store at room temperature.

What side effects may occur?

Evista has one very positive side effect: It lowers total cholesterol and LDL ("bad") cholesterol. It does not affect HDL ("good") cholesterol or trigly-ceride levels.

The unwanted side effects of Evista cannot be predicted. If any develop or change in intensity, inform your doctor as soon as possible. Only your doctor can determine if it is safe for you to continue taking Evista.

■ *More common side effects may include:*
Abdominal pain, arthritis, breast pain, chest pain, depression, fever, flu symptoms, gas, gynecological problems, hot flashes, increased cough, indigestion, infection, inflammation of the throat and sinus passages, insomnia, joint pain, leg cramps, muscle ache, nausea, rash, stomach and intestinal problems, sweating, swelling, urinary tract infection, vomiting, weight gain

■ *Less common side effects may include:*
Laryngitis, migraine, pneumonia

Why should this drug not be prescribed?

Evista is not for use by women who are—or could become—pregnant. You should also avoid this drug if you have a history of blood clot formation, including deep vein thrombosis (blood clot in the legs), pulmonary embolism (blood clot in the lungs), and retinal vein thrombosis (blood clot in the retina of the eye), since Evista increases the risk of clots. Avoid the drug, too, if it gives you an allergic reaction.

Special warnings about this medication

Because of Evista's tendency to promote clots, you should not take it during long periods of immobilization such as recovery from surgery or prolonged bed rest, or for 72 hours beforehand. If you are scheduled for surgery, make sure the doctor is aware that you are taking Evista.

For the same reason, if you are going on a trip where your movement will be restricted, make a point of periodically getting up and walking around.

Evista is not needed prior to menopause and shouldn't be taken until menopause has passed. It has not been studied in premenopausal women and its use is not recommended.

Use Evista with caution if you have congestive heart failure, a liver condition, or cancer. Be cautious, too, if you've had breast cancer in the past; the drug's effect in this situation is unknown.

If you develop unusual uterine bleeding or breast problems while taking Evista, tell your doctor immediately.

Evista will not cure hot flashes. (In fact, it may cause them.) Nevertheless, never combine Evista with estrogen hormones.

Possible food and drug interactions
when taking this medication
If Evista is taken with certain other drugs, the effects of either could be increased, decreased, or altered. It is especially important to check with your doctor before combining Evista with the following:

Cholestyramine (Questran)
Clofibrate (Atromid-S)
Diazepam (Valium)
Diazoxide (Proglycem)
Ibuprofen (Advil, Motrin, Nuprin)
Indomethacin (Indocin)
Naproxen (Aleve, Anaprox, Naprosyn)
Warfarin (Coumadin)

Special information
if you are pregnant or breastfeeding
Evista can harm a developing baby. Do not use if you are or may become pregnant. Also avoid breastfeeding while taking Evista.

Recommended dosage

POSTMENOPAUSAL WOMEN

The recommended dosage is one 60-milligram tablet once a day.

Overdosage
There have not been any reports of overdose with Evista. However, any medication taken in excess can have serious consequences. If you suspect an overdose, seek medical attention immediately.

Brand name:

EXGEST LA

See Entex LA, page 455.

Generic name:

FAMCICLOVIR

See Famvir, page 482.

Generic name:

FAMOTIDINE

See Pepcid, page 935.

Brand name:

FAMVIR

Pronounced: FAM-veer
Generic name: Famciclovir

Why is this drug prescribed?
Famvir tablets are used to treat herpes zoster, commonly referred to as "shingles," in adults. Shingles is a painful rash with raised, red pimples on the trunk of the body, usually the back. Because it is caused by the same virus that causes chickenpox, only people who have had chickenpox can get shingles.

Famvir is also prescribed to treat genital herpes that keeps flaring up.

Most important fact about this drug
Famvir is most effective if started within the first 48 hours after shingles first appears; treatment should be started at the first sign or symptom of genital herpes. Famvir treatment may not be effective if it is delayed more than 72 hours after the herpes zoster rash first appears or more than 6 hours after genital herpes becomes evident. Thus, it is important to see your doctor as soon as possible after symptoms appear.

How should you take this medication?
For maximum benefit, take Famvir for the full time of treatment, even if your symptoms begin to clear up. Do not, however, take Famvir more often or for a longer time than your doctor directs.

You may take Famvir with meals or in between.

■ *If you miss a dose...*
Take the forgotten dose as soon as you remember. If it is almost time for your next dose, skip the one you missed and go back to your regular schedule. Never take 2 doses at the same time.

■ *Storage instructions...*
Store at room temperature.

What side effects may occur?
Side effects cannot be anticipated. If any develop or change in intensity, inform your doctor as soon as possible. Only your doctor can determine if it is safe for you to continue taking Famvir.

■ *More common side effects may include:*
Constipation, diarrhea, dizziness, fatigue, fever, headache, nausea, vomiting

■ *Less common side effects may include:*
Abdominal pain, back pain, chills and fever, gas, indigestion, injury, insomnia, irritated sinuses, itching, joint pain, loss of appetite, pain, prickling or burning sensation of the skin, sleepiness, sore throat, upper respiratory infection

There have been infrequent cases of hallucinations, hives, and rash, and some people—especially older adults—may experience confusion, including delirium and disorientation.

Why should this drug not be prescribed?
Do not take Famvir if you are sensitive to it or have ever had an allergic reaction to it.

Special warnings about this medication
Famvir speeds healing of shingles and genital herpes, but it is not a cure. It may not prevent transmission of genital herpes to others, so you should avoid sexual intercourse whenever you have symptoms of the disease.

If you have any kidney problems, be sure your doctor knows about them before prescribing Famvir for you.

Possible food and drug interactions when taking this medication
If Famvir is taken with certain other drugs, the effects of either could be increased, decreased, or altered. It is especially important to check with your

doctor before combining Famvir with probenecid (Benemid), a drug used to treat gout (a type of arthritis).

Special information
if you are pregnant or breastfeeding

The effects of Famvir during pregnancy have not been adequately studied. If you are pregnant or plan to become pregnant, inform your doctor immediately. Famvir should be used during pregnancy only when the benefit to the mother clearly outweighs the potential risk to the baby. Famvir may appear in breast milk, and could affect a nursing infant. If this drug is essential to your health, your doctor may advise you to discontinue breastfeeding until your treatment with Famvir is finished.

Recommended dosage

ADULTS

Herpes Zoster
The usual adult dose is 500 milligrams every 8 hours for 7 days.

Recurrent Genital Herpes
The usual dose is 125 milligrams twice a day for 5 days.

CHILDREN

Safety and effectiveness in children under the age of 18 have not been established.

Overdosage

Any medication taken in excess can have serious consequences. If you suspect an overdose, seek medical attention immediately.

Brand name:

FASTIN

Pronounced: FAS-tin
Generic name: Phentermine hydrochloride
Other brand names: Adipex-P, Ionamin, Oby-Cap

Why is this drug prescribed?

Fastin, an appetite suppressant, is prescribed for short-term use (a few weeks) as part of an overall diet plan for weight reduction. Fastin should be used along with a behavior modification program.

Most important fact about this drug
Always remember that Fastin is an aid to, not a substitute for, good diet and exercise. Take Fastin only as directed by your doctor. Do not take it more often or for a longer time than your doctor has ordered. Fastin can lose its effectiveness after a few weeks.

How should you take this medication?
Take Fastin about 2 hours after breakfast. Do not take it late in the evening because it may keep you from sleeping.

Take Adipex-P before breakfast or up to 2 hours after breakfast. Tablets can be broken in half, if necessary.

Take Ionamin before breakfast or 10 to 14 hours before you go to bed. Ionamin capsules should be swallowed whole.

- *If you miss a dose...*
  Skip the missed dose completely; then take the next dose at the regularly scheduled time.

- *Storage instructions...*
  Store at room temperature.

What side effects may occur?
Side effects cannot be anticipated. If any develop or change in intensity, inform your doctor as soon as possible. Only your doctor can determine if it is safe for you to continue taking this medication.

- *Side effects may include:*
  Changes in sex drive, constipation, diarrhea, dizziness, dry mouth, exaggerated feelings of depression or elation, headache, high blood pressure, hives, impotence, inability to fall or stay asleep, increased heart rate, overstimulation, restlessness, stomach or intestinal problems, throbbing heartbeat, tremors, unpleasant taste

Why should this drug not be prescribed?
If you are sensitive to or have ever had an allergic reaction to phentermine hydrochloride or other drugs that stimulate the nervous system, you should not take this medication. Make sure your doctor is aware of any drug reactions you have experienced.

Do not take this drug if you have hardening of the arteries, symptoms of heart or blood vessel disease, an overactive thyroid gland, the eye condition known as glaucoma, or moderate to severe high blood pressure. Also avoid this drug if you are agitated, have ever abused drugs, or have taken an MAO inhibitor, including antidepressant drugs such as Nardil and Parnate, within the last 14 days.

Special warnings about this medication

Fastin may affect your ability to perform potentially hazardous activities. Therefore, you should be extremely careful if you have to drive a car or operate machinery.

You can become psychologically dependent on this drug. Consult your doctor if you rely on this drug to maintain a state of well-being.

If you stop taking Fastin suddenly after you have taken high doses for a long time, you may find you are extremely fatigued or depressed, or that you have trouble sleeping.

If you continually take too much of any appetite suppressant it can cause severe skin disorders, a pronounced inability to fall or stay asleep, irritability, hyperactivity, and personality changes.

Even if your blood pressure is only mildly high, be careful taking this drug.

Possible food and drug interactions
when taking this medication

This drug may react badly with alcohol. Avoid alcoholic beverages while you are taking it.

If Fastin is taken with certain other drugs, the effects of either can be increased, decreased, or altered. It is especially important that you check with your doctor before combining Fastin with the following:

Drugs classified as MAO inhibitors, including the antidepressants Nardil and Parnate
Diabetes medications such as insulin and Micronase
High blood pressure medications such as guanethidine (Ismelin)

Special information
if you are pregnant or breastfeeding

The effects of Fastin during pregnancy have not been adequately studied. If you are pregnant, plan to become pregnant, or are breastfeeding, notify your doctor immediately.

Recommended dosage

ADULTS

Fastin or Oby-Cap
The usual dosage is 1 capsule approximately 2 hours after breakfast. One capsule should suppress your appetite for 12 to 14 hours.

Adipex-P
The usual dose is 1 capsule or tablet a day, taken before breakfast or up to 2 hours after breakfast. Some people need only half a tablet each day. Others may find it more effective to take half a tablet twice daily.

Ionamin
The usual dose is 1 capsule a day, taken before breakfast or 10 to 14 hours before bedtime.

CHILDREN

This drug is not recommended for use in children under 12 years of age.

Overdosage

Any medication taken in excess can have serious consequences. An overdose of Fastin can be fatal. If you suspect an overdose, seek emergency medical treatment immediately.

■ *Symptoms of Fastin overdose may include:*
Abdominal cramps, aggressiveness, confusion, diarrhea, exaggerated reflexes, hallucinations, high or low blood pressure, irregular heartbeat, nausea, panic states, rapid breathing, restlessness, tremors, vomiting

Fatigue and depression may follow the stimulant effects of Fastin.

In cases of fatal poisoning, convulsions and coma usually precede death.

Generic name:

FELBAMATE

See Felbatol, page 487.

Brand name:

FELBATOL

Pronounced: FELL-ba-tohl
Generic name: Felbamate

Why is this drug prescribed?

Felbatol, a relatively new epilepsy medication, is used alone or with other drugs to treat partial seizures with or without generalization (seizures in which consciousness may be retained or lost). It is also used with other medications to treat seizures associated with Lennox-Gastaut syndrome (a childhood condition characterized by brief loss of awareness and muscle tone).

Felbatol is prescribed only when other medications have failed to control severe cases of epilepsy.

Most important fact about this drug
When taking Felbatol, be alert for signs of a very rare but dangerous side effect called aplastic anemia, in which the red blood cell count declines drastically. Warning signs include weakness, fatigue, and a tendency to easily bruise or bleed. Be on the watch, also, for signs of liver problems such as yellowing of the skin or eyes. There have been reports of fatal cases of liver failure among people taking Felbatol.

How should you take this medication?
Take this medication exactly as prescribed by your doctor. Felbatol should not be stopped suddenly. This could increase the frequency of your seizures.

If you are taking Felbatol liquid, shake well before using.

■ *If you miss a dose...*
Take the forgotten dose as soon as you remember. If it is almost time for your next dose, skip the one you missed and go back to your regular schedule. Never take a double dose.

■ *Storage instructions...*
Felbatol should be stored in a tightly closed container, at room temperature, away from excessive heat and moisture.

What side effects may occur?
Side effects cannot be anticipated. If any develop or change in intensity, notify your doctor as soon as possible. Only your doctor can determine if it is safe for you to continue taking Felbatol.

■ *Side effects in adults taking Felbatol alone may include:*
Acne, anxiety, constipation, diarrhea, double vision, ear infection, facial swelling, fatigue, headache, inability to fall or stay asleep, indigestion, loss of appetite, menstrual irregularities, nausea, nasal inflammation, rash, upper respiratory infection, urinary tract infection, vomiting, weight decrease

■ *Side effects in adults taking Felbatol with other medication may include:*
Abdominal pain, abnormal stride, abnormal taste, abnormal vision, anxiety, chest pain, constipation, depression, diarrhea, dizziness, double vision, dry mouth, fatigue, fever, headache, inability to fall or stay asleep, indigestion, lack of muscle coordination, loss of appetite, muscle pain, nausea, nervousness, pins and needles, rash, sinus inflammation, sleepiness, sore throat, stupor, tremor, upper respiratory infection, vomiting

■ *Side effects in children taking Felbatol with other medication may include:*
Abnormal stride, abnormal thinking, abnormally small pupils (pinpoint pupils), constipation, coughing, diarrhea, ear infection, fatigue, fever, headache, hiccups, inability to control urination, inability to fall or stay asleep, indigestion, lack of muscle coordination, loss of appetite, mood changes, nausea, nervousness, pain, rash, red or purple spots on skin, sleepiness, sore throat, taste changes, unstable emotions, upper respiratory infection, vomiting, weight decrease

Why should this drug not be prescribed?
If you are sensitive to or have ever had an allergic reaction to Felbatol or similar drugs, or if you have ever had any blood abnormalities or liver problems, do not take this medication. Make sure your doctor is aware of any drug reactions you have experienced.

Special warnings about this medication
Remember to watch for signs of aplastic anemia. (See "Most important fact about this drug.") If you have ever had liver problems, be sure to tell your doctor.

Expect your doctor to monitor your response carefully when you start taking Felbatol and to check your liver function every 1 or 2 weeks.

Possible food and drug interactions
when taking this medication
If you are taking Felbatol with certain other drugs, the effects of either could be increased, decreased, or altered. It is especially important to check with your doctor before combining Felbatol with other epilepsy drugs, such as Dilantin, Depakene, Depakote, Tegretol, and phenobarbital.

Special information
if you are pregnant or breastfeeding
The effects of Felbatol during pregnancy have not been adequately studied. If you are pregnant or plan to become pregnant, inform your doctor immediate-

ly. Felbatol appears in breast milk and could affect a nursing infant. If this medication is essential to your health, your doctor may advise you to discontinue breastfeeding until your treatment is finished.

Recommended dosage

ADULTS 14 YEARS OF AGE AND OVER

Whether Felbatol is taken alone or with other antiepileptic drugs, the usual starting dose is 1,200 milligrams per day divided into smaller doses and taken 3 or 4 times daily. Your doctor may gradually increase your daily dose to as much as 3,600 milligrams.

If you are already taking a drug to control your epilepsy, your doctor will reduce its dosage when you add Felbatol.

CHILDREN WITH LENNOX-GASTAUT SYNDROME (2 TO 14 YEARS)

The usual dose is 15 milligrams per 2.2 pounds of body weight per day divided into smaller doses taken 3 or 4 times daily. Your doctor may gradually increase your child's dose to 45 milligrams per 2.2 pounds of body weight per day. The doctor will reduce the amount of any other epilepsy drug your child is taking when starting Felbatol.

Overdosage

Any medication taken in excess can have serious consequences. If you suspect an overdose, seek medical treatment immediately.

■ *Symptoms of Felbatol overdose may include:*
Mild stomach upset, unusually fast heartbeat

Brand name:

FELDENE

Pronounced: FELL-deen
Generic name: Piroxicam

Why is this drug prescribed?

Feldene, a nonsteroidal anti-inflammatory drug, is used to relieve the inflammation, swelling, stiffness, and joint pain associated with rheumatoid arthritis and osteoarthritis (the most common form of arthritis). It is prescribed both for sudden flare-ups and for long-term treatment.

Most important fact about this drug
In a few patients on long-term therapy, Feldene can cause stomach ulcers and bleeding. Warning signs include severe abdominal or stomach cramps, pain or burning in the stomach, and black, tarry stools. Inform your doctor immediately if you develop any of these symptoms.

How should you take this medication?
To avoid digestive side effects, take Feldene with food or an antacid, and with a full glass of water. Never take it on an empty stomach.

Take this medication exactly as prescribed by your doctor. Avoid alcohol and aspirin while taking this drug.

- *If you miss a dose...*
  If you forget to take a dose, take it as soon as you remember. If it is almost time for your next dose, skip the one you missed and go back to your regular schedule. Never take 2 doses at the same time.

- *Storage instructions...*
  Store at room temperature. Protect from light and heat.

What side effects may occur?
Side effects cannot be anticipated. If any develop or change in intensity, inform your doctor as soon as possible. Only your doctor can determine if it is safe for you to continue taking Feldene.

- *More common side effects may include:*
  Abdominal pain or discomfort, anemia, constipation, diarrhea, dizziness, fluid retention, gas, general feeling of ill health, headache, heartburn, indigestion, inflammation inside the mouth, itching, loss of appetite, nausea, rash, ringing in ears, sleepiness, stomach upset, vertigo

- *Less common or rare side effects may include:*
  Abdominal bleeding, severe allergic reactions, angioedema (swelling of lips, face, tongue and throat), black stools, blood in the urine, blurred vision, bruising, colicky pain, congestive heart failure (worsening of), depression, dry mouth, eye irritations, fatigue, fever, flu-like symptoms, hepatitis, high blood pressure, hives, inability to sleep, joint pain, labored breathing, low or high blood sugar, nervousness, nosebleed, serum sickness (fever, painful joints, enlarged lymph nodes, skin rash), skin allergy to sunlight, skin eruptions, Stevens-Johnson syndrome (blisters in the mouth and eyes), sweating, swollen eyes, vomiting, vomiting blood, weight loss or gain, wheezing, worsening of angina, yellow eyes and skin

Why should this drug not be prescribed?

If you are sensitive to or have ever had an allergic reaction to Feldene, aspirin, or similar drugs, or if you have had asthma attacks caused by aspirin or other drugs of this type, you should not take this medication. Make sure that your doctor is aware of any drug reactions that you have experienced.

Special warnings about this medication

If you have heart disease, or high blood pressure, or other conditions that cause fluid retention, use this drug with caution. Feldene can increase water retention.

This drug should be used with caution if you have kidney or liver disease; it can cause liver inflammation in some people.

Drugs such as Feldene may cause eye disturbances in some people. If you develop visual problems, notify your eye doctor.

Possible food and drug interactions
when taking this medication

If Feldene is taken with certain other drugs, the effects of either could be increased, decreased, or altered. It is especially important to check with your doctor before combining Feldene with the following:

Anticoagulants (blood thinners such as Coumadin)
Aspirin
Lithium

Special information
if you are pregnant or breastfeeding

Feldene is not recommended for use in nursing mothers or pregnant women. If you are pregnant or plan to become pregnant, inform your doctor immediately.

Recommended dosage

ADULTS

Rheumatoid Arthritis and Osteoarthritis:
The usual dose is 20 milligrams a day in one dose. Your doctor may want you to divide this dose into smaller ones. You will not feel Feldene's full effects for 7 to 12 days, although some relief of symptoms will start to occur soon after you take the medication.

CHILDREN

The safety and effectiveness of Feldene have not been established in children.

Overdosage

Although there are no specific symptoms of a Feldene overdose, any medication taken in excess can have serious consequences. If you suspect an overdose, seek medical attention immediately.

Generic name:

FELODIPINE

See Plendil, page 974.

Brand name:

FEMSTAT

Pronounced: FEM-stat
Generic name: Butoconazole nitrate

Why is this drug prescribed?

Femstat Vaginal Cream cures yeast-like fungal infections of the vulva and vagina.

Most important fact about this drug

To obtain maximum benefit, it is important that you continue to use Femstat Vaginal Cream during menstruation and that you finish using all of the medication, even if your symptoms have disappeared.

How should you use this medication?

Use this medication exactly as prescribed. To keep it from getting on your clothing, wear a sanitary napkin. Do not use a tampon; it will absorb the drug. Do not douche unless your doctor tells you to do so.

While using Femstat, wear cotton underwear or pantyhose with a cotton crotch. Avoid synthetic fabrics such as rayon and nylon.

To apply Femstat:

1. Following the instructions, fill the applicator that comes with the vaginal cream to the level indicated; the cream also comes in a prefilled applicator.
2. Lie on your back with your knees drawn up.
3. Gently insert the applicator high into the vagina and push the plunger.
4. Withdraw the applicator and discard it.

To avoid reinfection, refrain from intercourse during treatment or ask your partner to use a condom.

■ *If you miss a dose...*
Insert it as soon as you remember. If it is almost time for your next dose, skip the one you missed and go back to your regular schedule.

■ *Storage instructions...*
Store at room temperature, away from heat. Do not freeze.

What side effects may occur?
Side effects cannot be anticipated. If any develop or change in intensity, inform your doctor as soon as possible. Only your doctor can determine if it is safe for you to continue using Femstat.

■ *Side effects may include:*
Itching of the fingers, soreness, swelling, vaginal discharge, vulvar itching, vulvar or vaginal burning

Why should this drug not be prescribed?
If you are sensitive to or have ever had an allergic reaction to butoconazole nitrate or any other ingredients in Femstat Cream, you should not use this medication. Make sure your doctor is aware of any drug reactions you have experienced.

Special warnings about this medication
If your symptoms persist, or if you become irritated or have an allergic reaction while using this medication, notify your doctor.

If this is the first time you have had vaginal itching and discomfort, see your doctor before using Femstat to be sure it is the right medication to use.

Do not use Femstat Cream if you have abdominal pain, a fever, or a vaginal discharge with a foul odor; instead, see your doctor.

If your infection doesn't clear up in 3 days, call your doctor. The problem may not be a yeast infection.

If your symptoms come back within 2 months, call your doctor. It could be a sign of pregnancy or a condition such as AIDS or diabetes.

Do not use this product if you have diabetes, have tested positive for HIV, or have AIDS.

Femstat Cream may damage condoms and diaphragms. Employ another method of birth control while you are using this product.

This product is for vaginal use only. Avoid getting it in your eyes or mouth.

**Possible food and drug interactions
when taking this medication**
No interactions with other drugs have been reported.

**Special information
if you are pregnant or breastfeeding**
You should not use Femstat if you are pregnant or think you may be pregnant.
It is not known whether this drug appears in breast milk. If Femstat is
essential to your health, your doctor may advise you to discontinue
breastfeeding until your treatment is finished.

Recommended dosage

ADULTS

The recommended dose is 1 applicatorful of cream inserted in the vagina at
bedtime for 3 days.

CHILDREN

Femstat Cream should not be used by girls under 12 years of age.

Overdosage
No overdosage has been reported.

Generic name:

FEXOFENADINE

See Allegra, page 36.

Generic name:

FINASTERIDE FOR BALDNESS

See Propecia, page 1016.

Generic name:

FINASTERIDE FOR PROSTATE PROBLEMS

See Proscar, page 1023.

Brand name:

FIORICET

Pronounced: fee-OAR-i-set
Generic ingredients: Butalbital, Acetaminophen, Caffeine
Other brand names: Anolor 300, Esgic, Esgic- Plus

Why is this drug prescribed?
Fioricet, a strong, non-narcotic pain reliever and relaxant, is prescribed for the relief of tension headache symptoms caused by muscle contractions in the head, neck, and shoulder area. It combines a sedative barbiturate (butalbital), a non-aspirin pain reliever (acetaminophen), and caffeine.

Most important fact about this drug
Mental and physical dependence can occur with the use of barbiturates such as butalbital when these drugs are taken in higher than recommended doses over long periods of time.

How should you take this medication?
Take Fioricet exactly as prescribed. Do not increase the amount you take without your doctor's approval.

■ *If you miss a dose...*
Take it as soon as you remember. If it is almost time for your next dose, skip the one you missed and go back to your regular schedule. Never take 2 doses at the same time.

■ *Storage instructions...*
Store at room temperature in a tight, light-resistant container.

What side effects may occur?
Side effects cannot be anticipated. If any develop or change in intensity, inform your doctor as soon as possible. Only your doctor can determine if it is safe for you to continue taking Fioricet.

■ *More common side effects may include:*
Abdominal pain, dizziness, drowsiness, intoxicated feeling, light-headedness, nausea, sedation, shortness of breath, vomiting

■ *Less common or rare side effects may include:*
Agitation, allergic reactions, constipation, depression, difficulty swallowing, dry mouth, earache, exaggerated feeling of well-being, excessive

sweating, excessive urination, excitement, fainting, fatigue, fever, flatulence, headache, heartburn, heavy eyelids, high energy, hot spells, itching, leg pain, mental confusion, muscle fatigue, numbness, rapid heartbeat, ringing in the ears, seizure, shaky feeling, skin redness and/or peeling, sluggishness, stuffy nose, tingling

Why should this drug not be prescribed?

If you are sensitive to or have ever had an allergic reaction to barbiturates, acetaminophen, or caffeine, you should not take this medication. Make sure that your doctor is aware of any drug reactions that you have experienced.

Unless you are directed to do so by your doctor, do not take this medication if you have porphyria (an inherited metabolic disorder affecting the liver or bone marrow).

Special warnings about this medication

Fioricet may cause you to become drowsy or less alert; therefore, driving or operating dangerous machinery or participating in any hazardous activity that requires full mental alertness is not recommended until you know your response to this drug.

If you are being treated for severe depression or have a history of severe depression or drug abuse, consult with your doctor before taking Fioricet.

Use this drug with caution if you are elderly or in a weakened condition, if you have liver or kidney problems, or if you have severe abdominal trouble.

Possible food and drug interactions
when taking this medication

Butalbital slows the central nervous system (CNS) and intensifies the effects of alcohol and other CNS depressants. Use of alcohol with this drug may also cause overdose symptoms. Avoid alcoholic beverages while taking Fioricet.

If Fioricet is taken with certain other drugs, the effects of either could be increased, decreased, or altered. It is especially important to check with your doctor before combining Fioricet with the following:

Antihistamines such as Benadryl
Drugs known as monoamine oxidase inhibitors, including the anti-
   depressants Nardil and Parnate
Drugs to treat depression such as Elavil
Major tranquilizers such as Haldol and Thorazine
Muscle relaxants such as Flexeril
Narcotic pain relievers such as Darvon

Sleep aids such as Halcion

Tranquilizers such as Xanax and Valium

Special information
if you are pregnant or breastfeeding

If you are pregnant or plan to become pregnant, inform your doctor immediately. Fioricet can affect a developing baby. It also appears in breast milk. If this medication is essential to your health, your doctor may advise you to discontinue breastfeeding your baby until your treatment is finished.

Recommended dosage

ADULTS

The usual dose of Fioricet is 1 or 2 tablets taken every 4 hours as needed. Do not exceed a total dose of 6 tablets per day.

The usual dose of Esgic-Plus is 1 tablet every 4 hours as needed. Do not take more than 6 tablets a day.

CHILDREN

The safety and effectiveness of Fioricet have not been established in children under 12 years of age.

OLDER ADULTS

Fioricet may cause excitement, depression, and confusion in older people. Therefore, your doctor will prescribe a dose individualized to suit your needs.

Overdosage

Symptoms of Fioricet overdose can be due to its barbiturate or its acetaminophen component.

■ *Symptoms of barbiturate poisoning may include:*
Coma, confusion, drowsiness, low blood pressure, shock, slow or troubled breathing

Overdose due to the acetaminophen component of Fioricet may cause kidney and liver damage, blood disorders, or coma due to low blood sugar. Massive doses may cause liver failure.

■ *Symptoms of liver damage include:*
Excess perspiration, feeling of bodily discomfort, nausea, vomiting

If you suspect an overdose, seek emergency medical treatment immediately.

Brand name:

FIORINAL

Pronounced: fee-OR-i-nahl
Generic ingredients: Butalbital, Aspirin, Caffeine
Other brand name: Isollyl

Why is this drug prescribed?

Fiorinal, a strong, non-narcotic pain reliever and muscle relaxant, is prescribed for the relief of tension headache symptoms caused by stress or muscle contraction in the head, neck, and shoulder area. It combines a non-narcotic, sedative barbiturate (butalbital) with a pain reliever (aspirin) and a stimulant (caffeine).

Most important fact about this drug

Barbiturates such as butalbital can be habit-forming if you take them over long periods of time.

How should you take this medication?

For best relief, take Fiorinal as soon as a headache begins.

Take the medication with a full glass of water or food to reduce stomach irritation. Do not take this medication if it has a strong odor of vinegar.

Take Fiorinal exactly as prescribed. Do not increase the amount you take without your doctor's approval, or take the drug for longer than prescribed.

- *If you miss a dose...*
  If you take Fiorinal on a regular schedule, take the forgotten dose as soon as you remember. If it is almost time for your next dose, skip the one you missed and go back to your regular schedule. Do not take 2 doses at once.

- *Storage instructions...*
  Store at room temperature. Keep the container tightly closed.

What side effects may occur?

Side effects cannot be anticipated. If any develop or change in intensity, inform your doctor as soon as possible. Only your doctor can determine if it is safe for you to continue taking Fiorinal.

- *More common side effects may include:*
  Dizziness, drowsiness

- *Less common or rare side effects may include:*
  Gas, light-headedness, nausea, skin problems, vomiting

Why should this drug not be prescribed?

If you are sensitive to or have ever had an allergic reaction to barbiturates, aspirin, caffeine, or other sedatives and pain relievers, you should not take this medication. The aspirin in Fiorinal, in particular, can cause a severe reaction in someone allergic to it. Make sure your doctor is aware of any drug reactions you have experienced.

Unless you are directed to do so by your doctor, do not take this medication if you have porphyria (an inherited metabolic disorder affecting the liver or bone marrow).

Because aspirin, when given to children and teenagers suffering from flu or chickenpox, can cause a dangerous neurological disease called Reye's syndrome, do not use Fiorinal under these circumstances.

Fiorinal contains aspirin. If you have a stomach (peptic) ulcer or a disorder affecting the blood clotting process, you should not take Fiorinal. Aspirin may irritate the stomach lining and may cause bleeding.

Special warnings about this medication

Fiorinal may make you drowsy or less alert; therefore, you should not drive or operate dangerous machinery or participate in any hazardous activity that requires full mental alertness until you know your response to this drug.

Taking more of this drug than your doctor has prescribed may cause dependence and symptoms of overdose.

Be especially careful with Fiorinal if you are an older person or in a weakened condition, if you have any kidney, liver, or intestinal problems or an enlarged prostate gland, or if you have had a head injury. Also be cautious if you have a thyroid problem, blood clotting difficulties, or a urinary disorder.

Possible food and drug interactions
when taking this medication

Butalbital decreases the activity of the central nervous system and intensifies the effects of alcohol. Avoid drinking alcohol while you are taking Fiorinal.

If Fiorinal is taken with certain other drugs, the effects of either could be increased, decreased, or altered. It is especially important to check with your doctor before combining Fiorinal with the following:

Acetazolamide (Diamox)
Beta-blocking blood pressure drugs such as Inderal and Tenormin
Blood-thinning drugs such as Coumadin
Drugs known as MAO inhibitors, such as the antidepressants Nardil and
  Parnate
Insulin
Mercaptopurine (Purinethol)
Methotrexate (Rheumatrex)
Narcotic pain relievers such as Darvon and Percocet
Nonsteroidal anti-inflammatory drugs such as Naprosyn and Motrin
Oral contraceptives
Oral diabetes drugs such as Micronase
Probenecid (Benemid)
Sleep aids such as Halcion and Nembutal
Steroid medications such as prednisone
Sulfinpyrazone (Anturane)
Theophylline (Theo-Dur, others)
Tranquilizers such as Librium, Valium, and Xanax
Valproic acid (Depakene, Depakote)

Special information
if you are pregnant or breastfeeding

The effects of Fiorinal during pregnancy have not been adequately studied. If
you are pregnant or plan to become pregnant, inform your doctor immediately. If you take aspirin late in your pregnancy it could cause bleeding in you or
your baby, or could delay the baby's birth. Aspirin, butalbital, and caffeine
appear in breast milk. If this medication is essential to your health, your
doctor may advise you to discontinue breastfeeding until your treatment with
this medication is finished.

Recommended dosage

ADULTS

The usual dose of Fiorinal is 1 or 2 tablets or capsules taken every 4 hours.
You should not take more than 6 tablets or capsules in a day.

CHILDREN

The safety and effectiveness of Fiorinal have not been established in children.

Overdosage

Any medication taken in excess can have serious consequences. If you
suspect an overdose, seek medical attention immediately.

- *Symptoms of an overdose of Fiorinal are mainly attributed to its barbiturate component. These symptoms may include:*
  Coma, confusion, drowsiness, low blood pressure, shock, slow or troubled breathing

- *Symptoms attributed to the aspirin and caffeine components of Fiorinal may include:*
  Abdominal pain, deep, rapid breathing, delirium, high fever, inability to fall or stay asleep, rapid or irregular heartbeat, restlessness, ringing in the ears, seizures, tremor, vomiting

Brand name:

FIORINAL WITH CODEINE

Pronounced: fee-OR-i-nahl with KO-deen
Generic ingredients: Butalbital, Codeine phosphate,
*   Aspirin, Caffeine*

Why is this drug prescribed?
Fiorinal with Codeine, a strong narcotic pain reliever and muscle relaxant, is prescribed for the relief of tension headache caused by stress and muscle contraction in the head, neck, and shoulder area. It combines a sedative-barbiturate (butalbital), a narcotic pain reliever and cough suppressant (codeine), a non-narcotic pain and fever reliever (aspirin), and a stimulant (caffeine).

Most important fact about this drug
Barbiturates such as butalbital and narcotics such as codeine can be habit-forming when taken in higher than recommended doses over long periods of time.

How should you take this medication?
Take Fiorinal with Codeine with a full glass of water or food to reduce stomach irritation. Do not take this medication if it has a strong odor of vinegar.

Take Fiorinal with Codeine exactly as prescribed. Do not increase the amount you take without your doctor's approval.

Do not take it more frequently than your doctor has prescribed.

- *If you miss a dose...*
  If you take the drug on a regular schedule, take the forgotten dose as soon as you remember. If it is almost time for your next dose, skip the one you missed and go back to your regular schedule. Do not take 2 doses at once.

- *Storage instructions...*
  Store at room temperature. Keep the container tightly closed.

What side effects may occur?
Side effects cannot be anticipated. If any develop or change in intensity, inform your doctor as soon as possible. Only your doctor can determine if it is safe for you to continue taking Fiorinal with Codeine.

- *More common side effects may include:*
  Abdominal pain, dizziness, drowsiness, nausea

- *Additional side effects, which can be caused by this drug's components, may include:*
  Anemia, blocked air passages, hepatitis, high blood sugar, internal bleeding, intoxicated feeling, irritability, kidney damage, lack of clotting, light-headedness, peptic ulcer, stomach upset, tremors

Why should this drug not be prescribed?
If you are sensitive to or have ever had an allergic reaction to butalbital, codeine, aspirin, caffeine, or other pain relievers, you should not take this medication. Make sure your doctor is aware of any drug reactions you have experienced.

Unless you are directed to do so by your doctor, do not take this medication if you have: a tendency to bleed too much, severe vitamin K deficiency, severe liver damage, nasal polyps (growths or nodules), asthma due to aspirin or other nonsteroidal anti-inflammatory drugs such as Motrin, swelling due to fluid retention, peptic ulcer, or porphyria (an inherited metabolic disorder affecting the liver and bone marrow).

Because aspirin, when given to children and teenagers with chickenpox or flu, can cause a dangerous neurological disease called Reye's syndrome, do not use Fiorinal with Codeine under these circumstances.

Special warnings about this medication
Fiorinal with Codeine may make you drowsy or less alert; therefore, you should not drive or operate dangerous machinery or participate in any

hazardous activity that requires full mental alertness until you know how this drug affects you.

Codeine may cause unusually slow or troubled breathing and may increase the pressure caused by fluid surrounding the brain and spinal cord in people with head injury. Codeine also affects brain and spinal cord function and makes it hard for the doctor to see how people with head injuries are doing.

If you have chronic (long-lasting or frequently recurring) tension headaches and your prescribed dose of Fiorinal with Codeine does not relieve the pain, consult with your doctor. Taking more of this drug than your doctor has prescribed may cause dependence and symptoms of overdose.

Aspirin can cause internal bleeding in people with ulcers or bleeding disorders.

Codeine can hide signs of severe abdominal problems.

If you have ever developed dependence on a drug, consult with your doctor before taking Fiorinal with Codeine.

If you are being treated for a kidney, liver, or blood clotting disorder, consult with your doctor before taking Fiorinal with Codeine.

If you are older or in a weakened condition, be very careful taking Fiorinal with Codeine. You should also be careful if you have Addison's disease (an adrenal gland disorder), if you have difficulty urinating, if your prostate gland is enlarged, or if your thyroid gland is not working well.

**Possible food and drug interactions
when taking this medication**
Fiorinal with Codeine reduces the activity of the central nervous system and intensifies the effects of alcohol. Use of alcohol with this drug may also cause overdose symptoms. Therefore, use of alcohol should be avoided.

If Fiorinal with Codeine is taken with certain other drugs, the effects of either could be increased, decreased, or altered. It is especially important to check with your doctor before combining Fiorinal with Codeine with the following:

Acetazolamide (Diamox)
Antidepressant drugs such as Elavil, Nardil, and Parnate
Antigout medications such as Benemid and Anturane
Antihistamines such as Benadryl
Beta-blocking blood pressure drugs such as Inderal and Tenormin

Blood-thinning drugs such as Coumadin
Divalproex (Depakote)
Insulin
6-Mercaptopurine (Purinethol)
Methotrexate (Rheumatrex)
Narcotic pain relievers such as Darvon and Vicodin
Nonsteroidal anti-inflammatory drugs such as Motrin and Indocin
Oral contraceptives
Oral diabetes drugs such as Micronase
Sleep aids such as Nembutal and Halcion
Steroid drugs such as prednisone
Theophylline (Theo-Dur, others)
Tranquilizers such as Librium, Xanax, and Valium
Valproic acid (Depakene)

Special information
if you are pregnant or breastfeeding

The effects of Fiorinal with Codeine during pregnancy have not been adequately studied. If you are pregnant or plan to become pregnant, inform your doctor immediately. Butalbital, aspirin, caffeine, and codeine appear in breast milk. If this medication is essential to your health, your doctor may advise you to discontinue breastfeeding until your treatment with this medication is finished.

Recommended dosage

ADULTS

The usual dose of Fiorinal with Codeine is 1 or 2 capsules taken every 4 hours. Do not take more than 6 capsules per day.

CHILDREN

The safety and effectiveness of butalbital have not been established in children under 12 years of age.

Overdosage

Symptoms of an overdose of Fiorinal with Codeine are mainly attributed to its barbiturate and codeine ingredients.

■ *Symptoms attributed to the barbiturate ingredient of Fiorinal with Codeine may include:*
Coma, confusion, dizziness, drowsiness, low blood pressure, shock, slow or troubled breathing

- *Symptoms attributed to the codeine ingredient of Fiorinal with Codeine may include:*
  Convulsions, loss of consciousness, pinpoint pupils, troubled and slowed breathing

- *Symptoms attributed to the aspirin ingredient of Fiorinal with Codeine may include:*
  Abdominal pain, deep, rapid breathing, delirium, high fever, restlessness, ringing in the ears, seizures, vomiting

Though caffeine poisoning occurs only at very high doses, it can cause delirium, insomnia, irregular heartbeat, rapid heartbeat, restlessness, and tremor.

If you suspect an overdose of Fiorinal with Codeine, seek emergency medical treatment immediately.

Brand name:

FLAGYL

Pronounced: FLAJ-ill
Generic name: Metronidazole
Other brand name: Protostat

Why is this drug prescribed?
Flagyl is an antibacterial drug prescribed for certain vaginal and urinary tract infections in men and women; amebic dysentery and liver abscess; and infections of the abdomen, skin, bones and joints, brain, lungs, and heart caused by certain bacteria.

Most important fact about this drug
Do not drink alcoholic beverages while taking Flagyl. The combination can cause abdominal cramps, nausea, vomiting, headaches, and flushing. It can also change the taste of the alcoholic beverage. When you have stopped taking Flagyl, wait at least 72 hours (3 days) before consuming any alcohol. Also avoid over-the-counter medications containing alcohol, such as certain cough and cold products.

How should you take this medication?
Flagyl works best when there is a constant amount in the blood. Take your doses at evenly spaced intervals, day and night, and try to avoid missing any.

If you are being treated for the sexually transmitted genital infection called trichomoniasis, your doctor may want to treat your partner at the same time, even if there are no symptoms. Try to avoid sexual intercourse until the infection is cured. If you do have sex, use a condom.

Flagyl can be taken with or without food. It may cause dry mouth. Hard candy, chewing gum, or bits of ice can help to relieve the problem.

- *If you miss a dose...*
  Take it as soon as you remember. If it is almost time for your next dose skip the one you missed and go back to your regular schedule. Do not take 2 doses at once.

- *Storage instructions...*
  Store at room temperature. Protect from light.

What side effects may occur?
Side effects cannot be anticipated. If any develop or change in intensity, tell your doctor immediately. Only your doctor can determine whether it is safe for you to continue taking Flagyl.

Two serious side effects that have occurred with Flagyl are seizures and numbness or tingling in the arms, legs, hands, and feet. If you experience either of these symptoms, stop taking the medication and call your doctor immediately.

- *More common side effects may include:*
  Abdominal cramps, constipation, diarrhea, headache, loss of appetite, nausea, upset stomach, vomiting

- *Less common side effects may include:*
  Blood disorders, confusion, dark urine, decreased sex drive, depression, difficulty sleeping, dizziness, dry mouth (or vagina or vulva), fever, flushing, furry tongue, hives, inability to hold urine, increased production of pale urine, inflamed mouth or tongue, inflammation of the rectum, irritability, lack of muscle coordination, metallic taste, occasional joint pain, pain during sexual intercourse, painful or difficult urination, pelvic pressure, rash, stuffy nose, vertigo, weakness, yeast infection (candida) in vagina

Why should this drug not be prescribed?
Flagyl should not be used during the first 3 months of pregnancy to treat vaginal infections. Do not take Flagyl if you have ever had an allergic reaction to or are sensitive to metronidazole or similar drugs. Tell your doctor about any drug reactions you have experienced.

Special warnings about this medication

If you experience seizures or numbness or tingling in your arms, legs, hands, or feet, remember that you should stop taking Flagyl and call your doctor immediately.

If you have liver disease, make sure the doctor is aware of it. Flagyl should be used with caution.

Active or undiagnosed yeast infections may appear or worsen when you take Flagyl.

Possible food and drug interactions
when taking this medication

Do not drink alcohol while taking Flagyl and for at least 72 hours after your last dose.

If Flagyl is taken with certain other drugs, the effects of either could be increased, decreased, or altered. It is especially important to check with your doctor before combining Flagyl with any of the following:

  Blood thinners such as Coumadin
  Cholestyramine (Questran)
  Cimetidine (Tagamet)
  Disulfiram (Antabuse)
  Lithium (Lithonate)
  Phenobarbital
  Phenytoin (Dilantin)

Special information
if you are pregnant or breastfeeding

The effects of Flagyl in pregnancy have not been adequately studied. If you are pregnant or plan to become pregnant, notify your doctor. This medication should be used during pregnancy only if it is clearly needed. Flagyl appears in breast milk and could affect a nursing infant. If Flagyl is essential to your health, your doctor may advise you to stop breastfeeding until your treatment is finished.

Recommended dosage

ADULT

Trichomoniasis

One-day treatment: 2 grams of Flagyl, taken as a single dose or divided into 2 doses (1 gram each) taken in the same day.

Seven-day course of treatment: 250 milligrams 3 times daily for 7 consecutive days.

Acute Intestinal Amebiasis (Acute Amebic Dysentery)
The usual dose is 750 milligrams taken by mouth 3 times daily for 5 to 10 days.

Amebic Liver Abscess
The usual dose is 500 milligrams or 750 milligrams taken by mouth 3 times daily for 5 to 10 days.

Anaerobic Bacterial Infections
The usual adult oral dosage is 7.5 milligrams per 2.2 pounds of body weight every 6 hours.

CHILDREN

Amebiasis
The usual dose is 35 to 50 milligrams for each 2.2 pounds of body weight per day, divided into 3 doses taken for 10 days.

The safety and efficacy of Flagyl for any other condition in children have not been established.

OLDER ADULTS

Your doctor will test to see how much medication is in your blood and will adjust your dosage if necessary.

Overdosage
Any medication taken in excess can have serious consequences. If you suspect an overdose, seek medical treatment immediately.

■ *Symptoms of Flagyl overdose may include:*
 Lack of muscle coordination, nausea, vomiting

Generic name:

FLAVOXATE

See Urispas, page 1317.

Generic name:

FLECAINIDE

See Tambocor, page 1189.

Brand name:

FLEXERIL

Pronounced: FLEX-eh-rill
Generic name: Cyclobenzaprine hydrochloride

Why is this drug prescribed?

Flexeril is a muscle relaxant prescribed to relieve muscle spasms resulting from injuries such as sprains, strains, or pulls. Combined with rest and physical therapy, Flexeril provides relief of muscular stiffness and pain.

Most important fact about this drug

Flexeril is not a substitute for the physical therapy, rest, or exercise that your doctor orders for proper healing. Although Flexeril relieves the pain of strains and sprains, it is not useful for other types of pain.

How should you take this medication?

Flexeril may be taken with or without food.

Flexeril should be used only for short periods (no more than 3 weeks). Since the type of injury that Flexeril treats should improve in a few weeks, there is no reason to use it for a longer period.

Flexeril may cause dry mouth. Sucking a hard candy, chewing gum, or melting ice chips in your mouth can provide temporary relief.

- *If you miss a dose...*
  Take it as soon as you remember, if it is within an hour or so of your scheduled time. If you do not remember until later, skip the missed dose and go back to your regular schedule. Do not take 2 doses at once.

- *Storage instructions...*
  Store away from heat, light, and moisture.

What side effects may occur?

Side effects cannot be anticipated. If any develop or change in intensity, inform your doctor as soon as possible. Only your doctor can determine if it is safe for you to continue taking Flexeril.

- *More common side effects may include:*
Dizziness, drowsiness, dry mouth

- *Less common or rare side effects may include:*
Abnormal heartbeats, abnormal sensations, abnormal thoughts or dreams, agitation, anxiety, bloated feeling, blurred vision, confusion, constipation, convulsions, decreased appetite, depressed mood, diarrhea, difficulty falling or staying asleep, difficulty speaking, disorientation, double vision, excitement, fainting, fatigue, fluid retention, gas, hallucinations, headache, heartburn, hepatitis, hives, increased heart rate, indigestion, inflammation of the stomach, itching, lack of coordination, liver diseases, loss of sense of taste, low blood pressure, muscle twitching, nausea, nervousness, palpitations, rash, ringing in the ears, severe allergic reaction, stomach and intestinal pain, sweating, swelling of the tongue or face, thirst, tingling in hands or feet, tremors, unpleasant taste in the mouth, urinating more or less than usual, vague feeling of bodily discomfort, vertigo, vomiting, weakness, yellow eyes and skin

Why should this drug not be prescribed?
You should not take this drug if you are taking an antidepressant drug known as an MAO inhibitor (such as Nardil or Parnate) or have taken an MAO inhibitor within the last 2 weeks. Also avoid Flexeril if you have ever had an allergic reaction to it, or if your thyroid gland is overactive.

In addition, you should not take Flexeril if you have recently had a heart attack or if you have congestive heart failure, or suffer from irregular heartbeat.

Special warnings about this medication
Flexeril may cause you to become drowsy or less alert; therefore, you should not drive or operate dangerous machinery or participate in any hazardous activity that requires full mental alertness until you know how this drug affects you.

You should use Flexeril with caution if you have ever been unable to urinate or if you have ever had the eye condition called glaucoma.

Possible food and drug interactions
when taking this medication
Serious, potentially fatal reactions may occur if you take Flexeril with an antidepressant drug known as an MAO inhibitor (such as Nardil or Parnate) or if it has been less than 2 weeks since you last took an MAO inhibitor. You should closely follow your doctor's advice regarding discontinuation of MAO inhibitors before taking Flexeril.

Avoid alcoholic beverages while taking Flexeril.

If Flexeril is taken with certain other drugs, the effects of either could be increased, decreased, or altered. It is especially important to check with your doctor before combining Flexeril with the following:

Antispasmodic drugs such as Donnatal or Bentyl
Barbiturates such as phenobarbital
Guanethidine (Esimil, Ismelin) and other high blood pressure drugs
Other drugs that slow the central nervous system, such as Halcion and Xanax

Special information
if you are pregnant or breastfeeding

The effects of Flexeril during pregnancy have not been adequately studied. If you are pregnant or plan to become pregnant, inform your doctor immediately. It is not known if Flexeril appears in breast milk. However, cyclobenzaprine is related to tricyclic antidepressants, and some of those drugs do appear in breast milk. If this medication is essential to your health, your doctor may advise you to discontinue breastfeeding your baby until your treatment is finished.

Recommended dosage

ADULTS

The usual dose is 10 milligrams 3 times a day. You should not take more than 60 milligrams a day.

CHILDREN

Safety and effectiveness of Flexeril have not been established for children under the age of 15.

Overdosage

Any medication taken in excess can have serious consequences. If you suspect a Flexeril overdose, seek medical attention immediately.

- *Symptoms of Flexeril overdose may include:*
  Agitation, coma, confusion, congestive heart failure, convulsions, dilated pupils, disturbed concentration, drowsiness, hallucinations, high or low temperature, increased heartbeats, irregular heart rhythms, muscle stiffness, overactive reflexes, severe low blood pressure, stupor, vomiting

High doses also may cause any of the conditions listed in "What Side Effects May Occur?"

Brand name:

FLOMAX

Pronounced: FLOW-maks
Generic name: Tamsulosin hydrochloride

Why is this drug prescribed?
Flomax is used to treat the symptoms of an enlarged prostate—a condition technically known as benign prostatic hyperplasia or BPH. The walnut-sized prostate gland surrounds the urethra (the duct that drains the bladder). If the gland becomes enlarged, it can squeeze the urethra, interfering with the flow of urine. This can cause difficulty in starting urination, a weak flow of urine, and the need to urinate urgently or more frequently. Flomax doesn't shrink the prostate. Instead, it relaxes the muscle around it, freeing the flow of urine and decreasing urinary symptoms.

Most important fact about this drug
Flomax can cause dizziness, especially when you first stand up. Be careful about driving, operating machinery, and performing any other hazardous task until you know how you react to the drug.

How should you take this medication?
Take Flomax once daily, half an hour after the same meal each day. Do not crush, chew, or open the capsule.

- *If you miss a dose...*
  Take it as soon as you remember. If it is almost time for your next dose, skip the one you missed and go back to your regular schedule. Do not take 2 doses at once.

If you miss several doses in a row, resume treatment with a dose of 1 capsule daily and check with your doctor on how to proceed.

- *Storage instructions...*
  Store at room temperature.

What side effects may occur?
Side effects cannot be anticipated. If any develop or change in intensity, inform your doctor as soon as possible. Only your doctor can determine if it is safe for you to continue taking Flomax.

- *More common side effects may include:*
  Abnormal ejaculation, back pain, chest pain, cough, diarrhea, dizziness, headache, infection, nausea, runny nose, sinus problems, sleepiness, sore throat, weakness

- *Less common side effects may include:*
  Decreased sex drive, dental problems, insomnia, vision problems

- *Rare side effects may include:*
  Fainting, low blood pressure upon standing, vertigo

Why should this drug not be prescribed?

If Flomax gives you an allergic reaction, you cannot take the drug.

Special warnings about this medication

Remember that, in a few men, Flomax can cause a drop in blood pressure upon first standing up, which in turn can lead to dizziness or fainting. Avoid driving and other hazardous tasks for 12 hours after your first dose or a dosage increase, and be careful to stand up slowly until you're sure the drug won't make you dizzy. If you do become dizzy, sit down until it passes.

Possible food and drug interactions
when taking this medication

If Flomax is taken with certain other drugs, the effects of either could be increased, decreased, or altered. It is especially important to check with your doctor before combining Flomax with any of the following:

Blood pressure drugs classified as alpha-blockers, such as Catapres
Cimetidine (Tagamet)
Warfarin (Coumadin)

Special information
if you are pregnant or breastfeeding

Flomax is for use only by men.

Recommended dosage

ADULT MEN

The recommended starting dose of Flomax is 1 capsule (0.4 milligram) daily, half an hour following the same meal each day. Your doctor may increase the dose to 2 capsules (0.8 milligram) once a day if needed.

Overdosage

Any medication taken in excess can have serious consequences. If you suspect an overdose, seek medical treatment immediately.

■ *Symptoms of Flomax overdose may include:*
Dizziness, fainting, headache

Brand name:

FLONASE

Pronounced: FLOW-naze
Generic name: Fluticasone propionate

Why is this drug prescribed?

Flonase is a remedy for the stuffy, runny, itchy nose that plagues many allergy-sufferers. It can be used either for seasonal attacks of hay fever or for year-round allergic conditions. Flonase is a steroid medication. It works by relieving inflammation within the nasal passages.

Most important fact about this drug

Flonase is not an instant cure. It may take a few days for the medication to start working; and you need to keep taking it regularly in order to maintain its benefits. While you are waiting for Flonase to take effect, neither increase the dose nor stop taking the medication.

How should you take this medication?

Flonase is taken in the nostrils. First, blow your nose. Then shake the spray bottle gently, tilt your head back, press one nostril closed, and insert the tip of the bottle a short way into the other nostril. Spray once, pull the tip of the bottle away from your nose, and inhale deeply through the treated nostril. Repeat with the other nostril.

■ *If you miss a dose...*
Take it as soon as you remember. If it is almost time for your next dose, skip the one you missed and go back to your regular schedule. Do not take 2 doses at once.

■ *Storage instructions...*
Flonase may be stored at room temperature or in the refrigerator.

What side effects may occur?

Side effects cannot be anticipated. If any develop or change in intensity, inform your doctor as soon as possible. Only your doctor can determine if it is safe for you to continue taking Flonase.

■ *Side-effects may include:*
Bad taste in mouth, bronchitis, congestion, dizziness, dry mouth, dry nose, eye problems, headache, hives, nasal irritation or burning, nasal sores, nausea, nosebleeds, runny nose, sinus problems, sneezing, sore throat, vomiting

Why should this drug not be prescribed?
If you have ever had an allergic reaction to Flonase or similar steroid inhalants such as Flovent, you should not take this medication.

Special warnings about this medication
If your symptoms do not improve after the first few days of Flonase therapy, check with your doctor. Never take more than the recommended dose. High doses of steroid medications such as Flonase can cause a condition known as Cushing's syndrome. Warning signs of this problem include weight gain and changes in the appearance of the face.

If you are being switched from an oral steroid tablet to Flonase, you may experience joint pain, muscle pain, weakness, depression, or fatigue while your body adjusts to the absence of steroid tablets and increases its own production of steroids.

People taking steroid medications run an increased risk of infections such as chickenpox and measles. If you are exposed to someone with either of these diseases and you have neither had the infection nor been vaccinated against it, contact your physician immediately.

In rare cases, Flonase can also cause a fungal infection in the nose. And steroid treatment can also make an existing infection worse. Be sure the doctor is aware of any infections you may have, including TB and viral infections of the eye.

Steroid medications can stunt growth. If your child is on Flonase therapy, the doctor should periodically check height and weight.

If you have recently had a nasal injury or ulcer, or had surgery on your nose, you should wait until you are fully healed before using Flonase.

Possible food and drug interactions
when taking this medication
The risk of developing Cushing's syndrome and other side effects increases when you take other steroid medications while using Flonase. Prednisone

and dexamethasone are examples of oral steroid medications. Certain asthma inhalers, skin creams, eye drops, and ear drops also may contain steroids.

Special information
if you are pregnant or breastfeeding

The effects of this drug during pregnancy have not been adequately studied. If you are pregnant or plan to become pregnant, inform your doctor immediately. It is not known whether Flonase appears in breast milk. If the drug is essential to your health, your doctor may advise you to stop nursing until your treatment is finished.

Recommended dosage

ADULTS

The usual starting dose is 2 sprays in each nostril once daily. (Some doctors may prescribe 1 spray in each nostril every 12 hours.) Once your symptoms are under control, your doctor may reduce the dose to 1 spray in each nostril once daily.

CHILDREN

Flonase is not recommended for children under the age of 12 unless advised by your doctor. For adolescents, the recommended starting dose is 1 spray in each nostril once a day. If symptoms do not improve in a few days, the dose can be increased to 2 sprays in each nostril once a day, then reduced again once symptoms have subsided.

Overdosage

Any medication taken in excess can have serious consequences. If you habitually use too much Flonase, you run the risk of developing Cushing's syndrome (see "Special warnings about this medication").

Brand name:

FLOXIN

Pronounced: FLOCKS-in
Generic name: Ofloxacin

Why is this drug prescribed?

Floxin is an antibiotic. It has been used effectively to treat lower respiratory tract infections, including chronic bronchitis and pneumonia, sexually transmitted diseases (except syphilis), pelvic inflammatory disease, and infections of the urinary tract, prostate gland, and skin.

Most important fact about this drug

Floxin kills a variety of bacteria, and is frequently used to treat infections in many parts of the body. However, you should stop taking the drug and notify your doctor immediately at the first sign of a skin rash or any other allergic reaction. Although quite rare, serious and occasionally fatal allergic reactions have been reported, some after only one dose. Signs of an impending reaction include swelling of the face and throat, shortness of breath, difficulty swallowing, rapid heartbeat, tingling, itching, and hives.

How should you take this medication?

You may take Floxin with or without food. Be sure to drink plenty of fluids while taking this medication.

Do not take mineral supplements, vitamins with iron or minerals, or antacids containing calcium, aluminum, or magnesium within 2 hours of taking Floxin.

Take Floxin exactly as prescribed. You need to complete the full course of therapy to obtain best results and decrease the risk of a recurrence of the infection.

■ *If you miss a dose...*
Take it as soon as you remember. If it is almost time for your next dose, skip the one you missed and go back to your regular schedule. Never take 2 doses at the same time.

■ *Storage instructions...*
Store at room temperature in a tightly closed container.

What side effects may occur?

Side effects cannot be anticipated. If any develop or change in intensity, inform your doctor as soon as possible. Only your doctor can determine if it is safe for you to continue taking Floxin.

■ *More common side effects may include:*
Diarrhea, difficulty sleeping, dizziness, headache, itching of genital area in women, nausea, vaginal inflammation, vomiting

■ *Less common or rare side effects may include:*
Abdominal pain and cramps, aggressiveness or hostility, agitation, anemia, anxiety, asthma, blood in the urine, blurred vision, body pain, bruising, burning or rash of the female genitals, burning sensation in the upper chest, changeable emotions, changes in thinking and perception, chest pain, confusion, conjunctivitis (pinkeye), continual runny nose, constipation, cough, decreased appetite, depression, difficult or labored breathing, disorientation, disturbed dreams, disturbed sense of smell, double vision, dry mouth, exaggerated sense of well-being, excessive perspiration, fainting, fatigue, fear, fever, fluid retention, frequent urination, gas, hallucinations, hearing disturbance or loss, hepatitis, hiccups, high or low blood pressure, high or low blood sugar, hives, inability to urinate, increased urination, indigestion, inflammation of the colon, inflammation or rupture of tendons, intolerance to light, involuntary eye movement, itching, joint pain, kidney problems, lack of coordination, light-headedness, liver problems, menstrual changes, muscle pain, nervousness, nightmares, nosebleed, pain, pain in arms and legs, painful or difficult urination, purple or red areas/spots on the skin, rapid heartbeat, rash, reddened skin, restlessness, ringing in the ears, seizures, sensitivity to light, severe allergic reaction, skin inflammation and flaking or eruptions, sleepiness, sleep problems, sore mouth or throat, speech difficulty, Stevens-Johnson syndrome (severe skin eruptions), stomach and intestinal upset or bleeding, taste distortion, thirst, throbbing or fluttering heartbeat, tingling or pins and needles, tremor, unexplained bleeding from the uterus, vaginal discharge, vaginal yeast infection, vague feeling of illness, vertigo, visual disturbances, weakness, weight loss, yellowing of eyes and skin

Why should this drug not be prescribed?
Do not take Floxin if you are sensitive to or have ever had an allergic reaction to it or other quinolone antibiotics such as Cipro and Noroxin.

Special warnings about this medication
Floxin, used in high doses for short periods of time, may hide or delay the symptoms of syphilis, but is not effective in treating syphilis. If you are taking Floxin for gonorrhea, your doctor will test you for syphilis and then perform a follow-up test after 3 months of treatment.

Convulsions, increased pressure in the head, psychosis, tremors, restlessness, light-headedness, nervousness, confusion, depression, nightmares, insomnia, and hallucinations have occasionally been reported with this type of antibiotic. If you experience any of these symptoms, stop taking the drug and contact your doctor immediately.

Floxin can cause a rupture in the muscle tendons in your hand, shoulder, or heel. If you notice any pain and inflammation in a tendon, rest and avoid exercise until you have seen your doctor.

If you are prone to seizures due to kidney disease, a brain disorder, or epilepsy, make sure your doctor knows about it. Floxin should be used with caution under these conditions.

If you have liver or kidney disease, your doctor will watch you closely while you are taking Floxin.

Avoid being in the sun too much; you can develop sun poisoning while you are taking Floxin.

Floxin may make you feel dizzy or light-headed. Be careful driving, operating machinery, or doing any activity that requires full mental alertness until you know how you react to this medication.

Safety has not been established for children under 18 years of age.

Possible food and drug interactions
when taking this medication

If Floxin is taken with certain other drugs, the effects of either could be increased, decreased, or altered. It is especially important to check with your doctor before combining Floxin with the following:

Antacids containing calcium, magnesium, or aluminum
Blood thinners such as Coumadin
Calcium supplements such as Caltrate
Cyclosporine (Sandimmune, Neoral)
Insulin
Iron supplements such as Feosol
Multivitamins containing zinc
Nonsteroidal anti-inflammatory drugs such as Motrin and Naprosyn
Oral diabetes drugs such as Diabinese and Micronase
Sucralfate (Carafate)
Theophylline-containing drugs, such as Theo-Dur

Special information
if you are pregnant or breastfeeding

The effects of Floxin during pregnancy have not been adequately studied. If you are pregnant or plan to become pregnant, inform your doctor immediately. This medication should not be used during pregnancy unless your doctor has determined that the benefit to you outweighs the risk to the unborn baby. Floxin appears in breast milk and could affect a nursing infant. If this medication is essential to your health, your doctor may advise you to stop breastfeeding until your treatment with Floxin is finished.

Recommended dosage

LOWER RESPIRATORY TRACT INFECTIONS

Worsening of Chronic Bronchitis
The usual dose is 400 milligrams every 12 hours for 10 days, for a total daily dose of 800 milligrams.

Pneumonia
The usual dose is 400 milligrams every 12 hours for 10 days, for a total daily dose of 800 milligrams.

SEXUALLY TRANSMITTED DISEASES

Gonorrhea
The usual dose is 400 milligrams taken once.

Infections of the Cervix or Urethra
The usual dose is 300 milligrams every 12 hours for 7 days, for a total daily dose of 600 milligrams.

PELVIC INFLAMMATORY DISEASE

The usual dose is 400 milligrams every 12 hours for 10 to 14 days, for a total daily dose of 800 milligrams.

MILD TO MODERATE SKIN INFECTIONS

The usual dose is 400 milligrams every 12 hours for 10 days, for a total daily dose of 800 milligrams.

URINARY TRACT INFECTIONS

Bladder Infections
The usual dose is 200 milligrams every 12 hours for a total daily dose of 400 milligrams. This dose is taken for 3 days for infections due to *E. coli* or *K. pneumoniae*. For infections due to other microbes, it is taken for 7 days.

Complicated Urinary Tract Infections
The usual dose is 200 milligrams every 12 hours for 10 days, for a total daily dose of 400 milligrams.

Prostatitis
The usual dose is 300 milligrams every 12 hours for 6 weeks, for a total daily dose of 600 milligrams.

Overdosage
Although no specific information is available, any medication taken in excess can have serious consequences. If you suspect an overdose, seek medical treatment immediately.

Generic name:

FLUCONAZOLE

See Diflucan, page 374.

Generic name:

FLUNISOLIDE

See AeroBid, page 21.

Generic name:

FLUOCINONIDE

See Lidex, page 671.

Generic name:

FLUOROMETHOLONE

See FML, page 523.

Generic name:

FLUOROURACIL

See Efudex, page 438.

Generic name:

FLUOXETINE

See Prozac, page 1037.

Generic name:

FLURAZEPAM

See Dalmane, page 309.

Generic name:

FLURBIPROFEN

See Ansaid, page 68.

Generic name:

FLUTAMIDE

See Eulexin, page 477.

Generic name:

FLUTICASONE

See Flonase, page 515.

Generic name:

FLUVASTATIN

See Lescol, page 649.

Generic name:

FLUVOXAMINE MALEATE

See Luvox, page 717.

Brand name:

FML

Generic name: Fluorometholone

Why is this drug prescribed?
FML is a steroid (cortisone-like) eye ointment that is used to treat inflammation of the eyelid and the eye itself.

Most important fact about this drug

Do not use FML more often or for a longer period of time than your doctor orders. Overuse can increase the risk of side effects and lead to eye damage. Also, if your eye problems return, do not use any leftover FML without first consulting your doctor.

How should you use this medication?

FML may increase the chance of infection from contact lenses. Your doctor may advise you to stop wearing your contacts while using this medication.

Use FML exactly as prescribed. Do not stop until your doctor advises you to do so. To avoid spreading infection, do not let anyone else use your prescription.

To administer FML eyedrops:

1. Wash your hands thoroughly.
2. Shake well before using.
3. Gently pull your lower eyelid down to form a pocket between your eye and eyelid.
4. Hold the eyedrop bottle on the bridge of your nose or on your forehead.
5. Do not touch the applicator tip to any surface, including your eye.
6. Tilt your head back and squeeze the medication into your eye.
7. Close your eyes gently. Keep them closed for 1 to 2 minutes.
8. Do not rinse the dropper.
9. Wait for 5 to 10 minutes before using a second eye medication.

■ *If you miss a dose...*
Apply it as soon as you remember. If it is almost time for your next dose, skip the one you missed and return to your regular schedule. Do not apply a double dose.

■ *Storage instructions...*
Store at room temperature. Protect from extreme heat.

What side effects may occur?

Side effects cannot be anticipated. If any develop or change in intensity, inform your doctor as soon as possible. Only your doctor can determine if it is safe for you to continue using FML.

■ *Side effects may include:*
Allergic reactions, blurred vision, burning/stinging, cataract formation, corneal ulcers, dilation of the pupil, drooping eyelids, eye inflammation and

infection including pinkeye, eye irritation, glaucoma, increased eye pressure, slow wound healing, taste alterations

Why should this drug not be prescribed?
Do not use FML if you have ever had an allergic reaction to or are sensitive to fluorometholone or similar drugs (anti-inflammatories and steroids) such as Decadron. Tell your doctor about any drug reactions you have experienced.

FML is not prescribed for patients with certain viral, fungal, and bacterial infections of the eye.

Special warnings about this medication
Prolonged use of FML may result in glaucoma (elevated pressure in the eye causing optic nerve damage and loss of vision), cataract formation (an eye disorder causing the lens of the eye to cloud up), or the development or worsening of eye infections.

Steroids such as FML have been known to cause punctures when used in the presence of diseases that cause thinning of the cornea or the sclera (tough, opaque covering at the back of the eyeball).

The use of a corticosteroid medication could hide the presence of a severe eye infection or cause the infection to become worse.

Internal pressure of the eye should be checked frequently by your doctor.

This medication should be used with caution after cataract surgery.

If pain or inflammation lasts longer than 48 hours, or becomes worse, discontinue use of FML and notify your doctor.

Possible food and drug interactions
when taking this medication
No interactions with food or other drugs have been reported.

Special information
if you are pregnant or breastfeeding
The effects of FML in pregnancy have not been adequately studied. If you are pregnant or plan to become pregnant, tell your doctor immediately. FML may appear in breast milk and could affect a nursing infant. If using FML is essential to your health, your doctor may advise you to stop breastfeeding until your treatment is finished.

Recommended dosage

ADULTS

FML Ointment
Apply a small amount of ointment (a ½-inch ribbon) between the lower eyelid and eyeball 1 to 3 times a day. During the first 24 to 48 hours, your doctor may increase the dosage to 1 application every 4 hours.

FML Liquifilm
Place 1 drop of suspension between the lower eyelid and eyeball 2 to 4 times a day. During the first 24 to 48 hours, the dosage may be increased to 1 application every 4 hours.

CHILDREN

The safety and effectiveness of FML have not been established in children under 2 years of age.

Overdosage
Overdosage with FML will not ordinarily cause severe problems. If FML is accidentally swallowed, drink fluids to dilute the medication.

Brand name:

FOSAMAX

Pronounced: FAH-suh-max
Generic name: Alendronate sodium

Why is this drug prescribed?
Fosamax is prescribed for the treatment of osteoporosis, the brittle-bone disease, in postmenopausal women and for Paget's disease, a painful weakening of the bones.

Most important fact about this drug
For Fosamax to be effective, you must take the tablets without food or other medications, exactly as directed.

How should you use this medication?
Fosamax is effective only when each tablet is taken with a full glass of water first thing in the morning, at least 30 minutes before the first food, beverage, or other medication. If you can wait longer before eating or drinking, the medication will be absorbed better. Do not lie down for at least 30 minutes after taking Fosamax and avoid chewing or sucking on the tablet; it can cause mouth sores.

You should take calcium and vitamin D supplements if you don't get enough in your diet. Avoid smoking and alcohol. Weight-bearing exercise can also strengthen bones.

■ *If you miss a dose...*
Take it as soon as you remember it. If it is almost time for the next dose, skip the one you missed and go back to your regular schedule.

■ *Storage instructions...*
Keep the container tightly closed and store at room temperature.

What side effects may occur?
Side effects cannot be anticipated. If any develop or change in intensity, inform your doctor as soon as possible. Only your doctor can determine if it is safe for you to continue using Fosamax.

■ *More common side effects may include:*
Abdominal pain, bone and joint pain, constipation, diarrhea, indigestion, muscle pain, nausea

■ *Less common side effects may include:*
Abdominal distention, acid backup, difficulty in swallowing, esophageal ulcers, gas, headache, vomiting

■ *Rare side effects may include:*
Changes in taste, inflammation of the stomach, rash, skin redness

Why should this drug not be prescribed?
You should not take Fosamax if the calcium level in your blood is low. Avoid Fosamax if it causes an allergic reaction.

Special warnings about this medication
Fosamax is not recommended for women on hormone replacement therapy, or for women with kidney problems.

Be sure to tell your doctor if you have trouble swallowing or have any digestive disease.

**Possible food and drug interactions
when taking this medication**
Combining aspirin with a Fosamax dose of more than 10 milligrams per day will increase the likelihood of stomach upset.

Calcium supplements such as Caltrate, antacids such as Riopan, and some other oral medications will interfere with the absorption of Fosamax, so wait at least 30 minutes after taking Fosamax before you take anything else.

Special information
if you are pregnant or breastfeeding

The effects of Fosamax during pregnancy and breastfeeding have not been adequately studied. If you are pregnant or plan to become pregnant, notify your doctor immediately. It is not known whether Fosamax appears in breast milk. The drug is not recommended for nursing mothers.

Recommended dosage

POSTMENOPAUSAL OSTEOPOROSIS

The usual dose is 10 milligrams once a day. Treatment continues for years.

PAGET'S DISEASE

The usual dose is 40 milligrams once a day for 6 months.

Overdosage

Any medication taken in excess can have serious consequences. If you suspect an overdose, seek medical attention immediately.

■ *Symptoms of Fosamax overdose may include:*
  Heartburn, inflammation of the esophagus or stomach, ulcer, upset stomach

Generic name:

FOSFOMYCIN

See Monurol, page 794.

Generic name:

FOSINOPRIL

See Monopril, page 790.

Brand name:

FULVICIN P/G

See Gris-PEG, page 545.

Generic name:

FUROSEMIDE

See Lasix, page 646.

Generic name:

GABAPENTIN

See Neurontin, page 832.

Brand name:

GANTRISIN

Pronounced: GAN-tris-in
Generic name: Sulfisoxazole

Why is this drug prescribed?

Gantrisin is a children's medication prescribed for the treatment of severe, repeated, or long-lasting urinary tract infections. These include pyelonephritis (bacterial kidney inflammation), pyelitis (inflammation of the part of the kidney that drains urine into the ureter), and cystitis (inflammation of the bladder).

This drug is also used to treat bacterial meningitis, and is prescribed as a preventive measure for children who have been exposed to meningitis.

Some middle ear infections are treated with Gantrisin in combination with penicillin or erythromycin.

Toxoplasmosis (parasitic disease transmitted by infected cats, their feces or litter boxes, and by undercooked meat) can be treated with Gantrisin in combination with pyrimethamine (Daraprim).

Malaria that does not respond to the drug chloroquine (Aralen) can be treated with Gantrisin in combination with other drug treatment.

Gantrisin is also used in the treatment of bacterial infections such as trachoma and inclusion inflammation conjunctivitis (eye infections), nocardiosis (bacterial disease affecting the lungs, skin, and brain), and chancroid (venereal disease causing enlargement and ulceration of lymph nodes in the groin).

Most important fact about this drug

Notify your doctor at the first sign of a reaction such as skin rash, sore throat, fever, joint pain, cough, shortness of breath, or other breathing difficulties, abnormal skin paleness, reddish or purplish skin spots or yellowing of the skin or whites of the eyes.

Rare but severe reactions, sometimes fatal, have occurred with the use of sulfa drugs such as Gantrisin. These reactions include sudden and severe liver damage, agranulocytosis (a severe blood disorder), and Stevens-Johnson syndrome (severe blistering).

Children taking sulfa drugs such as Gantrisin should have frequent blood counts.

How should you take this medication?
Be sure your child takes Gantrisin exactly as prescribed. It is important that the child drink plenty of fluids while taking this medication in order to prevent crystals in the urine and the formation of stones.

Gantrisin Pediatric Suspension should be shaken well before each dose. To ensure an accurate dose, ask your pharmacist for a specially marked measuring spoon.

Gantrisin, like other antibacterials, works best when there is a constant amount in the blood and urine. To help keep a constant level, try to make sure that your child does not miss any doses and takes them at evenly spaced intervals, around the clock.

■ *If you miss a dose...*
Give it as soon as you remember. If it is almost time for the next dose, skip the one you missed and go back to the regular schedule. Never take 2 doses at the same time.

■ *Storage instructions...*
Keep this medication in the container it came in, tightly closed. Store it at room temperature, away from moist places and direct light.

What side effects may occur?
Side effects cannot be anticipated. If any develop or change in intensity, inform your doctor as soon as possible. Only your doctor can determine if it is safe for your child to continue taking Gantrisin.

■ *Side effects may include:*
Abdominal bleeding, abdominal pain, allergic reactions, anemia and other blood disorders, angioedema (swelling of face, lips, tongue and throat), anxiety, bluish discoloration of the skin, chills, colitis, convulsions, cough, dark, tarry stools, depression, diarrhea, disorientation, dizziness,

drowsiness, enlarged salivary glands, enlarged thyroid, exhaustion, fainting, fatigue, fever, flushing, gas, hallucinations, headache, hearing loss, hepatitis, hives, inability to fall or stay asleep, inability to urinate, increased urination, inflammation of the mouth or tongue, itching, joint pain, kidney failure, lack of feeling or concern, lack of muscle coordination, lack or loss of appetite, low blood sugar, muscle pain, nausea, palpitations, presence of blood or crystals in urine, rapid heartbeat, reddish or purplish skin spots, retention of urine, ringing in the ears, sensitivity to light, serum sickness (fever, painful joints, enlarged lymph nodes, skin rash), severe skin welts or swelling, shortness of breath, skin eruptions, skin rash, swelling due to fluid retention, tingling or pins and needles, vertigo, vomiting, weakness, yellow eyes and skin

Why should this drug not be prescribed?

If your child is sensitive to or has ever had an allergic reaction to Gantrisin or other sulfa drugs, do not use this medication. Make sure your doctor is aware of any drug reactions the child has experienced.

Except in rare cases, doctors do not prescribe Gantrisin for infants less than 2 months of age. In addition, Gantrisin should never be taken by women at the end of pregnancy or those nursing a baby under 2 months.

Special warnings about this medication

If your child has impaired kidney or liver function, or severe allergies or bronchial asthma, make sure your doctor knows about it. Caution should be exercised when taking Gantrisin.

An analysis of urine and kidney function should be performed by your doctor during treatment with Gantrisin, especially if your child has a kidney problem.

If your child develops diarrhea while taking Gantrisin, notify your doctor.

Possible food and drug interactions
when taking this medication

If Gantrisin is taken with certain other drugs, the effects of either could be increased, decreased, or altered. It is especially important to check with your doctor before combining this drug with the following:

Blood-thinning drugs such as Coumadin
Methotrexate, an anticancer drug
Oral contraceptives
Oral diabetes drugs such as Micronase

Special information
if you are pregnant or breastfeeding
There are no adequate and well controlled studies in pregnant women. This medication should never be used during pregnancy unless the doctor has determined that the benefits outweigh the potential risks. Gantrisin appears in breast milk. If this medication is essential, the doctor may recommend against breastfeeding until treatment with this drug is finished.

Recommended dosage

CHILDREN

This medication should not be prescribed for infants under 2 months of age except in the treatment of congenital toxoplasmosis (a parasitic infection contracted by pregnant women and passed along to the fetus).

The usual dose for children 2 months of age or older is 150 milligrams per 2.2 pounds of body weight divided into 4 to 6 doses taken over 24 hours.

The usual starting dose is one-half of the regular dose, or 75 milligrams per 2.2 pounds of body weight divided into 4 to 6 doses taken over 24 hours. Doses should not exceed 6 grams over 24 hours.

Gantrisin pediatric suspension supplies a half-gram (500 milligrams) in each teaspoonful.

Overdosage
Any medication taken in excess can have serious consequences. If you suspect an overdose, seek emergency medical treatment immediately.

- *Symptoms of an overdose of Gantrisin include:*
  Blood or sediment in the urine, blue tinge to the skin, colic, dizziness, drowsiness, fever, headache, lack or loss of appetite, nausea, unconsciousness, vomiting, yellowing of skin and whites of eyes

Brand name:

GARAMYCIN OPHTHALMIC

Pronounced: gar-uh-MY-sin
Generic name: Gentamicin sulfate

Why is this drug prescribed?
Garamycin Ophthalmic, an antibiotic, is applied to the eye for treatment of infections such as conjunctivitis (pinkeye) and other eye infections.

Most important fact about this drug

To help clear up your infection completely, keep using Garamycin eyedrops or ointment for the full time of treatment, even if your symptoms have disappeared. Do not allow anyone else to use this medication, and do not save it for use on another infection.

How should you use this medication?

Use this medication exactly as prescribed. To administer Garamycin, follow these steps:

Eyedrops

1. Wash your hands thoroughly.
2. Gently pull your lower eyelid down to form a pocket between your eye and the lid.
3. Brace the eyedrop bottle on your forehead or on the bridge of your nose.
4. Do not touch the applicator tip to your eye or any other surface.
5. Close your eyes gently and keep them closed for a minute or two.
6. Do not rinse the dropper.
7. If you are using a second type of eyedrop, wait 5 to 10 minutes before applying it.

Eye Ointment

1. Wash your hands thoroughly.
2. Pull your lower eyelid down away from the eye to form a pocket.
3. Squeeze a thin strip of ointment into the pouch.
4. Avoid touching the tip of the tube to your eye or any other surface.
5. Close your eyes for a couple of minutes.
6. Wipe the tip of the tube with tissue and immediately replace the cap tightly.

Your vision may be blurred for a few minutes following application of the ointment.

■ *If you miss a dose...*
 Apply it as soon as you remember. If it is almost time for your next dose, skip the one you missed and go back to your regular schedule.

■ *Storage instructions...*
 Store away from heat and light. Do not freeze.

What side effects may occur?
Occasional eye irritation—with itching, redness and swelling—may occur with use of the eyedrops.

Occasional burning or stinging in the eye may occur with use of the ointment.

Why should this drug not be prescribed?
If you are sensitive to or have ever had an allergic reaction to Garamycin or certain other antibiotics, such as Tobrex, you should not take this medication. Make sure your doctor is aware of any drug reactions you have experienced.

Special warnings about this medication
Continued or prolonged use of this drug may result in a growth of bacteria or fungi that do not respond to this medication and can cause a second infection. Should this occur, notify your doctor.

Ophthalmic ointments may slow corneal healing.

Possible food and drug interactions
with this medication
No interactions have been reported.

Special Information
if you are pregnant or breastfeeding
There are no special recommendations for this medication. If you are pregnant or plan to become pregnant, ask your doctor for the best advice in your personal situation.

Recommended dosage

ADULTS AND CHILDREN

Garamycin Ophthalmic Solution
Put 1 or 2 drops into the affected eye every 4 hours. For severe infections, your doctor may increase your dosage up to a maximum of 2 drops once every hour.

Garamycin Ophthalmic Ointment
Apply a thin strip—about one-third inch—of ointment to the affected eye 2 or 3 times a day.

Overdosage

Although there is no information on overdose with Garamycin Ophthalmic products, any medication taken in excess can have serious consequences. If you suspect an overdose, seek medical attention immediately.

Brand name:

GAVISCON

See Antacids, page 71.

Brand name:

GELUSIL

See Antacids, page 71.

Brand name:

GEMCOR

See Lopid, page 688.

Generic name:

GEMFIBROZIL

See Lopid, page 688.

Brand name:

GENORA

See Oral Contraceptives, page 887.

Generic name:

GENTAMICIN

See Garamycin Ophthalmic, page 532.

Brand name:

GENUINE BAYER

See Aspirin, page 90.

Generic name:

GLIMEPIRIDE

See Amaryl, page 46.

Generic name:

GLIPIZIDE

See Glucotrol, page 540.

Brand name:

GLUCOPHAGE

Pronounced: GLEW-co-faje
Generic name: Metformin hydrochloride

Why is this drug prescribed?
Glucophage is an oral antidiabetic medication used to treat Type II (noninsulin-dependent) diabetes. Diabetes develops when the body proves unable to burn sugar and the unused sugar builds up in the bloodstream. Glucophage lowers the amount of sugar in your blood by decreasing sugar production and absorption and helping your body respond better to its own insulin, which promotes the burning of sugar. It does not, however, increase the body's production of insulin.

Most important fact about this drug
Always remember that Glucophage is an aid to, not a substitute for, good diet and exercise. Failure to follow a sound diet and exercise plan can lead to serious complications such as dangerously high or low blood sugar levels. Remember, too, that Glucophage is not an oral form of insulin and cannot be used in place of insulin.

How should you take this medication?
Do not take more or less of this medication than directed by your doctor. Glucophage should be taken with food to reduce the possibility of nausea or diarrhea, especially during the first few weeks of therapy.

■ *If you miss a dose...*
   Take it as soon as you remember. If it is almost time for your next dose, skip the one you missed and go back to your regular schedule. Never take 2 doses at the same time.

■ *Storage instructions...*
 Store it at room temperature.

What side effects may occur?
Side effects cannot be anticipated. If any develop or change in intensity, tell your doctor as soon as possible. Only your doctor can determine if it is safe for you to continue taking Glucophage.

If side effects from Glucophage occur, they usually happen during the first few weeks of therapy. Most side effects are minor and will go away after you've taken Glucophage for a while.

■ *More common side effects may include:*
 Abdominal bloating, diarrhea, gas, loss of appetite, metallic or unpleasant taste, nausea, vomiting

Glucophage, unlike other oral antidiabetics, does not usually cause hypoglycemia (low blood sugar). However, hypoglycemia remains a possibility, especially in older, weak, and undernourished people and those with kidney, liver, adrenal, or pituitary gland problems. The risk of hypoglycemia can be increased by missed meals, alcohol, other medications, fever, trauma, infection, surgery, or excessive exercise. To avoid hypoglycemia, you should closely follow the dietary and exercise plan suggested by your physician. If you feel hypoglycemia coming on, get some fast-acting sugar, such as a 4 to 6 ounce glass of fruit juice.

Glucophage can cause a serious side effect called lactic acidosis, a buildup of lactic acid in the blood. This problem is most likely to occur in people whose liver or kidneys are not working well. Although the condition is rare, it can be fatal. Lactic acidosis is a medical emergency that must be treated in a hospital.

■ *Symptoms of lactic acidosis may include:*
 Feeling very weak, tired, or uncomfortable, feeling cold, dizzy, or lightheaded, increasing sleepiness, muscle pain, slow or irregular heartbeat, trouble breathing, unexpected or unusual stomach discomfort

If you notice these symptoms, stop taking Glucophage and call your doctor right away.

Why should this drug not be prescribed?
Avoid Glucophage if it has ever given you an allergic reaction.

If you have congestive heart failure, do not take Glucophage. This condition increases your risk of developing lactic acidosis.

Do not take Glucophage if you are suffering from acute or chronic metabolic acidosis, including diabetic ketoacidosis (a life-threatening medical emergency caused by insufficient insulin and marked by excessive thirst, nausea, fatigue, pain below the breastbone, and fruity breath).

You should not take Glucophage for 2 days before and after having an X-ray procedure with an injectable contrast agent (radioactive iodine). Also, if you are going to have surgery, except minor surgery, you should stop taking Glucophage. Once you have resumed normal food and fluid intake, your doctor will tell you when you can go back to therapy with Glucophage.

If you have kidney or liver disease or develop serious conditions such as a heart attack, severe infection, or a stroke, do not take Glucophage.

You should not take Glucophage if you are seriously dehydrated, having lost a large amount of fluid from severe vomiting, diarrhea, or high fever.

Special warnings about this medication
Before you start therapy with Glucophage, and at least once a year thereafter, your doctor will do a complete assessment of your kidney function. If you develop kidney problems while on Glucophage, your doctor will discontinue this medication. If you are an older person, you will need to have your kidney function monitored more frequently, and your doctor may want to start you at a lower dosage.

If you are taking Glucophage, you should check your blood or urine periodically for abnormal sugar (glucose) levels. Your doctor will do annual blood checks to see if Glucophage is causing a vitamin B_{12} deficiency or any other blood problem.

It's possible that drugs such as Glucophage may lead to more heart problems than diet treatment alone, or diet plus insulin. If you have a heart condition, you may want to discuss this with your doctor. The effectiveness of any oral antidiabetic, including Glucophage, may decrease with time. This may be due to either a diminished responsiveness to the medication or a worsening of the diabetes.

Possible food and drug interactions
when taking this medication
If Glucophage is taken with certain other drugs, the effects of either could be increased, decreased, or altered. It is especially important to check with your doctor before combining Glucophage with the following:

Amiloride (Moduretic)
Calcium channel blockers (heart medications) such as Calan, Isoptin, and Procardia

Cimetidine (Tagamet)
Decongestant, airway-opening drugs such as Sudafed and Ventolin
Digoxin (Lanoxin)
Estrogens such as Premarin
Furosemide (Lasix) and other diuretics
Isoniazid (Rifamate), a drug used for tuberculosis
Major tranquilizers such as Thorazine
Morphine
Niacin (Slo-Niacin, Nicobid)
Oral contraceptives
Phenytoin (Dilantin)
Procainamide (Procan SR)
Quinidine (Quinidex)
Quinine
Ranitidine (Zantac)
Steroids such as prednisone (Deltasone)
Thyroid hormones (Synthroid)
Trimethoprim (Bactrim, Trimpex)
Vancomycin (Vancocin HCl)

Do not drink too much alcohol, since excessive alcohol consumption can cause low blood sugar and alcohol enhances some effects of this drug.

Special information
if you are pregnant or breastfeeding
If you are pregnant or plan to become pregnant, tell your doctor immediately. Glucophage should not be taken during pregnancy. Since studies suggest the importance of maintaining normal blood sugar (glucose) levels during pregnancy, your doctor may prescribe insulin injections instead.

It is not known whether Glucophage appears in human breast milk. Therefore, women should discuss with their doctors whether to discontinue the medication or to stop breastfeeding. If the medication is discontinued and if diet alone does not control glucose levels, then your doctor may consider insulin injections.

Recommended dosage
Your doctor will tailor your dosage to your individual needs.

ADULTS

The usual starting dose is one 500-milligram tablet twice a day, taken with morning and evening meals. Your doctor may increase your daily dose by 500 milligrams at weekly intervals, based on your response. Daily doses of greater than 2500 milligrams are not recommended. An alternative starting dose is one 850-milligram tablet a day, taken with the morning meal. Your doctor may increase this by 850 milligrams at 14-day intervals, to a maximum of 2550 milligrams a day.

The usual maintenance dose ranges from 1,500 to 2,550 milligrams daily.

OLDER ADULTS

Older people and those who are malnourished or in a weakened state are generally given lower doses of Glucophage because their kidneys may be weaker, making side effects more likely.

CHILDREN

The safety and effectiveness of Glucophage have not been established in children.

Overdosage

An overdose of Glucophage can cause lactic acidosis. (See "What Side Effects May Occur?") If you suspect a Glucophage overdose, seek emergency treatment immediately.

Brand name:

GLUCOTROL

Pronounced: GLUE-kuh-troll
Generic name: Glipizide
Other brand name: Glucotrol XL

Why is this drug prescribed?

Glucotrol is an oral antidiabetic medication used to treat Type II (non-insulin-dependent) diabetes. In diabetics either the body does not make enough insulin or the insulin that is produced no longer works properly.

There are actually two forms of diabetes: Type I insulin-dependent and Type II non-insulin-dependent. Type I usually requires insulin injections for life, while Type II diabetes can usually be treated by dietary changes and/or oral antidiabetic medications such as Glucotrol. Apparently, Glucotrol controls diabetes by stimulating the pancreas to secrete more insulin. Occasionally, Type II diabetics must take insulin injections on a temporary basis, especially during stressful periods or times of illness.

Most important fact about this drug

Always remember that Glucotrol is an aid to, not a substitute for, good diet and exercise. Failure to follow a sound diet and exercise plan can lead to serious complications, such as dangerously high or low blood sugar levels. Remember, too, that Glucotrol is *not* an oral form of insulin, and cannot be used in place of insulin.

How should you take this medication?
In general, to achieve the best control over blood sugar levels, Glucotrol should be taken 30 minutes before a meal. However, the exact dosing schedule as well as the dosage amount must be determined by your physician.

Glucotrol XL should be taken with breakfast. Swallow the tablets whole; do not chew, crush, or divide them. Do not be alarmed if you notice something that looks like a tablet in your stool—it will be the empty shell that has been eliminated.

■ *If you miss a dose...*
Take it as soon as you remember. If it is almost time for your next dose, skip the one you missed and go back to your regular schedule. Never take 2 doses at the same time.

■ *Storage instructions...*
Glucotrol should be stored at room temperature and protected from moisture and humidity.

What side effects may occur?
Side effects from Glucotrol are rare and seldom require discontinuation of the medication.

■ *More common side effects may include:*
Constipation, diarrhea, drowsiness, gas, hives, itching, low blood sugar, sensitivity to light, skin rash and eruptions, stomach pain

■ *Less common or rare side effects may include:*
Anemia and other blood disorders, yellow eyes and skin

Glucotrol and Glucotrol XL, like all oral antidiabetic drugs, can cause low blood sugar. This risk is increased by missed meals, alcohol, other medications, and/or excessive exercise. To avoid low blood sugar, you should closely follow the dietary and exercise regimen suggested by your physician.

■ *Symptoms of mild low blood sugar may include:*
Blurred vision, cold sweats, dizziness, fast heartbeat, fatigue, headache, hunger, light-headedness, nausea, nervousness

■ *Symptoms of more severe low blood sugar may include:*
Coma, disorientation, pale skin, seizures, shallow breathing

Ask your doctor what steps you should take if you experience mild hypoglycemia. If symptoms of severe low blood sugar occur, contact your doctor immediately. Severe hypoglycemia should be considered a medical emergency, and prompt medical attention is essential.

Why should this drug not be prescribed?
You should not take Glucotrol if you have had an allergic reaction to it previously.

Glucotrol will be stopped if you are suffering from diabetic ketoacidosis (a life-threatening medical emergency caused by insufficient insulin and marked by excessive thirst, nausea, fatigue, pain below the breastbone, and a fruity breath).

Special warnings about this medication
It's possible that drugs such as Glucotrol may lead to more heart problems than diet treatment alone, or diet plus insulin. If you have a heart condition, you may want to discuss this with your doctor.

If you are taking Glucotrol, you should check your blood and urine periodically for the presence of abnormal sugar (glucose) levels.

Even people with well-controlled diabetes may find that injury, infection, surgery, or fever results in a lack of control over their diabetes. In these cases, the physician may recommend that you stop taking Glucotrol temporarily and use insulin instead.

Glucotrol may not work well in patients with poor kidney or liver function.

In addition, the effectiveness of any oral antidiabetic, including Glucotrol, may decrease with time. This may occur because of either a diminished responsiveness to the medication or a worsening of the diabetes.

Be careful taking the extended-release form of the drug, Glucotrol XL, if you have any narrowing in your stomach or intestines. Also, if you have any stomach or intestinal disease, Glucotrol XL may not work as well.

Possible food and drug interactions
when taking this medication
It is essential that you closely follow your physician's dietary guidelines and that you inform your physician of any medication, either prescription or nonprescription, that you are taking. Specific medications that affect Glucotrol include:

Airway-opening drugs such as Sudafed
Antacids such as Mylanta
Aspirin
Chloramphenicol (Chloromycetin)
Cimetidine (Tagamet)
Clofibrate (Atromid-S)
Corticosteroids such as prednisone (Deltasone)
Diuretics such as HydroDIURIL
Estrogens such as Premarin
Fluconazole (Diflucan)
Gemfibrozil (Lopid)
Heart and blood pressure medications called beta blockers such as
    Tenormin and Lopressor
Heart medications called calcium channel blockers such as Cardizem
    and Procardia XL
Isoniazid (Nydrazid)
Itraconazole (Sporanox)
MAO inhibitors (antidepressant drugs such as Nardil)
Major tranquilizers such as Thorazine and Mellaril
Miconazole (Monistat)
Nicotinic acid (Nicobid)
Nonsteroidal anti-inflammatory drugs such as Motrin
Oral contraceptives
Phenytoin (Dilantin)
Probenecid (Benemid)
Rifampin (Rifadin)
Sulfa drugs such as Bactrim
Thyroid medications such as Synthroid
Warfarin (Coumadin)

Alcohol must be used carefully, since excessive alcohol consumption can
cause low blood sugar.

Special information
if you are pregnant or breastfeeding
The effects of Glucotrol during pregnancy have not been adequately
studied. Therefore, if you are pregnant, or planning to become pregnant,
you should take Glucotrol only on the advice of your physician. Since
studies suggest the importance of maintaining normal blood sugar
(glucose) levels during pregnancy, your physician may prescribe insulin
during pregnancy. To minimize the risk of low blood sugar in newborn
babies, Glucotrol, if taken during pregnancy, should be discontinued at

least one month before the expected delivery date. Although it is not known if Glucotrol appears in breast milk, other oral antidiabetics do. Because of the potential for hypoglycemia in nursing infants, your doctor may advise you either to discontinue Glucotrol or to stop nursing. If Glucotrol is discontinued and if diet alone does not control glucose levels, your doctor may prescribe insulin.

Recommended dosage

Dosage levels must be determined by each patient's needs.

ADULTS

Glucotrol

The usual recommended starting dose is 5 milligrams taken before breakfast. Depending upon blood glucose response, your doctor may increase the initial dose in increments of 2.5 to 5 milligrams. The maximum recommended daily dose is 40 milligrams; total daily dosages above 15 milligrams are usually divided into 2 equal doses that are taken before meals.

Glucotrol XL

The usual starting dose is 5 milligrams each day at breakfast. After 3 months, your doctor may increase the dose to 10 milligrams daily. The maximum recommended daily dose is 20 milligrams.

CHILDREN

The safety and effectiveness of this drug in children have not been established.

OLDER ADULTS

Older people or those with liver disease usually start Glucotrol therapy with 2.5 milligrams. They can start Glucotrol XL treatment with 5 milligrams.

Overdosage

An overdose of Glucotrol can cause low blood sugar. (See side effects section for symptoms.) Eating sugar or a sugar-based product will often correct the condition. Otherwise, seek medical attention immediately.

Generic name:

GLYBURIDE

See Micronase, page 763.

Brand name:

GLYNASE

See Micronase, page 763.

Brand name:

GRISACTIN

See Gris-PEG, page 545.

Generic name:

GRISEOFULVIN

See Gris-PEG, page 545.

Brand name:

GRIS-PEG

Pronounced: GRISS-peg
Generic name: Griseofulvin
Other brand names: Grisactin, Fulvicin P/G

Why is this drug prescribed?

Gris-PEG is prescribed for the treatment of the following ringworm infections:

Athlete's foot
Barber's itch (inflammation of the facial hair follicles)
Ringworm of the body
Ringworm of the groin and thigh
Ringworm of the nails
Ringworm of the scalp

Because Gris-PEG is effective for only certain types of fungal infections, before treatment your doctor may perform tests to identify the source of infection.

Most important fact about this drug

To clear up your infection completely, continue taking Gris-PEG as prescribed until your doctor tells you to stop. Although some improvement may appear within a few days, you need to take Gris-PEG for an extended period.

How should you take this medication?

To minimize stomach irritation and help your body absorb the drug, take Gris-PEG at meal times or with food or whole milk. If you are on a low fat diet, check with your doctor.

Observe good hygiene during treatment to help control infection and prevent reinfection.

- *If you miss a dose...*
  Take it as soon as you remember. If it is almost time for your next dose, skip the one you missed and go back to your regular schedule. Do not take 2 doses at once.

- *Storage instructions...*
  Store at room temperature in a tightly closed container. Protect from light. Keep the liquid from freezing.

What side effects may occur?

Side effects cannot be anticipated. If any develop or change in intensity, inform your doctor as soon as possible. Only your doctor can determine if it is safe for you to continue taking Gris-PEG.

- *More common side effects may include:*
  Hives, skin rashes

- *Less common side effects may include:*
  Confusion, diarrhea, dizziness, fatigue, headache, impairment of performance of routine activities, inability to fall or stay asleep, nausea, oral thrush (mouth inflammation), upper abdominal pain, vomiting

- *Rare side effects may include:*
  Menstrual irregularities, swelling, itching, and shedding of areas of skin, tingling sensation in hands and feet

Why should this drug not be prescribed?

If you are sensitive to or have ever had an allergic reaction to Gris-PEG or other drugs of this type, you should not take this medication. Make sure your doctor is aware of any drug reactions you have experienced.

Unless you are directed to do so by your doctor, do not take this medication if you have liver damage or porphyria (an inherited disorder of the liver or bone marrow).

Do not take Gris-PEG while pregnant.

Special warnings about this medication

Gris-PEG is similar to penicillin. Although penicillin-sensitive people have used Gris-PEG without difficulty, notify your doctor if you are sensitive to or allergic to penicillin.

Because Gris-PEG can make you sensitive to light, avoid exposure to intense natural or artificial sunlight.

Notify your doctor if you develop lupus erythematosus (a form of rheumatism) or a lupus-like condition. Signs and symptoms of lupus include arthritis, red butterfly rash over the nose and cheeks, tiredness, weakness, sensitivity to sunlight, and skin eruptions.

If you are being treated with Gris-PEG for an extended period of time, your doctor should perform regular tests, including periodic monitoring of kidney function, liver function, and blood cell production.

Gris-PEG has not been proved safe and effective for the prevention of fungal infections.

Gris-PEG may decrease the effectiveness of birth-control pills. Use additional protection while you are taking Gris-PEG.

Men should wait at least 6 months after finishing therapy with griseofulvin before they father a child.

Women should avoid becoming pregnant while they are taking the drug.

Possible food and drug interactions
when taking this medication

Gris-PEG may intensify the effects of alcohol. If you drink alcohol while taking this medication, your heart may start beating faster and your skin may be flushed.

If Gris-PEG is taken with certain other drugs, the effects of either could be increased, decreased, or altered. It is especially important to check with your doctor before combining Gris-PEG with the following:

Blood-thinning drugs such as Coumadin
Barbiturates such as phenobarbital
Oral contraceptives

Special information
if you are pregnant or breastfeeding

Do not take Gris-PEG if you are pregnant. If you become pregnant while taking this drug, notify your doctor immediately. There is a potential hazard to the developing baby.

If you are breastfeeding, consult with your doctor before taking Gris-PEG.

Recommended dosage

The usual treatment periods for various ringworm infections are:

Ringworm of the scalp—4 to 6 weeks
Ringworm of the body—2 to 4 weeks
Athlete's foot—4 to 8 weeks

The usual treatment period, depending on the rate of growth, for ringworm of the fingernails is at least 4 months and for ringworm of the toenails at least 6 months.

ADULTS

Ringworm of the Body, Groin and Thigh, Scalp
The usual dosage is 375 milligrams a day taken as a single dose or divided into smaller doses, as determined by your doctor.

Athlete's Foot, Ringworm of the Nails
The usual dosage is 750 milligrams a day divided into smaller doses, as determined by your doctor.

CHILDREN

A single daily dose is effective in children with ringworm of the scalp.

The usual dosage is 3.3 milligrams per pound of body weight per day. This means that children weighing 35 to 60 pounds will take 125 to 187.5 milligrams a day, and children weighing more than 60 pounds will take 187.5 to 375 milligrams a day.

No dosage has been established for children 2 years of age and under.

Overdosage
Any medication taken in excess can have dangerous consequences. If you suspect an overdose of Gris-PEG, seek emergency medical treatment immediately.

Generic name:

GUAIFENESIN WITH CODEINE

See Tussi-Organidin NR, page 1294.

Generic name:

GUAIFENESIN WITH PHENYLPROPANOLAMINE

See Entex LA, page 455.

Generic name:

GUANABENZ

See Wytensin, page 1365.

Generic name:

GUANFACINE

See Tenex, page 1206.

Brand name:

GYNE-LOTRIMIN

Pronounced: GUY-nuh-LOW-trim-in
Generic name: Clotrimazole
Other brand names: Lotrimin, Mycelex, Mycelex-7

Why is this drug prescribed?

Clotrimazole, the active ingredient in these medications, is used to treat fungal infections. In preparations for the skin, it is effective against ringworm, athlete's foot, and jock itch. In vaginal creams and tablets, it is used against vaginal yeast infections. In lozenge form, it is prescribed to treat oral yeast infections and to prevent them in people with weak immune systems.

Most important fact about this drug

Keep using this medicine for the full time of treatment, even if the infection seems to have disappeared. If you stop too soon, the infection could return. You should continue using the vaginal forms of this medicine even during your menstrual period.

How should you take this medication?

Keep all forms of this medicine away from your eyes.

Before applying the skin preparations, be sure to wash your hands. Massage the medication gently into the affected area and the surrounding skin.

If you are taking Mycelex troches, place the lozenge in your mouth and let it dissolve slowly for 15 to 30 minutes. Do not chew the lozenge or swallow it whole.

If you are using a vaginal cream or tablet, use the following administration technique:

1. Load the applicator to the fill line with cream, or unwrap a tablet, wet it with warm water, and place it in the applicator as shown in the instructions you receive with the product.
2. Lie on your back with your knees drawn up.
3. Gently insert the applicator high into the vagina and push the plunger.
4. Withdraw the applicator and discard it if disposable, or wash with soap and water.

To keep the vaginal medication from getting on your clothing, wear a sanitary napkin. Do not use a tampon because it will absorb the medicine. Wear underwear or pantyhose with a cotton crotch—avoid synthetic fabrics such as nylon or rayon. Do not douche unless your doctor tells you to do so.

■ *If you miss a dose...*
Make up for it as soon as you remember. If it is almost time for the next dose, skip the one you missed and go back to your regular schedule.

■ *Storage instructions...*
Store at room temperature, away from heat, light, and moisture.

What side effects may occur?
Side effects cannot be anticipated. If any develop or change in intensity, inform your doctor as soon as possible. Only your doctor can determine if it is safe for you to continue using this medication.

■ *Side effects may include:*
Blistering, burning, hives, irritated skin, itching, peeling, reddened skin, stinging, swelling due to fluid retention

■ *Side effects of clotrimazole vaginal preparations may include:*
Abdominal/stomach cramps/pain, burning/irritation of penis of sexual partner, headache, pain during sexual intercourse, skin rash, hives, vaginal burning, vaginal irritation, vaginal itching, vaginal soreness during sexual intercourse

An unpleasant mouth sensation has been reported by some people taking Mycelex.

Why should this drug not be prescribed?
You should not be using this medication if you have had an allergic reaction to any of its ingredients.

Special warnings about this medication
Contact your doctor if you experience increased skin irritations (such as redness, itching, burning, blistering, swelling, or oozing).

Check with your doctor before using this medication on a child.

In general, if your symptoms have not improved within 2 to 4 weeks of treatment, notify your doctor.

Clotrimazole vaginal preparations should not be used if you have abdominal pain, fever, or a foul-smelling vaginal discharge. Contact your doctor immediately.

While using the vaginal preparations, either avoid sexual intercourse or make sure your partner uses a condom. This will prevent reinfection. Oils used in some vaginal preparations can weaken latex condoms or diaphragms. To find out whether you can use your medication with latex products, check with your pharmacist.

Possible food and drug interactions
when taking this medication
None have been reported.

Special information
if you are pregnant or breastfeeding
The use of clotrimazole during the first trimester of pregnancy has not been adequately studied. It should be used during the first trimester only if clearly needed. Do not use clotrimazole at any time during pregnancy without the advice and supervision of your doctor.

It is not known whether clotrimazole appears in breast milk. Nursing mothers should use this medication cautiously and only when clearly needed.

Recommended dosage

LOTRIMIN

Adults and Children

Wash your hands before and after you use Lotrimin. Apply in the morning and evening. Use enough Lotrimin to massage into the affected area.

Symptoms usually improve during the first week of treatment with Lotrimin.

GYNE-LOTRIMIN CREAM

Adults

Fill the applicator with the cream and insert 1 applicatorful into the vagina every day, preferably at bedtime. Repeat this procedure for 7 consecutive days.

MYCELEX TROCHE

Adults

The recommended dosage is 1 troche slowly dissolved in the mouth 5 times daily for 14 consecutive days. For prevention, the recommended dose is 1 troche 3 times daily.

Overdosage

Although any medication used in excess can have serious consequences, an overdose of clotrimazole is unlikely. If you suspect an overdose, however, seek medical help immediately.

Brand name:

HABITROL

See Nicotine Patches, page 835.

Brand name:

HALCION

Pronounced: HAL-see-on
Generic name: Triazolam

Why is this drug prescribed?

Halcion is used for short-term treatment of insomnia. It is a member of the benzodiazepine class of drugs, many of which are used as tranquilizers.

Most important fact about this drug

Sleep problems are usually temporary, requiring treatment for only a short time, usually 1 or 2 days and no more than 1 to 2 weeks. Insomnia that lasts longer than this may be a sign of another medical problem. If you find you need this medicine for more than 7 to 10 days, be sure to check with your doctor.

How should you take this medication?

Take this medication exactly as directed; never take more than your doctor has prescribed.

As with all prescription medications, never share Halcion with anyone else.

To help avoid upset stomach, Halcion can be taken with food.

■ *If you miss a dose...*
Take Halcion only as needed.

■ *Storage instructions...*
Keep this medication in the container it came in, tightly closed, and out of reach of children. Store it at room temperature.

What side effects may occur?

Side effects cannot be anticipated. If any develop or change in intensity, inform your doctor as soon as possible. Only your doctor can determine if it is safe for you to continue taking Halcion.

■ *More common side effects may include:*
Coordination problems, dizziness, drowsiness, headache, light-headedness, nausea/vomiting, nervousness

■ *Less common or rare side effects may include:*
Aggressiveness, agitation, behavior problems, burning tongue, changes in sexual drive, chest pain, confusion, congestion, constipation, cramps/pain, delusions, depression, diarrhea, disorientation, dreaming abnormalities, drowsiness, dry mouth, exaggerated sense of well-being, excitement, fainting, falling, fatigue, hallucinations, impaired urination, inappropriate behavior, incontinence, inflammation of the tongue and mouth, irritability, itching, loss of appetite, loss of sense of reality, memory impairment, memory loss (e.g. traveler's amnesia), menstrual irregularities, morning "hangover" effects, muscle spasms in the shoulders or neck, nightmares, rapid heart rate, restlessness, ringing in the ears, skin inflammation, sleep

disturbances including insomnia, sleepwalking, slurred or difficult speech, stiff awkward movements, taste changes, tingling or pins and needles, tiredness, visual disturbances, weakness, yellowing of the skin and whites of the eyes

Why should this drug not be prescribed?

You should not take this drug if you are pregnant or if you have had an allergic reaction to it or to other benzodiazepine drugs such as Valium.

Also avoid Halcion if you are taking the antifungal medications Nizoral or Sporanox, or the antidepressant Serzone.

Special warnings about this medication

When Halcion is used every night for more than a few weeks, it loses its effectiveness to help you sleep. This is known as tolerance. Also, it can cause dependence, especially when it is used regularly for longer than a few weeks or at high doses.

Abrupt discontinuation of Halcion should be avoided, since it has been associated with withdrawal symptoms (convulsions, cramps, tremor, vomiting, sweating, feeling ill, perceptual problems, and insomnia). A gradual dosage tapering schedule is usually recommended for patients taking more than the lowest dose of Halcion for longer than a few weeks. The usual treatment period is 7 to 10 days.

If you develop unusual and disturbing thoughts or behavior during treatment with Halcion, you should discuss them with your doctor immediately.

"Traveler's amnesia" has been reported by patients who took Halcion to induce sleep while traveling. To avoid this condition, do not take Halcion on an overnight airplane flight of less than 7 to 8 hours.

You may suffer increased anxiety during the daytime while taking Halcion.

When you first start taking Halcion, until you know whether the medication will have any "carry over" effect the next day, use extreme care while doing anything that requires complete alertness such as driving a car or operating machinery.

After discontinuing the drug, you may experience a "rebound insomnia" for the first 2 nights—that is, insomnia may be worse than before you took the sleeping pill.

You should be aware that anterograde amnesia (forgetting events after an injury) has been associated with benzodiazepine drugs such as Halcion.

You should be cautious about using this drug if you have liver or kidney problems, lung problems, or a tendency to temporarily stop breathing while you are asleep.

Possible food and drug interactions
when taking this medication

Avoid alcoholic beverages and grapefruit juice.

If Halcion is taken with certain other drugs, the effects of either could be increased, decreased, or altered. It is especially important to check with your doctor before combining Halcion with the following:

Amiodarone (Cordarone)
Antidepressant medications, including "tricyclic" drugs such as Elavil
    and such MAO inhibitors as Nardil and Parnate
Antihistamines such as Benadryl and Tavist
Barbiturates such as phenobarbital and Seconal
Cimetidine (Tagamet)
Clarithromycin (Biaxin)
Cyclosporine (Sand-immune Neoral)
Diltiazem (Cardizem)
Ergotamine (Cafergot)
Erythromycin (E.E.S., PCE, E-Mycin, others)
Fluvoxamine (Luvox)
Isoniazid (Nydrazid)
Itraconazole (Nizoral)
Ketoconazole (Sporanox)
Narcotic painkillers such as Demerol
Major tranquilizers such as Mellaril and Thorazine
Nefazodone (Serzone)
Nicardipine (Cardene)
Nifedipine (Adalat)
Other tranquilizers such as BuSpar, Valium, and Xanax
Oral contraceptives
Paroxetine (Paxil)
Ranitidine (Zantac)
Seizure medications such as Dilantin and Tegretol
Sertraline (Zoloft)
Verapamil (Calan)

Special information
if you are pregnant or breastfeeding

Since benzodiazepines have been associated with damage to the developing baby, you should not take Halcion if you are pregnant, think you may be pregnant, or are planning to become pregnant; or if you are breastfeeding.

Recommended dosage

ADULTS

The usual dose is 0.25 milligram before bedtime. The dose should never be more than 0.5 milligram.

CHILDREN

Safety and effectiveness for children under the age of 18 have not been established.

OLDER ADULTS

To decrease the possibility of oversedation, dizziness, or impaired coordination, the usual starting dose is 0.125 milligram. This may be increased to 0.25 milligram if necessary.

Overdosage

Any medication taken in excess can have serious consequences. Severe overdosage of Halcion can be fatal. If you suspect an overdose, seek medical help immediately.

- *Symptoms of Halcion overdose may include:*
  Apnea (temporary cessation of breathing), coma, confusion, excessive sleepiness, problems in coordination, seizures, shallow or difficult breathing, slurred speech

Brand name:

HALDOL

Pronounced: HAL-dawl
Generic name: Haloperidol

Why is this drug prescribed?

Haldol is used to reduce the symptoms of mental disorders such as schizophrenia. It is also prescribed to control tics (uncontrolled muscle contractions of face, arms, or shoulders) and the unintended utterances that mark Gilles de la Tourette's syndrome. In addition, it is used in short-term treatment of children with severe behavior problems, including hyperactivity and combativeness.

Some doctors also prescribe Haldol to relieve severe nausea and vomiting caused by cancer drugs, to treat drug problems such as LSD flashback and

PCP intoxication, and to control symptoms of hemiballismus, a condition that causes involuntary writhing of one side of the body.

Most important fact about this drug
Haldol may cause tardive dyskinesia—a condition characterized by involuntary muscle spasms and twitches in the face and body. This condition can be permanent, and appears to be most common among the elderly, especially women. Ask your doctor for information about this possible risk.

How should you take this medication?
Haldol may be taken with food or after eating. If taking Haldol in a liquid concentrate form, you will need to dilute it with milk or water.

You should not take Haldol with coffee, tea, or other caffeinated beverages, or with alcohol.

Haldol causes dry mouth. Sucking on a hard candy or ice chips may help alleviate the problem.

■ *If you miss a dose...*
Take it as soon as you remember. Take the rest of the doses for that day at equally spaced intervals. Do not take 2 doses at once.

■ *Storage instructions...*
Store away from heat, light, and moisture in a tightly closed container. Do not freeze the liquid.

What side effects may occur?
Side effects cannot be anticipated. If any side effects develop or change in intensity, inform your doctor as soon as possible. Only your doctor can determine if it is safe for you to continue taking Haldol.

■ *Side effects may include:*
Abnormal secretion of milk, acne-like skin reactions, agitation, anemia, anxiety, blurred vision, breast pain, breast development in males, cataracts, catatonic (unresponsive) state, chewing movements, confusion, constipation, coughing, deeper breathing, dehydration, depression, diarrhea, dizziness, drowsiness, dry mouth, epileptic seizures, exaggerated feeling of well-being, exaggerated reflexes, excessive perspiration, excessive salivation, hair loss, hallucinations, headache, heat stroke, high fever, high or low blood pressure, high or low blood sugar, impotence, inability to urinate, increased sex drive, indigestion, involun-

tary movements, irregular menstrual periods, irregular pulse, lack of muscular coordination, liver problems, loss of appetite, muscle spasms, nausea, Parkinson-like symptoms, persistent abnormal erections, physical rigidity and stupor, protruding tongue, puckering of mouth, puffing of cheeks, rapid heartbeat, restlessness, rigid arms, feet, head, and muscles, rotation of eyeballs, sensitivity to light, skin rash, skin eruptions, sleeplessness, sluggishness, swelling of breasts, twitching in the body, neck, shoulders, and face, vertigo, visual problems, vomiting, wheezing or asthma-like symptoms, yellowing of skin and whites of eyes

Why should this drug not be prescribed?

You should not take Haldol if you have Parkinson's disease or are sensitive to or allergic to the drug.

Special warnings about this medication

You should use Haldol cautiously if you have ever had breast cancer, a severe heart or circulatory disorder, chest pain, the eye condition known as glaucoma, seizures, or any drug allergies.

Temporary muscle spasms and twitches may occur if you suddenly stop taking Haldol. Follow your doctor's instructions closely when discontinuing the drug.

This drug may impair your ability to drive a car or operate potentially dangerous machinery. Do not participate in any activities that require full alertness if you are unsure of your reaction to Haldol.

Haldol may make your skin more sensitive to sunlight. When spending time in the sun, use a sunscreen or wear protective clothing.

Avoid exposure to extreme heat or cold. Haldol interferes with the body's temperature-regulating mechanism, so you could become overheated or suffer severe chills.

Possible food and drug interactions
when taking this medication

Extreme drowsiness and other potentially serious effects can result if Haldol is combined with alcohol, narcotics, painkillers, sleeping medications, or other drugs that slow down the central nervous system.

If Haldol is taken with certain other drugs, the effects of either could be increased, decreased, or altered. It is especially important to check with your doctor before combining Haldol with the following:

Antiseizure drugs such as Dilantin or Tegretol
Antispasmodic drugs such as Bentyl and Cogentin
Blood-thinning medications such as Coumadin
Certain antidepressants, including Elavil, Tofranil, and Prozac
Epinephrine (EpiPen)
Lithium (Lithonate)
Methyldopa (Aldomet)
Propranolol (Inderal)
Rifampin (Rifadin)

Special information
if you are pregnant or breastfeeding

The effects of Haldol during pregnancy have not been adequately studied. Pregnant women should use Haldol only if clearly needed. If you are pregnant or plan to become pregnant, inform your doctor immediately. Haldol should not be used by women who are breastfeeding an infant.

Recommended dosage

ADULTS

Moderate Symptoms
The usual dosage is 1 to 6 milligrams daily. This amount should be divided into 2 or 3 smaller doses.

Severe Symptoms
The usual dosage is 6 to 15 milligrams daily, divided into 2 or 3 smaller doses.

CHILDREN

Children younger than 3 years old should not take Haldol.

For children between the ages of 3 and 12, weighing approximately 33 to 88 pounds, doses should start at 0.5 milligram per day. Your doctor will increase the dose if needed.

For Psychotic Disorders
The daily dose may range from 0.05 milligram to 0.15 milligram for every 2.2 pounds of body weight.

For Non-Psychotic Behavior Disorders and Tourette's Syndrome
The daily dose may range from 0.05 milligram to 0.075 milligram for every 2.2 pounds of body weight.

OLDER ADULTS

In general, older people take dosages of Haldol in the lower ranges. Older adults (especially older women) may be more susceptible to tardive dyskinesia—a possibly irreversible condition marked by involuntary muscle spasms and twitches in the face and body. Consult your doctor for information about these potential risks.

Doses may range from 1 to 6 milligrams daily.

Overdosage

Any medication taken in excess can have serious consequences. If you suspect an overdose, seek medical help immediately.

■ *Symptoms of Haldol overdose may include:*
Catatonic (unresponsive) state, coma, decreased breathing, low blood pressure, rigid muscles, sedation, tremor, weakness

Brand name:

HALFPRIN

See Aspirin, page 90.

Generic name:

HALOPERIDOL

See Haldol, page 556.

Brand name:

HELIDAC THERAPY

Pronounced: HEL-i-dak
Generic ingredients: Bismuth subsalicylate, Metronidazole, Tetracycline hydrochloride

Why is this drug prescribed?

Helidac is a drug combination that cures the infection responsible for most stomach ulcers. Although ulcers used to be blamed on stress and spicy food, doctors now know that a germ called *Helicobacter pylori* is the actual culprit in a majority of cases.

Most important fact about this drug

You need to take all of the Helidac pills 4 times each day for 14 days. (You should also be taking an acid blocker such as Zantac, Pepcid, or Tagamet.) If you fail to stick to this regimen, the infection may not be cured.

How should you take this medication?

There are four pills in each dose of Helidac. The two pink tablets (bismuth subsalicylate) should be chewed and swallowed. The white tablet (metronidazole) and the orange and white capsule (tetracycline) should be swallowed whole. Be sure to drink plenty of fluid with each dose—and especially at bedtime—to prevent irritation.

■ *If you miss a dose...*
Take the next dose at the appointed time and continue with your regular schedule until the medication is used up. Do not try to "catch up" by doubling a dose. If you miss more than four doses, contact your physician.

■ *Storage instructions...*
Store at room temperature.

What side effects may occur?

Side effects cannot be anticipated. If any develop or change in intensity, inform your doctor as soon as possible. Only your doctor can determine if it is safe for you to continue taking Helidac.

■ *More common side effects may include:*
Abdominal pain, diarrhea, nausea

■ *Less common side effects may include:*
Appetite loss, black bowel movements, constipation, dizziness, insomnia, pain, prickly feeling, rectal discomfort, upper respiratory infection, vomiting, weakness

■ *Rare side effects may include:*
Arthritis, bleeding in the stomach or intestines, dry mouth, fainting, gas, general feeling of illness, heart attack, high blood pressure, indigestion, inflamed mouth or tongue, nervousness, rash, sensitivity to light, trouble swallowing

Why should this drug not be prescribed?

Do not take Helidac if you have ever had an allergic reaction to any of the following medications:

    Aspirin
    Pepto-Bismol (bismuth subsalicylate)
    Flagyl (metronidazole)
    Tetracycline
    Vibramycin (doxycycline)

Helidac is not for use by children and pregnant or nursing women. The tetracycline part of the therapy can harm a developing baby, stunt a child's growth, and interfere with tooth development.

You should also avoid Helidac if you have kidney or liver disease.

Special warnings about this medication

Don't be alarmed if your tongue and/or bowel movements turn black while you are taking Helidac. This a harmless side effect of the bismuth subsalicylate part of the therapy.

The tetracycline part of Helidac therapy increases the risk of getting a bad sunburn. Limit your exposure to the sun. If you notice a reddening of your skin, stop taking Helidac and call your doctor.

If you develop a headache and blurred vision, numbness and tingling in the arms and legs, or seizures, stop taking Helidac and call your doctor immediately. Also report any infection that develops and be sure your doctor is aware of any infection or blood disorder you already have.

Possible food and drug interactions
when taking this medication

Combining aspirin with Helidac sometimes causes ringing in the ears. If this happens, check with your doctor. You may need to temporarily stop taking aspirin.

During Helidac therapy, alcoholic beverages can cause abdominal cramps, nausea, vomiting, headache, and flushing. Avoid alcohol until at least 1 day after finishing Helidac.

For 1 hour before and 2 hours after each dose of Helidac, avoid eating dairy products. They can interfere with the medication's absorption.

Since Helidac can interfere with oral contraceptives, you should use an additional form of birth control during Helidac therapy.

Certain other drugs may also interact. Check with your doctor before combining Helidac with any of the following:

    Antacids containing aluminum, calcium, or magnesium
    Blood-thinning drugs such as warfarin (Coumadin)
    Cimetidine (Tagamet)

Diabetes medications such as insulin and glyburide (Micronase)
Disulfiram (Antabuse)
Iron (including vitamins that contain iron)
Lithium (Lithonate)
Penicillin
Phenobarbital
Phenytoin (Dilantin)
Probenecid (Benemid)
Sodium bicarbonate (baking soda)
Sulfinpyrazone (Anturane)
Zinc (including vitamins that contain zinc)

Special information
if you are pregnant or breastfeeding
Do not undertake Helidac therapy during this period.

Recommended dosage

ADULTS

Take all 4 Helidac pills 4 times daily, with each meal and at bedtime.

Overdosage
An overdose of the bismuth subsalicylate part of Helidac can be fatal. The other components can have serious consequences as well.

■ *Symptoms of Helidac overdose may include:*
Confusion, coma, convulsions, coordination problems, diarrhea, fast heartbeat, high fever, lethargy, nausea, numbness or pain in the arms and legs, rapid breathing, ringing in the ears, severe heart and lung problems, vomiting

If you suspect an overdose, seek medical attention immediately.

Brand name:

HISMANAL

Pronounced: HISS-man-al
Generic name: Astemizole

Why is this drug prescribed?
Hismanal is an antihistamine prescribed to relieve hay fever and to treat chronic hives. Hismanal is for long-term use; it will not provide immediate relief.

Most important fact about this drug
Never take more than the prescribed dose of Hismanal in an attempt to speed its action. Higher doses have been known to cause dangerously irregular heartbeats.

How should you take this medication?
Hismanal should be taken on an empty stomach—for example, 1 hour before you eat or 2 hours after eating. Taking the drug with food may make it less effective.

- *If you miss a dose...*
  Take it as soon as you remember. If it is almost time for your next dose, skip the one you missed and go back to your regular schedule. Never take 2 doses at the same time.

- *Storage instructions...*
  Store at room temperature. Protect from moisture.

What side effects may occur?
Side effects cannot be anticipated. If any develop or change in intensity, inform your doctor as soon as possible. Only your doctor can determine if it is safe for you to continue taking Hismanal.

- *More common side effects may include:*
  Drowsiness, dry mouth, fatigue, headache, increase in appetite, weight gain

- *Less common side effects may include:*
  Asthma-like symptoms, burning, prickling, or tingling, depression, diarrhea, dizziness, fluid retention, hepatitis, inflammation of the eyelids, itching, joint pain, muscle pain, nausea, nervousness, nosebleed, palpitations, sensitivity to light, skin rash, sore throat, stomach and intestinal pain

- *Rare side effects may include:*
  Low blood pressure

Why should this drug not be prescribed?
Avoid Hismanal if you have a known allergy to it.

Special warnings about this medication

Rare—but serious—heart-related side effects have been reported when Hismanal is used with erythromycin (PCE, E-Mycin), ketoconazole (Nizoral), or itraconazole (Sporanox). If you are taking these medicines, do not take Hismanal. The same reaction can be caused by combining Hismanal with a large dose of quinine. However, the amount of quinine in tonic water is too small to cause the problem under ordinary circumstances.

If you are being treated for a lower respiratory tract disease such as asthma or for liver or kidney disease, consult with your doctor before taking Hismanal.

Possible food and drug interactions
when taking this medication

Taking this drug with food can decrease its effectiveness.

If Hismanal is taken with certain other drugs, the effects of either may be increased, decreased, or altered. It is especially important to check with your doctor before combining Hismanal with the following:

Alcohol
Antibiotics such as Flagyl
Antifungal drugs such as Diflucan, Nizoral, and Sporanox
Drugs that affect heart rhythms such as Vascor, Elavil, and Thorazine
"Macrolide" antibiotics such as Zithromax, Biaxin, E-Mycin, PCE, and
    Tao
Quinine

See "Special warnings about this medication" for more information.

Special information
if you are pregnant or breastfeeding

The effects of Hismanal during pregnancy have not been adequately studied. Therefore, this medication should be prescribed only when the benefits of therapy outweigh any potential risk to the fetus. It is not known whether Hismanal appears in breast milk. If this medication is essential to your health, your doctor may advise you to stop nursing your baby until your treatment with this drug is finished.

Recommended dosage

ADULTS

The usual dose for adults and children 12 years and over is 10 milligrams (1 tablet) once daily.

CHILDREN

Safety and effectiveness in children under 12 have not been established.

Overdosage

Hismanal is generally safe; however, large amounts may cause serious symptoms. If you suspect an overdose, get medical help immediately.

■ *Symptoms of Hismanal overdose may include:*
  Cardiac arrest, fainting, irregular heartbeat, seizures

Brand name:

HIVID

Pronounced: HIV-id
Generic name: Zalcitabine

Why is this drug prescribed?

Hivid is one of the drugs used against the human immunodeficiency virus (HIV)—the deadly cause of AIDS. HIV does its damage by slowly undermining the immune system, finally leaving the body without any defense against infection. Hivid staves off collapse of the immune system by interfering with the virus's ability to reproduce.

Hivid is often combined with one of the new protease inhibitors (Crixivan, Invirase, and Norvir) as part of the "cocktail" of drugs that has proven so effective in halting or even reversing the progress of HIV. Hivid can also be combined with the HIV drug Retrovir, provided you have not already been taking Retrovir for more than 3 months. For people with advanced cases of HIV, Hivid is sometimes prescribed by itself when other drugs don't work or can't be tolerated.

Most important fact about this drug

Although Hivid can slow the progress of HIV, it is not a cure. You may continue to develop complications, including frequent infections. Even if you feel better, regular physical exams and blood counts by your doctor are highly advisable. Also be sure to notify your doctor immediately if you experience any changes in your general health.

How should you take this medication?
Hivid should be taken every 8 hours, exactly as prescribed. It is important to keep levels of the drug in your body as constant as possible, so be sure to take every scheduled dose. Never take more than the prescribed dose; nerve disorders could result.

■ *If you miss a dose...*
Take it as soon as you remember. If it is almost time for the next dose, skip the one you missed and go back to your regular schedule. Never take 2 doses at once.

■ *Storage instructions...*
Store at room temperature in a tightly closed bottle.

What side effects may occur?
Although side effects can never be predicted, they are more likely—and more apt to be severe—in people with an advanced case of HIV. If any side effects develop or change in intensity, inform your doctor as soon as possible. Only your doctor can determine if it is safe for you to continue using Hivid.

■ *More common side effects may include:*
Abdominal pain, fatigue, hives, itching, mouth sores and inflammation, nausea and vomiting, rash, tingling, burning, numbness, or pain in the hands and feet

■ *Less common side effects may include:*
Constipation, convulsions, diarrhea, fever, headache

There have been isolated reports of an extremely wide variety of additional problems occurring during Hivid therapy. Whether these problems were caused by the drug remains unclear. Nevertheless, it's wise to check with your doctor whenever any unexplained symptom develops.

Why should this drug not be prescribed?
If Hivid gives you an allergic reaction, you cannot use this medication.

Special warnings about this medication
If you have an advanced case of HIV, there is a one-in-three chance that Hivid will cause a serious nerve disorder called peripheral neuropathy. The

first signs of this problem are numbness, tingling, and burning pain in the hands and feet. Check with your doctor as soon as any of these symptoms develop. If you continue to take Hivid, they will be followed by episodes of intense, sharp, shooting pain or severe, continuous, burning pain—and the condition could become irreversible. If Hivid is stopped promptly, the symptoms will gradually disappear.

Much more rarely, Hivid has been known to cause a dangerous inflammation of the pancreas (pancreatitis), especially in people who have previously had the problem. The chief signs are bouts of severe abdominal pain—usually lasting for days—accompanied by nausea and vomiting. If these symptoms develop, call your doctor without delay. Hivid therapy must be discontinued permanently.

Other rare but dangerous side effects to watch for include liver failure, weakening of the heart, and ulcers in the mouth and the canal to the stomach (esophagus). Kidney disease increases the risk of these side effects. If you've ever had kidney, liver, or heart problems, or tend to abuse alcohol, be sure your doctor is aware of the situation.

Remember that Hivid does not eliminate HIV from the body. The infection can still be passed to others through sexual contact or blood contamination.

Possible food and drug interactions
when taking this medication
A number of drugs can cause peripheral neuropathy and should not be taken with Hivid. The list includes:

Chloramphenicol (Chloromycetin)
Cisplatin (Platinol)
Dapsone
Disulfiram (Antabuse)
Ethionamide (Trecator-SC)
Glutethimide
Gold
Hydralazine (Ser-Ap-Es)
Iodoquinol (Yodoxin)
Isoniazid (Nydrazid)
Metronidazole (Flagyl)
Nitrofurantoin (Macrodantin)
Phenytoin (Dilantin)
Ribavirin (Virazole)
Vincristine (Oncovin)

Several other drugs should be either avoided or taken with caution while on Hivid therapy. Check with your doctor before taking the following:

Aminoglycosides such as Garamycin
Amphotericin B (Fungizone)
Antacids containing magnesium and aluminum, including Maalox and Mylanta
Cimetidine (Tagamet)
Didanosine (Videx)
Foscarnet (Foscavir)
Metoclopramide
Pentamidine (Pentam 300)
Probenecid (Benemid)

Special information
if you are pregnant or breastfeeding

The safety of Hivid during pregnancy has not been adequately studied. Take contraceptive measures while using Hivid. If you are pregnant or plan to become pregnant, notify your doctor immediately.

Do not breastfeed your baby. HIV can be passed to an infant through breast milk.

Recommended dosage

ADULTS

The usual dose, alone or in combination with Retrovir, is one 0.750 milligram tablet every 8 hours. Your doctor may adjust the dosage if you have kidney problems or are taking other HIV medications.

CHILDREN

Safety and effectiveness have not been established for children under 13.

Overdosage

Any medication taken in excess can have serious consequences. If you suspect an overdose, seek medical attention immediately.

- *Symptoms of Hivid overdose may include:*
  Drowsiness, vomiting, numbness, tingling, burning, and pain in the arms and legs

Brand name:

HUMULIN

See Insulin, page 610.

Brand name:

HYDERGINE

Pronounced: HY-der-jeen
Generic name: Ergoloid mesylates

Why is this drug prescribed?
Hydergine helps relieve symptoms of declining mental capacity, thought to be related to aging or dementia, seen in some people over age 60. The symptoms include reduced understanding and motivation, and a decline in self-care and interpersonal skills.

Most important fact about this drug
It may take several weeks or more for Hydergine to produce noticeable results. In fact, your doctor may need up to 6 months to determine whether the drug is right for you. Keep taking your regular doses even if you feel no effect.

How should you take this medication?
Take Hydergine exactly as prescribed.

- *If you miss a dose...*
  Skip the dose you missed and go back to your regular schedule. Do not take 2 doses at once. If you miss 2 or more doses in a row, consult your doctor.

- *Storage instructions...*
  Store at room temperature. Protect from heat and light. Do not freeze capsules or oral solution.

What side effects may occur?
Side effects cannot be anticipated. If any develop or change in intensity, notify your doctor as soon as possible. Only your doctor can determine whether it is safe to continue taking Hydergine.

■ *Side effects may include:*
Stomach upset, temporary nausea

Why should this drug not be prescribed?
Do not use Hydergine if you have ever had an allergic reaction to or are sensitive to the drug, or if you have a mental disorder.

Special warnings about this medication
Since the symptoms treated with Hydergine are of unknown origin and may change or evolve into a specific disease, your doctor will make a careful diagnosis before prescribing Hydergine and then watch closely for any changes in your condition.

**Possible food and drug interactions
when taking this medication**
No interactions have been reported.

**Special information
if you are pregnant or breastfeeding**
Hydergine is not intended for use by women of childbearing age.

Recommended dosage

ADULTS

The usual dose of Hydergine is 1 milligram, 3 times a day.

Overdosage
Any medication taken in excess can have serious consequences. If you suspect an overdose of Hydergine, seek medical attention immediately.

Brand name:

HYDROCET

See Vicodin, page 1337.

Generic name:

HYDROCHLOROTHIAZIDE

See HydroDIURIL, page 572.

Generic name:

HYDROCHLOROTHIAZIDE WITH TRIAMTERENE

See Dyazide, page 425.

Generic name:

HYDROCODONE WITH ACETAMINOPHEN

See Vicodin, page 1337.

Generic name:

HYDROCODONE WITH CHLORPHENIRAMINE

See Tussionex, page 1291.

Generic name:

HYDROCODONE WITH IBUPROFEN

See Vicoprofen, page 1340.

Generic name:

HYDROCORTISONE

See Anusol-HC, page 77.

Brand name:

HYDRODIURIL

Pronounced: High-dro-DYE-your-il
Generic name: Hydrochlorothiazide
Other brand name: Esidrix

Why is this drug prescribed?
HydroDIURIL is used in the treatment of high blood pressure and other conditions that require the elimination of excess fluid (water) from the body. These conditions include congestive heart failure, cirrhosis of the liver, corticosteroid and estrogen therapy, and kidney disorders. When used for high blood pressure, HydroDIURIL can be used alone or with other high blood pressure medications. HydroDIURIL contains a form of thiazide, a diuretic

that prompts your body to produce and eliminate more urine, which helps lower blood pressure.

Most important fact about this drug
If you have high blood pressure, you must take HydroDIURIL regularly for it to be effective. Since blood pressure declines gradually, it may be several weeks before you get the full benefit of HydroDIURIL; and you must continue taking it even if you are feeling well. HydroDIURIL does not cure high blood pressure; it merely keeps it under control.

How should you take this medication?
Take HydroDIURIL exactly as prescribed by your doctor.

- *If you miss a dose...*
  If you forget a dose, take it as soon as you remember. If it is almost time for your next dose, skip the one you missed and go back to your regular schedule. Never take 2 doses at the same time.

- *Storage instructions...*
  Keep container tightly closed. Protect from light, moisture, and freezing cold. Store at room temperature.

What side effects may occur?
Side effects cannot be anticipated. If any develop or change in intensity, inform your doctor as soon as possible. Only your doctor can determine if it is safe for you to continue taking HydroDIURIL.

- *Side effects may include:*
  Abdominal cramping, diarrhea, dizziness upon standing up, headache, loss of appetite, low blood pressure, low potassium (leading to symptoms such as dry mouth, excessive thirst, weak or irregular heartbeat, muscle pain or cramps), stomach irritation, stomach upset, weakness

- *Less common or rare side effects may include:*
  Anemia, blood disorders, changes in blood sugar, constipation, difficulty breathing, dizziness, fever, fluid in the lung, hair loss, high levels of sugar in the urine, hives, hypersensitivity reactions, impotence, inflammation of the lung, inflammation of the pancreas, inflammation of the salivary glands, kidney failure, muscle spasms, nausea, rash, reddish or purplish spots on the skin, restlessness, sensitivity to light, skin disorders including Stevens-Johnson syndrome (blisters in the mouth and eyes),

skin peeling, tingling or pins and needles, vertigo, vision changes, vomiting, yellow eyes and skin

Why should this drug not be prescribed?

If you are unable to urinate, you should not take this medication.

If you are sensitive to or have ever had an allergic reaction to HydroDIURIL or similar drugs, or if you are sensitive to sulfa or other sulfonamide-derived drugs, you should not take this medication.

Special warnings about this medication

Diuretics can cause your body to lose too much potassium. Signs of an excessively low potassium level include muscle weakness and rapid or irregular heartbeat. To boost your potassium level, your doctor may recommend eating potassium-rich foods or taking a potassium supplement.

If you are taking HydroDIURIL, your kidney function should be given a complete assessment, and should continue to be monitored.

If you have liver disease, diabetes, gout, or lupus erythematosus (a form of rheumatism), HydroDIURIL should be used with caution.

If you have bronchial asthma or a history of allergies, you may be at greater risk for an allergic reaction to this medication.

Dehydration, excessive sweating, severe diarrhea or vomiting could deplete your body's fluids and cause your blood pressure to become too low. Be careful when exercising and in hot weather.

Possible food and drug interactions
when taking this medication

HydroDIURIL may increase the effects of alcohol. Do not drink alcohol while taking this medication.

If HydroDIURIL is taken with certain other drugs, the effects of either could be increased, decreased, or altered. It is especially important to check with your doctor before combining HydroDIURIL with the following:

Barbiturates such as phenobarbital
Cholestyramine (Questran)
Colestipol (Colestid)
Corticosteroids such as prednisone and ACTH
Digoxin (Lanoxin)
Drugs to treat diabetes such as insulin or Micronase
Lithium (Lithonate)
Narcotics such as Percocet
Nonsteroidal anti-inflammatory drugs such as Naprosyn

Norepinephrine (Levophed)
Other high blood pressure medications such as Aldomet
Skeletal muscle relaxants, such as tubocurarine

Special information
if you are pregnant or breastfeeding

The effects of HydroDIURIL during pregnancy have not been adequately studied. If you are pregnant or plan to become pregnant, inform your doctor immediately. HydroDIURIL appears in breast milk and could affect a nursing infant. If this medication is essential to your health, your doctor may advise you to discontinue breastfeeding until your treatment is finished.

Recommended dosage

Dosage should be adjusted to each individual's needs. The smallest dose that is effective should be used.

ADULTS

Water Retention

The usual dose is 25 milligrams to 100 milligrams per day. Your doctor may tell you to take the drug in a single dose or to divide the total amount into more than one dose. Your doctor may put you on a day on, day off schedule or some other alternate day schedule to suit your needs.

High Blood Pressure

The usual dose is 25 milligrams as a single dose. Your doctor may increase the dose to 50 milligrams, as a single dose or divided into 2 doses. Dosages should be adjusted when used with other high blood pressure medications.

CHILDREN

Dosages for children should be adjusted according to weight, generally 0.5 to 1 milligram per pound of body weight in 1 or 2 doses per day. Infants under 2 years should not receive more than 37.5 milligrams per day, and children aged 2 to 12 should not get more than 100 milligrams a day. Infants under 6 months may need 1.5 milligrams per pound per day in 2 doses.

Under 2 years

Based on age and body weight, the daily dosage is 12.5 milligrams to 37.5 milligrams per day.

2 to 12 years

The daily dosage, based on body weight, is 37.5 milligrams to 100 milligrams.

HydroDIURIL tablets come in strengths of 25, 50 and 100 milligrams.

Overdosage
Any medication taken in excess can cause symptoms of overdose. If you suspect an overdose, seek medical attention immediately.

- *Symptoms of HydroDIURIL overdose may include:*
  Dry mouth, excessive thirst, muscle pain or cramps, nausea and vomiting, weak or irregular heartbeat, weakness and dizziness

Generic name:

HYDROMORPHONE

See Dilaudid, page 382.

Generic name:

HYDROXYCHLOROQUINE

See Plaquenil, page 967.

Generic name:

HYDROXYZINE

See Atarax, page 96.

Brand name:

HYGROTON

Pronounced: HIGH-grow-ton
Generic name: Chlorthalidone
Other brand name: Thalitone

Why is this drug prescribed?
Hygroton is a diuretic (water pill) used to treat high blood pressure and fluid retention associated with congestive heart failure, cirrhosis of the liver (a disease of the liver caused by damage to its cells), corticosteroid and estrogen therapy, and kidney disease. When used for high blood pressure, Hygroton may be used alone or in combination with other high blood pressure medications. Diuretics help your body produce and eliminate more urine, which helps lower blood pressure.

Most important fact about this drug

If you have high blood pressure, you must take Hygroton regularly for it to be effective. Since blood pressure declines gradually, it may be several weeks before you get the full benefit of Hygroton; and you must continue taking it even if you are feeling well. Hygroton does not cure high blood pressure; it merely keeps it under control.

How should you take this medication?

Diuretics such as Hygroton increase urination; therefore Hygroton should be taken in the morning.

Do not interchange Hygroton or generic chlorthalidone with Thalitone without consulting your doctor or pharmacist.

Hygroton may be taken with food. Take it exactly as prescribed.

- *If you miss a dose...*
  Take it as soon as you remember. If it is almost time for the next dose, skip the one you missed and go back to your regular schedule. Do not take 2 doses at the same time.

- *Storage instructions...*
  Store at room temperature.

What side effects may occur?

Side effects cannot be anticipated. If any side effects develop or change in intensity, tell your doctor immediately. Only your doctor can determine whether it is safe to continue taking Hygroton.

- *Side effects may include:*
  Allergic reaction, anemia, changes in blood sugar, change in potassium levels (causing such symptoms as dry mouth, excessive thirst, weak or irregular heartbeat, and muscle pain or cramps), constipation, cramping, diarrhea, dizziness, dizziness upon standing up, flaky skin, headache, hives, impotence, inflammation of the pancreas, itching, loss of appetite, low blood pressure, muscle spasms, nausea, rash, restlessness, sensitivity to light, stomach irritation, tingling or pins and needles, vision changes, vomiting, weakness, yellow eyes and skin

Why should this drug not be prescribed?

If you are unable to urinate or if you have ever had an allergic reaction to or are sensitive to chlorthalidone or other sulfa drugs, do not take Hygroton.

Special warnings about this medication

Diuretics can cause your body to lose too much potassium. Signs of an excessively low potassium level include muscle weakness and rapid or irregular heartbeat. To boost your potassium level, your doctor may recommend eating potassium-rich foods or taking a potassium supplement.

Tell your doctor if you have ever had an allergic reaction to other diuretics or if you have asthma, kidney or liver disease, gout, or lupus.

If you have a history of bronchial asthma, you are more likely to have an allergic reaction to Hygroton.

Be careful in hot weather not to become dehydrated. Contact your doctor if you experience excessive thirst, tiredness, restlessness, muscle pains or cramps, nausea, vomiting, or increased heart rate or pulse.

This medication may aggravate lupus erythematosus, a disease of the connective tissue.

Avoid prolonged exposure to sunlight.

Possible food and drug interactions
when taking this medication

Drinking alcohol may increase the chance of dizziness. Do not drink alcohol while taking this medication.

If Hygroton is taken with certain other drugs, the effects of either could be increased, decreased, or altered. It is especially important to check with your doctor before combining Hygroton with the following:

Appetite-control medicines such as Tenuate
Cholestyramine (Questran)
Colestipol (Colestid)
Decongestants (medicines for colds, cough, hay fever, or sinus)
Digitalis (Lanoxin)
Insulin
Lithium (Lithonate)
Oral diabetes drugs such as Micronase
Other high blood pressure medications such as Catapres and Aldomet
Steroids such as prednisone

Special information
if you are pregnant or breastfeeding

Information is not available about the safety of Hygroton during pregnancy. If you are pregnant or plan to become pregnant, inform your doctor immediately. Hygroton may appear in breast milk and could affect a nursing infant. If

Hygroton is essential to your health, your doctor may advise you to stop breastfeeding until your treatment is finished.

Recommended dosage
Your doctor will tailor your individual dose to the lowest possible amount that delivers a satisfactory response.

Once desired control of blood pressure or fluid retention has been achieved, your doctor may adjust your dose downward.

HIGH BLOOD PRESSURE

Hygroton
The usual initial dosage is a single dose of 25 milligrams. Your doctor may increase the dose to 100 milligrams once daily.

Thalitone
The usual initial dose is a single dose of 15 milligrams. Your doctor may increase the dose to 45 to 50 milligrams once daily.

FLUID RETENTION

Hygroton
The usual recommended initial dose is 50 to 100 milligrams daily or 100 milligrams every other day. Some people may require up to 150 to 200 milligrams at these intervals.

Thalitone
The usual initial dose is 30 to 60 milligrams daily or 60 milligrams on alternate days. Some people may require up to 90 to 120 milligrams at these intervals.

Overdosage
Any medication taken in excess can have serious consequences. If you suspect an overdose, seek medical treatment immediately.

■ *Symptoms of Hygroton overdose may include:*
Confusion, dizziness, nausea, weakness

Generic name:

HYOSCYAMINE

See Levsin, page 656.

Brand name:

HYTONE

See Anusol-HC, page 77.

Brand name:

HYTRIN

Pronounced: HIGH-trin
Generic name: Terazosin hydrochloride

Why is this drug prescribed?
Hytrin is prescribed to reduce high blood pressure. It may be used alone or in combination with other blood pressure lowering drugs, such as HydroDIURIL (a diuretic) or Inderal, a beta blocker.

Hytrin is also prescribed to relieve the symptoms of benign prostatic hyperplasia or BPH. BPH is an enlargement of the prostate gland that surrounds the urinary canal. It leads to the following symptoms:

- a weak or interrupted stream when urinating
- a feeling that you cannot empty your bladder completely
- a feeling of delay when you start to urinate
- a need to urinate often, especially at night
- a feeling that you must urinate right away

Hytrin relaxes the tightness of a certain type of muscle in the prostate and at the opening of the bladder. This can reduce the severity of the symptoms.

Most important fact about this drug
If you have high blood pressure, you must take Hytrin regularly for it to be effective. Since blood pressure declines gradually, it may be several weeks before you get the full benefit of Hytrin; and you must continue taking it even if you are feeling well. Hytrin does not cure high blood pressure; it merely keeps it under control.

How should you take this medication?
You may take Hytrin with or without food. Take your first dose at bedtime. Do not take more than the 1 milligram your doctor has prescribed.

- If you miss a dose...
  Take it as soon as you remember. If it is almost time for the next dose, skip the one you missed and go back to your regular schedule. Do not take 2 doses at the same time.

- *Storage instructions...*
  Store at room temperature in a cool, dry place. Protect from light.

What side effects may occur?
Side effects cannot be anticipated. If any develop or change in intensity, inform your doctor as soon as possible. Only your doctor can determine if it is safe for you to continue taking Hytrin.

- *More common side effects may include:*
  Difficult or labored breathing, dizziness, headache, heart palpitations, light-headedness upon standing, nausea, pain in the arms and legs, sleepiness, stuffy nose, swollen wrists and ankles, weakness

If these symptoms persist, tell your doctor. Your dosage of Hytrin may be higher than needed.

- *Less common or rare side effects may include:*
  Anxiety, back pain, blurred vision, bronchitis, conjunctivitis (inflamed eyes), constipation, decreased sex drive, depression, diarrhea, dimmed vision, dry mouth, facial swelling, fainting, fever, flu or cold symptoms (cough, sore throat, runny nose), fluid retention, frequent urination, gas, gout, impotence, inability to hold urine, increased heart rate, indigestion, inflamed sinuses, insomnia, irregular heartbeat, itching, joint pain and inflammation, low blood pressure, muscle aches, nasal inflammation, nervousness, nosebleed, numbness or tingling, painful lasting erection, pain in the abdomen, chest, neck, or shoulder, rash, ringing in the ears, severe allergic reaction, sweating, urinary tract infection, vertigo, vision changes, vomiting, weight gain

Why should this drug not be prescribed?
Do not take Hytrin if you are sensitive to it or have ever had an allergic reaction to it.

Special warnings about this medication
When your blood pressure falls in response to Hytrin, you may faint. Other less severe reactions include dizziness, heart palpitations, light-headedness, and drowsiness. You are also likely to feel dizzy or faint whenever you rise from a sitting or lying position; this should disappear as your body becomes accustomed to Hytrin. If your occupation is such that these symptoms might cause serious problems, make sure your doctor knows this from the start; he or she will increase your Hytrin dosage very cautiously.

Regardless of your occupation, avoid driving, climbing, and other hazardous tasks at the following times:

- For 12 hours after your first dose of Hytrin
- With each new dosage increase
- When you re-start Hytrin after any treatment interruption

If you are taking Hytrin for benign prostatic hyperplasia, remember that although Hytrin helps relieve the symptoms of BPH, it does NOT change the size of the prostate, which may continue to grow. You may still need surgery in the future. In addition, it *is* possible to have BPH and prostate cancer at the same time.

If you develop the side effect called priapism—a painful erection that last for hours—call your doctor without delay. The condition can lead to impotence if not treated immediately.

Possible food and drug interactions
when taking this medication

If Hytrin is taken with certain other drugs, the effects of either could be increased, decreased, or altered. It is especially important to check with your doctor before combining Hytrin with the following:

Nonsteroidal anti-inflammatory painkillers such as Motrin and Naprosyn
Other blood pressure medications, such as Dyazide, Vasotec, Calan, and Verelan

Special information
if you are pregnant or breastfeeding

The effects of Hytrin during pregnancy have not been adequately studied. If you are pregnant or plan to become pregnant, notify your doctor immediately. Hytrin is not recommended during pregnancy unless the benefit outweighs the potential risk to the unborn baby. It is not known whether Hytrin appears in breast milk. Because many drugs do appear in breast milk, your doctor may advise you to stop breastfeeding until your treatment with this drug is finished.

Recommended dosage

ADULTS

High Blood Pressure

The usual initial dose is 1 milligram at bedtime. Your doctor may slowly increase the dose until your blood pressure has been lowered sufficiently. The usual recommended dosage range is 1 milligram to 5 milligrams taken once a day; however, some people may benefit from doses as high as 20 milligrams per day.

Benign Prostatic Hyperplasia

The starting dose is 1 milligram at bedtime. Your doctor will gradually increase the dose to 10 milligrams, taken once a day, usually for at least 4 to 6 weeks. A few men have needed a dose of 20 milligrams a day.

If you stop taking Hytrin for several days or longer, your doctor will re-start your treatment with 1 milligram at bedtime.

CHILDREN

Safety and effectiveness of Hytrin in children have not been established.

Overdosage

If you take too much Hytrin, dizziness, light-headedness, and fainting may occur within 90 minutes. A large overdose may lead to shock. If you suspect an overdose of Hytrin, seek medical attention immediately.

Brand name:

HYZAAR

Pronounced: HIGH-zahr
Generic ingredients: Losartan potassium and
  Hydrochlorothiazide

Why is this drug prescribed?

Hyzaar is a combination medication used in the treatment of high blood pressure. One component, losartan, belongs to a new class of blood pressure medications that work by preventing the hormone angiotensin II from constricting the blood vessels, thus allowing blood to flow more freely and keeping the blood pressure down. The other component, hydrochlorothiazide, is a diuretic that increases the output of urine, removing excess fluid from the body and thus lowering blood pressure.

Most important fact about this drug

You must take Hyzaar regularly for it to be effective. Since blood pressure declines gradually, it may be several weeks before you get the full benefit of Hyzaar, and you must continue taking it even if you are feeling well. Hyzaar does not cure high blood pressure; it merely keeps it under control.

How should you take this medication?

Hyzaar may be taken with or without food. Take Hyzaar exactly as directed. Try to take it at the same time each day so that it is easier to remember.

- *If you miss a dose...*
  Take the forgotten dose as soon as you remember. If it is almost time for your next dose, skip the one you missed and go back to your regular schedule.

- *Storage instructions...*
  Keep in a tightly closed container at room temperature. Protect from light.

What side effects may occur?
Side effects cannot be anticipated. If any develop or change in intensity, inform your doctor as soon as possible. Only your doctor can determine if it is safe for you to continue taking Hyzaar.

- *More common side effects include:*
  Dizziness, upper respiratory infection

- *Less common side effects include:*
  Abdominal pain, back pain, cough, fluid retention and swelling, heart palpitations, sinus inflammation, skin rash

Why should this drug not be prescribed?
If you have ever had an allergic reaction to losartan, hydrochlorothiazide, or sulfa drugs, you should not take this medication. If you are unable to urinate, do not take Hyzaar.

Special warnings about this medication
If you are taking Hyzaar and have kidney disease, your doctor will watch your kidney function carefully.

Hyzaar can cause low blood pressure, especially if you are also taking another diuretic. You may feel light-headed or faint, especially during the first few days of therapy. If these symptoms occur, contact your doctor. Your dosage may need to be adjusted or discontinued. If you actually faint, stop taking the medication until you have talked to your doctor.

If you have liver or kidney disease, diabetes, gout, or lupus erythematosus, Hyzaar should be used with caution. This drug may bring out hidden diabetes. If you are already taking insulin or oral diabetes drugs, your medication may have to be adjusted. If you have bronchial asthma or a history of allergies, you may be at greater risk for an allergic reaction to this medication.

Excessive sweating, severe diarrhea or vomiting could deplete your body fluids and cause your blood pressure to drop too low. Be careful when exercising and in hot weather. Call your doctor if your mouth becomes dry, you feel weak or tired or sluggish, you are unusually thirsty, you feel restless or confused, you ache all over, your heart starts beating faster, or you are nauseated.

Possible food and drug interactions when taking this medication

Hyzaar may increase the effects of alcohol. Avoid alcohol while taking this medication.

If Hyzaar is taken with certain other drugs, the effects of either could be increased, decreased, or altered. It is especially important to check with your doctor before taking Hyzaar with the following:

Barbiturates such as phenobarbital and Seconal
Cholestyramine (Questran)
Colestipol (Colestid)
Corticosteroids (Prednisone)
Insulin
Ketoconazole (Nizoral)
Lithium (Eskalith, Lithobid)
Narcotic painkillers such as Demerol, Tylenol with Codeine, and Percocet
Nonsteroidal anti-inflammatory drugs such as Aleve, Anaprox, and Motrin
Other blood pressure-lowering drugs such as Procardia XL and Tenormin
Oral diabetes drugs such as Diabinese, DiaBeta, and Glucotrol
Potassium supplements such as Slow-K
Salt substitutes containing potassium
Sulfaphenazole
Troleandomycin (Tao)

Special Information if you are pregnant or breastfeeding

When used in the second or third trimester of pregnancy, Hyzaar can cause injury or even death to the unborn child. Stop taking Hyzaar as soon as you know you are pregnant. If you are pregnant or plan to become pregnant, tell your doctor immediately. Hyzaar appears in breast milk and can affect the nursing infant. If this medication is essential to your health, your doctor may advise you to stop breastfeeding while you are taking Hyzaar.

Recommended dosage

ADULTS

The usual starting dose of Hyzaar is 1 tablet once daily (losartan 50 milligrams/hydrochlorothiazide 12.5 milligrams).

If your blood pressure does not respond to this dose, after about 3 weeks the dose may be increased to 2 tablets once daily. Taking more than 2 tablets daily is not recommended.

CHILDREN

The safety and effectiveness of Hyzaar in children have not been studied.

Overdosage

Any medication taken in excess can have serious consequences. Information concerning Hyzaar overdosage is limited. However, extremely low blood pressure and abnormally rapid or slow heartbeat may be signs of an overdose. Other signs may include dryness and thirst, overall weakness and tiredness, restlessness and confusion, muscle pains, nausea, and vomiting.

If you suspect an overdose, seek medical attention immediately.

Generic name:

IBUPROFEN

See Motrin, page 795.

Brand name:

ILETIN

See Insulin, page 610.

Brand name:

ILOSONE

See Erythromycin, Oral, page 461.

Brand name:

IMDUR

Pronounced: IM-duhr
Generic name: Isosorbide mononitrate
Other brand names: Ismo, Monoket

Why is this drug prescribed?

Imdur is prescribed to prevent angina pectoris (crushing chest pain that results when partially clogged arteries restrict the flow of needed oxygen-rich blood to the heart muscle). This medication does not relieve angina attacks already underway.

Most important fact about this drug
Imdur may cause severe low blood pressure (possibly marked by dizziness or fainting), especially when you are standing or if you sit up quickly. People taking blood pressure medication or those who have low blood pressure should use Imdur with caution.

How should you take this medication?
To maintain this drug's protective effect, it is important that you take it exactly as prescribed.

Take Imdur once a day, when you get up in the morning. It may be taken with or without food. Imdur tablets should not be crushed or chewed. Swallow them with half a glass of liquid.

Do not switch to another brand of isosorbide mononitrate without consulting your doctor or pharmacist.

■ *If you miss a dose...*
Take it as soon as you remember. If it is almost time for your next dose, skip the one you missed and go back to your regular schedule. Do not take 2 doses at the same time.

■ *Storage instructions...*
Store at room temperature.

What side effects may occur?
Side effects cannot be anticipated. If any develop or change in intensity, tell your doctor as soon as possible. Only your doctor can determine if it is safe for you to continue taking Imdur.

Headache is the most common side effect; usually, aspirin or acetaminophen will relieve the pain. The headaches associated with Imdur usually subside within a short time after treatment with the drug begins. Check with your doctor if your headaches persist or become more intense. Another common side effect is dizziness.

■ *Less common or rare side effects may include:*
Abdominal pain, abnormal hair texture, abnormal heart sounds, abnormal or terrifying dreams, abnormal vision, acne, anemia, anxiety, back pain, bacterial infection, black stools, breast pain, bronchitis, chest pain,

confusion, constipation, coughing, decreased sex drive, depression, diarrhea, difficult or labored breathing, difficulty concentrating, diminished sense of touch, drooping eyelid, dry mouth, earache, excessive amount of urine, fatigue, fever, fluid retention and swelling, flu-like symptoms, flushing, frozen shoulder, gas, general feeling of illness, heart attack, heart failure, heart murmur, hemorrhoids, high blood pressure, hot flashes, impotence, inability to sleep, increased mucus from the lungs, increased sweating, indigestion, inflamed eyes, inflammation of the stomach, inflammation of the tongue, inflammation of the vagina, intolerance of light, irregular heartbeat, itching, joint pain, kidney stones, leg ulcer, loose stools, low blood pressure, migraine, muscle and/or bone pain, muscle weakness, nasal or sinus inflammation, nausea, nervousness, palpitations (throbbing or fluttering heartbeat), paralysis, perforated eardrum, pneumonia, purple or red spots on the skin, rapid heartbeat, rash, ringing in the ears, severe pain in calf muscles during walking, sleepiness, slow heartbeat, sore throat, stomach ulcer with or without bleeding, stuffy nose, tingling or pins and needles, tremor, twisted neck, urinary tract infection, varicose veins, vertigo, viral infection, vomiting, weakness, wheezing, worsening of angina pectoris, yeast infection

Why should this drug not be prescribed?

You should not take Imdur if you have had a previous allergic reaction to it or to other heart medications containing nitrates or nitrites. Your doctor will probably not prescribe Imdur if you have had a recent heart attack or congestive heart failure. If the doctor decides that this medication is essential, your heart function and blood pressure will need to be closely monitored to avoid potential side effects.

Special warnings about this medication

Do not abruptly stop taking this medication. Follow your doctor's plan for a gradual withdrawal.

Since Imdur can cause dizziness, you should be careful while driving, operating machinery, or performing other tasks that demand concentration.

Nitrate-type medications such as Imdur may aggravate angina caused by certain heart conditions.

Do not try to avoid a headache by changing your dose. If your headache stops, it may mean the drug has lost its effectiveness.

Be sure to tell your doctor about any medical conditions you have before starting Imdur therapy.

Possible food and drug interactions
when taking this medication
If Imdur is taken with certain other drugs, the effects of either could be increased, decreased, or altered. Extreme low blood pressure with dizziness and fainting upon standing up may occur if Imdur is taken with calcium-blocking blood pressure medications such as Calan, Cardizem, and Procardia.

Alcohol may interact with Imdur and cause a swift decrease in blood pressure, possibly resulting in light-headedness.

Special information
if you are pregnant or breastfeeding
The effects of Imdur during pregnancy have not been adequately studied. If you are pregnant or plan to become pregnant, tell your doctor immediately. Imdur should be used during pregnancy only if it is clearly needed.

It is not known whether Imdur appears in breast milk. If the drug is essential to your health, your doctor may advise you to stop nursing until your treatment is finished.

Recommended dosage

ADULTS

The usual starting dose is 30 milligrams (taken as a single 30-milligram tablet or as one-half of a 60-milligram tablet) or 60 milligrams once a day.

After several days, your doctor may increase the dose to 120 milligrams (a single 120-milligram tablet or two 60-milligram tablets) once daily.

Your doctor may further adjust the dosage according to your response to the medication.

CHILDREN

Safety and effectiveness of Imdur in children have not been established.

Overdosage
Any medication taken in excess can have serious consequences. Severe overdosage of Imdur can be fatal. If you suspect an overdose, seek medical help immediately.

■ *Symptoms of Imdur overdose may include:*
Air hunger, bloody diarrhea, coma, confusion, difficulty breathing, fainting, fever, nausea, palpitations, paralysis, pressure in the head, profuse sweating, seizures, skin either cold and clammy or flushed, slow heartbeat, throbbing headache, vertigo, visual disturbances, vomiting

Generic name:

IMIPRAMINE

See Tofranil, page 1249.

Brand name:

IMITREX

Pronounced: IM-i-trex
Generic name: Sumatriptan succinate

Why is this drug prescribed?
Imitrex is prescribed for the treatment of a migraine attack with or without the presence of an aura (visual disturbances, usually sensations of halos or flickering lights, which precede an attack). The injectable form is also used to relieve cluster headache attacks. (Cluster headaches come on in waves, then disappear for long periods of time. They are limited to one side of the head, and occur mainly in men.)

Imitrex cuts headaches short. It will not reduce the number of attacks you experience.

Most important fact about this drug
Imitrex should be used only to treat an acute, classic migraine attack or a cluster headache. It should not be used for certain unusual types of migraine.

How should you take this medication?
Imitrex should be taken as soon as your symptoms appear, but may be used at any time during an attack.

Imitrex Injection is administered just below the skin with an autoinjector (self-injection device). Choose a site where the skin is thick enough to take the full length of the needle (1/4 inch). Avoid injecting Imitrex into a muscle or a vein. Your doctor should instruct you on how to use the autoinjector and how to dispose of the empty syringes. You should also read the instruction pamphlet that comes with the medication.

You can take a second injection if your headache returns; however, never take more than 2 injections within 24 hours, and be sure to wait 1 hour between doses.

Imitrex tablets should be swallowed whole, with liquid.

If you have had no relief 2 hours after taking Imitrex Tablets, you may take a second dose of up to 100 milligrams, if your doctor advises it. If the headache returns, you may take additional doses at intervals of at least 2 hours. You should not take more than 300 milligrams in one day. If your headache returns after you have had an Imitrex Injection, you may take single Imitrex Tablets, at intervals of at least 2 hours, up to a maximum of 200 milligrams in a day.

■ *If you miss a dose...*
Imitrex is *not* for regular use. Take it only during an attack.

■ *Storage instructions...*
Store Imitrex away from heat and light, at room temperature, in the case provided. If your medication has expired (the expiration date is printed on the treatment pack), throw it away as instructed, but keep the autoinjector. If your doctor decides to stop your treatment, do not keep any leftover medicine unless your doctor tells you to. Throw away your medicine as instructed.

What side effects may occur?
Side effects cannot be anticipated. If any develop or change in intensity, inform your doctor as soon as possible. Only your doctor can determine if it is safe for you to continue taking Imitrex.

■ *More common side effects may include:*
Burning sensation, dizziness or vertigo, feeling of heaviness, feeling of tightness, flushing, mouth and tongue discomfort, muscle weakness, neck pain and stiffness, numbness, pressure sensation, redness at the site of injection, sore throat, tingling, warm/hot sensation

■ *Less common or rare side effects may include:*
Abdominal discomfort, agitation, allergic reactions (severe), anxiety, changes in heart rhythm, cold sensation, difficult or painful urination, difficulty swallowing, drowsiness/calmness, eye irritation, fatigue, feeling strange, general feeling of illness, headache, hives, itching, jaw discomfort, muscle cramps, muscle pain or tenderness, pressure in chest, rapid and throbbing heartbeat, rash, rise in blood pressure (temporary), shortness of breath, sinus or nasal discomfort, sweating, tight feeling in head, tightness in chest, vision changes

In addition to the above side effects, people taking Imitrex for cluster headache may experience nausea, a "pins and needles" sensation, vomiting, or wheezing.

Why should this drug not be prescribed?

If you are sensitive to or have had an allergic reaction to sumatriptan you should not use this drug again. Make sure your doctor is aware of any drug reactions you have experienced.

Imitrex should not be used if you have certain types of heart or blood vessel disease, including angina (crushing chest pain) or a history of heart attack, if you suffer from uncontrolled high blood pressure, or within 24 hours of taking a medication containing ergotamine (often used in other migraine medications) or drugs such as D.H.E. 45 Injection and Sansert.

Special warnings about this medication

Your doctor may administer the first dose of Imitrex in the office. Although extremely rare, serious heart problems have occurred in people with heart disease when receiving this medication, and you should be carefully observed after the initial dose to make sure this medication is safe for you to use. Tell your doctor if you have high blood pressure, high cholesterol, or diabetes, if you smoke, if there is heart disease in your family, or if you have gone through menopause.

Be careful not to inject Imitrex into a vein. This can cause a serious heart irregularity.

If your fingers turn pale, then blue, after a dose of Imitrex, you may have a circulatory problem such as hardening of the arteries. Be sure to let your doctor know.

This medication should not be used for other types of migraine headache. If the first dose does not relieve your symptoms, your doctor will re-evaluate you; you may not have migraine or cluster headache.

If your headache does not feel like any you have been experiencing, do not take Imitrex.

Use Imitrex cautiously if you have liver or kidney disease. Also, if you have any trouble with your eyes, tell your doctor.

Imitrex has not been tested in children or adults over age 65.

Although very rare, severe and even fatal allergic reactions have occurred in people taking Imitrex. Such reactions are more likely in people who have several allergies. In rare cases, people have suffered seizures after taking Imitrex.

Possible food and drug interactions
while taking this medication

If Imitrex is taken with certain other drugs, the effects of either may be increased, decreased, or altered. It is important to check with your doctor before combining Imitrex with the following:

Drugs classified as MAO inhibitors, including the antidepressants Nardil and Parnate
Ergot-containing drugs such as Cafergot and Ergostat
Fluoxetine (Prozac)
Fluvoxamine (Luvox)
Paroxetine (Paxil)
Sertraline (Zoloft)

Special information
if you are pregnant or breastfeeding

The effects of Imitrex during pregnancy have not been adequately studied. If you are pregnant or plan to become pregnant, inform your doctor immediately. Imitrex does appear in breast milk and could affect a nursing infant. If this medication is essential to your health, your doctor may advise you to discontinue breastfeeding until your treatment with Imitrex is finished.

Recommended dosage

IMITREX INJECTION

The maximum single recommended adult dose is 6 milligrams injected under the skin.

The maximum recommended dose that may be given within 24 hours is two 6 milligram injections taken at least 1 hour apart.

IMITREX TABLETS

The usual adult dose is one 25-milligram tablet taken with water or other liquid. The most you should take at one time is 100 milligrams, and the most you should take in 1 day is 300 milligrams. Doses should be spaced at least 2 hours apart.

If you have liver disease, you should not take more than 50 milligrams of Imitrex Tablets at one time.

Overdosage

Any medication taken in excess can have serious consequences. If you suspect an overdose, seek medical attention immediately.

- *Symptoms of Imitrex overdose may include:*
  Bluish tinge to the skin, convulsions, dilated pupils, inactivity, lack of
  coordination, paralysis, redness in the arms and legs, skin changes at the
  site of injection, slow breathing, sluggishness, tremor

Brand name:

IMODIUM

Pronounced: i-MOH-dee-um
Generic name: Loperamide hydrochloride

Why is this drug prescribed?
Imodium is prescribed for the control and relief of symptoms of diarrhea not
known to be caused by a specific germ, and for diarrhea associated with
long-term inflammatory bowel disease. This drug is also prescribed for
reducing the volume of discharge from an ileostomy (a surgical opening of
the small intestine onto the abdominal wall for purposes of elimination).

Some doctors also prescribe Imodium, along with antibiotics such as Septra
or Bactrim, to treat traveler's diarrhea.

Most important fact about this drug
If your diarrhea does not stop after a couple of days, if you have blood in your
stools, or a fever develops, notify your doctor immediately.

How should you take this medication?
Do not take more than the prescribed dose of this medication.

Imodium may cause dryness of the mouth. Sucking on a hard candy or
chewing gum can help relieve the problem.

- *If you miss a dose...*
  If you are taking Imodium on a regular schedule for chronic diarrhea and
  miss a dose, take it as soon as you remember then take the remaining
  doses for that day at evenly spaced intervals. However, if you are not
  having diarrhea, skip the missed dose completely.

- *Storage instructions...*
  Imodium should be stored at room temperature.

What side effects may occur?
Side effects reported from the use of Imodium are difficult to distinguish from
symptoms associated with diarrhea. Those reported, however, were more
commonly observed during the treatment of long-lasting diarrhea.

■ *Side effects may include:*
Abdominal distention, abdominal pain or discomfort, allergic reactions, including skin rash, constipation, dizziness, drowsiness, dry mouth, nausea and vomiting, tiredness

Why should this drug not be prescribed?
If you are sensitive to or have ever had an allergic reaction to Imodium, you should not take this medication. Make sure that your doctor is aware of any drug reactions that you have experienced.

Unless you are directed to do so by your doctor, do not take Imodium if constipation must be avoided.

Special warnings about this medication
Imodium may cause drowsiness and/or dizziness. You should exercise extra caution while driving or performing tasks requiring mental alertness.

Imodium is not good for all types of diarrhea. It is not prescribed for acute dysentery (an inflammation of the intestines characterized by abdominal pain, watery—sometimes bloody—stools, and fever, caused by bacteria, viruses, or parasites).

Dehydration can be a problem when you have diarrhea. It is important that you drink plenty of fluids while taking Imodium.

Use special caution when giving Imodium to a young child. Response to the drug can be unpredictable.

If you have a liver problem, your doctor should closely watch for signs of central nervous system reactions, such as drowsiness or convulsions.

If you have colitis and develop abdominal distention, constipation or an intestinal blockage, notify your doctor immediately. The use of Imodium should be discontinued.

Possible food and drug interactions
when taking this medication
There are no reported food or drug interactions.

Special information
if you are pregnant or breastfeeding
The effects of Imodium during pregnancy have not been adequately studied. If you are pregnant or plan to become pregnant, notify your doctor. It is not known whether Imodium appears in breast milk. If this medication is

essential to your health, your doctor may advise you to discontinue breastfeeding until your treatment is finished.

Recommended dosage

ADULTS

Severe Diarrhea
The recommended starting dosage is 2 capsules (4 milligrams) followed by 1 capsule (2 milligrams) after each unformed stool. Daily dosage should not exceed 8 capsules (16 milligrams). Improvement should be observed within 48 hours.

Long-Lasting or Frequently Recurring Diarrhea
The recommended starting dosage is 2 capsules (4 milligrams) followed by 1 capsule (2 milligrams) after each unformed stool until diarrhea is controlled, after which the dosage of Imodium should be reduced by your doctor to meet your individual needs. When the ideal daily dosage has been established, this amount may then be given as a single dose or in divided doses. The average maintenance dosage is 2 to 4 capsules per day, not to exceed 8 capsules. If improvement is not observed after treatment with 8 capsules (16 milligrams) per day for at least 10 days, notify your doctor.

CHILDREN

Imodium is not recommended in children under 2 years of age.

Severe Diarrhea
In children 2 to 5 years of age or 44 pounds or less, the nonprescription liquid medication (Imodium A-D) should be used. For children between the ages of 6 and 12, either Imodium capsules (2 milligrams per capsule) or Imodium A-D Liquid (1 milligram per teaspoonful) may be used.

For children 2 to 12 years of age, the following schedule for capsules or liquid will usually fulfill starting dosage requirements:

   2 to 5 years (28-44 pounds):
      1 milligram (1 teaspoonful of Imodium A-D liquid) taken 3 times a
      day (3 milligrams daily)

   6 to 8 years (45-66 pounds):
      2 milligrams taken 2 times a day (4 milligrams daily)

   8 to 12 years (67 pounds and over):
      2 milligrams taken 3 times a day (6 milligrams daily)

After the first day of treatment, additional Imodium doses (1 milligram per 22 pounds of body weight) should be given only after a loose stool. The total daily dosage should not exceed the recommended dosages for the first day.

Long-Lasting or Frequently Recurring Diarrhea
A dosage has not been established for children with long-lasting or frequently recurring diarrhea.

Overdosage
Any medication taken in excess can have serious consequences. If you suspect an Imodium overdose, seek medical attention immediately.

■ *Symptoms of an Imodium overdose may include:*
Constipation, drowsiness, lethargy and depression, nausea

Generic name:

INDAPAMIDE

See Lozol, page 711.

Brand name:

INDERAL

Pronounced: IN-der-al
Generic name: Propranolol hydrochloride
Other brand name: Inderal LA

Why is this drug prescribed?
Inderal, a type of medication known as a beta blocker, is used in the treatment of high blood pressure, angina pectoris (chest pain, usually caused by lack of oxygen to the heart due to clogged arteries), changes in heart rhythm, prevention of migraine headache, hereditary tremors, hypertrophic subaortic stenosis (a condition related to exertional angina), and tumors of the adrenal gland. It is also used to reduce the risk of death from recurring heart attack.

When used for the treatment of high blood pressure, it is effective alone or combined with other high blood pressure medications, particularly thiazide-type diuretics. Beta blockers decrease the force and rate of heart contractions, reducing the heart's demand for oxygen and lowering blood pressure.

Most important fact about this drug

If you have high blood pressure, you must take Inderal regularly for it to be effective. Since blood pressure declines gradually, it may be several weeks before you get the full benefit of Inderal; and you must continue taking it even if you are feeling well. Inderal does not cure high blood pressure; it merely keeps it under control.

How should you take this medication?

Inderal works best when taken before meals. Take it exactly as prescribed, even if your symptoms have disappeared.

Try not to miss any doses. If this medication is not taken regularly, your condition may worsen.

■ *If you miss a dose...*
Take it as soon as you remember. If it is within 8 hours of your next scheduled dose, skip the one you missed and go back to your regular schedule. Never take 2 doses at the same time.

■ *Storage instructions...*
Store at room temperature in a tightly closed, light-resistant container. Protect from freezing or excessive heat.

What side effects may occur?

Side effects cannot be anticipated. If any develop or change in intensity, inform your doctor as soon as possible. Only your doctor can determine if it is safe for you to continue taking Inderal.

■ *Side effects may include:*
Abdominal cramps, colitis, congestive heart failure, constipation, decreased sexual ability, depression, diarrhea, difficulty breathing, disorientation, dry eyes, fever with sore throat, hair loss, hallucinations, headache, light-headedness, low blood pressure, lupus erythematosus (a disease of the connective tissue), nausea, rash, reddish or purplish spots on the skin, short-term memory loss, slow heartbeat, tingling, prickling in hands, tiredness, trouble sleeping, upset stomach, visual changes, vivid dreams, vomiting, weakness, worsening of certain heartbeat irregularities

Why should this drug not be prescribed?

If you have inadequate blood supply to the circulatory system (cardiogenic shock), certain types of irregular heartbeat, a slow heartbeat, bronchial asthma, or severe congestive heart failure, you should not take this medication.

Special warnings about this medication

If you have a history of congestive heart failure, your doctor will prescribe Inderal cautiously.

Inderal should not be stopped suddenly. This can cause increased chest pain and heart attack. Dosage should be gradually reduced.

If you suffer from asthma or other bronchial conditions, coronary artery disease, or kidney or liver disease, this medication should be used with caution.

Ask your doctor if you should check your pulse while taking Inderal. This medication can cause your heartbeat to become too slow.

This medication may mask the symptoms of low blood sugar or alter blood sugar levels. If you are diabetic, discuss this with your doctor.

Notify your doctor or dentist that you are taking Inderal if you have a medical emergency, and before you have surgery or dental treatment.

Possible food and drug interactions
when taking this medication

If Inderal is taken with certain other drugs, the effects of either could be increased, decreased, or altered. It is especially important to check with your doctor before combining Inderal with the following:

Alcohol
Aluminum hydroxide gel (Amphojel)
Antipyrine (Auralgan)
Calcium-blocking blood pressure drugs such as Cardizem, Procardia, and Calan
Certain high blood pressure medications such as Diupres and Ser-Ap-Es
Chlorpromazine (Thorazine)
Cimetidine (Tagamet)
Epinephrine (EpiPen)
Haloperidol (Haldol)
Insulin
Lidocaine (Xylocaine)
Nonsteroidal anti-inflammatory drugs such as Motrin and Naprosyn
Oral diabetes drugs such as Micronase
Phenobarbitone
Phenytoin (Dilantin)
Rifampin (Rifadin)
Theophylline (Theo-Dur and others)
Thyroid medications such as Synthroid

Special information
if you are pregnant or breastfeeding

The effects of Inderal during pregnancy have not been adequately studied. If you are pregnant or plan to become pregnant, inform your doctor immediately. Inderal appears in breast milk and could affect a nursing infant. If this medication is essential to your health, your doctor may advise you to discontinue breastfeeding until your treatment with this medication is finished.

Recommended dosage

ADULTS

All dosages of Inderal, for any problem, must be tailored to the individual. Your doctor will determine when and how often you should take this drug. Remember to take it exactly as directed.

Hypertension

The usual starting dose is 40 milligrams 2 times a day. This dose may be in combination with a diuretic. Dosages are gradually increased to between 120 milligrams and 240 milligrams per day for maintenance. In some cases, a dose of 640 milligrams per day may be needed. Depending on the individual, maximum effect of this drug may not be reached for a few days or even several weeks. Some people may do better taking this medication 3 times a day.

Angina Pectoris

The usual daily dosage is 80 milligrams to 320 milligrams, divided into 2, 3, or 4 smaller doses. When your treatment is being discontinued, your doctor will reduce the dosage gradually over a period of several weeks.

Irregular Heartbeat

The usual dose is 10 milligrams to 30 milligrams 3 or 4 times a day, before meals and at bedtime.

Heart Attack

The usual daily dosage is 180 milligrams to 240 milligrams divided into smaller doses. The usual maximum dose is 240 milligrams, although your doctor may increase the dose when treating heart attack with angina or high blood pressure.

Migraine
The usual starting dosage is 80 milligrams per day divided into smaller doses. Dosages can be increased gradually to between 160 milligrams and 240 milligrams per day. If this dose does not relieve your symptoms in 4 to 6 weeks, your doctor will slowly take you off the drug.

Tremors
The usual starting dose is 40 milligrams, 2 times per day. Symptoms will usually be relieved with a dose of 120 milligrams per day; however, on occasion, dosages of 240 milligrams to 320 milligrams per day may be necessary.

Hypertrophic Subaortic Stenosis
The usual dose is 20 milligrams to 40 milligrams, 3 to 4 times a day, before meals and at bedtime.

Before Adrenal Gland Surgery
The usual dose is 60 milligrams a day divided into smaller doses for 3 days before surgery in combination with an alpha-blocker drug.

Inderal may also be taken by people with inoperable tumors in doses of 30 milligrams a day, divided into smaller doses.

CHILDREN

Inderal will be carefully individualized for use in children and is used only for high blood pressure. Doses in children are calculated by body weight, and range from 2 milligrams to 4 milligrams per 2.2 pounds daily, divided into 2 equal doses. The maximum dose is 16 milligrams per 2.2 pounds per day.

If treatment is stopped, this drug must be gradually reduced over a 7- to 14-day period.

Inderal is also available in a sustained-release formulation, called Inderal LA, for once-a-day dosing.

Overdosage
No specific information on Inderal overdosage is available; however, overdose symptoms with other beta blockers include:

Extremely slow heartbeat, irregular heartbeat, low blood pressure, severe congestive heart failure, seizures, wheezing

Any medication taken in excess can have serious consequences. If you suspect an overdose, seek medical attention immediately.

Brand name:

INDERIDE

Pronounced: IN-deh-ride
Generic ingredients: Inderal (Propranolol hydrochloride),
  Hydrochlorothiazide
Other brand name: Inderide LA

Why is this drug prescribed?

Inderide is used in the treatment of high blood pressure. It combines a beta blocker (Inderal) with a thiazide diuretic (hydrochlorothiazide). Beta blockers decrease the force and rate of heart contractions, thus lowering blood pressure. Diuretics help your body produce and eliminate more urine, which also helps lower blood pressure.

Most important fact about this drug

You must take Inderide regularly for it to be effective. Since blood pressure declines gradually, it may be several weeks before you get the full benefit of Inderide; and you must continue taking it even if you are feeling well. Inderide does not cure high blood pressure; it merely keeps it under control.

How should you take this medication?

Take Inderide exactly as prescribed, even if your symptoms have disappeared.

Try not to miss any doses. If this medication is not taken regularly, your condition may worsen.

- *If you miss a dose...*
  Take it as soon as you remember. If the next dose is within 8 hours, skip the one you missed and go back to your regular schedule. Do not take 2 doses at the same time.

- *Storage instructions...*
  Store at room temperature in a tightly closed container, protected from moisture, freezing, and excessive heat.

What side effects may occur?

Side effects cannot be anticipated. If any develop or change in intensity, inform your doctor as soon as possible. Only your doctor can determine if it is safe for you to continue taking Inderide.

- *Side effects may include:*
  Allergic reactions (including fever, rash, aching and sore throat), anemia,

blood disorders, blurred vision, constipation, congestive heart failure, cramps, decreased mental clarity, depression, diarrhea, difficulty breathing, difficulty sleeping, disorientation, dizziness, dizziness when standing, dry eyes, emotional changeability, exhaustion, fatigue, hair loss, hallucinations, headache, high blood sugar, hives, increased skin sensitivity to sunlight, inflammation of the large intestine or the pancreas, inflammation of the salivary glands, light-headedness, loss of appetite, low blood pressure, lupus erythematosus (a connective tissue disease), male impotence, muscle spasms, nausea, restlessness, short-term memory loss, slow heartbeat, stomach irritation, sugar in the urine, tingling or pins and needles, upset stomach, vertigo, visual disturbances, vivid dreams, vomiting, weakness, wheezing, yellow eyes and skin

Why should this drug not be prescribed?

If you have inadequate blood supply to the circulatory system (cardiogenic shock), certain types of irregular heartbeat, slow heartbeat, bronchial asthma, or congestive heart failure, you should not take this medication.

Do not take Inderide if you are unable to urinate or if you are sensitive to or have ever had an allergic reaction to any of its ingredients or to sulfa drugs.

Special warnings about this medication

Inderide should not be stopped suddenly. This can cause chest pain and even heart attack. Dosage should be gradually reduced.

Diuretics can cause your body to lose too much potassium. Signs of an excessively low potassium level include muscle weakness and rapid or irregular heartbeat. To boost your potassium level, your doctor may recommend eating potassium-rich foods or taking a potassium supplement.

If you suffer from asthma, seasonal allergies or other bronchial conditions, or kidney or liver disease, your doctor will prescribe this medication with caution.

This medication may mask the symptoms of low blood sugar or alter blood sugar levels. If you are diabetic, discuss this with your doctor.

If you have a history of allergies or bronchial asthma, you are more likely to have an allergic reaction to Inderide.

Inderide may interfere with the screening test for glaucoma (excessive pressure in the eyes) and pressure within the eyes may increase when the medication is stopped.

Notify your doctor or dentist that you are taking Inderide if you have a medical emergency, and before you have surgery or dental treatment.

Possible food and drug interactions when taking this medication

If Inderide is taken with certain other drugs, the effects of either could be increased, decreased, or altered. It is especially important to check with your doctor before combining Inderide with the following:

ACTH (adrenocorticotropic hormone)
Alcohol
Aluminum hydroxide gel (Amphojel)
Antipyrine (Auralgan)
Calcium-blocking blood pressure drugs such as Calan, Cardizem, and Procardia XL
Certain blood pressure medications such as Diupres and Ser-Ap-Es
Chlorpromazine (Thorazine)
Cimetidine (Tagamet)
Corticosteroids such as prednisone
Digitalis (Lanoxin)
Epinephrine (EpiPen)
Haloperidol (Haldol)
Insulin
Lidocaine (Xylocaine)
Nonsteroidal anti-inflammatory drugs such as Motrin
Norepinephrine (Levophed)
Oral diabetes drugs such as Micronase
Phenobarbitone
Phenytoin (Dilantin)
Rifampin (Rifadin)
Theophylline (Theo-Dur)
Thyroid medications such as Synthroid

Special information if you are pregnant or breastfeeding

The effects of Inderide during pregnancy have not been adequately studied. If you are pregnant or plan to become pregnant, inform your doctor immediately. Inderide appears in breast milk and could affect a nursing infant. If Inderide is essential to your health, your doctor may advise you to discontinue breastfeeding until your treatment is finished.

Recommended dosage

ADULTS

Your doctor will tailor your dosage according to your response to Inderide's main ingredients.

The usual dose is one Inderide tablet, 2 times per day.

Your doctor may use this medication in combination with other high blood pressure drugs to achieve the desired effect.

This drug is also available in a sustained-release formulation, called Inderide LA, for once-a-day dosing.

CHILDREN

The safety and effectiveness of this drug in children have not been established.

OLDER ADULTS

Your doctor will adjust your dosage with extra caution.

Overdosage

Any medication taken in excess can have severe consequences. If you suspect an overdose, seek medical attention immediately.

- *Symptoms of Inderide overdose may include:*
    Coma, extremely slow heartbeat, heart failure, increased urination, irritation and overactivity of the stomach and intestines, low blood pressure, sluggishness, stupor, wheezing

Generic name:

INDINAVIR

See Crixivan, page 289.

Brand name:

INDOCIN

Pronounced: IN-doh-sin
Generic name: Indomethacin

Why is this drug prescribed?
Indocin, a nonsteroidal anti-inflammatory drug, is used to relieve the inflammation, swelling, stiffness and joint pain associated with moderate or severe rheumatoid arthritis and osteoarthritis (the most common form of

arthritis), and ankylosing spondylitis (arthritis of the spine). It is also used to treat bursitis, tendinitis (acute painful shoulder), acute gouty arthritis, and other kinds of pain.

Most important fact about this drug
You should have frequent checkups with your doctor if you take Indocin regularly. Ulcers or internal bleeding can occur without warning.

How should you take this medication?
Indocin should be taken with food or an antacid, and with a full glass of water. Never take on an empty stomach.

Take this medication exactly as prescribed by your doctor.

If you are using Indocin for arthritis, it should be taken regularly.

If you are taking the liquid form of this medicine, shake the bottle well before each use.

Indocin SR capsules should be swallowed whole, not crushed or broken.

Do not lie down for about 20 to 30 minutes after taking Indocin. This helps prevent irritation that could lead to trouble in swallowing.

If you are using the suppository form of this medicine:

1. If the suppository is too soft to insert, hold it under cool water or chill it before removing the wrapper
2. Remove the foil wrapper and moisten your rectal area with cool tap water.
3. Lie down on your side and use your finger to push the suppository well up into the rectum. Hold your buttocks together for a few seconds.
4. Indocin suppositories should be kept inside the rectum for at least 1 hour so that all of the medicine can be absorbed by your body.

■ *If you miss a dose...*
   Take the forgotten dose as soon as you remember. If it is time for your next dose, skip the one you missed and return to your regular schedule. Never take a double dose.

■ *Storage instructions...*
   The liquid and suppository forms of Indocin may be stored at room temperature. Keep both forms from extreme heat, and protect the liquid from freezing.

What side effects may occur?
Side effects cannot be anticipated. If any develop or change in intensity inform your doctor as soon as possible. Only your doctor can determine if it is safe for you to continue taking Indocin.

■ *More common side effects may include:*
Abdominal pain, constipation, depression, diarrhea, dizziness, fatigue, headache, heartburn, indigestion, nausea, ringing in the ears, sleepiness or excessive drowsiness, stomach pain, stomach upset, vertigo, vomiting

■ *Less common or rare side effects may include:*
Anemia, anxiety, asthma, behavior disturbances, bloating, blurred vision, breast changes, changes in heart rate, chest pain, coma, congestive heart failure, convulsions, decrease in white blood cells, fever, fluid in lungs, fluid retention, flushing, gas, hair loss, hepatitis, high or low blood pressure, hives, itching, increase in blood sugar, insomnia, kidney failure, labored breathing, light-headedness, loss of appetite, mental confusion, muscle weakness, nosebleed, peptic ulcer, problems in hearing, rash, rectal bleeding, Stevens-Johnson syndrome (skin peeling), stomach or intestinal bleeding, sweating, twitching, unusual redness of skin, vaginal bleeding, weight gain, worsening of epilepsy, yellow eyes and skin

Why should this drug not be prescribed?
If you are sensitive to or have ever had an allergic reaction to Indocin, aspirin, or similar drugs, or if you have had asthma attacks caused by aspirin or other drugs of this type, you should not take this medication. Make sure that your doctor is aware of any drug reactions that you have experienced.

Do not use Indocin suppositories if you have a history of rectal inflammation or recent rectal bleeding.

Special warnings about this medication
Indocin prolongs bleeding time. If you are taking blood-thinning medication, this drug should be taken with caution.

Your doctor should prescribe the lowest possible effective dose. The incidence of side effects increases as dosage increases.

Peptic ulcers and bleeding can occur without warning.

This drug should be used with caution if you have kidney or liver disease, and it can cause liver inflammation in some people.

Do not take aspirin or any other anti-inflammatory medications while taking Indocin, unless your doctor tells you to do so.

If you have heart disease or high blood pressure, this drug can increase water retention.

This drug can mask the symptoms of an existing infection.

Indocin may cause you to become drowsy or less alert; therefore, driving or operating dangerous machinery or participating in any hazardous activity that requires full mental alertness is not recommended.

Possible food and drug interactions
when taking this medication
If Indocin is taken with certain other drugs, the effects of either could be increased, decreased or altered. It is especially important to check with your doctor before combining Indocin with the following:

Aspirin
Beta-blockers such as the blood pressure medications Tenormin and
    Inderal
Blood-thinning medicines such as Coumadin
Captopril (Capoten)
Cyclosporine (Sandimmune)
Diflunisal (Dolobid)
Digoxin (Lanoxin)
Lithium (Eskalith)
Loop diuretics (Lasix)
Other nonsteroidal anti-inflammatory drugs such as Advil, Aleve, and
    Motrin
Potassium-sparing water pills such as Aldactone
Probenecid (Benemid, ColBENEMID)
The anticancer drug methotrexate
Thiazide-type water pills such as Diuril
Triamterene (Dyazide)

Special information
if you are pregnant or breastfeeding
The effects of Indocin during pregnancy have not been adequately studied. If you are pregnant or plan to become pregnant inform your doctor immediately. Indocin appears in breast milk and could affect a nursing infant. If this medication is essential to your health, your doctor may advise you to discontinue breastfeeding until your treatment with this medication is finished.

Recommended dosage

ADULTS

This medication is available in liquid, capsule, and suppository form. The following dosages are for the capsule form. If you prefer the liquid form, ask your doctor to make the proper substitution. Do not try to convert the medication or dosage yourself.

Moderate to Severe Rheumatoid Arthritis, Osteoarthritis, Ankylosing Spondylitis

The usual dose is 25 milligrams 2 or 3 times a day, increasing to a total daily dose of 150 to 200 milligrams. Your doctor should monitor you carefully for side effects when you are taking this drug.

Your doctor may prescribe a single daily 75-milligram capsule of Indocin SR in place of regular Indocin.

Bursitis or Tendinitis

The usual dose is 75 to 150 milligrams daily divided into 3 to 4 small doses for 1 to 2 weeks, until symptoms disappear.

Acute Gouty Arthritis

The usual dose is 50 milligrams 3 times a day until pain is reduced to a tolerable level (usually 3 to 5 days). Your doctor will advise you when to stop taking this drug for this condition. Keep him informed of its effects on your symptoms.

CHILDREN

The safety and effectiveness of Indocin have not been established in children under 14 years of age. However, your doctor may decide that the benefits of this medication outweigh any potential risks.

OLDER ADULTS

Your doctor will adjust the dosage as needed.

Overdosage

Any medication taken in excess can cause symptoms of overdose. If you suspect an overdose seek medical attention immediately.

■ *The symptoms of Indocin overdose may include:*
Convulsions, disorientation, dizziness, intense headache, lethargy, mental confusion, nausea, numbness, tingling or pins and needles, vomiting

Generic name:

INDOMETHACIN

See Indocin, page 605.

Generic name:

INSULIN

Pronounced: IN-suh-lin
Available formulations:
Insulin, Human:
  Humulin
Insulin, Human Isophane Suspension:
  Humulin N
Insulin, Human NPH:
  Novolin N
Insulin, Human Regular:
  Novolin R
  Humulin BR & R
  Velosulin Human
Insulin, Human Regular and Human NPH mixture:
  Humulin 70/30
  Novolin 70/30
Insulin, Human, Zinc Suspension:
  Humulin L & U
  Novolin L
Insulin, NPH:
  NPH Iletin I (also II, Beef; II, Pork)
  NPH Insulin
Insulin, Zinc Crystals:
  NPH Iletin I
Insulin, Regular:
  Iletin I Regular (also II, Beef; II, Pork)
  Regular Insulin
  Velosulin
Insulin, Zinc Suspension:
  Iletin I, Lente
  Protamine, Zinc and Iletin
  Iletin I, Semilente
  Iletin I
  Lente Insulin
  Ultralente Insulin

Why is this drug prescribed?
Insulin is prescribed for diabetes mellitus when this condition does not improve with oral medications or by modifying your diet. Insulin is a hormone produced by the pancreas, a large gland that lies near the stomach. This hormone is necessary for the body's correct use of food, especially sugar. Insulin apparently works by helping sugar penetrate the cell wall, where it is then utilized by the cell. In people with diabetes, the body either does not make enough insulin, or the insulin that is produced cannot be used properly.

There are actually two forms of diabetes: Type I insulin-dependent and Type II non-insulin-dependent. Type I usually requires insulin injection for life, while Type II diabetes can usually be treated by dietary changes and/or oral antidiabetic medications such as Diabinese and Glucotrol. Occasionally, Type II diabetics must take insulin injections on a temporary basis, especially during stressful periods or times of illness.

The various insulin brands above differ in several ways: in the source (animal, human, or genetically engineered), in the time requirements for the insulin to take effect, and in the length of time the insulin remains working.

Regular insulin is manufactured from beef and pork pancreas, begins working within 30 to 60 minutes, and lasts for 6 to 8 hours. Variations of insulin have been developed to satisfy the needs of individual patients. For example, zinc suspension insulin is an intermediate-acting insulin that starts working within 1 to 1½ hours and lasts approximately 24 hours. Insulin combined with zinc and protamine is a longer-acting insulin that takes effect within 4 to 6 hours and lasts up to 36 hours. The time and course of action may vary considerably in different individuals or at different times in the same individual. The genetically engineered insulin lispro injection works faster and for a shorter length of time than human regular insulin and should be used along with a longer-acting insulin. It is available only by prescription.

Animal-based insulin is a very safe product. However, some components may cause an allergic reaction (see "What side effects may occur?"). Therefore, genetically engineered human insulin has been developed to lessen the chance of an allergic reaction. It is structurally identical to the insulin produced by your body's pancreas. However, some human insulin may be produced in a semi-synthetic process that begins with animal-based ingredients, which may cause an allergic reaction.

Most important fact about this drug
Regardless of the type of insulin your doctor has prescribed, you should follow carefully the dietary and exercise guidelines he or she has recommended. Failure to follow these guidelines or to take your insulin as prescribed may result in serious and potentially life-threatening complications such as hypoglycemia (lowered blood sugar levels).

How should you take this medication?
Take your insulin exactly as prescribed, being careful to follow your doctor's dietary and exercise recommendations.

- *If you miss a dose...*
  Your doctor should tell you what to do if you miss an insulin injection or meal.

- *Storage instructions...*
  Store insulin in a refrigerator (but not in the freezer) or in another cool, dark place. Do not expose insulin to heat or direct sunlight.

Some brands of prefilled syringes can be kept at room temperature for a week or a month. The vial or cartridge of genetically engineered insulin lispro can be kept unrefrigerated for up to 28 days. Check your product's label. Never use insulin after the expiration date which is printed on the label and carton.

What side effects may occur?
While side effects from insulin use are rare, allergic reactions or low blood sugar (sometimes called "an insulin reaction") may pose significant health risks. Your doctor should be notified if any of the following occur:

- *Mild allergic reactions:*
  Swelling, itching or redness at the injection site (usually disappears within a few days or weeks)

- *More serious allergic reactions:*
  Fast pulse, low blood pressure, perspiration, rash over the entire body, shortness of breath, shallow breathing, or wheezing

Other side effects are virtually eliminated when the correct dose of insulin is matched with the proper diet and level of physical activity. Low blood sugar may develop in poorly controlled or unstable diabetes. Consuming sugar or a sugar-containing product will usually correct the condition, which can be brought about by taking too much insulin, missing or delaying meals, exercising or working more than usual, an infection or illness, a change in the body's need for insulin, drug interactions, or consuming alcohol.

- *Symptoms of low blood sugar include:*
  Abnormal behavior, anxiety, blurred vision, cold sweat, confusion, depressed mood, dizziness, drowsiness, fatigue, headache, hunger, inability to concentrate, light-headedness, nausea, nervousness, personality changes, rapid heartbeat, restlessness, sleep disturbances, slurred speech, sweating, tingling in the hands, feet, lips, or tongue, tremor, unsteady movement

Contact your physician if these symptoms persist.

- *Symptoms of more severe low blood sugar include:*
  Coma, disorientation

Remember, too, the symptoms associated with an under-supply of insulin, which can be brought on by taking too little of it, overeating, or fever and infection.

- *Symptoms of insufficient insulin include:*
  Drowsiness, flushing, fruity breath, heavy breathing, loss of appetite, rapid pulse, thirst

If you are ill, you should check your urine for ketones (acetone), and notify your doctor if the test is positive. This condition can be life-threatening.

Why should this drug not be prescribed?
Insulin should be used only to correct diabetic conditions.

Special warnings about this medication
Wear personal identification that states clearly that you are diabetic. Carry a sugar-containing product such as hard candy to offset any symptoms of low blood sugar.

Do not change the type of insulin or even the model and brand of syringe or needle you use without your physician's instruction. Failure to use the proper syringe may lead to improper dosage levels of insulin.

If you become ill from any cause, especially with nausea and vomiting or fever, your insulin requirements may change. It is important to eat as normally as possible. If you have trouble eating, drink fruit juices, soda, or clear soups, or eat small amounts of bland foods. Test your urine and/or blood sugar and tell your doctor at once. If you have severe and prolonged vomiting, seek emergency medical care.

If you are taking insulin, you should check your glucose levels with home blood and urine testing devices. If your blood tests consistently show above-normal sugar levels or your urine tests consistently show the presence of sugar, your diabetes is not properly controlled, and you should tell your doctor.

To avoid infection or contamination, use disposable needles and syringes or sterilize your reusable syringe and needle carefully.

Always keep handy an extra supply of insulin as well as a spare syringe and needle.

Possible food and drug interactions
when taking this medication
Follow your physician's dietary guidelines as closely as you can and inform your physician of any medication, either prescription or non-prescription, that you are taking. Specific medications, depending on the amount present, that affect insulin levels or its effectiveness include:

ACE inhibitors such as the blood pressure medications Capoten and
    Lotensin
Anabolic steroids such as Anadrol-50
Appetite suppressants such as Tenuate
Aspirin
Beta-blocking blood pressure medicines such as Tenormin and Lopressor
Diuretics such as Lasix and Dyazide
Epinephrine (EpiPen)
Estrogens such as Premarin
Isoniazid (Nydrazid)
Major tranquilizers such as Mellaril and Thorazine
MAO inhibitors (drugs such as the antidepressants Nardil and Parnate)
Niacin (Nicobid)
Octreotide (Sandostatin)
Oral contraceptives
Oral drugs for diabetes such as Diabinese and Orinase
Phenytoin (Dilantin)
Steroid medications such as prednisone
Sulfa antibiotics such as Bactrim and Septra
Thyroid medications such as Synthroid

Use alcohol carefully, since excessive alcohol consumption can cause low blood sugar. Don't drink unless your doctor has approved it.

Special information
if you are pregnant or breastfeeding

Insulin is considered safe for pregnant women, but pregnancy may make managing your diabetes more difficult.

Properly controlled diabetes is essential for the health of the mother and the developing baby; therefore, it is extremely important that pregnant women follow closely their physician's dietary and exercise guidelines and prescribing instructions.

Since insulin does not pass into breast milk, it is safe for nursing mothers. It is not known whether genetically engineered insulin lispro appears in breast milk.

Recommended dosage

Your doctor will specify which insulin to use, how much, when, and how often to inject it. Your dosage may be affected by changes in food, activity, illness, medication, pregnancy, exercise, travel, or your work schedule. Proper control of your diabetes requires close and constant cooperation with your doctor. Failure to use your insulin as prescribed may result in serious and potentially fatal complications.

Some insulins should be clear, and some have a cloudy precipitate. Find out what your insulin should look like and check it carefully before using.

Genetically engineered insulin lispro injection should not be used by children under age 12.

Overdosage

An overdose of insulin can cause low blood sugar (hypoglycemia). Symptoms include:

Depressed mood, dizziness, drowsiness, fatigue, headache, hunger, inability to concentrate, irritability, nausea, nervousness, personality changes, rapid heartbeat, restlessness, sleep disturbances, slurred speech, sweating, tingling, tremor, unsteady movements

■ *Symptoms of more severe low blood sugar include:*
   Coma, disorientation, pale skin, seizures

Your doctor should be contacted immediately if these symptoms of severe low blood sugar occur.

Eating sugar or a sugar-based product will often correct the condition. If you suspect an overdose, seek medical attention immediately.

Brand name:

INTAL

Pronounced: IN-tahl
Generic name: Cromolyn sodium
Other brand name: Nasalcrom

Why is this drug prescribed?
Intal contains the antiasthmatic/antiallergic medication cromolyn sodium.

Different forms of the drug are used to manage bronchial asthma, to prevent asthma attacks, and to prevent and treat seasonal and chronic allergies.

The drug works by preventing certain cells in the body from releasing substances that can cause allergic reactions or prompt too much bronchial activity. It also helps prevent bronchial constriction caused by exercise, aspirin, cold air, and certain environmental pollutants such as sulfur dioxide.

Most important fact about this drug
Intal does not help an acute asthma attack. When taken to prevent severe bronchial asthma, it can be 4 weeks before you feel its maximum benefit, though some people get relief sooner. Do not discontinue the inhalation capsules or nasal solution abruptly without the advice of your doctor.

How should you take this medication?
Intal capsules should not be swallowed. They are for inhalation using the Spinhaler turbo-inhaler. The contents of 1 capsule are usually inhaled 4 times daily at regular intervals. Wash the Spinhaler in warm water at least once a week; dry thoroughly. Replace the Spinhaler every 6 months.

Intal nebulizer solution should be inhaled using a power-operated nebulizer equipped with an appropriate face mask or mouthpiece. Hand-operated nebulizers are not suitable. It is important that the solution be inhaled at regular intervals, usually 4 times per day.

Intal aerosol spray can be used either for chronic asthma or to prevent an asthma attack. For chronic asthma, it must be inhaled at regular intervals, as directed by your doctor, usually 2 sprays inhaled 4 times daily. To prevent an asthma attack caused by exercise, cold air, or other irritants, the usual dose of 2 inhalation sprays should be taken between 10 and 60 minutes before exercising or exposure to cold or pollutants.

Nasalcrom nasal solution should be used with a metered nasal spray device, which should be replaced every 6 months. Blow your nose to clear your nasal passages before administering the spray. The nasal solution is used for nasal congestion due to seasonal or chronic allergies. For seasonal allergies, treatment is more effective if begun before the start of the allergy season. Treatment should then continue throughout the season. For year-round allergies, treatment may be required for up to 4 weeks before results are seen. Your doctor may find it necessary to add other allergy medications, such as antihistamines or decongestants, during initial treatment.

■ *If you miss a dose...*
Take it as soon as you remember. Then take the rest of that day's doses at equally spaced intervals. Do not take 2 doses at once.

■ *Storage instructions...*
Store at room temperature, away from light and heat. Keep the ampules in their foil pouch until you are ready to use them.

What side effects may occur?
Side effects cannot be anticipated. If any develop or change in intensity, inform your doctor as soon as possible. Only your doctor can determine if it is safe for you to continue taking Intal.

■ *More common side effects may include:*
Cough, nasal congestion or irritation, nausea, sneezing, throat irritation, wheezing

■ *Less common or rare side effects may include:*
Angioedema (swelling of face around lips, tongue, and throat, swollen arms and legs), bad taste in mouth, burning in chest, difficulty swallowing, dizziness, ear problems, headache, hives, joint swelling and pain, nosebleed, painful urination or frequent urination, postnasal drip, rash, severe allergic reaction, swollen glands, swollen throat, teary eyes, tightness in throat

Why should this drug not be prescribed?
If you are sensitive to or have ever had an allergic reaction to cromolyn sodium or lactose, you should not take this medication. Make sure your doctor is aware of any drug reactions you have experienced.

Special warnings about this medication

Asthma symptoms may recur if the recommended dosage of Intal is reduced or discontinued. Intal has no role in the treatment of an acute asthmatic attack once it has begun. Obtain medical help immediately if you experience a severe attack.

If you have liver or kidney problems, your doctor may have to reduce the dosage or even take you off the drug altogether.

When using the capsules, you may accidentally inhale some powder, which can irritate your throat or make you cough. Try rinsing your mouth or taking a drink of water immediately before and/or after using the Spinhaler.

If your heartbeat is ever irregular or if you have any other kind of heart trouble, be sure your doctor knows about it before you use Intal aerosol spray.

Intal aerosol spray may not help you if your attack has been brought on by exercise.

Possible food and drug interactions
when taking this medication

If you are taking other prescription or nonprescription drugs, discuss this with your doctor to determine if these drugs would interact with Intal.

Special information
if you are pregnant or breastfeeding

The effects of Intal during pregnancy have not been adequately studied. If you are pregnant or plan to become pregnant, inform your doctor immediately. It is not known whether Intal appears in breast milk. As with all medication, a nursing woman should use this drug only after careful consultation with her doctor.

Recommended dosage

INTAL CAPSULES FOR INHALATION
INTAL NEBULIZER SOLUTION

Adults and Children 2 Years Old and Over

For management of bronchial asthma, the usual dosage is 20 milligrams (1 capsule or ampule) inhaled 4 times daily at regular intervals, using the Spinhaler turbo-inhaler or power-operated nebulizer. If you have chronic asthma, this drug's effectiveness depends on your taking it regularly, as directed, and only after an attack has been controlled and you can inhale adequately.

For the prevention of an acute attack following exercise or exposure to cold, dry air or environmental irritants, the usual dose is 1 capsule or ampule inhaled shortly before exposure to the irritant. You may repeat the inhalation as needed for continued protection during prolonged exposure.

INTAL INHALER AEROSOL SPRAY

Adults and Children 5 Years Old and Over
For the management of bronchial asthma, the usual starting dose is 2 metered sprays taken at regular intervals, 4 times daily. This is the maximum dose that should be taken, and lower dosages may be effective in children. This drug should be used only after an asthma attack has been controlled and you can inhale adequately.

For the prevention of an acute asthma attack following exercise, exposure to cold air or environmental agents, the usual dose is inhalation of 2 metered sprays shortly (10 to 15 minutes but not more than 60 minutes) before exposure to the irritant.

NASALCROM NASAL SOLUTION

Adults and Children 6 Years Old and Over
For the prevention and treatment of allergies caused by exposure to certain irritants, the usual dosage is 1 spray in each nostril 3 to 4 times per day at regular intervals, using the metered spray device. Your doctor may have you use the spray 6 times a day if you need it.

Overdosage
Any medication taken in excess can have serious consequences. If you suspect an overdose, seek medical attention immediately.

▪ *Symptoms of Intal overdose may include:*
  Difficulty breathing, heart failure, low blood pressure, slow heartbeat

Brand name:

INVIRASE

Pronounced: IN-vir-ace
Generic name: Saquinavir mesylate

Why is this drug prescribed?
Invirase is used in the treatment of advanced human immunodeficiency virus (HIV) infection. HIV causes the immune system to break down so that it can

no longer fight off other infections. This leads to the fatal disease known as acquired immune deficiency syndrome (AIDS).

Invirase belongs to a new class of HIV drugs called protease inhibitors, which work by interfering with an important step in the virus's reproductive cycle. Invirase is used in combination with other HIV drugs called nucleoside analogues (Retrovir or Hivid, for example). The combination produces an increase in the immune system's vital CD4 cells (white blood cells) and reduces the amount of virus in the bloodstream.

Most important fact about this drug
Invirase will not cure an HIV infection. You will continue to face the possibility of complications, including opportunistic infections (rare infections that develop only when the immune system falters, such as certain types of pneumonia, tuberculosis, and fungal infections). Therefore, it is important that you remain under the care of a doctor and keep all your follow-up appointments.

How should you take this medication?
Take this medication exactly as prescribed by your doctor. Do not share this medication with anyone and do not exceed your recommended dosage. Take Invirase within 2 hours after a full meal. This allows the drug to be properly absorbed by your body. Your doctor will perform laboratory tests before you start therapy with Invirase and at regular intervals during your therapy to see how you are reacting to the medication.

■ *If you miss a dose...*
Take it as soon as possible. If it is almost time for your next dose, skip the one you missed and go back to your regular schedule. Never take a double dose.

■ *Storage instructions...*
Store Invirase at room temperature in a tightly closed bottle.

What side effects may occur?
Side effects cannot be anticipated. If any develop or change in intensity, tell your doctor as soon as possible. Only your doctor can determine if it is safe for you to continue taking Invirase.

■ *Possible side effects may include:*
Abdominal discomfort and pain, appetite disturbance, diarrhea, dizziness, headache, indigestion, mouth sores, muscle and bone pain, nausea, numbness in the arms and legs, tingling or "pins and needles" sensation, weakness

Why should this drug not be prescribed?
If you suffer an allergic reaction to Invirase or any of its components, you will not be able to use this drug.

Special warnings about this medication
Invirase has been studied for only a limited period of time and only in patients with advanced HIV infections. Its long-term effects are still unknown.

This medication does not reduce the risk of transmission of HIV to others through sexual contact or blood contamination. Therefore, you should continue to avoid practices that could give HIV to others.

Possible food and drug interactions when taking this medication
If Invirase is taken with certain other drugs, the effects of either could be increased, decreased, or altered. It is especially important to check with your doctor before combining Invirase with the following:

Astemizole (Hismanal)
Calcium channel blockers (blood pressure medications such as Calan, Verelan, Cardizem, and Procardia)
Carbamazepine (Tegretol)
Cisapride (Propulsid)
Clindamycin (Cleocin)
Dapsone (a drug used to treat leprosy)
Dexamethasone (Decadron)
Phenobarbital (Donnatal)
Phenytoin (Dilantin)
Quinidine (Quinidex)
Rifabutin (Mycobutin)
Rifampin (Rifadin)
Terfenadine (Seldane)
Triazolam (Halcion)

Be sure to tell your doctor and pharmacist about all the medications (both prescription and over-the-counter) that you are presently taking. Alert them, too, whenever you *stop* taking a medication.

Special information if you are pregnant or breastfeeding
The effects of Invirase during pregnancy have not been adequately studied. If you are pregnant or plan to become pregnant, tell your doctor immediately.

Do not breastfeed. HIV appears in breast milk and can be passed to a nursing infant.

Recommended dosage

ADULTS

The recommended dosage is 600 milligrams (three 200-milligram capsules), taken 3 times a day within 2 hours after a full meal. Daily doses lower than 600 milligrams 3 times a day are not recommended, since they will not have the same antiviral activity. You should also be taking Retrovir, Hivid, or another antiviral drug as directed.

CHILDREN

The safety and effectiveness of Invirase in children younger than 16 years of age have not been established.

Overdosage
There have been no reports of Invirase poisoning. However, any medication taken in excess can have serious consequences. If you suspect an overdose, seek emergency medical treatment immediately.

Brand name:

IONAMIN

See Fastin, page 484.

Generic name:

IPRATROPIUM

See Atrovent, page 102.

Brand name:

ISMO

See Imdur, page 586.

Brand name:

ISOLLYL

See Fiorinal, page 499.

Generic name:

ISOMETHEPTENE, DICHLORALPHENAZONE, AND ACETAMINOPHEN

See Midrin, page 767.

Brand name:

ISOPTIN

See Calan, page 170.

Brand name:

ISOPTO CARPINE

See Pilocar, page 965.

Brand name:

ISORDIL

Pronounced: ICE-or-dill
Generic name: Isosorbide dinitrate
Other brand name: Sorbitrate

Why is this drug prescribed?
Isordil is prescribed to relieve or prevent angina pectoris (suffocating chest pain). Angina pectoris occurs when the arteries and veins become constricted and sufficient oxygen does not reach the heart. Isordil dilates the blood vessels by relaxing the muscles in their walls. Oxygen flow improves as the vessels relax, and chest pain subsides.

In swallowed capsules or tablets, Isordil helps to increase the amount of exercise you can do before chest pain begins.

In chewable or sublingual (held under the tongue) tablets, Isordil can help relieve chest pain that has already started or prevent pain expected from a strenuous activity such as walking up a hill or climbing stairs.

Most important fact about this drug
Isordil may cause severe low blood pressure (possibly marked by dizziness or fainting), especially when you stand or sit up quickly. People taking diuretic

medication or those who have low blood pressure should use Isordil with caution.

How should you take this medication?

Swallowed capsules or tablets should be taken on an empty stomach. While regular tablets may be crushed for easier use, sustained- or prolonged-release products should not be chewed, crushed or altered.

Chewable tablets should be chewed thoroughly and held in the mouth for a couple of minutes. Do not eat, drink, smoke, or use chewing tobacco while a sublingual tablet is dissolving.

This drug's effectiveness is closely linked to the dose, so follow your doctor's instructions carefully.

■ *If you miss a dose...*
If you are taking this drug regularly, take the forgotten dose as soon as you remember. If your next dose is within 2 hours—or 6 hours for controlled-release tablets and capsules—skip the one you missed and go back to your regular schedule. Do not take 2 doses at once.

■ *Storage information...*
Store at room temperature in a tightly closed container, away from light.

What side effects may occur?

Side effects cannot be anticipated. If any develop or change in intensity, inform your doctor as soon as possible. Only your doctor can determine if it is safe for you to continue taking Isordil.

Headache is the most common side effect; usually, standard headache treatments with over-the-counter pain products will relieve the pain. The headaches associated with Isordil usually subside within 2 weeks after treatment with the drug begins. Do not change your dose to avoid the headache. At a dose that eliminates headaches, the drug may not be as effective against angina.

■ *Other common side effects may include:*
Dizziness, light-headedness, low blood pressure, weakness

■ *Less common or rare side effects may include:*
Collapse, fainting, flushed skin, high blood pressure, nausea, pallor, perspiration, rash, restlessness, skin inflammation and flaking, vomiting

Why should this drug not be prescribed?

You should not take Isordil if you have had a previous allergic reaction to it or to other nitrates or nitrites.

Special warnings about this medication

You should use Isordil with caution if you have anemia, the eye condition called glaucoma, a previous head injury or heart attack, heart disease, low blood pressure, or thyroid disease.

If you stop using Isordil, you should follow your doctor's plan for a gradual withdrawal schedule. Abruptly stopping this medication could result in additional chest pain.

Some people may develop a tolerance to Isordil, which causes its effects to be reduced over time. Tell your doctor if you think Isordil is starting to lose its effectiveness.

Possible food and drug interactions
when taking this medication

If Isordil is taken with certain other drugs, the effects of either could be increased, decreased, or altered.

Extreme low blood pressure (marked by dizziness, fainting, and numbness) may occur if you take Isordil with certain other high blood pressure drugs such as Cardizem and Procardia.

Alcohol may interact with Isordil and produce a swift decrease in blood pressure, possibly causing dizziness and fainting.

Special information
if you are pregnant or breastfeeding

The effects of Isordil in pregnancy have not been adequately studied. Isordil should be used only when the benefits of therapy clearly outweigh the potential risks to the developing baby. If you are pregnant or plan to become pregnant, inform your doctor immediately. It is not known if Isordil appears in breast milk; therefore, nursing mothers should use Isordil with caution.

Recommended dosage

Because you can develop a tolerance to this drug, your doctor may schedule a daily period of time when you do not take any drug.

ADULTS

The usual sublingual starting dose for the treatment of angina pectoris is 2.5 milligrams to 5 milligrams. Your doctor will increase this initial dose gradually until the pain subsides or side effects prove bothersome.

The usual sublingual starting dose for the prevention of an impending attack of angina pectoris is usually 5 or 10 milligrams every 2 to 3 hours.

To prevent chronic stable angina pectoris, the usual starting dose for swallowed, immediately released Isordil is 5 to 20 milligrams. Your doctor may increase this initial dose to 10 to 40 milligrams every 6 hours.

To prevent chronic stable angina pectoris with controlled-release Isordil, the usual initial dose is 40 milligrams. Your doctor may increase this dose from 40 to 80 milligrams given every 8 to 12 hours.

CHILDREN

The safety and effectiveness of Isordil have not been established for children.

Overdosage

Any medication taken in excess can have serious consequences. Severe overdosage of Isordil can be fatal. If you suspect an overdose, seek medical help immediately.

■ *Symptoms of Isordil overdose may include:*
Bloody diarrhea, coma, confusion, convulsions, fainting, fever, flushed and perspiring skin (later cold and blue), nausea, palpitations, paralysis, rapid decrease in blood pressure, rapid, then difficult and slow breathing, slow pulse, throbbing headache, vertigo, visual disturbances, vomiting

Generic name:

ISOSORBIDE DINITRATE

See Isordil, page 623.

Generic name:

ISOSORBIDE MONONITRATE

See Imdur, page 586.

Generic name:

ISOTRETINOIN

See Accutane, page 7.

Generic name:

ISRADIPINE

See DynaCirc, page 431.

Generic name:

ITRACONAZOLE

See Sporanox, page 1155.

Brand name:

KADIAN

See MS Contin, page 799.

Brand name:

KAON-CL

See Micro-K, page 760.

Brand name:

K-DUR

See Micro-K, page 760.

Brand name:

KEFLEX

Pronounced: KEF-lecks
Generic name: Cephalexin hydrochloride
Other brand name: Keftab

Why is this drug prescribed?
Keflex and Keftab are cephalosporin antibiotics. They are prescribed for bacterial infections of the respiratory tract including middle ear infection, bone, skin, and the reproductive and urinary systems. Because they are effective for only certain types of bacterial infections, before beginning treatment your doctor may perform tests to identify the organisms causing the infection.

Keflex is available in capsules and an oral suspension form for use in children. Keftab, available only in tablet form, is prescribed exclusively for adults.

Most important fact about this drug

If you are allergic to either penicillin or cephalosporin antibiotics in any form, consult your doctor *before taking Keflex*. There is a possibility that you are allergic to both types of medication and if a reaction occurs, it could be extremely severe. If you take the drug and feel signs of a reaction, seek medical attention immediately.

How should you take this medication?

Keflex may be taken with or without meals. However, if the drug upsets your stomach, you may want to take it after you have eaten.

Take Keflex at even intervals around the clock as prescribed by your doctor.

If you are taking the liquid form of Keflex, use the specially marked spoon to measure each dose accurately.

To obtain maximum benefit, it is important that you finish taking all of this medication, even if you are feeling better.

- *If you miss a dose...*
  Take it as soon as you remember. If it is almost time for the next dose, and you take 2 doses a day, take the one you missed and the next dose 5 to 6 hours later. If you take 3 or more doses a day, take the one you missed and the next dose 2 to 4 hours later, or double the next dose. Then go back to your regular schedule.

- *Storage instructions...*
  Store capsules and tablets at room temperature. Store the liquid suspension in a refrigerator; discard any unused medication after 14 days.

What side effects may occur?

Side effects cannot be anticipated. If any develop or change in intensity, inform your doctor as soon as possible. Only your doctor can determine if it is safe for you to continue taking Keflex.

- *More common side effects may include:*
  Diarrhea

- *Less common or rare side effects may include:*
  Abdominal pain, agitation, colitis (inflammation of the large intestine), confusion, dizziness, fatigue, fever, genital and rectal itching, hallucina-

tions, headache, hepatitis, hives, indigestion, inflammation of joints, inflammation of the stomach, joint pain, nausea, rash, seizures, severe allergic reaction, skin peeling, skin redness, swelling due to fluid retention, vaginal discharge, vaginal inflammation, vomiting, yellowing of skin and whites of eyes

Why should this drug not be prescribed?

If you are sensitive to or have ever had an allergic reaction to the cephalosporin group of antibiotics, you should not use this medication. Make sure your doctor is aware of any drug reactions you have experienced.

Special warnings about this medication

If you have a history of stomach or intestinal disease, especially colitis, check with your doctor before taking Keflex.

If you have ever had an allergic reaction, particularly to drugs, be sure to tell your doctor.

If diarrhea occurs while taking cephalexin, check with your doctor before taking a remedy. Certain diarrhea medications (for instance, Lomotil) may increase your diarrhea or make it last longer.

Prolonged use of Keflex may result in an overgrowth of bacteria that do not respond to the medication, causing a secondary infection. Your doctor will monitor your use of this drug on a regular basis.

If you have a kidney disorder, check with your doctor before taking Keflex. You may need a reduced dose.

If you are diabetic, it is important to note that Keflex may cause false results in tests for urine sugar. Notify your doctor that you are taking this medication before being tested. Do not change your diet or dosage of diabetes medication without first consulting with your doctor.

If your symptoms do not improve within a few days, or if they get worse, notify your doctor immediately.

Do not give this medication to other people or use it for other infections before checking with your doctor.

Possible food and drug interactions
when taking this medication

If Keflex is taken with certain other drugs, the effects of either could be increased, decreased, or altered. It is especially important to check with your doctor before combining Keflex with the following:

Certain diarrhea medications such as Lomotil
Oral contraceptives

Special information
if you are pregnant or breastfeeding

The effects of Keflex during pregnancy have not been adequately studied. If you are pregnant or plan to become pregnant, notify your doctor immediately. Keflex appears in breast milk and could affect a nursing infant. If this medication is essential to your health, your doctor may advise you to discontinue breastfeeding until your treatment is finished.

Recommended dosage

ADULTS

Throat, Skin, and Urinary Tract Infections

The usual adult dosage is 500 milligrams taken every 12 hours. Cystitis (bladder infection) therapy should be continued for 7 to 14 days.

Other Infections

The usual recommended dosage is 250 milligrams taken every 6 hours. For more severe infections, larger doses may be needed, as determined by your doctor.

CHILDREN

Keflex

The usual dose is 25 to 50 milligrams for each 2.2 pounds of body weight per day, divided into smaller doses.

For strep throat in children over 1 year of age and for skin infections, the dose may be divided into 2 doses taken every 12 hours. For strep infections, the medication should be taken for at least 10 days. Your doctor may double the dose if your child has a severe infection.

For middle ear infection, the dose is 75 to 100 milligrams per 2.2 pounds per day, divided into 4 doses.

Keftab

Safety and effectiveness have not been established in children.

Overdosage

Any medication taken in excess can have serious consequences.

If you suspect an overdose, seek emergency medical treatment immediately.

- *Symptoms of Keflex overdose may include:*
  Blood in the urine, diarrhea, nausea, upper abdominal pain, vomiting

Brand name:

KEFTAB

See Keflex, page 627.

Generic name:

KETOCONAZOLE

See Nizoral, page 849.

Generic name:

KETOPROFEN

See Orudis, page 898.

Generic name:

KETOROLAC

See Toradol, page 1263.

Brand name:

KLONOPIN

Pronounced: KLON-uh-pin
Generic name: Clonazepam

Why is this drug prescribed?

Klonopin is used alone or along with other medications to treat convulsive disorders such as epilepsy. It is also prescribed for panic disorder—unexpected attacks of overwhelming panic accompanied by fear of recurrence. Klonopin belongs to a class of drugs known as benzodiazepines.

Most important fact about this drug

Klonopin works best when there is a constant amount in the bloodstream. To keep blood levels as constant as possible, take your doses at regularly spaced intervals and try not to miss any.

How should you take this medication?

Klonopin should be taken exactly as prescribed by your doctor.

Take Klonopin exactly as prescribed. If you are taking it for panic disorder and you find it makes you sleepy, your doctor may recommend a single dose at bedtime.

■ *If you miss a dose...*
If it is within an hour after the missed time, take the dose as soon as you remember. If you do not remember until later, skip the dose and go back to your regular schedule. Never take 2 doses at the same time.

■ *Storage instructions...*
Store at room temperature away from heat, light, and moisture.

What side effects may occur?
Side effects cannot be anticipated. If any develop or change in intensity, inform your doctor as soon as possible. Only your doctor can determine if it is safe for you to continue taking Klonopin.

■ *More common side effects in seizure disorders may include:*
Behavior problems, drowsiness, lack of muscular coordination

■ *Less common or rare side effects in seizure disorders may include:*
Abnormal eye movements, anemia, bed wetting, chest congestion, coated tongue, coma, confusion, constipation, dehydration, depression, diarrhea, double vision, dry mouth, excess hair, fever, fluttery or throbbing heartbeat, "glassy-eyed" appearance, hair loss, hallucinations, headache, inability to fall or stay asleep, inability to urinate, increased sex drive, involuntary rapid movement of the eyeballs, loss of or increased appetite, loss of voice, memory loss, muscle and bone pain, muscle weakness, nausea, nighttime urination, painful or difficult urination, partial paralysis, runny nose, shortness of breath, skin rash, slowed breathing, slurred speech, sore gums, speech difficulties, stomach inflammation, swelling of ankles and face, tremor, uncontrolled body movement or twitching, vertigo, weight loss or gain

Klonopin can also cause aggressive behavior, agitation, anxiety, excitability, hostility, irritability, nervousness, nightmares, sleep disturbances, and vivid dreams.

■ *Side effects due to rapid decrease or abrupt withdrawal from Klonopin may include:*
Abdominal and muscle cramps, behavior disorders, convulsions, depressed feeling, hallucinations, restlessness, sleeping difficulties, tremors

- *More common side effects in panic disorder may include:*
  Allergic reaction, constipation, coordination problems, depression, dizziness, fatigue, inflamed sinuses or nasal passages, flu, memory problems, menstrual problems, nervousness, reduced thinking ability, respiratory infection, sleepiness, speech problems

- *Less common or rare side effects in panic disorder may include:*
  Abdominal pain/discomfort, abnormal hunger, acne, aggressive reaction, anxiety, apathy, asthma attack, bleeding from the skin, blood clots, bronchitis, burning sensation, changes in appetite, changes in sex drive, confusion, coughing, difficulty breathing, dizziness when standing, ear problems, emotional changeability, excessive dreaming, excitement, fever, flushing, fluttery or throbbing heartbeat, frequent bowel movements, gas, general feeling of illness, gout, hair loss, hemorrhoids, hoarseness, increased salivation, indigestion, infections, inflamed stomach and intestines, lack of attention, lack of sensation, leg cramps, loss of taste, male sexual problems, migraine, motion sickness, muscle pain/cramps, nightmares, nosebleed, overactivity, pain (anywhere in the body), paraylsis, pneumonia, shivering, skin problems, sleep problems, sneezing, sore throat, swelling with fluid retention, swollen knees, thick tongue, thirst, tingling/pins and needles, tooth problems, tremor, twitching, upset stomach, urinary problems, vertigo, vision problems, weight gain or loss, yawning

Why should this drug not be prescribed?
If you are sensitive to or have ever had an allergic reaction to Klonopin or similar drugs, such as Librium and Valium, you should not take this medication. Make sure your doctor is aware of any reactions you have experienced.

You should not take this medication if you have severe liver disease or the eye condition known as acute narrow angle glaucoma.

Special warnings about this medication
Klonopin may cause you to become drowsy or less alert; therefore, you should not drive or operate dangerous machinery or participate in any hazardous activity that requires full mental alertness until you know how this drug affects you.

If you have several types of seizures, this drug may increase the possibility of grand mal seizures (epilepsy). Inform your doctor if this occurs. Your doctor may wish to prescribe an additional anticonvulsant drug or increase your dose.

Klonopin can be habit-forming and can lose its effectiveness as you build up a tolerance to it. You may experience withdrawal symptoms—such as convulsions, hallucinations, tremor, and abdominal and muscle cramps—if you stop using this drug abruptly. Discontinue or change your dose only in consultation with your doctor.

Possible food and drug interactions
when taking this medication
Klonopin slows the nervous system and its effects may be intensified by alcohol. Do not drink while taking this medication.

If Klonopin is taken with certain other drugs, the effects of either could be increased, decreased, or altered. It is especially important to check with your doctor before combining Klonopin with the following:

Antianxiety drugs such as Valium
Antidepressant drugs such as Elavil, Nardil, Parnate, and Tofranil
Barbiturates such as phenobarbital
Carbamazepine (Tegretol)
Major tranquilizers such as Haldol, Navane, and Thorazine
Narcotic pain relievers such as Demerol and Percocet
Oral antifungal drugs such as Fungizone, Mycelex, Mycostatin
Other anticonvulsants such as Dilantin, Depakene, and Depakote
Sedatives such as Halcion

Special information
if you are pregnant or breastfeeding
Avoid Klonopin if at all possible during the first 3 months of pregnancy; there is a risk of birth defects. When taken later in pregnancy, the drug can cause other problems, such as withdrawal symptoms in the newborn. If you are pregnant or plan to become pregnant, inform your doctor immediately. Klonopin appears in breast milk and could affect a nursing infant. If this medication is essential to your health, you should not breastfeed until your treatment with this medication is finished.

Recommended dosage

SEIZURE DISORDERS

Adults
The starting dose should be no more than 1.5 milligrams per day, divided into 3 doses. Your doctor may increase your daily dosage by 0.5 to 1 milligram every 3 days until your seizures are controlled or the side effects become too bothersome. The most you should take in 1 day is 20 milligrams.

SEIZURE DISORDERS

Children
The starting dose for infants and children up to 10 years old or up to 66 pounds should be 0.01 to 0.03 milligram—no more than 0.05 milligram—per 2.2 pounds of body weight daily. The daily dosage should be given in 2 or 3 smaller doses. Your doctor may increase the dose by 0.25 to 0.5 milligram every 3 days until seizures are controlled or side effects become too bad. If the dose cannot be divided into 3 equal doses, the largest dose should be given at bedtime. The maximum maintenance dose is 0.1 to 0.2 milligram per 2.2 pounds daily.

PANIC DISORDER

Adults
The startng dose is 0.25 milligram twice a day. After 3 days, your doctor may increase the dose to 1 milligram daily. Some people need as much as 4 milligrams a day.

PANIC DISORDER

Children
For panic disorder, safety and effectiveness have not been established in children under age 18.

Overdosage
Any medication taken in excess can have serious consequences. If you suspect an overdose, seek medical attention immediately.

■ *The symptoms of Klonopin overdose may include:*
   Coma, confusion, sleepiness, slowed reaction time

Brand name:

KLOR-CON

See Micro-K, page 760.

Brand name:

K-TAB

See Micro-K, page 760.

Brand name:

KWELL

Pronounced: QUELL
Generic name: Lindane

Why is this drug prescribed?

Kwell cream and lotion are used to treat scabies, a contagious skin disease caused by an almost invisible organism known as the "itch mite." Kwell shampoo is used to treat people with head lice and pubic (crab) lice and their eggs.

Most important fact about this drug

Use Kwell only as directed by your doctor. Using too much or applying it more often than directed can result in seizures or even death, particularly in the young. Read the "Instructions to Patients" information sheet accompanying the Kwell package before using. If you have any questions, call your doctor.

How should you use this medication?

CREAM AND LOTION

Shake the lotion well before using. Apply cream or lotion in a thin layer to dry skin, starting from the neck and working down, including the soles of your feet (unless otherwise directed by your doctor), and rub in thoroughly. Trim your nails and apply the medication under the nails with a toothbrush, then throw the toothbrush away. If you take a warm bath or shower before using Kwell, dry your skin thoroughly and let it cool completely before applying the medication. Leave the cream or lotion on for no less than 8 and no more than 12 hours (usually overnight), then take a shower or bath to wash it off thoroughly. Apply only once, and use only enough to cover the body in a thin layer.

SHAMPOO

Before applying Kwell shampoo, wash your hair with regular shampoo, without conditioners, then rinse it and dry it completely. Shake the shampoo well, then apply directly to dry hair, without adding water. Work thoroughly into your hair and leave it on for 4 minutes. After 4 minutes, add a little water until you have a good lather. Immediately rinse all the lather away. Do not let the lather touch any other part of the body any more than necessary. Towel-dry your hair. Remove nits (eggs) with a nit comb or tweezers. If you are using Kwell on another person, try to keep it off your skin as much as possible. If you are using Kwell on more than one person, wear rubber gloves (this applies especially to pregnant women and nursing mothers).

■ *If you miss a dose...*
Use Kwell only once per infection. Multiple applications are dangerous.

■ *Storage instructions...*
Store away from heat and direct light. Keep out of the reach of children.

What side effects may occur?
Side effects are extremely rare, but can be serious. If any develop, contact your doctor as soon as possible.

■ *Side effects may include:*
Convulsions, dizziness, seizures, skin eruptions, skin rash

Why should this drug not be prescribed?
If you are sensitive to or have ever had an allergic reaction to Kwell or any of its ingredients, do not use it again. Do not use Kwell on premature infants, their skin is more sensitive and more drug could be absorbed into the body. Do not use Kwell if you have any kind of seizure disorder; and do not use the cream or lotion for Norwegian scabies (an extremely contagious skin disease with a thin, flaky, rash).

Special warnings about this medication
Be careful to avoid contact with your eyes. If any Kwell does get in your eyes, immediately flush them with cold water; if they become irritated or you have an allergic reaction, call your doctor.

Do not swallow Kwell. If you accidentally swallow any, call your doctor or your local poison control center immediately. Do not allow your child to apply Kwell without close adult supervision.

Be sure to cover an infant's hands and feet during treatment with Kwell cream or lotion to prevent the child from sucking or licking the medication.

Do not use Kwell on open wounds such as cuts or sores unless directed by your doctor. After one application of Kwell cream or lotion, your itching may continue for several weeks. The itching is quite normal and does not require a reapplication of Kwell. You will not usually need a second treatment with Kwell shampoo, but if you find living lice in your hair 7 days after treatment, call your doctor. You may need retreatment.

Wash all recently worn clothing, underwear and pajamas, used sheets, pillow cases, and towels in very hot water or have them dry cleaned.

Use Kwell cream or lotion cautiously on young children and the elderly because their skin may absorb more of the medication. To avoid reinfection, make sure that any sexual partners are treated at the same time that you are. Kwell cannot be used to prevent scabies or lice, since no effects remain after it has been washed off.

Possible food and drug interactions
when taking this medication
Oils may cause more Kwell to be absorbed through the skin into the body, possibly causing serious side effects. Therefore, do not use oils, creams, or ointments at the same time you are using Kwell cream or lotion and do not use oil treatments or oil-based hair dressings or conditioners immediately before and after you apply Kwell shampoo.

Special information
if you are pregnant or breastfeeding
If you are pregnant, follow your doctor's directions carefully. Do not use more Kwell than your doctor recommends, and do not use it more than twice during your pregnancy.

If you are breastfeeding, be sure to check with your doctor before using Kwell. Small amounts pass into breast milk, so even though Kwell has not been found to cause problems in nursing infants, your doctor may have you give up breastfeeding for 4 days after using Kwell.

Recommended dosage

CREAM AND LOTION

Adults and children aged 6 and over
Use 1 to 2 ounces. Apply only once; and do not leave on for more than 12 hours.

Children under age 6
Use 1 ounce (half of a 2-ounce container). Apply only once.

SHAMPOO

Use 1 ounce (1/2 bottle) for short hair, 1 1/2 ounces (3/4 bottle) for medium-length hair, and 2 ounces (1 bottle) for long hair. Do not use more than 2 ounces.

Overdosage
Any medication used in excess can have serious consequences. If you suspect an overdose, seek medical attention immediately.

- *Symptoms of Kwell overdose may include:*
Convulsions, dizziness

Generic name:

LABETALOL

See Normodyne, page 857.

Generic name:

LACTULOSE

See Chronulac Syrup, page 223.

Brand name:

LAMICTAL

Pronounced: LAM-ic-tal
Generic name: Lamotrigine

Why is this drug prescribed?
Lamictal is prescribed to control partial seizures in people with epilepsy. It is used in combination with other antiepileptic medications such as Tegretol and Depakene.

Most important fact about this drug
You may develop a rash during the first 2 to 8 weeks of Lamictal therapy, particularly if you are also taking Depakene. If this happens, notify your doctor immediately. The rash could become severe and even dangerous, particularly in children. A slight possibility of this problem remains for up to 6 months.

How should you take this medication?
Take Lamictal exactly as prescribed by your doctor. Taking more than the prescribed amount can increase your risk of developing a serious rash. Do not stop taking this medication without first discussing it with your doctor. An abrupt halt could increase your seizures. Your doctor can schedule a gradual reduction in dosage.

- *If you miss a dose...*
Take it as soon as you remember. If it is almost time for your next dose, skip the one you missed and go back to your regular schedule. Do not take 2 doses at once.

- *Storage instructions...*
  Store in a tightly closed container at room temperature. Keep dry and protect from light.

What side effects may occur?
Side effects cannot be anticipated. If any develop or change in intensity, tell your doctor as soon as possible. Only your doctor can determine if it is safe for you to continue taking Lamictal.

- *More common side effects may include:*
  Blurred vision, dizziness, double vision, headache, nausea, rash, sleepiness, uncoordinated movements, vomiting

- *Less common side effects may include:*
  Abdominal pain, accidental injury, anxiety, constipation, depression, diarrhea, fever, "flu-like" symptoms, increased cough, inflammation of vagina, irritability, painful menstruation, sore throat, tremor

- *Rare side effects may include:*
  Absence of menstrual periods, chills, confusion, dry mouth, ear pain, emotional changes, heart palpitations, hot flashes, joint disorders, memory decrease, mind racing, muscle weakness, muscle spasm, poor concentration, ringing in ears, sleep disorder, speech disorder

Why should this drug not be prescribed?
If you are sensitive to or have ever had an allergic reaction to Lamictal, you should not take this medication. Make sure your doctor is aware of any drug reactions you have experienced.

Special warnings about this medication
Lamictal may cause some people to become drowsy, dizzy, or less alert. Do not drive or operate dangerous machinery or participate in any activity that requires full mental alertness until you are certain the drug does not have this kind of effect on you. Remember to be alert for development of any type of rash, especially during the first 2 to 8 weeks of treatment.

Be sure to tell your doctor about any medical problems you have before starting therapy with Lamictal. If you have kidney or liver disease, or heart problems, Lamictal should be used with caution.

Lamictal may cause vision problems. If any develop, notify your doctor immediately. Also be quick to call your doctor if you develop a fever or have any other signs of an allergic reaction. Notify your doctor, too, if your seizures get worse.

Possible food and drug interactions
when taking this medication

Lamictal is not used alone; it is combined with other medications used to treat epilepsy, including the following:

Carbamazepine (Tegretol)
Phenobarbital (Donnatal, Quadrinal, others)
Phenytoin (Dilantin)
Primidone (Mysoline)
Valproic acid (Depakene)

Be sure to check with your doctor before combining any other drugs with your seizure medications. Lamictal, in particular, may inhibit the action of sulfa drugs such as Bactrim, Proloprim, and Septra.

Special information
if you are pregnant or breastfeeding

The effects of Lamictal during pregnancy have not been adequately studied. If you are pregnant or plan to become pregnant, tell your doctor immediately. Lamictal should be used during pregnancy only if clearly needed. Lamictal appears in breast milk. Because the effects of Lamictal on an infant exposed to this medication are unknown, breastfeeding is not recommended.

Recommended dosage

ADULTS

Lamictal combined with Tegretol, Dilantin, Phenobarbital, and Mysoline:
One 50-milligram dose per day for 2 weeks, then two 50-milligram doses per day, for 2 weeks. After that, your doctor will have you take a total of 300 milligrams to 500 milligrams a day, divided into 2 doses.

Lamictal combined with Depakene and any of the above medications:
One 25-milligram dose every other day for 2 weeks, then 25 milligrams once a day for 2 weeks. After that, the doctor will prescribe a total of 100 milligrams to 150 milligrams a day, divided into 2 doses. You should not take more than 25 milligrams every other day because of the increased risk of rash with this combination of drugs.

CHILDREN

Safety and effectiveness of Lamictal in children below the age of 16 have not been established.

Overdosage

Any medication taken in excess can have serious consequences. If you suspect an overdose, seek medical treatment immediately. There has been little experience with Lamictal overdose. However, the following symptoms might be seen.

■ *Symptoms of Lamictal overdose may include:*
  Coma, dizziness, headache, sleepiness

Generic name:

LAMIVUDINE

See Epivir, page 458.

Generic name:

LAMOTRIGINE

See Lamictal, page 639.

Brand name:

LANOXIN

Pronounced: la-NOCKS-in
Generic name: Digoxin

Why is this drug prescribed?

Lanoxin is used in the treatment of congestive heart failure, irregular heartbeat, and other heart problems. It improves the strength and efficiency of your heart, which leads to better circulation of blood and reduction of the uncomfortable swelling that is common in people with congestive heart failure. Lanoxin is in a class of drugs known as digitalis glycosides.

Most important fact about this drug

You should not stop taking Lanoxin without first consulting your doctor. A sudden absence of the drug could cause a serious change in your heart function. You will probably have to take Lanoxin for a long time—possibly for the rest of your life.

How should you take this medication?
Lanoxin usually is taken once daily. To help you remember your dose, try to take it at the same time every day, for instance when brushing your teeth in the morning or going to bed at night.

If you are taking the liquid form of Lanoxin, use the specially marked dropper that comes with it.

It's best to take this medicine on an empty stomach. However, if this upsets your stomach, you can take Lanoxin with food.

Avoid taking this medicine with high-bran/high-fiber foods, such as certain breakfast cereals.

Do not change from one brand of this drug to another without first consulting your doctor or pharmacist.

Your doctor may ask you to check your pulse rate while taking Lanoxin. Slowing or quickening of your pulse could mean you are developing side effects to your prescribed dose. The amount of Lanoxin needed to help most people is very close to the amount that could cause serious problems from overdose, so monitoring your pulse can be very important.

■ *If you miss a dose...*
If you remember within 12 hours, take it immediately. If you remember later, skip the dose you missed and go back to your regular schedule. Never take 2 doses at the same time. If you miss doses 2 or more days in a row, consult your doctor.

■ *Storage instructions...*
Store this medication at room temperature in the container it came in, tightly closed, and away from moist places and direct light. Keep out of reach of children. Digitalis-type drugs such as Lanoxin are a major cause of accidental poisoning in the young.

What side effects may occur?
Side effects cannot be anticipated. If any develop or change in intensity, inform your doctor as soon as possible. Only your doctor can determine if it is safe for you to continue taking Lanoxin.

■ *Side effects may include:*
Apathy, blurred vision, breast development in males, change in heartbeat, diarrhea, dizziness, headache, loss of appetite, lower stomach pain, nausea, psychosis, rash, vomiting, weakness, yellow vision

Why should this drug not be prescribed?

If you are sensitive to or have ever had an allergic reaction to Lanoxin or other digitalis preparations, you should not take this medication. Make sure your doctor is aware of any drug reactions you have experienced.

Lanoxin should not be taken by people with the heart irregularity known as ventricular fibrillation.

Lanoxin should not be used, alone or with other drugs, for weight reduction. It can cause irregular heartbeat and other dangerous, even fatal, reactions.

Special warnings about this medication

Tell the doctor that you are taking Lanoxin if you have a medical emergency and before you have surgery or dental treatment.

Even if you have no symptoms, do not change your dose or discontinue the use of Lanoxin before consulting with your doctor.

Possible food and drug interactions
when taking this medication

In general, you should avoid nonprescription medicines, such as antacids; laxatives; cough, cold, and allergy remedies; and diet aids, except on professional advice.

If Lanoxin is taken with certain other drugs, the effects of either can be increased, decreased, or altered. It is especially important to check with your doctor before combining Lanoxin with the following:

Airway-opening drugs such as Proventil and Ventolin
Alprazolam (Xanax)
Amiloride (Midamor)
Amiodarone (Cordarone)
Antacids such as Maalox and Mylanta
Antibiotics such as neomycin, tetracycline, erythromycin, and
    clarithromycin
Beta-blocking blood pressure drugs such as Tenormin and Inderal
Calcium (injectable form)
Calcium-blocking blood pressure drugs such as Calan SR, Cardizem, and
    Procardia
Certain anticancer drugs such as Neosar
Cholestyramine (Questran)
Colestipol (Colestid)
Cyclosporine (Sandimmune)
Diphenoxylate (Lomotil)
Disopyramide (Norpace)

Heartbeat-regulating drugs such as Quinidex
Indomethacin (Indocin)
Itraconazole (Sporanox)
Kaolin-pectin
Metoclopramide (Reglan)
Propafenone (Rythmol)
Propantheline (Pro-Banthine)
Rifampin (Rifadin)
Steroids such as Decadron and Deltasone
Succinylcholine (Anectine)
Sucralfate (Carafate)
Sulfasalazine (Azulfidine)
Thyroid hormones such as Synthroid
Water pills such as Lasix

Special information
if you are pregnant or breastfeeding
The effects of Lanoxin during pregnancy have not been adequately studied. If you are pregnant or plan to become pregnant, inform your doctor immediately. Lanoxin appears in breast milk and could affect a nursing infant. If this medication is essential to your health, your doctor may advise you to discontinue breastfeeding.

Recommended dosage
Your doctor will determine your dosage based on several factors: (1) the disease being treated; (2) your body weight; (3) your kidney function; (4) your age; and (5) other diseases you have or drugs you are taking.

ADULTS

If you are receiving Lanoxin for the first time, you may be rapidly "digitalized" (a larger first dose may be taken, followed by smaller maintenance doses), or gradually "digitalized" (maintenance doses only), depending on your doctor's recommendation. A typical maintenance dose might be a 0.125 milligram or 0.25 milligram tablet once daily, but individual requirements vary widely. The exact dose will be determined by your doctor, based on your needs.

CHILDREN

Infants and young children usually have their daily dose divided into smaller doses; children over age 10 need adult dosages in proportion to body weight as determined by your doctor.

Overdosage
Suspected overdoses of Lanoxin must be treated immediately; you should contact your doctor or emergency room without delay.

■ *Symptoms of Lanoxin overdose include:*
Abdominal pain, diarrhea, irregular heartbeat, loss of appetite, nausea, very slow pulse, vomiting

In infants and children, irregular heartbeat is the most common sign of overdose.

Generic name:

LANSOPRAZOLE

See Prevacid, page 1000.

Brand name:

LASIX

Pronounced: LAY-six
Generic name: Furosemide

Why is this drug prescribed?
Lasix is used in the treatment of high blood pressure and other conditions that require the elimination of excess fluid (water) from the body. These conditions include congestive heart failure, cirrhosis of the liver, and kidney disease. When used to treat high blood pressure, Lasix is effective alone or in combination with other high blood pressure medications. Diuretics help your body produce and eliminate more urine, which helps lower blood pressure. Lasix is classified as a "loop diuretic" because of its point of action in the kidneys.

Lasix is also used with other drugs in people with fluid accumulation in the lungs.

Most important fact about this drug
Lasix acts quickly, usually within 1 hour. However, since blood pressure declines gradually, it may be several weeks before you get the full benefit of Lasix; and you must continue taking it even if you are feeling well. Lasix does not cure high blood pressure; it merely keeps it under control.

How should you take this medication?
Take this medication exactly as prescribed by your doctor.

■ *If you miss a dose...*
Take the forgotten dose as soon as you remember. If it is almost time for your next dose, skip the one you missed and go back to your regular schedule. Never take 2 doses at the same time.

■ *Storage instructions...*
Keep this medication in the container it came in, tightly closed, and away from direct light. Store at room temperature.

What side effects may occur?
Side effects cannot be anticipated. If any develop or change in intensity, inform your doctor as soon as possible. Only your doctor can determine if it is safe for you to continue taking Lasix.

■ *Side effects may include:*
Anemia, blood disorders, blurred vision, constipation, cramping, diarrhea, dizziness, dizziness upon standing, fever, headache, hearing loss, high blood sugar, hives, itching, loss of appetite, low potassium (leading to symptoms like dry mouth, excessive thirst, weak or irregular heartbeat, muscle pain or cramps), muscle spasms, nausea, rash, reddish or purplish spots on the skin, restlessness, ringing in the ears, sensitivity to light, skin eruptions, skin inflammation and flaking, stomach or mouth irritation, tingling or pins and needles, vertigo, vision changes, vomiting, weakness, yellow eyes and skin

Why should this drug not be prescribed?
If you are sensitive to or have ever had an allergic reaction to Lasix or diuretics, or if you are unable to urinate, you should not take this medication.

Special warnings about this medication
Lasix can cause your body to lose too much potassium. Signs of an excessively low potassium level include muscle weakness and rapid or irregular heartbeat. To improve your potassium level, your doctor may prescribe a potassium supplement or recommend potassium-rich foods, such as bananas, raisins, and orange juice.

Make sure the doctor knows if you have kidney disease, liver disease, diabetes, gout, or the connective tissue disease, lupus erythematosus. Lasix should be used with caution.

If you are allergic to sulfa drugs, you may also be allergic to Lasix.

If you have high blood pressure, avoid over-the-counter medications that may increase blood pressure, including cold remedies and appetite suppressants.

Your skin may be more sensitive to the effects of sunlight.

**Possible food and drug interactions
when taking this medication**
If Lasix is taken with certain other drugs, the effects of either could be increased, decreased, or altered. It is especially important to consult with your doctor before taking Lasix with any of the following:

Aminoglycoside antibiotics such as Garamycin
Aspirin and other salicylates
Ethacrynic acid (Edecrin)
Indomethacin (Indocin)
Lithium (Lithonate)
Norepinephrine (Levophed)
Other high blood pressure medications such as Hytrin and Cardura
Sucralfate (Carafate)

**Special information
if you are pregnant or breastfeeding**
The effects of Lasix during pregnancy have not been adequately studied. If you are pregnant or plan to become pregnant, inform your doctor immediately. Lasix appears in breast milk and could affect a nursing infant. If this medication is essential to your health, your doctor may advise you to discontinue breastfeeding until your treatment is finished.

Recommended dosage
Your doctor will adjust the dosages of this strong diuretic to meet your specific needs.

ADULTS

Fluid Retention
You will probably be started at a single dose of 20 to 80 milligrams. If needed, the same dose can be repeated 6 to 8 hours later, or the dose may be increased. Your doctor may raise the dosage by 20 milligrams or 40 milligrams with each successive administration— each 6 to 8 hours after the previous dose—until the desired effect is achieved. This dosage is then taken once or twice daily thereafter. Your doctor should monitor you carefully using laboratory tests. The maximum daily dose is 600 milligrams.

High Blood Pressure
The usual starting dose is 80 milligrams per day divided into 2 doses. Your doctor will adjust the dosages and may add other high blood pressure medications if Lasix is not enough.

CHILDREN

The usual initial dose is 2 milligrams per 2.2 pounds of body weight given in a single oral dose. The doctor may increase subsequent doses by 1 to 2 milligrams per 2.2 pounds. Doses are spaced 6 to 8 hours apart. A child's dosage will be adjusted to the lowest needed to achieve maximum effect, and should not exceed 6 milligrams per 2.2 pounds.

Overdosage
Any medication taken in excess can have serious consequences. An overdose of Lasix can cause symptoms of severe dehydration. If you suspect an overdose, seek medical attention immediately.

- **Symptoms of Lasix overdose may include:**
  Dry mouth, excessive thirst, low blood pressure, muscle pain or cramps, nausea and vomiting, weak or irregular heartbeat, weakness or drowsiness

Generic name:

LATANOPROST

See Xalatan, page 1368.

Brand name:

LESCOL

Pronounced: LESS-cahl
Generic name: Fluvastatin sodium

Why is this drug prescribed?
Lescol is a cholesterol-lowering drug. Your doctor may prescribe Lescol if you have been unable to reduce your blood cholesterol level sufficiently with a low-fat, low-cholesterol diet alone.

Most important fact about this drug
Lescol is usually prescribed only if diet, exercise, and weight loss fail to bring your cholesterol levels under control. It's important to remember that Lescol

is a supplement—not a substitute—for those other measures. To get the full benefit of the medication, you need to stick to the diet and exercise program prescribed by your doctor. All these efforts to keep your cholesterol levels normal are important because together they may lower your risk of heart disease.

How should you take this medication?
If you've been prescribed a small, single dose per day, take it at bedtime. A large dosage may be divided into 2 smaller doses and taken twice a day. You may take Lescol with or without food.

■ *If you miss a dose...*
If you miss a dose of this medication, take it as soon as you remember. However, if it is almost time for your next dose, skip the one you missed and go back to your regular schedule. Do not take 2 doses at the same time.

■ *Storage instructions...*
Store at room temperature. Protect from direct light and excessive heat. Keep out of reach of children.

What side effects may occur?
Side effects cannot be anticipated. If any develop or change in intensity, tell your doctor as soon as possible. Only your doctor can determine if it is safe for you to continue taking Lescol.

■ *More common side effects may include:*
Abdominal pain, accidental injury, back pain, diarrhea, flu-like symptoms, headache, indigestion, joint pain, muscle pain, nasal inflammation, nausea, sore throat, upper respiratory infection

■ *Less common side effects may include:*
Allergy, arthritis, constipation, coughing, dizziness, dental problems, fatigue, gas, inflamed sinuses, insomnia, rash

Why should this drug not be prescribed?
Do not take Lescol while pregnant or nursing. Also avoid Lescol if you are experiencing liver problems, or if you have ever been found to be excessively sensitive to it.

Special warnings about this medication
Because Lescol may damage the liver, your doctor may order a blood test to check your liver enzyme levels before you start taking this medication. Blood

tests will probably be done at 6 and 12 weeks after you start Lescol therapy and periodically after that. If your liver enzymes rise too high, your doctor may tell you to stop taking Lescol. Your doctor will monitor you especially closely if you have ever had liver disease or if you are, or have ever been, a heavy drinker.

Since Lescol may cause damage to muscle tissue, be sure to tell your doctor of any unexplained muscle pain, tenderness, or weakness right away, especially if you also have a fever or feel sick. Your doctor may want to do a blood test to check for signs of muscle damage. If your blood test shows signs of muscle damage, your doctor may suggest discontinuing this medication.

If your risk of muscle and/or kidney damage suddenly increases because of major surgery or injury, or conditions such as low blood pressure, severe infection, or seizures, your doctor may tell you to stop taking Lescol for a while.

Be sure to tell your doctor about any medical conditions you may have before starting therapy with Lescol.

Possible food and drug interactions
when taking this medication
If you take Lescol with certain drugs, the effects of either could be increased, decreased, or altered. It is especially important to check with your doctor before combining Lescol with the following:

Cholestyramine (Questran)
Cimetidine (Tagamet)
Clofibrate (Atromid-S)
Cyclosporine (Sandimmune, Neoral)
Digoxin (Lanoxin, Lanoxicaps)
Erythromycin (E-Mycin, E.E.S.)
Gemfibrozil (Lopid)
Ketoconazole (Nizoral)
Omeprazole (Prilosec)
Ranitidine (Zantac)
Rifampin (Rifadin)
Spironolactone (Aldactone, Aldactazide)

Special information
if you are pregnant or breastfeeding
You must not become pregnant while taking Lescol. This medication lowers cholesterol, and cholesterol is needed for a baby to develop properly.

Because of the possible risk of birth defects, your doctor will prescribe Lescol only if you are highly unlikely to get pregnant while taking this medication. If you do become pregnant while taking Lescol, stop taking the drug and notify your doctor right away.

Lescol does appear in breast milk. Therefore, Lescol could cause severe side effects in a nursing baby. Do not take Lescol while breastfeeding your baby.

Recommended dosage
Your doctor will put you on a cholesterol-lowering diet before starting treatment with Lescol. You should continue on this diet while you are taking Lescol.

ADULTS

The usual starting dose is 20 to 40 milligrams per day, taken as a single dose at bedtime. The usual range after that is 20 to 80 milligrams per day. At the 80-milligram level, the dosage will be split into two 40-milligram doses taken 2 times a day. After 4 weeks of therapy with Lescol, your doctor will check your cholesterol level and adjust your dosage if necessary.

Combined Drug Therapy
If you are taking Lescol with another cholesterol medication such as Questran, make sure you take the other drug at least 2 hours before your dose of Lescol.

CHILDREN

The safety and effectiveness of Lescol in children under 18 years old have not been established. Do not give Lescol to children under 18 years of age.

Overdosage
Although no specific information about Lescol overdose is available, any medication taken in excess can have serious consequences. If you suspect an overdose of Lescol, seek medical attention immediately.

Brand name:

LEVAQUIN

Pronounced: LEAV-ah-kwin
Generic name: Levofloxacin

Why is this drug prescribed?
Levaquin cures a variety of bacterial infections, including several types of sinus infection and pneumonia. It is also prescribed for flare-ups of chronic

bronchitis, acute kidney infections, certain urinary infections, and mild to moderate skin infections. Levaquin is a member of the quinolone family of antibiotics.

Most important fact about this drug

Levaquin has been known to cause dangerous allergic reactions as soon as you take the first dose. Stop taking the drug and call your doctor immediately if you develop any of the following warning signs:

Skin rash, hives, or any other skin reaction
Rapid heartbeat
Difficulty swallowing or breathing
Swelling of the face, lips, tongue, or throat

How should you take this medication?

Take your complete prescription exactly as directed, even if you begin to feel better. If you stop taking Levaquin too soon, the infection may come back.

You may take Levaquin at mealtimes or in-between, but you should avoid taking it within 2 hours of the following:

Aluminum or magnesium antacids such as Maalox, Mylanta, or Gaviscon
Iron supplements such as Ferro-Sequels or Feosol
Any multivitamin preparation containing zinc
The ulcer medication Carafate

Be sure to drink plenty of fluid while taking Levaquin.

■ *If you miss a dose...*
Take it as soon as you remember. If it is almost time for your next dose, skip the one you missed and go back to your regular schedule. Do not take 2 doses at once.

■ *Storage instructions...*
Store at room temperature. Keep container tightly closed.

What side effects may occur?

Side effects cannot be anticipated. If any develop or change in intensity, tell your doctor as soon as possible. Only your doctor can determine if it is safe for you to continue taking Levaquin.

■ *Side effects may include:*
Abdominal pain, anxiety, bad taste, constipation, diarrhea, dizziness, fatigue, gas, general feeling of illness, headache, hives, indigestion,

itching, lack of appetite, nausea, nervousness, rash, sleeplessness and sleep disorders, sweating, swelling, tremors, vaginal discharge, vaginal inflammation, vomiting, yeast infection

Why should this drug not be prescribed?
If any other quinolone antibiotic—such as Cipro, Floxin, Maxaquin, Noroxin, or Penetrex—has ever given you an allergic reaction, avoid Levaquin.

Special warnings about this medication
In rare cases, Levaquin has caused convulsions and other nervous disorders. If you develop any warning signs of a nervous reaction—ranging from restlessness and tremors to depression and hallucinations—stop taking this medication and call your doctor.

Hypersensitivity to quinolone antibiotics can, in rare instances, lead to severe illnesses ranging from blood disorders to liver or kidney failure. The first sign of a developing problem is often a rash; so you should stop taking Levaquin and check with your doctor when any type of skin disorder appears. Remember, too, that an immediate allergic reaction is also a possibility (see "Most important fact about this drug").

A case of diarrhea during Levaquin therapy could signal development of the potentially dangerous condition known as pseudomembranous colitis, an inflammation of the bowel. Call your doctor for treatment at the first sign of a problem.

Stop taking Levaquin, avoid exercise, and call your doctor if you develop pain, inflammation, or a rupture in a tendon. Quinolone antibiotics have been known to cause tendon rupture during and after therapy.

If you have a kidney condition, make sure the doctor is aware of it. Your dosage may need to be lowered.

Possible food and drug interactions
when taking this medication
Nonsteroidal anti-inflammatory drugs such as Advil, Motrin, and Naprosyn can increase the risk of a nervous reaction to Levaquin. Also, check with your doctor before combining Levaquin with an oral diabetes drug such as Glucotrol, Micronase, or Orinase; changes in blood sugar levels could result.

If you are taking the asthma drug, theophylline, or the blood-thinning drug, Coumadin, make sure the doctor is aware of it. Other quinolone antibiotics have been known to interact with these medications.

Special information
if you are pregnant or breastfeeding

The effects of this drug during pregnancy have not been adequately studied. If you are pregnant or plan to become pregnant, inform your doctor immediately. Levaquin is likely to appear in breast milk and could harm a nursing infant. If the drug is essential to your health, your doctor may advise you to stop nursing until your treatment is finished.

Recommended dosage

ADULTS

Respiratory and skin infections
The usual dose is 500 milligrams once a day.

Kidney and urinary infections
The usual dose is 250 milligrams once a day

CHILDREN

Not for children under 18. Levaquin might damage developing bones and joints.

Overdosage

Levaquin is not especially poisonous. However, an overdose could still be dangerous. If you suspect one, seek emergency treatment immediately.

■ *Symptoms of Levaquin overdose may include:*
Breathlessness, lack of movement, poor coordination, tremors, convulsions, collapse

Brand name:

LEVBID

See Levsin, page 656.

Brand name:

LEVLEN

See Oral Contraceptives, page 887.

Generic name:

LEVOBUNOLOL

See Betagan, page 147.

Generic name:

LEVOFLOXACIN

See Levaquin, page 652.

Brand name:

LEVOTHROID

See Synthroid, page 1178.

Generic name:

LEVOTHYROXINE

See Synthroid, page 1178.

Brand name:

LEVOXYL

See Synthroid, page 1178.

Brand name:

LEVSIN

Pronounced: LEV-sin
Generic name: Hyoscyamine sulfate
Other brand names: Anaspaz, Levbid, Levsinex

Why is this drug prescribed?

Levsin is an antispasmodic medication given to help treat various stomach, intestinal, and urinary tract disorders that involve cramps, colic, or other painful muscle contractions. Because Levsin has a drying effect, it may also be used to dry a runny nose or to dry excess secretions before anesthesia is administered.

Together with morphine or other narcotics, Levsin is prescribed for the pain of gallstones or kidney stones. For inflammation of the pancreas, Levsin may be used to help control excess secretions and reduce pain. Levsin may also be taken in Parkinson's disease to help reduce muscle rigidity and tremors and to help control drooling and excess sweating.

Doctors also give Levsin as part of the preparation for certain diagnostic x-rays (for example, of the stomach, intestines, or kidneys).

Levsin comes in several forms, including regular tablets, tablets to be dissolved under the tongue, sustained-release capsules (Levsinex Timecaps) and sustained-release tablets (Levbid), liquid, drops, and an injectable solution.

Most important fact about this drug
Levsin may make you sweat less, causing your body temperature to increase and putting you at the risk of heatstroke. Try to stay inside as much as possible on hot days, and avoid warm places such as very hot baths and saunas.

How should you take this medication?
If you take Levsin for a stomach disorder, you may also need to take antacid medication. However, antacids make Levsin more difficult for the body to absorb. To minimize this problem, take Levsin before meals and the antacid after meals.

Take Levsin exactly as prescribed. Although the sublingual tablets (Levsin/SL) are designed to be dissolved under the tongue, they may also be chewed or swallowed. The regular tablets should be swallowed. Levbid extended-release tablets should not be crushed or chewed.

Levsin can cause dry mouth. For temporary relief, suck on a hard candy or chew gum.

■ *If you miss a dose...*
Take it as soon as you remember. If it is almost time for your next dose, skip the one you missed and go back to your regular schedule. Do not take 2 doses at once.

■ *Storage instructions...*
Store at room temperature.

What side effects may occur?
Side effects cannot be anticipated. If any side effects develop or change in intensity, tell your doctor immediately. Only your doctor can determine whether it is safe for you to continue taking Levsin.

■ *Side effects may include:*
Allergic reactions, bloating, blurred vision, confusion, constipation, decreased sweating, dilated pupils, dizziness, drowsiness, dry mouth, excitement, headache, hives, impotence, inability to urinate, insomnia, itching, heart palpitations, lack of sense of taste, nausea, nervousness, rapid heartbeat, skin reactions, speech problems, vomiting, weakness

Why should this drug not be prescribed?
Do not take Levsin if you have ever had an allergic reaction to it or similar drugs such as scopolamine. Also, you should not be given Levsin if you have any of the following:

Bowel or digestive tract obstruction or paralysis
Glaucoma (excessive pressure in the eyes)
Myasthenia gravis (a disorder in which muscles become weak and tire easily)
Ulcerative colitis (severe bowel inflammation)
Urinary obstruction

Levsin is not appropriate if you have diarrhea, especially if you have a surgical opening to the bowels (an ileostomy or colostomy).

Special warnings about this medication
Be careful using Levsin if you have an overactive thyroid gland, heart disease, congestive heart failure, irregular heartbeats, high blood pressure, or kidney disease.

Because Levsin may make you dizzy or drowsy, or blur your vision, do not drive, operate other machinery, or do any other hazardous work while taking this medication.

While you are taking Levsin, you may experience confusion, disorientation, short-term memory loss, hallucinations, difficulty speaking, lack of coordination, coma, an exaggerated sense of well-being, decreased anxiety, fatigue, sleeplessness and agitation. These symptoms should disappear 12 to 48 hours after you stop taking the drug.

Possible food and drug interactions
when taking this medication
If Levsin is taken with certain other drugs, the effects of either drug could be increased, decreased, or altered. It is especially important to check with your doctor before combining Levsin with the following:

Amantadine (Symmetrel)
Antacids
Antidepressant drugs such as Elavil, Nardil, Parnate, and Tofranil
Antihistamines such as Benadryl
Major tranquilizers such as Thorazine and Haldol
Other antispasmodic drugs such as Bentyl
Potassium supplements such as Slow-K

Special information
if you are pregnant or breastfeeding

If you are pregnant or plan to become pregnant, inform your doctor immediately. Although it is not known whether Levsin can cause birth defects, pregnant women should avoid all drugs except those necessary to health.

Levsin appears in breast milk. Your doctor may ask you to forgo breastfeeding when taking this drug.

Recommended dosage

LEVSIN AND LEVSIN/SL TABLETS

Levsin tablets should be swallowed. Levsin/SL tablets may be placed under the tongue, swallowed, or chewed.

Adults and Children 12 Years of Age and Older

The usual dose is 1 to 2 tablets every 4 hours or as needed. Do not take more than 12 tablets in 24 hours.

Children 2 to Under 12 Years of Age

The usual dose is one-half to 1 tablet every 4 hours or as needed. Do not give a child more than 6 tablets in 24 hours.

LEVSIN ELIXIR

Adults and Children 12 Years of Age and Older

The recommended dosage is 1 to 2 teaspoonfuls every 4 hours or as needed, but no more than 12 teaspoonfuls in 24 hours.

Children 2 to 12 Years of Age

Dosage is by body weight. Doses may be given every 4 hours or as needed. Do not give a child more than 6 teaspoonfuls in 24 hours.

Weight	Dose
22 pounds	1/4 teaspoon
44 pounds	1/2 teaspoon
88 pounds	3/4 teaspoon
110 pounds	1 teaspoon

LEVSIN DROPS

Adults and Children 12 Years of Age and Older

The recommended dosage is 1 to 2 milliliters every 4 hours or as needed, but no more than 12 milliliters in 24 hours.

Children 2 to 12 Years of Age

The usual dosage is one-quarter to 1 milliliter every 4 hours or as needed. Do not give a child more than 6 milliliters in 24 hours.

Children under 2 Years of Age

Your doctor will determine the dosage based on body weight. The doses may be repeated every 4 hours or as needed.

Weight	Usual Dose	Do Not Exceed in 24 Hours
7.5 pounds	4 drops	24 drops
11 pounds	5 drops	30 drops
15 pounds	6 drops	36 drops
22 pounds	8 drops	48 drops

LEVSINEX TIMECAPS

Adults and Children 12 Years of Age and Older

The recommended dosage is 1 to 2 capsules every 12 hours. Your doctor may adjust the dosage to 1 capsule every 8 hours if needed. Do not take more than 4 capsules in 24 hours.

LEVBID EXTENDED-RELEASE TABLETS

Adults and Children 12 Years of Age and Older

The dosage is 1 to 2 tablets every 12 hours. The tablets are scored so that you can break them in half if your doctor wants you to. Do not crush or chew them. You should not take more than 4 tablets in 24 hours.

Overdosage

Any medication taken in excess can have serious consequences. If you suspect an overdose, seek medical attention immediately.

- *Symptoms of Levsin overdose may include:*
  Blurred vision, dilated pupils, dizziness, dry mouth, excitement, headache, hot dry skin, nausea, swallowing difficulty, vomiting

Brand name:

LEVSINEX

See Levsin, page 656.

Brand name:

LEXXEL

Pronounced: LECKS-ell
Generic ingredients: Enalapril maleate, Felodipine

Why is this drug prescribed?

Lexxel is used to treat high blood pressure. It combines two blood pressure drugs: an ACE inhibitor and a calcium channel blocker. The ACE inhibitor (enalapril) lowers blood pressure by preventing a chemical in your blood called angiotensin I from converting to a more potent form that narrows the blood vessels and increases salt and water retention. The calcium channel blocker (felodipine) also works to keep the blood vessels open, and eases the heart's workload by reducing the force and rate of your heartbeat.

Lexxel can be prescribed alone or in combination with other blood pressure medicines, especially water pills (diuretics) such as HydroDIURIL or Esidrix.

Most important fact about this drug

Doctors usually prescribe Lexxel for patients who have been taking one of its components—enalapril (Vasotec) or extended-release felodipine (Plendil)—without showing improvement. Like other blood pressure medications, Lexxel must be taken regularly for it to be effective. Since blood pressure declines gradually, it may be 1 or 2 weeks before you get the full benefit of Lexxel; and you must continue taking it even if you are feeling well. Lexxel does not cure high blood pressure; it merely keeps it under control.

How should you take this medication?

Lexxel can be taken with or without food. Remember, however, that a high-fat meal can reduce its effectiveness, and that grapefruit juice increases its impact.

Swallow Lexxel tablets whole. Do not crush, divide, or chew them.

- *If you miss a dose...*
  Take it as soon as you remember. If it is almost time for your next dose, skip the one you missed and go back to your regular schedule. Never take 2 doses at the same time.

- *Storage instructions...*
  Store at room temperature. Keep the container tightly closed and protect from light and humidity.

What side effects may occur?

Side effects cannot be anticipated. If any develop or change in intensity, inform your doctor as soon as possible. Only your doctor can determine if it is safe for you to continue taking Lexxel.

- *More common side effects may include:*
  Dizziness, headache, swelling

- *Less common side effects may include:*
  Cough, fatigue, flushing, lack of strength

- *Rare side effects may include:*
  Abdominal pain, agitation, chest pain, constipation, diarrhea, difficulty breathing, drowsiness, dry mouth or throat, dry skin, facial swelling, fainting, gas, gout, hair loss, heartburn, hot flashes, impotence, increased pressure within the eyes, indigestion, insomnia, itching, joint swelling, nausea, neck pain, nervousness, poor coordination, rash, rectal pain, respiratory congestion, skin swelling, slow heartbeat, sore throat, tingling sensation, tremor, vomiting

Why should this drug not be prescribed?

Avoid Lexxel if you have ever had an allergic reaction to it, or have ever developed a swollen throat and difficulty swallowing (angioedema) while taking similar drugs such as Capoten, Vasotec, or Zestril. Make sure your doctor is aware of the incident.

Special warnings about this medication

Call your doctor immediately if you begin to suffer angioedema while taking Lexxel. Warning signs include swelling of the face, lips, tongue, or throat; swelling of the arms and legs; and difficulty swallowing or breathing.

Bee or wasp venom given to prevent an allergic reaction to stings may cause a severe allergic reaction to Lexxel. Kidney dialysis can also prompt an allergic reaction to the drug.

Lexxel sometimes causes a severe drop in blood pressure. The danger is especially great if you have been taking water pills (diuretics), or if you have heart disease, kidney disease, or a potassium or salt imbalance. Excessive sweating, severe diarrhea, and vomiting are also a threat. They can rob the body of water, causing a dangerous drop in blood pressure. If you feel light-headed or faint, have chest pain, or feel your heart racing, contact your doctor immediately.

Because another of the ACE inhibitors, Capoten, has been known to cause serious blood disorders, your doctor will check your blood regularly while you are taking Lexxel. If you develop signs of infection such as a sore throat or a fever, you should contact your doctor at once—an infection could be a signal of blood abnormalities.

Lexxel may also affect the liver; and your doctor will need to adjust your dosage with extra care if you are over 65 or have liver disease. Report these symptoms of liver problems to your doctor immediately: a generally run-down feeling, pain in the upper right abdomen, or yellowing of the skin or the whites of your eyes.

If you suffer from heart failure or kidney disease, make certain that your doctor knows about it. Lexxel should be used with caution under these circumstances.

Some people taking Lexxel develop a dry, nagging cough. This will go away when you stop taking the drug. Others are troubled by swollen gums. Good dental hygiene makes this less likely.

**Possible food and drug interactions
when taking this medication**

If Lexxel is taken with certain other drugs, the effects of either could be increased, decreased, or altered. It is especially important to check with your doctor before combining Lexxel with the following:

Blood pressure medicines known as beta-blockers, including Lopressor, Inderal, and Tenormin
Cimetidine (Tagamet)

Diuretics such as Lasix or HydroDIURIL

Diuretics that leave potassium in the body, such as Aldactone, Midamor, and Dyrenium

Epilepsy medications such as Dilantin, phenobarbital, and Tegretol

Grapefruit juice

High-fat meals

Lithium (Eskalith, Lithobid)

Potassium supplements such as K-Lyte, K-Tabs, and Slow-K

Because Lexxel tends to increase your potassium level, avoid potassium-containing salt substitutes unless your doctor approves.

Special information
if you are pregnant or breastfeeding

Do not take Lexxel during pregnancy. When taken during the final 6 months, the ACE inhibitor in Lexxel can cause birth defects, prematurity, and death in the developing or newborn baby. If you are pregnant, inform your doctor immediately.

Lexxel may appear in breast milk and could affect a nursing infant. If this medication is essential to your health, your doctor may advise you to stop breastfeeding.

Recommended dosage

ADULTS

The usual starting dose is 1 tablet once a day. If there is no change in your blood pressure after 1 or 2 weeks, the doctor may increase your dose to 2 tablets daily.

CHILDREN

The safety and effectiveness of Lexxel in children have not been established.

OLDER ADULTS

If you are over 65, your doctor may have to monitor your blood pressure closely at the beginning of treatment, and adjust your dose with care.

Overdosage

Any medication taken in excess can have serious consequences. If you suspect an overdose, seek medical treatment immediately.

■ *Symptoms of Lexxel overdose may include:*
Low blood pressure, rapid heartbeat

Brand name:

LIBRAX

Pronounced: LIB-racks
Generic ingredients: Chlordiazepoxide hydrochloride,
  Clidinium bromide
Other brand name: Clindex

Why is this drug prescribed?

Librax is used, in combination with other therapy, for the treatment of peptic ulcer, irritable bowel syndrome (spastic colon), and acute enterocolitis (inflammation of the colon and small intestine). Librax is a combination of a benzodiazepine (chlordiazepoxide) and an antispasmodic medication (clidinium).

Most important fact about this drug

Because of its sedative effects, you should not operate heavy machinery, drive, or engage in other hazardous tasks that require you to be mentally alert while you are taking Librax.

How should you take this medication?

Take Librax as directed by your doctor. Other therapy may be prescribed to be used at the same time.

Librax can make your mouth dry. For temporary relief, suck a hard candy or chew gum.

Take Librax before meals and at bedtime.

- *If you miss a dose...*
  Take it as soon as you remember. If it is almost time for your next dose, skip the one you missed and go back to your regular schedule. Do not take 2 doses at once.

- *Storage instructions...*
  Store away from heat, light, and moisture.

What side effects may occur?

Side effects cannot be anticipated. If any develop or change in intensity, inform your doctor as soon as possible. Only your doctor can determine if it is safe for you to continue taking Librax.

- *Side effects may include:*
  Blurred vision, changes in sex drive, confusion, constipation, drowsiness, dry mouth, fainting, lack of coordination, liver problems, minor menstrual

irregularities, nausea, skin eruptions, swelling due to fluid retention, urinary difficulties, yellowing of skin and eyes

Why should this drug not be prescribed?

You should not take this drug if you have glaucoma (elevated pressure in the eye), prostatic hypertrophy (enlarged prostate), or a bladder obstruction. If you are sensitive to or have ever had an allergic reaction to Librax or any of its ingredients, you should not take this medication. Make sure your doctor is aware of any drug reactions you have experienced.

Special warnings about this medication

Librax can be habit-forming and has been associated with drug dependence and addiction. Be very careful taking this medication if you have ever had problems with alcohol or drug abuse. Never take more than the prescribed amount.

In addition, you should not stop taking Librax suddenly, because of the risk of withdrawal symptoms (convulsions, cramps, tremors, vomiting, sweating, feeling depressed, and insomnia). If you have been taking Librax over a long period of time, your doctor will have you taper off gradually.

The elderly are more likely to develop side effects such as confusion, excessive drowsiness, and uncoordinated movements when taking Librax. The doctor will probably prescribe a low dose.

Long-term treatment with Librax may call for periodic blood and liver function tests.

Possible food and drug interactions when taking this medication

If Librax is taken with certain other drugs, the effects of either can be increased, decreased, or altered. It is especially important to check with your doctor before combining Librax with the following:

Antidepressant drugs known as MAO inhibitors, such as Nardil and Parnate
Blood-thinning drugs such as Coumadin
Certain diarrhea medications such as Donnagel and Kaopectate
Ketoconazole (Nizoral)
Major tranquilizers such as Stelazine and Thorazine
Potassium supplements such as Micro-K

In addition, you may experience excessive drowsiness and other potentially dangerous side effects if you combine Librax with alcohol or other drugs, such as Benadryl and Valium, that make you drowsy.

Special information
if you are pregnant or breastfeeding
Several studies have found an increased risk of birth defects if Librax is taken during the first 3 months of pregnancy. Therefore, Librax is rarely recommended for use by pregnant women. If you are pregnant, plan to become pregnant, or are breastfeeding, inform your doctor immediately.

Recommended dosage

ADULTS

The usual dose is 1 or 2 capsules, 3 or 4 times a day before meals and at bedtime.

OLDER ADULTS

Your doctor will have you take the lowest dose that is effective.

Overdosage
Any medication taken in excess can have serious consequences. A severe overdose of Librax can be fatal. If you suspect an overdose, seek medical help immediately.

- *Symptoms of Librax overdose may include:*
  Blurred vision, coma, confusion, constipation, excessive sleepiness, excessively dry mouth, slow reflexes, urinary difficulties

Brand name:

LIBRITABS

See Librium, page 667.

Brand name:

LIBRIUM

Pronounced: LIB-ree-um
Generic name: Chlordiazepoxide
Other brand name: Libritabs

Why is this drug prescribed?
Librium is used in the treatment of anxiety disorders. It is also prescribed for short-term relief of the symptoms of anxiety, symptoms of withdrawal in

acute alcoholism, and anxiety and apprehension before surgery. It belongs to a class of drugs known as benzodiazepines.

Most important fact about this drug

Librium is habit-forming and you can become dependent on it. You could experience withdrawal symptoms if you stopped taking it abruptly (see "What side effects may occur?"). Discontinue or change your dose only on advice of your doctor.

How should you take this medication?

Take this medication exactly as prescribed.

■ *If you miss a dose...*
Take it as soon as you remember if it is within an hour or so of your scheduled time. If you do not remember until later, skip the dose you missed and go back to your regular schedule. Do not take 2 doses at once.

■ *Storage instructions...*
Store away from heat, light, and moisture.

What side effects may occur?

Side effects cannot be anticipated. If any develop or change in intensity, inform your doctor as soon as possible. Only your doctor can determine if it is safe for you to continue taking Librium.

■ *Side effects may include:*
Confusion, constipation, drowsiness, fainting, increased or decreased sex drive, liver problems, lack of muscle coordination, minor menstrual irregularities, nausea, skin rash or eruptions, swelling due to fluid retention, yellow eyes and skin

■ *Side effects due to rapid decrease or abrupt withdrawal from Librium include:*
Abdominal and muscle cramps, convulsions, exaggerated feeling of depression, sleeplessness, sweating, tremors, vomiting

Why should this drug not be prescribed?

If you are sensitive to or have ever had an allergic reaction to Librium or similar tranquilizers, you should not take this medication.

Anxiety or tension related to everyday stress usually does not require treatment with Librium. Discuss your symptoms thoroughly with your doctor.

Special warnings about this medication

Librium may cause you to become drowsy or less alert; therefore, you should not drive or operate dangerous machinery or participate in any hazardous activity that requires full mental alertness until you know how you react to this drug.

If you are severely depressed or have suffered from severe depression, consult with your doctor before taking this medication.

This drug may cause children to become less alert.

If you have a hyperactive, aggressive child taking Librium, inform your doctor if you notice contrary reactions such as excitement, stimulation, or acute rage.

Consult with your doctor before taking Librium if you are being treated for porphyria (a rare metabolic disorder) or kidney or liver disease.

Possible food and drug interactions
when taking this medication

Librium is a central nervous system depressant and may intensify the effects of alcohol or have an additive effect. Do not drink alcohol while taking this medication.

If Librium is taken with certain other drugs, the effects of either can be increased, decreased, or altered. It is especially important to check with your doctor before combining Librium with the following:

Antacids such as Maalox and Mylanta
Antidepressant drugs known as MAO inhibitors, including Nardil and
    Parnate
Barbiturates such as phenobarbital
Blood-thinning drugs such as Coumadin
Cimetidine (Tagamet)
Disulfiram (Antabuse)
Levodopa (Larodopa)
Major tranquilizers such as Stelazine and Thorazine
Narcotic pain relievers such as Demerol and Percocet
Oral contraceptives

Special information
if you are pregnant or breastfeeding

Do not take Librium if you are pregnant or planning to become pregnant. There may be an increased risk of birth defects. This drug may appear in breast milk and could affect a nursing infant. If the medication is essential to your health, your doctor may advise you to discontinue breastfeeding until your treatment with the drug is finished.

Recommended dosage

ADULTS

Mild or Moderate Anxiety
The usual dose is 5 or 10 milligrams, 3 or 4 times a day.

Severe Anxiety
The usual dose is 20 to 25 milligrams, 3 or 4 times a day.

Apprehension and Anxiety before Surgery
On days preceding surgery, the usual dose is 5 to 10 milligrams, 3 or 4 times a day.

Withdrawal Symptoms of Acute Alcoholism
The usual starting oral dose is 50 to 100 milligrams; the doctor will repeat this dose, up to a maximum of 300 milligrams per day, until agitation is controlled. The dose will then be reduced as much as possible.

CHILDREN

The usual dose for children 6 years of age and older is 5 milligrams, 2 to 4 times per day. Some children may need to take 10 milligrams, 2 or 3 times per day. The drug is not recommended for children under 6.

OLDER ADULTS

Your doctor will limit the dose to the smallest effective amount in order to avoid oversedation or lack of coordination. The usual dose is 5 milligrams, 2 to 4 times per day.

Overdosage

Any medication taken in excess can cause symptoms of overdose. If you suspect an overdose, seek medical attention immediately.

■ *The symptoms of Librium overdose may include:*
Coma, confusion, sleepiness, slow reflexes

Brand name:

LIDEX

Pronounced: LYE-decks
Generic name: Fluocinonide
Other brand name: Dermacin

Why is this drug prescribed?
Lidex is a steroid medication that relieves the itching and inflammation of a wide variety of skin problems, including redness and swelling.

Most important fact about this drug
When you use Lidex, you inevitably absorb some of the medication through your skin and into the bloodstream. Too much absorption can lead to unwanted side effects elsewhere in the body. To keep this problem to a minimum, avoid using large amounts of Lidex over large areas, and do not cover it with airtight dressings such as plastic wrap or adhesive bandages unless specifically told to by your doctor.

How should you use this medication?
Lidex is for use only on the skin. Be careful to keep it out of your eyes. If the medication gets in your eyes and causes irritation, immediately flush your eyes with a large amount of water.

Apply Lidex as directed by your doctor. Do not use more of the medication than suggested by your doctor.

■ *If you miss a dose...*
Apply it as soon as you remember. If it is almost time for the next dose, skip the one you missed and go back to your regular schedule.

■ *Storage instructions...*
Store at room temperature. Avoid excessive heat.

What side effects may occur?
Side effects cannot be anticipated. If any develop or change in intensity, inform your doctor immediately. Only your doctor can determine if it is safe for you to continue using Lidex.

■ *Side effects may include:*
Acne-like eruptions, burning, dryness, excessive hair growth, infection of the skin, irritation, itching, lack of skin color, prickly heat, skin inflammation, skin loss or softening, stretch marks

Why should this drug not be prescribed?

You should not be using Lidex if you are allergic to any of its components.

Special warnings about this medication

Do not use Lidex more often or for a longer time than your doctor ordered. If enough of the drug is absorbed through the skin, it may produce unusual side effects, including increased sugar in your blood and urine and a group of symptoms called Cushing's syndrome, characterized by a moon-shaped face, emotional disturbances, high blood pressure, weight gain, and growth of body hair in women.

Some factors that may increase absorption include:

Using bandages over the area where the medication is applied;
Using the medication over a large area of skin or on broken skin; or
Using the medication for an extended period of time.

Children may absorb a proportionally greater amount of steroid drugs and may be more sensitive to the effects of these drugs. Avoid covering a treated area with waterproof diapers or plastic pants. They can increase absorption of Lidex.

■ *Effects experienced by children may include:*
Bulges on the head
Delayed weight gain
Headache
Slow growth

Lidex should be discontinued if irritation develops, and another treatment should be used.

Extended treatment time with any steroid product may cause skin to waste away. This may also occur with short-term use on the face, armpits, and skin creases.

Possible food and drug interactions
when taking this medication

No interactions have been reported with Lidex.

Special information
if you are pregnant or breastfeeding

Pregnant women should not use steroids on the skin in large amounts or for long periods of time. During pregnancy, these medications should be used only if the possible gains outweigh the possible risks to the baby.

Steroids do appear in breast milk. Women who breastfeed an infant should use them cautiously.

Recommended dosage

ADULTS

Lidex is applied to the affected areas in a thin film 2 to 4 times a day. If hair covers the infected area, part the hair so that the medication can be applied directly.

CHILDREN

Children should be given the smallest effective dose.

Overdosage

Lidex can be absorbed in amounts large enough to have temporary effects on the adrenal, hypothalamic, and pituitary glands.

- *Some effects of steroid drugs may include:*
  Abnormal sugar levels in urine, excessive blood sugar levels, symptoms of Cushing's syndrome

- *Symptoms of Cushing's syndrome may include:*
  Easily bruised skin, increased blood pressure, mood swings, water retention, weak muscles, weight gain

If you suspect a Lidex overdose, seek medical help immediately.

Generic name:

LINDANE

See Kwell, page 636.

Brand name:

LIPITOR

Pronounced: LIP-ih-tor
Generic name: Atorvastatin calcium

Why is this drug prescribed?

Lipitor is a cholesterol-lowering drug. Your doctor may prescribe it along with a special diet if your blood cholesterol level is high enough to put you in danger of heart disease, and you have been unable to lower your cholesterol by diet alone.

The drug works by helping to clear harmful low density lipoprotein (LDL) cholesterol out of the blood and by limiting the body's ability to form new LDL cholesterol.

Most important fact about this drug
Lipitor is usually prescribed only if diet, exercise, and weight loss fail to bring your cholesterol levels under control. It's important to remember that Lipitor is a supplement—not a substitute—for those other measures. To get the full benefit of the medication, you need to stick to the diet and exercise program prescribed by your doctor. All these efforts to keep your cholesterol levels normal are important because they may lower your risk of heart disease.

How should you take this medication?
Lipitor should be taken once a day, with or without food. You can take it in the morning or the evening, but should hold to the same time each day. The drug generally begins working within 2 weeks.

For an even greater cholesterol-lowering effect, your doctor may prescribe Lipitor along with a different kind of lipid-lowering drug such as Questran or Colestid. It's important to avoid taking the two drugs at the same time of day. Take Lipitor at least 1 hour before or 4 hours after the other drug.

■ *If you miss a dose...*
Take the forgotten dose as soon as you remember. If it is almost time for your next dose, skip the one you missed and go back to your regular schedule. Do not take 2 doses at the same time.

■ *Storage instructions...*
Store at room temperature.

What side effects may occur?
Side effects cannot be anticipated. If any develop or change in intensity, inform your doctor as soon as possible. Only your doctor can determine if it is safe for you to continue taking Lipitor. The side effects of Lipitor—if any develop—are usually mild.

■ *Side effects may include:*
Abdominal pain, allergic reaction, back pain, changes in eyesight, cold, constipation, diarrhea, dry eyes, dry skin, flu symptoms, gas, hair loss, headache, heartburn, indigestion, inflammation of sinus and nasal

passages, itching, joint pain, leg cramps, muscle aching or weakness, purple or red spots on the skin, rash, sore throat, urinary problems, vomiting, weakness

Why should this drug not be prescribed?
Never take Lipitor during pregnancy or while breastfeeding. You should also avoid Lipitor if you have liver disease, or if the drug gives you an allergic reaction.

Special warnings about this medication
There is a slight chance of liver damage from Lipitor, so your doctor may order a blood test to check your liver function before you start taking the drug, again 6 weeks and 12 weeks after you begin therapy or your dosage is increased, and every 6 months thereafter. If the tests reveal a problem, you may have to stop using the drug.

Drugs like Lipitor have occasionally been known to damage muscle tissue, so be sure to tell your doctor immediately if you notice any unexplained muscle tenderness, weakness, or pain, especially if you also have a fever or feel sick. Your doctor may want to do a blood test to check for signs of muscle damage.

Possible food and drug interactions
when taking this medication
If you take Lipitor with certain other drugs, the effects of either could be increased, decreased, or altered. It is especially important to check with your doctor before combining Lipitor with any of the following:

Cimetidine (Tagamet)
Cyclosporine (Sandimmune, Neoral)
Digoxin (Lanoxin)
Erythromycin (E.E.S., Erythrocin, others)
Fluconazole (Diflucan)
Gemfibrozil (Lopid)
Itraconazole (Sporanox)
Ketoconazole (Nizoral)
Niacin (Nicobid, Nicolar)
Oral contraceptives
Spironolactone (Aldactone, Aldactazide)

Special information
if you are pregnant or breastfeeding
Developing babies need plenty of cholesterol, so this cholesterol-lowering drug should never be used during pregnancy. In fact, your doctor is unlikely

to prescribe Lipitor if there is even a chance that you may become pregnant. If you do conceive while taking this drug, notify your doctor right away. Lipitor does make its way into breast milk, so you should not take the drug while breastfeeding your baby.

Recommended dosage

You need to follow a standard cholesterol-lowering diet before starting Lipitor, and should continue following it throughout your therapy.

ADULTS

The usual starting dose is 10 milligrams once a day, with or without food. The doctor will check your cholesterol levels every 2 to 4 weeks and adjust the dose accordingly. The maximum recommended daily dose is 80 milligrams.

CHILDREN

Use in children is rare. The drug has never been prescribed for children under 9 years of age.

Overdosage

Although no specific information about Lipitor overdose is available, any medication taken in excess can have serious consequences. If you suspect an overdose of Lipitor, seek medical attention.

Generic name:

LISINOPRIL

See Zestril, page 1390.

Generic name:

LISINOPRIL WITH HYDROCHLOROTHIAZIDE

See Zestoretic, page 1386.

Generic name:

LITHIUM

See Lithonate, page 677.

Brand name:

LITHOBID

See Lithonate, page 677.

Brand name:

LITHONATE

Pronounced: LITH-oh-nate
Generic name: Lithium carbonate
Other brand names: Cibalith-S (lithium citrate), Eskalith,
  Lithobid, Lithotabs

Why is this drug prescribed?

Lithonate is used to treat the manic episodes of manic-depressive illness, a condition in which a person's mood swings from depression to excessive excitement. A manic episode may involve some or all of the following symptoms:

Aggressiveness
Elation
Fast, urgent talking
Frenetic physical activity
Grandiose, unrealistic ideas
Hostility
Little need for sleep
Poor judgment

Once the mania subsides, Lithonate treatment may be continued over the long term, at a somewhat lower dosage, to prevent or reduce the intensity of future manic episodes.

Some doctors also prescribe lithium for premenstrual tension, eating disorders such as bulimia, certain movement disorders, and sexual addictions.

Most important fact about this drug

If the Lithonate dosage is too low, you will derive no benefit; if it is too high, you could suffer lithium poisoning. You and your doctor will need to work together to find the correct dosage. Initially, this means frequent blood tests to find out how much of the drug is actually circulating in your bloodstream. As long as you take Lithonate, you will need to watch for side effects. Signs of lithium poisoning include vomiting, unsteady walking, diarrhea, drowsiness, tremor, and weakness. Stop taking the drug and call your doctor if you have any of these symptoms.

How should you take this medication?

To avoid stomach upset, take Lithonate immediately after meals or with food or milk.

Do not change from one brand of lithium to another without consulting your doctor or pharmacist. Take the drug exactly as prescribed.

While taking Lithonate, you should drink 10 to 12 glasses of water or fluid a day. To minimize the risk of harmful side effects, eat a balanced diet that includes some salt and lots of liquids. If you have been sweating a great deal or have had diarrhea, make sure you get extra liquids and salt.

If you develop an infection with a fever, you may need to cut back on your Lithonate dosage or even quit taking it temporarily. While you are ill, keep in close touch with your doctor.

Long-acting forms of lithium, such as Eskalith CR or Lithobid, should be swallowed whole. Do not chew, crush, or break.

If you are taking a syrup form of lithium, such as Cibalith-S, dilute it with fruit juice or another flavored beverage. You may obtain a specially marked measuring spoon from your pharmacist to ensure an accurate dose.

- *If you miss a dose...*
  Ask your doctor what to do; requirements vary for each individual. Do not take 2 doses at once.

- *Storage instructions...*
  Store at room temperature.

What side effects may occur?

The possibility of side effects varies with the level of lithium in your bloodstream. If you experience unfamiliar symptoms of any kind, inform your doctor as soon as possible.

- *Side effects that may occur when you start taking lithium include:*
  Discomfort, frequent urination, hand tremor, mild thirst, nausea

■ *Side effects that may occur at a high dosage include:*
Diarrhea, drowsiness, lack of coordination, muscular weakness, vomiting

Why should this drug not be prescribed?
Although your doctor will be cautious under certain conditions, lithium may be prescribed for anyone.

Special warnings about this medication
Lithonate may affect your judgment or coordination. Do not drive, climb, or perform hazardous tasks until you find out how this drug affects you.

Your doctor will prescribe Lithonate with extra caution if you have a heart or kidney problem, brain or spinal cord disease, or a weak, run-down, or dehydrated condition.

Also make sure your doctor is aware of any medical problems you may have, including diabetes, epilepsy, thyroid problems, Parkinson's disease, and difficulty urinating.

You should be careful in hot weather to avoid activities that cause you to sweat heavily. Also avoid drinking large amounts of coffee, tea, or cola, which can cause dehydration through increased urination. Do not make a major change in your eating habits or go on a weight loss diet without consulting your doctor. The loss of water and salt from your body could lead to lithium poisoning.

Possible food and drug interactions
when taking this medication
If Lithonate is taken with certain other drugs, the effects of either could be increased, decreased, or altered. It is especially important to check with your doctor before combining Lithonate with the following:

ACE-inhibitor blood pressure drugs such as Capoten or Vasotec
Acetazolamide (Diamox)
Amphetamines such as Dexedrine
Antidepressant drugs that boost serotonin levels, including Paxil, Prozac, and Zoloft
Anti-inflammatory drugs such as Indocin and Feldene
Bicarbonate of soda
Caffeine (No-Doz)
Calcium-blocking blood pressure drugs such as Calan and Cardizem
Carbamazepine (Tegretol)
Diuretics such as Lasix or HydroDIURIL

Fluoxetine (Prozac)
Iodine-containing preparations such as potassium iodide (Quadrinal)
Major tranquilizers such as Haldol and Thorazine
Methyldopa (Aldomet)
Metronidazole (Flagyl)
Phenytoin (Dilantin)
Sodium bicarbonate
Tetracyclines such as Achromycin V and Sumycin
Theophylline (Theo-Dur, Quibron, others)

Special information
if you are pregnant or breastfeeding

The use of Lithonate during pregnancy is usually not recommended because of the possibility that it might cause birth defects. If you are pregnant or plan to become pregnant, inform your doctor immediately.

Lithonate is excreted in breast milk and is considered potentially harmful to a nursing infant. If this medication is essential to your health, your doctor may advise you to discontinue breastfeeding while you are taking it.

Recommended dosage

ADULTS

Acute Episodes

The usual dosage is a total of 1,800 milligrams per day. Immediate-release forms are taken in 3 doses per day; long-acting forms are taken twice a day. The usual dose of syrup is 2 teaspoons, taken 3 times a day.

Your doctor will individualize your dosage according to the levels of the drug in your blood. Your blood levels will be checked at least twice a week when the drug is first prescribed and on a regular basis thereafter.

Long-term Control

Dosage will vary from one individual to another, but a total of 900 milligrams to 1,200 milligrams per day is typical. Immediate-release forms are taken in 3 or 4 doses per day; long-acting forms are taken two or three times a day. The usual dose of syrup is 1 teaspoon 3 or 4 times a day.

Blood levels in most cases should be checked every 2 months.

CHILDREN

Safety and effectiveness of Lithonate in children under 12 years of age have not been established.

OLDER ADULTS

Older people often need less Lithonate and may show signs of overdose at a dosage younger people can handle well.

Overdosage

Any medication taken in excess can have serious consequences. If you suspect symptoms of an overdose of Lithonate, seek medical attention immediately.

The harmful levels are close to those that will treat your condition. Watch for early signs of overdose, such as diarrhea, drowsiness, lack of coordination, vomiting, and weakness. If you develop any of these signs, stop taking the drug and call your doctor.

Brand name:

LITHOTABS

See Lithonate, page 677.

Brand name:

LODINE

Pronounced: LOW-deen
Generic name: Etodolac

Why is this drug prescribed?

Lodine, a nonsteroidal anti-inflammatory drug, is available in regular and extended-release forms (Lodine XL). Both forms are used to relieve the inflammation, swelling, stiffness, and joint pain of osteoarthritis (the most common form of arthritis) and rheumatoid arthritis. Regular Lodine is also used to relieve pain in other situations.

Most important fact about this drug

You should have frequent checkups with your doctor if you take Lodine regularly. Ulcers or internal bleeding can occur without warning.

How should you take this medication?

Your doctor may ask you to take Lodine with food or an antacid, and with a full glass of water. Never take it on an empty stomach.

Take this medication exactly as prescribed by your doctor.

You should see results in 1 to 2 weeks.

If you are using Lodine for arthritis, it should be taken regularly.

■ *If you miss a dose...*
Take the forgotten dose as soon as you remember. If it is almost time for the next dose, skip the one you missed and go back to your regular schedule. Never try to "catch up" by doubling the dose.

■ *Storage instructions...*
Store at room temperature. Protect capsules from moisture. Protect Lodine tablets from light; protect Lodine XL tablets from excessive heat and humidity.

What side effects may occur?
Side effects cannot be anticipated. If any develop or change in intensity, inform your doctor as soon as possible. Only your doctor can determine if it is safe for you to continue taking Lodine.

■ *More common side effects may include:*
Abdominal pain, black stools, blurred vision, chills, constipation, depression, diarrhea, dizziness, fever, gas, increased frequency of urination, indigestion, itching, nausea, nervousness, rash, ringing in ears, painful or difficult urination, vomiting, weakness

■ *Less common or rare side effects may include:*
Abdominal bleeding, abnormal intolerance of light, anemia, asthma, blood disorders, congestive heart failure, dry mouth, fainting, flushing, hepatitis and other liver problems, high blood pressure, high blood sugar in some diabetics, hives, inability to sleep, inflamed blood vessels, inflammation of mouth or upper intestine, kidney problems, including kidney failure, loss of appetite, peptic ulcer, rapid heartbeat, rash, severe allergic reactions, skin disorders including increased pigmentation, sleepiness, Stevens-Johnson syndrome (peeling skin), sweating, swelling (fluid retention), thirst, visual disturbances, yellowed skin and eyes

Why should this drug not be prescribed?
If you are sensitive to or have ever had an allergic reaction to Lodine, or if you have had asthma attacks, hives, or other allergic reactions caused by aspirin or other nonsteroidal anti-inflammatory drugs such as Motrin, you

should not take this medication; it might cause a severe allergic reaction. Make sure your doctor is aware of any drug reactions you have experienced; and be careful about taking this drug if you have asthma—even if you've never had a drug reaction before. If you do suffer an allergic reaction, call for emergency help immediately.

Special warnings about this medication

Peptic ulcers and bleeding can occur without warning. You may have other problems with bleeding as well.

Call your doctor if you have any signs or symptoms of stomach or intestinal ulcers or bleeding, blurred vision or other eye problems, skin rash, weight gain, or fluid retention and swelling.

This drug should be used with caution if you have kidney or liver disease; and it can cause liver inflammation in some people.

Do not take aspirin or any other anti-inflammatory medications while taking Lodine, unless your doctor tells you to do so.

If you are taking Lodine over an extended period of time, your doctor should check your blood for anemia.

This drug can increase water retention. Use with caution if you have heart disease or high blood pressure.

Possible food and drug interactions
when taking this medication

If Lodine is taken with certain other drugs, the effects of either could be increased, decreased, or altered. It is especially important to check with your doctor before combining Lodine with the following:

Aspirin
Cyclosporine (Sandimmune, Neoral)
Digoxin (Lanoxin)
Lithium (Lithobid, others)
Methotrexate
Phenylbutazone (Butazolidin)
The blood-thinning drug warfarin (Coumadin)

Special information
if you are pregnant or breastfeeding

The effects of Lodine during pregnancy have not been adequately studied. However, you should definitely not take it in late pregnancy. If you are pregnant or plan to become pregnant, inform your doctor immediately. Lodine may appear in breast milk and could affect a nursing infant. If this medication is essential to your health, your doctor may advise you to discontinue breastfeeding until your treatment with this medication is finished.

Recommended dosage

ADULTS

General Pain Relief
Take 200 to 400 milligrams every 6 to 8 hours as needed. Ordinarily, you should not take more than 1,000 milligrams a day, although your doctor may increase the dose to 1,200 milligrams a day if absolutely necessary.

Osteoarthritis and Rheumatoid Arthritis
The starting dose of Lodine is 300 milligrams 2 or 3 times a day, or 400 or 500 milligrams twice a day. The usual daily maximum ranges from 600 to 1,000 milligrams, although your doctor may prescribe as much as 1,200 milligrams a day if necessary.

The usual dose of Lodine XL is 400 to 1,000 milligrams taken once a day.

Your doctor will stick with the lowest dose that proves effective.

CHILDREN
The safety and effectiveness of Lodine have not been established in children.

Overdosage
Any medication taken in excess can cause symptoms of overdose. If you suspect an overdose, seek medical attention immediately.

- **Symptoms of Lodine overdose may include:**
  Drowsiness, lethargy, nausea, stomach pain, vomiting

Brand name:

LOESTRIN

See Oral Contraceptives, page 887.

Generic name:

LOMEFLOXACIN

See Maxaquin, page 727.

Brand name:

LOMOTIL

Pronounced: loe-MOE-till
Generic ingredients: Diphenoxylate hydrochloride, Atropine
sulfate

Why is this drug prescribed?
Lomotil is used, along with other drugs, in the treatment of diarrhea.

Most important fact about this drug
Lomotil is not a harmless drug, so never exceed your recommended dosage.
An overdose could be fatal.

How should you take this medication?
Lomotil can be habit-forming. Take it exactly as prescribed.

Be sure to drink plenty of liquids to replace lost body fluids. Eat bland foods,
such as cooked cereals, breads and crackers.

Lomotil may cause dry mouth. Suck on a hard candy or chew gum to relieve
this problem.

- *If you miss a dose...*
  Take it as soon as you remember. If it is almost time for your next dose,
  skip the one you missed and go back to your regular schedule. Do not take
  2 doses at once.

- *Storage instructions...*
  Store away from heat, light, and moisture. Keep the liquid from freezing.

What side effects may occur?
Side effects cannot be anticipated. If any develop or change in intensity,
inform your doctor as soon as possible. Only your doctor can determine if it
is safe for you to continue taking Lomotil.

- *Side effects may include:*
  Abdominal discomfort, confusion, depression, difficulty urinating, dizziness, dry mouth and skin, exaggerated feeling of elation, fever, flushing,
  general feeling of not being well, headache, hives, intestinal blockage,
  itching, lack or loss of appetite, nausea, numbness of arms and legs, rapid
  heartbeat, restlessness, sedation/drowsiness, severe allergic reaction,
  sluggishness, swelling due to fluid retention, swollen gums, vomiting

Why should this drug not be prescribed?
If you are sensitive to or have ever had an allergic reaction to the

ingredients of Lomotil, diphenoxylate or atropine, you should not take this medication. Make sure your doctor is aware of any drug reactions you have experienced.

Unless you are directed to do so by your doctor, do not take Lomotil if you have obstructive jaundice (a disease in which bile made in the liver does not reach the intestines because of a bile duct obstruction such as gallstones). Do not take Lomotil if you have diarrhea associated with pseudomembranous enterocolitis (inflammation of the intestines) or an infection with enterotoxin-producing bacteria (an enterotoxin is a poisonous substance that affects the stomach and intestines).

Special warnings about this medication
Certain antibiotics such as Ceclor, Cleocin, PCE and Achromycin V may cause diarrhea. Lomotil can make this type of diarrhea worse and longer-lasting. Check with your doctor before using Lomotil while taking an antibiotic.

Lomotil may cause drowsiness or dizziness. Therefore, you should not drive a car, operate dangerous machinery, or participate in any hazardous activity that requires full mental alertness until you know how this drug affects you.

Lomotil slows activity of the digestive system; this can result in a buildup of fluid in the intestine, which may worsen the dehydration and imbalance in normal body salts that usually occur with diarrhea.

If you have severe ulcerative colitis (an inflammation of the intestines), your doctor will want to monitor your condition while you are taking this drug. If your abdomen becomes distended, or enlarged, notify your doctor.

Use Lomotil with extreme caution if you have kidney and liver disease or if your liver is not functioning normally.

Lomotil should be used with caution in children, since side effects may occur even with recommended doses, especially in children with Down's syndrome (congenital mental retardation).

Since addiction to diphenoxylate hydrochloride is possible at high doses, you should never exceed the recommended dosage.

Possible food and drug interactions
when taking this medication
Lomotil may intensify the effects of alcohol. It's better not to drink alcohol while taking this medication.

If Lomotil is taken with certain other drugs, the effects of either could be increased, decreased, or altered. It is especially important to check with your doctor before combining Lomotil with the following:

Barbiturates (anticonvulsants and sedatives such as phenobarbital)
MAO inhibitors (antidepressants such as Nardil and Parnate)
Tranquilizers (such as Valium and Xanax)

Special information
if you are pregnant or breastfeeding

The effects of Lomotil during pregnancy have not been adequately studied. If you are pregnant or plan to become pregnant, notify your doctor immediately. Lomotil appears in breast milk and could affect a nursing infant. If this medication is essential to your health, your doctor may advise you to discontinue breastfeeding until your treatment is finished.

Recommended dosage

ADULTS

The recommended starting dosage is 2 tablets 4 times a day or 2 regular teaspoonfuls (10 milliliters) of liquid 4 times per day.

Once your diarrhea is under control, your doctor may reduce the dosage; you may need as little as 5 milligrams (2 tablets or 10 milliliters of liquid) per day.

You should see improvement within 48 hours. If your diarrhea persists after you have taken 20 milligrams a day for 10 days, the drug is not likely to work for you.

CHILDREN

Lomotil is not recommended for children under 2 years of age.

Your doctor will take into account your child's nutritional status and degree of dehydration before prescribing this drug.

In children under 13, use only Lomotil liquid and administer with the plastic dropper. The recommended starting dosage is 0.3 to 0.4 milligram per 2.2 pounds of body weight per day, divided into 4 equal doses. The following provides approximate starting dosage recommendations for children:

2 years (24-31 pounds):
    1.5-3.0 milligrams, 4 times daily
3 years (26-35 pounds):
    2.0-3.0 milligrams, 4 times daily
4 years (31-44 pounds):
    2.0-4.0 milligrams, 4 times daily

5 years (35-51 pounds):
    2.5-4.5 milligrams, 4 times daily
6-8 years (38-71 pounds):
    2.5-5.0 milligrams, 4 times daily
9-12 years (51-121 pounds):
    3.5-5.0 milligrams, 4 times daily

Your doctor may reduce the dosage as soon as symptoms are controlled. A maintenance dosage may be as low as one-quarter of the starting dose. If your child does not show improvement within 48 hours, Lomotil is unlikely to work.

Overdosage

An overdose of Lomotil can be dangerous and even fatal. If you suspect an overdose, seek medical attention immediately.

■ *Symptoms of Lomotil overdose may include:*
Coma, dry skin and mucous membranes, enlarged pupils of the eyes, extremely high body temperature, flushing, involuntary eyeball movement, lower than normal muscle tone, pinpoint pupils, rapid heartbeat, restlessness, sluggishness, suppressed breathing

Suppressed breathing may be seen as late as 30 hours after an overdose.

Brand name:

LO/OVRAL

See Oral Contraceptives, page 887.

Generic name:

LOPERAMIDE

See Imodium, page 594.

Brand name:

LOPID

Pronounced: LOH-pid
Generic name: Gemfibrozil
Other brand name: Gemcor

Why is this drug prescribed?

Lopid is prescribed, along with a special diet, for treatment of people with very high levels of serum triglycerides (a fatty substance in the blood) who are at risk of developing pancreatitis (inflammation of the pancreas) and who do not respond adequately to a strict diet.

This drug can also be used to reduce the risk of coronary heart disease in people who have failed to respond to weight loss, diet, exercise, and other triglyceride- or cholesterol-lowering drugs.

Most important fact about this drug
Lopid is usually prescribed only if diet, exercise, and weight-loss fail to bring your cholesterol levels under control. It's important to remember that Lopid is a supplement—not a substitute—for these other measures. To get the full benefit of the medication, you need to stick to the diet and exercise program prescribed by your doctor. All these efforts to keep your cholesterol levels normal are important because together they may lower your risk of heart disease.

How should you take this medication?
Take this medication 30 minutes before the morning and evening meal, exactly as prescribed.

■ *If you miss a dose...*
Take it as soon as you remember. If it is almost time for the next dose, skip the one you missed and go back to your regular schedule. Do not take 2 doses at the same time.

■ *Storage instructions...*
Store at room temperature.

What side effects may occur?
Side effects cannot be anticipated. If any develop or change in intensity, inform your doctor as soon as possible. Only your doctor can determine if it is safe for you to continue taking Lopid.

■ *More common side effects may include:*
Abdominal pain, acute appendicitis, constipation, diarrhea, eczema, fatigue, headache, indigestion, nausea/vomiting, rash, vertigo

■ *Less common or rare side effects may include:*
Anemia, blood disorders, blurred vision, confusion, convulsions, decreased male fertility, decreased sex drive, depression, dizziness, fainting, hives, impotence, inflammation of the colon, irregular heartbeat, itching, joint pain, laryngeal swelling, muscle disease, muscle pain, muscle weakness,

painful extremities, sleepiness, tingling sensation, weight loss, yellow eyes and skin

Why should this drug not be prescribed?

There is a slight possibility that Lopid may cause malignancy, gallbladder disease, abdominal pain leading to appendectomy, or other serious, possibly fatal, abdominal disorders. This drug should not be used by those who have only mildly elevated cholesterol levels, since the benefits do not outweigh the risk of these severe side effects.

If you are sensitive to or have ever had an allergic reaction to Lopid or similar drugs such as Atromid-S, you should not take this medication. Make sure your doctor is aware of any drug reactions you have experienced.

Unless you are directed to do so by your doctor, do not take this medication if you are being treated for severe kidney or liver disorders or gallbladder disease.

Special warnings about this medication

Excess body weight and excess alcohol intake may be important risk factors leading to unusually high levels of fats in the body. Your doctor will probably want you to lose weight and stop drinking before he or she tries to treat you with Lopid.

Your doctor will probably do periodic blood level tests during the first 12 months of therapy with Lopid because of blood diseases associated with the use of this medication.

Liver disorders have occurred with the use of this drug. Therefore, your doctor will probably test your liver function periodically.

If you are being treated for any disease that contributes to increased blood cholesterol, such as an overactive thyroid, diabetes, nephrotic syndrome (kidney and blood vessel disorder), dysproteinemia (excess of protein in the blood), or obstructive liver disease, consult with your doctor before taking Lopid.

Lopid should begin to reduce cholesterol levels during the first 3 months of therapy. If your cholesterol is not lowered sufficiently, this medication should be discontinued. Therefore, it is important that your doctor check your progress regularly.

The use of this medication may cause gallstones leading to possible gallbladder surgery. If you develop gallstones, your doctor will have you stop taking the drug.

The use of this drug may be associated with myositis, a muscle disease. If you have muscle pain, tenderness, or weakness, consult with your doctor. If myositis is suspected, your doctor will stop treating you with this drug.

Possible food and drug interactions
when taking this medication

If Lopid is taken with certain other drugs, the effects of either could be increased, decreased, or altered. It is especially important to check with your doctor before combining Lopid with the following:

Blood-thinning drugs such as Coumadin
Fluvastatin (Lescol)
Lovastatin (Mevacor)
Pravastatin (Pravachol)
Simvastatin (Zocor)

Special information
if you are pregnant or breastfeeding

The effects of Lopid during pregnancy have not been adequately studied. If you are pregnant or plan to become pregnant, inform your doctor immediately. Because this medication causes tumors in animals, it may have an effect on nursing infants. If Lopid is essential to your health, your doctor may advise you to discontinue breastfeeding until your treatment with Lopid is finished.

Recommended dosage

ADULTS

The recommended dose is 1,200 milligrams divided into 2 doses, given 30 minutes before the morning and evening meals.

CHILDREN

Safety and effectiveness of Lopid have not been established for use in children.

OLDER ADULTS

This drug should be used with caution by older adults.

Overdosage

There have been no reported cases of overdose with Lopid. However, should you suspect a Lopid overdose, seek medical attention immediately.

Brand name:

LOPRESSOR

Pronounced: low-PRESS-or
Generic name: Metoprolol tartrate

Why is this drug prescribed?

Lopressor, a type of medication known as a beta blocker, is used in the treatment of high blood pressure, angina pectoris (chest pain, usually caused by lack of oxygen to the heart due to clogged arteries), and heart attack. When prescribed for high blood pressure, it is effective when used alone or in combination with other high blood pressure medications. Beta blockers decrease the force and rate of heart contractions, thereby reducing the demand for oxygen and lowering blood pressure.

Occasionally doctors prescribe Lopressor for the treatment of aggressive behavior, prevention of migraine headache, and relief of temporary anxiety.

Most important fact about this drug

If you have high blood pressure, you must take Lopressor regularly for it to be effective. Since blood pressure declines gradually, it may be several weeks before you get the full benefit of Lopressor; and you must continue taking it even if you are feeling well. Lopressor does not cure high blood pressure; it merely keeps it under control.

How should you take this medication?

Lopressor should be taken with food or immediately after you have eaten.

Take Lopressor exactly as prescribed, even if your symptoms have disappeared.

Try not to miss any doses. If this medication is not taken regularly, your condition may worsen.

- *If you miss a dose...*
  If it is within 4 hours of your next dose, skip the one you missed and go back to your regular schedule. Never take 2 doses at the same time.

- *Storage instructions...*
  Store at room temperature in a tightly closed container, away from light. Protect from moisture.

What side effects may occur?
Side effects cannot be anticipated. If any develop or change in intensity, inform your doctor as soon as possible. Only your doctor can determine if it is safe for you to continue taking Lopressor.

■ *More common side effects may include:*
Depression, diarrhea, dizziness, itching, rash, shortness of breath, slow heartbeat, tiredness

■ *Less common or rare side effects may include:*
Blurred vision, cold hands and feet, confusion, congestive heart failure, constipation, difficult or labored breathing, dry eyes, dry mouth, gas, hair loss, headache, heart attack, heartburn, low blood pressure, muscle pain, nausea, nightmares, rapid heartbeat, ringing in the ears, short-term memory loss, stomach pain, swelling due to fluid retention, trouble sleeping, wheezing, worsening of heart irregularities

Why should this drug not be prescribed?
If you have a slow heartbeat, certain heart irregularities, low blood pressure, inadequate output from the heart, or heart failure, you should not take this medication.

Special warnings about this medication
If you have a history of congestive heart failure, Lopressor should be used with caution.

Do not stop Lopressor abruptly. This can cause increased chest pain and heart attack. Dosage should be gradually reduced.

If you suffer from asthma, seasonal allergies or other bronchial conditions, or liver disease, this medication should be used with caution.

Ask your doctor if you should check your pulse while taking Lopressor. This medication can cause your heartbeat to become too slow.

This medication may mask some symptoms of low blood sugar in diabetics or alter blood sugar levels. If you are diabetic, discuss this with your doctor.

Lopressor may cause you to become drowsy or less alert; therefore, driving or operating dangerous machinery or participating in any hazardous activity that requires full mental alertness is not recommended until you know how you respond to this medication.

Notify your doctor or dentist that you are taking Lopressor if you have a medical emergency, or before you have surgery or dental treatment.

Notify your doctor if you have any difficulty in breathing.

Possible food and drug interactions
when taking this medication

If Lopressor is taken with certain other drugs, the effects of either could be increased, decreased, or altered. It is especially important to check with your doctor before combining Lopressor with certain high blood pressure drugs such as reserpine (Ser-Ap-Es).

■ *Other medications that might interact with Lopressor include:*

Albuterol (Proventil, Ventolin)
Amiodarone (Cordarone)
Barbiturates such as phenobarbital
Calcium channel blockers such as Calan and Cardizem
Cimetidine (Tagamet)
Ciprofloxacin (Cipro)
Clonidine (Catapres)
Epinephrine (EpiPen)
Hydralazine (Apresoline)
Insulin
Nonsteroidal anti-inflammatory drugs such as Motrin and Indocin
Oral diabetes drugs such as Glucotrol and Micronase
Prazosin (Minipress)
Quinidine (Quinaglute)
Ranitidine (Zantac)
Rifampin (Rifadin)

Special information
if you are pregnant or breastfeeding

The effects of Lopressor during pregnancy have not been adequately studied. If you are pregnant or plan to become pregnant, inform your doctor immediately. Lopressor appears in breast milk and could affect a nursing infant. If this medication is essential to your health, your doctor may advise you to discontinue breastfeeding until your treatment with this medication is finished.

Recommended dosage

ADULTS

Dosages of Lopressor should be individualized by your doctor. It should be taken with or immediately following meals.

Hypertension
The usual starting dosage is a total of 100 milligrams a day taken in 1 or 2 doses, whether taken alone or with a diuretic. Your doctor may gradually increase the dosage up to 400 milligrams a day. Generally, the effectiveness of each dosage increase will be seen within a week.

Angina Pectoris
The usual starting dosage is a total of 100 milligrams a day taken in 2 doses. Your doctor may gradually increase the dosage up to 400 milligrams a day.

Generally, the effectiveness of each dosage increase will be seen within a week. If treatment is to be discontinued, your doctor will withdraw the drug gradually over a period of 1 to 2 weeks.

Heart Attack
Lopressor can be used for treatment of heart attack both in the hospital during the early phases and after the individual's condition has stabilized. Your doctor will determine the dosage according to your needs.

CHILDREN

The safety and effectiveness of Lopressor have not been established in children.

Overdosage
Any medication taken in excess can cause symptoms of overdose. If you suspect an overdose, seek medical attention immediately.

- *The symptoms of Lopressor overdose may include:*
  Asthma-like symptoms, heart failure, low blood pressure, slow heartbeat

Brand name:

LOPROX

Pronounced: LOW-prox
Generic name: Ciclopirox olamine

Why is this drug prescribed?
Loprox is prescribed for the treatment of the following fungal skin infections:

Athlete's foot
Fungal infection of the groin (jock itch)
Fungal infection of non-hairy parts of the skin

Candidiasis (yeastlike fungal infection of the skin, nails, mouth, vagina, and lungs)

Tinea versicolor—infection of the skin that is characterized by brown or tan patches on the trunk.

Loprox is available in cream and lotion forms.

Most important fact about this drug
Loprox is for external treatment of skin infections. Do not use Loprox in the eyes.

How should you use this medication?
Use this medication for the full treatment time even if your symptoms have improved. Notify your doctor if there is no improvement after 4 weeks.

Shake Loprox lotion vigorously before each use.

■ *If you miss a dose...*
Apply the forgotten dose as soon as you remember. If it is almost time for your next dose, skip the one you missed and go back to your regular schedule.

■ *Storage instructions...*
Store at room temperature.

What side effects may occur?
Loprox rarely causes side effects. If any develop or change in intensity, inform your doctor as soon as possible. Only your doctor can determine if it is safe for you to continue using Loprox.

■ *Rare side effects may include:*
Burning, itching, worsening of infection symptoms

Why should this drug not be prescribed?
If you are sensitive to or have ever had an allergic reaction to ciclopirox olamine or any other ingredient in Loprox, you should not take this medication. Make sure your doctor is aware of any drug reactions you have experienced.

Special warnings about this medication
If the affected area of skin shows signs of increased irritation (redness, itching, burning, blistering, swelling, oozing), notify your doctor.

Avoid the use of airtight dressings or bandages.

Special information
if you are pregnant or breastfeeding
The effects of Loprox during pregnancy have not been adequately studied. If you are pregnant or plan to become pregnant, inform your doctor immediately. It is not known whether this drug appears in breast milk. If this medication is essential to your health, your doctor may advise you to discontinue breastfeeding your baby until your treatment is finished.

Recommended dosage

ADULTS

Gently massage Loprox into the affected and surrounding skin areas 2 times a day, in the morning and evening. For most infections, improvement usually occurs within the first week of treatment. People with tinea versicolor usually show signs of improvement after 2 weeks of treatment.

CHILDREN

Safety and effectiveness have not been established in children under 10 years of age.

Overdosage
Any medication taken in excess can have serious consequences. If you suspect an overdose, seek medical treatment immediately.

Brand name:

LOPURIN

See Zyloprim, page 1419.

Brand name:

LORABID

Pronounced: LOR-a-bid
Generic name: Loracarbef

Why is this drug prescribed?
Lorabid is used to treat mild-to-moderate bacterial infections of the lungs, ears, throat, sinuses, skin, urinary tract, and kidneys.

Most important fact about this drug
If you have ever had an allergic reaction to Lorabid, penicillin, cephalosporins, or any other drug, be sure your doctor is aware of it before you take Lorabid.

You may experience a severe reaction if you are sensitive to penicillin-type medications.

How should you take this medication?

Take Lorabid at least 1 hour before or 2 hours after eating. It is best to take your medication at evenly spaced intervals, day and night.

Do not stop taking your medication even if you begin to feel better after a few days. If you stop taking your medicine too soon, your symptoms may return. If you have a "strep" infection, you should take your medication for at least 10 days.

■ *If you miss a dose...*
Take it as soon as possible. This will help keep a constant amount of medicine in your system. If it is almost time for your next dose, skip the one you missed and go back to your regular schedule. Do not take 2 doses at once.

■ *Storage instructions...*
Lorabid can be stored at room temperature. The liquid form can be kept in the refrigerator, but not in the freezer. Discard any unused portion.

What side effects may occur?

Side effects cannot be anticipated. If any develop or change in intensity, tell your doctor as soon as possible. Only your doctor can determine if it is safe for you to continue taking Lorabid.

■ *More common side effects in children may include:*
Diarrhea, inflamed, runny nose, vomiting

■ *Less common or rare side effects in children may include:*
Headache, loss of appetite, rash, sleepiness

■ *More common side effects in adults may include:*
Diarrhea, headache

■ *Less common side effects in adults may include:*
Abdominal pain, nausea, rhinitis, skin rashes, vaginitis (inflammation of the vaginal tissues), vomiting, yeast infection

■ *Rare side effects may include:*
Blood disorders, dizziness, hives, insomnia, itching, loss of appetite, nervousness, red bumps on skin, sleepiness, vasodilation (widening of the blood vessels)

■ *Side effects for other drugs of this class may include:*
Allergic reactions (sometimes severe), anemia, blood disorders, hemorrhage, kidney problems, serum sickness (fever, skin rash, joint pain, swollen lymph nodes), skin peeling

Why should this drug not be prescribed?
If you are allergic to penicillin, cephalosporins, or other medications, you should not take Lorabid. Make sure you tell your doctor about any drug reactions you have experienced.

Special warnings about this medication
As with many antibiotics, Lorabid can cause colitis—an inflammation of the bowel. This condition can range from mild to life-threatening. If you develop diarrhea while taking Lorabid, notify your doctor, and do not take any diarrhea medication without your doctor's approval.

Prolonged use of Lorabid may result in development of bacteria that do not respond to the medication, leading to a second infection. Because of this danger, you should not use any left-over Lorabid for later infections, even if they have similar symptoms. Take Lorabid only when your doctor prescribes it for you.

If you have known or suspected kidney problems, your doctor will perform blood tests to check your urine and kidney function before and during Lorabid therapy.

Possible food and drug interactions
when taking this medication
If Lorabid is taken with certain other drugs, the effects of either could be increased, decreased, or altered. It is especially important to check with your doctor before combining Lorabid with the following:

Diuretics such as Lasix and Bumex
Probenecid (the gout medication Benemid)

Special information
if you are pregnant or breastfeeding
The effects of Lorabid during pregnancy have not been adequately studied. If you are pregnant or plan to become pregnant, tell your doctor immediately.

Lorabid should be used during pregnancy only if clearly needed. It is not known whether Lorabid appears in human breast milk. Your doctor will determine whether it is safe for you to take Lorabid while breastfeeding.

Recommended dosage

ADULTS (13 YEARS AND OLDER)

Bronchitis
The usual dose is 200 to 400 milligrams every 12 hours for 7 days.

Pneumonia
The usual dose is 400 milligrams every 12 hours for 14 days.

Sinusitis
The usual dose is 400 milligrams every 12 hours for 10 days.

Skin and Soft Tissue Infections
The usual dose is 200 milligrams every 12 hours for 7 days.

Streptococcal Pharyngitis ("Strep Throat") and Tonsillitis
The usual dose is 200 milligrams every 12 hours for 10 days. For strep throat, take Lorabid for at least 10 days.

Bladder Infections
The usual dose is 200 milligrams every 24 hours for 7 days.

Kidney Infections
The usual dose is 400 milligrams every 12 hours for 14 days.

If you have impaired kidney function, your doctor will adjust the dosage according to your needs.

CHILDREN (6 MONTHS TO 12 YEARS OF AGE)

Otitis Media
This infection of the middle ear should be treated with the suspension. Do not use the pulvules.

The dose is based on body weight. The usual dose is 30 milligrams of liquid per 2.2 pounds of body weight per day in divided doses (half the dose every 12 hours), for 10 days.

Streptococcal Pharyngitis (Strep Throat) and Tonsillitis
The dose is based on body weight. The usual dose is 15 milligrams per 2.2 pounds of body weight per day in divided doses (half the dose every 12 hours), for at least 10 days.

Impetigo (Skin Infection)
The dose is based on body weight. The usual dose is 15 milligrams of liquid per 2.2 pounds of body weight per day in divided doses (half the dose every 12 hours), for 7 days.

Overdosage
Any medication taken in excess can have serious consequences. If you suspect an overdose, seek medical attention immediately.

■ *Symptoms of Lorabid overdose may include:*
  Diarrhea, nausea, stomach upset, vomiting

Generic name:

LORACARBEF

See Lorabid, page 697.

Generic name:

LORATADINE

See Claritin, page 230.

Generic name:

LORATADINE WITH PSEUDOEPHEDRINE

See Claritin-D, page 232.

Generic name:

LORAZEPAM

See Ativan, page 99.

Brand name:

LORCET

See Vicodin, page 1337.

Brand name:

LORTAB

See Vicodin, page 1337.

Generic name:

LOSARTAN

See Cozaar, page 287.

Generic name:

LOSARTAN WITH HYDROCHLOROTHIAZIDE

See Hyzaar, page 583.

Brand name:

LOTENSIN

Pronounced: Lo-TEN-sin
Generic name: Benazepril hydrochloride

Why is this drug prescribed?
Lotensin is used in the treatment of high blood pressure. It is effective when used alone or in combination with thiazide diuretics. Lotensin is in a family of drugs called ACE (angiotensin-converting enzyme) inhibitors. It works by preventing a chemical in your blood called angiotensin I from converting into a more potent form that increases salt and water retention in your body. Lotensin also enhances blood flow throughout your blood vessels.

Most important fact about this drug
You must take Lotensin regularly for it to be effective. Since blood pressure declines gradually, it may be several weeks before you get the full benefit of Lotensin; and you must continue taking it even if you are feeling well. Lotensin does not cure high blood pressure; it merely keeps it under control.

How should you take this medication?
Lotensin can be taken with or without food. Do not use salt substitutes containing potassium.

Take Lotensin exactly as prescribed. Suddenly stopping Lotensin could cause your blood pressure to increase.

- *If you miss a dose...*
  Take the forgotten dose as soon as you remember. If it is almost time for the next dose, skip the one you missed and go back to your regular schedule. Never try to "catch up" by doubling the dose.

- *Storage instructions...*
  Store at room temperature in a tightly closed container. Protect from light.

What side effects may occur?
Side effects cannot be anticipated. If any develop or change in intensity, inform your doctor as soon as possible. Only your doctor can determine if it is safe for you to continue taking Lotensin.

- *More common side effects may include:*
  Cough, dizziness, fatigue, headache, high potassium levels (dry mouth, excessive thirst, weak or irregular heartbeat, muscle pain or cramps), nausea

If you develop swelling of your face, around the lips, tongue, or throat; swelling of arms and legs; sore throat, fever, and chills; or difficulty swallowing, you should contact your doctor immediately. You may need emergency treatment.

- *Less common or rare side effects may include:*
  Allergic reactions, anxiety, arthritis, asthma, blisters, bronchitis, chest pain, constipation, dark tarry stool containing blood, decreased sex drive, difficulty sleeping, dizziness when standing, fainting, fluid retention, flushing, impotence, infection, inflammation or peeling of the skin, inflammation of the stomach or pancreas, itching, joint pain, low blood pressure, muscle pain, nervousness, pounding heartbeat, rash, sensitivity to light, shortness of breath, sinus inflammation, sweating, swelling of arms, legs, face, tingling or pins and needles, urinary infections, vomiting, weakness

Why should this drug not be prescribed?
If you are sensitive to or have ever had an allergic reaction to Lotensin or other angiotensin-converting enzyme (ACE) inhibitors, do not take this medication.

Special warnings about this medication
Your kidney function should be assessed when you start taking Lotensin and then monitored for the first few weeks. If you are on kidney dialysis, your doctor may need to use a different medication.

Lotensin can cause low blood pressure, especially if you are also taking a diuretic. You may feel light-headed or faint, especially during the first few days of therapy. If these symptoms occur, contact your doctor. Your dosage may need to be adjusted or discontinued.

If you have congestive heart failure, this drug should be used with caution.

Do not use potassium supplements or salt substitutes containing potassium without talking to your doctor first.

If you develop a sore throat or fever, you should contact your doctor immediately. It could indicate a more serious illness.

Excessive sweating, dehydration, severe diarrhea, or vomiting could make you lose too much water, causing your blood pressure to become too low.

Possible food and drug interactions
when taking this medication

If Lotensin is taken with certain other drugs, the effects of either could be increased, decreased, or altered. It is especially important to check with your doctor before combining Lotensin with the following:

Diuretics such as Lasix and HydroDIURIL
Lithium (Lithonate)
Potassium supplements such as Slow-K
Potassium-sparing diuretics such as Moduretic and Dyazide

Special information
if you are pregnant or breastfeeding

Lotensin can cause injury or death to developing and newborn babies, especially if taken during the second and third trimesters of pregnancy. If you are pregnant or plan to become pregnant and are taking Lotensin, contact your doctor immediately to discuss the potential hazard to your unborn child. Minimal amounts of Lotensin appear in breast milk. If this medication is essential to your health, your doctor may advise you to discontinue breastfeeding until your treatment with this medication is finished.

Recommended dosage

ADULTS

For people not taking a diuretic drug, the usual starting dose is 10 milligrams, once a day. Regular total dosages range from 20 to 40 milligrams per day either taken in a single dose or divided into 2 equal doses. The maximum dose is 80 milligrams per day. Your doctor will closely monitor the effect of this drug and adjust it according to your individual needs.

For people already taking a diuretic, the diuretic should be stopped, if possible, 2 to 3 days before taking Lotensin. This reduces the possibility of fainting or light-headedness. If blood pressure cannot be controlled by Lotensin alone, then diuretic use should begin again. If the diuretic cannot be discontinued, the starting dosage of Lotensin should be 5 milligrams.

For people with reduced kidney function, the dosages should be individualized according to the amount of reduced function. The usual starting dose in these instances is 5 milligrams per day, adjusted upwards to a maximum of 40 milligrams per day. If you are on kidney dialysis, your doctor may need to use a different medication.

CHILDREN

The safety and effectiveness of Lotensin have not been established in children.

Overdosage

Although there is no specific information available, a sudden drop in blood pressure would most likely be the primary symptom of Lotensin overdose. If you suspect a Lotensin overdose, seek medical attention immediately.

Brand name:

LOTREL

Pronounced: LOW-trel
Generic names: Amlodipine and Benazepril Hydrochloride

Why is this drug prescribed?

Lotrel is used in the treatment of high blood pressure. It is a combination medicine that is used when treatment with a single drug has not been successful or has caused side effects.

One component, amlodipine, is a calcium channel blocker. It eases the workload of the heart by slowing down the passage of nerve impulses and hence the contractions of the heart muscle. This improves blood flow through the heart and throughout the body and reduces blood pressure. The other component, benazepril, is an angiotensin-converting enzyme (ACE) inhibitor. It works by preventing the transformation of a hormone called angiotensin I into a more potent substance that increases salt and water retention in your body.

Most important fact about this drug

You must take Lotrel regularly for it to be effective. Since blood pressure declines gradually, it may take 1 to 2 weeks for the full effect of Lotrel to be seen. Even if you are feeling well, you must continue to take the medication. Lotrel does not cure high blood pressure; it merely keeps it under control.

How should you take this medication?
Take Lotrel exactly as prescribed by your doctor. Try to take your medication at the same time each day, such as before or after breakfast, so that it is easier to remember.

- *If you miss a dose...*
  Take it as soon as you remember. However, if it is almost time for your next dose, skip the one you missed and go back to your regular schedule. Do not take 2 doses at once.

- *Storage instructions...*
  Store at room temperature. Store away from moisture and light; avoid excessive heat.

What side effects may occur?
Side effects cannot be anticipated. If any develop or change in intensity, tell your doctor as soon as possible. Only your doctor can determine if it is safe for you to continue taking Lotrel.

If you develop swelling of your face, around the lips, tongue, or throat; swelling of arms and legs; or difficulty swallowing, you should contact your doctor immediately. You may need emergency treatment.

- *More common side effects may include:*
  Cough

- *Less common side effects may include:*
  Abdominal pain, anxiety, back pain, bloating and gas, constipation, cramps, decreased sex drive, diarrhea, dizziness, dry mouth, excessive urination, fluid retention and swelling, flushing, headache, hot flashes, impotence, insomnia, muscle and bone pain, muscle cramps, nausea, nervousness, rash, skin disorders, sore throat, tremor, weakness and fatigue

- *Rare side effects may include:*
  Anemia, blisters that leave dark spots on the skin, heart attack, pancreatitis (inflammation of the pancreas), worsening of angina pectoris (crushing chest pain)

Why should this drug not be prescribed?

If you are sensitive to or have ever had an allergic reaction to amlodipine, benazepril, or any angiotensin-converting enzyme (ACE) inhibitors, do not take this medication.

Special warnings about this medication

Your kidney function should be assessed when you start taking Lotrel, then monitored for the first few weeks.

Lotrel can cause low blood pressure, especially if you are taking high doses of diuretics. You may feel light-headed or faint, especially during the first few days of therapy. If these symptoms occur, contact your doctor. Your dosage may need to be adjusted or discontinued.

If you have congestive heart failure, use this drug with caution. If you have kidney disease or severe liver disease, diabetes, lupus erythematosus, or scleroderma (a rare disease affecting the blood vessels or connective tissue), use Lotrel with caution.

Excessive sweating, severe diarrhea, or vomiting could make you lose too much water, causing a severe drop in blood pressure. If you notice a yellow coloring to your skin or the whites of your eyes, stop taking the drug and notify your doctor immediately. You could be developing liver problems.

If you develop a persistent, dry cough, tell your doctor. It may be due to the medication and, if so, will disappear if you stop taking Lotrel. In a medical emergency and before you have surgery, notify your doctor or dentist that you are taking Lotrel.

Possible food and drug interactions
when taking this medication

If Lotrel is taken with certain other drugs, the effects of either could be increased, decreased, or altered. It is especially important to check with your doctor before combining Lotrel with the following:

  Lithium (Eskalith, Lithobid)
  Potassium supplements (Slow-K)
  Potassium-sparing water pills such as Aldactazide, Moduretic, and
    Maxzide
  Other water pills such as Diuril, Lasix, HydroDIURIL

Special information
if you are pregnant or breastfeeding

Lotrel can cause injury or death to developing and newborn babies, especially if taken during the second and third trimesters of pregnancy. If you are pregnant and are taking Lotrel, contact your doctor immediately to discuss the potential hazard to your unborn child. Minimal amounts of benazepril appear in breast milk. If this medication is essential to your health, your doctor may advise you to discontinue breastfeeding while you are taking Lotrel.

Recommended dosage

ADULTS

Your doctor will closely monitor the effects of this drug and adjust the dosage according to your blood pressure response. For small, older, frail, or liver-impaired individuals, the usual starting dose is a capsule containing 2.5 milligrams amlodipine and 10 milligrams benazepril.

CHILDREN

Safety and effectiveness in children have not been established.

Overdosage

Any medication taken in excess can have serious consequences. Although there is no specific information available, a sudden drop in blood pressure and rapid heartbeat would be the primary symptoms of a Lotrel overdose. If you suspect an overdose, seek medical attention immediately.

Brand name:

LOTRIMIN

See Gyne-Lotrimin, page 549.

Brand name:

LOTRISONE

Pronounced: LOE-trih-sone
Generic ingredients: Clotrimazole, Betamethasone
  dipropionate

Why is this drug prescribed?

Lotrisone, a combination of a steroid (betamethasone) and an antifungal drug (clotrimazole), is used to treat skin infections caused by fungus, such as athlete's foot, jock itch, and ringworm of the body.

Betamethasone treats symptoms (such as itching, redness, swelling, and inflammation) that result from fungus infections, while clotrimazole treats the cause of the infection by inhibiting the growth of certain yeast and fungus organisms.

Most important fact about this drug

When you use Lotrisone, you inevitably absorb some of the medication through your skin and into the bloodstream. Too much absorption can lead to unwanted side effects elsewhere in the body. To keep this problem to a minimum, avoid using large amounts of Lotrisone over wide areas, and do not cover it with airtight dressings such as plastic wrap or adhesive bandage unless specifically told to by your doctor.

How should you use this medication?

Wash your hands before and after applying Lotrisone. Gently massage it into the affected area and surrounding skin twice a day, in the morning and evening. Do not get it in your eyes.

Use Lotrisone for the full time prescribed, even if your condition has improved.

Lotrisone should be applied sparingly to the groin area, and it should not be used for longer than 2 weeks. Wear loose-fitting clothing.

- *If you miss a dose...*
  Apply it as soon as you remember. If it is almost time for your next dose, skip the one you missed and go back to your regular schedule.

- *Storage instructions...*
  Store at room temperature.

What side effects may occur?

Side effects cannot be anticipated. If any develop or change in intensity, inform your doctor as soon as possible. Only your doctor can determine if it is safe for you to continue using Lotrisone.

- *More common side effects may include:*
  Blistering, hives, infection, irritated skin, itching, peeling, reddened skin, skin eruptions and rash, stinging, swelling due to fluid retention, tingling sensation

- *Less common side effects may include:*
  Acne, burning, dryness, excessive hair growth, inflamed hair follicles, inflamed skin, irritated skin around mouth, loss of skin color, softening of the skin, streaks in the skin

Why should this drug not be prescribed?

You should not use Lotrisone if you are sensitive to clotrimazole or betamethasone or any of its other ingredients, or to similar steroid and antifungal medications.

Special warnings about this medication

Steroid drugs (such as betamethasone) can affect the functioning of the adrenal, hypothalamic, and pituitary glands and temporarily produce sugar in the urine, excessive blood sugar levels, and a disorder called Cushing's syndrome. Symptoms of Cushing's syndrome include easily bruised skin, increased blood pressure, low potassium levels, low sex hormone levels, mood swings, water retention, weak muscles, and weight gain.

Do not take Lotrisone internally and be sure to keep it away from your eyes.

If you are using Lotrisone to treat jock itch (tinea cruris) or a fungal infection of the skin, called tinea corporis, and there has been no improvement after 1 week, notify your doctor.

If you are using Lotrisone to treat athlete's foot (tinea pedis), notify your doctor if there is no improvement after 2 weeks of treatment.

Do not use Lotrisone for any condition other than the one for which it was prescribed, and do not use it for longer than 4 weeks.

Lotrisone is not for use on diaper rash.

Possible food and drug interactions
when taking this medication

No interactions have been reported.

Special information
if you are pregnant or breastfeeding

Pregnant women should not use steroid drugs in large amounts or for prolonged periods of time. The effects of Lotrisone during pregnancy have not been adequately studied. The medication should be used during pregnancy only if the potential benefits justify the potential risk to the developing baby. It is not known whether Lotrisone appears in breast milk. Nursing mothers should use Lotrisone with caution and only when clearly needed.

Recommended dosage

ADULTS AND CHILDREN OVER 12 YEARS OLD

"Jock Itch" (Tinea Cruris) or Fungal Skin Infections (Tinea Corporis)

Gently massage Lotrisone into the affected and surrounding skin areas twice a day, in the morning and the evening, for 2 weeks. Lotrisone should be applied sparingly to the groin area. Notify your doctor if there has been no improvement after 1 week of treatment.

Athlete's Foot (Tinea Pedis)

Gently massage Lotrisone into the affected and surrounding skin areas twice a day, in the morning and the evening, for 4 weeks. Notify your doctor if there has been no improvement after 2 weeks of treatment.

CHILDREN

The safety and effectiveness of Lotrisone have not been established for children under 12 years of age. Children may absorb proportionally larger amounts of topical Lotrisone and be more sensitive to its effects than are adults.

Overdosage

Any medication used in excess can have serious consequences. A serious overdose of Lotrisone, which is applied to the skin, is unlikely. However, seek medical help immediately if you suspect an overdose.

Generic name:

LOVASTATIN

See Mevacor, page 751.

Brand name:

LOZOL

Pronounced: LOW-zoll
Generic name: Indapamide

Why is this drug prescribed?

Lozol is used in the treatment of high blood pressure, either alone or in combination with other high blood pressure medications. Lozol is also used to relieve salt and fluid retention. During pregnancy, your doctor may prescribe Lozol to relieve fluid retention caused by a specific condition or when fluid retention causes extreme discomfort that is not relieved by rest.

Most important fact about this drug
If you have high blood pressure, you must take Lozol regularly for it to be effective. Since blood pressure declines gradually, it may be several weeks before you get the full benefit of Lozol; and you must continue taking it even if you are feeling well. Lozol does not cure high blood pressure; it merely keeps it under control.

How should you take this medication?
Take Lozol exactly as prescribed by your doctor. Suddenly stopping Lozol could cause your condition to worsen.

Lozol is best taken in the morning.

■ *If you miss a dose...*
Take the forgotten dose as soon as you remember. If it is almost time for your next dose, skip the one you missed and go back to your regular schedule. Never take 2 doses at the same time.

■ *Storage instructions...*
Store Lozol at room temperature. Protect from excessive heat. Keep the container tightly closed.

What side effects may occur?
Side effects cannot be anticipated. If any side effects develop or change in intensity, tell your doctor immediately. Only your doctor can determine whether it is safe to continue taking Lozol. Most side effects are mild and temporary.

■ *More common side effects may include:*
Agitation, anxiety, back pain, dizziness, headache, infection, irritability, muscle cramps or spasms, nasal inflammation, nervousness, numbness in hands and feet, pain, tension, weakness, fatigue, loss of energy or tiredness

■ *Less common or rare side effects may include:*
Abdominal pain or cramps, blurred vision, chest pain, conjunctivitis, constipation, cough, depression, diarrhea, dizziness when standing up too quickly, drowsiness, dry mouth, excessive urination at night, fluid retention, flu-like symptoms, flushing, fluttering heartbeat, frequent urination, hives, impotence or reduced sex drive, indigestion, insomnia,

irregular heartbeat, itching, light-headedness, loss of appetite, nausea, nervousness, premature heart contractions, production of large amounts of pale urine, rash, runny nose, sore throat, stomach irritation, tingling in hands and feet, vertigo, vomiting, weakness, weak or irregular heartbeat, weight loss

Why should this drug not be prescribed?

Avoid using Lozol if you are unable to urinate or if you have ever had an allergic reaction or are sensitive to indapamide or other sulfa-containing drugs.

Special warnings about this medication

Diuretics such as Lozol can cause the body to lose too much salt and potassium, especially among elderly women. Signs of an excessively low potassium level include muscle weakness and rapid or irregular heartbeat. To boost your potassium level, your doctor may recommend eating potassium-rich foods or taking a potassium supplement.

The risk of potassium loss increases when larger doses are used, if you have cirrhosis, or if you are also using corticosteroids or ACTH. Your doctor should check your blood regularly, especially if you have an irregular heartbeat or are taking heart medications.

Lozol should be used with care if you have gout or high uric acid levels, liver disease, diabetes, or lupus erythematosus, a disease of the connective tissue.

This medication should be used with caution if you have severe kidney disease. Your kidney function should be given a complete assessment and should continue to be monitored.

In general, diuretics should not be taken if you are taking lithium, as they increase the risk of lithium poisoning.

Possible food and drug interactions
when taking this medication

If Lozol is taken with certain other drugs, the effects of either could be increased, decreased, or altered. It is especially important to check with your doctor before combining Lozol with the following:

Lithium (Eskalith)
Norepinephrine (a drug used to treat cardiac arrest and to maintain blood pressure)
Other high blood pressure medications such as Aldomet and Tenormin

Special information
if you are pregnant or breastfeeding
If you are pregnant or plan to become pregnant, tell your doctor immediately. No information is available about the safety of Lozol during pregnancy.

Lozol may appear in breast milk and could affect a nursing infant. If Lozol is essential to your health, your doctor may advise you to stop breastfeeding until your treatment is finished.

Recommended dosage

ADULTS

High Blood Pressure
The usual starting dose is 1.25 milligrams as a single daily dose taken in the morning. If Lozol does not seem to be working for you, your doctor may gradually increase your dosage up to 5 milligrams taken once a day.

Fluid Buildup in Congestive Heart Failure
The usual starting dose is 2.5 milligrams as a single daily dose taken in the morning. Your doctor may increase your dosage to 5 milligrams taken once daily.

Overdosage
Any medication taken in excess can have serious consequences. If you suspect an overdose, seek medical treatment immediately.

■ *Symptoms of Lozol overdose may include:*
   Electrolyte imbalance (potassium or salt depletion due to too much fluid loss), nausea, stomach disorders, vomiting, weakness

Brand name:

LURIDE

Pronounced: LUHR-ide
Generic name: Sodium fluoride

Why is this drug prescribed?
Luride is prescribed to strengthen children's teeth against decay during the period when the teeth are still developing.

Studies have shown that children who live where the drinking water contains a certain level of fluoride have fewer cavities than others. Fluoride helps prevent cavities in three ways: by increasing the teeth's resistance to dissolving on contact with acid, by strengthening teeth, and by slowing down the growth of mouth bacteria.

Luride may be given to children who live where the water fluoride level is 0.6 parts per million or less.

Most important fact about this drug

Before Luride is prescribed, it is important for the doctor to know the fluoride content of the water your child drinks every day. Your water company, or a private laboratory, can tell you the level of fluoride in your water.

How should you take this medication?

Give your child Luride exactly as prescribed by your doctor. It is preferable to give the tablet at bedtime after the child's teeth have been brushed. The youngster may chew and swallow the tablet or simply suck on it until it dissolves. The liquid form of this medicine is to be taken by mouth only. It may be dropped directly into the mouth or mixed with water or fruit juice. Always store Luride drops in the original plastic dropper bottle.

■ *If you miss a dose...*
Give it as soon as you remember. If it is almost time for the next dose, skip the one you missed and go back to your regular schedule. Do not give 2 doses at once.

■ *Storage instructions...*
Store at room temperature away from heat, light, and moisture. Keep the liquid from freezing.

What side effects may occur?

Side effects cannot be anticipated. If any develop, tell your doctor immediately. Only your doctor can determine whether it is safe for your child to continue taking Luride.

In rare cases, Luride may cause an allergic rash or some other unexpected effect.

Why should this drug not be prescribed?

Your child should not take Luride if he or she is sensitive to it or has had an allergic reaction to sodium fluoride in the past.

Your child should not take the 1-milligram strength of Luride if the drinking water in your area contains 0.3 parts per million of fluoride or more. He or she should not take the other forms of Luride if the water contains 0.6 parts per million of fluoride or more.

Special warnings about this medication

Do not give full-strength tablets (1 milligram) to children under the age of 6. Do not give the half-strength tablets (0.5 milligram) to children under 3, or to children under 6 when your drinking water fluoride content is 0.3 parts per million or more. Do not give the quarter-strength tablets (0.25 milligrams) to children under 6 months, or to children under 3 years when fluoride content is 0.3 parts per million or more.

Possible food and drug interactions
when taking this medication

Avoid giving your child Luride with dairy products. The calcium in dairy products may interact with the fluoride to create calcium fluoride, which the body cannot absorb well.

Recommended dosage

Since this drug is used to supplement water with low fluoride content, consult your physician to determine the proper amount based on the local water content. Also check with your doctor if you move to a new area, change to bottled water, or begin using a water-filtering device. Dosages are determined by both age and the fluoride content of the water.

INFANTS AND CHILDREN

The following daily dosages are recommended for areas where the drinking water contains fluoride at less than 0.3 parts per million:

Children 6 Months to 3 Years of Age
1 quarter-strength (0.25 milligram) tablet or half a dropperful of liquid

3 to 6 Years of Age
1 half-strength (0.5 milligram) tablet or 1 dropperful of liquid

6 to 16 Years of Age
1 full-strength (1 milligram) tablet or 2 droppersful of liquid

For areas where the fluoride content of drinking water is between 0.3 and 0.6 parts per million, the recommended daily dosage of the tablets is one-half the above dosages. Dosage of the liquid should be reduced to half a dropperful for children ages 3 to 6 and 1 dropperful for children over 6.

Overdosage

Any medication taken in excess can have serious consequences. Taking too much fluoride for a long period of time may cause discoloration of the teeth. Notify your doctor or dentist if you notice white, brown, or black spots on the teeth.

Swallowing large amounts of fluoride can cause burning in the mouth and a sore tongue, followed by diarrhea, nausea, salivation, stomach cramping and pain, and vomiting sometimes with blood.

Brand name:

LUVOX

Pronounced: LOO-voks
Generic name: Fluvoxamine maleate

Why is this drug prescribed?
Luvox is prescribed for obsessive compulsive disorder. An obsession is marked by continual, unwanted thoughts that prevent proper functioning in everyday living. Compulsive behavior is typified by ritualistic actions such as repetitive washing, repeating certain phrases, completing steps in a process over and over, counting and recounting, checking and rechecking to make sure that something has not been forgotten, excessive neatness, and hoarding of useless items.

Most important fact about this drug
Before starting therapy with Luvox, be sure your doctor knows what medications you are taking—both prescription and over-the-counter—since combining Luvox with certain drugs may cause serious or even life-threatening effects. You should never take Luvox with the antihistamines Seldane and Hismanal or the heartburn medication Propulsid. You should also avoid taking Luvox within 14 days of taking any antidepressant drug classified as an MAO inhibitor, including Nardil and Parnate.

How should you take this medication?
Take this medication only as directed by your doctor.

Luvox may be taken with or without food.

■ *If you miss a dose...*
If you are taking 1 dose a day, skip the missed dose and go back to your regular schedule. If you are taking 2 doses a day, take the missed dose as soon as possible, then go back to your regular schedule. Never take 2 doses at the same time.

■ *Storage instructions...*
Store at room temperature and protect from humidity.

What side effects may occur?
Side effects cannot be anticipated. If any develop or change in intensity, tell your doctor immediately. Only your doctor can determine if it is safe for you to continue taking Luvox.

■ *More common side effects may include:*
Abnormal ejaculation, abnormal tooth decay and toothache, anxiety, blurred vision, constipation, decreased appetite, diarrhea, dizziness, dry mouth, feeling "hot or flushed," "flu-like" symptoms, frequent urination, gas and bloating, headache, heart palpitations, inability to fall asleep, indigestion, nausea, nervousness, sleepiness, sweating, taste alteration, tremor, unusual tiredness or weakness, upper respiratory infection, vomiting

■ *Less common side effects may include:*
Abnormal muscle tone, agitation, chills, decreased sex drive, depression, difficult or labored breathing, difficulty swallowing, extreme excitability, impotence, inability to urinate, lack of orgasm, yawning

Why should this drug not be prescribed?
If you are sensitive to or have ever had an allergic reaction to Luvox or similar drugs, such as Prozac and Zoloft, do not take this medication. Make sure your doctor is aware of any drug reactions you have experienced.

Never combine Luvox with Seldane, Hismanal, or Propulsid, or take it within 14 days of taking an MAO inhibitor such as Nardil or Parnate. (See "Most important fact about this drug.")

Special warnings about this medication
You should discuss all your medical problems with your doctor before starting therapy with Luvox, as certain physical conditions or diseases may affect your reaction to Luvox.

If you suffer from seizures, use this medication cautiously. If you experience a seizure while taking Luvox, stop taking the drug and call your doctor immediately.

If you have or have ever had suicidal thoughts, be sure to tell your doctor, as your dosage may need to be adjusted.

If you have a history of mania (excessively energetic, out-of-control behavior), use this medication cautiously.

If you have liver disease, your doctor will adjust the dosage.

Luvox may cause you to become drowsy or less alert and may affect your judgment. Therefore, avoid driving, operating dangerous machinery, or participating in any hazardous activity that requires full mental alertness until you know your reaction to this medication.

If you develop a rash or hives, or any other allergic-type reaction, notify your physician immediately.

Possible food and drug interactions
when taking this medication

Do not drink alcohol while taking this medication. If you smoke, be sure to tell your doctor before starting Luvox therapy, as your dosage may need adjustment.

If Luvox is taken with certain other drugs, the effects of either could be increased, decreased, or altered. It is especially important to check with your doctor before combining Luvox with the following:

Anticoagulant drugs such as Coumadin
Antidepressant medications such as Anafranil, Elavil, and Tofranil, as
    well as the MAO inhibitors Nardil and Parnate
Blood pressure medications known as beta blockers, including Inderal
    and Lopressor
Carbamazepine (Tegretol)
Cisapride (Propulsid)
Clozapine (Clozaril)
Diazepam (Valium)
Diltiazem (Cardizem)
Lithium (Lithonate)
Methadone (Dolophine)
Phenytoin (Dilantin)
Quinidine (Quinidex)
Theophylline (Theo-Dur)
Tranquilizers and sedatives such as Halcion, Valium, Versed, and Xanax
Tryptophan

Special information
if you are pregnant or breastfeeding

The effects of Luvox in pregnancy have not been adequately studied. If you are pregnant or plan to become pregnant, consult your doctor immediately. Luvox passes into breast milk and may cause serious reactions in a nursing baby. If this medication is essential to your health, your doctor may advise you to discontinue breastfeeding until your treatment with Luvox is finished.

Recommended dosage

ADULTS

The usual starting dose is one 50-milligram tablet taken at bedtime.

Your doctor may increase your dose, depending upon your response. The maximum daily dose is 300 milligrams. If you take more than 100 milligrams a day, your doctor will divide the total amount into 2 doses; if the doses are not equal, you should take the larger dose at bedtime.

CHILDREN

The safety and effectiveness of Luvox have not been established in children under age 18.

Overdosage

Any medication taken in excess can have serious consequences. If you suspect an overdose, seek medical attention immediately.

■ *Symptoms of Luvox overdose may include:*
Breathing difficulties, changes in pulse rate, coma, convulsions, diarrhea, dizziness, drowsiness, low blood pressure, liver problems, vomiting

Brand name:

MAALOX

See Antacids, page 71.

Brand name:

MACROBID

See Macrodantin, page 720.

Brand name:

MACRODANTIN

Pronounced: Mack-row-DAN-tin
Generic name: Nitrofurantoin
Other brand name: Macrobid

Why is this drug prescribed?

Nitrofurantoin, an antibacterial drug, is prescribed for the treatment of urinary tract infections caused by certain strains of bacteria.

Most important fact about this drug
Breathing disorders have occurred in people taking nitrofurantoin. The drug can cause inflammation of the lungs marked by coughing, difficulty breathing, and wheezing. It has also been known to cause pulmonary fibrosis (an abnormal increase in fibrous tissue of the lungs). This condition can develop gradually without symptoms and can be fatal. An allergic reaction to this drug is also possible and may occur without warning. Symptoms include a feeling of ill health and a persistent cough. However, all these reactions occur rarely and generally in those receiving nitrofurantoin therapy for 6 months or longer.

Sudden and severe lung reactions are characterized by fever, chills, cough, chest pain, and difficulty breathing. These acute reactions usually occur within the first week of treatment and subside when therapy with nitrofurantoin is stopped.

Your doctor should monitor your condition closely, especially if you are receiving long-term treatment with this medication.

How should you take this medication?
To improve absorption of the drug, nitrofurantoin should be taken with food.

Follow your doctor's instructions carefully. Take the full amount prescribed, even if you are feeling better.

This medication works best if your urine is acidic. Ask your doctor whether you should be taking special measures to assure its acidity.

Nitrofurantoin may turn the urine brown.

■ *If you miss a dose...*
Take the forgotten dose as soon as you remember, then space out the rest of the day's doses at equal intervals.

■ *Storage instructions...*
Store at room temperature. Protect from light and keep the container tightly closed.

What side effects may occur?
Side effects cannot be anticipated. If any develop or change in intensity, inform your doctor as soon as possible. Only your doctor can determine if it is safe for you to continue taking nitrofurantoin.

■ *More common side effects may include:*
Lack or loss of appetite, nausea, vomiting

■ *Less common or rare side effects may include:*
Abdominal pain/discomfort, blue skin, chills, confusion, cough, chest pain, depression, diarrhea, difficulty breathing, dizziness, drowsiness, exaggerated sense of well-being, eye disorder, fever, hair loss, headache, hepatitis, hives, inflammation of the nerves causing symptoms of numbness, tingling, pain, or muscle weakness, intestinal inflammation, involuntary eye movement, irregular heartbeat, itching, itchy red skin patches, joint pain, muscle pain, peeling skin, psychotic reactions, rash, severe allergic reactions, skin inflammation with flaking, skin swelling or welts, vertigo, yellowing of the skin and whites of the eyes, weakness

Why should this drug not be prescribed?
If you are sensitive to or have ever had an allergic reaction to nitrofurantoin or other drugs of this type, such as Furoxone, you should not take this medication. Make sure that your doctor is aware of any drug reactions that you have experienced.

Unless you are directed to do so by your doctor, do not take this medication if you have poor kidneys, producing little or no urine.

Nitrofurantoin should not be taken at term of pregnancy or during labor and delivery; it should not be given to infants under 1 month of age.

Special warnings about this medication
Tell your doctor if you have any unusual symptoms while you are taking this drug.

Fatalities have been reported from hepatitis (liver disease) during treatment with nitrofurantoin. Long-lasting, active hepatitis can develop without symptoms; therefore, if you are receiving long-term treatment with this drug, your doctor should test your liver function periodically.

Fatalities from peripheral neuropathy—a disease of the nerves—have also been reported in people taking nitrofurantoin. Conditions such as a kidney disorder, anemia, diabetes mellitus, a debilitating disease, or a vitamin B deficiency make peripheral neuropathy more likely. If you develop symptoms such as muscle weakness or lack of sensation, check with your doctor immediately.

If you experience diarrhea, tell your doctor. It may be a sign of serious intestinal inflammation.

Hemolytic anemia (destruction of red blood cells) has occurred in people taking nitrofurantoin.

Continued or prolonged use of this drug may result in growth of bacteria that do not respond to it. This can cause a renewed infection, so it is important that your doctor monitor your condition on a regular basis.

Possible food and drug interactions
when taking this medication
If nitrofurantoin is taken with certain other drugs, the effects of either could be increased, decreased, or altered. It is especially important to check with your doctor before combining nitrofurantoin with the following:

Magnesium trisilicate (Gaviscon Antacid Tablets)
The gout drugs Benemid and Anturane, and other drugs that increase
    the amount of uric acid in the urine

Special information
if you are pregnant or breastfeeding
The safety of nitrofurantoin during pregnancy and breastfeeding has not been established. Nitrofurantoin does appear in human breast milk. If you are pregnant or breastfeeding or you plan to become pregnant or breastfeed, inform your doctor immediately.

Recommended dosage
Treatment with nitrofurantoin should be continued for 1 week or for at least 3 days after obtaining a urine specimen free of infection. If your infection has not cleared up, your doctor should re-evaluate your case.

ADULTS

The recommended dosage of Macrodantin is 50 to 100 milligrams taken 4 times a day. For long-term treatment, your doctor may reduce your dosage to 50 to 100 milligrams taken at bedtime.

The recommended dosage of Macrobid is one 100 milligram capsule every 12 hours for 7 days.

CHILDREN

This medication should not be prescribed for children under 1 month of age.

The recommended daily dosage of Macrodantin for infants and children over 1 month of age is 5 to 7 milligrams per 2.2 pounds of body weight, divided into 4 doses over 24 hours.

For the long-term treatment of children, the doctor may prescribe daily doses as low as 1 milligram per 2.2 pounds of body weight taken in 1 or 2 doses per day.

The dosage of Macrobid for children over 12 years of age is one 100 milligram capsule every 12 hours for 7 days. Safety and effectiveness have not been established for children under 12.

Overdosage
An overdose of nitrofurantoin does not cause any specific symptoms other than vomiting. If vomiting does not occur soon after an excessive dose, it should be induced.

If you suspect an overdose, seek emergency medical treatment immediately.

Brand name:

MATERNA

See Stuartnatal Plus, page 1163.

Brand name:

MAVIK

Pronounced: MA-vick
Generic name: Trandolapril

Why is this drug prescribed?
Mavik controls high blood pressure. It is effective when used alone or combined with other high blood pressure medications such as diuretics that help rid the body of excess water. Mavik is in a family of drugs known as ACE (angiotensin converting enzyme) inhibitors. It works by preventing a chemical in your blood called angiotensin I from converting into a more potent form that increases salt and water retention in your body. ACE inhibitors also expand your blood vessels, further reducing blood pressure.

Most important fact about this drug
You will get the full benefit of Mavik within a week; but you must continue taking it regularly to maintain the effect. Mavik does not cure high blood pressure, it merely keeps it under control.

How should you take this medication?
Mavik can be taken with or without food. Try to make Mavik part of your regular daily routine. If you take it at the same time each day—for example, right after breakfast—you will be less likely to forget a dose.

- *If you miss a dose...*
Take it as soon as you remember. However, if it is almost time for your next dose, skip the one you missed and go back to your regular schedule.

- *Storage instructions...*
Mavik may be stored at room temperature.

What side effects may occur?
Side effects cannot be anticipated. If any develop or change in intensity, tell your doctor as soon as possible. Only your doctor can determine if it is safe for you to continue taking Mavik.

- *Side effects may include:*
Abdominal pain, anxiety, bloating, chest pain, constipation, cough, cramps, decreased sex drive, diarrhea, difficult or labored breathing, dizziness, drowsiness, fainting, flushing, fluid retention, gout, impotence, indigestion, insomnia, itching, low blood pressure, muscle cramps, nosebleed, pains in arms and legs, palpitations, pins and needles, rash, severe skin disease, slowed heartbeat, swelling of face and lips, swelling of tongue and throat, swelling of arms or legs, throat inflammation, upper respiratory infection, vertigo, vomiting, yellow eyes and skin

Why should this drug not be prescribed?
If you have ever had an allergic reaction to Mavik or similar drugs such as Capoten or Vasotec, you should not take this medication. Make sure your doctor is aware of any drug reactions you have experienced.

Special warnings about this medication
If you develop signs of an allergic reaction, such as swelling of the face, lips, tongue, or throat and difficulty swallowing (or swelling of the arms and legs), you should stop taking Mavik and contact your doctor immediately. You may need emergency treatment. Desensitization treatments with bee or wasp venom make an allergic reaction more likely. Kidney dialysis also increases the danger.

When prescribing Mavik, your doctor will perform a complete assessment of your kidney function and will continue to monitor your kidneys.

If you have congestive heart failure, your blood pressure may drop sharply after the first few doses of Mavik and you may feel light-headed for a time. Your doctor should monitor you closely when you start taking this medication and when your dosage is increased.

High doses of diuretics combined with Mavik may cause excessively low blood pressure. Your doctor may need to reduce your diuretic dose to avoid this problem.

Mavik sometimes affects the liver. If you notice a yellow coloring to your skin or the whites of your eyes, stop taking Mavik and notify your doctor immediately.

Dehydration may cause a drop in blood pressure. If you do not drink enough water, perspire a lot, or suffer vomiting or diarrhea, notify your doctor immediately.

Also contact your doctor promptly if you develop a sore throat or fever. It could indicate a more serious illness.

If you develop a persistent, dry cough, tell your doctor. It may be due to the medication and, if so, will disappear if Mavik is discontinued.

Heart and circulatory problems, diabetes, lupus erythematosus, and kidney disease are all reasons for using Mavik with care. Also be sure to tell your doctor or dentist that you are taking Mavik if you are planning any type of surgery.

Possible food and drug interactions
when taking this medication
If Mavik is taken with certain other drugs, the effects of either could be increased, decreased, or altered. It is especially important to check with your doctor before combining Mavik with the following:

Diuretics such as HydroDIURIL
Diuretics that spare the body's potassium, such as Aldactone, Dyazide, and Moduretic
Lithium (Lithonate)
Potassium preparations such as Micro-K and Slow-K

Also check with your doctor before using potassium-containing salt substitutes.

Special information
if you are pregnant or breastfeeding
ACE inhibitors such as Mavik can cause injury and even death to the developing baby when used during the last 6 months of pregnancy. At the first sign of pregnancy, stop taking Mavik and contact your doctor immediately.

Mavik may appear in breast milk and could affect a nursing infant. Do not take this medication while you are nursing.

Recommended dosage

ADULTS

The usual starting dose if you are not taking a diuretic is 1 milligram once a day; African-Americans should start on 2 milligrams once a day.

Depending on your blood pressure response, your doctor may increase your dosage at 1-week intervals, up to 2 to 4 milligrams once a day. If your blood pressure still does not respond, your dosage may be increased to 4 milligrams twice a day and the doctor may add a diuretic to your regimen.

If you are already taking a diuretic, your doctor will have you stop taking it 2 to 3 days before you start treatment with Mavik. If your diuretic should not be stopped, your starting dose of Mavik will be 0.5 milligram. A starting dose of 0.5 milligram daily is also recommended for people with liver or kidney disease.

CHILDREN

The safety and effectiveness of Mavik in children have not been established.

Overdosage

Any medication taken in excess can have serious consequences. The most likely effects of a Mavik overdose are light-headedness or dizziness due to a sudden drop in blood pressure. If you suspect an overdose, seek medical attention immediately.

Brand name:

MAXAQUIN

Pronounced: MAX-ah-kwin
Generic name: Lomefloxacin hydrochloride

Why is this drug prescribed?

Maxaquin is a quinolone antibiotic used to treat lower respiratory infections, including chronic bronchitis, and urinary tract infections, including cystitis (inflammation of the inner lining of the bladder). Maxaquin is also given before bladder surgery and prostate biopsy to prevent the infections that sometimes follow these operations.

Most important fact about this drug

During and following treatment, Maxaquin causes sensitivity reactions in people exposed to sunlight or sunlamps. The reactions can occur despite use of sunscreens and sunblocks, and can be prompted by shaded or diffused light or exposure through glass. Avoid even indirect sunlight while taking Maxaquin and for several days following therapy.

How should you take this medication?
It is important to finish your prescription of Maxaquin completely. If you stop taking your medication too soon, your symptoms may return.

Maxaquin may be taken with or without food. Take it with a full 8-ounce glass of water; and be sure to drink plenty of fluids while on this medication.

You can reduce the risk of a reaction to sunlight by taking Maxaquin in the evening (at least 12 hours before you will be exposed to the sun).

- *If you miss a dose...*
  Take it as soon as you remember. If it is almost time for your next dose, skip the one you missed and go back to your regular schedule. Do not take 2 doses at the same time.

- *Storage instructions...*
  Store at room temperature.

What side effects may occur?
Side effects cannot be anticipated. If any develop or change in intensity, tell your doctor as soon as possible. Only your doctor can determine if it is safe for you to continue taking Maxaquin.

- *More common side effects may include:*
  Headache, nausea

- *Less common side effects may include:*
  Diarrhea, dizziness, sensitivity to light

- *Rare side effects may include:*
  Abdominal pain, abnormal or terrifying dreams, abnormal vision, agitation, allergic reaction, altered taste, angina pectoris (crushing chest pain), anxiety, back pain, bleeding between menstrual periods, bleeding in the stomach and intestines, blood clots in the lungs, blood in the urine, blue skin color, chest pain, chills, coma, confusion, conjunctivitis (pinkeye), constipation, convulsions, cough, decreased heat tolerance, depression, difficult or labored breathing, difficulty swallowing, dry mouth, earache, eye pain, facial swelling, fainting, fatigue, fluid retention and swelling, flu-like symptoms, flushing, gas, general feeling of illness, gout, harsh, high-

pitched sound during breathing, heart attack, heart failure, high blood pressure, hives, inability to sleep, increased appetite, increased mucus from the lungs, increased sweating, indigestion, inflammation in the male genital area, inflammation of the stomach and intestines, inflammation of the vagina, irregular heartbeat, itching, joint pain, lack of urine, leg cramps, loss of appetite, loss of sense of identity, low blood pressure, low blood sugar, lung infection or other problems, muscle pain, nervousness, nosebleed, overactivity, pain in the genital-rectal area, problems with urination, purple or red spots on the skin, rapid heartbeat, rash, ringing in the ears, skin disorders, skin eruptions or peeling, sleepiness, slow heartbeat, thirst, tingling or a "pins and needles" feeling, tongue discoloration, tremor, vaginal yeast infection, vertigo, vomiting, weakness, wheezing, white or yellow vaginal discharge

Why should this drug not be prescribed?

If you are sensitive to or have ever had an allergic reaction to Maxaquin or other quinolone antibiotics such as Cipro and Floxin, you should not take this medication. Make sure your doctor is aware of any drug reactions you have experienced.

Special warnings about this medication

Use Maxaquin cautiously if you have disorders such as epilepsy, severe hardening of the arteries in the brain, and other conditions that can lead to seizures. Maxaquin may cause convulsions.

In rare cases, people taking antibiotics similar to Maxaquin have experienced severe, even fatal reactions, sometimes after only one dose. These reactions may include confusion, convulsions, difficulty breathing, hallucinations, hives, itching, light-headedness, loss of consciousness, rash, restlessness, swelling in the face or throat, tingling, and tremors. If you develop any of these symptoms, stop taking Maxaquin immediately and seek medical help.

If other antibiotics have given you diarrhea, or it develops while you are taking Maxaquin, be sure to tell your doctor. Maxaquin may cause inflammation of the bowel, ranging from mild to life-threatening.

Maxaquin may cause dizziness or light-headedness and may impair your ability to drive a car or operate potentially dangerous machinery. Do not participate in any activities that require full alertness until you know how Maxaquin affects you.

Maxaquin can cause rupture of muscle tendons. If you notice any pain or inflammation, stop exercising the affected tendon until your doctor has examined you.

Possible food and drug interactions when taking this medication

If Maxaquin is taken with certain other drugs, the effects of either could be increased, decreased, or altered. It is especially important to check with your doctor before combining Maxaquin with the following:

Antacids containing magnesium or aluminum, such as Maalox or Gaviscon
Caffeine (including coffee, tea, and some soft drinks)
Cimetidine (Tagamet)
Cyclosporine (Sandimmune and Neoral)
Probenecid (Benemid)
Sucralfate (Carafate)
Theophylline (Theo-Dur)
Warfarin (Coumadin)
Vitamins or products containing iron or zinc

Special information if you are pregnant or breastfeeding

The effects of Maxaquin in pregnancy have not been adequately studied. If you are pregnant or plan to become pregnant, notify your doctor immediately. It is not known if Maxaquin appears in breast milk. Because many drugs do make their way into breast milk, your doctor may have you stop nursing while you are taking Maxaquin.

Recommended dosage

ADULTS

Chronic Bronchitis
The usual dosage is 400 milligrams once a day for 10 days.

Cystitis
The usual dosage is 400 milligrams once a day for 10 days.

Complicated Urinary Tract Infections
The dosage is 400 milligrams once a day for 14 days.

People With Impaired Renal Function or Cirrhosis
Your doctor will adjust the dosage according to your needs.

People on Dialysis
The recommended dosage for people on dialysis is 400 milligrams, followed by daily maintenance doses of 200 milligrams (one half tablet) once a day for the duration of treatment.